# Fundamentals of
# Clinical Supervision

# Fundamentals of Clinical Supervision

JANINE M. BERNARD
*Fairfield University*

RODNEY K. GOODYEAR
*University of Southern California*

**ALLYN AND BACON**
Boston London Toronto Sydney Tokyo Singapore

Managing Editor: Susan Badger
Series Editorial Assistant: Dana Lamothe
Production Coordinator: Lisa Feder
Editorial-Production Service: York Production Services
Cover Administrator: Linda Dickinson
Cover Designer: Suzanne Harbison
Manufacturing Buyer: Louise Richardson

Copyright © 1992 by Allyn and Bacon
A Division of Simon & Schuster, Inc.
160 Gould Street
Needham Heights, Massachusetts 02194

**Library of Congress Cataloging-in-Publication Data**
Bernard, Janine M.
     Fundamentals of clinical supervision / Janine M. Bernard, Rodney
K. Goodyear.
          p.     cm.
     Includes index.
     ISBN 0-205-12869-6
     1. Psychotherapists — Supervision of.   2. Counselors — Supervision
of.   3. Clinical psychologists — Supervision of.     I. Goodyear,
Rodney K.   II. Title
     RC480.5.B455     1992
     362.2′0425′0683 — dc 20                                              91-12290
                                                                          CIP

Printed in the United States of America

10  9  8  7  6  5  4  3          96  95  94  93

*To Dick and Karen*

# CONTENTS

# References                                                    243

# Appendices

# PREFACE

Clinical supervision has been practiced as long as has psychotherapy. Yet supervision only recently has begun to receive sustained attention by educators and researchers. Consequently, whereas students of psychotherapy have had a substantial body of literature from which to draw, students of supervision have been less fortunate. This textbook is intended to supplement the still-small clinical supervision literature.

In thinking about this text, we first had to grapple with the problem that each mental health profession seems to have developed its own supervision literature. Although each of these separate fields of literature has much to offer supervisors in *all* professions, its availability generally has been restricted to those in the particular profession. Therefore, we undertook to review what we considered to be the best supervision literature from several disciplines. Our intent was for this book to reflect the fields of counseling, psychology, social work, and marriage and family therapy. (Some literature from psychiatry is covered as well but to a more limited extent.)

Because our goal is to help promote supervision in general, we have blended these fields of literature. With the exception of live supervision, which typically is associated with marriage and family therapy, we have tended not to identify particular resources as a "contribution from psychology" or a "contribution from social work." Rather, this textbook integrates the knowledge that has been produced by these different disciplines and leads the reader through conceptual and practical topics that are of interest to all clinical supervisors regardless of their particular professional lens.

Another of our goals was to write a book that would be equally useful as a textbook for the student of supervision and as a professional resource for the supervision practitioner. We intended that the book be both scholarly (accomplished through a comprehensive review of the literature) and pragmatic (accomplished through our choice of topics and manner of writing).

This book does not defend any one approach to studying or practicing clinical supervision; instead it attempts to present a comprehensive view of the field and the issues that are central to supervision practice. There are other resources for the reader who is interested in a particular conceptual map of supervision (e.g., Stoltenberg and Delworth's book describing a developmental model of supervision) or supervision related to one discipline (e.g., Kadushin's book on social work supervision; Liddle, Breunlin, and Schwartz's book on family therapy supervision).

Chapter 1 defines supervision and differentiates it from other related professional activities, including training. It is intended to establish a foundation for the chapters that follow.

Writing Chapter 2 was a particular challenge. In it, we attempted to pull together the various conceptual approaches to clinical supervision. We expect that of all the chapters in the book, this chapter may cause the most varied reactions. It also will be the most vulnerable to obsolescence as the field becomes more theoretically sophisticated. Despite these potential difficulties, we considered a chapter of this sort to be imperative. If it stimulates debate, so much the better.

Chapter 3 puts us back on less controversial ground. It considers the various roles of the clinical supervisor as well as the dimensions, responsibilities, and outcomes that correspond to each. Incorporated into our discussion is the interface of the supervisor's personal world view and professional role definitions.

The following three chapters might be seen as a unit in that they each cover a particular mode of supervision. Chapter 4 is a comprehensive review of the methods used for the individual case conference, ranging from self-report and the use of process notes to videotape usage and live observation. Chapter 5 focuses on group supervision and offers the reader a rationale for the use of group supervision, a review of the dynamics that determine the success of the group, and different models for use in supervision groups. Finally, Chapter 6 is devoted to live supervision, a relatively novel model. Its history, methods, and unique advantages and challenges are considered.

Chapters 7, 8, and 9 address the professional responsibilities of clinical supervisors. Chapter 7 is devoted to the crucial task of evaluation. Considered in the chapter are favorable conditions for evaluation, criteria, methods of delivery, and the issue of subjectivity. Chapter 8, dealing with ethical and legal issues, continues our theme of professional responsibility. Throughout this chapter, therapy dimensions that the supervisor must oversee and ethical and legal issues that are endemic to supervision are differentiated. Both are reviewed in detail, along with some of the leading legal precedents that determine accepted practice today. Finally, Chapter 9 completes this trilogy by taking a serious look at the administrative responsibilities and organizational skills that are paramount for clinical supervision. In this chapter we take the position that a supervisor who is clinically outstanding but ignores structure and the need to take time to plan supervision will have only partial or random influence on supervisees. But when all the standards of professional

competence presented in these three chapters are employed *along with* advanced clinical skill as a supervisor, supervisees are apt to have an outstanding learning experience.

Chapter 10 and 11 consider both intrapersonal (e.g., personal attributes) and interpersonal (e.g., cultural attributes) as they may affect supervision process and outcomes. Chapter 10 acknowledges that the supervisee and the supervisor meet one another with well-developed personalities and that individual histories might complicate the supervisory process. Entitled "Supervision Issues and Dilemmas," this chapter offers the supervisor both theory and empirical findings to help find satisfactory solutions to idiosyncratic difficulties.

Chapter 11 expands the scope of the supervisor's responsibility to include awareness of the group identity of the supervisee and of the need to confront the challenges of multicultural supervision. Of all the topics included in this book, we see the area of multicultural interactions to be the least chartered, even for many seasoned supervisors. Therefore, to a greater extent than in other chapters, we have supplemented information from supervision literature on the topic with material from therapy literature. Knowing that the supervisor always must function with two levels in mind—those of therapy and supervision—our goal was to make this chapter a primer in multicultural training and supervision for the supervisor whose own training did not include this important dimension.

Finally, Chapter 12 picks up where Chapter 2 left off. Having employed empirical literature throughout the textbook to support our assertions, we conclude the book with a comprehensive look at how we have arrived at our present knowledge and how we might improve this knowledge base. This chapter is based on the premise that we need better research to arrive at credible supervision theory. For that reason, both methodology and content are considered.

The textbook's appendixes are in the service of our goal of offering a comprehensive text. Appendix A contains the Standards for Counselor Supervision endorsed by the Association for Counselor Education and Supervision and the American Association for Counseling and Development. These standards can serve as a checklist for the training of clinical supervisors.

Appendix B is the complete manual for a two-day workshop in clinical supervision. This manual can be used for in-service training of novice or seasoned supervisors. (It has been used successfully with both populations.) Alternatively, the eight sessions can be infused into a more traditional course in clinical supervision as the experiential component. Appendix C consists of selected instruments for evaluating supervisors and supervisees.

Finally, Appendix D reproduces the complete transcripts of the supervision videotapes produced by Rod Goodyear and featuring the supervision of Erving Polster, Carl Rogers, Rudolph Ekstein, Norman Kagan, and Albert Ellis. With the exception of the Rogers's ses-

sion, this is the first time these transcripts appear in print.

In short, this book is a product of some of the energy found in the supervision field today. Our hope is that with this book we will lend even more energy to the continuing development of that field.

It is a pleasure to conclude this preface by acknowledging our sincere appreciation to those who, in one way or another, have contributed to the development of this book. First, we wish to thank our families for their patient forebearance. DiAnne Borders, Patricia Wolleat, and Elaine Johnson provided reviews that were invaluable in guiding revisions. Allyson Haley deserves acknowledgment for her volunteered service. And, finally, thanks are due to those who provided specific suggestions for and critiques of Chapter 12: DiAnne Borders, P. Paul Heppner, Elizabeth Holloway, and Everett Worthington.

March 1991                              Janine M. Bernard
                                        Rodney K. Goodyear

# CHAPTER 1

# INTRODUCTION

The person who wishes to become a mental health professional commits to training that is relatively extensive. That training is multifaceted and includes formal course work in therapy-related theory and research; laboratory courses in which basic helping skills are taught; personal growth experiences of one type or another; and, certainly, actual practice in providing interventions. Additionally, noviatiates in every discipline are required to take formal course work specific to their particular discipline: psychological testing and research methods for counselors and psychologists, medical training for psychiatrists, social welfare policies and services for social workers, and systematic paradigms for family therapists.

Professional training at its most basic level, however, is a process of inculcating in the trainee two distinct realms of knowledge (Schön, 1983). The first includes formal theories and observations that have been confirmed or are confirmable by research. The second is the knowledge and accompanying skills that have accrued through the professional experiences of practitioners. Both types of knowledge are essential, for each complements the other.

Too often, however, these two realms of knowledge seem unconnected, despite the considerable attention that has been given to articulating a scientist-practitioner model that integrates the two (e.g., Claiborn, 1987). In universities the first realm is typically regarded as that of "real" knowledge. But if asked, most practitioners and trainees likely would indicate that they prefer practitioner-generated knowledge. This knowledge feels more real, relevant,

and accessible to them. It is verifiable with their own experience.

In fact, it is their actual clinical experiences that students in the mental health disciplines are most likely to regard as the meat of their professional training. This seems true regardless of the student's specific discipline (see, for example, Henry, Sims, & Spray, 1971). But if such training is to be adequate, the developing professional needs to do more than simply spend time with clients. Client contact must be monitored by supervisors who can use it as the basis for imparting the practitioner-based knowledge of the field.

The helping professional who has gained experience *without* the benefit of supervision is likely to have acquired skills and work habits that are at variance with usual standards of practice. It has been the experience of many of us who have provided clinical training that the most troublesome trainee is often the one who has extensive unsupervised human service experience—gained, for example, in a drug or alcohol treatment setting—and has returned to school for more formal training. Such trainees tend to have unwarranted confidence in and commitment to their own idiosyncratic approaches.

Hill, Charles, and Reed (1981) reported empirical data that seem to support this. In their study, previous counseling experience was found *not* to accelerate the clinical progress of students in a doctoral-level psychology program. In studies of the progression of trainees through hypothesized developmental stages, both Wiley and Ray (1986) and Reising and Daniels (1983) found that although *supervised* counseling experience correlated with the supervisory needs of trainees, unsupervised experience did not. Yet another study that supports this is that of Bradley and Olson (1980), who examined clinical psychology students' felt competence as psychotherapists. Of all the variables they examined as possible correlates (e.g., total number of hours of therapy conducted, amount of therapy course work), only two variables were related to felt-competence: the number of hours of formal supervision in which the students participated and the number of supervisors they had.

Supervision, then, must accompany client-contact experiences if students in the mental health professions are to acquire the necessary practice skills and conceptual ability. Its importance is attested to by the extent to which licensing, credentialing, and accrediting bodies require applicants to have supervision experience. States stipulate amounts and types of supervision applicants for licenses are to accrue; often this runs into thousands of hours. The same is true of such independent credentialing groups as the Academy of Certified Social Workers, the American Board of Professional Psychology, the Council for the Accreditation of Counseling and Related Educational Programs (CACREP), and the American Association for Marriage and Family Therapists. CACREP, for example, requires that a student completes a combined total of 1000 hours of practicum and internship and receives weekly a minimum of 1 hour of individual and 1.5 hours of group supervision each week during this period.

Licensing and credentialing groups, however, are intended to govern the individual professional. Another category of institutions, accrediting bodies, governs the training programs that prepare practitioners, specifying the scope, content, and quality of training. Like the licensing and credentialing groups, the accrediting groups stipulate amounts and conditions of supervision. The American Psychological Association, for example, requires that students receive 400 hours of practicum

experience, of which 75 hours must be in formally scheduled supervision, prior to their predoctoral internship (American Psychological Association, 1986).

But this supervised training experience is not limited to the period in which the trainee is enrolled in a formal degree program. States almost invariably stipulate a particular amount of supervised clinical experience that must be acquired after completing the degree. In addition to the appropriate licensure, many agencies also require newly hired professionals to be supervised to ensure the quality of care for their clients.

Whereas supervision is an essential component in the preparation of competent mental health professionals, it also is essential as a means of protecting the welfare of clients seen by these trainees. The work of trainees has real consequences in the lives of the people for whom they care. Although we wish those consequences always to be positive, that simply is not the case. Supervisors, then, are obligated to monitor the quality of care provided to clients by trainees.

In summary, then, supervision is a means of transmitting the skills, knowledge, and attitudes of a particular profession to the next generation in that profession. It also is an essential means of ensuring that clients receive a certain minimum quality of care while trainees work with them to gain their skills.

Because supervision is such an essential aspect of professional training and because so much of it is required, it should not be surprising that it is one of the more frequent activities of mental health professionals. Over a decade ago, Garfield and Kurtz (1976) found that supervision was fifth in a list of activities in which clinical psychologists engaged, ranking ahead of such activities as group therapy and research. Similar results have emerged in recent studies of counseling psychologists (e.g., Fitzgerald & Osipow, 1986; Watkins, Lopez, Campbell, & Himmell, 1936), and Kadushin (1976) reported that, depending on their field of practice, between 12.6 percent and 20 percent of social workers have some supervisory responsibilities.

But this frequently used and essential intervention is distinct from other interventions. As we shall discuss, supervision has elements in common with other interventions such as teaching, therapy, and consultation but is unique among them. For this reason its practitioners should receive specific preparation. Yet in their survey of new supervisors, McColley and Baker (1982) found that only 20 percent had taken a course or seminar in supervision; about 50 percent had *some* training in supervision. Similarly, Hess and Hess (1983) found that ongoing training of supervisors occurs in only about 40 percent of psychology internship training sites.

One hindrance to the development of more universal training of supervisors has been the fact that so many mental health professionals have taken on the role of supervisor without formal preparation. Although they lack specific training in it, they are *doing* supervision — typically believing they are pretty good at it. Consequently, they are more inclined to believe that if they have learned it without formal preparation, then their students and trainees can as easily do so. These faculty and field supervisors often serve as role models for trainees, who may receive mixed messages about the ·ctual importance of supervision training.

But increasing attention has been given to the training of supervisors. An exciting and relatively recent development has been the implementation of standards and procedures for certifying supervisors. Within the counseling profession, for example, the Association for Counselor Education and Supervision (ACES) has authored a Standards for Counselor Supervision (ACES, 1988; see Appendix A), and the American Association for Marriage and Family Therapy has a supervisor membership category that requires specified training.

This book is intended for mental health professionals, regardless of their specific discipline, who are preparing to become clinical supervisors. Supervision researchers and writers in the various disciplines often have ignored the related literature available in the books and journals of sister disciplines; even those who are aware of this and attempt broad reviews of supervision literature sometimes will treat it as if it were comprised of separate literatures (e.g., Loganbill, Hardy, & Delworth, 1982). Yet despite the unique histories and traditions of each discipline, there are certain essential processes and issues in supervision that are common to all. This book focuses on those commonalties.

## SUPERVISION DEFINED

We have heard colleagues assert that the term *supervision* derives from the "super" vision that supervisors allegedly possess. Although this definition of the term is glib, it does suggest a wish that many supervisors must entertain. Moreover, there is a small grain of truth to the idea of having super vision: Supervisors do seem to gain a clarity of perspective about the counseling or therapy precisely because they are not one of the parties involved. In this, they work from a unique vantage point that is not afforded the therapist.

Levenson (1984) indicated this when he observed that in the ordinary course of his work as a therapist, he spent a considerable time perplexed, confused, bored, and "at sea." But "when I supervise, all is clear to me" (p. 153). He reported finding that theoretical and technical difficulties were surprisingly clear to him. Moreover, he maintained that he found that those of his supervisees who seemed confused most of the time reported that they attained a similar clarity when they supervise. He speculated that this is "an odd, seductive aspect of the phenomenology of the supervisory process itself" (p. 154) that occurs because it is an intervention at a different level of abstraction than therapy.

Despite this, however, supervisors do not have super vision. Nor does this definition of the term capture supervision's essential meaning. The definition of supervision is simply "to oversee" (Merriam-Webster Dictionary, 1974). In fact, this is what clinical supervisors do. But this definition is too inclusive to suggest the actual functions of those who supervise trainees in the mental health disciplines. It encompasses the activities of a great number of other professionals, including possibly administrative supervisors in business and industry; its range even could extend to such groups as financial auditors and probation officers.

The working definitions of supervision that have been offered by various authors differ considerably as a result of such factors as the author's discipline and training focus. Our intent in this book is to offer a definition that is specific enough to be helpful but at the same time broad enough to encompass the multiple roles, disciplines, and settings associated with supervision. Before offering that definition, it might be useful to consider two definitions that have been offered.

Loganbill et al. (1982) define supervision as "an intensive, interpersonally focused one-to-one relationship in which one person is designated to facilitate the development of therapeutic competence in the other person" (p. 4). In contrast to the definition of supervision as "to oversee," which was too broad and inclusive to be helpful, this one suggests a focus more narrow and restrictive than that which we intend to maintain in this book. For example, in their consideration of supervision as something that occurs only in the context of a one-to-one relationship, Loganbill et al. (1982) overlooked group supervision. Group supervision, however, is a modality that clinical supervisors employ quite frequently (Holloway & Johnston, 1985).

In declaring their goal to be the development of the trainee's therapeutic competence, Loganbill et al. (1982) leave no room for supervising other psychological services such as psychoeducation or career counseling. Although a large portion of this book focuses on the supervision of psychotherapy, we believe many of the essential issues and processes remain the same in the supervision of other psychological interventions. Finally, the Loganbill et al. (1982) definition does not acknowledge explicitly the client-protective function of supervision.

Hart's (1982) definition more closely approximates the definition we intend to consider although it, too, seems to suggest a one-to-one focus. Hart states that supervision is "an ongoing educational process in which one person in the role of supervisor helps another person in the role of the supervisee acquire appropriate professional behavior through an examination of the supervisee's professional activities" (p. 12).

For this book, we are offering the following working definition of supervision: An intervention that is provided by a senior member of a profession to a junior member or members of that same profession. This relationship is evaluative, extends over time, and has the simultaneous purposes of enhancing the professional functioning of the junior member(s), monitoring the quality of professional services offered to the clients she, he, or they see(s), and serving as a gatekeeper for those who are to enter the particular profession.

This succinct definition merits further explication. It is useful to break it into its component parts for a more extended consideration of each part. Prior to doing this, however, we wish to offer a brief discussion of the terms we will use in this book. Because we are writing for a multidisciplinary audience and terminology differs somewhat across the several mental health disciplines, we believe it is important to do this for the sake of clarity.

We have chosen to use *trainee* and *supervisee* interchangeably and will occasionally intend *therapist* to designate this same role as a means of acknowledging the increasing frequency of postgraduate supervision. Similarly, we will use *counseling, therapy,* and *psychotherapy* throughout the book to refer to the same intervention. Although it is possible in some instances to distinguish among them, Patterson (1986) has pointed out that usually such distinctions are artificial and serve little function. Finally, throughout most of the book we will follow the convention suggested by Rogers (1951) of referring to the recipient of therapeutic services as a *client*.

In the section that follows, we will make distinctions between supervision and several interventions with which it has overlapping purposes and processes. We wish to make a special mention here, however, about what we perceive to be the distinction between supervision and training. Both are essential components in the imparting of therapeutic skills, and often the boundaries between them do seem to blur. In fact, they often are treated together in reviews of literature (e.g., Matarazzo & Patterson, 1986). Training differs from supervision, however, in that it has a more limited scope and focuses on specific skills (e.g., how to offer restatements of client affect and content). Also, training often takes place in laboratory courses rather than in real clinical settings. We will not use the terms interchangeably.

We turn now to offering a more complete explication of our working definition of supervision. Each of the following sections addresses a specific element of that definition.

### Supervision Is a Distinct Intervention

Supervision is an intervention as are education, psychotherapy, and mental health consultation. Although there are ways in which it overlaps substantially with these other interventions, it is unique.

*Education Versus Supervision.* Like education, a purpose of supervision is to teach; the role of the supervisee is that of a learner (notice the title of the classic Ekstein and Wallerstein book, *The teaching and learning of psychotherapy,* 1972). Moreover, education and supervision are alike in that there is an evaluative aspect to the intervention. Each ultimately serves a gatekeeping function, regulating who is legitimized to enter the world of work in a chosen area.

In education, however, there typically is an explicit curriculum with teaching goals that are imposed uniformly on everyone. Education in this sense certainly does occur in clinical preparation. In fact, training (to impart specific skills such as the ability to reflect feelings) is an example of this. But even though the focus of supervision at its broadest level (to prepare competent practitioners) might seem to point to common goals, the actual intervention is tailored to meet the needs of individual trainees and their clients.

*Counseling Versus Supervision.* There are also elements of counseling, or therapy, in supervision. That is, the supervisor may help the supervisee to examine aspects of his or her behavior, thoughts, or feelings that are stimulated by a client, particularly when these may act as barriers to the work with the client. Any therapeutic intervention with the trainee, however, should be *only* in the service of helping the trainee to become more effective with clients: To provide therapy that has broader goals is an ethical problem.

There are differences, too. For example, clients generally are free to enter therapy or not; when they do, they usually have a voice in choosing their therapists. Trainees, on the other hand, are not given a choice about whether to receive supervision and often have no voice in whom their supervisor is to be.

It may be that the single most important difference between therapy and supervision resides in the evaluative responsibilities of the supervisor. Although few would maintain that counseling or therapy is or could be entirely value free, most therapists do resist actively imposing their values on clients or making explicit evaluations of them. On the other hand, supervisees are evaluated against criteria that are imposed on them by others.

*Consultation Versus Supervision.* Mental health consultation is yet another intervention that overlaps with supervision. In fact, for senior professionals supervision often evolves into consultation. That is, the experienced therapist might meet informally on an occasional basis with a colleague to get ideas about how to handle a particularly difficult client or to regain needed objectivity. We all encounter blind spots in ourselves, and it is to our benefit to get help in this manner.

But despite the similarities, there are distinctions between consultation and supervision. Caplan (1970), for example, has suggested several of these. One distinction is that the parties in the consultation relationship often are not of the same professional discipline (e.g., a social worker might consult with a teacher about a child's problem). Another distinction is that consultation is more likely to be a one-time-only event than is supervision.

Two consultation-supervision distinctions echo distinctions already made between therapy and supervision. One is that supervision is more likely imposed whereas consultation is typically freely sought. More significantly, there is no evaluative role for the consultant — Caplan (1970) maintained that the relationship was between two equals — whereas evaluation is one of the defining attributes of supervision.

In summary, then, specific aspects of such related interventions as education, therapy, and consultation also are present as components of supervision. That is, certain skills of teachers, therapists, and consultants are common in supervision as well. But although there are common skills across these several interventions, the manner in which they are arrayed is different in each intervention.

Martin (1990) makes some useful remarks about skills that have implications for thinking about supervision and its relationship to the interventions of counseling, education, and consultation.

> *The word* skill *has a specific meaning. It is an ability that can be perfected by training and exercise of the ability itself, usually without much regard to the particular context in which it may be put to use. Thus, dribbling a basketball is a skill; so too is typing or enunciation of words and phrases in oral speech. Of course, matters are complicated somewhat by the fact that any skill typically can be subdivided into various subskills. Skills also can be combined with other skills, at a similar level and category, to comprise more inclusive skills. Nonetheless, there is much more to playing basketball, writing meaningful prose, or effective public speaking than dribbling, typing or enunciating. (p. 403)*

To put this into a context relevant to this book, supervision should be thought of as an intervention that is comprised of multiple skills, many of which are common to other forms of intervention. Yet their configuration is such that it makes supervision unique among psychological interventions. Moreover, there is at least one phenomenon — that of parallel, or reciprocal, processes (see, for example, Doehrman, 1976; Searles, 1955) — that is unique to supervision and distinguishes it from other interventions. (Parallel processes are discussed in Chapter 2.)

## Monitoring of Client Care

Although the teaching and learning of goals of supervision are the usual focus of supervision literature, it is important that supervisors never lose sight of the fact that the monitoring of client care is an essential supervision goal. In fact, Loganbill et al (1982) correctly maintain that this is the supervisor's *paramount* responsibility. Blocher (1983) stated it bluntly when he observed that clients "are not expendable laboratory animals to be blithely sacrificed in the name of training" (p. 29). If a sense of professional responsibility is not enough motivation to keep the supervisor focused on monitoring quality of client care, then self-interest should be: As we will discuss in Chapter 10, the concept of vicarious liability is that the supervisor can be held liable for any harm done by a supervisee.

It is useful to remember that the original purpose of clinical supervision was to monitor the quality of care given the clients. Supervision in the mental health disciplines almost certainly began with social work supervision, which "dates from the nineteenth century Charity Organization Societies in which paid social work agents supervised the moral treatment of the poor by friendly visitors" (Harkness & Poertner, 1989, p. 115). The focus of this supervision was on the *client*.

Eisenberg (1956) notes that the first known call for supervision to focus on the professional rather than exclusively on the client was expressed by Zilphia Smith in 1901. Such a shift in focus apparently had occurred briefly during the depression of 1893 in the face of large caseloads. This supervisory focus did not become the norm, however, until approximately the time of the depression of the 1930s when supervisors were influenced by the combination of large caseloads, the influence of Freud's new psychology, and a greater emphasis on the professional training of social workers (Harkness & Poertner, 1989).

But despite its importance, the need to ensure quality of client care is one job demand with a particular potential for causing dissonance in the supervisor. Most of the time, supervisors are able to perceive themselves as allies of their supervisees. Yet they also must be prepared, if they see harm being done to clients, to risk bruising the egos of their supervisees — or, in extreme cases, even to be an instrument in steering the supervisee from the

profession. From the perspective of supervisees, especially those with autonomy conflicts, this aspect of supervision can lead to what Kadushin (1976) spoke of as "snooper vision."

### Supervisors and Supervisees Are of the Same Profession

The widely acknowledged purpose of supervision is to facilitate supervisees' development of therapeutic and case management skills. Certainly this is essential. Moreover, it is possible to accomplish this purpose when the supervisory dyad is comprised of members of two different disciplines (e.g., a marital and family therapist supervising the work of a counselor). Although this results in technical competence, it is an arrangement that overlooks the socialization function that supervision serves. Trainees are developing a sense of professional identity, and it is best acquired through association with senior members of the trainees' own professional discipline. Ekstein and Wallerstein (1972) point to this when they note that if all a training program were to do was to provide its trainees with all the basic psychotherapeutic skills, it would have fallen short. They note that skill acquisition is not enough: "What would still be missing is a specific quality in the psychotherapist that makes him [or her] into a truly professional person, a quality we wish to refer to as his [or her] professional identity" (p. 65).

If one consequence of supervision is that supervisees are socialized into a profession, this must be accomplished by supervisors serving as role models. It follows, then, that most of the supervisors with whom a supervisee works be of the profession in which the supervisee intends to be a member. Social work students should receive supervision from social workers; counseling psychology students should receive supervision from counseling psychologists; and so on. Most state laws that govern the licensure of mental health professions stipulate that applicants have a certain portion of their supervised clinical hours from supervisors of a like profession. Ekstein and Wallerstein (1972) observe that this is normative. The major exception occurs with multidisciplinary training institutes that offer postgraduate preparation in a specific approach (e.g., psychoanalytic, Jungian, rational emotive, strategic).

It is true that counseling or psychotherapy provides a nexus for the several mental health professions. Certain therapeutic skills are common across all of these groups; it is possible for members of one mental health profession to be helpful to members of another mental health profession. At the same time, however, each of the professions is in some way distinct, with its own history and philosophy; each also has functions more common to it than to the others. These professional traditions and world views are passed on through the mentoring relationship of the supervisory relationship. As we already have discussed, one distinction Caplan (1970) offers between consultation and supervision centers on whether the interactants are of the same profession.

In a cautionary tale of the adverse consequences of using members of one profession to supervise new members of another profession, Albee (1970) invoked the metaphor of the cuckoo: The cuckoo is a bird that lays its eggs in the nests of other birds who then raise the offspring as their own. His case in point was clinical psychology, which had used the Veterans Administration system as a primary base of training in the decades following World War II. From Albee's perspective, this was unfortunate, for the clinical psychology fledglings were put in the care of psychiatrists who then socialized them into their way of viewing the world. Albee asserted that a consequence of this pervasive practice was that clinical psychology lost some of what was unique to it as its members incorporated the perspectives of psychiatry.

**Supervision Is Evaluative**

We already have mentioned several times that evaluation is an aspect of supervision that stands as one of its hallmarks, distinguishing it from both counseling, or therapy, and consultation. Evaluation is implicit in supervisors' mandate to safeguard clients—both those currently being seen by trainees and those who will be seen by trainees who finish the training program.

Evaluation is also a tool in that it provides the supervisor with an important source of interpersonal influence. For example, although most trainees have a very high degree of intrinsic motivation to learn and to use feedback to self-correct, evaluation can provide an additional, extrinsic motivation to change or evolve, particularly to those supervisees who might not be as self-monitoring as they should be.

But despite its importance as a component of supervision, both supervisor and supervisee can experience evaluation with discomfort. Supervisors, for example, were trained first in the more nonevaluative role of counselor or therapist. Indeed, they may well have been attracted to the field because of this aspect. The role of evaluator can be not only new but uncomfortable.

Doehrman (1976) has addressed some of the facts of life imposed on the supervisee by evaluation:

> *Students are not only taught psychotherapy by their supervisors, they are also evaluated by them. The criteria for evaluating students' performances tend to be subjective and ambiguous, in large part because the skills being evaluated are highly complex, intensely personal, and difficult to measure. Students know that their psychological health, interpersonal skills, and therapeutic competence are being judged against unclear standards. . . . Supervisors are thus not only admired teachers but feared judges who have real power. (pp. 10–11).*

Evaluation, then, is an important, integral component of supervision and one that is often the source of problems for supervisors and supervisees alike. For these reasons we have devoted an entire chapter of this book to the topic of evaluation. Although there is no way in which evaluation could, or should, be removed from supervision, there are ways to enhance its usefulness and to minimize problems attendant to it. These will be discussed.

**Supervision Extends Over Time**

The final element of our definition of supervision is that it is an intervention that extends over time. This distinguishes supervision from training, which might be brief, as in, for example, a workshop intended to impart a specific skill; it also distinguishes supervision from consultation, which might be very time limited as one professional seeks the help of another to gain or regain objectivity in working with a client.

The fact that it is ongoing allows the supervisor-supervisee relationship to grow and develop. Indeed, some supervision theorists have focused particular attention on the growing, developing nature of this relationship. The particular focus of Mueller and Kell's (1972) book, for example, was on the process of resolving the relationship conflicts that inevitably arise between supervisor and supervisee. Their belief was that successful conflict resolution strengthens and advances the relationship. This is similar to Bordin's (1983) proposition that supervision involves a working alliance similar to that which is present in therapy—one in which there are both weakenings and repairs that cumulatively affect the supervisor-supervisee relationship and the work that the two accomplish. It is perhaps significant that the working alliance is a lens through which researchers increasingly are beginning to view the supervisory relationship.

## CONCLUSION

Issues raised in this chapter will be discussed in much greater detail in the chapters that follow. Additionally, certain other issues will be introduced. For example, because we live in a society that is increasingly diverse, it is important that supervisors have sensitivity to racial, ethnic, and gender issues that may affect their work. This is the focus of Chapter 11.

We mentioned earlier the two realms of knowledge (Schön, 1983) that are the basis of professional training: the theory and research that are the focus of university training and the knowledge derived from practitioners' experiences. We said, also, that these are not and should not be distinct, for they are actually complementary. We should note here that our own preference is for a scientist-practitioner perspective. Material in this book, therefore, will be drawn from both realms of knowledge with the belief that each informs the other. In fact, the concluding chapter outlines some ideas about how supervision research should take from the richness of the observations and hunches of practitioners; practitioners, in turn, should be able to draw from research findings to enrich their work as supervisors.

# CHAPTER 2

# CONCEPTUALIZING SUPERVISION

Clinical supervision remains a relatively new professional domain (Leddick & Bernard, 1980; Liddle, Breunlin, Schwartz, & Constantine, 1984; Loganbill, Hardy, & Delworth, 1982). Still in its adolescence, supervision is growing energetically, and sometimes randomly, as a science and practice. As a consequence, the literature is rich with options for both the practitioner and the researcher but often seems to lack order and continuity.

Supervision practices traditionally have paralleled those of psychotherapy (Leddick & Bernard, 1980). Supervisors relied on their therapy training to find answers to supervision problems. But one index of the growing maturity of the science and practice of supervision is that new models are emerging that are independent of psychotherapy. (Few of these proposed models, however, have yet been subjected to empirical scrutiny [Russell, Crimmings, & Lent, 1984].)

In the face of all these developments, graduate training programs have been slow to offer comprehensive supervision education and training, even to doctoral students. Instead, they have often continued to rely on an apprenticeship form of supervision, a practice that may or may not give ample attention to underlying assumptions and conceptualizations. Although there is value in such an approach, its effects can be serendipitous; it is incomplete as an educational or training model. As Hart (1982) noted, "one can imitate an outstanding supervisor, but without theory or a conceptual model one does not really understand the process of supervision" (p. 27). Hart then suggested that every supervisor has had to become a theorist in that many have been forced to practice without the luxury of having studied conceptual models.

The conceptualization of supervision parallels that of therapy in that therapists are required to come to grips with multiple approaches that are based on competing beliefs. Supervisors are even more likely than therapists, however, to have a blended orientation. In part, this is because supervisors work from *both* therapeutic and educational models. At the same time, supervisors are less likely to be able to articulate their conceptual assumptions than are therapists, even if they are no less consistent in their practice. This is because the training of therapists has been more grounded in theoretical content than has been that of supervisors.

This chapter will consider the conceptualization of supervision in some depth. Prior to embarking on this task, however, we would like to isolate one view of supervision from the others because it is the "no model" form of supervision. By this we mean that the supervisor has failed to address the role of supervisor as different from the role of therapist. This is not the same as the supervisor who uses a theory of psychotherapy to define supervision. The latter believes that the trainee will be influenced to learn based on the same principles that lead a client to change. The no-model practitioner has not yet made a conceptual leap to supervision and has identified no assumptions, goals, or behaviors that are unique to supervision. The only assumption made by this approach is that a good therapist will make a good supervisor.

Assuming this is analogous to assuming that a good athlete will make a good coach or, in some cases, a good sports announcer. But yet we can all look to our favorite sport to find data that tell us that this is not always the case. The great players tend not to become the great coaches and vice versa. On the other hand, most great coaches have played the game, and some of them have played quite well. It is because of this close but not quite perfect relationship between therapy and supervision that the no-model form of supervision still exists and yet has been found insufficient for most practitioners.

In short, some supervisors engage in a process they refer to as supervision without any awareness of the knowledge base that is specific to that intervention. To us, such supervisors seem analogous to the paraprofessional therapist who has learned some of the rudimentary skills of helping but lacks an adequate conceptual understanding of the process.

Figure 2.1 represents one way to depict the growth of the clinical supervision field and the interconnectedness among various conceptualizations. We have identified two general types of supervision models: those that are grounded in psychotherapy theory and practice and those that have been developed independently from psychotherapy to speak specifically to the process of supervision. This is, of course, but one map of the playing field. Others might dispute its boundaries. For example, there has been considerable debate about the actual underpinnings of the various conceptual models (e.g., Holloway, 1987; Stoltenberg & Delworth, 1988). Although no map will find universal agreement, there is utility in having one. The one depicted in Figure 2.1 will be used as the basis for organizing this chapter.

The five approaches to conceptualizing supervision that we will discuss are psychotherapy based, developmental, model based, personal growth, and parallel process and iso-morphism. The order of presentation reflects our beliefs about the relative importance of each to our present understanding of clinical supervision. As we will emphasize in Chapter 12, however, this by no means exhausts the possible conceptualizations of supervision. Rather, this chapter reflects only our present understanding of a young field. Chapter 12 is intended to help direct the reader to some of the kinds of issues that must be addressed for the field to continue to mature theoretically.

Finally, although we have attempted in Figure 2.1 to identify connections among certain perspectives on supervision, the text of the chapter will not parallel that attempt. In part, this is a function of the supervision literature that has been more concerned with the proliferation of ideas than with the task of consolidation. Also, although we may identify in Figure 2.1 a theoretical antecedent of a later development in the field (e.g., person-centered and Gestalt therapies as antecedents of personal growth supervision), we perceive each development to be more distinct from its origins than connected. Therefore, we allow each perspective to stand on its own merit.

## PSYCHOTHERAPY-BASED SUPERVISION

We are using a very specific definition of the *psychotherapy-based* supervisor. Although all supervisors incorporate psychological theory into their work, the psychotherapy-based supervisor is one whose supervision is based totally and consistently on the supervisor's theory of psychotherapy or counseling. This includes hypothesizing about the trainees in terms of normal and abnormal personality, or family, development. Such hypotheses are used much less by supervisors who rely on conceptual models of supervision.

At this juncture we would like to make the point that drawing from psychotherapy theory is not the same as developing a theory of supervision. Although applied to the supervisory process, these theories have not been

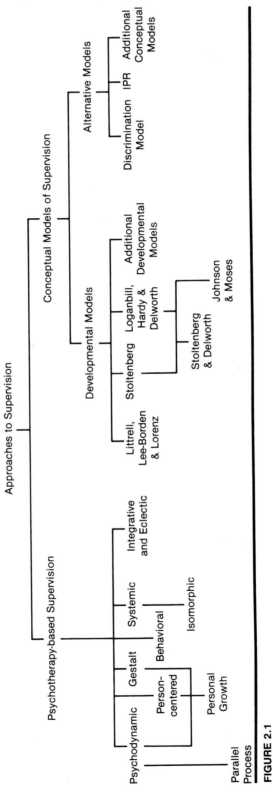

**FIGURE 2.1**

12

developed within the context of supervision. Therefore, although much of the supervision literature reflects this type of therapy-to-supervision extrapolation, there are substantial limits to it (see Chapter 12 for a more extended discussion). Additionally, we believe there are fewer purely psychotherapy-based supervisors than one might think — most seem to incorporate other approaches into their supervision.

Those psychotherapy approaches that have addressed supervision include the psychodynamic school, the person-centered school, the behavioral school, and, more recently, the systemic school. In addition to the theoretical orientations named, we will consider eclectic or integrative approaches to supervision.

Although one initially might believe that developmental theory constitutes another psychotherapy-based school, this generally is not the case. Most developmental supervision models have drawn from such other areas as cognitive structure to conceptualize development (see, for example, Holloway's 1987 critique). Therefore, we have decided to treat developmental supervision as a type of conceptual model.

## Psychodynamic Supervision

Supervision from the psychodynamic perspective has the longest history in the helping professions of working with both individuals and families. This is not only because Freud preceded the creators of other therapeutic approaches, but also because supervision has always been integrated into the analytic training model. In order to take on the responsibility of clients and be up to the task of reacting appropriately to transference and countertransference issues, therapists themselves by necessity needed to undergo analysis and participate later in control analysis supervisions.

For both therapy and supervision, resistance to change in the psychodynamic framework is understood to be the reaction to conflict caused by intrapsychic conflict. Of course, for the client and the trainee, this conflict is outside of conscious awareness. Therefore, the task for supervisors is to help trainees understand their inner (and repressed) conflicts just as this is the therapists' task with clients.

But as Ekstein and Wallerstein (1972) asserted, supervision is not therapy. Its purpose is to teach, and the reason for working closely with trainees is to have them learn how to understand the dynamics of resolving conflict (Mueller & Kell, 1972) for the benefit of future work with clients. Moldawsky (1980) explained the instructional motive of control analysis another way:

> *The necessity is based on the observation that anxiety in the patient induces anxiety in the therapist, and unless the therapist is open to the experience, he/she will defend against the anxiety by characterological or symptomatic defenses and will unconsciously encourage repression in the patient, rather than exposure. (p. 126)*

Stated simply, the supervisor, using a process similar to therapy, teaches the trainee to be open to experience. Moldawsky goes on to say that the therapist ultimately must learn the "analytic attitude" (p. 126), which includes patience, trust in the analytic process, interest in the client, and respect for the power and tenacity of client resistance. An assumption of psychodynamic supervision is that the best way for the trainee to learn these qualities is by receiving the same in the supervisory relationship.

Although the goals of supervision are intended to be separate from the goals of therapy, the boundaries between the two often become blurred. Mueller and Kell (1972) stated that "the heart of supervision consists of a series of deepening, recycling excursions into [the trainee's] personality and the anxiety and conflicts generated through intense interaction" (p. viii). Ekstein and Wallerstein (1972) expected both emotional and behavioral change as a result of supervision. This is reinforced by Mueller and Kell (1972) who shared the term *impasse* with the Gestaltists and expected supervisees both to arrive at and struggle through psychological blocks to supervision. They predicted that this would happen through identification with the supervisor. In short, it is expected that trainees will resist change, that supervision will call for personal exploration into deep-seated conflicts (Russell, Crimmings, & Lent, 1984), and that trainees will leave the supervisory relationship as different persons from when they entered. Goals aside, much of the above sounds more like therapy than not.

Moldawsky (1980) addressed this confusion between therapy and supervision. His resolution was to structure his remarks to trainees in a manner that was less intrusive into their personal lives. He might, therefore, point to the trainee's resistance but not search for the roots of the resistance in the trainee's past. The latter, he argued, should happen in analysis, not in supervision. This middle of the road position is possibly more representative of present-day psychodynamic supervision.

An additional concept that is important to psychodynamic supervision is that of parallel process. According to this principle, the conflicts between therapists and clients will be reenacted between supervisors and therapists. Because of recent developments in the supervision discipline, we believe parallel process has emerged as a perspective in its own right, and we will address it separately. However, its roots are clearly in psychodynamic supervision theory.

The following is an excerpt from a psychodynamic supervision session presented by Fleming and Benedek (1966). Although brief and out of context, it will give you an example of the tone taken by one psychodynamic supervisor. Prior to this excerpt, the trainee and

supervisor were discussing how the trainee handled the client's wish that he not be addressed by name in therapy. (S is the supervisor; T, the therapist)

S: *Yes, but actually what did you do?*
T: *I cut off his flow of association.*
S: *Not only did you cut off his flow of associations but you defended yourself against analyzing his transference reaction. When he tells you, "I wish you wouldn't call me anything," that means, "I wish that you would not become something for me, but would remain nothing, nobody, just an institution—analysis." Now that doesn't exist. You have to become somebody. You were just as afraid of the closeness as he was. And so you responded to his feeling, "O.K., you leave me alone and I'll leave you alone," and so on.*
T: *I didn't follow up what we thought was so important last time: his formulation of his relationship problem.*
S: *Well, relationship is the major problem for everybody. I think that you actually cling to that, defending yourself against how sick that boy is. He's afraid of his sadism and criminality, homosexuality and otherwise, and you say, "O.K., that is all a relationship problem." You always protect yourself against how ill that boy is; this time you really defended yourself against his transference reactions to you. You accept his defenses. Now, you see, there is nothing wrong in accepting his defenses, but you have to think why you do accept his defenses. Why are you so afraid of his illness? (p. 93)*

For an additional example, see Appendix D, which includes a transcript of Rudolph Ekstein conducting supervision from a psychodynamic perspective. Ekstein is a noted psychoanalyst who has written extensively about both psychotherapy and supervision. In fact, his book with Wallerstein (Ekstein & Wallerstein, 1972) is regarded as one of the seminal works in supervision.

## Person-centered Supervision

Over 25 years ago, Patterson (1964) said that client-centered supervision was an influencing process that incorporated elements of teaching and therapy even though it was neither. More recently, Carl Rogers seemed to be leaning more toward therapy. In an interview with Goodyear, he stated,

> *I think my major goal is to help the therapist to grow in self-confidence and to grow in understanding of himself or herself, and to grow in understanding the therapeutic process. And to that end, I find it very fruitful to explore any difficulties the therapist may feel he or she is having working with the client. Supervision for me becomes a modified form of the therapeutic interview. (Hackney & Goodyear, 1984, p. 283)*

Later in the same interview, Goodyear asked Rogers how he differentiated supervision from therapy. He answered,

> *I think there is no clean way. I think it does exist on a continuum. Sometimes therapists starting in to discuss some of the problems they're having with a client will look deeply into themselves and it's straight therapy. Sometimes it is more concerned with problems of the relationship and that is clearly supervision. But in that sense, too, I will follow the lead, in this case, the lead of the therapist. The one difference is I might feel more free to express how I might have done it than I would if I were dealing with a client. (p. 285)*

It is clear from Rogers's words that he did not stray too far from his counseling theory in his supervision. He felt it was as equally necessary to establish facilitating conditions for the trainee as it was for the client. Rice (1980) described person-centered supervision as relying on a theory of process in the context of relationship. The successful person-centered supervisor must have a profound trust that trainees have within themselves the ability and motivation to grow and explore both the therapy situation and the self. This is the same type of trust that the therapist must have, for without it, person-centered therapy or supervision is doomed (Rice, 1980).

Regardless of the ongoing debate as to whether the facilitative conditions are "necessary and sufficient" (Rogers, 1957), the tenets of this theory of psychotherapy have been incorporated into most training programs as "basic responding skills" (Hackney & Goodyear, 1984). Rogers and his followers taught us to listen and to communicate our understanding in a way that most of us had not experienced prior to our training as professional helpers. But person-centered supervision is more than listening and responding; it is believing in the phenomenological process to such an extent that the wisdom of giving advice or instruction becomes a moot issue. It is stepping into the experience of those we wish to influence. It is a mirror and a paradox.

The following is a segment of a supervision session in which Carl Rogers works with Harold Hackney after having viewed 25 minutes of a videotaped therapy session Hackney conducted. Prior to this segment, Hackney expressed feeling compelled to direct the session in order to know what focus to take to move the client along. Rogers reacts to this.

R: *And the focus is really up to you?*

H: *I've been assuming some responsibility for it, yes.*

R: *Did you ever express that to her?*

H: *Not in so many words. I'm sure that on a couple of occasions I've asked her "What is it you'd really like to see happen as a result of counseling?" But I think I've done that indirectly.*

R: *Almost as if you've been drawing the answers from her rather than expressing your own feeling of uncomfortableness.*

H: *I think that's fair, yes. I think that is what I've been doing.*

R: *Sort of wish she would answer your questions for you.*

H: *Probably that's part of it. I think a part of me also would like for her to discover some self-direction maybe. Maybe I'm believing in that too much at this point. But yes, I've been trying to pull it out of her rather than to express myself. I think what you're hitting on there may be one of the, the qualities of this relationship that we have—that, ah, that I'm removed in it, a bit.*

R: *In the portion we saw of the interview, any particular things trouble you there?*

H: *I think she was working well, there, in that part, uh, I wish it were like that more often.*

R: *What do you feel about your own function? (Hackney & Goodyear, 1984, pp. 288-290)*

As the reader certainly will note, Rogers used several reflective comments to bring out the therapist and allow him to confront his own behavior. This is consistent with a person-centered therapy style. (The complete transcript of this supervision session can be found in Appendix D.)

## Behavioral Supervision

Behaviorism, based on learning theory, is well established in psychology, counseling, and social work (Linehan, 1980). Behavior therapy began by manipulating overt behavior, but soon cognitive behaviorism emerged to correct negative and self-defeating thinking (Beck, 1976; Ellis, 1974; Mahoney, 1974, 1977; Meichenbaum, 1977), and sociobehaviorism evolved for the treatment of families (Everett & Koerpel, 1986). Additionally, the systemic therapies, especially strategic family therapy, have obvious behavioral underpinnings. Whether working with the individual or with a larger system, the behavioral supervisor, like the behavioral therapist, operates on the assumption that both adaptive and maladaptive behaviors are learned and maintained through the systematic delivery of conditioning and reinforcement procedures (Russell et al., 1984). It is probably no surprise that behavioral supervisors have been more specific and more systematic than supervisors of other orienta-

tions in their presentation of the goals and processes of supervision.

As reported elsewhere (Leddick & Bernard, 1980), Wolpe, Knopp, and Garfield (1966) were among the first to outline procedures for behavioral supervision. They listed three distinct alternatives to accomplish this: an apprenticeship model that they favored but found time consuming, an ongoing seminar that would involve instruction and case presentations, and an intensive training session that would add demonstrations of techniques and role playing with peers to didactic instruction. Those of us involved in the training of helping professionals can see the impact these thinkers had on supervisors who followed them. In fact, most training programs incorporate some form of skills training, and as Hackney (1971) recommended, most receive training prior to seeing their first client.

In the past two decades, many behavioral training or supervision models have been put forth (Boyd, 1978; Delaney, 1972; Jakubowski-Spector, Dustin, & George, 1971; Levine & Tilker, 1974; Lineham, 1980; Schmidt, 1979). As Boyd (1978) stated, most behavioral models represent variations of the following four propositions:

1. *Proficient therapist performance is more a function of learned skills than a "personality fit." The purpose of supervision is to teach appropriate therapist behaviors and extinguish inappropriate behavior[s].*
2. *The therapist's professional role consists of identifiable tasks, each one requiring specific skills. Training and supervision should assist the trainee in developing these skills, applying and refining them.*
3. *Therapy skills are behaviorally definable and are responsive to learning theory, just as are other behaviors.*
4. *Supervision should employ the principles of learning theory within its procedures. (p. 89)*

The supervisory methods typically described by behavioral supervisors include establishing a trusting relationship, skill analysis and assessment, setting goals for the trainee, construction and implementation of strategies to accomplish goals, and follow-up evaluation and generalization of learning (Bradley, 1989). Additionally, Schmidt (1979), translating cognitive behaviorism to supervision, attempted to correct the trainee's negative self-statements that could have interfered with his or her therapy.

In summary, the behavioral supervisor defines the potential of the trainee as the potential to learn rather than the more phenomenological potential to "grow." Also, the supervisor takes at least part of the responsibility for learning to occur. Once the trainee has participated in identifying those skills that need to be learned, it is the supervisor as expert who can guide the trainee into the correct learning environment. Such is the supervision contract.

An example of behavioral supervision follows. In this simulation, the trainee is working with a client who, among other things, reports being very nervous and highly irritable with her small child.

S: *What are you planning to do in your next session?*

T: *Well, Eve says that she wants to try to find a job, but she's a wreck by mid-morning. So, she keeps putting it off until the next day. I've thought of suggesting that she arrange for someone to take care of her little boy one day a week and on that day she can job hunt. I also think she might benefit from some relaxation techniques.*

S: *I think those are both good ideas, if your client agrees. Have you ever used systematic relaxation techniques with a client?*

T: *No, I've only read about them. I was hoping you could help me with them.*

S: *Of course; I'd be happy to. I'll model them first; then you can try it with me.*

*(After modeling and practice)*

S: *How do you think you did?*

T: *I think I got the order right and presented it*

okay, but I think I rushed the whole thing a bit.

S: *Good. That's pretty much how I saw it. The pacing really was the only thing that needed improvement. The rest was fine. Why don't you rehearse again at home and audiotape it. I'll listen to the tape and give you additional feedback.*

As an example of supervision from a cognitive behaviorist standpoint, Appendix D includes a supervision session conducted by Albert Ellis.

## Systemic Supervision

Liddle and Halpin (1978) reviewed the family therapy supervision literature and found that "formal theories of supervision training have not crystallized and hence the reader is faced with the task of abstracting personally useful information from the array of literature" (p. 78). More recently, Everett and Koerpel (1986) reviewed the supervision literature and reported that the process of supervision "remains fragmented, blurred, and undeveloped" (p. 66). As a result of these and similar assertions in the family therapy field, systemic supervisors have been encouraged, at least by some authors, to be therapy based (Storm & Heath, 1985).

McDaniel, Weber, and McKeever (1983) reviewed the structural, strategic, Bowenian, and experiential schools of systemic family therapy and argued that supervision in these schools should be theoretically consistent. If the goal of the therapy, therefore, was to maintain a clear boundary between therapist and family (and between parents and children in the family), then there should be a clear boundary between the supervisor and the therapist. Furthermore, if therapy focused on family of origin issues, then the therapist must be encouraged to relate training to his or her own family of origin issues.

Some discussion has ensued regarding the appropriateness of therapy-based supervision when the therapy upon which supervision is based is nonegalitarian, if not overtly manipulative. Strategic family therapy supervision has become a case in point. Many strategic directives are paradoxical in nature or, at the very least, do not rely on the insight of the recipient. Strategic supervisors have asked themselves, therefore, if strategic interventions are appropriate for trainees.

To date, at least as reflected in the scant literature on the topic, the answer seems to be yes. Storm and Heath (1982) reported that their supervisees expected their supervisors to use strategic interventions with them. However, when supervisors were caught using such an approach, the reaction of supervisees was negative. In other words, supervisees were comfortable with the notion that they might need to be manipulated in order to learn, but they expected the manipulation to be very clever and subtle. This begs the question about what to do as supervisees gain in their own clinical skill.

Protinsky and Preli (1987) offered at least a partial solution to this dilemma. In their discussion of strategic supervision, they proposed that interventions, although admittedly manipulative, follow the development of the trainee. Therefore, as the trainee gained in therapeutic skill, the supervisor would create a situation in which the trainee would enter more of an egalitarian relationship with the supervisor. Protinsky and Preli mirrored Storm and Heath's issue of supervisee awareness, stating that "the best strategic supervisory interventions seem to be those that remain out of the awareness of the supervisee. This out-of-awareness prevents self-reflexive thinking and is useful in producing behavior change in the supervisee" (p. 23). They went on to suggest, however, that once a supervisee had made the breakthrough that the intervention called for, it was appropriate, if not desirable, for the supervisor to initiate a discussion aimed at supervisee insight.

Protinsky and Preli offered seven examples of strategic supervisory interventions

ranging from the use of paradox to "graduating to equality" (p. 22). The following example was described as the use of an aversive reframe. The therapist in the example had been working with a family made up of an acting-out adolescent, a meek and submissive mother, and an arrogant and abrasive father. The therapist had repeatedly gotten caught in struggles with the father. The supervisor had attempted to explain the situation systemically, pointing out the circular nature of the sequence (i.e., adolescent acts out, mother acts overwhelmed, father acts abrasive, therapist reacts to father), but there had been no progress to that point. In a postsession meeting the supervisor suddenly changed her position and framed the therapist's protection of the mother as positive. Who would not protect a woman from such an abrasive man? She then left without discussing the case further. The trainee was a social worker who had previously stated that she prided herself on her objectivity. Therefore, the reframe was aversive and succeeded in angering her.

The therapist at first complained to the other trainees how mistaken the supervisor was. She did not like to be perceived as protecting the mother and stated that she would never knowingly do such a thing. At the next session, however, she modified her behavior so that she could prove that she was objective. By reacting more positively toward the father and refraining from protecting the mother, the therapist was then able to use effective strategic interventions.

## Eclectic or Integrative Supervision

In one study (Goodyear & Robyak, 1982), 60 percent of the participating supervisors reported being eclectic. This is consistent with other findings about therapists' orientations (e.g., Garfield & Kurtz, 1976). It also stands to reason that seasoned practitioners will find value in more than one orientation when there has been no reported indication that any theory is superior to another in accomplishing the goals of therapy or supervision.

Being eclectic or integrative does not mean that the supervisor has less emphasis on psychological theory. In fact, it is the fear of being perceived as operating within a theoretical vacuum that has led recent authors to prefer the term *integrative* to *eclectic*.

Being eclectic implies being ungrounded and potentially operating from incompatible theoretical positions. This should be distinguished from *technical eclecticism* in which one may remain theoretically consistent but draw from a variety of techniques, even those that may originate from opposing camps.

Integrative connotes the combining of more than one orientation and doing so with a good deal of consistency. Of course, there are supervisors who correctly are more eclectic than integrative, but we would argue that their conceptualization of their work is not theoretical in nature but more likely to be in one of the categories we will discuss later. (See Garfield & Kurtz [1977] for a useful consideration of types of eclectic and integrative therapists.)

Our review of the literature only further confuses the semantic issue. Russell et al. (1984) described as eclectic the Discrimination Model (Bernard, 1979) that we would describe as atheoretical. On the other hand, Everett (1980) presented as integrative an approach to family therapy that includes not only theoretical input from both the systems and psychodynamic schools but also concepts such as personal growth and professional socialization. Therefore, Everett clearly was using the term *integrative* to mean more than a theoretical blending. To make matters more confusing, Halgin (1986) introduced the phrase "pragmatic blending" to describe his supervision approach that integrates psychodynamic, interpersonal, person-centered, and behavioral techniques.

At this point it is fair to ask what exactly is an integrative approach? As a point of departure, an integrative approach must incorporate theoretical loyalty to at least two theories. One integrative approach that is quite prominent in the literature is humanist behaviorism, combining some person-centered and behavioral concepts and interventions. It must be noted, however, that the theoretical underpinnings of these two theories are contradictory and it is likely that the supervisor relies more heavily on one theory for conceptualization and the other for working style. Perhaps the only truly integrative approaches are those that already fall within a larger framework — for example, behavioral and cognitive behavioral therapies; Lazarus's (1976) Multimodal Behavior Therapy with another behavioral therapy; or strategic and structural family therapies, both of which are systemic. If one views developmental concepts as a separate theoretical orientation, then many supervisors blend a developmental view with another theoretical orientation. Finally, we believe many supervisors are not as equally integrative in their supervision as they might be in therapy. For example, the same person might blend the behavioral and systemic orientations in therapy but be behavioral only (or systemic only) in supervision. In fact, in our literature search we found only one example of a truly eclectic approach to supervision (Ponerotto & Zander, 1984), and this was because the authors followed Lazarus's already eclectic multimodal approach as their model. Therefore, the supervisor is "seen as flexible, adaptable, and technically eclectic" (p. 40).

Because of the confusion in the literature, it might be difficult for supervisors to determine if they are truly integrative. Again, integrative supervisors, like all psychotherapy-based supervisors, do not go beyond their special blending of psychotherapy theory to define and deliver supervision. Therefore, we expect there to be few pure integrative supervisors. Rather, we expect that most supervisors blend some psychotherapy concepts with other conceptual models. Such models will be discussed in other sections of this chapter.

## Conclusions About
## Psychotherapy-based Supervision

*Assumptions.* At least three assumptions seem to emerge in discussions of the different therapeutic approaches to supervision. These are:

1. The psychotherapy theory being used describes human learning in a comprehensive manner that can be applied equally to the instructional goals of the trainee and the developmental and remedial goals of the client.
2. There is nothing significantly different between the trainee and the client that would challenge the utility of the theory for either.
3. All theories of psychotherapy are as applicable to the supervisory context as they are to the therapy context.

*Advantages.* Patterson (1983) has asserted that supervision is more advantageous when the trainee and the supervisor share the same theoretical orientation. We believe that supervisors who employ a psychotherapy-based approach have at least the following advantages:

1. Modeling is maximized when supervisors use the same theoretical approach as they try to teach.
2. The trainee experiences the theory first-hand and will know better the probable reaction of clients to the theoretical approach.
3. Theory is more integrated into training when the supervisor is psychotherapy based.

*Disadvantages.* Psychotherapy-based approaches to supervision also have disadvantages. Among them are the following:

1. Such an approach requires that the trainee be committed beforehand to a theoretical orientation that matches the supervisor's.
2. In graduate training, the psychotherapy-based supervisor may not meet the needs of all students. This may pose an ethical dilemma.
3. If a student in training discovers a different, more preferable orientation, problems may arise.
4. If the supervisor treats the trainee in a way similar to the treatment of a client, there is the possibility that the trainee might feel or behave like a client.

## DEVELOPMENTAL APPROACHES
## TO SUPERVISION

Our second major category for conceptualizing supervision is the developmental approach. As is depicted in Figure 2.1, the various developmental models contribute greatly to what we have labeled as the conceptual model perspective of supervision. The similarity all conceptual models have with each other is their central focus on supervisees and their interactions with supervisors. Conceptual models, therefore, have an advantage over psychotherapy-based models in that they do not have to make the leap from the assumptions of therapy to those of supervision.

Holloway's (1987) comment that "developmental models of supervision have become the *Zeitgeist* of supervision thinking and research" (p. 209) still rings true. In the tremendous growth in the supervision literature in recent years, by far the most visible theme has been that of the developmentalist. This has been the case in the psychiatric, psychological, counseling, and social work fields (Worthington, 1984) but less so in the marriage and family therapy field (Everett & Koerpel, 1986).

Borders (1986) argued that the developmental model of supervision "describes counselor growth as a series of sequential, hierarchical stages, each requiring different supervision interventions" (p. 9). To their credit, developmental supervisors have conducted and stimulated an impressive body of research on the efficacy of the developmental model. Therefore, for this discussion we will be able to draw upon both conceptual and empirical contributions and the critical relationship they have to each other.

Different authors have waded through the developmental literature in different ways. Borders (1986) divided models into three categories: those that focus on the role of the supervisor (e.g., Littrell, Lee-Borden, & Lorenz, 1979), those that focus on the dynamics of the trainee (e.g., Loganbill et al., 1982), and those that focus on the learning environment of supervision (e.g., Stoltenberg, 1981). Russell et al. (1984) divided developmental models into two categories: those in the Eriksonian tradition that offer definitive linear stages of development (e.g., Hogan, 1964; Stoltenberg, 1981; Littrell et al., 1979) and those that propose a step-by-step process for conflict resolution or skill mastery, a process that is repeated as the trainee faces more complicated issues (e.g., Ekstein & Wallerstein, 1972; Mueller & Kell, 1972; Loganbill et al., 1982). Holloway (1987), in her challenging review of the five most frequently cited developmental models, divided them into those that have linked their origins to psychosocial developmental theory (e.g., Blocher, 1983; Loganbill et al., 1982; Stoltenberg, 1981) and those that have not (e.g., Hogan, 1964; Littrell et al., 1979). Finally, in an extremely comprehensive review of developmental models and the empirical studies spawned by these models, Worthington (1987) divided the literature into two groups: the models and studies that have addressed supervision of the developing counselor (e.g., Hill, Charles, & Reed, 1981; Loganbill et al., 1982; Stoltenberg, 1981) and those that have taken the complementary tack of addressing supervision by the developing supervisor (e.g., Alonso, 1983; Hess, 1986).

As the reader can gather, developmental models have certain assumptions in common but vary in their application of those assumptions. We have chosen to review a few of the models briefly so that both the commonalities and the diversity of developmental models can emerge.

Littrell et al. (1979) proposed a four-stage model that attempted to match the supervisor's behavior to the developmental needs of the trainee. The first stage is characterized by relationship building, goal setting, and contracting the conditions of supervision. During the second stage, the supervisor fluctuates between a counselor role and a teacher role as the trainee is faced with affective issues and skill deficits. The third stage requires that the supervisor adopts the more collegial role of consultant as the trainee gains confidence and expertise. The fourth and final stage is for the trainee to become a self-supervisor and take responsibility as the "principle designer of his or her learning" (p. 134). The supervisor, we assume, becomes a more distant consultant at this time.

Stoltenberg (1981) also defined four stages, or "levels," in his Complexity Model. He described the trainee at each level and the optimum supervision environment required at that level in order to meet the trainee's needs. Level one depicts a trainee who is dependent on the supervisor, imitative, lacking in self- and other awareness, and limited by categorical thinking and little experience. The supervisory environment for this level should offer instruction, interpretation, support, and structure. Autonomy should be encouraged within the limits of the level. Level two is characterized by a dependency-autonomy conflict. As awareness increases, there is a striving for independence, fluctuating motivation, more assertion, and less imitation. The environment should offer less structure and instruction. The supervisor should model high autonomy, support, ambivalence, giving clarification only when asked. Level three is one of conditional dependency. The trainee is more differentiated, motivated, insightful, and empathic. The supervisor should treat the trainee more as a peer and allow for autonomy. There should be mutual sharing, exemplification, and confrontation. Level four describes the "master counselor" who is skilled not only interpersonally and cognitively but also professionally. At this point supervision, if continued, is collegial.

Loganbill et al. (1982) described the first comprehensive model of counselor development in the literature (Holloway, 1987). Loganbill and her colleagues chose Chickering's (1969) developmental tasks of youth and redefined them into eight professional issues for helpers: competence, emotional awareness, autonomy, identity, respect for individual differences, purpose and direction, personal motivation, and professional ethics. For each of these issues the trainee might be at one of three stages or in transition between stages. The stages are stagnation (unawareness, dualistic thinking, extreme dependence), confusion (instability, conflict, fluctuation of feeling regarding ability of self and supervisor), and integration (calm reorganization, refreezing of attitudes, realistic view of self and supervisor). As defined by the model, the supervisor's role is to assess each trainee for each issue and to attempt to move the trainee to the next stage of development. The supervisor's repertoire of interventions include facilitating, confronting, conceptualizing, prescribing, and catalyzing (getting things moving). (The use of this model is described more fully in Chapter 4.)

More recently, Johnson and Moses (1988) proposed another model based on Chickering's vectors. According to these authors, each vector is comprised of a cognitive, emotional, and behavioral dimension. Supervision assessment, therefore, should include a determination of which of the three areas represented the need for supervisee growth. Furthermore, Johnson and Moses defined the supervisor's role as the balancing of different activities of support and challenge, thereby stimulating supervisees to reach their potential but not overwhelming them with unattainable expectations. (The discussion of the develop-

mental case conference in Chapter 4 will offer more of the contribution of Johnson and Moses.)

Finally, Stoltenberg and Delworth (1987) revised Stoltenberg's (1981) earlier developmental model and borrowed from the contributions of Loganbill et al. (1982). Stoltenberg and Delworth described three developmental levels of the trainee over eight dimensions: intervention skills, assessment techniques, interpersonal assessment, client conceptualization, individual differences, theoretical orientation, treatment goals and plans, and professional ethics. Three structures are proposed in the model to trace the progress of trainees through the levels on each of the dimensions. These structures are the trainee's awareness of self and others, motivation toward the developmental process, and the amount of dependency or autonomy displayed by the trainee.

A developmental approach to supervision is appealing for at least two reasons: It makes sense intuitively (most of us think we are better than when we began), and it is hopeful, therefore diminishing the evaluative component that many supervisors find troublesome. The attributes that make this approach attractive, however, may be the same that blind their advocates to competing explanations of what goes on in supervision. Most empirical investigations of developmental models of supervision report "partial," or "some," support (e.g., Borders, 1989c; Krause & Allen, 1988; Reising & Daniels, 1983; Miars, Tracey, Ray, Cornfeld, O'Farrell, & Gelso, 1983). A smaller number of studies (e.g., Fisher, 1989; Moy & Goodman, 1984) found no support for developmental theory. Perhaps the assumptions of developmental models are, as yet, only partially salient. In other words, perhaps there is a developmental process that we experience intuitively but are still only in the beginning stages of operationalizing.

Russell et al. (1984) criticized most developmental models as being too simplistic. They implied that the development of the professional helper involves a great deal more than these models suggest. Holloway (1987) put forth a similar view and suggested that supervision is only one event in the trainee's professional and personal life, and it is perhaps not the most important event. Holloway asserted that it is too early to assume a predictable development paradigm.

> *Although researchers are interpreting their results as tentatively supporting a developmental model, lack of developmental-specific methodology, confinement to the supervisory experience as a source of information, predominant use of structured self-report questionnaires, and lack of evidence of distinct, sequential stages in trainee's growth reflect the prematurity of such claims. (p. 215)*

In subsequent publications (Holloway, 1988; Stoltenberg & Delworth, 1988) a dialogue was established that will further our understanding of the cognitive constructs and behavioral and affective components of different levels of therapeutic competence as well as the training prerequisites at each level.

In his excellent review of empirical studies based on developmental models, Worthington (1987) addressed both what is known and what is missing regarding supervision from the developmental perspective. To summarize Worthington's findings, we list the following points:

1. There is some support for general developmental models.
2. In general, perceptions of supervisors and trainees have been broadly consistent with developmental theories (Reising & Daniels, 1983; Wiley, 1982; Miars et al., 1983; Worthington & Roehlke, 1979; Heppner & Roehlke, 1984).
3. The behavior of supervisors changes as trainees gain experience (Raphael, 1982; Rickards, 1984; Holloway & Wampold, 1983).
4. The supervision relationship changes as

counselors gain experience (Heppner & Handley, 1982; Dodenhoff, 1982).
5. There are differences in skillfulness in supervision among supervisors (Cross & Brown, 1983; Heppner & Handley, 1981; Worthington, 1984b; Worthington & Stern, 1985; Zucker & Worthington, 1986).
6. Supervisors do not become more competent as they gain experience (Marikis, Russell, & Dell, 1985; Worthington, 1984b; Zucker & Worthington, 1986).

Because supervision from a developmental perspective is far more conceptual than stylistic (that is, the supervisor's behavior will necessarily change based on the assessment of the supervisee's level), it is difficult to give a brief example of a typical supervision session from this orientation. (Added to this is our earlier point that having a developmental framework does not negate the possibility of being psychotherapy based. Therefore, depending on the theoretical orientation of the supervisor, supervision sessions will differ.) A common occurrence for the clinical supervisor is to work with trainees at different developmental levels, which may or may not pose problems. Our example, therefore, considers this kind of situation.

> *Patricia is one of five students enrolled in a beginning practicum. The supervisor uses a combination of individual and group supervision. Although Patricia has no more experience than other students, she shows superior natural ability to do therapy. Additionally, the ability to apply the didactic material she has been taught is equally impressive. Patricia has virtually no experience in the role of helper, but her initial interviews are of a quality that the supervisor hopes for by the end of the practicum experience.*

Among the questions that the supervisor needs to address are the following: What issues might arise in the group as a result of the difference between Patricia and the other students? Is Patricia's presence an advantage or a complication? Should the group be approached differently because of Patricia's presence? Does the fact that none of the six students have any actual experience counteract Patricia's superiority? Should Patricia be allowed to waive this practicum and move on to a more advanced training experience?

As this brief example illustrates, developmental issues are relevant not only to individual supervision but also to group supervision.

## Supervisor Development

Although not as central to the developmental dialogue, supervisor development is also an assumption of the developmental models. Referring back to Worthington (1987), we note that several of the studies he reported made inferences regarding supervisor development even though those that attempted to record change based on supervisor experience failed to do so. Despite these empirical findings Hess (1986, 1987) described supervisor development as having three stages: a beginning stage characterized by the difficulty of role-status change and a focus more on the client than the counselor and on techniques that will produce client change, an exploration stage in which the supervisor begins to identify with the role of supervisor and becomes more knowledgeable regarding supervision dynamics, and a confirmation of supervisor identity stage in which the central focus is on the supervisee's learning agenda.

It is not surprising that we are only now developing models of supervisor development and that these lack empirical validation. Only as training for clinical supervisors increases and our knowledge base regarding supervision per se grows should we expect to see differences between those who are applying these concepts as novices and those who have grown beyond their training.

## Conclusions About the Developmental Approach

### *Assumptions*

1. There is a beginning point, if not an ending point, of learning to be a professional helper.
2. Individual learning styles and personality types can be subsumed under a developmental model.
3. There is a logical sequence of stages through which trainees pass in their development.
4. The order of developmental stages are approximately the same for every trainee.

### *Advantages*

1. Hypothetically, supervisors can track trainees' progress, allowing them to determine when training is completed.
2. Because of the atheoretical nature of developmental models, they can be used with several theoretical approaches to psychotherapy.
3. Developmental models focus not only on the trainee's development but also on the supervisor's development.

### *Disadvantages*

1. Developmental models potentially disallow certain things. For example, at certain times and under certain circumstances an advanced trainee might need conditions associated with beginning trainees.
2. Most models do not adequately accommodate for divergent developmental paths.
3. The models do not address relapse or "no progress."

## ALTERNATIVE CONCEPTUAL MODELS OF SUPERVISION

Referring once again to Figure 2.1, we have grouped in this section all conceptual models that are not developmental in nature. By default, then, this section is the most diverse of those in this chapter.

There are many more models of supervision than there are theories of psychotherapy. In part, this reflects the more specific nature of models. Some models have attempted to pair different techniques for accomplishing one or several goals of supervision (e.g., Kagan, 1976, 1980; Spice & Spice, 1976). Other models help the supervisor track the supervision process (e.g., Bernard, 1979); still others attempt to address both case conceptualization and intervention choice (e.g., Howard, Nance, & Myers, 1986). For our purposes here, we will attempt to limit our attention to models that are fairly comprehensive, that is, those that could conceivably represent an *approach* to supervision rather than a supervision *technique*.

Models do not replace theories of psychotherapy. Some models draw from a single theoretical orientation or a combination of theories; others do not. Those that do not are atheoretical, that is, they are designed to be useful within several theoretical orientations. It is up to the supervisor to determine if a particular model has a different premise than his or her psychotherapy theory. Models also are less ambitious than theories. They tend not to try to be more than what they are—a package, of sorts, of either ideas or techniques that will be useful in supervision. Supervisors who are attracted to models tend to be more integrative in their approach to both therapy and supervision. They also are more likely to focus on the teaching aspect of supervision and to see the context of supervision less like therapy than psychotherapy-based supervisors.

Models of supervision have flooded the professional literature in recent years. They are too numerous and too diverse to be covered here in any comprehensive fashion. Rather, we will review a brief sample of models to give the reader an idea of the variety available to the supervisor and focus more fully on Interpersonal Process Recall, which draws from the phenomenological world view and stresses a combination of techniques, and the Discrimination Model, which is atheoretical and conceptual only. None of the models in this section will reflect a developmental perspective of either the trainee's growth or the process of supervision because this focus already has been discussed separately.

An example of a supervision model that draws on a blend of theoretical orientations is Webb's (1983) Life Model, which combines ego psychology and communications theory into a conceptual framework devised to understand the training needs for competent clinical practitioners. Webb included 15 guidelines for supervisors that enable them to promote competence in their trainees. Each guideline includes a principle, an application, and a rationale. For example, guideline ten states:

> Principle: *Permit and encourage disagreement.*
> Application: *Urge supervisees to give reasons for his or her views.*
> Rationale: *Expect supervisee to have own opinions; supervisee may be more knowledgeable in some areas than supervisor. (p. 49)*

Richardson and Bradley (1984) applied the principles of microtraining (Ivey, 1971) to the training of counselor supervisors. In both microtraining and microsupervision, learning is accomplished by breaking down complex therapist or supervisor behavior into specific skills that are then modeled, practiced, and evaluated. This model relies heavily on behavioral theory and is more often used for training at the prepracticum or paraprofessional levels than for supervisor training.

An interesting alternative model is Sharon's (1986) ABCX Model, which is based on work done by Hill (1958) and McCubbin and Patterson (1983). Sharon's conceptualization of the supervision process is quite complex (parts of it read like a geometry text) but worthwhile. ABCX stands for event, perception of event, resources to meet the event, and effective change. The particular value of this model is that it addresses in detail the potential, and common, occurrences of differences among clients, therapists, and supervisors at each of the four points.

Finally, Zimmerman, Collins, and Bach (1986) suggested a model based on one critical variable: the birth order of the trainee. They proposed that ordinal position affects cognitive style and relationship processes and that supervision goals should focus on this variable.

As this small sample indicates, the literature is varied, if not confusing, as supervision models continue to proliferate.

### Interpersonal Process Recall (IPR)

Kagan's (1976, 1980) highly regarded model was one of the first to take advantage of modern technology (see Chapter 4). Although some of IPR appears behavioral because of the use of videotape replays and practice for the role of inquirer, the model aligns itself closely with a phenomenological philosophy in that "people are the best authority on their own dynamics and the best interpreter of their own experience" (1980, pp. 279–280).

IPR began as a therapy model in which the reviewing of therapy sessions on videotape by both therapist and client allowed for new insights into the therapeutic relationship. Soon, however, IPR was favored as a training and supervision device without the client present, and the supervisor and therapist worked with the videotape stimuli. More recently, IPR has been used for issues that affect the supervision relationship as well as those that affect the therapy relationship (Bernard, 1981, 1989).

Kagan (1980) developed his own conceptual base for his model. He identified two basic tenets: People need each other, and people

learn to fear each other. From these conflicting states emerge the approach-avoidance behaviors most people display in their search for intimacy. From the therapist's standpoint, Kagan proposed that "extensive covert analysis, especially when accompanied by anxiety, limits one's ability to attend to the other" (p. 275). Therefore, the use of IPR allows an immediacy after the session that was not possible during the session. This rather paradoxical phenomenon is possible only because therapists (or supervisors) are reexperiencing the sessions and are allowing their insights to emerge from within themselves. Thus, the phenomenological base is established. (See Appendix D for a transcript of IPR supervision.)

### The Discrimination Model

The purpose of the Discrimination Model (Bernard, 1979) is to give supervisors a cognitive map by which to track the focus of supervision and to determine the best supervisory vehicle for accomplishing supervision goals. The model describes three separate foci for supervision: the trainee's process skills (what the trainee is doing in the session that is observable by the supervisor), the trainee's conceptualization skills (how the trainee understands what is occurring in the session, identifies patterns, or chooses interventions), and the trainee's personalization skills (how the trainee interfaces a personal style with the role of the therapist at the same time that the trainee attempts to keep therapy uncontaminated by personal issues). More recently, Lanning (1986) added a fourth focus area, professional behavior (that which reflects an ability to adhere to commonly accepted professional practice).

The supervisor must make a judgment about the trainee's abilities within each focus area. Once this has been done, the supervisor must choose a role that will accomplish the supervision goals. The roles available to the supervisor are those of teacher, counselor, or consultant. There are many reasons for choosing a role, but the worst reason is habit or personal preference, indiscriminate of the trainee's needs. The developmentalists tend to pair roles with the sophistication of the trainees, matching the teaching role with the novice supervisee and the consultant role with the advanced supervisee (Littrell et al., 1979; Stoltenberg, 1981). Although there is a sound defense for this approach, the Discrimination Model takes a less static view of the supervisor's role, believing there is value in using each role at all supervision levels. (The Discrimination Model will be presented more fully in Chapter 3.)

### Conclusions About Conceptual Models of Supervision

#### Assumptions
1. Supervision is a process separate from therapy and requires a different conceptual framework.
2. Models do not interact with theoretical perspectives in a negative fashion.
3. Models add clarity to the supervision process.
4. Different models have different objectives and are not interchangeable.

#### Advantages
1. Models are more flexible than theories. They can be modified easily.
2. Models are easier than theories to test empirically because they tend to be more specific.
3. Models can help supervisors to vary their approaches and be used as a safeguard against stagnation.
4. Models can help simplify the supervision process and give the supervisor and supervisee a common language.

#### Disadvantages
1. The supervisor can rely on models to the exclusion of clear theoretical premises.

2. Because of their usual deemphasis on psychotherapeutic theory, inconsistent models can be forced together and may confuse the trainee.
3. Models can be gimmicky and can allow the supervisor to sidestep serious encounters with the trainee.

### PERSONAL GROWTH SUPERVISION

As the primary focus of supervision, personal growth has as long a history as psychotherapy itself. Although no longer the predominant model in the professional literature, personal growth still is a valued and visible force. The roots of the personal growth orientation are firmly in the schools of psychoanalysis and phenomenology. Other theoretical approaches, however, have borrowed this belief that supervision should be therapeutic (e.g., the experiential arm of the systemic school). We present the personal growth perspective as a separate conceptual approach to supervision because it crosses several theoretical orientations and can become the focus of supervision in its own right.

A major premise of the personal growth approach is that "by its nature, supervision is person-centered" (Hennessy, 1979, p. 2). In other words, there is no way to attend to the needs and growth potential of the client while skipping over those same needs in the trainee. Furthermore, a keen sense of self-awareness, insight, and control of one's own feelings and behavior are necessary if one is to be empathic and understanding with clients (Middleman & Rhodes, 1985). These twin abilities of understanding oneself and being able to use the self in therapy are keys to this approach.

Loganbill et al. (1982) took a slightly different approach and paired effectiveness in therapy with letting go of the belief that everything is personally intact with the trainee. Supervisor and trainee share with the client the knowledge that they are "unfinished products." In other words, growth is the inevitable by-product of the context of therapy whether one is therapist or client, and there is no reason to assume that such growth will terminate. Similarly, Altucher (1967) stated that "learning to be a counselor is both an emotional and intellectual experience, and of the two, the emotional part is the most crucial" (p. 165). Therefore, personal growth is necessary to be good as a therapist and is also necessary as a reaction to the learning process itself.

Even when one or all of these assumptions are accepted, there is some disagreement among supervisors about the proper place for personal growth in supervision. Some adhere to the position that the trainee should be in therapy during, but away from, supervision. Others believe that personal growth must be integrated into supervision. Real advocates go further and say that even the experienced therapist should not be satisfied at a high-level psychological plateau (Hennessy, 1979) but should continue to strive for personal growth. We will look at the first two of these options more closely.

Hart (1982) discussed the ongoing debate as to whether personal growth is the responsibility of training institutions. Most authors who advocate therapy as part of training for either individual or family therapists are more ambiguous about whether therapy should be done by persons inside or outside the training program (Kaslow, 1977; Liddle & Halpin, 1978; Loganbill et al., 1982). In a similar vein, Wampler and Strupp (1976) reported that 67 percent of APA-accredited clinical training programs actively encouraged personal therapy but only 4 percent required it. The impression one gets from the literature is that therapy should be done elsewhere. When therapy is suggested as part of training, we would agree. This type of arrangement, however, is schizophrenic as a supervision philosophy in that personal growth is required but not under the supervision of the program. As such, it must be viewed as a quasi-personal-growth model of supervision.

Those programs with a clearer and more consistent model are recognized by two characteristics: Personal growth is part of supervision, and therapy is differentiated from supervision that is therapeutic. Twenty-five years ago, Truax and Carkhuff (1967) advocated "quasi-group therapy" for trainees in which personal conflicts caused by training would be resolved. Truax and Carkhuff warned that training programs needed to offer high levels of what they called "core conditions." Essentially, these are the same conditions Rogers saw as necessary for therapy. Although not as clear (and perhaps not as forthright) in their goals, many training programs continue to use group process courses in a similar way.

Boyd (1978) made a distinction between experiential supervision and psychotherapeutic supervision. The former includes no attempt to have trainees learn about their personal dynamics. Rather, the supervisor offers a therapeutic relationship that facilitates self-growth and learning. Boyd was leery of this approach and echoed Liddle and Halpin's (1978) reservation that there is relatively no research to support such an approach. Psychotherapeutic supervision, on the other hand, has as its explicit goal the learning of the trainee. Boyd listed four goals for psychotherapeutic supervision.

1. *Dynamic awareness. This includes awareness of both interpersonal and intrapersonal issues and patterns.*
2. *Understanding dynamic contingencies. Once the trainee is aware, he or she must become cognizant of what stimulates personal dynamics and how they are played out.*
3. *A change in dynamics. Troublesome inter and intrapersonal dynamics are targeted for change.*
4. *Therapeutic utilization of dynamics. The trainee must not only learn to control his or her dynamics but become adept at using "self" for the betterment of the client. (pp. 43–47)*

As an example of personal growth supervision, we have chosen an excerpt from Erving Polster's supervision session with Harold Hackney (the complete transcript is presented in Appendix D). Although Polster is a Gestaltist (and this, therefore, could be considered a psychotherapy-based session), it is clear that his focus during the session is the supervisee and his personal growth.

> *H: A couple of sessions back, I had just gotten my hair cut, or had had it styled; and she came in, and about a third of the way through the session, she said, "You know, you look better than I've ever seen you look."*
>
> *P: Unhuh.*
>
> *H: Well, I got embarrassed and just sort of brushed it aside.*
>
> *P: You're a very handsome man, you know.*
>
> *H: Well, thanks.*
>
> *P: I feel it. You got embarrassed . . . ?*
>
> *H: Yes.*
>
> *P: I'd like to know about your embarrassment. Also, how did you feel about my saying you were handsome?*

We invite the reader to compare this excerpt with those presented for psychodynamic and person-centered supervisions. What differences do you perceive? What elements do they have in common? If you find few differences among them stylistically, how are the goals different for each? Are these distinctions exact enough for them to be considered different conceptual models of supervision?

## Conclusions About Personal Growth Supervision

### Assumptions

1. The trainee's personal issues will necessarily spill over into therapy.
2. Trainees can work on their personal issues and the issues of their clients during the same time frame.

3. It is virtually impossible to be therapeutic with another about issues that one has not resolved for oneself.

### Advantages

1. The trainee gains at two levels: the personal level and the professional level.
2. If the trainee has any personal issues that are too great to be overcome and will hamper the trainee's performance as a therapist, these will most likely become apparent.
3. Because the trainee's personal issues are addressed in supervision, empathy for the experience of clients remains high.

### Disadvantages

1. The trainee might become so engrossed in personal issues so as to neglect the client's issues.
2. The trainee might avoid certain topics in supervision because they represent problematic personal areas.
3. The supervisor who enjoys the role of therapist must fight the tendency to turn the trainee into a client.

## PARALLEL PROCESS OR ISOMORPHISM AS THE FOCUS OF SUPERVISION

As we stated earlier, the concept of parallel process has its roots in psychodynamic supervision; more specifically, its roots are found in the concepts of transference and countertransference (Friedman, 1983). First introduced by Searles (1955), who referred to it as the "reflection process" between therapy and supervision, the concept has been expanded more recently (Mueller & Kell, 1972; Mueller, 1982; Ekstein & Wallerstein, 1972) and has appeared as a key concept in virtually every major writing on the topic of supervision. Simply stated, parallel process refers to the common phenomenon of the dynamics in supervision replicating those that occurred in the trainee's therapy. Or as Friedlander, Siegel, and Brenock (1989) described the concept, "trainees unconsciously present themselves to their supervisors as their clients have presented to them. The process reverses when the trainee adopts attitudes and behaviors of the supervisor in relating to the client" (p. 149).

In recent years, the premise of parallel process has been adopted and expanded by systemic family therapists, especially those of the structural or strategic schools. Haley (1976) has been given credit for spearheading this development (Liddle & Saba, 1983). Choosing the term *isomorphism,* systemic supervisors have focused on the interrelational and structural similarities between therapy and supervision rather than the intrapsychic parallels. Both psychodynamic and systemic schools, however, view these concepts as relevant to supervision regardless of theoretical orientation. In their review, Russell et al. (1984) concurred that several authors from a variety of theoretical positions have addressed dynamics that resemble one or both of these concepts. Because parallel processes and isomorphism have become foci of supervision separate from any necessary adherence to their theoretical roots, we include them as a unique conceptual focus of supervision rather than infuse them into our discussions of psychotherapy-based supervision.

For our purposes here, we will treat parallel process and isomorphism separately. Although we view them as two sides of the same coin, we believe the focus each offers is, and should remain, a separate contribution. At the same time, however, their basic similarities place them in the same conceptual framework as a supervision approach.

As is the case with approaches covered in the other sections of this chapter, most supervisors will blend this approach with at least one other. As will be discussed later, however, some supervisors view the metaphor of parallel process as a total approach to supervision.

## Parallel Process

Russell et al. (1984) identified the supervisory value of the parallel process framework as twofold:

> *First, as the supervisee becomes aware of the parallels in the relationships with the client and the supervisor, understanding of the client's psychological maladjustment is increased. Second, the supervisee's understanding of the therapeutic process grows in that the supervisee learns how to respond therapeutically to the client just as the supervisor has responded to the supervisee. (p. 629)*

Mueller (1982) stated that parallel process cannot be denied anymore than transference can be denied.

Traditionally it was assumed that parallel process was a bottom up, or transference only, phenomenon. The trainee would replay conflict from a therapeutic relationship in the supervisory relationship, and this would be out of the trainee's consciousness (Mueller & Kell, 1972). Explanations for the occurrence vary:

1. Trainees identify with clients and, therefore, produce reactions in their supervisors that they themselves felt with their clients (Russell et al., 1984).
2. The parallel chosen (unconsciously) by the trainee reflects the initial impasse formed between the client and the trainee (Mueller & Kell, 1972).
3. Through a natural screening process, the trainee selects part of the client's problem that parallels one that the trainee shares (Mueller & Kell, 1972).
4. Through lack of skill, the trainee is prone to those aspects of the client's problem that parallel his or her specific learning problems in supervision (Ekstein & Wallerstein, 1972).

Ekstein and Wallerstein added that parallel process is a "never-ending surprise," based on the "irrational expectation that the teaching and learning of psychotherapy should consist primarily of rational elements" (p. 177). The flavor of this comment, however, is that the irrationality comes from the trainee. With Doehrman's (1976) research came the realization that parallel process was bidirectional, thereby involving countertransference as well as transference. The supervisor was as likely as the trainee to initiate a dynamic that would be played out in the trainee's therapy. Thus, there has been more discussion recently of top-down parallel process. Mueller (1982) stated that a problem that begins in supervision must be settled there. Williams (1987) called the ability of the supervisor to recognize personal feelings in relation to the trainee the "art of arts" within supervision.

Once it was established that the supervisor was not above the phenomenon, it was a small step for supervisors to realize the training implications of parallel processes. Ekstein and Wallerstein (1972) pointed out that an authoritative style from the supervisor focusing on the giving of information would cloud parallel patterns. More recently, Mueller (1982) referred to parallel process as a "powerful supervisory vehicle" (p. 44) that must be integrated into the assessment and intervention aspects of supervision. Mueller implied that this is best done when the supervisor, like a good parent, can create a context for the trainee to experience the joy of disco ering a direction for therapy rather than telling the trainee how to proceed. The model assumes, then, that the trainee will be inclined to create a similar context for the client.

Although it is sparse, McNeill and Worthen (1989) identified some empirical support that parallel process does occur between therapy and supervision (see, especially, Doehrman, 1971; Friedlander, Siegel, & Brenock, 1989). There is, however, a great deal yet to be learned about this phenomenon. Two research questions are suggested by Friedlander et al. (1989): Are parallel processes more likely to occur in different formats (e.g., live

observation versus taped playback versus simply recounting what occurred), and is their occurrence related to supervisor style (e.g., relationship oriented versus task oriented)?

Parallel process, therefore, seems to be an important conceptual approach to supervision, at least as one perspective for the supervisor to consider when supervision dynamics seem inconsistent with what was expected. McNeill and Worthen (1989), however, cautioned that too much focus on the process of supervision might become tiresome for trainees and that, in general, more advanced trainees are most likely to benefit from a discussion of transference and countertransference. Finally, Vargas (1989) noted that when supervisor, therapist, and client represent different cultural backgrounds, parallel processes will reflect multicultural issues.

The example of parallel process that follows was recalled by Friedman (1983):

*[A] mother and child were being seen by the same student therapist for a diagnostic assessment. The student described the mother as being very unfocused and disorganized, so that she had a hard time keeping the mother on track . . . Mother presented herself as very undifferentiated and presented members of her family in the same way, e.g., speaking of Michael, Jr. and Michael Sr. as Michael. In mother's mind, all the children appeared to be unseparated so that when the student asked about the developmental history of M. Jr., mother would speak of all the children in her undifferentiated way.*

*The student in her supervisory hour, and this was after several earlier sessions with the mother, reported that even after she had seen M. Jr. twice she was unable to visualize the boy's face and could not recall any of his features . . . The student found this very disconcerting . . . The student had been so caught up in her counter-transference reaction to the mother, that this well-organized, well-sructured, competent student . . . experienced the child as being as undifferentiated as did the mother. (pp. 9–10)*

Abroms (1977) offers a transition from this to our next section. Abroms referred to "metatransference," which, as defined by Abroms, is very similar, if not identical, to parallel process. In discussing this phenomenon, Abroms came as close as anyone to blending the concepts of parallel process and isomorphism: "To think in terms of metatransference is to think in parallel structures at different levels of abstraction, that is, to recognize the multilevel, isomorphic mirroring of interactional processes" (p. 93).

### Isomorphism

Hofstadter (1979) offered the following definition of isomorphism:

> *The word "isomorphic" applies when two complex structures can be mapped onto each other, in such a way that to each part of one structure there is a corresponding part in the other structure, where "corresponding" means that the two parts play similar roles in their respective structures. This usage of the word "isomorphic" is derived from a more precise notion in mathematics. (p. 49)*

For systems therapists, isomorphism refers to the "recursive replication" (Liddle et al., 1984) that occurs between therapy and supervision. The focus is interrelational and not intrapsychic. As Liddle and Saba (1983) suggested, the two fields, therapy and supervision, constantly influence and are influenced by each other; both are interpersonal systems with properties of all systems, including boundaries, hierarchies, and subsystems, each with its own distinct characteristics. There is no linear reality in this construct, only reverberations. Content is important but not nearly so important as repeating patterns.

Because supervision is viewed as the isomorph of therapy, Liddle et al. (1984) suggested that the same rules apply to both, including the need to join with both clients and trainees, the need for setting goals and thinking in stages, the importance of appreciating contextual sensitivity, and the charge of challenging realities. In other words, like advocates of parallel process, those who adhere to the isomorphic relationship between therapy and supervision view it as dictating intervention and not as a descriptive construct alone. "It suggests that trainers would do well to understand and intentionally utilize with their trainees the same basic principles of change employed in therapy" (p. 141).

If supervisors are aware of this process, they will watch for dynamics in supervision that reflect the initial assessments they have made about what is transpiring in therapy. In that way, the assessments are either verified or called into question. Because the client (family) is usually a group and many systemic supervisors prefer team supervision, the interactions are easily replicated. For example, an overwhelmed parent will appeal to the trainee for help while other family members sit expectantly, which will be followed by an overwhelmed trainee appealing to the supervisor for help while other team members sit expectantly. When intervening into the therapeutic system (trainee plus family), it is important that there be consistency down the hierarchy. For example, Haley (1987) recommended that if the goal is for the parents to be firm with their teenager, then the therapist must be firm with the parents, and to complete the isomorph, the supervisor must be firm with the therapist. In this way, content and process are matched and communicate the same message throughout the interconnected systems.

Liddle and Saba (1983) argued that live supervision, by requiring risk taking and experiential behavior on the part of the therapist, parallels structural family therapy where family members are actively put in direct contact with each other. Live supervision, therefore, is an isomorphically correct form of supervision for structural family therapy. Knowing a good metaphor when they saw one, Liddle and Saba (1982) described an introductory course in marriage and family therapy where the content and process of the course was designed to follow all the rules for the progression of family therapy. The authors noted that matching process and content right from the start of training makes for a much more powerful learning experience.

The following illustrates the isomorphic relationship between therapy and supervision:

> *Ted is seeing the Doyles for marriage counseling. There is a supervision team observing the session. The Doyles have been married for 20 years. They have no children. Mr. Doyle has fought depression through most of his adult life. Mrs. Doyle tells how hard it has been to help him, only to have her efforts go nowhere. She cries intermittently. It is obvious watching Ted that he is feeling this couple's plight. In the supervision room, there is virtually no movement. The team mirrors the sadness and despair of the couple. Halfway through the session, Ted excuses himself to consult with the team . . . As Ted is seated, Bill turns to him and says, "Boy what do you do for them at this point?" Ted shrugs and looks around for help.*

In addition to recognizing the isomorphic nature of what is transpiring, the supervisor must (1) determine how to approach the team, (2) predict Ted's role in the group, and (3) decide on an intervention that wil' not only help to stimulate Ted and the team but also serve to initiate a direction for Ted to take with the Doyle's.

## Conclusions About Parallel Processes and Isomorphism

### Assumptions

1. Parallels between therapy and supervision are not random phenomena.
2. What the supervisor models for the trainee will empower the trainee to do the same with the client.
3. All trainees are susceptible to these dynamics.

### Advantages

1. It helps the supervisor not to take personally the negative behaviors of the trainee in supervision.
2. Dynamics in supervision give the supervisor clues to what is transpiring in therapy and vice versa.
3. Through information giving and modeling, the supervisor has two vehicles for influencing trainees.

### Disadvantages

1. The supervisor may fail to detect important differences between the therapy context and the supervisory context (Liddle & Saba, 1983).
2. Trainees might not be able to transfer what is learned (experienced) in one context to the other.
3. Supervision might be limited to those transactions that occur in therapy.

## CONCLUSION

In this chapter we have led the reader through a maze of alternative conceptualizations of the supervision process. In so doing, our purpose has been both to present the more important perspectives on supervision and to provide a map (Figure 2.1) of the maze in which they are found.

The earliest conceptualizations of clinical supervision were extrapolations from psychotherapy theories. More recently, specific supervision models have been developed independent of psychotherapy. None of these perspectives, however, has received adequate empirical attention. Therefore, the burgeoning supervision literature contains more and more of what we do not know.

Subsequent chapters will address many issues and tasks that are relatively independent of theory. We will, however, return to theory in the final chapter on research. Theory and research are, after all, mutually dependent. In that chapter, we will consider ways in which supervision has been conceptualized, then suggest next steps in the development of a supervision science that will include both theory and research.

# CHAPTER 3

# SUPERVISOR ROLES

In seeking to explain the often substantial differences in behavior that exist from one supervisor to another, Friedlander and Ward (1984) offered the model depicted in Figure 3.1. It suggests the multiple determinants of supervisory technique. Each of its concentric rectangles is successively less broad and encompassing; at the same time, each has more direct influence on the technique the supervisor actually employs. This model also makes clear visually that terms such as *role, theory, focus,* and *technique* are *not* interchangeable. Not all authors have been clear about these distinctions.

In the Friedlander and Ward model, *assumptive world* refers to the person's past professional and life experience, training, values, and general outlook on life. It influences the

supervisor's choice of *theoretical orientation* (e.g., systemic, psychoanalytic, eclectic), which in turn influences the choice of *style-role.* Style-role determines *strategy-focus,* which in turn influences choice of *format* (e.g., live supervision, group supervision). Format, then, influences *technique.* In short, the model assumes the following path of causal influence: assumptive world → theoretical orientation → style-role → strategy-focus → format → technique.

Figure 3.1 shows the relationship this chapter has to those that immediately preceded it and to those that follow. Whereas Chapter 2 discussed theories and models of supervision (approximately the second level of the Friedlander and Ward model), Chapters 4, 5, and 6 will address strategies, format, and techniques. The purpose of this chapter is to consider the various roles available to supervisors as well as both their antecedents and effects. We also will give particular attention to the Discrimination Model (Bernard, 1979) as an explicit and parsimonious means of considering supervisor roles. Finally, we briefly will consider two other topics: supervisee roles and problems arising from role conflicts.

Although this chapter is rooted in a single level of the Friedlander and Ward model, we should acknowledge that we will in two instances consider phenomena appropriate to other levels of that model. In discussing metaphors underlying roles, we will be addressing the supervisor's assumptive world, and in discussing the Discrimination Model, we briefly will consider possible supervisory foci. Each of these moves to other levels of the model,

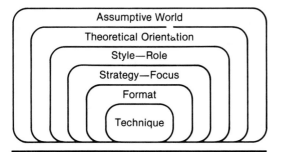

**FIGURE 3.1** Interrelated sources of variability among supervisors*

*From Friedlander, M. L., & Ward, L. G. (1984). Development and validation of the supervisory styles inventory. *Journal of Counseling Psychology, 31,* 541–557. Copyright © (1984) by the American Psychological Association. Reprinted by permission.

however, is in the service of providing a broadened understanding of supervisor roles.

## THE CONSTELLATION OF POSSIBLE SUPERVISOR ROLES

There is no universal role for supervisors. In fact, the goals of supervision *demand* substantial role flexibility. The title Danskin (1957) chose for his article over three decades ago, "A role-ing counselor gathers no moss," may seem glib. At the same time, though, it does convey an important message not only about the essential value of thinking in terms of roles but also about the importance of role flexibility in counseling. We believe this same message pertains in supervision.

The nature of this role flexibility was suggested by Douce (1989), who asserted that "supervision is a separate skill similar to teaching—but different; similar to counseling—but different; and similar to consulting—but different" (p. 5). This seems like virtually the same point suggested by the title of Ekstein's (1964) article, "Supervision of psychotherapy: Is it teaching? Is it administration? Or is it therapy?"

There are a number of professional roles available to supervisors, and the greater the experience levels of the supervisors, the greater the number of roles from which they can draw (Stoltenberg & Delworth, 1988). We would argue that the more such roles are available to employ, the better.

The Friedlander and Ward (1984) model depicted in Figure 3.1 suggests that a major determinant of a supervisor's role is the theoretical orientation. Corsini (1981) identified 240 theories of counseling and psychotherapy for which published material existed. Fortunately, supervision has not reached that level of diversity (or confusion). Even so, there have evolved a number of different perspectives from which to conceptualize the work of the supervisor. As is the case with the theories of counseling and psychotherapy, none has claim

to "the truth." Almost all seem to have some merit and must be judged according to their usefulness.

As was explained in Chapter 2, for each supervision model there are particular hypotheses about the processes and phenomena that supervisors might be expected to encounter. Each also suggests, either implicitly or explicitly, the roles that the supervisor might be expected to fill, the aspects of the trainee's work on which the supervisor might be expected to focus, and the circumstances under which the supervisor might attend to these respective roles and foci.

Returning to the Friedlander and Ward (1984) model (Figure 3.1), we can see that it is reasonable to infer that the supervisor's theoretical orientation is itself influenced by the supervisor's assumptive world. This certainly would include the basic metaphors used by the supervisor. These metaphors also have affected and been affected by the supervisor's personal and professional history. Because of the importance of metaphor, we will give it specific consideration as a determinant of theory, and ultimately a role.

### Roles and Metaphors

Most of us recognize metaphor as a phenomenon of speech and language. We all know it, for example, as an essential component of poetry. Yet metaphor operates at multiple levels of behavior and is not strictly limited to the verbal domain. Mental health professionals, in fact, base much of their work on the assumption that a person's previous life experiences can and often do function metaphorically for current ones.

Such metaphoric functioning provides the mechanism by which transference and countertransference reactions occur. Sullivan (1953) used the term *parataxic distortion* to address the everyday counterpart of this. The essential idea is that Person A, by virtue of some shared characteristics with Person B, is responded to (affectively, behaviorally, or cognitively) as if she or he *were* Person B. In other words, particular life experiences and patterns serve us as a something of a template: Our perceptions and responses to a new situation are organized and structured as they were in a previous similar situation. Because of their apparent similarities, we then respond to the new situation *as if* it were the earlier one.

Not only do mental health practitioners employ metaphor in their interventions, they also draw on particular root metaphors to define their professional roles. Kopp (1971), for example, has drawn from various sources to describe several basic metaphors that find expression as roles that therapists adopt. Among these are the priest or shaman; the Zen master; and Socrates, who saw himself as "midwife to the ideas of others" (Kopp, 1971). Kopp also discussed ways in which children's stories such as *The Wizard of Oz* (Baum, 1956) can serve as metaphors for psychotherapy. There are, of course, many other metaphors to define the work of therapists. Common among these are the therapist as healer, the therapist as scientist, and the humanistic notion of the therapist as cotraveler on the journey of life. The list of possible metaphors for therapists is long.

If the roles and behaviors of clients and therapists are in part metaphoric expressions of other life experiences, this almost certainly must be the case for the supervisor and supervisee. Supervision is, after all, a higher-order intervention that almost invariably is conducted by senior professionals who bring to it a history of training and experience. In their day-to-day professional practice, particular ways of perceiving and behaving have become deeply ingrained through frequent use. Consequently, these response patterns are likely to be invoked as the professional enters the new situation of supervision.

*Supervisor-Supervisee as Parent-Child.* Family metaphors seem to be particularly available in supervision, and the most basic of these is the parent-child relationship. Lower (1972), for example, employed this metaphor in referring to the unconscious parent-child fantasies that he believed are stimulated by the supervisory situation itself.

Many theorists, of course, have employed this metaphor of the parent-child relationship as a way to think about therapy. As it may apply to supervision, the metaphor simultaneously is both *less* and *more* appropriate than for therapy. It is less appropriate in that personal growth is not a primary goal of the supervision intervention as it is in therapy; rather, it is an instrumental goal that works in the service of making the trainee a better therapist. It is more appropriate, on the other hand, in that supervision is an evaluative relationship as is parenting, and therapy presumably is not.

Just knowing that they are being evaluated often is sufficient to trigger in supervisees an expectation of a guilt-punishment sequence that recapitulates early parent-child interactions. Supervisors can through their actions intensify such transference responses in supervisees, triggering perceptions of themselves as good or bad parents. We have heard, for example, of instances in which supervisors posted publicly in the staff lounge the names of trainees who had too many client no-shows. The atmosphere created in a situation such as this easily can establish supervisory staff as feared parents.

Another parallel between parent-child and supervisor-supervisee relationships is that status, knowledge, maturity, and power differences between the participants eventually will begin to disappear. The parties who today are supervisor and supervisee can expect that one day they will relate to one another as peers and colleagues.

The parent-child metaphor also is suggested in the frequent use of developmental metaphors to describe supervision. Hillerbrand's (1989) suggestion that supervisors begin to consider the theorizing of Vygotsky

(1978) is an example of this. The following description of Vygotsky's thinking really derives at the most basic level from the manner in which parents teach life tasks to their children.

> *[Vygotsky] proposed that cognitive skills are acquired through social interaction. Unskilled persons learn cognitive skills by assuming more and more responsibility from experts during performance (what he called "expert scaffolding"). Novices first observe an expert's cognitive activity while the experts do most of the work. As novices begin to perform the skills, they receive feedback from the experts on their performance; as they learn to perform the skill correctly, they begin to assume more responsibility for the cognitive skill. Finally, novices assume the major responsibility for the cognitive skill, and experts become passive observers.* (Hillerbrand, 1989, p. 294).

*Sibling and Master-Apprentice Metaphors.* A second family metaphor that can pertain in supervision is that of older and younger siblings. For many supervisory dyads, this probably is more appropriate than the parent-child metaphor. The supervisor is farther along on the same path that is being traveled by the supervisee. As such, the supervisor is in a position to show the way in a nurturing, mentoring relationship. But as with siblings, issues of competence sometimes can trigger competition over who is more skilled or more brilliant in understanding the client.

Alonso (1985) discussed the sibling metaphor in supervision, maintaining that it is the young supervisor who is more likely to be perceived as an older sibling. Different metaphors pertain to those at other life stages; for example, a very senior supervisor might function as a benevolent grandparent.

Yet another metaphor that has been used with some frequency is that of the relationship between a master craftsperson and an apprentice. Such relationships have existed for hundreds, perhaps thousands, of years and are perpetuated in supervision. In these relationships, the master craftsperson serves as mentor to the person who aspires to enter the occupation, showing the apprentice the skills, procedures, and culture of that occupation. In this manner the master craftsperson also helps to perpetuate the craft. Eventually, after what is usually a stipulated period of apprenticeship, the apprentice becomes a peer of the craftsperson.

These metaphors, particularly those of parent or sibling, occur at fundamental and often primitive levels. Because they influence in an immediate and felt way, they have special, and probably ongoing, influence on the supervisory relationship. Moreover, such metaphors probably operate outside the awareness of the supervisor.

Other metaphors operate at higher levels of abstraction and probably are more appropriate to consider as possible influences on supervision. By this we mean those professional roles that already have been mastered by supervisors in earlier professional work and, therefore, become metaphors or templates for their work as supervisors. Ekstein and Wallerstein (1972) addressed this point in stating that

> *[t]he one confronted with something new will try at first to reduce the new to the familiar. The psychotherapist who becomes a teacher of psychotherapy will frequently be tempted to fall back on skills that represent prior acquisitions. He [or she] will thus try to convert the teaching relationship into a therapeutic relationship.* (pp. 254–255)

**Four Assumptions About Supervisor Roles**

Before going further with our discussion about the roles supervisors might employ in their work, we would like to offer some basic assumptions. Four in particular seem foundational for considering supervisory roles.

*Assumption One.* The first assumption is that treating supervision as a metaphor for something else and consequently employing a role from that previous something is not only a fact of life but also a desirable occurrence. At the same time we believe it is important that the supervisor understand the *as if* nature of the metaphor and not take it literally. For example, one metaphor from which supervisors might draw is that of therapist. This does not mean that supervisors should treat the supervisees in *exactly* the same manner as they do clients, only that certain behaviors and attitudes of the therapist are taken selectively into the supervisory situation.

*Assumption Two.* Our second assumption is that role flexibility is essential to good supervision. This means both that the effective supervisor will have available a repertoire of roles from which to draw and that the supervisor will change roles as the situation dictates. To the extent that the supervisor becomes frozen in a particular role, the supervisor's effectiveness is compromised.

No matter what the intended intervention, no effective human service professional will respond the same to each and every person who seeks help. The same also is true of supervision. For example, it often is helpful to adopt a directive style of supervision with supervisees. But the supervisor who would employ that style with *all* supervisees would be acting detrimentally to those who need to work out their issues on their own. The analogy would be to a carpenter who had only a single tool (e.g., a hammer) for use in *all* situations, even those that called for another type of tool. To complete the analogy, the goal for supervisors is to first outfit themselves with a complete tool kit and then have the flexibility to use all those tools. The tool kit to which we refer consists of the different roles a supervisor might adopt.

*Assumption Three.* Our third assumption is that the roles taken by a supervisor will be responsive to the context in which supervision occurs. In particular, the setting in which the supervision intervention occurs will influence

the roles of both the supervisor and supervisee. For example, all clinical supervisors, regardless of setting, are ethically responsible simultaneously for ensuring clients' welfare *and* for enhancing the skill and cognitive development of the trainee. Yet the relative emphasis given these two goals may differ somewhat from setting to setting, according to the mission of the particular unit. In service agencies that sponsor training, for example, client welfare needs are more likely to be the premier goal. College and university training programs, on the other hand, have an explicit training intent and the primary attention is more likely to be on the trainee's cognitive and skill development. The roles of supervisors in service agencies and educational programs consequently will vary as a function of their working in either of these settings.

Friedlander and Ward (1984) offered data that support our assertion that context will influence supervision. They found that both supervisors and supervisees reported that the supervisory style they called "interpersonally sensitive" was used more often in outpatient settings than in inpatient settings. It seems logical, of course, that when the clients have less severe problems (that is, are in outpatient settings), the supervisors can attend more to the relationships between them and their supervisees.

The findings of Tracey, Ellickson, and Sherry (1989) also seem relevant to this discussion of the influence of supervision context. Tracey et al. concluded from their data on supervision environments and client problem types that "in cases of high trainee anxiety (like with suicidal clients), there is relatively little diversity in what trainees prefer. In these cases, almost all trainees prefer structure" (p. 342).

*Assumption Four.* Our fourth assumption is that there is a particular perceptual set that underlies *all* supervisor roles. This set differs from what is used in other professional roles, especially in that of therapist.

Liddle (1988) discussed the transition from therapist to supervisor as a role development process involving several evolutionary steps. An essential early step in this process is for the emerging supervisor to make a shift in focus. That is, the supervisor eventually must realize that the purpose of supervision is neither to treat the client indirectly through the trainee nor to provide psychotherapy to the trainee.

Borders (1989c) discussed this same step in the supervisor-to-be's professional evolution. She maintained that the supervisor-to-be must make a cognitive shift in the transition from the role of counselor or therapist to that of supervisor. To illustrate how difficult this often is for new supervisors, she gave the example of a supervisor-trainee she was supervising who persisted for some time in referring to his supervisee as "my client." Until he was able to correctly label the trainee's role in relation to himself, his perceptual set remained that of a therapist.

This shift, then, requires the supervisor to give up doing what might be called "therapy by proxy" or "therapy by remote control." We note, however, that the pull to do this may always remain present even though unexpressed in practice. In part this is reinforced by supervisors' mandate to act always as monitors of client care, vigilant about how the client is functioning. Similarly, the longer the person has functioned as a therapist, the harder it may be to make the necessary shift in perspective.

Borders (1989c), in fact, observed that

*untrained professionals don't necessarily make this shift on their own, simply as a result of experience as a supervisor. As a matter of fact, some "experienced" professionals seem to have more difficulty changing their thinking than do doctoral students and advanced master's students in academic courses. (p. 2)*

In light of this assertion, it is especially interesting to consider Carl Rogers's statement: "Often when I . . . hear a tape of an interview . . . my feeling quite strongly is 'Move out of that chair. Let me take over.' " (Hackney & Goodyear, 1984, p. 285)

## THE DISCRIMINATION MODEL

A number of attempts have been made to identify roles a supervisor might adopt. The range of possibilities is suggested in Table 3.1, which depicts supervisory roles and models taken from four different sources. This depiction helps to illustrate both that there is variability in the roles that have been identified *and*

**TABLE 3.1**    Summary of Four Selected Categorizations of Supervisor Roles*

| Holloway (1984) | Hess (1980) | Littrell et al. (1979) | Hart (1982) |
| --- | --- | --- | --- |
| instructor | teacher | teaching | skill development |
| counselor | therapist | counseling/therapeutic | personal development |
| consultant | — | consulting | — |
| monitor | monitor | — | — |
| colleague | colleague-peer | — | — |
| — | case reviewer | — | — |
| — | instructor | — | — |
| — | — | self-supervising | — |
| — | — | — | integrative |

*Although Hart (1982) and Littrell et al. (1979) discuss models rather than roles, they imply roles in their models.

that there is some consensus for a few of the roles. (Notice, incidentally, that some authors have discussed *models* but imply *roles*.)

Of the available considerations of supervisory roles, we will describe the Discrimination Model (Bernard, 1979) in more detail. The Discrimination Model has been found to be useful for novice supervisors (e.g., Douce, 1989) primarily because of its parsimony and versatility. It can be understood as involving three basic supervisor roles (therapist, teacher, and consultant) and three basic foci (process, conceptualization, and personalization). The supervisor who works from this model, therefore, has nine possible choice points from which to choose in responding to a supervisee.

The Discrimination Model is *situation specific*. In fact, it is called the discrimination model precisely because it implies that the supervisor will use it to tailor a response to the particular supervisee's needs. This means that the supervisor's roles and foci should change not only *across* sessions but also *within* any particular session. This is consistent with our assertion earlier in this chapter that effective supervision requires role flexibility of the supervisor. Therefore, we now extend our argument to include flexibility of focus as well. Table 3.2 suggests possible examples of how this model might work. To better understand that table and the Discrimination Model itself, some elaboration is necessary.

### Supervisor Focus

The roles of therapist, teacher, and consultant must seem relatively clear-cut, for they are metaphoric expressions of the work performed by most mental health professionals. Less familiar, perhaps, is the idea of foci, or learning, dimensions. In the Discrimination Model (Bernard, 1979) three foci are proposed that, together, might be seen as comprising the primary ability domains of a competent therapist. In this manner they suggest an outline for supervision of any given trainee.

In the following section we will discuss the three foci suggested by the Discrimination Model: process skills, personalization skills, and conceptualization skills. They will be ordered from most to least overt. That is, process skills are expressed most overtly and, therefore, are most readily observable; personalization skills include those that are both overt and covert; conceptualization skills are those that are most covert and lest directly observable.

Process skills are those that most of us understand as involving therapeutic technique and strategy. It is important to recognize, however, that this focus is on the actual *implementation* of such skills rather than on the planning or anticipation of them. The latter falls within the focus of conceptualization. Illustrative examples of process skills include

*(a) ability to open an interview smoothly, (b) competence in the use of reflection, probes, restatement, summaries, or interpretations, (c) helping clients say what is on their minds, (d) using nonverbal communication to enhance verbal communication, (e) successfully implementing intervention strategies, and, (f) achieving interview closure. (Bernard, 1979, p. 61–62)*

Personalization refers to the more personal aspects of the trainee's experience. Certainly the trainee's countertransference responses fall within this domain. There are, however, a number of other possible examples of issues to be addressed within this focus, including

*(a) the [trainee's] comfort in assuming some authority in the counseling relationship and taking responsibility for his or her specialized knowledge and skills, (b) the ability of the [trainee] to hear challenges by the client or feedback from the supervisor without becoming overly defensive, (c) the ability to be comfortable with the [trainee's] own feelings, values, and attitudes, as well as those of the client, and, (d) the ability to have a fundamen-*

**TABLE 3.2**    The Discrimination Model*

| Focus of Supervision | SUPERVISOR ROLE | | |
| --- | --- | --- | --- |
| | *Teacher* | *Counselor* | *Consultant* |
| Process | S-ee would like to use systematic desensitization with a client but has never learned the technique. | S-ee is able to use a variety of process skills, but with one client uses question asking as his primary style. | S-ee finds her clients reacting well to her humor and would like to know more ways to use humor in counseling. |
| | S-or teaches the S-ee relaxation techniques, successive approximation, hierarchy building, and the desensitization process. | S-or attempts to help S-ee determine the effect of this client on him, which limits his use of skills in therapy sessions. | S-or works with S-ee to identify different uses of humor in counseling and to practice these. |
| Conceptualization | S-ee is unable to recognize themes and patterns of client thought either during or following therapy sessions. | S-ee is unable to set realistic goals for her client who requests assertion training. | S-ee would like to use a different model for case conceptualization. |
| | S-or uses transcripts of therapy sessions to teach S-ee to identify thematic client statements (e.g., blaming, dependence). | S-or helps S-ee relate her discomfort to her own inability to be assertive in several relationships. | S-or discusses several models for S-ee to consider. |
| Personalization | S-ee is unaware her preference for a close seating arrangement intimidates the client. | S-ee is unaware that his female client is attracted to him sexually. | S-ee would like to feel more comfortable working with older clients. |
| | S-or assigns the reading of proximity studies in the literature. | S-or attempts to help S-ee confront his own sexuality and his resistance to recognizing sexual cues from women. | S-or and S-ee discuss developmental concerns of older people. |

*S-or is supervisor; S-ee is supervisee. Adapted from Bernard, J. M. (1979). Supervisor training: A discrimination model. *Counselor Education and Supervision, 19,* 60–69. Copyright (1979) by the American Association for Counseling and Development. Adapted by permission.

*tal respect for the client. (Bernard, 1979, p. 62-63)*

Most of the counselor's covert behaviors fall under the general category of conceptualization. That is, conceptualization is a cognitive skill that reflects deliberate thinking and case analysis by the trainee. It involves

*(a) the ability to understand what the client is saying, (b) the skill in identifying themes in the client's messages, (c) the skill to recognize appropriate and inappropriate goals for the client, (d) skill in choosing strategies that are appropriate to the client's expressed goals, and (e) skill in recognizing even subtle improvement by the client. (Bernard, 1979, p. 62).*

We suspect that anyone who has been supervised knows that trainees' comfort levels often are greatest when their supervisors choose to focus on conceptualization. After all, to focus on conceptualization usually means the spotlight is primarily on the client; discussion is diverted from a consideration of the trainee's own strengths and weaknesses.

We do not wish to imply, however, that addressing trainees' conceptualization skills is wrong. In fact, Loganbill and Stoltenberg (1983), concerned that trainees' conceptualization skills are given too little systematic attention, developed a supervision format they use to address this focus. They have employed this format, summarized in Table 3.3, with practicum students in two different university settings as a way of helping to develop their conceptualization skills. Loganbill and Stoltenberg reported that they require trainees to follow this format in a step-by-step fashion in initial sessions of individual supervision; trainees also are to use this format in presenting cases to the practicum group. But just as Loganbill and Stoltenberg developed this conceptualization format for their own training purposes, other supervisors might modify it according to their needs or preferences.

All three foci, personalization, process, and conceptualization, should be in the super-

visor's repertoire and be invoked when appropriate. The problems arise either when the supervisor adopts one focus at the expense of the supervisee's more salient needs or when the supervisor is rigid in using one particular focus.

We note at the same time, however, that although supervisors may have a preferred focus, it is not possible to attend *exclusively* to only one. In any given supervision session, all three foci invariably are invoked, even when one or two are given little emphasis. Figure 3.2 suggests the approximate way this works: If the apexes of the triangle each represent one of the three foci, it can be seen that although supervisor X may focus primarily on process skills, supervisor Y is more balanced in the use of the foci; both, however, will address *each* of the foci (learning dimensions) to some extent.

The emphasis given to a particular focus is determined by several factors, including theoretical orientation and supervisee's level of development. For example, supervisors of beginning trainees might expect to focus predominantly on process skills whereas supervisors of more advanced students might expect to offer more balanced supervision across foci. But regardless of the reasons for a supervisor's preference among the foci (e.g., theoretical orientation, students' developmental level), the preferred focus typically will suggest the criteria the supervisor uses in evaluating the trainee. For example, if the supervisor's preferred focus is on the trainee's personalization skills, then issues of personhood are more likely to be used in evaluating the supervisee than will be true of the supervisor whose preferred focus is on process skills.

## Conclusions About the Discrimination Model

Our own professional experience as supervisors and as trainers of supervisors has been that the Discrimination Model is quite useful

**TABLE 3.3**  Loganbill and Stoltenberg's Format for Case Conceptualization*

| Content Area | Description of Content Area | | |
| --- | --- | --- | --- |
| Identifying Data | 1. age | | 5. living situation |
| | 2. sex | | 6. manner of dress |
| | 3. race | | 7. physical appearance |
| | 4. marital status | | 8. general self-presentation |
| Presenting Problem | This includes a listing of the problem areas, from the client's perspective, noting particularly the client's view of their order of importance. Suggested items to focus upon: <br> 1. Was there a precipitating set of circumstances? <br> 2. How long has the problem(s) persisted? <br> 3. Has this problem occurred before? What were the circumstances then? | | |
| Relevant History | This will vary in comprehensiveness, according to depth and length of treatment, and will vary in focus according to theoretical orientation and specific nature of the problem(s). | | |
| Interpersonal Style | This should include a description of the client's orientation toward others in his or her environment and should include two sections: <br> 1. Is there an overall posture s/he takes toward others? What is the nature of his/her typical relationships? Karen Horney's conceptualization may be helpful here: <br>   a. moving toward (dependency, submission) <br>   b. moving against (aggressive, dominance) <br>   c. moving away (withdrawal) <br> Is there a tendency toward one or the other polarity of dominance vs. submission, love vs. hate? <br> 2. How is the client's interpersonal stance manifested specifically within the therapeutic dyad? What is the client's interpersonal orientation toward the therapist? | | |
| Environmental Factors | This might include: <br> 1. elements in the environment that function as *stressors* to the client, both those centrally related to the problem and those more peripheral. <br> 2. elements in the environment that function as *support* for the client (e.g., friends, family, living accommodations, recreational activities, financial situation) | | |
| Personality Dynamics | 1. Cognitive factors: Included are any data relevant to thinking and mental processes, such as: <br>   a. intelligence <br>   b. mental alertness <br>   c. persistence of negative cognitions <br>   d. positive cognitions <br>   e. nature and content of fantasy life <br>   f. level of insight—client's "psychological mindedness" or ability to be aware and observant of changes in feeling state and behavior and client's ability to place his/her behavior in some interpretive scheme and to consider hypotheses about his/her own and others' behavior <br>   g. capacity for judgment—client's ability to make decisions and carry out the practical affairs of daily living <br> 2. Emotional factors: <br>   a. typical or most common emotional states <br>   b. mood during interview <br>   c. appropriateness of affect <br>   d. range of emotions the client has the capacity to show <br>   e. cyclical aspects of the client's emotional life | | |

**TABLE 3.3**   Loganbill and Stoltenberg's Format for Case Conceptualization* (*cont.*)

| Content Area | Description of Content Area |
|---|---|
| | 3. Behavioral factors:<br>  a. psychosomatic symptoms<br>  b. other physical related symptoms<br>  c. existence of persistent habits or mannerisms<br>  d. sexual dysfunctioning<br>  e. eating patterns<br>  f. sleeping patterns |
| Therapist's Conceptualization of the Problem | This will include a summary of the therapist's view of the problem. It should include only the most central and core dynamics of the client's personality and note in particular the inter-relationships between the major dynamics. What are the common themes? What ties it all together? This is a synthesis of all the above data and the essence of the conceptualization. |

*This table was adapted from Figure 1 (p. 237) in Loganbill, C., & Stoltenberg, C. (1983). The case conceptualization format: A training device for practicum. *Counselor Education and Supervision, 22,* 235–242. Copyright (1983) by the American Association for Counseling and Development. Adapted by permission.

in the supervisor's own conceptualization. But we do not intend to offer it as the perfect model. Like all others, it has both strengths and weaknesses. We will conclude this section of the chapter by discussing several of these.

Because it suggests both roles and foci, the Discrimination Model is more inclusive than most models that have addressed supervisor roles. In fact, the Discrimination Model is rooted in a technical eclecticism. The strength of this is that it frees the user to be broadly flexible in responding to the supervisee. On the other hand, a possible limitation is that it is not driven by any particular theoretical approach, as the Friedlander and Ward model depicted in Figure 3.1 suggests should be the case. When theory is removed as a causal force, there are fewer signposts for the supervisor to use in selecting roles and foci.

The fact is, though, that supervisors never can or will divorce themselves totally from the influence of their theoretical beliefs. Moreover, they often will invoke theory as a rationalization for what actually is personal idiosyncrasy. Gizynski (1978), for example, observed that the supervisor easily can mistakenly believe that style is not a manifestation of personality characteristics but rather "a distil-

lation of his [or her] accumulated experience in clinical intervention" (p. 207). But whether it is theory or rationalization, the net result is to block the flexibility demanded of the supervisor to fully use the Discrimination Model.

A second point is that the Discrimination Model is concerned specifically with the *training* aspects of supervision. Therefore, it does not directly address the role of monitor (see, for example, Table 3.1), which is important as a means to ensure quality of client care.

A third point is that the Discrimination Model has some empirical support. Russell, Crimmings, and Lent (1984) correctly have noted that very little research has been done to test models of supervision that suggest supervisor roles. A strength of the Discrimination

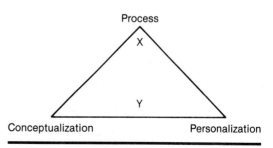

**FIGURE 3.2**   Depiction of the use of supervisory foci

Model is that it may be the most researched of these models. During the past decade, a number of studies either have explicitly tested the Discrimination Model or have employed it as a way to frame research questions (e.g., Ellis & Dell, 1986; Ellis, Dell, & Good, 1988; Glidden & Tracey, 1989; Goodyear, Abadie, & Efros, 1984; Goodyear & Robyak, 1982; Stenack & Dye, 1982; Yager, Wilson, Brewer, & Kinnetz, 1989). The model seems generally to have been supported in the various findings of these studies.

Interestingly, the role of consultant has remained somewhat elusive in these studies. For example, Goodyear et al. (1984) found that a sample of experienced supervisors were able to differentiate among the supervision sessions of four major psychotherapy theorists according to their use of the teacher and counselor roles but not the consultant role. Similarly, the counselor and teacher roles were validated, but the consultant role was not, in a factor analytic study by Stenack and Dye (1982). In multidimensional scaling studies by Ellis and Dell (1986) and Glidden and Tracey (1989) the teaching and counseling roles were found to anchor opposite ends of a single dimension; the consultant role did not clearly emerge from their data. This is curious because the idea of the consultant role for supervisors is intuitively appealing, especially in work with more advanced supervisees (e.g., Gurk & Wicas, 1979). One possible explanation is that the consultant role is "fuzzier" than the others. Although it is frequently endorsed, there is not the common understanding of it that is true of the counselor and teacher roles.

## SUPERVISEE ROLES

Our primary emphasis in this chapter has been on the supervisor's possible roles and foci. Implicit, though, has been the assumption that the roles a supervisor employs are effective to the extent that the trainee adheres to a complementary role. Holloway (1984), for example, is one who has offered an explicit link between specific supervisor and supervisee roles.

Although supervision is a learning rather than a healing process, it might be instructive to consider the four conditions Frank (1973) hypothesized to be required for successful healing:

1. An emotionally charged and confiding relationship
2. A setting in which patients' expectancies for help and confidence in the therapist's role as healer are strengthened
3. A rationale or conceptual scheme that plausibly explains symptoms and prescribes a procedure for their resolution
4. A set of procedures or rituals, in which both client and therapist engage, that they believe to be the means of helping the client meet its goals

With only relatively minor modifications, these same four conditions of change seem to typify supervision. It is, after all, an intervention that occurs in the context of a relationship of some intensity and in a socially sanctioned setting. Also, supervisors work from and believe in a particular theoretical model and engage in a set of procedures and rituals (e.g., live supervision, listening to tapes, giving feedback) that they believe will have the effect of enhancing supervisees' work. Essential to success is that the supervisee share the supervisor's belief in both the model being used and the rituals appropriate to that model. Bordin (1983) noted that the strength of a supervisor-supervisee working alliance depends, in part, on such shared expectations.

But although such supervisor-supervisee complementarity is typical, it is not universal. Occasionally, for example, the supervisor deliberately may adopt a role that is not complementary to that of the supervisee. Blocher (1983), for example, advocated deliberate mismatching as a means to encourage supervisee growth and development. Noncomplementary roles also can be adopted for less deliberate reasons. One of these might be the differing expectations each person brings into the relationship. Such mismatching also might occur when supervisees simply are uninformed about the appropriate roles they are to assume as supervisee.

To anticipate mismatches that may occur because of differing expectations between supervisor and supervisee, initial negotiation, or contracting, is useful. When the issue is that the supervisee simply does not know what the role options are — as might be the case with a beginning supervisor — role induction procedures can be effective. That is, the trainee can be educated about the expected role of supervisee by, for example, discussions and videotaped role modeling. Although little research has been done to investigate the effectiveness of this procedure in supervision, its effectiveness with therapy clients has been demonstrated (e.g., Garfield, 1986; Kaul & Bednar, 1986).

## ROLE CONFLICTS

Most mental health professionals are sensitive to the fact that dual relationships are problematic and to be avoided as much as possible. But what is a dual relationship if not one in which there is a role conflict, or to use Robiner's (1982) term, role "diffusion"? Another way to conceptualize this problem is as one of violations of boundaries across subsystems.

Certain of these role conflicts, or dual relationships, are more obvious and, therefore, perhaps easier to anticipate and head off than others. For example, most mental health professionals recognize it is wrong for members of a supervisory dyad also to be sexual partners

(e.g., Hall, 1988) or for students in a training program also to serve as clients to other members of that program (Patrick, 1989). In these cases, the conflict is between a supervision-appropriate role and one that is *not* supervision appropriate.

Other role conflicts — particularly those that are both supervision appropriate but have competing or antagonistic goals — are more difficult to avoid, even by the best intentioned and most alert supervisor. For example, the supervisor who draws from a counselor role may intend to increase the supervisee's development by encouraging the supervisee to be self-disclosing and open. At the same time, however, the supervisor also functions in the role of evaluator. It is conceivable, therefore, that material the supervisor gains by encouraging supervisee self-disclosure may lead to the conclusion that the trainee simply is not suited for this line of work. The consequent actions the supervisor may then take in the role of evaluator can be antithetical to the supervisee's personal and professional development, the training goals of the intervention.

It is not possible, then, for supervisors to fully avoid role conflicts. They can be alert to the adoption of extrasupervision roles (e.g., lover) that are certain to cause role conflict. Supervisors also can attenuate, to some extent, the effects of supervision-appropriate role conflicts by informing the supervisee at the outset of the relationship about the possibility of such conflicts and their consequences. At the same time, supervisors should know that these preventive approaches still fall short of constituting informed consent in its best sense, for trainees are not given a choice about receiving supervision. Ultimately, there is no substitute for the supervisor remaining vigilant against the possible occurrence of dual relationship problems and being prepared to minimize that intrusion. We will consider these and similar issues more fully in Chapters 7 and 8.

## CONCLUSION

There are a number of factors that influence the roles supervisors might employ, including their comfort with roles they have taken in other professional contexts. The major theme of this chapter, however, has been that a supervisor must have available both a range of possible roles and the flexibility to employ them deliberately, according to the supervisee's particular needs.

The Discrimination Model was proposed as one means of considering supervisor roles central to the training aspects of supervision. Several of its strengths and limitations were noted.

Although most of the chapter focused on supervisor roles, supervisee roles were discussed briefly. The chapter then concluded with a consideration of some problems of role conflicts.

# CHAPTER 4

# THE INDIVIDUAL CASE CONFERENCE: METHODS AND TECHNIQUES

Having described a context for supervision in the first three chapters, we are now prepared to consider how clinical supervision is carried out. This chapter on individual supervision is only one of three chapters that will look at the process of supervision. It will be followed by chapters on group supervision and live supervision.

Individual supervision is still considered the cornerstone of professional development. Although most supervisees will experience some form of group supervision in their training and some may have an opportunity to work within a live supervision paradigm, virtually all supervisees will experience individual supervision sessions. Whether these individual conferences will produce memories and insights that will linger long into the supervisee's career or will frustrate or perhaps even bore the supervisee has something to do with the supervisor's skill in choosing and using a variety of supervision methods. At this point in the history of the helping professions there are many different techniques from which the supervisor can choose to conduct an individual case conference. This chapter will outline these different techniques, and will address their advantages and occasional disadvantages.

Although all of the supervision interventions described in this chapter are appropriate for individual conferences, many of them also could be applied within a group supervision context. Chapter 5, Group Supervision, however, focuses on strategies that rely on group dynamics for their implementation.

Finally, we will make one cautionary remark. When writing a textbook of this sort, each chapter becomes an artificial compartmentalization of one aspect of the whole. The gestalt, so to speak, is violated. Although this cannot be avoided, it seems particularly problematic as we consider methods and techniques of supervision. Of all the many aspects of clinical supervision, methods of supervision is the most vulnerable to abuse. That is, it is possible to conduct supervision using a great many different formats without stepping back to consider the bigger picture, — a conceptual base, an evaluation plan, ethical constraints, and so on. We urge the reader, therefore, to view this chapter not in isolation but in the context of other concepts presented in this book.

## CRITERIA FOR CHOOSING SUPERVISION INTERVENTIONS

A supervisor's choice of method is influenced by a number of factors both rational and irrational. The supervisor might believe that without an audiotape or videotape of therapy there is no real way to know what has transpired between trainees and their clients. Or the supervisor might be adamant that self-report is the only form of supervision that provides a glimpse at the supervisee's internal reasoning. The list can, and indeed does, go on. Borders and Leddick (1987) listed six reasons for choosing different supervision methods (p. 28).

1. *The supervisee's learning goals.* Although novice trainees may introduce learning goals, usually the advanced trainee is more articulate about supervision needs. For example, a supervisee who has received only one type of supervision (e.g., self-report) may request direct observation as part of a new supervision contract. Obviously, the supervisee must possess some ability to self-evaluate in order to identify appropriate learning goals.

2. *The supervisee's experience level and developmental issues.* It is the wisdom of the profession as well as the results of empirical investigation that trainees desire more structure early in their clinical work and less structure as their experience grows (Rabinowitz, Heppner, & Roehlke, 1986; Tracey, Ellickson, & Sherry, 1989; Worthington & Roehlke, 1979). Loganbill, Hardy, and Delworth's (1982) model more specifically evaluates trainees on several target issues to determine their developmental position. Tracey et al. (1989) considered trainee personality variables as these related to an acceptance or rejection of structure in supervision. The results of such evaluations, then, would help determine the focus and method of intervention.

3. *The supervisee's learning style.* One of the appealing assumptions of Neurolinguistic Programming (Grinder & Bandler, 1976) was that people vary in how they use and relate to the different senses. We process information idiosyncratically, and this affects how we communicate and, certainly, how we learn. Whether a student is visual or auditory, global or specific, or theatrical or reticent results in different ways of learning and knowing. There are ample supervision methods to meet the needs of a wide variety of trainees.

4. *The supervisor's goals for the supervisee.* Assuming that some assessment has oc-

curred, supervisors will decide what each trainee lacks in terms of clinical ability and will design supervision to compensate for the deficit.

5. *The supervisor's theoretical orientation.* Although some supervision methods may be attractive in their own right, they may simply not be compatible with some theoretical positions. For example, live supervision is antithetical to person-centered therapy.

6. *The supervisor's own learning goals for the supervisory experience.* Supervisors might want to improve their supervisory abilities. If a supervisor has relied heavily on one type of supervision process, there is a real danger of becoming stagnant or of individual trainees being fit to the method rather than the reverse. Adding new supervisory methods will allow the supervisor to grow in the practice of supervision, as important a process to good supervision as continued growth in the practice of therapy.

As one might assume, decisions about the process of supervision are not a one-time occurrence. The supervisor may avoid certain methods because of theoretical differences with the underlying premises of those methods, but within the supervisor's comfort range there may be a variety of methods from which to choose. An additional aid for the supervisor in determining what method to use in a given situation is to pinpoint the immediate function of supervision. There are three general functions of supervision interventions (Borders, Bernard, Dye, Fong, Henderson, & Nance, undated): assessing the learning needs of the supervisee; changing, shaping or supporting the supervisee's behavior; and evaluating the performance of the supervisee. Although the majority of supervision falls within the second function, supervisors are continually reassessing their supervisee's learning needs and evaluating their progress. As these separate functions are being addressed, the supervisor might find that different methods fit the approach to one function better than others. For example, a supervisor might choose to watch a videotape of a supervisee in order to assess that person's skills but rely on process notes to accomplish the second function of attempting to change, support, or redirect the supervisee's work.

## Art and Science

The helping professions have engaged in the art-versus-science argument for some time. It is our position that this argument is fruitless and too often is founded on stereotypical understandings of what it means to be either an artist or a scientist. In fact, as scientist practitioners, we believe that the effective supervisor should be *both*. The ideal is the supervisor who has the creativity of an artist and demonstrates the critical thinking of the scientist (see, for example, Claiborn, 1987).

The supervisor who functions only as a technician is quite another matter. Expensive video equipment and intercom systems do not make a supervisor. Many supervisors seem convinced that they will change their supervision process as soon as they find time to set up equipment (or order it), organize their case conferences, catch up on their reading, and so on. Many of those who do accomplish these goals trust that the technology alone will suffice as supervision.

At the same time, talented supervisors limit their potential impact if they do not take advantage of modern supervision aids. Our point is that if supervisors are to benefit from supervision technology, they must make a conscious decision to do this and then give themselves the time it requires to implement different supervision strategies. There is little question that planning is required to use certain supervision methods. Our hope is that su-

pervisors employ the creativity of an artist and the critical thinking of a scientist to guide their planning for and use of technology.

## METHODS, FORMS, AND TECHNIQUES OF SUPERVISION

With technology becoming more sophisticated every day and with the helping professions exhibiting a heightened interest in supervision, different techniques, methods, and paradigms for conducting supervision are evolving at a rapid pace. Because of the dynamic nature of the field, therefore, we do not presume to present an inclusive list of supervision interventions. Rather, we hope to present an appreciation for the diversity of choices that have been spawned during supervision's growth spurt, some rationale for using different methods, and the findings on their relative strengths and weaknesses as reported in the literature.

Borders (1989c) identified one issue endemic to all supervision case conferences situations, that being the challenge to think like a supervisor rather than a therapist. She contends that seasoned practitioners tend to continue to be fascinated by therapy issues, thus focusing on client issues rather than the learning and developmental needs of their supervisees. As part of a training package to help supervisors make the shift, Borders suggested that supervisors observe or listen to a trainee's counseling session and take notes on the content. The supervisors are then asked to peruse their notes looking for the relative amount of attention they paid to the supervisee's behaviors versus the client's behaviors. In other words, have they focused on the therapist's interventions or have they assumed their former practitioner stance and focused on the client? Other aids suggested by Borders include planning for supervision by considering learning goals for supervisees, writing case notes on supervision sessions that focus on supervisory goals and outcomes, and asking for feedback from supervisees to make certain that their supervision needs are being met.

The remainder of this chapter has been designed to advance from methods that allow least direct observation by the supervisor to those that allow the most. Therefore, self-report begins our list as a case conference that relies on the supervisee's recollections of therapy as the source of information to be used for supervision.

## Self-Report

Although it is a simple form of supervision in one sense, we consider self-report to be a difficult method to perform well. In fact, some of the best and the worst supervision can be found within the domain of self-report. Under supervisors who excel at their art, supervisees will be challenged conceptually and personally and will learn a great deal. Many supervisors relying on self-report, however, have fallen into stagnation; supervision becomes pro forma, with little difference evident from session to session or from supervisee to supervisee.

The professional literature has given relatively little attention to self-report in the past two decades, focusing much more in earnest on the technological forms of supervision. Self-report, however, continues to be a commonly used form of supervision, especially in the field. This is in sharp contrast to training programs that rely more and more heavily on more active forms of supervision. The implications of this dichotomy between the training of helping professionals and their ultimate employment sites has not been addressed sufficiently by the helping professions. While there is some expectation among training institutions and accrediting agencies that the field will follow the ground-breaking work that has been done in the area of clinical supervision, the immediate future is more likely to put new practitioners in the position of trying to make

relevant the supervisory experience they acquired while in training as they experience a very different form of supervision in their jobs.

Because self-report is the grandfather of supervision forms, there also is a tendency to return to it when other supervisory processes become tiresome. In fact, Hess and Hess (1983) reported that even among APA-accredited internship sites where doctoral candidates were trained in supervision, the most frequent form of supervision of supervision was the individual conference without audiovisual aids. The second most frequent form of supervision of supervision was "none."

At its best, self-report is an intense tutorial relationship in which the therapist fine-tunes both case conceptualization ability and personal knowledge as it relates to each therapist-client relationship. Although Dowling's (1984) study was not based strictly on the self-report format, she nevertheless sought to determine how clinical students in speech and language pathology viewed their supervisory conferences both in terms of what was typical and what was ideal. Seventy-six students at three different levels of clinical experience were asked to rate 18 different items as describing either what typically occurred in supervision and/or what they found most valuable. Five of the items on the questionnaire were considered to reflect direct supervisory interventions; nine were seen as indirect; and four were viewed as neither (see Table 4.1). Overall, typical supervisory conferences were seen as direct while ideal conferences were viewed primarily as indirect. The preference for indirect interventions increased with the experience of the clinician, reinforcing the notion that self-report is best used to challenge advanced supervisees rather than to instruct or guide novices.

Biggs (1988) supported the notion that self-report conferences should be cognitively challenging and confronted the competing sentiment that the supervisor should fill the

**TABLE 4.1** Individual Conference Rating Scale Item Delineation*

| | |
|---|---|
| 1. The supervisee asks many questions. | Indirect |
| 2. The supervisor provides justification for statements or suggestion. | Direct |
| 3. The supervisor uses conference time to discuss ways to improve materials. | Descriptive |
| 4. The supervisor offers suggestions on therapy techniques during the conference. | Direct |
| 5. The supervisor uses the supervisee's ideas in discussion during the conference. | Indirect |
| 6. The supervisor responds to statements, questions, or problems presented by the supervisee. | Indirect |
| 7. The supervisee uses the conference time to provide feedback to the supervisor about the clinical session. | Indirect |
| 8. The supervisor and supervisee participate in a teacher-student relationship. | Descriptive |
| 9. The supervisor uses a supportive style. | Indirect |
| 10. The supervisor helps the supervisee set realistic goals for the clients. | Indirect |
| 11. The supervisee verbalizes needs. | Indirect |
| 12. The supervisor uses conference time to discuss weaknesses in the supervisee's clinical behavior. | Direct |
| 13. The supervisor presents value judgments about the supervisee's clinical behavior. | Direct |
| 14. During the conference, the supervisee requests a written copy of the supervisor's behavioral observations. | Descriptive |
| 15. The supervisor and supervisee participate in a superior-subordinate relationship. | Direct |
| 16. The supervisor states the objectives of the conference. | Descriptive |
| 17. The supervisor asks the supervisee to analyze or evaluate something that has occurred or may occur in the clinical session. | Indirect |
| 18. The supervisor asks the supervisee to think about strategies that might have been done differently or that may be done in the future. | Indirect |

*From Dowling, S. (1988). Typical, ideal conferences: Perceptions as a function of training. *The Clinical Supervisor,* 6(2), 49–62. Copyright © (1988) by The Haworth Press, Inc., 10 Alice Street, New York, NY 13904. Reprinted by permission.

role of master therapist and that communication in the conference should be from expert to novice (Hess, 1980b). Biggs identified three conceptual tasks that should be addressed in the supervision conference: identifying how observations and inferences are used to provide the evidence for clinical judgments; describing and discussing major dimensions of the therapeutic relationship; and describing the assumptions regarding the client's personality, problem conditions, and choice of treatments. Biggs proceeded to elaborate on each task and its importance for supervision.

Holloway (1988) questioned Biggs's assumption that supervisees come to supervision with the skills necessary to take advantage of such a complex cognitive process. She further

doubted the wisdom of a supervision model that excludes direct observation, including the use of audio or videotape, thereby losing "the opportunity for (a) independent judgment regarding the client's problem, and (b) illustrating directly with the case in question how to draw inferences from client information" (p. 256). Holloway's point is well taken and underscores one of the key vulnerabilities of the self-report method: As a supervision strategy, it is only as good as the observational and conceptual abilities of the supervisee and the seasoned insightfulness of the supervisor. It seems, therefore, that self-report offers too many opportunities for failure if it represents the complete supervision plan. Williams (1988) perhaps said it best:

*It takes a master chess player to play without seeing the pieces; but that is what we attempt to do when we supervise merely by talk. Supervisors can be theoretically blind, and keep trying to apply the old solutions, only harder; and sometimes, they can be methodologically blind, and keep applying the same technique — verbal rationalization — only harder. (p. 22)*

## Process Notes

The above discussion of self-report did not assume the use of any form of systematic written documentation of the cases being presented in supervision or of therapeutic interventions. For supervisors who do not use more direct or active forms of supervision, case notes can provide a means of controlling the type of information offered in supervision.

Goldberg (1985) offered a helpful look at the advantages of process notes and audio- and videotape as different information sources for supervision. He observed that an obstacle to the development of clinical supervision has been the controversy between those who prefer to base their supervision on the introspection allowed by process notes and those who prefer their supervision to be based on direct access to the supervisee's clinical work. Goldberg supported Borders and Leddick's (1987) belief that the method should be based on the immediate learning needs of the supervisee and that supervisors need to avoid fixed styles in their supervision.

Many of the advantages of using process notes, according to Goldberg (1985), are similar to the advantages discussed under self-report. (Goldberg used individual dynamic psychotherapy as his point of reference, in which process notes are the supervisee's written explanation of the content of the therapy session, the interactional processes that occurred between therapist and client, the therapist's feelings about the client, and the rationale and manner of intervention.) Goldberg argued that process notes allow a wealth

of information to enter the supervisory session and, therefore, allow the supervisor an opportunity to track the supervisee's cognitive processes in ways that more active forms of supervision disallow. Goldberg also found value in the experiential component between supervisor and supervisee who are free from the distraction of media, and he predicted more worthwhile modeling of therapeutic conditions to occur when process notes, as opposed to media, are the focus of supervision.

Goldberg acknowledged that the use of process notes as the exclusive method of supervision might be more advantageous for the advanced supervisee. He reported the work of Muslin, Singer, Meusea, and Leahy (1968), who compared process notes based on therapy sessions with actual recordings of the sessions and found "gross distortions and deletions of information at a variety of levels" (Goldberg, 1985, p. 7). Therefore, for supervisees other than the most clinically astute, process notes will compromise the accuracy of the information being presented. In fact, supervisors might be well advised to view process notes more as metaphors of therapy than as literal accounts of what transpired. Again, this type of view parallels the supervision goals usually associated with self-report.

Being reminded of the limits of process notes does not underestimate their value, especially when used in conjunction with other supervision methods. Even a brief outline to track a therapy session can help both novice and experienced supervisees order their thinking in meaningful ways, allowing them to use their supervision time more fully. Schwartz (1981) suggested a one-page worksheet that family therapy trainees complete after each session to include

*(1) diagnosis and hypotheses (or changes in these) of the case based upon the previous session; (2) assessment of the previous session's goals, strategies and interventions; (3) goals (or changes in goals) for the case and for [the supervisee] based upon the previous session;*

*(4) specific objectives (therapist's) for the next session; and (5) strategies for attaining therapist's objectives for next session. (p. 90)*

A similar process notes outline is offered in Table 4.2

If the supervision goal is for the supervisee to learn to conceptualize the ecological reality of the client, then a more intensive, client- or system-centered outline can be followed. The Loganbill and Stoltenberg (1983) outline presented in Chapter 3 is an example of a tool to use for the conceptualization of individual clients (see Table 3.3). For family cases and a systemic approach to conceptualizing cases, the questions suggested by Resnikoff (1981) in Table 4.3 might be considered.

## Audiotaping

Although live observation and videotape have led to some of the more dramatic breakthroughs in the supervision process, the audiotape was first to revolutionize our perceptions of what could be accomplished in su-

**TABLE 4.3**   Questions to Delineate the Elements of Family Functioning*

1. What is the outward appearance of the family? (This item includes the positioning of family members in the therapy room.)
2. What is the cognitive functioning in the family? (This item includes the quality and clarity of communication.)
3. What repetitive, non-productive sequences do you notice?
4. What is the basic feeling state in the family and who carries it?
5. What individual roles reinforce family resistances and what are the most prevalent family defenses?
6. What subsystems are operative in the family?
7. Who carries the power of the family?
8. How are the family members differentiated from each other and what are the subgroup boundaries?
9. What part of the life cycle is the family experiencing and are the problem-solving methods stage-appropriate?
10. What are the evaluator's own reactions to the family?

*From Resnikoff, R. O. (1981) Teaching family therapy: Ten key questions for understanding the family as patient. *Journal of Marital and Family Therapy*, 7(2), 135–142. Copyright © (1981) by the American Association for Marriage and Family Therapy. Reprinted by permission.

**TABLE 4.2**   Progress Notes

1. What were your goals for this session?
2. Did anything happen *during* the session that caused you to reconsider your goals? How did you resolve this?
3. What was the major theme of the session? Was there any important content?
4. Describe the interpersonal dynamics between you and the client during the session?
5. How successful was the session?
6. What did you learn (if anything) about the helping process from this session?
7. What are your plans/goals for the next session?
8. What specific questions do you have for your supervisor regarding this and/or future sessions?

pervision. Without the facilities of a laboratory and without the funds, technological expertise, or necessary space to utilize videotape, the audiotape allowed therapists to transport an accurate (albeit partial) recording of therapy to a supervisor who was not present at the time the session occurred. The audiotape is still the most widely used source of information for supervisors who expect to have some sort of direct access to the work of their supervisees.

Indeed, in many counseling and therapy settings the audiotape is still the only practical means of direct supervision. Additionally, there is no empirical evidence that audiotape is inferior to videotape as a means of supervision as measured by supervisee performance skills (Ward, Kagan, & Krathwohl, 1972). For these reasons, we believe it is important that training programs not completely abandon the use of audiotape for more sophisticated technology. If trainees are not exposed to credible uses of audiotape in their clinical programs, they may forsake direct supervision of any kind in their professional positions when more costly supervision methods are not available.

The above notwithstanding, we also believe that audiotape can be used for the wrong reasons—for example, for the convenience of the supervisor when other options are available. Audiotape can also be used randomly, with little care about how to achieve maximum advantage from its employment.

When audiotape is first required of supervisees (especially if they have been relying on self-report or process notes), there is often some resistance that takes the form of "My clients won't be comfortable." This reaction is occasionally echoed at practicum or internship sites when a training institution asks for audiotapes of the supervisee's clinical work. As most experienced supervisors know, it is usually not the client but the trainee who is experiencing discomfort at the prospect of being scrutinized. The vast majority of clients are open to having their sessions audiotaped as long as they have an assurance that confidentiality will not be compromised and the supervisee's demeanor is not tense (implying danger) when presenting the topic of audiotaping.

Although it is assumed that trainees will be initially uncomfortable with the expectation of taping, at least one study (Bowman & Roberts, 1979) found no increase in anxiety for counseling trainees when taping for supervisory evaluation over that which was present when counseling without taping for evaluation. Most supervisees will report that there was initial anxiety but that it abated once taping became commonplace. For a minority of supervisees, the scrutiny is an issue, one that will lead either to some discussion about the trainee's overall readiness to take on the responsibility of clinical work or to an alternative supervisory method while the supervisee regains confidence. When audiotaping (or any other direct supervision method) seems to be escalating anxiety, we do not believe that more of the same is the solution.

***Planning Supervision.*** The least productive way to use an audiotape in supervision may be that which is depicted in the following vignette: The supervisee arrives with two or three audiotapes of recent counseling sessions, without having reviewed any of them privately. Because the supervisee has made no decision about which session to discuss during supervision, the supervisee spends several minutes telling the supervisor about the cases that are on tape. The supervisor eventually picks one tape, which the trainee must then rewind. The counseling session is played from the beginning until something strikes the supervisor as important.

Our point is simple: The process of supervision must be based on a plan, and it is the supervisor's responsibility to outline that plan. We do believe spontaneity is important, but it is unlikely to emerge when the supervision process has no vitality. Listening to an audiotape for 20 minutes with a supervisee saying "Gee, I guess the part I was talking about was further into the session than I realized" is one sure way to kill supervision vitality.

Audiotaped segments can be used in several ways. Goldberg (1985) identified several teaching goals that can be accomplished by using audiotape, including focusing on specific therapy techniques, helping the supervisee see the relationship between process and content, focusing on how things are said (paralanguage), and helping the supervisee differentiate between a conversational tone and a therapeutic one. Audiotape also can be used to provide an experiential moment for the supervisee if a segment of tape is chosen where it is obvious that the supervisee is struggling personally or interpersonally in the taped session.

During the initial phase of a supervision relationship, it may be advisable for the supervisor to listen to an entire therapy session prior to supervision in order to get an overview of the supervisee's ability and have control over what segment of tape will be chosen for supervision. It is important also to help the supervisee understand the rationale behind the choice of tape segment if this is not apparent. Preselected segments can be chosen by the supervisor for a variety of reasons:

1. To highlight the most productive part of the session
2. To highlight the most important part of the session
3. To highlight to part of the session where the supervisee is struggling the most
4. To underscore any number of content issues, including metaphors and recurring themes
5. To ask about a confusing part of the session, perhaps because paralanguage contradicts content
6. To focus attention on the point in the session where interpersonal dynamics were either particularly therapeutic or particularly strained

In other words, supervisors will almost always have in mind a teaching function when they preselect a section of audiotape for supervision.

This process should evolve, however, as the supervisee develops in conceptual ability and experience. Relatively quickly the supervisee can be preselecting the section of tape that will determine the direction of supervision. Often supervisees are just asked to choose a part of the session where they felt confused, lost, overwhelmed, or frustrated. The supervisor will then listen to the segment with them and proceed from there. If this format is used, the supervisee should be prepared to

- State the reason for selecting this part of the session for discussion in supervision
- Briefly state what transpired up to that point
- Explain what he or she was trying to accomplish at that point in the session
- Clearly state the specific help desired from the supervisor.

Although a valid supervision format, the same format used repeatedly may make supervision become stagnant. When the supervisee is repeatedly asked to select a troublesome tape segment, for example, the supervision may become skewed toward problems in therapy, with little opportunity for the supervisee to enjoy successes as a practitioner. Additionally, the supervisor has no way of knowing if there are more productive moments in therapy if difficult moments become the theme for supervision.

As an alternative between supervisor control and trainee control, the supervisor might assign a theme for the next session and have the supervisee be responsible for producing the segment of tape. For example, the supervisor might suggest that reframing would be of great help for a particular client or family and that the supervisee should try to reframe as often as possible in the next session and choose the most successful of these attempts to present in the next supervision session. In addition to using supervision to sharpen a skill, this strategy also allows the supervisor to connect technique to a therapy situation and to get data on the supervisee's self-evaluation ability. The types of assignments that can direct the use of audiotape are potentially limitless and can focus on the process of therapy, the conceptual issues in therapy, personal or interpersonal issues, and ethical dilemmas, among others; it also can reflect different supervisee developmental levels. In summary, careful preselection of an audiotape segment is perhaps the most crucial part of making the audiotape a powerful supervision tool.

***Dual Channel Supervision.***    Yet another use of audiotape that deserves special attention is Smith's (1984) dual channel supervision. Reacting to a need expressed by practicum students in counseling for direct supervision from the supervisor, Smith used stereophonic cassette recorders to combine live observation with audiotaped feedback. While observing sessions, Smith was able to react to moment-to-moment interactions between the counselor and client and record his feedback. After the session, the trainee could listen to the tape unobstructed by supervisor reactions by turning the balance control to the left channel or could listen to the tape with the supervisor's feedback by setting the balance control at the midpoint.

This use of audiotape has two distinct advantages: It forces the trainee to review the tape of the session in order to receive feedback, and it allows regularly scheduled supervision time to be focused on either conceptual issues or other global themes because the more specific bits of feedback have been taken care of on tape. The major disadvantage of this approach is that it makes it difficult for the supervisor to roam among several concurrent counseling sessions (Smith, 1984). There is nothing, however, to prevent the supervisor from signing on and off of a session for a period to time. This would still allow for the advantages of this model.

***The Written Critique of Audiotapes.***    Finally, the supervisor can combine a written analysis of an audiotape with individual supervision. Many supervisors choose to listen to tapes between supervision sessions rather than during them. This is especially true at the beginning of supervision. Rather than taking notes to use in a subsequent supervision session, the supervisor writes an analysis of the session that can be given to the student. Word processors make this chore somewhat more palatable, and the exercise forces the supervisor to conceptualize the feedback before the supervision session. Additionally, the critiques automatically become a record of supervision; they allow the supervisee to review comments made by the supervisor; and they can be a way of coordinating supervision if other supervisors are involved (e.g., a site supervisor could be sent a copy of the critique prepared by the university supervisor). In fact, critiques serve as excellent instructional materials for the training of supervisors in the planning and giving of feedback. It must be noted, however, that such written feedback does not replace either individual or group supervision.

### Videotape

Although the audiotape is still our backup, the videotape has certainly taken center stage as the technology of choice in supervision. Those who use videotape are firm about its superiority over audiotape (e.g., Broder & Sloman, 1982; Stoltenberg & Delworth, 1987). We want to emphasize, however, that many of the process variables we mentioned for using audiotape could be used with videotape, as well as the reverse.

With no intention of insulting our readers, we will point out that the videotape has one major advantage, the addition of the picture, and one major disadvantage, its bulk. To say that a picture is worth a thousand words is less trite when one sees a client that one has heard but not seen up to that time. A voice that is gruff matched with a persona that is gentle, a precise presentation of plot when the physical presentation is disorganization, the smiles, the nods, the looking away, the hand gestures all comprise a wealth of information. When the client is a family, the phenomena grow in algebraic proportions. In fact, experiencing an overload of data is one of the reasons that Goldberg (1985) and Hart (1982) suggested using videotape at later stages of supervision. But, as Rubinstein and Hammond (1982) aptly put it, "[p]aradoxically, the greatest limitation of videotape may result from what it best provides the supervisor—a wealth of material about the recorded session" (p. 161).

The bulk of the videotape (camera, recorder, and monitor) make it more likely to be used in group supervision, but there are notable exceptions to this (e.g., Interpersonal Process Recall). Regardless of the numbers involved, videotape supervision will take more room than working with audiotape. If one does supervision within the confines of a small, private office, feedback based on videotape may have to be foregone. Another drawback of using videotape is that a higher level of comfort with technology is required than with audiotape. If someone throws the wrong switch, the supervisor who does not like to tinker may be unduly frustrated by using videotape.

The associations trainees may make between videotaped supervision and commercial television can present yet another problem. Because television connotes entertainment, Munson (1983) saw the dual problem of observers not finding others' sessions entertaining enough and trainees feeling they must "perform" on videotape, thereby suffering from excessive "performance anxiety." The supervisor's role, according to Munson, includes structuring supervision so that observers are stimulated cognitively (usually by means of a specific task related to the videotaped segment) while at the same time attempting to safeguard the integrity of the trainee on tape.

Despite all of these valid cautions regarding the use of videotape in supervision, there is no question that our knowledge base and experiential alternatives have increased greatly as a result of this technology. With videotape, supervisees can literally see themselves in the role of helper, thus allowing them to be an observer of their work, which is not possible with

audiotape (Whiffen, 1982; Sternitzke, Dixon, & Ponterotto, 1988).

In an excellent discussion of the use of videotape in the supervision of marriage and family therapy, Breunlin, Karrer, McGuire, and Cimmarusti (1988) asserted that videotape supervision is very complex and should be used carefully. They argued that videotape supervision should be focused on the interaction between trainee and clients as well as the far more subtle internal processes experienced by the trainee during both the therapy session and the supervision session. To focus on one to the exclusion of the other would be an error, according to Breunlin et al. Furthermore, they stated that therapists can never be objective observers of their own roles separate from the family, (or individual) client, as this is an interactional impossibility. Breunlin et al., therefore, recommended six guidelines for working with both the cold accuracy of the videotape and the dynamic reality experienced by the supervisee (pp. 199–204). (We should note that the guidelines outlined by Breunlin et al. also apply to other methods of supervision.

1. *Focus videotape supervision by setting realistic goals for the supervised therapy session.* This has two advantages: It reduces the sense of information overload by narrowing down the field to those interventions that are connected to goals, and it increases the possibility that the supervisee will emerge from the session moderately satisfied because realistic goals are attainable. As Breunlin et al. expressed it, "[m]oderate satisfaction minimizes dread and the anxiety that distorts internal process, and also motivates the therapist to want to review the tape" (p. 200).

2. *Relate internal process across contexts.* The point here is that what the therapist experiences in the session is important to discuss in supervision. Furthermore, Breunlin et al. emphasized that supervi-

sors should allow therapists to disclose their perceptions first, rather than supervisors offering their own observations. Most important, however, is the issue of validating the internal processes of the therapist rather than forfeiting such discussions in favor of "strategy review." Interpersonal Process Recall (Kagan, 1976, 1980), as described later in this chapter, is an excellent model for meeting this guideline.

3. *Select tape segments that focus on remedial performance.* By this, the authors meant that the focus of corrective feedback should be on performance that the therapist has the ability to change. In other words, focusing on aspects of the therapist's personal style or skills that are too complex for immediate attainment will be nonproductive.

4. *Use supervisor comments to create a moderate evaluation of performance.* The authors relied on the research of Fuller and Manning (1973) to arrive at this guideline. The latter found that a moderate discrepancy between performance and the target goal is optimal for learning. Therefore, the supervisor must find videotape segments that are neither exemplary nor too far from the stated goal. We can begin to appreciate the kind of supervisor commitment that is required to use the suggestions of Breunlin et al.

5. *Refine goals moderately.* This guideline underscores the fact that videotape review must be seen in the larger context of supervisee development. Sometimes the multitude of possibilities that a review can generate are irrespective of the skill level of the therapist. Additionally, Breunlin et al. remind us that what appears easy when viewing a session can be far more difficult to pull off in therapy. Moderation, therefore, must remain the constant focus for the supervisor.

6. *Maintain a moderate level of arousal.* The

authors posited that attending to the first five guidelines will take care of the sixth. The supervisor, however, must always be cautious that the supervisee is stimulated to grow without becoming overly threatened. Therefore, the supervisor, as always, must be alert to multiple levels of experience.

Also addressing supervisee internal processes, Rubinstein and Hammond (1982) maintained that the supervisor who uses videotape must have a healthy respect for its power. There is no hiding from the stark reality of one's picture and voice being projected into the supervision room. Therefore, Rubinstein and Hammond cautioned that videotape should not be used unless there is a relatively good relationship between the supervisor and supervisee. We concur up to a point but also postulate that a good relationship can be formed in the process of using videotape sensitively. In addition, the supervisee will be far less camera shy if videotape was used in training prior to supervision. Rubinstein and Hammond made the fine suggestion that supervisors appear on videotape prior to having their supervisees do the same. This can serve many purposes, but especially attractive is dispelling the myth that supervisors conduct perfect therapy sessions. As all supervisors know, the insight and cleverness that is evidence in supervision is rarely matched in one's own therapy.

Finally, Rubinstein and Hammond suggested that the use of the videotape remain technologically simple. They are not in favor of split screens, superimposed images, or other such equipment capabilities, believing that it detracts from the lifelike experience of watching the taped session. In stark contrast to this opinion is the work done by Froehle (1984), who used a computer to track physiological data on the therapist while in the process of conducting Interpersonal Process Recall. Of course, decisions about using videotape reflect the supervisor's fascination, or lack thereof, with technology as well as the supervision goals. Every supervisor will develop a comfort level with technological advances, but the supervisor would still be wise to remember Rubinstein and Hammond's caution lest machinery and its multiple uses become the center of supervision.

*Interpersonal Process Recall (IPR).* Perhaps the most widely known supervision model using videotape is Interpersonal Process Recall (Kagan, 1976, 1980; Kagan & Krathwohl, 1967; Kagan, Krathwohl, & Farquhar, 1965; Kagan, Krathwohl, & Miller, 1963). As a result of a national survey of counselor education programs, Borders and Leddick (1988) found that IPR was one of only two clearly delineated methods of supervision taught in supervision courses, the other being live supervision.

As we stated in Chapter 2, IPR began as a therapy model and occasionally is still used as such; for our purposes here, however, we will confine our discussion to the use of IPR in supervision. Kagan (1980) asserted that there are many psychological barriers to complete communication and that these operate in therapy as they do in other daily interactions. Primary among these is the strongly socialized habit of behaving diplomatically. As a result, much of what a supervisee thinks, intuits, and feels during therapy is disregarded almost automatically because allowing such perceptions to surface would confront the predisposition to be diplomatic.

The purpose of IPR, then, is to give the supervisee a safe haven for these internal reactions. Kagan (1980) strongly maintained that all persons are "the best authority of their own dynamics and the best interpreter of their own experience" (pp. 279–280). Starting with this assumption, therefore, the supervisor's role becomes that of a facilitator to stimulate the awareness of the supervisee beyond the point at which it operated during the therapy session.

The process of IPR is relatively simple. The supervisor and trainee view a prerecorded videotape of a therapy session together. At any point at which either person feels that something is happening on tape, especially something that is not being addressed in the therapy session, the videotape is stopped (dual controls are helpful, but it is easy enough to signal the person holding the control to stop the tape). If the trainee stops the tape, the trainee will speak first, saying, for example, "I was getting really frustrated here. I didn't know what she wanted. We had been over all of this before. I thought it was resolved last week but here it is again." At that point it is essential that the supervisor not adopt a teaching role and instruct the trainee about what might have been done. Rather, the supervisor needs to allow the trainee the psychological space to investigate internal processes to some resolution. At the same time, the good facilitator, or "inquirer," as Kagan prefers to call it, can ask direct questions that are assertive, perhaps even confrontive. Some possible questions for the example are: What do you wish you had said to her? How do you think she might have reacted if you said those things to her? What kept you from saying what you wanted to say? If you had the opportunity now, how might you tell her what you are thinking and feeling? Once it is felt that the dynamics for the chosen segment of tape have been sufficiently reexamined, the tape is allowed to continue.

As one can certainly discern, this process is slow. Only a portion of a therapy session can be reviewed in this manner unless supervision is extended significantly. Therefore, choosing the most interpersonally weighted segment of videotape will be most productive for supervision purposes.

One caution is advisable: Because IPR puts interpersonal dynamics under a microscope, it is possible that they will be magnified to the extent of distortion (Bernard, 1981). In other words, what is a perfectly functional helping relationship can come to look somehow dysfunctional when overexposed, and as all persons in the helping professions know, some relationship dynamics are best left underexposed. We need not be in perfect sync with all our clients to be of help to them. The clinical skill comes in determining which interactions are important and which are not. IPR has no internal reasoning; therefore, it is up to the supervisor and supervisee to decide which interactions warrant exploration and which do not. Because the supervisee is usually more reticent than the supervisor, the supervisor will most often be left to make such decisions. Answering the following two questions may serve useful in selecting segments for IPR: From what I can observe, does this interaction seem to be interrupting the flow of therapy? From what I know of the trainee, would focusing on this interaction aid in his or her development as a mental health professional? Appendix B describes the inclusion of IPR in a training package for clinical supervisors.

## Live Observation

Live observation is a frequent form of supervision in many training programs; it is used less frequently in the field because of scheduling difficulties and structural constraints. We differentiate between live observation and live supervision, the former being a method of observing the supervisee but not interacting with supervisee during the session (except in cases of emergency) and the latter being a combination of observation and active supervision during the session. Because the involvement of the supervisor in live supervision represents a paradigm shift from all other supervisory methods, we treat it separately in Chapter 6.

Live observation offers several advantages over all other forms of supervision, with the exception of live supervision. First of all, there is a firm safeguard for client welfare when live observation is employed because the supervisor is immediately available to intervene in

case of an emergency. A second advantage of live observation is that it affords the supervisor a more complete picture of clients and supervisees than is attainable through the use of audiotape or videotape. When using the latter, for example, the camera position is often fixed throughout a session, giving only side views of both the client and the therapist or focusing on the client exclusively. Supervisors who have used both live observation and taping certainly can attest to the relatively firsthand experience that live observation provides.

A third, and perhaps most utilized, advantage of live observation is that it offers the utmost flexibility regarding the timing of the case conference. Should the supervisor choose to conduct supervision immediately after the therapy session, the trainee has the maximum amount of time available to use supervision in preparing for the next therapy session. Certainly the use of live observation will reduce the chances of a most frustrating situation where the supervisor is watching a videotape of a session only to be told that the trainee has seen the client again since the video was made. It is difficult to make supervision fresh when the therapy session is stale.

## Timing of Supervision

Regardless of the methods used to produce the material for the case conference, an additional matter, the timing of the conference, must be considered. Little has been said in the professional literature about the timing of supervision except to warn that supervision that is scheduled for convenience only (e.g., every Tuesday at 10:00 for one hour) may invite legal liability if there are no provisions for the occasion when the supervisee experiences a more pressing need for supervision (Cohen, 1979).

Couchon and Bernard (1984) conducted a study that examined how several variables were influenced by the timing of supervision. Among the variables that were considered were supervisor and counselor behavior in supervision, follow-through from supervision to counseling, client and counselor satisfaction with counseling, and counselor satisfaction with supervision. Three treatments were introduced: supervision within four hours prior to an upcoming counseling session, supervision the day before a specified counseling session, and supervision occurring more than two days before a specified counseling session.

Some provocative results emerged from this study. Perhaps the most surprising result was that the timing of supervision seemed to affect supervisor behavior in the supervision session more so than counselor behavior. Supervision the day before a specified counseling session was highly content oriented. Perhaps because the counseling session was still one day away, supervisors felt the permission to offer several alternative strategies for counselors to consider. The supervisor was more likely to adopt an instructional mode and, therefore, was doing more of the work in the supervision session. We do not know how much the supervisee actually learned in these supervision sessions, but follow-through to the subsequent counseling session was low. In other words, strategies discussed and approved by the supervisor in the supervision session were not acted upon in counseling to any significant degree. We can hypothesize that because information was so voluminous in supervision, the counselor was not able to prioritize or translate supervisory information into counseling strategies.

Supervision conducted within four hours of a subsequent session was quite different. With the press of the upcoming session, the supervisor was far less likely to offer content and, instead, adopted a more consultative role. Fewer strategies were discussed, more of the strategies were offered by the counselor than by the supervisor, and those that were suggested met with more supervisor approval. Furthermore, there was far more follow-through from supervision to counseling for this treatment condition. Therefore, we can

view supervision immediately before counseling to be more of a work session for the counselor with support from the supervisor as needed.

The third timing of supervision, more or less midway between counseling sessions, had no strong effects. Because other counseling sessions with other clients intervened and there was no immediate pressure to prepare for an upcoming session, the supervision conference was simply more diffuse in its content and follow-through.

The Couchon and Bernard study highlighted the importance of timing as a process variable in supervision. Depending on the developmental and learning needs of the supervisee, different timing of supervision might be appropriate. For example,

> a counselor who conceptualizes well but who implements ideas poorly might benefit more from supervision immediately before counseling. On the other hand, a counselor who performs well but who lacks conceptual ability might benefit from supervision conducted the day before counseling. (Couchon & Bernard, 1984, p. 18)

Contrary to the assumptions of many supervisors, the counselors in the Couchon and Bernard study were equally satisfied with supervision regardless of when supervision was offered. (Timing also did not affect client or counselor satisfaction with counseling.) It should be noted, however, that an important time for supervision, immediately after counseling, was not studied. We hypothesize that if there is a time that would get an elevated satisfaction rating, it would be immediately after counseling when the supervisee might benefit from support and reinforcement. This hypothesis is supported in part by Smith (1984), who found that practicum students evaluated postsession supervisor feedback as the most effective among several choices. But postsession was not clearly defined and may or may not have occurred immediately after counseling.

Additionally, regardless of supervisee satisfaction, the amount and kind of learning resulting from this timing of supervision is unknown.

Conducting supervision during therapy will be discussed in Chapter 6 when we consider live supervision.

## Techniques Derived from Developmental Models

Our discussion thus far has focused on the methods used by the supervisor to obtain the data that will be used in the case conference. All of these methods are as relevant to the supervisor with a developmental focus as to other supervisors. However, two developmental models offer schemata for supervisee assessment and supervisor intervention that are equally relevant to our discussion of the case conference. We should note that for both models, the authors have not specified what methods were used to provide supervision material (i.e., process notes, audiotapes, etc.); therefore, the reader can assume that different methods should be considered to implement these authors' suggestions.

*The Loganbill, Hardy, and Delworth Model.* As we stated in Chapter 2, the Loganbill et al. model is a comprehensive approach to the process of supervision. Regardless of the source of supervision material, the supervisor will be tracking the supervisee on the eight variables in Table 4.4 to determine whether the supervisee is at the point of *stagnation, confusion,* or *integration.* Loganbill et al. defined stagnation for the novice trainee as naive unawareness and for the more advanced supervisee as being stagnant or "stuck." In either case, the supervisee is unlikely to move beyond this stage without some intervention from the supervisor. Confusion, marked by erratic cognitive and behavioral fluctuations, disorganization, and dependency on the supervisor indicate that the supervisee has moved beyond stagnation for the supervision issue in question. Finally, integration is apparent when the supervisee once again becomes comfortable

**TABLE 4.4**    Assessment of Supervisee Stage Level*

| Critical Issues in Supervision | Stage One Stagnation | Stage Two Confusion | Stage Three Integration |
|---|---|---|---|
| 1. *Issues of competence.* Skills. Technique. Mastery. | | | |
| 2. *Issues of Emotional Awareness.* Knowing oneself. Awareness of feelings. | | | |
| 3. *Issues of Autonomy.* Sense of self. Independence. Self-directedness. | | | |
| 4. *Issues of Identity.* Theoretical consistency. Synthesized theoretical identity. Conceptual integration. | | | |
| 5. *Issues of Respect for Individual Differences.* Tolerance. Non-judgmentalness. Acceptance of others. | | | |
| 6. *Issues of Purpose and Direction.* Setting goals. Direction in counseling. Appropriate long-term or short-term goals. | | | |
| 7. *Issues of Personal Motivation.* Personal meaning. Reward satisfaction. | | | |
| 8. *Issues of Professional Ethics.* Values. | | | |

*From Loganbill, C., Hardy, E., & Delworth, U. (1982). Supervision: A conceptual model. *The Counseling Psychologist, 10*(1), 3–42. Copyright © (1982) by Division 17 of the American Psychological Association. Reprinted by permission of Sage Publications, Inc.

and has attained a level of emotional and cognitive comfort with a significant new learning.

Obviously, the work of the supervisor is to help supervisees get beyond stagnation or confusion for any of the eight supervision issues. Table 4.4 depicts what could become a worksheet for supervision as the supervisee is assessed and then tracked for developmental progress. As the third component of their model, Loganbill et al. (1982) delineated five categories of supervisor interventions to assist the supervisee in making the transition from a lower stage to the next higher stage. (The authors did not pair certain interventions with specific transition points; rather, they viewed them as the repertoire from which the supervisor can choose to accomplish a desired end.)

1. *Facilitative interventions* are as much a set of assumptions and attitudes as direct interventions. They are supervisee centered and help promote the natural developmental process. Inherent in this category is the belief that with support and reflective activity, the supervisee can learn and change.
2. *Confrontive interventions* are a type of intervention that "brings together two things for examination and comparison" (p. 33). The discrepancy can be internal to the supervisee, for example, a conflict between feelings and behavior, or it can be a discrepancy between the supervisee and an external actuality, for example, the supervisor seeing client dynamics in a way very different from how they have been perceived by the supervisee.
3. *Conceptual interventions* occur whenever the supervisor is asking the supervisee to think analytically or theoretically. Loganbill et al. cautioned the supervisor to take learning styles into consideration as some supervisees grasp theory through experience whereas others need a theoretical grounding prior to experience.
4. *Prescriptive interventions* take the form of coaching the supervisee to either perform certain behaviors or delete certain behaviors. This is the most direct intervention category described by Loganbill et al. Therefore, they warned that prescriptive interventions could thwart supervisee development if used too liberally or when a more conservative approach might be substituted. (We will find a similar caution in our discussion of live supervision in Chapter 6.) Client welfare is a frequent rationale for using prescriptive interventions.
5. *Catalytic interventions* include those supervisor statements that are "designed to get things moving" (p. 35). Although the authors noted that in one sense all supervision interventions are catalytic, they also argued that catalytic interventions are qualitatively different from each of the other four. When a supervisor uses a catalytic intervention, the supervisor is seizing the moment to bring additional meaning to the supervisory process. Loganbill et al. offered two examples of catalytic interventions: helping the supervisee to appreciate realistic client potential for change and, thereby, setting appropriate goals (a buffer, the authors asserted, from burnout); and encouraging the supervisee to experiment with new roles in the therapeutic relationship.

To summarize, the process of developmental supervision using the Loganbill et al. (1982) model begins by assessing the supervisee on eight dimensions as either stagnant, confused, or integrated. Then the supervisor relies on combinations of the five supervisor intervention categories to bring the supervisee to integration on as many dimensions as possible. The source of supervision information on which the supervisor relies will depend on the issue, some needing direct observation whereas others are more contemplative in nature.

*The Johnson and Moses Model.* More recently, Johnson and Moses (1988) proposed a second developmental map that has high utility for the supervisor conducting a developmental case conference. Similar to Loganbill et al. (1982), they relied on Chickering's vectors but collapsed personal motivation and professional ethics into one category they called "integrity," thus leaving them with seven instead of eight dimensions on which to track the supervisee.

From this point on, Johnson and Moses depart from the Loganbill et al. model. Rather than using the concepts of stagnation, confusion, and integration, they noted that the supervisee must master each vector on three dimensions: *cognitive, affective,* and *behavioral.* They made the point that a supervisee might be comfortable intellectually with, say, working with a minority client and may understand multicultural ideology. But this same supervisee might be less ready emotionally to cross cultures, or the supervisee's behavior with the minority client might be well intentioned but grossly inadequate.

Finally, Johnson and Moses depicted the supervisor's role as having to choose between *support* or *challenge* in working with the supervisee once dimension and vector have been determined. If there is too little challenge, the supervisee might slip into stagnation (borrowing from the Loganbill et al. model); too much challenge and too little support, the supervisee may get discouraged or defensive. The choice between challenge and support was seen by Johnson and Moses as the most critical decision the supervisor makes. Once this decision is made, Johnson and Moses referred to the Bernard (1979) schema of roles (teacher, consultant, counselor) as being the primary choices for the supervisor to help the supervisee attain the desired growth.

## Instruction

Instruction is far more likely to be used in the initial training of the helping professional than in supervision. But although we cannot conceive of a situation where instruction ever would be adequate as the only form of supervision, there are times when the most efficient and productive form of supervision is some type of direct instruction. The most obvious example of this is when the supervisee is ready to learn more advanced skills, skills that were not considered essential for the novice supervisee but that are highly useful once the supervisee is prepared to learn them. Paradoxical interventions are an example of sophisticated skills that would probably require additional instruction once a trainee is more advanced.

Obviously instruction will be based primarily on the client load carried by a trainee. Hawthorne (1987) argued that all of the trainee's field experiences can be put to an educational purpose. But even if one prefers less of a teaching role in supervision, a random client load will certainly lead the trainee to a need for new techniques. With laboratory courses being hard-pressed to cover the basics, it is most likely (and desirable) that more instruction is conducted once clinical work commences.

Microtraining (Ivey, 1971; Ivey & Authier, 1978) is most widely utilized in training programs as a systematic approach to teaching therapeutic skills. As described by Forsyth and Ivey (1980), the four steps of microtraining are quite straightforward:

1. *Teach one skill at a time.* When done as part of supervision, the trainee must understand that the skill about to be learned will later be placed in the context of treatment objectives. In other words, one skill may be a small part of the entire therapeutic intervention, but, nonetheless, it is important to be executed adroitly. Furthermore, if the technique is complex (e.g., paradox or systematic desensitization), each part of the technique will be taught separately, pulling it all together at the end.

2. *Present the skill.* Modeling is an impor-

tant part of microtraining and can consist of a live demonstration by the supervisor or a taped enactment of the target skill. Explaining the skill verbally is not an adequate presentation.

3. *Practice the skill.* Again, it is not sufficient for the trainee to see the skill performed and then be expected to accomplish it competently in the next counseling session. The trainee must be allowed to practice the skill in the supervisory context. Better yet, the trainee's efforts should be videotaped or audiotaped so that the power of self-modeling (Hosford, 1981) can be integrated into the instruction. Practicing the skill will necessitate a sequence of role-plays and/or reverse role-plays. If done in individual supervision, this means that the supervisor must be willing to invest in each part of the role-play and that the supervisee must be sufficiently comfortable with the supervisor to put their relationship aside for the sake of the practice session. It is because of this latter complication, that supervisors may choose to steer away from microtraining in individual supervision, preferring it as a group supervision model.

4. *Allow for mastery.* The most common mistake made in instruction of clinical skills is to allow the trainee to terminate practice prior to mastery. Of course in this context, mastery is a relative term and means a level at which the supervisor is comfortable that the skill will contribute to a successful therapeutic intervention. Only when mastery has been achieved should the supervisee be asked to use the skill in treatment. If mastery is not accomplished, it can either mean that enough time has not been given to the task, the modeling was insufficient, or the skill is beyond the capacity of the trainee at that time. As noted by Breunlin et al. (1988), the latter would be the more serious supervision error because it may move

the trainee from a moderate amount of anxiety to a level that can block learning.

Lambert and Arnold (1987) substituted *feedback* for *mastery* as the fourth element for efficient learning. It makes sense that the clarity and accuracy of supervisor feedback as the supervisee practices a skill is essential for learning. Additionally, a combination of feedback and practice most assuredly presents the supervisee with the greatest opportunity for mastery.

As part of the training laboratory outlined in Appendix B, there are additional guidelines for using microtraining in supervision and in the training of supervisors.

## SUPERVISION OF SUPERVISION

All of the methods and techniques presented as forms of supervision can also be used to conduct supervision of supervision. There is little in the professional literature on the process of supervision of supervision; however, some examples are available using, for example, Interpersonal Process Recall (e.g., Bernard, 1989), microtraining (e.g., Richardson & Bradley, 1984), and live supervision (e.g., Constantine, Piercy, & Sprenkle, 1984; Heath & Storm, 1985). This is an area of research that begs attention.

## RESEARCH ON THE USE OF SUPERVISION METHODS

We have reported relevant empirical findings as they related to different methods of supervision. A few studies have attempted to track the helping professions for their use of different methods of supervision. We would like to consider these now briefly.

Before we begin, however, it seems important to note the paucity of research in the area of supervision process. It is another statement of the youth of clinical supervision as an area of academic interest that so few studies have attempted to investigate its methods; instead, the process of supervision is taken for granted. As we mentioned earlier, Borders and Leddick (1988) reviewed counselor education programs to determine what was being covered in supervision courses. Although a substantial number of topics were identified, only two could be identified as supervision techniques, Interpersonal Process Recall and live supervision. In contrast, however, the practice of supervision that was required of supervisors in training was much more extensive and included conducting case conferences, using audiotape and videotape, and group supervision, among others. Therefore, although supervisors in training were asked to utilize different supervisory methods, they received no training in using the methods, which reflects a continuation of the tradition of learning while doing.

Hess and Hess (1983) reviewed 151 APA-accredited predoctoral internship sites to determine the form supervision was taking in these highly credible settings. By far the most frequent form of supervision offered to interns was individual supervision. (It is unclear whether these conferences were based on anything other than self-report.) The next four

methods in order of frequency were supervision seminar, audiotape, videotape, and group supervision (p. 506).

In addition to their interest in the type of supervision received, Hess and Hess also wanted to know if interns were themselves trained in clinical supervision. This seems to us to be an important issue because supervision is usually considered to be the domain of the person holding the doctoral degree. Hess and Hess found that only one-third of the internship sites offered such training. The frequency of procedures used to train the interns in psychotherapy supervision comprised a slightly different rank ordering: individual supervision of supervision, vertical teams (e.g., a senior postdoctoral fellow who supervises a predoctoral intern), group supervision, structured seminar, live observation, assigned readings, videotapes, and audiotapes. Note that the use of videotapes and audiotapes are much further down the list for supervision of supervision than they were for supervision of therapy. Our assumption is that this is more a consequence of convenience than of any assumption that these methods are not as viable in one context as the other.

## CONCLUSION

As the supervisor conducts individual supervision, many options are available regarding the form that supervision will take. Much of this will be determined by prior experience, interest in experimenting with different methods, and perceived supervisee need. All methods carry with them opportunities and opportunities bypassed. The quality of supervision is intimately related to the decisions about meth-

ods. But presently there is not sufficient empirical evidence to either encourage or reject the use of any of the available methods. Clearly supervisors need not only to expand their repertoire but also to systematically study their methods and techniques. In this way they can best serve both their supervisees and their profession.

# CHAPTER 5

# GROUP SUPERVISION

Individual supervision historically has been the cornerstone for training in the helping professions. Chapter 4 reviewed a variety of means of conducting individual supervision. This chapter will consider the other principal alternative, that of conducting supervision with more than one person.

Although many of the procedures described in Chapter 4 can and have been used in the context of a group, they fall short of group supervision when the focus remains on the individual trainee. In order to qualify as group supervision, therefore, the procedure must depend on the interaction of group members and must have at its core the dynamics of group process, including the delicate balance between individual growth and development and group growth and development.

## WHY SUPERVISE IN GROUPS?

Holloway and Johnston (1985) criticized the indiscriminate use of group supervision, noting the lack of research to support the desirability of group supervision. We do not quarrel with the argument that there needs to be more research on the topic of group supervision. But there seem to be several learning objectives that are better accomplished with a group modality, and there is no question that groups are more efficient and cost-effective than one-on-one supervision. We believe these alone are justification for conducting group supervision while waiting for more definitive empirical findings. Furthermore, to abandon group supervision would be to reinforce what McCarthy, DeBell, Kanuha, and McLeod (1988) consider a myth, that individual super-

vision is superior. As this chapter will point out, however, there are additional reasons to support the group format for supervision.

Defenders of group supervision often argue that its use can help avoid trainee dependence, which more likely results from individual supervision (Getzel & Salmon, 1985; Parihar, 1983). Additionally, group supervision can diminish the hierarchical issues between the supervisor and trainee by encouraging more input in case analysis from other trainees (Allen, 1976; Cohen, Gross, & Turner, 1976). Sansbury (1982) was of the opinion that the group is a more natural setting for a greater variety of behavioral and experiential supervision strategies that, when combined with cognitive interaction, offer the trainee a more comprehensive supervision experience. We concur and add that the use of group supervision can help bridge the gap between the classroom, where most of the trainee's cognitive understanding of therapy occurs, and the practice of therapy itself, which often is accompanied by a sense of intellectual and emotional isolation.

Similarly, Hillerbrand (1989) offered a substantial argument for group supervision that is based on research on collaborative learning and cognitive skill acquisition. Assuming that trainees need to acquire the skills to conceptualize client issues accurately, make inferences, and convert these inferences into a therapeutic plan, there is evidence that "skills are enhanced by the novice's verbalization of his or her cognitive processes in the presence of other novices" (Hillerbrand, 1989, p. 294). Furthermore, Hillerbrand cited evidence that novices can learn conceptually from each other more efficiently than they can from an expert. This finding suggests that the group modality is superior to individual supervision for some purposes.

Evaluation of a trainee also can be influenced by the group supervision process. In Chapter 7 we discuss the situation where a trainee seems blocked in his/her own work but is still an intelligent and insightful member of a supervision group. Seeing this allows the supervisor to view the trainee's difficulties in a different way (e.g., either fear or isomorphism) from what might be the case if individual supervision were used exclusively. In other words, group supervision allows the supervisor to see a supervisee perform in a relatively ego-protected environment, at least when another supervisee's clinical work is the focus. Additionally, the trainee can experience the positive feedback from the group when the trainee's insights are particularly astute. Conversely, Kadushin (1985) noted that group supervision also can help supervisees put their failures in perspective. When group members see each other's struggles, they are less likely to personalize their own frustrations with the learning process. Group supervision, therefore, gives supervisees a broader context by which to judge themselves.

Hart (1982) offered yet another rationale for group supervision. The increase in group counseling in many settings makes the group modality for supervision appropriate to mirror the supervisee's direct service activity.

A final justification for the use of group supervision is the belief that trainees can offer each other a variety of perspectives that no single supervisor could provide. When this is a principal rationale for group supervision, it reduces not only trainee isolation but also supervisor isolation. Too many supervisors get caught in the trap of believing they must provide all the answers for their trainees and be equally effective with each trainee regardless of the personalities or learning styles involved. Supervisors who choose a group modality because of their belief in the collective wisdom

of the group will find their trainees more willing to risk their opinions in supervision (Cohen et al., 1976). These supervisors also will be modeling the spirit of consultation by asking trainees to trust each other's abilities to be helpful colleagues. From the supervisee's vantage point, a safety in numbers might allow a supervisee to challenge the opinion of the supervisor, something the supervisee might be less likely to do in an individual conference (Kadushin, 1985).

To this point, we have confined our discussion to justifiable reasons for group supervision; however, there also are reasons that are not justifiable. Perhaps the least justifiable reason for group supervision is expediency. Although often among the reasons for group supervision, if this is the only justification for group supervision, it will work against the overall goals of both the supervisor and the supervisees. Moreover, when the rationale for any type of supervision is not grounded in a solid training philosophy, it usually fails, at least in part. In the group modality, the result is often individual supervision attempted in a group rather than group supervision.

A final point about rationale needs to be made. Regardless of the enthusiasm expressed by certain authors about the possibilities of group supervision, none that we found suggested the replacement of individual supervision with group supervision, except perhaps in the case of postgraduate peer supervision. Working with supervisees as a group was consistently viewed as a supplement to individual supervision or to follow individual supervision in the course of training and, most often, beyond training. Acknowledging the supplemental, rather than central, place of group supervision provides an important context for this chapter.

## CONCEPTUALIZING GROUP SUPERVISION

Before we study the actual process of supervision groups, we want to consider the different ways they can be conceptualized. Although admittedly some supervisors begin supervision groups without giving attention to what can and should be accomplished in the group, most supervisors begin with certain assumptions. The professional literature on group supervision reflects not only a great deal of overlap in conceptual plans but also some distinct differences between conceptual plans. The primary way that the literature conceptualizes group supervision is to outline different legitimate activities for the group. Sansbury (1982) found four justifiable group supervision activities:

1. Teaching interventions directed at the entire group
2. Presenting specific case-oriented information, suggestions, or feedback
3. Focusing on affective responses of a particular supervisee as the feelings pertain to the client
4. Processing the group's interaction and development, which can be used to facilitate supervisee exploration, openness, and responses. (p. 54)

Getzel and Salmon (1985) differed from Sansbury in that they focused on the relationship between the supervisee and the client. They also included the supervision group's interpersonal relationships as a legitimate focus as well as supervisor-supervisee relationships and the supervisee's relationships to the organization (either a training program or mental health setting).

In their review of group supervision literature, Holloway and Johnston (1985) found reference to groups that addressed one of three areas: didactic material, case conceptualization, and interpersonal process material. Holloway and Johnston pointed out that groups devoted exclusively to an interpersonal process focus were more common during the inception of training programs in the helping professions and have much less credibility at the present time. In a similar review of the options available to the group supervisor, Wilbur, Roberts-Wilbur, Hart, and Betz (undated) de-

fined three distinct categories: The task process group modality, which seems to be a combination of didactic and case conceptualization material; the psycho-process modality, which seems to parallel the intrapsychic growth expected in the interpersonal process group; and the socio-process modality, which parallels the interpersonal relationship growth expected in the interpersonal process group.

Kruger, Cherniss, Maher, and Leichtman (1988) attempted to develop an instrument that could track the activity of supervision groups. In doing so, these authors defined the main activity of groups as problem solving and divided this activity into clarifying problems, designing counseling programs, action planning, and evaluating, all of which could be subsumed under case conceptualization. Additionally, Kruger et al. identified "counselor problems" as a nonproblem solving activity, a category defined as "verbal behavior that helped the team [group] understand or reduce team members' social or affective problems" (p. 336). This final focus again seems akin to interpersonal process activity, blending both individual and group development.

Finally, Shulman (1982) conceptualized the supervision of staff groups (in a work setting) as falling into four categories. Two of the categories are quite clear, the one being staff meetings, which we would not include under group supervision, the other being in-service training, which Shulman uses to describe the introduction of new didactic material to supervisees. Shulman, however, differentiated case consultation and group supervision for his last two categories, referring to the former as focusing on the client and the latter as focusing on supervisee growth. Shulman saw these as discrete categories because the former may occur even for the seasoned professional who may need consultation for a particular client whereas the latter assumes less experienced supervisees who are developing in their professional identity. Furthermore, whereas the case consultation group remains fairly faithful to the task of case analysis, the group supervision groups can focus on a variety of topics central to supervisee development, including "job management skills and professional practice skills, impact skills, and learning skills" (p. 224).

Table 5.1 depicts these authors' conceptualization of group supervision. We have identified five discrete categories (didactic presentations, case conceptualization, supervisee individual development, group development, and organization issues) and one less discrete category (supervisee-supervisor issues), which might legitimately be subsumed under group development. This chapter will give particular attention to case conceptualization, supervisee individual development, and group development. Didactic presentations and organizational issues will not be a specific focus because they are not as generic to group supervision as it has developed in recent years.

Therefore, for our purposes here, we define group supervision as the regular meeting of a group of supervisees with a designated supervisor for the purpose of furthering their understanding of themselves as clinicians, or their clients, or of service delivery in general

and who are aided in this endeavor by their interactions with each other and with their supervisor in the context of group process.

## GROUP PROCESS

Regardless of the agenda for a particular group, the group will experience a life of its own, typically referred to as group process, and follow predictable stages. In this section, we will consider some global group process issues and then apply them to the tasks of group supervision.

Corey and Corey (1987) described four principal stages in the life of a group: the initial stage, the transition stage, the working stage, and the ending stage. They also recommended that some consideration be given to a pregroup stage and a postgroup stage.

### Pregroup Stage

Corey and Corey (1987) described the pregroup stage as a planning stage. As we will discuss more thoroughly in Chapter 9, the supervisor who takes ample time to plan and

**TABLE 5.1**    Group Supervision Activities

| | Didactic Presentations | Case Conceptualization | Individual Development | Group Development | Organizational Issues | Supervisor-Supervisee Issues |
|---|---|---|---|---|---|---|
| Sansbury (1982) | X | X | X | X | | |
| Getzel & Salmon (1985) | | | X | X | X | X |
| Holloway & Johnston (1985) | X | X | X | X | | |
| Wilbur et al. (1987) | X | X | X | X | | |
| Kruger et al. (1988) | | X | X | X | | |
| Shulman (1982) | X | X | X | X | | |

organize the supervision experience will begin that experience with a distinct advantage. In addition to other issues, the supervisor must question the use of the group modality per se, knowing that some objectives will be enhanced by the use of group supervision while others will be frustrated.

During the pregroup stage, the supervisor should be considering all contingencies for the group that lie ahead. Therefore, the list of items to be considered is quite long. Among those issues outlined by Corey and Corey are a screening process for members of the group, a clearly defined purpose for the group, ground rules for the group and a structure for its process, the risks inherent to group activity, leader and member expectations, a plan for evaluating the outcome of the group, and practical questions like How large will the group be? Will it be voluntary or involuntary? Open or closed? and Where will group meetings occur?

Depending on the circumstances, some of these issues will appear to be more fundamental than others. For example, a training program with a group supervision component as part of the internship will, perhaps, give very little attention to the screening process for the group and to whether the group is voluntary (it isn't). Rather, the training program itself serves as a screening process from admissions criteria to the successful completion of prerequisites to internship. What appears to be a moot issue, therefore, is simply covered in an alternative fashion. Our point is that all groups, whether part of a training program or a supervision group in an agency (voluntary or not), should be cognizant of pregroup concerns and make sure that they are attended to in some fashion (Hamlin & Timberlake, 1982; Roth, 1986).

The screening of group members has received some attention in supervision literature. More specifically, there is some debate as to whether a homogenous group or a heterogeneous group is more advantageous for group members. For novices, there seems to be a case for relative homogeneity. When trainees are more or less in the same boat they are more likely to empathize with each other and trust building is more easily accomplished. Furthermore, in a homogenous group one's relative strength can be more readily appreciated because experience level does not cloud individual talent. It may be the case, for example, that one trainee is more likely to take a risk by using a novel intervention whereas another leads the group in case conceptualization ability. Although an awareness of relative strengths can feed an atmosphere of competition, it also can enhance self-awareness. The responsibility of the supervisor is to have trainees identify their baseline strengths and build from there.

When supervision occurs after training in a work setting, a heterogeneous group is more likely to be the case. Chaiklin and Munson (1983) noted that this type of situation causes supervision to be diluted because it takes much longer to present cases. They also imply that it is the more experienced practitioners that lose when the group is mixed. Parihar (1983) also found heterogeneity to be a disadvantage in that different experience levels meant very different expectations that supervisees brought to supervision. Therefore, the group supervisor would be bound to make compromises in a mixed group, leading to some level of dissatisfaction with the experience. Allen (1976) echoed these concerns and identified lack of homogeneity as a major drawback for supervision groups in mental health settings.

Wendorf, Wendorf, and Bond (1985) were more positive about the heterogeneous group, arguing that it is more realistic and allows different group members to adopt more responsible roles as they are ready. In the meantime, more experienced clinicians can be taking appropriate leadership positions and modeling higher level functioning for those less experienced. Getzel and Salmon (1985) also asserted that too much homogeneity will stifle the exact benefits hoped for in group supervision, including spontaneity. Furthermore, they pointed out that homogeneity of cultural background can produce an undesirable situation, especially if the clientele being served is culturally diverse. Finally, homogeneity of experience but not of perspective was recommended by Schreiber and Frank (1983) for experienced clinicians in private practice pursuing peer supervision. In discussing their position, the authors stated that "[o]ur sense was that at a more advanced state in career development these differences [in perspective and expertise] are welcomed and perceived as edifying. By this time each of us was secure enough about our skills to feel comfortable with a peer having another approach in which she was expert" (p. 31).

Because homogeneity versus heterogeneity is an unresolved issue for group supervision, the supervisor must consider the makeup of the group carefully and attempt to compensate for the disadvantages of either situation through group structure and ground rules.

Group structure and ground rules provide group members with the sense of safety that is needed if they are to risk exposing their clinical work in front of their peers. Structure may seem a mundane topic, but it can influence the group process significantly. For example, if attendance at all meetings is not mandated, the supervisee who does not come the week after presenting a difficult case will cause others to worry that their feedback might have been too confrontive. This not only will affect the group session with the missing member but also will affect the quality of feedback given to this member upon return if it is not addressed in the group.

Another matter involving structure is the means by which cases will be presented (which was a major focus of Chapter 4). If this is left totally up to group members, some may begin by presenting audio- or videotapes only to find other members relying on self-report. This allows some members to remain safe while others have been exposed, directly affecting

the cohesion and trust being developed in the group.

On the other hand, if structure is too rigid, it can create its own tension by stifling spontaneity and fitting some members far better than others. The supervisor, therefore, needs not only to create an initial structure but also to monitor its effect on the group and be prepared to alter or abandon part of the group's structure based on group feedback. (Requesting feedback is itself a structural matter.)

Some rather obvious components of structure, such as the size of the group and the frequency and place of meetings, are more of an issue for voluntary supervision groups than of those in training programs, which are often directed by professional standards of preparation. For example, in their discussion of peer supervision groups, Chaiklin and Munson (1983) recommended groups of six to twelve members, and Schreiber and Frank (1983) suggested at least seven members. Both sets of authors found that any fewer were disruptive because of absences and drop-outs.

How often the group meets will also affect group process; meeting once a month, for instance, might make it difficult to arrive at a viable atmosphere, whereas meeting twice a week might be untenable for some members and cause resentment. Marks and Hixon (1986) found that groups that met weekly (as opposed to biweekly) provided their members with the most growth, including "an increased willingness to deal with feelings associated with the treatment process, and a marked decrease in anxiety due to an increase in trust" (p. 422). By contrast, groups that met biweekly remained more cognitive and formal.

Whether the group meets on common ground (e.g., the work site) or rotates meeting place (e.g., one meeting at each member's home) will affect the feelings group members have about each other and accelerate or delay cohesion. Structure, therefore, is deserving of the supervisor's and member's attention.

Ground rules are essential if the group is to serve any consistent purpose. A ground rule of openness and respect can be achieved at the outset if the supervisor states his or her expectations of the group and asks members to do the same. It goes without saying that the supervisor must respond to the expectations put forward by group members or else closedness and disrespect will be communicated. This is not to say that all supervisees' expectations will be sound or appropriate. Nevertheless, time needs to be given to a rational explanation of why some objectives will be honored, whereas others will not.

Among the ground rules mentioned by Corey and Corey (1987) are those that pertain to confidentiality, the responsibility of each member, level of participation, and protection of members from undue peer pressure and intimidation. Many of the ground rules for group supervision have to do with how clinical material will be presented and processed. For example, Munson (1983) put forward the following guidelines for case presentations:

1. The supervisor should present a case first.
2. The supervisee should be granted time to prepare the case for presentation.
3. The presentation should be based on written or audiovisual material.
4. The presentation should be built around questions to be answered.
5. The presentation should be organized and focused.
6. The presentation should progress from client dynamics to practitioner dynamics. (p. 104)

Munson also outlined ground rules for supervisors, suggesting that supervisors avoid presentation of several cases in a short session, presentation of specific problems rather than the case in context, presentation of additional problems in a single case, discussion of therapist dynamics preceding case dynamics, and intervention expectations beyond the capabilities of the therapist (p. 104). Not all supervi-

sors would agree with each of these guidelines. It is important, however, that there be ground rules for each supervision group and that these be communicated in a clear fashion to each member.

Perhaps the most common ground rules for group supervision have to do with the offering of feedback to each other as a result of case presentation. These ground rules can be suggested by the supervisor but should receive some level of group consensus. Table 5.2 is one

**TABLE 5.2** Guidelines for Case Conference

As you view or listen to a counseling session
1. Note what the *counselor* did.
   a. What were things you liked about the counselor's approach? (No one likes to hear criticism right off the bat.)
   b. What seemed to be the client's reaction to the counselor's behavior?
   c. What would you have added to the session?
   d. What things did the counselor do that you might have done in a different way?
   e. Were there any things in the session done by the counselor that you think were unhelpful? If so, what do you believe should have been done instead?
2. Note what the *client* did.
   a. What do you think of this client and the client's concerns?
   b. What themes were evident?
   c. Were there any inconsistencies that confused you?
   d. Did the client's input seem to make things clearer?
3. Note what the *session* accomplished.
   a. Given what you know about this client, did the session accomplish any process goals or outcome goals?
   b. What would you say was the major accomplishment of this session?
   c. What would you say was the major flaw of this session?
   4. If this were your client, what would be reasonable and productive goals for the next session? *How would you accomplish these goals?*

such set of ground rules that helps the group members to organize their thoughts and provide feedback in a focused way.

A final pregroup stage task is to decide if indeed group supervision is the modality of choice. We have already listed some of the advantages of group supervision. There are, of course, limitations too. The learning available to each group member in group supervision may be too diffuse to be worthwhile (Hamlin & Timberlake, 1982). Furthermore, an overpowering group member might rob others of their instructional needs, or the structure itself might fit a majority of members but offer virtually nothing to a minority of them (Parihar, 1983).

*Limitations of Group Supervision.* Corey and Corey (1987) listed five limitations of group work, which we believe can be applied to group supervision as well (p. 93).

1. Groups are not cure-alls. Some supervisors believe too much in group process, assuming that all training and personal needs can be accomplished in a group setting. Group members can share this faulty assumption, especially if they have had a powerful group experience in another context.
2. There is often a subtle pressure to conform to group norms and expectations. Although groups can validate us and give us the realization that we are not alone, they can accomplish just the opposite if our perceptions are different from our peers (Allen, 1976). Especially for the novice, it can be very difficult to risk sharing an alternative way of conceptualizing therapy or a novel intervention if this has not been advocated by the group or by the supervisor.
3. Some people become hooked on groups and make the group experience an end in itself. In relation to supervision groups, this can occur when the personal growth of supervisees or the development of the group itself overshadow the needs of clients. Supervisors and members must always keep in mind that supervision groups are a means to an end and not an end in themselves.
4. Not all people are suited to groups. Even among helping professionals (who, it is assumed, are comfortable with other people), the group format may not be the most beneficial for training purposes. We have assumed that all practitioners must be comfortable in group settings. Although it might be argued that the practitioner cannot afford to be inept as a group leader, this does not mean that the group is each person's natural setting. Some room for individual preference and aptitude must be evident in the expectations of supervision.
5. Some people have made the group a place to ventilate their miseries and be rewarded for baring their soul. For the highly manipulative supervisee, the group offers an arena to stay protected by seeming to risk. In other words, a supervisee can be the first to put forth sensitive material, only to keep sympathies high and feedback low. Especially in groups of helping professionals who have a calling to take care of others, this can be a successful way to manipulate, at least initially.

Kadushin (1985) offered two additional admonitions regarding group supervision that warrant our attention.

1. "The group conference has to be directed to the general, common needs of all the supervisees and the special, particular needs of none" (p. 400). Although this might be overstated, there is a distinct danger that the training needs of the strongest supervisee, or the weakest, or the one whose field placement is nontraditional, or the minority supervisee, etc., might be sacrificed for the more generic goals of the group.
2. Just as there is strength in numbers, there

also is the potential to hide in numbers. There are ways to get through a group supervision session without ever being exposed. This is far less likely, if not impossible, in individual supervision.

Once all of the issues raised above have been considered and resolved, at least in theory, the supervisor is ready to begin a supervision group.

## Initial Stage

The initial stage of the group is the state at which the supervisor begins to address many of the issues considered in the pregroup stage. For some groups this will be a honeymoon stage where good planning pays off. For other groups this will be a time of great frustration for members trying to figure out ambiguous rules and for supervisors assuming that members are being resistant. If the initial stage is troublesome, it is probably wise for the supervisor to view this as feedback regarding the readiness of the group to begin. If the structure is adequate and expectations and goals are clear, the atmosphere in the group should be positive and expectant. But if screening was inadequate or ground rules are understated or nonexistent, the group will react randomly and often destructively. Although not the optimal time to address pregroup issues, the supervisor who is in the position of overseeing a chaotic initial stage of group supervision might do well to back up and negotiate each item with the group until some resolution is accomplished.

On the other hand, some resistance is natural at this stage (Corey & Corey, 1987) and should not cause an overreaction by the supervisor. Even if the preparation has been adequate, group members cannot be expected to jump into the water without getting some idea of the temperature. Perhaps the first thing that the supervisor should do to counteract early resistance is to communicate acceptance of each member's caution. Beyond that, Corey and Corey suggested that the leader (supervisor) focus on sharing responsibility as soon as possible with group members regarding the direction of the group and each person's contribution and work to find a balance between too much structure and too little.

For example, if supervisees appear particularly timid (which can be a result of previous group or supervisory experiences or simply the group's personality), the supervisor could introduce a highly structured case presentation. Wilbur and Roberts-Wilbur (undated) have devised such a structure that distracts supervisees from some of their more personal issues and seems, in our experience, to work very well with groups that approach the task of case conferences in an overly cautious fashion.

The structured group supervision model (SGS) is presented in Table 5.3

## The Transition Stage

Whether or not it is true in all cases, group theory hypothesizes that any group will struggle through a transition stage before it moves on to the working stage (Corey & Corey, 1987). The transition stage will be characterized by anxiety, defensiveness and resistance, a struggle for control, conflict, challenges to the leader (supervisor), and confrontation. (We will deal with several of these topics at length in Chapter 10.) Assuming that supervision and the exposure that comes along with it threatens supervisees at some level, the transition stage will be the working out of that threat.

Bauman (1972) listed several trainee "games" that are played in order to avoid supervision.

1. Submission: "I'll do anything you say. I have no opinion of my own."
2. Turning the table: "What do you think the client meant by that statement? How do you handle resistant clients? When is depression serious?"
3. "I'm no good": "I just can't do anything right. Maybe I'm in the wrong profession."

**TABLE 5.3**   Schemata of the Steps of the Structured Group Supervision Model*

| | |
|---|---|
| Step 1: Plea for Help | The supervisee states what assistance is being requested from the supervision group. The supervisee provides group with summary information relating to the request for assistance. Information may be in the form of audio or videotaped material, a written summary, or verbal communication. Following the presentation of the summary information, supervisee makes Plea for Help statement, e.g., "I need help with . . ." |
| Step 2: Question Period | The supervision group members ask the supervisee questions about the information presented in Step 1. This step allows group members to obtain additional information or clarify any misperceptions concerning the summary information. One at a time, in an orderly manner, group members ask one question at a time of the supervisee. The process is repeated until there are no more questions. |
| Step 3: Feedback/Confrontation | Group supervision members respond to the information provided in Steps 1 and 2 by stating how they would handle the supervisee's issue, problem, client, etc. During this step, the supervisee remains silent but may take notes regarding the comments or suggestions. When giving feedback, group members again proceed one at a time stating how they would handle the supervisee's dilemma. First person is used, e.g., "If this were my client, I would . . ." The process is repeated until there is no additional feedback. |
| Pause or Break | There is a 10 to 15 minute break between Steps 3 and 4. Group members should not converse with the supervisee during this break. This is time for the supervisee to reflect on the group's feedback and to prepare for Step 4. |
| Step 4: Response Statement | The group members remain silent and the supervisee, in round robin fashion, responds to each group member's feedback. The supervisee tells group member which of their statements were helpful, which were not helpful, and why they were beneficial or not. |
| Optional Step 5: Discussion | The supervisor may conduct a discussion of the four step process, summarize, react to feedback offered, process group dynamics, etc. |

*Developed by Wilbur, M. P., & Roberts-Wilbur, J. (Undated). Unpublished table.

4. Helplessness: "I've only had three clients. I couldn't possibly handle this case."
5. Projection: "Things were going fine until I heard you enter the observation room. It's really your fault that I'm so unnatural in my counseling."

Liddle (1986) reminds us that resistance is not just contrariness but an attempt to avoid a perceived threat. She listed five possible sources of threat in supervision: evaluation anxiety, performance anxiety (living up to one's expectations of oneself), personal issues (e.g., having unresolved feelings about one's mother as one is treating a client with a similar issue), deficits in the supervisory relationship, and anticipated consequences (e.g., resisting the learning of empathic responses because one is afraid of stimulating client emotion.)

Corey and Corey (1987) suggested a two-pronged approach for the supervisor when transition behaviors become evident: support and confrontation. They stress that overly negative confrontation might alienate supervisees even more, but support only might communicate the erroneous impression that the supervisor considers the supervisees to be too fragile to handle honest feedback. Either extreme will prolong the transition phase and discourage entry into the working stage.

It is not always easy to balance support and confrontation skillfully. The wise supervisor might allow the supervision group to help find the balance. By sharing leadership responsibilities early in the life of the group, the supervisor can take the position of filling in the gaps rather than being the sole feedback provider. For example, the group may be structured in a way that supervisees offering feedback to a peer are evaluated on the quality of their feedback, but the supervisee presenting a case is off the hook for the day (unless, perhaps, something potentially damaging has been done in therapy by the supervisee). This serves two purposes: It allows the supervisor to monitor the group's readiness to be confrontive; and it allows group members an opportunity to be articulate about their insights, rather than the supervisor being the sole therapy expert in the group. This kind of structure will really pay off in the working stage of the group.

Others have taken a more intrapsychic view of the transition stage of supervision groups, assuming that "nonwork styles" (Bion, 1961) of group members are derived from unconscious issues with their primary group, the family (Abels, 1977; Cooper & Gustafson, 1985). "When adults' group behavior unfolds, it is all too apparent that a group character is emerging which dramatizes (in the here and now) patterned roles, sets of expectations, and tests all deriving from family group experiences" (Cooper & Gustafson, 1985, p. 7). Cooper and Gustafson attributed the homeostatic quality of supervision groups to these patterned responses outside of the supervisee's awareness, including the handing over of inordinate authority over oneself to the supervisor out of unconscious respect for one's parents. Of course, in addition to family loyalties, there have been family sacrifices, and the

supervisee may react negatively to any feedback of a personal nature that comes from an authority figure.

Although homeostasis is a powerful force, so too is the immediacy and power of the group. Lewin's (1952) force field analysis depicts any social group in a relative state of equilibrium as experiencing forces that promote change and growth and forces that retard change. If the supervisor can successfully move the supervisee beyond "nonwork," change and growth can occur. "The group supervision learning, in a nutshell, exposes and permits questioning and revision of family group loyalty paradigms" (Cooper & Gustafson, 1985, p. 9). The method suggested for breaking through the transition phase is not to conduct "pseudo group therapy," but rather to work to empower supervisees. Cooper and Gustafson stated that trying to reject the role of expert outright will only result in resistance. Rather, they suggested that the supervisor actively court the discriminating potential of each supervisee.

> In other words, the leader [supervisor] must demonstrate the capacity to be disloyal to the unconscious and submissive pressure of the supervisees. This could involve agreeing with incomplete ideas, encouraging emotions before they are thought out, being willing to go out on a limb and be wrong, and generally helping create an atmosphere which courts intellectual disloyalty. (p. 14)

In wrestling with the same issue, Abels (1977) contended that when homeostasis is evident, something different needs to be done if the group is to move in a productive direction. Abels described six ways that the supervisor can restructure the group supervision experience to promote movement.

1. We can restructure roles by minimizing the status of expert, leader, parent figure, versus the beginner, novice, infant, dope.
2. We can restructure our message: All people are worthy of respect. No one is

more deserving, not even the supervisor. No one is to be a scapegoat, not even the destructive member.

3. We can restructure the norms by clarifying the contract, the ground rules, the expectations, and reasoning ability.

4. We can restructure other persons' understanding of the situation by giving new knowledge about ourselves, others, and the situation.

5. We can restructure our ways of thinking to include viewing the consequences of our actions, not merely our goals. (p. 192)

Abels relied on the pronoun *we* in order to underscore the transactional nature of group supervision, which is, of course, both its strength and its challenge. By working with group members, however, by

> *examining but not yielding to the nonwork patterns played out by the members, by maintaining the thrust of the contract, by insisting on inquiry and evidence, by raising the consciousness of the members about their patterns of reasoning and the paradoxes of perception and interpretation, the supervision can help transform the patterns into more constructive and productive ones. (p. 193)*

### The Working Stage

In a way, the working stage is a slight misnomer in that by the time one arrives at it, the more demanding work of group supervision has been done. Rather than the exhausting work of protecting oneself or trying to pry through another's resistance, the work of the group at this stage is the energizing variety that is characterized by a commitment to explore and examine one's own therapeutic efforts. Supervisees present cases that show them stretching the upper limits of their skill, rather than cases that are too clear or too impossible to elicit critical comments.

Of course, there are group process issues still to be addressed at this stage. The group might plateau on occasions or regress (Corey & Corey, 1987). The supervisor might rely too much on one particular structure or technique (e.g., exclusive use of audiotape or one particular method of discussing cases). The sensitive supervisor will be watching for signs of nonwork returning and will change direction, ask the group for feedback, or offer the group some process feedback if this occurs. On the other hand, the supervisor must understand the importance of a recycling of issues if, in fact, they are being understood and confronted at new levels. What might feel like an old theme revisited, might be a theme understood for the first time.

Borders (1989b) offered a structured group model that can breathe life into a stagnated process. Relying on videotape for the presentation of cases, Boders requires supervisees to present specific questions about the client or the session and to ask for specific feedback. Other group members are then assigned one of four tasks to direct their observation of the videotape segment, depending on the issues raised by the supervisee. The first of these is a focused observation. A peer might be asked to focus on the use of one type of skill (e.g., confrontation) or one aspect of the session, such as the relationship between the counselor and client. Borders points out that all four tasks can be used to develop the skills of the observer. In other words, the observer who has a tendency to quicken the pace of sessions might be asked to observe the pace of the videotaped session.

The second option described by Borders is role taking. An observer can be asked to be an alter ego of sorts and take the role of the counselor or client or can be asked to add dimension to the session by taking the role of a significant person in the client's life (e.g., a parent or spouse). For family sessions, the assignment could be to represent the family member who refuses to come to therapy. After the videotape has been shown, the observer gives feedback from the perspective of the represented person.

Borders's third task is to observe the session from a particular theoretical orientation. One observer could be assigned this task, or several observers could be looking at a session from different theoretical perspectives. For example, a school counseling intern could be asked to observe another supervisee's school counseling session from a systemic perspective. This exercise helps supervisees not only apply theory to practice but also bring forth underlying assumptions about problem formation and resolution.

The final assignment is for an observer to watch the session with a descriptive metaphor in mind. Borders reports that this approach has been particularly helpful when the issue is the interpersonal dynamics between the client and counselor or the counselor feeling stuck. For example, an observer might be asked to think of a road map and describe the direction counseling is taking or to view the counselor-client relationship within the context of a movie and describe each person's part in the drama.

The role of the supervisor in Borders's model is to be a moderator and process commentator. As moderator the supervisor keeps the group on task, choreographs the experience, and summarizes feedback. As process commentator, the supervisor attends to immediate group dynamics. For both roles Borders emphasizes the need for the supervisor to be cognizant of the developmental level of the supervisees, novice counselors needing more direction and structure and more advanced supervisees being able to take on more responsibility. The model, therefore, requires a good deal of supervisor flexibility.

*Indeed, the success of this approach depends on the supervisor's artistry in recognizing a needed and appropriate intervention, assigning tasks to particular peer group members, and orchestrating the feedback. Often working at several levels, the supervisor helps a productive learning experience to unfold. (pp. 5–6)*

Another challenge for the supervisor at the work stage is to convince supervisees of

the benefit of making new, more sophisticated mistakes. Once a supervisee has mastered enough therapeutic knowledge to coast, it can be difficult to convince that person to return to a more vulnerable position. We believe that it is important to pair the encouragement to experiment with the freedom to falter. For example, if a trainee has accomplished all reasonable goals for completion of the internship, it is important to tell the trainee that this is so and that there will be no negative consequences (e.g., a lower grade) for attempting to learn new things and making some mistakes in the process. A similar kind of assurance can be made in the workplace. (We will discuss how evaluation can aid or detract from learning in Chapter 7.)

Finally, when one is in the working stage, individual differences should be more apparent. Because there is more group cohesion, there is less of a need for group conformity. For example, each person's brand of humor should be more evident at this stage as should personal philosophies of life and of helping. When a supervision group is working well, there are no stars (not even the supervisor) and no dunces. Rather, each supervisee is known for his or her particular talents, idiosyncratic ways of viewing clients, and personal supervision goals. Everyone has something to gain from the group and something to offer the group.

As we already have asserted, the kind of work that is done at the working stage is more challenging than demanding. Some groups, however, never get to this stage and continue to hang on to some aspect of the transition stage. Probably all groups have some element of nonwork throughout their life span. Shulman (1982) referred to the supervision group's "culture" as an important concept to keep in mind. The culture is that gestalt that makes the group feel different from all other groups. The culture is created by an evolving set of norms and rules. These are not ground rules specified by the supervisor but are the rules that are not addressed and, therefore, potentially more powerful. One such rule might be Give feedback, but don't make anyone angry. Although benign enough in the initial stages of group supervision, such a rule, if more powerful than the injunction to be honest, will carry a non-work flavor into some of the work of the group. It is rewarding when the culture of the supervision group is called into question by a supervisee, but if this does not occur, it is ultimately up to the supervisor to be aware of and to confront the limitations brought about by certain aspects of the group's culture.

## The Ending Stage

Because there are time-limited supervision groups and ongoing supervision groups, it is appropriate that we discuss each separately in terms of endings.

*The Time-Limited Group.*   Many supervision groups, both on and off campus, are determined by the academic year. For practicum and internship groups, the supervision experience can be one of weeks, rather than months or years. Especially when the life of the supervision group is predetermined to be one semester — a mere 15 or so weeks — the ending of the group will feel premature to almost everyone. Additionally, toward the conclusion of the semester there will be a sense of urgency in managing the termination of each supervisee's client load that will typically override any consideration of the closure issues in the group itself.

Although understandable, it is a mistake to end a supervision group without allowing the group to process this phase. In one respect, all groups should begin with an eye to ending just as should all therapy relationships. The goals of the group should be specific enough to be noticed when they have been achieved so that supervisees can feel a sense of accomplishment upon ending. At the same time, the supervisor needs to help supervisees put their learning into context to help alleviate any panic at ending the supervision experience. We are referring to the naive assumption that most trainees have upon entering supervision that they will feel totally competent upon its completion. We know, of course, that training is only the beginning of practitioners' learning of their trade. (For this reason, supervision among experienced practitioners is becoming more and more prevalent.) A discussion of this reality is an important aspect of closing out group supervision. Equally important is giving each supervisee some direction regarding the learning to be accomplished in the immediate future. This may need to be done individually, but certainly some supervision groups will have developed sufficiently to handle this task in the group context. The point is that a time-limited experience is just that: limited in both time and opportunity to learn. Therefore, supervisees must be evaluated knowing that the amount of time given to them is most likely insufficient for their needs and that it is essential for them to leave the supervision experience with a plan for self-improvement. A part of each supervisee's plan for self-improvement will most likely be the securing of additional supervision. An important culminating experience, therefore, would be to crystallize what can be learned from supervision and how to go about securing appropriate supervision.

One aspect of time-limited supervision that can be frustrating for the supervisor is the near universal tendency to divest oneself from the group when the end is in sight. Supervisees who are simultaneously approaching closure with their clients will complain that their clients have stopped working. Often these same supervisees will be unaware that they are working less with each other in the supervision group. The need for psychological distance in order to cope with the loss of both people and a valuable process is important to address in the group as supervisees handle multiple closure experiences.

*The Ongoing Supervision Group.* A danger of the ongoing supervision group is that it might fizzle out rather than end. Just like a relationship that fizzles out, the group that terminates in this fashion is left with unfinished business and perhaps an inadequate understanding of what caused the ending to occur. In order to avoid this, it is advisable to schedule at the outset of the group a time at which the group will evaluate itself. Like all social systems, groups need markers in order to appreciate their development. A scheduled evaluation can provide this kind of marker, giving group members an opportunity to reestablish norms, refocus their energies, disband, or continue with virtually no change.

The kind of ending we are suggesting may be an appointed time when the group reviews the assumptions and decisions that were made in the pregroup phase. It is a time when as many things as possible become negotiable, including ground rules and the process of supervision itself. It is a time for supervisees to evaluate their individual development and their level of commitment and contribution to the goals of the group. It is a time for the supervisor to evaluate the amount of responsibility that has been shared with group members, the process that has been in place, and the feasibility of continuance.

There are several ways that endings can be added to the life of a group. One way is to freeze membership for a certain amount of time — say one year — at which time some members might leave and others might enter. The change of membership gives the group a chance to start over, in a sense. Another way is for the process of the group itself to change. For example, a supervisor might decide that it is time for the group to change from a supervisor-led group to a peer supervision group. This juncture could be planned as an ending. Time also can be manipulated to produce a marker. A break of four to six weeks could be planned to occur every six months in order to encourage an evaluation and renegotiation

period prior to, or immediately after, the break. Each group will find its own way to end once the importance of ending is appreciated.

## Postgroup Stage

Corey and Corey (1987) reminded group leaders that they might be called upon to offer postgroup consultation and referrals. They also stressed the importance of evaluation. We believe this is important for the clinical supervisor also to consider. Depending upon the supervisor, consultation, referral, and networking will often occur after group supervision has ended. A follow-up study of a supervision experience, however, often is not done except in academic programs that do a systematic survey of their graduates, which typically is not specific enough to aid clinical supervisors in improving their work. We encourage evaluation based on pregroup planning as an essential way to ensure that supervisors continue to develop professionally as they aid their supervisees to do so.

Thus far, our discussion pertains to most supervision groups. But we now devote the rest of this chapter to a special kind of group, the peer supervision group.

## PEER GROUP SUPERVISION

In Chapter 1 we differentiated supervision from consultation, noting that the former included evaluation and was an ongoing relationship. In this section we deviate slightly from our definition of supervision in that peer supervision does not include formal evaluation. At the same time, it is not consultation because it is ongoing, and group members feel more accountable to each other than they might in a consulting relationship. In fact, peer group supervision seems to be a growing phenomenon and an important ingredient to the vitality of the mental health professions.

Anyone who has been in the helping professions for a while has heard colleagues talk about the problem of isolation and the fear of practitioner burnout along with the fear of becoming stale. In more recent years, professional organizations have highlighted the need for continuing supervision, often incorporating the expectation of posttraining supervision into certification requirements. But there comes a time when a person has met the profession's designated criteria, and that person is far more likely to be a supervisor than a supervisee. For an increasing number of professionals, the alternative to receiving no additional supervision has come in the form of peer group supervision.

Peer supervision has received only modest coverage in the professional literature. In one study, though, Lewis, Greenburg, and Hatch (1988) found that in a national sample of psychologists in private practice, 23 percent were members of peer supervision groups, 24 percent had belonged to such a group in the past, and 61 percent expressed desire to belong to a group if one were available. The reasons for joining peer groups (in order of importance) were (1) suggestions for problem cases, (2) discussing ethical or professional issues, (3) countering isolation, (4) sharing information, (5) exploring problematic feelings or attitudes toward clients, (6) learning or mastering therapeutic techniques, (7) support for stress in private practice, (8) countering burnout, and (9) exposure to other theoretical approaches.

Peer supervision groups can be either developed from supervisor-led groups to peer groups or conceived as peer supervision groups from the outset. In either case, at the point that peers attempt to offer each other supervision (or consultation, as some authors prefer to call it), certain conditions must exist if the process is to be successful. Chaiklin and Munson (1983) noted that a sincere desire to improve clinical skills is, of course, the primary condition for peer supervision. They also favored the model of a peer group beginning with a supervisor whose role is to work him or herself out of a job. For practitioners

working in mental health settings, the second major condition is administrative backing (Chaiklin & Munson, 1983; Marks & Hixon, 1986). If peer supervision is not viewed as valuable and cost-effective by administrators and if this is not communicated by the provision of space and time to conduct supervision meetings, the agency peer group will certainly falter.

The independent peer group (that is, outside of any employment setting) has probably the greatest potential for compatibility among its members because such a group tends to be formed by professionals who already know and respect each other. For the peer group formed within an institution, there may be some history to overcome among some of the members, such as political entanglements, competitiveness, or personality issues (Hamlin & Timberlake, 1982). Additionally, lack of homogeneity of experience is far more likely for the agency group, which means that the group will most likely veer toward either the most experienced members or the least experienced members, potentially frustrating the other members of the group.

Regardless of the initial compatibility of the peer group, however, the group stages outlined by Corey and Corey (1987) will still occur and need attention. It is a common error of professionals who already are comfortable with one another to forgo the planning stage for the group until issues begin to arise. Another potential for all supervision groups, but more so with peer groups, is differential contact among its members outside of supervision. Ground rules may need to be outlined regarding any processing of supervision outside of the group so as not to drain off energy that legitimately belongs within the group.

## The Process of Peer Supervision Groups

Peer supervision groups tend to be more informal than other types of supervision groups (Lewis et al., 1988). This might be considered an error, at least in the beginning. Without the direction of a designated leader, structure can give the group some measure of stability as it is finding its particular rhythm.

Part of the structure must be a plan for handling the leadership of the group. Although leaderless by definition, peer groups have realized that ignoring the issue of leadership gives rise to competitiveness (Schreiber & Frank, 1983). Therefore, most groups rotate the leadership role, with one person directing each meeting. Leader may concern themselves with group leadership issues only or may be asked to take responsibility for secretarial issues arising as a result of the meeting, including communicating with absent members about the next meeting, keeping records of supervision meetings and actions taken, and so on.

The peer supervision process also includes a plan for case presentation. Typically one or two cases is the maximum that can be reasonably discussed at one meeting. Marks and Hixon (1986) suggested that the presenter come prepared with two or three questions about the case to direct the group's discussion. They also suggested that a process observer be appointed who is neither the presenter nor the designated leader. This person would give feedback at the end of the supervision meeting about the group process that was observed, including "a statement regarding the group's ability to stay task-oriented, its adherence to ground rules, what group building may have occurred and the participation level of the group members" (p. 241).

## Advantages and Disadvantages

Those practitioners who participate in peer supervision groups are far more laudatory than critical. There is every reason to assume, therefore, that the numbers of peer supervision groups will grow. Among the advantages ascribed to peer supervision groups are the following (Hamlin & Timberlake, 1982; Lewis et al., 1986; Marks & Hixon, 1986; Schreiber & Frank, 1983; Wendorf et al., 1985):

1. They help clinicians to remain reflective about their work and offer clinicians options beyond their individual frameworks.
2. They offer the type of environment that is especially attractive to adult learners.
3. They provide a forum for the reexamination of familiar experiences (e.g., early terminations or working with one particular ethnic group.
4. They provide a peer review process that maintains high standards for practice, thus reducing the risk of ethical violations.
5. They provide a forum for transmitting new information, thus providing continuing education for members.
6. They provide the continuity necessary for serious consultation.
7. They can provide some of the therapeutic factors often attributed to group process, including reassurance, validation, and a sense of belonging. As a result, they can reduce the potential for burnout.
8. They enable clinicians to become more aware of countertransference issues and parallel process.
9. They provide supervision that is less likely to be compromised by conflicts with authority figures because feedback is offered by peers rather than an "expert."

The major limitation reported by members of peer supervision groups came from agency groups (Marks & Hixon, 1986). Because group members might form their own coalitions, interagency communication might not be facilitated. Also, when group members must work with each other outside of the group, they may be reticent to self-disclose and be less trustful in the group. Finally, the structure of the group may be inflexible in dealing with the crisis situations that are bound to occur occasionally in agencies. Allen

(1976) mentioned one additional disadvantage of peer groups; they may limit the amount of individual supervision sought by the group members. Marks and Hixon (1986), however, found that peer group supervision strengthened individual supervision by "pointing out its gaps" (p. 423).

Group supervision is a cost-effective form of supervision that offers the supervisee the benefits of peer relationships, exposure to a greater number of cases, and vicarious as well as direct learning. There is little doubt that group supervision will continue to be an important supplement to individual supervision. Therefore, we would be well advised to give this vital form of supervision more empirical attention while we develop and utilize group supervision models.

# CHAPTER 6

# LIVE SUPERVISION

In Chapters 4 and 5 we reviewed the various forms that individual and group supervision can take. That material addressed supervision as most mental health professionals understand it. For our final chapter that considers the process of supervision, we move on to live supervision.

Live supervision represents a paradigmatic shift from either individual supervision or group supervision; therefore, it cannot be considered a subgroup of either even though live supervision can be carried out with a lone supervisor or with a group (team) of supervisees. The paradigmatic shift essentially consists of two components: The distinction between therapy and supervision seems less pronounced than in traditional supervision, and the role of the supervisor is significantly changed to include both coaching and cotherapist dimensions. As a result of these essential differences, the process of live supervision and its advantages and drawbacks are distinctly different from other forms of supervision. This chapter will address the evolution of live supervision, describe its process both with and without a team, note the advantages and disadvantages for both forms of live supervision, and address the empirical findings, about its effectiveness that are available.

No other form of supervision has received so much professional attention in the past decade as has live supervision. With its roots firmly in family therapy, it continues to be identified primarily with family therapy institutes and academic programs. Nichols (1984) referred to live supervision as the "hallmark of family therapy" (p. 89) and more recently Lewis and Rohrbaugh (1989) commented that

"the literature suggests that the one-way mirror may be as basic to family therapy as the couch was to psychoanalysis" (p. 323). Other mental health disciplines have borrowed a little or a lot from live supervision practices; no specialty, however, has been as affected by this—or perhaps any other supervision method—as has family therapy. In fact, live supervision in the form of team supervision has become as much a family therapy delivery system as a supervision method.

Before we continue, we need to define some terms and explain our treatment of different aspects of the live supervision phenomenon. Live supervision began as an intensive method for working with an individual trainee (or perhaps two trainees working as cotherapists). In more recent years, the team form of live supervision has gained in momentum. The team is a group of therapists or trainees, with or without a supervisor, who work as a group on their cases. Because of the significantly different dynamics between live supervision without a team and team supervision, we will discuss the former first and team supervision later in this chapter. Furthermore, although live supervision can be, and is, used as a method to supervise trainees working with individual clients, it is still most often associated with family therapy. Therefore, in our discussion we will follow suit and assume that the client is a family.

Finally, we will not attempt to make clear distinctions between training or supervision (with the trainee as the focus) and intervention (with the family system as the focus) even though we are aware that such distinctions often are made in the literature on live supervision. It easily could be argued that the distinction between training and service delivery is artificial and more a matter of supervisor priority. Live supervision has brought the dual levels of supervision more into focus by attending to both levels more or less concurrently.

Live supervision was initiated by Jay Haley and Salvadore Minuchin (Simon, 1982) in the late 1960s as a result of a rather singular project. At the time, both were invested in treating poor families but were not enamored with the idea of trying to teach middle class therapists what it was like to be poor. Therefore, they decided to recruit people from poor communities with no more than a high school education and train them to work with other poor families. Because of the real need to protect the families being treated, Haley and Minuchin devised a live supervision model in which they could guide the new therapists as they worked. The result? In Haley's words, "Actually they did very well. We worked with them in live supervision, 40 hours a week for two years. Nobody has ever been trained that intensely" (Simon, 1982, p. 29).

As we mentioned earlier, live supervision combines direct observation of the therapy session with some method that enables the supervisor to communicate with, and thereby influence the work of, the supervisee. Therefore, the supervisor is simultaneously in charge of both training the therapist and controlling the course and, ultimately, the outcome of therapy (Lewis, 1988). (It should be noted that some family therapy trainers offer alternative ways to conceptualize what is occurring during live supervision. For example, deShazer [1984] and others have opted to view the therapist, supervisor, and family as all part of one therapy system rather than to look at the supervisor's control over therapy, which is considered too linear a view.)

The well-documented advantage of live supervision is that through this form of coaching by a more experienced clinician, there is a much greater likelihood that therapy will go well. There also is an assumption that the supervisee will learn more efficiently and, perhaps, more profoundly as a result of these successful therapy sessions. To return to our coaching metaphor, it is better to be coached and to win the game than to be playing independently and suffer defeat.

In addition to the training function of live supervision, there is a built-in safeguard for client welfare. Because the supervisor is immediately accessible, clients are cared for more directly. This also allows trainees to work with more challenging cases, cases that might be too difficult for them if another form of supervision were being used (Cormier & Bernard, 1982).

Much has been written about the technology of live supervision, especially about different methods for communicating with the supervisee. Because most of the literature on live supervision assumes one or another method of performing live supervision, we will begin by reviewing the different technologies used to communicate with supervisees; we also will consider the messages given by supervisors during live supervision. Once we have explored how live supervision is conducted, we will back up to consider some of the guidelines, or parameters, of live supervision and trainee developmental issues.

## METHODS OF LIVE SUPERVISION

Bubenzer, Mahrle, and West (1987) listed six methods used to conduct live supervision: **bug-in-the-ear**, **monitoring**, **in vivo**, **walk-in**, **phone-in**, and **consultation**. We will discuss each of these briefly, as well as a seventh, **sending a written message** to the family (Goodman, 1985).

### The Bug-in-the-Ear

With some exceptions (e.g., Gallant & Thyer, 1989), the bug-in-the-ear (BITE) seems a less favored form of live supervision technology. BITE consists of a wireless earphone that is worn by the supervisee through which the supervisor can coach the supervisee during the therapy session. It has two major advantages. First, it allows the supervisor to make minor adjustments (e.g., "Get them to talk to each other") or to briefly reinforce the therapist (e.g., "Excellent") without interrupting the flow of the therapy session. In fact, much of what can be communicated through BITE might not warrant a more formal interruption of the session. Second, it protects the therapy relationship more fully because the families are unaware which comments are the direct suggestion of the supervisor (Alderfer, 1983, as cited in Gallant & Thyer).

The disadvantages of BITE flow from its advantages. Because BITE is seemingly so nonintrusive, it can be overused by the supervisor and can be a distraction to the supervisee who is trying to track the family as well as take in advice from the supervisor. As the flip side to supervisor overuse, BITE encourages trainee dependence on the supervisor, discouraging spontaneity. Finally, it is a less crisp form of live supervision that can produce awkward moments. For example, the trainee who is attempting to listen to a supervision comment might need to interrupt the family in order to focus on the supervisory input. Furthermore, because family members do not know when the supervisee is receiving input, the device itself can produce ambivalent feelings because of the secrecy it symbolizes.

## Monitoring

Monitoring is the second form of live supervision, and it, too, is used minimally. Monitoring is the process whereby the supervisor observes the session and intervenes directly into the session if the therapist is in difficulty (Minuchin & Fishman, 1981). By implication, therefore, monitoring can be either a way to safeguard client welfare (in which case it is re-

ally not live supervision per se but something that many supervisors might do if they felt a sense of urgency) or a form of live supervision that is less sensitive to the dynamics between therapist and family. Conversely, an advantage of monitoring, assuming that the supervisor takes over when entering the room, is that it allows the supervisor to directly experience the family dynamics. Often what looks or feels one way from the safety of the observation booth is quite different in the presence of the client system. Therefore, by having the supervisor experience what the therapist experiences enhances their mutual understanding of the intensity of family process. A final advantage of monitoring is that it allows the trainee to benefit from the modeling provided by the supervisor working with the family.

## In Vivo

In vivo has some similarity to monitoring in that it allows clients to see the supervisor in operation. Rather than taking over for the therapist, however, the supervisor consults with the therapist in view of the clients. With in-vivo supervision, there is an assumption that the family deserves to have access to all information, including a discussion of interventions. Seen from a different angle, the conversation between the supervisor and the therapist can itself constitute an intervention by heightening the family's awareness of particular dynamics, especially when dynamics are therapeutically reframed for the benefit of the family.

## The Walk-in

A final intervention that has similar characteristics to the two previous ones is the walk-in. The supervisor enters the room at some deliberate moment, interacts with both the therapist and the clients, and then leaves. The walk-in does not imply an emergency, nor does it imply the kind of collegiality that is evident with in-vivo supervision. A walk-in, therefore, can be used to redirect therapy and to establish certain dynamics between the supervisor and the family or the therapist and the family. As a result, it can be viewed as more of a therapy intervention than either monitoring or in-vivo supervision. All three methods of supervision that involve having the supervisor enter the therapy room are more intrusive in the therapy relationship than those methods that follow.

**Phone-ins and Consultation Breaks**

The most common forms of live supervision are phone-ins and consultation breaks. These methods are similar in that they both interrupt therapy for the therapist to receive input from the supervisor. There is little opportunity for the therapist to react to the intervention, however, when it is phoned-in using an intercom system. In the consultation break, the therapist leaves the therapy room to consult with the supervisor when the supervisor alerts the therapist by, for example, knocking on the door; when the therapist feels the need to consult; or at a predetermined point in the therapy hour. The therapist then has an opportunity to clarify what the supervisor is suggesting prior to returning to the therapy room.

**Sending a Written Message**

Sending in a written message is usually not a separate form of live supervision; rather, it is a way for the supervisor either to send a message directly to the client without entering the therapy room or to serve as an aid to the therapist when the wording of the intervention is very important. When the intervention is multifaceted or paradoxical, the wording can be critical. Also, a written message to the family can be taken home, allowing it to be an extension of therapy between sessions.

Some supervisors are firmly committed to one method of live supervision. For example,

Todtman, Bobele, and Strano (1988) implied that the phone is the most desirable method because it is culturally familiar to the client system. They also commented that it is less intrusive than a supervisor walking into the therapy room but stops therapy nonetheless, avoiding the confusion that can occur when using the bug-in-the-ear. Others feel equally strong about the advantages of a consultation break during the session. Most of the literature on live supervision, however, underplays the method used for live supervision, focusing instead on guidelines for the intervention or directive, parameters that must be respected when using live supervision, the acculturation of supervisees to live supervision, and supervisee issues while working within the live supervision framework.

**THE LIVE SUPERVISION INTERVENTION**

As we have already stated, the core of live supervision is that it allows the supervisor an opportunity to communicate with the supervisee or client system during therapy. We have referred to these communications as messages; they also can be referred to as the *supervisory intervention* or *supervisor directives*. For our purposes here, the terms are interchangeable. Because phone-ins and consultation breaks are the most frequently utilized forms of live supervision (Kaplan, 1987), we will limit our discussion of interventions to those that are compatible with these methods.

**Telephone Directives**

As is the case for all live supervision interventions, telephone directives should be used conservatively; Furthermore, they should be brief, concise, and generally action oriented (Haley, 1987a; Lewis & Rohrbaugh, 1989; Rickert & Turner, 1978; Wright, 1986). Depending on the developmental level of the supervisee, a verbatim directive might be given (e.g., "Ask the mother 'What is your worst fear about

Thomas if he continues with his present crowd?' ") or, for the more advanced trainee, a more flexible directive might be given (e.g., "Reframe Mom's behavior as concern") (Rickert & Turner, 1978; Wright, 1986).

Two generally accepted guidelines (Wright, 1986) include avoiding process statements (or keeping them very brief) and not exceeding two instructions per phone-in. Wright, however, asserted that it is sometimes strategically wise to begin an intervention with positive reinforcement of what has transpired in the session up to the present. In other words, taking the time to say "You're really doing a terrific job keeping Dad from taking over" might be worth the time and increase the supervisee's investment in carrying out future interventions. Our only caution about this is aimed at highly reactive supervisees who might be so sensitive to the supervisor's comments that it would be difficult for them to listen carefully to what follows the compliment.

Lewis and Rohrbaugh (1989) found that supervisors who use phone-ins felt there were four additional parameters to consider: The timing of the phone-in is as important as its content; "the wording, phrasing, and attitude that the supervisor conveys during a phone-in should parallel how he or she wants the therapist to interact with the family" (p. 324); the numbers of phone-ins should be monitored; and the supervisee should be free to work the directives into the session when the supervisee feels the timing is right.

Haley (1987a) has offered one additional guideline for live supervision: If the supervisee needs more clarification than can be provided with a phone call, the supervisee should leave the room for a consultation break.

## The Consultation Break

Even if a phone system is available to the supervisor, a consultation break may be the method of choice. In addition to the supervisee's need for clarification, consultation will be preferred if it is the opinion of the supervisor that

1. The intervention will be lengthy and the supervisee will need some extra time to absorb it (Rickert & Turner, 1978);
2. The supervisee will need a rationale for the intervention, which is not accomplished well using the phone-in (Rickert & Turner, 1978);
3. The supervisee will profit from the opportunity to react to the intervention, perhaps to be sure that it is understood or compatible with how the supervisee is experiencing the family;
4. It will be important to check out some impressions with the supervisee as part of forming the intervention.

When consultation is used, it is essential that the supervisor be attentive to the amount of time the conference takes away from therapy. There is a momentum to the therapy session that is dulled by a live supervision conference. This momentum must be considered as part of the formula for successful live supervision. If the therapist remains out of the therapy room for too long, the intervention that is carried back to the client might be moot. A partial exception to this admonition is if the client system has been forewarned that a lengthy consultation is part of the therapy hour. In fact, when strategic family therapy is being implemented, the consultation break may take place somewhere near the halfway mark of the therapy hour and the supervisee might return to the session only to deliver the final directive, usually in the form of a homework assignment.

The practice of live supervision consultation breaks can lead to creative improvisations even when live supervision is not available. For example, two colleagues of ours worked in a family clinic on the same evening, seeing families back to back. No supervisors or other therapists were available for consultation. Therefore, they decided to each leave their sessions thirty minutes into the hour and to consult with each other about what was going on. Neither had observed the other, so they spent a few minutes describing what had transpired. Although relying on self-report, this form of live consultation allowed them to be of help to each other without adding time to either of their loads (Ritchie & Storm, personal communication).

Other therapists who have been exposed to the use of consultation breaks have found it helpful to take a break during their therapy sessions even when there is no one to consult. As many practitioners know, a moment or two away from the dynamics of the therapy system can lead to highly therapeutic insights.

## PRESESSION PLANNING AND POSTSESSION DEBRIEFING

Although the interaction between the supervisor and the therapy system is the core of live supervision, what comes before and after are the underpinnings of the successful implementation of the model. Especially because of the level of activity involved in live supervision, there is a necessity for groundwork to be done in order for the activity during the session to remain meaningful.

As one might suppose, the goal of the presession is to prepare the trainee for the upcoming therapy session. If there has been a prior session, there will be some speculation about what the family might bring to this session. The supervisor will have two goals in the presession: to prepare the trainee for the upcoming session and to focus on the trainee's own learning goals as they pertain to the upcoming session. Piercy stated that he wants his trainees to show evidence of having a "theoretical map" and then to be able to "tie it to a practical understanding of how to bring about change" (West, Bubenzer, & Zarski, 1989, p. 27). Additionally, trainees are often asked to attempt a particular technique (e.g., to raise

the intensity of the interactions between family members), or they may be asked if they have something particular that they would like the supervisor to observe. In other words, it is important that both the supervisee and the supervisor complete the presession with some clarity about their roles for the therapy session.

On the other hand, Okun argued that family therapy "cannot be organized like a lesson plan" (West et al., 1989, p. 27). Families will force both trainees and supervisors to be spontaneous even if they are adequately prepared for the session. Both Piercy and Okun also noted that the developmental level of the trainee will be reflected in the presession just as it is in the therapy session. The supervisor will be more active with the novice trainee in terms of both helping to provide a conceptual overview and in planning for immediate interventions. Once the trainee has gained in experience, it is expected that the supervisor will take a more consultative position (West et al., 1989).

The postsession debriefing allows the trainee and the supervisor to discuss what transpired in the session. Because they were both involved in the therapy but held different vantage points, this is an important time to share perceptions, review the effectiveness of interventions, offer feedback, and address any unfinished business from the session as a precursor to planning the next session.

If homework has been assigned to the family, this is also a time to consider ways in which the family might respond to the assignment and begin to consider future interventions based on the family's response. In other words, the successful postsession will leave the trainee with some food for thought to consider prior to the next presession (West et al., 1989).

Now that we have described the general process of live supervision, we want to turn to an appraisal of some of the parameters of live supervision.

## PARAMETERS OF LIVE SUPERVISION

In his seminal article, Montalvo (1973) listed six guidelines for live supervision that continue to be relevant today.

> 1. *Supervisor and supervisee agree that a supervisor can either call the supervisee out, or that the latter can come out for feedback when he [sic] wishes.*
> 2. *Supervisor and supervisee, before settling down to work, agree on defined limits within which both will operate. [For example, the supervisor outlines under what condition, if any, the supervisee can reject the supervisor's intervention.]*
> 3. *The supervisor endeavors not to inhibit the supervisee's freedom of exploration and operation too much, but, if he does so, the supervisee is expected to tell him.*
> 4. *The mechanism for establishing direction is routine talks before and after the session. [Montalvo felt strongly that the family should not be privy to these discussions and that efforts to "democratize" the therapy process have not proven useful. To date, there is no uniform opinion among family therapy theorists about this issue.]*
> 5. *The supervisor tries to find procedures that best fit the supervisee's style and preferred way of working.*
> 6. *The beginner should understand that at the start he may feel as if he is under remote control. (pp. 343–345)*

These guidelines reflect Montalvo's structural family therapy bias. The wisdom of the guidelines, however, lies in both their clarity regarding the supervision hierarchy and their respect for the integrity, if not the ego, of the supervisee. Insufficient attention to one of these issues can result in an unsatisfactory experience with live supervision.

In addition to setting clear guidelines, there are other steps the supervisor can take to ensure trainee readiness for live supervision. Rickert and Turner (1978), among others, noted that more advanced clinicians will have the most difficulty acclimating to the live supervision model. Because they have experienced other forms of supervision, their idea of what supervision entails as well as their autonomy is being confronted, assuming that they found other methods of supervision to be less intrusive. Regardless, the supervisor would be wise to be sensitive to the differences between supervisees for whom all supervision is new and those for whom live supervision only is new.

Bubenzer et al (1987) made four suggestions to help desensitize supervisees to live supervision. Using phone-ins as their method, they suggested that supervisors first show new supervisees videotapes of family sessions during which the phone rings and the session is interrupted. By doing this, trainees are able to observe how clients react when the phone rings and how things proceed afterward. This is often one of the first concerns for new trainees. Second, new supervisees are allowed to be observers while live supervision is being conducted with other counselors. They are encouraged to ask the supervisor any questions as things proceed. Third, hypothetical cases are presented to the trainees for them to practice the consecutive stages of pretreatment (or presession planning), counseling-during-session, and posttreatment (or postsession debriefing). At that time the possible use of phone-ins are discussed. Finally, again through role-play of hypothetical cases, the supervisees conduct sessions, following through on their plans, and experience phone-ins during the sessions as previously discussed. With the amount of anxiety that can surround supervision of any type, the idea of allowing a trial run as described by Bubenzer et al. makes intuitive sense.

Once the therapist becomes used to the idea of the inevitability of being interrupted during therapy and knows what form that will take, the pressure is on the supervisor to be concise and helpful. Berger and Dammann

(1982) offered two astute observations about the supervisor's reality versus the supervisee's reality during live supervision. Because of the one-way mirror separating them, the supervisor "will see patterns more quickly and will be better able to think about them—to think meta to them—then the therapist will" (p. 338). Secondly, "the supervisor will lack accurate information as to the intensity of the family affect. This becomes readily apparent if the supervisor enters the room to talk with the family" (pp. 338–339).

There are outgrowths to each of these perceptual differences. Because of the advantage the supervisor enjoys by being behind the one-way mirror, a common reaction for the therapist, according to Berger and Dammann, is to "feel stupid" (p. 338) once something is called to the therapist's attention. The reason, of course, that the trainee feels stupid is because what is pointed out seems painfully obvious but is something that eluded the trainee during the therapy session. The wise supervisor will prepare supervisees for this reaction and allow them opportunities to experience firsthand the cleverness that comes from being at a safe distance from the therapy interaction.

Regarding the intensity issue, the supervisee might rightfully feel that the supervisor does not understand the family if the supervisor is underestimating the intensity of family affect. It is for this reason—the direct contact with the family that is experienced primarily by the supervisee—that Berger and Dammann supported others who believed that, except for an emergency, "the supervisor proposes and the therapist disposes" (p. 339).

Gershenson and Cohen (1978) also noted that the relationship between the trainee and the supervisor can begin on rocky ground because of the vulnerability felt by the trainee. This vulnerability can be experienced as anxiety and resistance, persecutory fantasies, and anger (Gershenson & Cohen, 1978). It could be conjectured that at this stage, the trainee is reacting to the unfair advantage of the super-

visor (behind the one-way mirror) along with extreme embarrassment at the mediocrity of his or her own performance. Fortunately, this initial stage seems to be short-lived for most trainees. According to Gershenson and Cohen (1978) a second stage follows that is characterized by high emotional investment in the process and perceiving the supervisor as a supporter rather than a critic. We can assume that this stage also represents a heightened dependence on the supervisor. Finally, a third stage emerges in which "the directions of our supervisor became less important as techniques to be implemented and instead served as a stimulus to our own thinking . . . [w]e reached a point at which we were able to initiate our own therapeutic strategies" (p. 229).

## ADVANTAGES, DISADVANTAGES, AND ISSUES

Some of the advantages of live supervision have already been delineated. With this form of supervision, supervisees can experience more successful implementation of different techniques during the therapy hour and will see their clients improve more rapidly. Hypothetically, then, what might be learned in months of more traditional supervision can be learned in weeks using live supervision. Furthermore, because of the direct involvement of the highly skilled supervisor, clients assigned to trainees will receive better treatment (Rickert & Turner, 1978). Another advantage is that the therapist can be assigned more challenging cases sooner because the supervisor is, in effect, also assigned to the case. Of course, the difficulty of the case must be considered carefully. Too difficult a therapy case will mean that the trainee is simply the voice of the supervisor and little more. The supervisor must be astute regarding the developmental level of the trainee and determine what cases are within the trainee's grasp. A similar advantage to live supervision is that the trainee is more likely to risk more in conducting therapy because of the knowledge that the supervisor is there to help with interventions (Berger & Dammann, 1982).

Another set of advantages has to do with the trainee's relationship with the supervisor and the trainee's observations about therapy. Because the supervisor often will share responsibility for interventions, the supervisor is far more vulnerable than in other forms of supervision. Especially if a verbatim directive is given, the supervisor cannot come back later and say "You misunderstood the intent of my comment." This kind of sharing of responsibility, when it occurs, will reduce the distance between supervisor and trainee.

Furthermore, live supervision keeps the supervisor aware that what looks relatively simple from behind the mirror is far more complicated when enacted. This too will aid in the supervisor-trainee relationship. Perhaps more importantly, when trainees are extracted from the family during the session, they can be made aware of the extent to which they have become entrenched in the family's system. Proponents of live supervision believe that such entrenchment is inevitable (if not desirable if therapists are to understand the parameters of the family), but only live supervision offers an opportunity for the trainee to move in and out of the family system.

Finally, the trainee's view of the process of therapy will also be affected by live supervision as therapy will unfold far more systematically. When the supervisor gives a rationale for an intervention, predicts reactions, and proves to be right, the therapist experiences firsthand the predictability of patterns once they have been comprehended. This is an exciting moment for the therapist; fortunately, it is balanced by those moments when clients react unpredictably, thus ensuring our sense of fallibility as helpers.

The most noted disadvantages of live supervision are the time it demands of supervisors (although the efficiency with which supervisees are trained has been reported to

offset this initial time commitment), the cost of facilities, the problem of scheduling cases to accommodate all those who are to be involved, and the potential reactions of clients and trainees to this unorthodox form of supervision. Additionally, Schwartz, Liddle, and Breunlin (1988) have returned to one of Montalvo's (1973) initial concerns and have alerted supervisors to the tendency of "robotization" in using live supervision. Unless the supervisor is highly systematic in giving the trainee more and more autonomy, live supervision can produce clinicians who show little initiative or creativity during therapy and who conceptualize inadequately. This potential disadvantage of live supervision has been echoed by others (e.g., Kaplan, 1987; Montalvo, 1973; Rickert & Turner, 1978; Wright, 1986). Schwartz et al. (1988) noted that both critics and proponents of live supervision are concerned about how live supervision underplays the therapist's own observations and intuitions in favor of the supervisor's.

In addition to the danger of the supervisor dominating therapy through live supervision, there is some danger that the supervisor will suggest "dramatic, yet inappropriate, interventions" (Goodman, 1985, p. 48). In other words, Goodman acknowledged the very human possibility of the supervisor showing off in front of trainees. Even if an intervention is appropriate, the supervisor must determine whether it is one that the trainee can carry off successfully. If not, the supervisor is trying to do therapy through the supervisee, rather than conducting live supervision.

Additionally, if live supervision is the only method used within a training program, it may not adequately prepare trainees for working in the far more isolated world of the mental health professions. In other words, even if the supervisor is attentive to trainee developmental levels, live supervision represents a paradigmatic shift not only from other supervision forms but also from the typical autonomy of therapists' responsibilities. Again, this disadvantage is serious only when all of a person's training has been completed within the context of live supervision.

Finally, live supervision operationalizes what behaviorists would call punishment in that interruptions are made mostly when something is going wrong. Although it is certainly possible, it is less likely that the therapist will be phoned or called out of the therapy room for the sole purpose of receiving praise.

## TEAM SUPERVISION

To this point we have focused on the supervisor-therapist relationship in live supervision. More and more, however, live supervision has become synonymous with team supervision, that is, live supervision with other trainees (in addition to the supervisor) behind the one-way mirror. Although team therapy was originally developed by seasoned practitioners (peers) as a means to study and improve their trade, it has become increasingly popular as a method of training even novice practitioners (e.g., Haley, 1987a). Team supervision also can take on a variety of forms. Defining the two most common forms, Roberts (1983) differentiated between supervisor guided live supervision, in which the supervisor is the only, or primary, person from the team who offers direction to the trainee, and the collaborative team model (also described by Sperling et al., 1986), in which, although the supervisor offers initial direction, team members are encouraged to take more and more responsibility for the direction of therapy as time goes on. For our purposes here, we believe that supervisor guided live supervision, as described by Roberts, differs very little from live supervision as it has been presented thus far in this chapter, the only difference being that observers have an opportunity to learn vicariously while the supervisor is working with the supervisee. Therefore, we will focus our attention on the collaborative team model, where supervisees are actively involved in the progress of

therapy and in the development of the supervisee.

Briefly described, the process of team supervision has a group of trainees present with the supervisor behind the one-way mirror during the therapy session. Typically, one trainee will serve as the therapist for a case while the rest of the group works as team members along with the supervisor. As with supervisor only live supervision, the technology most frequently used in team supervision is the phone. The other common method of communication is consultation in the observation room.

Therefore, while the therapist is working with the family, the team is observing interactions, metacommunication, and so on to arrive at some sort of decision regarding the direction therapy should go. The observation room is as busy, if not busier, than the therapy room. The team members have the luxury of being one step removed, allowing them to see the entire therapeutic system, including the therapist. The assumption is that this more objective posture will aid the conceptualization process. Team supervision also allows the supervisor to do a great deal of teaching while therapy is being conducted and to culminate an important clinical lesson with a timely intervention sent to the family through the therapist. Team supervision, therefore, becomes therapy, supervision, and classroom, all in one.

In order to facilitate the activity and efficiency of the team, it is sometimes helpful to assign specific tasks to different team members (West, Bubenzer, & Zarski, 1989). These tasks can be assigned by the supervisor or, if the therapist is looking for specific feedback, by the therapist. For example, the therapist trainee who is concerned about her ability to maintain appropriate boundaries within the session might ask one team member to observe only this aspect of the session.

Bernstein, Brown, and Ferrier (1984) presented a model describing what they considered essential roles in team supervision: the *therapist,* the person who will sit with the family during the session and will remain attuned to the mechanics of running the session; the *taskmaster,* the member of the team assigned to direct the conference and keep the team from deviating from the agreed upon structure for analyzing the information being produced by the family while ensuring an atmosphere conducive to creativity and spontaneity; and the *historian,* the person responsible for maintaining the threads of continuity across and within treatment sessions.

The supervisor can organize the team to accomplish any number of goals. One member could be asked to observe one member of the family or one relationship (e.g., father-child) or to track one theme, such as what happens in the family when feelings are introduced. Such assignments allow the supervisor to teach the importance of particular dynamics for progress in therapy. Furthermore, the supervisor can assign tasks to specific team members that represent their training goals. For instance, the team member who has a difficult time joining with children in therapy sessions can be asked to observe another trainee's joining style with children. The team, therefore, offers not only the advantage of in-session assistance but also numerous and rich possibilities for learning and postsession feedback.

## Novel Forms of Team Supervision

As many practitioners have discovered, once the traditional mold of therapy has been broken, the possibilities for reconstructing both therapy and supervision, and a combination of the two, are innumerable. There have been several variations on the theme of the therapeutic team, each carrying with it new assumptions and parameters for both therapy and supervision.

For example, Olson and Pegg (1979) described what they referred to as Direct Open Supervision (DOS). In their model the team is present in the therapy room and is used in therapy as needed. For example, Olson and Pegg described one case where the husband and wife would do battle whenever they tried to negotiate. Two team members were asked to role-play one of their arguments and then to model some negotiating behaviors. Following this, the couple gave feedback about what they thought they could use from the role-play and what would not work for them. At the end of the session, the team processes what transpired in the therapy session with the family present. No private deliberations are allowed in this model. Whatever team members and the supervisor have to say to each other is heard by the family. This model, therefore, firmly represents a democratic view of therapy.

An even busier model than DOS is the "Pick-a-Dali Circus" (PDC) (Landau & Stanton, 1983; Stanton & Stanton, 1986), in which all team members (including the therapist) are asked to play a variety of roles in order to highlight family dynamics and push the family toward resolution. "In many ways, PDC is like theatre of the absurd. Team members respond singularly, in couples or small groups, or in unison, in an ongoing, flowing way during the session. They may physically situate themselves at different places in the room, change their positions, leave the room alone or in groups to observe through a one-way mirror, and so on, in accordance with the therapeutic stratagem of the moment" (Stanton & Stanton, 1986, p. 171). We assume that careful preparation and a highly regarded supervisor are necessary elements for the successful implementation of PDC, lest therapy becomes theatre of the absurd.

Finally, Brodsky and Myers (1986) presented a model similar to those that have already been described but designed for individual clients. Again, the entire team is present in the room for what the authors called In Vivo Rotation. A client contracts for 13 weekly sessions. For the first four to six sessions, the supervisor conducts therapy with the trainees observing, followed by each trainee taking a turn in the therapist role for the next several weeks. The supervisor again assumes the role of therapist for the final session.

Each session follows three phases. During the first, the therapist works with the client for 45 minutes. Next, the therapist joins the observers (in view of the client) for a 30 minute discussion of what has transpired in therapy, including client dynamics and therapist technique. The therapist then rejoins the client for 15 minutes, and they process the issues raised by the observation group. At no time are observers allowed to intervene directly with the client. Although the authors reported substantial benefits from the use of In Vivo Rotation, they admitted that it is not for everyone.

Because it is not possible to cover adequately all the dynamics to be considered for these various team models, we will use as our reference for the rest of the chapter the standard model where the team and supervisor are positioned behind the one-way mirror with the therapist and client group in the therapy room.

## Team Dynamics

With the variety of opportunities offered by team supervision, it is perhaps not surprising that a team approach involves some initial issues and complications not typically associated with other forms of supervision. The most central of these is the cohesion of the group that will form the team (deShazer, 1985). Wendorf (1984) suggested that before the team attempts to work as a unit in offering therapy, they come together as a group through a careful examination of group process.

Referring back to Chapter 5 and our discussion of group dynamics (Corey & Corey, 1987), one can surmise that Wendorf would not recommend that the team take on cases until they had reached the working stage. In order to help the team understand each member's needs and agendas, Wendorf recommended that the group alternate between meetings with a supervisor and meetings with peers only. His experience has been that team members will relate to each other differently depending on whether the supervisor is present and that prior to doing therapy, the team needs to know as much as possible about each member.

As might be expected, Wendorf's recommendations are not universally accepted. Theoretical compatibility among team members has been viewed as another essential ingredient for success (Cade, Speed, & Seligman, 1986). Although another type of supervision group might be enhanced by participants coming from widely varying assumptions about therapy, this is far less true with a therapeutic team. Because there is a limited amount of time within a session for the team to confer and recommend an intervention, there needs to be enough theoretical compatibility to allow the team to work efficiently. (Later in this chapter we will present an opposing view as argued by Markowski and Cain [1983].)

***In-session (Midsession) Dynamics.*** The therapist's right to accept or reject the intervention is an ongoing issue, and one that is exacerbated with a team. Unlike the situation with a solitary supervisor where a trainee might be asked to carry out an intervention even though not totally committed to it, the dynamic is more complicated when a group of peers is primarily responsible for the intervention. Even if the supervisor is supportive of the team's direction, it is more important for the trainee to be in agreement with the directive than it is when no team exists. If not, the therapist will eventually feel manipulated by his or her peers, and team dynamics might eventually override the goal of providing exemplary therapy.

Heath (1982) asserted that it is the supervisor's responsibility to choreograph the input from the team to the therapist and to be sure that the intervention is compatible with the therapist's style, "unless the style has become part of the problem" (p. 192). Heath also acknowledged that prior to the in-session conference, the supervisor may be confronted with competitiveness among team members, an understandable phenomenon when the role of therapist is curtailed in favor of the team approach to therapy and training.

A final issue that should receive attention prior to the actual therapy session is which, and how many, team members will be allowed to formulate interventions for the therapist. When consultation is the method used, this is less of an issue, especially if there is a designated taskmaster to translate the group discussion into an intervention. However, when directives are phoned in or the therapist is called into the consultation room to receive the directive rather than to confer with the team, will several members of the team be allowed to be involved in the interchange or just one? This may seem like a minor issue, but it is probably one of the most critical process issues for a team if relations between the therapist and the team are to remain intact. Once again, it is up to the supervisor to monitor the busyness of the observation room and the readiness of individual team members to participate in a more direct fashion.

***Pre- and Postsessions.*** Because of the complexity and intensity of team supervision during the therapy session, it is vital to have planning sessions and debriefing sessions. Liddle and Schwartz (1983) maintained that the presession conference should address family considerations, trainee considerations, relationship considerations, and teaching considerations. If the team goes into the session knowing pretty well what is to be accomplished with the family and what the trainee will be working on personally, the during-session consultations should serve the function of

"mid-course corrections to the general session plan" (p. 478). Additionally, giving time in the presession to team dynamics, taking time to convey a respect for the position and perspective of the therapist, and addressing how this particular session dovetails with overall training goals will prepare the team for the intensity and activity of team supervision.

The postsession conference is equally important. Regardless of the amount of planning that has occurred, team members, especially the therapist, will have a need to debrief. Heath (1982) suggested that the supervisor allow the therapist to suggest a format for the discussion. In addition to a general discussion of the session, including a discussion of hypotheses and goals, the postsession should include some feedback to the therapist and feedback to the team (Heath, 1982). Heath also maintained that emotional reactions on the part of different team members can be appropriate to address if they enhance the process but that criticism be offered only if paired with alternative action. In a similar vein, Cade et al. (1986) stated that

> [t]he therapist will often need time to "disengage" mentally and emotionally from the family before feeling able to consider what the team has to offer. The advantages of multiple perspectives can become a disadvantage if the therapist becomes swamped with ideas, particularly where these are conflicting ideas arising out of conflicting frameworks. (pp. 112–113)

Finally, the supervisor should help the team address the session that just occurred as it fits in the larger context of training (Liddle & Schwartz, 1983) and direct team members' thinking for the next scheduled presession.

***Advantages and Disadvantages of Team Supervision.*** As is the case in peer supervision groups, those supervisees and seasoned practitioners who have been involved in therapeutic teams tend to be strong advocates of the process. Among the advantages delineated are the following (Cade et al., 1986; Quinn, Atkinson, & Hood, 1985; Speed, Seligman, Kingston, & Cade, 1982; Sperling et al., 1985):

1. Team work appears to be highly satisfying. "Family therapy is always difficult, sometimes nerve-wracking and sometimes depressing; working in teams can be creative, highly supportive, challenging and very often fun" (Speed et al., 1982, p. 283).
2. When a crisis occurs within a case, the therapist can attend to the immediate needs of the client, while the team wrestles with conceptualizing the case.
3. As with other forms of group supervision, the therapeutic team reinforces the value of case consultation.
4. The model requires that team members work on their feet, thus training them to arrive at therapeutic interventions more quickly. This ability aids team members in their therapy away from the team.
5. The team model automatically multiplies the numbers of interesting cases with which each team member has the opportunity to work.
6. The team itself can be used to enhance therapeutic goals. For example, a team split can be used as the intervention (Sperling et al., 1985), where the team is said to be in disagreement behind the mirror and sends in two opposing courses of action. This allows the therapist to stay in a neutral position and help the family look at alternatives while acknowledging that there is more than one valid way to proceed.
7. A group of therapists is more likely to take greater risks and operate at a more creative level than an individual therapist. For highly intransigent cases, creative approaches to intervention might be called for if the client system is to improve.

Although the team model is intriguing and dynamic, there are certain disadvantages and pitfalls to be considered and for the supervisor to avoid (Cade et al., 1986; Wendorf, Wendorf, & Bond, 1985).

1. Because of the intensity of the team's efforts, the group can find itself heading toward group therapy instead of group processing.
2. It is very difficult for competitive team members to resist using the therapy sessions to prove their conceptual superiority. This not only means that team members are competing with each other instead of supporting each other but also means that sometimes interventions sent in to families are unduly complicated or clever and not necessarily the most productive for accomplishing therapeutic goals.
3. Because of the high level of group cohesiveness that typically is associated with therapeutic teams, members can become overprotective and fail to challenge each other. For peer team groups, members might drop from the team rather than pursue a different line of thinking.
4. If a team is a subunit of an agency or a training program, the members of the team can pose a threat to other staff members. "A mystique can develop around what a particular team is 'up to.' Other staff feel 'put down' or patronized when in discussion with team members who can somehow convey that they are in possession of 'the truth' " (Cade et al., 1986, pp. 114–115). At the very least, team members will share a common experience not available to others, thus promoting an atmosphere of an "in" group and an "out" group.
5. For a team that has a long span of time to work together, there is a danger of becoming the "other family." We believe, as did Cade et al., that every group has a limited creative life span, at least without the impetus of new members or a change of con-

text. Supervisors need to be sensitive to systemic dynamics within teams as well as within client groups.

6. Finally, it seems to us that team supervision is as much a closed system as some other forms of supervision. By this we mean that there is definitely some self-selection among those supervisors who choose team supervision as their method of choice. They might, for example, be somewhat more theatrical than other supervisors, or perhaps they enjoy therapy more than supervision. Regardless, training programs that wed themselves entirely to team supervision might be discriminating against some of their trainees unknowingly—trainees who are equally talented but more traditional in their approaches to therapy. One way to compensate for this pitfall is to vary one's approaches to supervision. We think the Quinn et al. (1985) "stuck-case clinic" is an excellent approach to team supervision. Rather than having the team consider all cases (and thereby running the risk of overkill for some cases), each team member is charged with bringing his or her most difficult case to the team. As a result, the team's time is spent efficiently, and those therapists who excel in other forms of supervision but are less inclined to the team approach a. ? not seen as weak therapists.

## RESEARCH AND LIVE SUPERVISION

Because live supervision is a relatively new form of supervision in the helping professions and one that has been documented well in the literature, it is possible to observe its evolution. Live supervision began as a dramatic and paradigm-provoking method of supervision, enjoyed a substantial honeymoon period, and only now is being challenged both conceptually and empirically. For example, as stated earlier, it has been suggested by several authors (e.g., Haley, 1987a; Heath, 1982; Hovestadt, Fenell, & Piercy, 1983; Liddle & Halpin, 1978) that family therapists receive superior training when live supervision is the method of choice (especially team supervision). But at least one empirical investigation (Fenell, Hovestadt, & Harvey, 1986) comparing live (team) supervision to delayed feedback found no differences in the skill level of trainees based on type of supervision they received.

Another belief of those using live supervision is that the initial discomfort of the process for trainees and clients will disappear once therapy is in progress. But, as a result of a follow-up study designed to gather reactions of both groups, Piercy, Sprenkle, and Constantine (1986) found that almost one-third (32 percent) of trainees would have preferred no observers of their therapy, and family members reported discomfort with the model in certain situations. Although comfort level was impeded, it is important to note that for these therapists and families, the outcome of therapy did not seem to be affected by their negative feelings. Clearly, much more of this type of research needs to be done to either support, revise, or confront the practice of live supervision (and all other forms of supervision, for that matter).

As stated earlier in this chapter, the most documented form of supervision in recent years is live supervision. Like other forms of supervision, however, the literature reflects more accolades than critical analyses of the delivery of live supervision. But two notable exceptions are studies done by McKenzie, Atkinson, Quinn, and Heath (1986) and Lewis and Rohrbaugh (1989), both of which looked at the frequency of use of live supervision. This is an important issue given the centrality of live supervision to much of the family therapy training literature. McKenzie et al. conducted a national survey of AAMFT-approved supervisors to determine what form of supervision they used most and what form they believed to be most productive. The results showed some discrepancies. From the supervisors' perspective, the most effective form of supervision was live supervision with immediate feedback. But the most frequently used method of supervision was listening to an audiotape, followed by relying on written process notes. Different forms of live supervision ranked from seventh through tenth in frequency even though only 33 percent of the sample reported not using live supervision at all. Furthermore, only 8.5 percent of the respondents thought that process notes were an effective form of supervision, despite the high rate of use.

In a similar study with a smaller sample, Lewis and Rohrbaugh (1989) surveyed all of the AAMFT family therapists in Virginia to determine how live supervision was being carried out. To the authors' surprise, less than one-third of the respondents used live supervision.

Lewis and Rohrbaugh offered two competing hypotheses about the low number of supervisors using live supervision: The one-third figure is encouraging because it is a sign that live supervision is "catching on;" "the field is more diverse and less epistemologically pure than many realize or would like to believe" (p. 326). Certainly this is an important issue for the marriage and family therapy field to resolve.

It is important to notice that the McKenzie et al. (1986) study found two-thirds of their supervisors using live supervision, whereas Lewis and Rohrbaugh (1989) found only one-third.

Lewis and Rohrbaugh correctly cautioned that Virginia might not be representative of the rest of the country. Also, the former study surveyed only approved supervisors, whereas the Virginia study included AAMFT clinical members and associate members who were offering supervision as part of their professional duties. It could be hypothesized, therefore, that approved supervisors use live supervision more frequently. One delineation that neither study addressed was the number of supervisors who were in training settings versus those who were in mental health delivery settings. We believe this to be an important missing datum, especially if, as we assume, live supervision is far more prevalent in training settings.

## LIVE SUPERVISION IN MENTAL HEALTH SETTINGS

Although we concede that live supervision has just begun to be scrutinized empirically, we also consider it to be a major breakthrough in the practice of supervision, and one that will continue to influence training programs, at least in the foreseeable future. Rather troublesome, therefore, is the dichotomy between the extensive use of live supervision in training and its minimal use in mental health settings. This is troublesome for at least three reasons: If live supervision is indeed considered the supervision method of choice, the majority of one's career will be denied this most direct form of supervision; graduates of marriage and family therapy training programs may find their subsequent supervision pro forma and inadequate; and as stated earlier, training programs might eventually be criticized for not providing their students with supervision that will translate to future work sites.

For these reasons alone, we consider it important to report the experiences of those mental health settings that have attempted to incorporate live supervision into their functioning. There are very few references in the literature to this type of activity other than to those settings that were developed as specialized marriage and family therapy clinics, such as the Ackerman Institute or the Philadelphia Child Guidance Clinic. We will report the experiences of two public agencies that introduced live supervision to their operation, one agency subscribing to systemic framework, one committed to diverse conceptual frameworks.

We might assume that live supervision is

easier to implement if the staff already operates within a systemic framework. Based on Lewis's (1988) discussion, it seems that this assumption is valid. Lewis described the infusion of live supervision into a rural public mental health and substance abuse agency. Although the problems of the clients varied greatly, the staff and agency had adopted a systemic orientation. It is possible, therefore, that several staff members had experienced live supervision prior to their employment. Lewis reported no resistance to the live supervision paradigm, either from clinical staff, administration, or clients. He does, however, make a distinction between live supervision and live consultation, which we will discuss in the next section.

Markowski and Cain (1983), on the other hand, reported the introduction of live supervision to a community mental health center staffed by clinicians of various theoretical persuasions. The goal of the mental health center was to increase the skill of a group of core staff in marriage and family therapy. Therefore, an outside consultant was hired to conduct live (team) supervision one-half day per week for the purpose of helping this core staff acquire sufficient competence to function without the consultant. An additional incentive for the staff was meeting the criteria for state certification as marriage and family therapists. For this eclectic staff, it was critical that the consultant was supportive of different clinical orientations so that the integrity of the staff members was protected.

Markowski and Cain reported that the bug-in-the-ear was an unsatisfactory method for their teams (two were formed) and that consultations became the method of choice. We assume that the range of theoretical positions in the team required the kind of give and take that is possible during consultations but not possible using BITE. In time Markowski and Cain also found that team members became more sensitive to their differences and were better able to suggest interventions that fit the therapist's own style and therapeutic assumptions. Therefore, it might be argued that in this case, live supervision made the members of a diverse staff more respectful of their individual contributions, rather than clones of the supervisor as some authors have feared.

Although a positive experience, Markowski and Cain recounted difficulties, too, especially as they related to record keeping, the necessity of separating services, and the acceptance of the individual illness model by third party insurers. The authors concluded that if there is respect and administrative support for such a program, "both the individual and the systems models can co-exist in productive harmony" (p. 44).

## LIVE SUPERVISION: TRAINING, SUPERVISION OR CONSULTATION

It is unorthodox to end a chapter with a definition of terms. We would, however, like to introduce the notion that live supervision introduces a paradigmatic shift not only for the practice of supervision but also for the very meaning of the word *supervision* itself.

Recently, a colleague of ours stated that she believed live supervision was the only legitimate method of supervision for a training program. Her next comment was "I can't train with any other form of supervision." Although some would consider hers an extreme position, our colleague was underscoring the real contribution of live supervision: its training function.

On the other end of the spectrum, Lewis (1988) argued that when a live supervision team is made up of colleagues, the model they are using is better referred to as live consultation. In contrast, Lewis defined live supervision as "a situation where one supervisor is clearly in charge of both training and the therapist as well as the course and, ultimately, the outcome of therapy" (p. 87). Therefore, if the therapist has the right to accept or reject the suggestions of the team, the model becomes, by definition, one of consultation rather than supervision.

Perhaps it is the more contemplative aspect of supervision that live supervision does not address. As we stated in Chapter 1, there are a variety of definitions of supervision, not all of which emphasize the same parts of the over-seeing function. Live supervision fits our definition of supervision in that it is conducted by a senior person in an evaluative relationship with the dual responsibility of enhancing professional functioning and ensuring client welfare. For others, however, the pre- and postsessions might be viewed as supervision, whereas the actual therapy session is either training or something else.

We are certainly not prepared to make any definitive statements here about the language used to describe live or team supervision.

Rather, we see the awkwardness of the language as a metaphor for the paradigmatic shift that live supervision represents or, perhaps, some indication that we have more to learn about supervision in all of its forms. The literature certainly provides many more accolades about what live supervision does than what it does not do. Knowing that any method of learning is incomplete, we must realize that there is more to discover. As yet, we have no evidence that certain supervision approaches are superior, except as based on the convincing arguments of their proponents. As we will discuss in Chapter 12, the supervision field will be driven by those questions that recent theorists and practitioners have given us, questions that have to do with the most efficient and productive ways for us to accomplish our supervision responsibilities.

# CHAPTER 7

# CLINICAL EVALUATION

Evaluation troubles most clinical supervisors. Some view it as a necessary evil; a few see it as antithetical to the helping professions (Cohen, 1987). Whether in an academic setting or in a field setting, many supervisors experience conflict between their role as therapist and the evaluation component of their role as supervisor. As experienced therapists, they have learned to work with clients at various stages or levels of development. Progress is defined in the client's terms. Except in the most global sense, external criteria are avoided. Therapists are taught that unless they can accept clients unconditionally or can appreciate that clients' symptomatic behaviors are the best they can put forth at the time, they will do their clients little good. Furthermore, each therapist has had to learn that client goals can be much less ambitious than a therapist's goals for them. If the presenting problem is under control, it is probably time to terminate even if the client is not a fully functioning human being.

In supervision, many of the working conditions reflect those in therapy, and yet there is an essential paradigmatic difference. Even if the supervisor wanted to use the trainee's progress as the critical variable for evaluation, responsibility to the profession and to future clients would preclude this. The supervisor must be able to evaluate the trainee as compared to some external set of criteria that the supervisor views as endemic to therapeutic practice. But isn't it also important to suspend judgment until the trainee has had an opportunity to gain some experience and benefit from feedback? Yes; this brings us to an important difference between formative evaluation and summative evaluation (Levy, 1983).

Formative evaluation represents the bulk of the supervisor's work with the trainee and is the ongoing feedback that is, or should be, targeted at the trainee's level of ability, with an eye to the next learning step. Formative evaluation does not feel like evaluation because it stresses process and progress, not outcome. But it is important to remember that there is an evaluative message in all supervision (Kadushin, 1976). When supervisors tell trainees that an intervention was successful, they are evaluating. When supervisors say nothing, trainees will either decide that their performance was exemplary or too awful to discuss. In other words, by virtue of the relationship, evaluation is a constant variable in supervision. Some of the supervisor's evaluative comments are sent (encoded) by the supervisor to the trainee; others are received (decoded) by the trainee and may or may not be an accurate understanding of the supervisor's assessments. Because we are always communicating, an evaluative message can always be inferred.

Summative evaluation, on the other hand, is what many of us mean when we discuss evaluation. This is the moment of truth when the supervisor steps back, takes stock, and decides how the trainee measures up. Although this is when the trainee is likely to feel most anxious, often the supervisor's weaknesses are apparent at this juncture. Because supervisors must determine whether trainees measure up, they must first decide against what they are measuring trainees. Furthermore, the trainee should possess the same yardstick. In truth, summative evaluations are trying times because often they are disconnected from what has come before in the supervision relationship. Either because of lack of organization or lack of a clear set of standards, the supervisor conducts summative evaluation in a vague or biased way. A supervisor who is helpful and articulate during the formative contacts can appear rushed and insecure at a summative conference. We believe that the real work of summative evaluation comes prior to the summative conference. Therefore, with clear guidelines that are communicated to the trainee and used to guide supervision, much of the discomfort of the summative conference can be avoided.

Our optimistic assertion notwithstanding, we want to acknowledge that our profession is plagued with a certain degree of ambiguity that limits us as evaluators. We still are unsure about what in therapy is therapeutic. People on waiting lists frequently get well as fast as those in treatment (Bloom, 1984). Furthermore, all supervisors have seen trainees introduce what clearly looked like the wrong therapeutic approach only to have it work. Finally, many therapists have been evaluated incorrectly, resulting in much wasted time as they tried to change something that didn't need changing or valued something that should have been discarded. All of these factors further complicate our perception of evaluation. Kadushin (1985) addressed this situation by pointing out that

> . . . many supervisors question the legitimacy of evaluation and lack a sense of entitlement. They do not think they should or can judge another. Further, they are oppressed by conflicting, ambiguous evidence of performance and by imprecise, vague standards available for judging performance. Not feeling 'without sin,' they are reluctant to cast the first stone. (p. 338)

These two factors then, the incompatibility of evaluation and the therapeutic model and the ambiguity of the field at large, represent the burden of evaluation. Supervisors have two choices for managing this burden:

They can throw their hands up and minimize the function of evaluation in their supervision; or they can work to counteract both burdensome factors by thoughtful planning, structuring, intervening, and communicating. The rest of this chapter can be viewed as a preventive model for those who would like to face evaluation head-on, to lessen its bite by taking it out of the threatening background and putting it in the foreground, where it can be viewed openly and within an ongoing working relationship.

## FAVORABLE CONDITIONS FOR EVALUATION

A major problem with evaluation in the helping professions is that it hits so close to home. Therapy is a very human activity; therefore, to be lacking in therapeutic skills can be perceived as being a less than adequate human being. For this reason, and because of the vulnerability accompanying any evaluation process, it is so important to do all that is possible to create favorable conditions when evaluating. Favorable conditions not only make evaluation more palatable but also become part of the evaluation process itself. As Ekstein and Wallerstein (1972) noted, when the context of supervision is favorable, the trainee stops asking How can I avoid criticism? and starts asking How can I make the most of this supervision time?

Several authors have addressed the conditions that make evaluation a more positive experience. In addition to our own thoughts, the following list of conditions draws from the work of Ekstein and Wallerstein (1972), Fox (1983), Kadushin (1985), and Mathews (1986).

1. Supervisors must remember that supervision is an unequal relationship. No amount of empathy will erase the fact that supervisors' reactions to supervisees will have consequences for them, some of which may be negative. Being sensitive to

the position of the trainee will make supervisors more compassionate evaluators.

2. Clarity adds to a positive context. Supervisors need to state clearly their administrative, as well as clinical, roles. Who will be privy to the feedback supervisors give trainees? Will the supervisor be making decisions regarding the trainee's continuation in a graduate program or job? If not, what is the supervisor's relationship to the persons who make those decisions? For example, most graduate programs conduct periodic student reviews. At these reviews the evaluation by the clinical supervisor often is weighed more heavily than other evaluations. Students should be aware, at the very least, that their performance in the clinical component of the program will be discussed by the total faculty at some point in the future.

3. Defensiveness should be addressed openly. Supervision makes trainees feel naked, at least initially. It is natural, if not desirable, that they attempt to defend themselves. Some will defend by trying to outguess the supervisor. Others will appear vulnerable and helpless. The truth is that all trainees are vulnerable, and supervisors need to be sensitive to this fact and not hold that vulnerability against them. Rather, supervisors can introduce appropriate and inappropriate defensive tactics as a legitimate topic for discussion. "Games" frequently played by trainees (Bauman, 1972; Kadushin, 1968; see Chapter 10) can be described. If asked, trainees usually can tell what type of defense they are most likely to use. If the supervisor then follows such a disclosure with "What should I do when you play 'I'm no good'?" the beginnings of an honest, working relationship have been established.

4. Evaluation procedures should be spelled out in advance. Whatever structure has been decided upon, it should be known by the trainee. Differences between formative and summative evaluation should be explained. Among the procedural topics that should be included are the projected length of the supervisory relationship, the preferred methods of supervision and how these will be used, any additional sources that will be used to determine the trainee's progress, the frequency of supervision conferences, and how the evaluation will be used.

5. Evaluation should be a mutual process and a continuous process. The trainee should be actively involved in determining what is to be learned. In a sense the supervisor is there to serve the trainee, and this contractual dimension should not get lost. Also, the formative aspect of evaluation should be the most active. Although both parties know that there must be a taking stock down the road, the process of learning and the evaluation of the learning should not feel static.

6. There should be enough flexibility so that some down time will not jeopardize a summative evaluation. Kadushin (1985) made the excellent observation that outside reality will sometimes interfere with a trainee's performance. Therefore, supervisors' evaluations should take this into account. Especially in a profession that attracts second career adults, it is important that supervisors balance their expectations with the knowledge that, for trainees as well as for themselves, children have crises, elderly parents need care, and spouses lose or change jobs. Life does not always accommodate supervisees' career aspirations. In a Type A world, we all need to learn that the best laid plans are vulnerable to the unexpected. Supervisors model an important attitude when they are accepting of life's impositions on their supervisees. It is equally important to leave enough space in a training schedule to accommodate life's predictable lack of

predictability. There are times when the best advice a supervisor can give a trainee is that the trainee should postpone internship (or that extra project) until his or her personal life regains some semblance of normality. Learning to appreciate the balance between professional demands and personal demands is an important lesson for all of us in the helping professions. Of course, these comments do not fit the supervisee whose life is perpetually in crisis. That is a different evaluation issue.

7. The background to evaluation must be a strong administrative structure. Whether in an educational or work setting, supervisors must know that their evaluations will stick. Nothing is as frustrating and damaging as when a supervisor risks the consequences of a negative evaluation only to have this overturned by a superior in the organization. When this happens, more often than not, one of two things has happened. Either due process was not followed, or the supervisor did not have a clear sense of the administrative structure beforehand. In other words, the supervisor assumed that he or she would be backed up without bothering to check. Or, the supervisor did not have the political savvy to inform his or her superiors prior to the evaluation, both to warn them and to make sure the process would be supported.

   Whether or not the supervisor is correct in the evaluation can be a moot issue if the trainee's rights were not protected, or appeared not to be protected, during the evaluation process. One of our colleagues gave a student an unsatisfactory evaluation after a counseling practicum only to have the evaluation overturned by the department's grievance committee. The reason for their decision was that although the faculty member had met with the student regularly to give him feedback (therefore, according to the faculty mem-

ber, the student was well warned), the content of these sessions had not been recorded in writing. The student denied foreknowledge of an impending negative evaluation and had to be given the benefit of the doubt. (We will outline appropriate procedures for evaluation later in this chapter.)

The supervisor is not the only one who needs administrative support. Supervisees also must know that there is a place to go if they think an evaluation is unfair or incomplete. On university campuses, the grievance committee is usually the administrative body of choice once the head of the department has been consulted; in employment settings, the supervisor's immediate superior is the appropriate person. If there is no such protective body or person, it is up to the supervisor to establish some sort of safeguard for the supervisee. Supervision objectives will be greatly handicapped if anyone in the system feels trapped. A strong administrative structure offers the same kind of security to supervisees that a strong, and reasonable, parental system offers children. We do not mean to infantilize supervisees, but we do believe that it is appropriate for the organization to acknowledge their subordinate positions and build in appropriate safeguards.

8. Making stars of trainees should be avoided. Whether a supervisor is working with one trainee or several, it is important to resist overreacting to the person who shows unusual potential. We are not implying that one should withhold positive feedback or be dishonest. Rather, we believe that supervisors often react too quickly and by evaluating too quickly set their trainees and themselves up to fail. If supervision occurs in a group, morale is hurt when it becomes obvious that "Mom likes you best!" As Munson (1983) pointed out, supervisees need to know

that they are doing well almost as much as children need to know that they are loved. When early distinctions are inferred among trainees, the natural competition in such a setting can become neurotic. On the contrary, when the group is challenged to insure that everyone wins, the atmosphere is energetic and supportive.

Some trainees will enter supervision expecting to be recognized and treated as stars. It is the supervisor, however, who makes it happen by relying on initial impressions and forgetting that some therapy skills can only be assessed accurately over the long term. Whether a trainee wears well will be terribly important to the trainee's future colleagues, supervisors, and clients. This cannot be determined in a few weeks, regardless of the strength of the trainee's entry behavior.

9. Supervisees need to witness the professional development of their supervisors. As a supervisor, the best way to do this is to invite feedback and use it. Trainees feel empowered if they sense that they have something valuable to offer their supervisor. Additionally, the supervisor's involvement and sharing of continuing education activities models for trainees the need for continuing expansion in the work of therapy. Presenting new ideas that the supervisor is struggling with gives a much more accurate picture of the profession than playing the part of an all-knowing guru. Also, presenting some tentativeness in thinking will remind the supervisor to be tentative about the work of trainees. Supervisors must constantly remind themselves that they do not deal in a profession of facts, but of concepts.

As Haley (1987) noted, therapists develop hypotheses about clients' problems so that they can have some idea about how to work with those clients. The hypotheses, however, are not reality; at best they are a metaphor of reality. With Ha-

ley's distinction in mind, it is important for supervisors to remember that all of their conceptualizations, including the assessments of their trainees, are subject to change in the future, perhaps the not too distant future.

10. Supervisors must always keep an eye to the relationship. As we have discussed elsewhere in this book, the relationship interacts with all aspects of supervision. Evaluation is potentially the most difficult aspect of supervision when the relationship has become too close or is strained. In fact, it is the reality of evaluation that behooves the supervisor to maintain both a positive and a supportive relationship with the trainee — yet one that is professional, not personal. If for whatever reasons relationships are strained, supervisors must ask themselves whether they can evaluate objectively enough. (No evaluation is totally objective; the goal is to keep objective standards in mind while superimposing subjective impressions.) Some personalities clash and the best intentions do not make the initial dislike for the trainee, or for the supervisor, disappear. The trainee should not bear the brunt of this kind of situation. Whenever supervision is conducted, there should be some thought given to the possibility of strong incompatibility, and at least a sketchy plan should be in place for how to resolve such a problem.

11. No one who does not enjoy supervising should supervise. For this final condition, we refer to the point we made at the beginning of this chapter. Evaluation is difficult, even for those supervisors who love the challenge of supervision. For the supervisor who is supervising for any lesser reason, evaluation may feel like too great a burden. When this is the case, the supervisor will short change the trainee and give perfunctory evaluations or will avoid the task, especially if the evaluation could

be confrontive. Supervisors always have many other responsibilities to use as rationalizations for keeping a trainee at an arm's length. It is not difficult to find a helping professional who can attest to the frustration of getting little or no constructive feedback from a supervisor. Whenever a trainee is denied appropriate supervision and evaluation, the professional community is diminished.

## CRITERIA FOR EVALUATION

If favorable conditions for supervisors exist, then the work of supervision can begin with a reasonable promise for success. The mistake frequently made by supervisors is to assume that establishing proper conditions *is* the work of supervision, and they disregard the essential step of deciding on criteria for successful completion of the supervision contract. Criteria are more often established during the early phases of training. Yet even with advanced trainees or in ongoing supervisory relationships, it is important to have goals stated and to determine what evidence will be accepted as having met those goals. In this section, we will consider the process of establishing criteria and the complementary activity of goal setting. We also will look at evaluation instruments and their relationship to evaluation criteria.

Although the supervisee should be involved in determining training objectives, the responsibility of identifying criteria ultimately falls to the supervisor. Supervisors must delineate the behaviors that they pair with being a competent helping professional, decide the level of competence they expect from supervisees, communicate these expectations to their supervisees, and refer to these same behaviors at the end of supervision during the summative conference.

All supervisors have certain things they look for in a trainee even if they have not articulated their criteria to their supervisees or to themselves. For example, many supervisors consider the writing of reports to be a valuable skill but not as important as clinical ability. Additionally, criteria for each supervisor will change somewhat as the supervisor changes. Criteria may also change depending on the setting. For instance, a site supervisor might value autonomy in a supervisee far more than a university supervisor would. Regardless, all supervisors should spend time evaluating their own criteria for successful clinical practice. Furthermore, these criteria should be reevaluated regularly and should be adjusted (when possible) to accommodate the goals of individual supervisees.

Different authors have put forth different sets of criteria for evaluation. In our training programs, we have identified four general categories for evaluation: general clinical ability, both case conceptualization and intervention delivery; written work, including case notes as well as formal reports; ability to be supervised; and professional behavior.

Addressing the employment situation for social workers, Kadushin (1985) listed seven criteria:

1. *Ability to establish and maintain meaningful, effective, appropriately professional relationships with the client system*
2. *Social work process — knowledge and skills*
3. *Orientation to agency administration — objectives, policies, and procedures*
4. *Relationship to, and use of, supervision*
5. *Staff and community relationship*
6. *Management of work requirements and work load*
7. *Professionally related attributes and attitudes (pp. 359–361)*

Grann, Hendricks, Hoop, Jackson, and Traunstein (1986) have devised a rating form of 14 items that are divided into four criteria categories: the student and learning, the student and the agency, the student and society, and the student and the client. The exact number of criteria doesn't really matter as long as there are more than one or two and no more than eight or ten. In other words, the criteria must not be so global as to be useless and must be a small enough number to be manageable. It should be communicated to the student that these are the criteria that will be evaluated at the end of supervision (or at the next summative conference if supervision is to be ongoing). From these criteria, the supervisee's learning goals should be established.

Sometimes a baseline must be established before goals can be established. Using the Evaluation of Counselor Behaviors form (Appendix B), for example, we can track the trainee until we can determine where learning needs to occur. At that time, we give baseline feedback and discuss supervision goals. Note that the evaluation form in Appendix B focuses mostly on the counseling relationship and mentions written work and professional behavior only superficially. Therefore, this form could not be used exclusively for criteria establishment or summative evaluation.

Fox (1983) advised that supervision goals be specific; explicit; feasible in regard to capacity, opportunity, and resources; realistic for the trainee; seen in light of constraints; related to the task formulated; modifiable over time; measurable; and ordered into priority. We would underscore these guidelines.

As supervisors, we must be careful not to overload our trainees with too many learning objectives at one time. As is suggested in Appendix B, Session 1, supervisors need to be trained to take notes freely while observing a therapy session and then pare them down to a few essential topics for supervision. By limiting the number of topics, supervisors are far more likely to have trainees hear and incorporate their feedback.

Munson (1983) also stressed the need for simplicity during the work phase of supervision. Without discarding global criteria and with immediate goals in mind, Munson suggested a four-cell grid for evaluating a trainee's session with a client. Munson introduced two

axes, patient distress and therapist effectiveness, which are presented in Table 7.1. He begins a supervisory session by having the therapist choose the cell that best identifies how the therapist perceived the session. The therapist's choices are *smooth sailing* (low client distress, high therapist effectiveness), *heavy going* (high client distress, high therapist effectiveness), *floundering* (high client distress, low therapist effectiveness), and *coasting* (low client distress, low therapist effectiveness). Munson makes the point that even when the session was smooth sailing, it becomes an important datum for supervision. High therapist effectiveness should not be devalued because the client is experiencing little distress.

We made brief mention of the level of expertise for each criterion. The more explicit the supervisor can be about the level that is expected of the trainee, the better. Put succinctly, the supervisor must decide what is adequate for the supervisee to be given a positive evaluation. Additionally, it should be suggested what performance is clearly below standards and what level of performance is considered as meeting the highest standards. The issue of level can be addressed easily through the use of Likert scales as in the Evaluation of Counselor Behaviors form. If this is done, however, the supervisor must be consistent in using the scale. If a trainee comes into

**TABLE 7.1**  Therapist Perception of Session*

| PATIENT DISTRESS | THERAPIST EFFECTIVENESS | |
|---|---|---|
| | *Low* | *High* |
| Low | Coasting | Smooth Sailing |
| High | Floundering | Heavy Going |

*From Munson, C. E. (1983). *An introduction to clinical social work supervision.* New York: The Haworth Press., Copyright © by The Haworth Press, 10 Alice Street, New York, NY 13904. Reprinted by permission.

supervision with superior ability in several areas, the Likert scale ratings should reflect this. Some supervisors use such a scale differently, deciding that no supervisee should receive a score higher than a certain number (e.g., 5) until the supervisory experience is at least half complete. If this is the supervisor's policy, it is important that the supervisee know this. When the supervisor uses it in this way, however, the supervisor bypasses the issue of level of accomplishment.

Another way to approach this problem is described by Paravonian (1981). Preservice counseling students were given performance standards reflecting four levels for each skill they were expected to acquire. Grades were determined by how many levels the student acquired during the supervision experience; an A reflected the attainment of level four (which subsumed levels 1, 2, and 3) for a majority of skills.

Having a usable evaluation instrument or outline is half the battle of criteria evaluation. The literature is filled with references to the difficulty of establishing criteria for evaluation and the even more difficult task of measuring them. We believe there are many useful ways to organize therapeutic practice and, therefore, do not presume to offer a definitive list of criteria. Rather, we stress that regardless of the criteria identified, the summative evaluation should relate directly to these same criteria. It is not unheard of for supervisors to find themselves hunting for an evaluation form at the end of the supervisory relationship as if the form had no relationship to the formative sessions that preceded. On the contrary, whatever is to be used at the end of supervision to summarize the trainee's progress should be introduced early in supervision and used throughout supervision for intermittent feedback.

## THE PROCESS OF EVALUATION

By introducing evaluation criteria and forms, we have addressed the beginning and the end

of evaluation. Process defines how supervisors do their business between these two markers and how they incorporate the issue of evaluation from the beginning of supervision to its completion. Process also defines the means by which supervisors obtain the data they use to make their assessments, a topic more completely addressed in Chapters 4, 5, and 6.

Each supervisory conference can, and perhaps should, end with a plan of action for goal attainment and a time frame for completion of the plan (Kadushin, 1985). In the same way, each conference should begin with an update on progress toward the goals set in the previous session. Middleman and Rhodes (1985) suggested that formative evaluation occur often enough for changes to be suggested with enough time to implement before the summative evaluation. In other words, evaluation should be fluid and relevant throughout the supervision experience, not just at the beginning and the end.

The medium used for supervision also affects the evaluation process. Each method of supervision—whether process notes, self-report, audio- or videotapes of therapy sessions, or live supervision—influences evaluation differently. Live supervision can pose a particular problem if the supervisor is considered a part of the team of observers. Haley (1987), however, suggested that the supervisor keep the hierarchy clear and not allow the role of supervisor to be diffused by live supervision. Some supervisors rely heavily on group supervision and may even encourage some form of peer evaluation among trainees. This approach provides markedly different information than that gathered from, for example, self-report. When the ultimate responsibility to evaluate is paramount in the supervisor's awareness, the supervisor will seek supplemental data if it is needed to arrive at a balanced evaluation.

Supervisees can be at a disadvantage when the form of supervision changes from one setting to another. For example, Collins and Bogo (1986) have observed that early training experiences (on campus) tend to use a considerable amount of technology, whereas field supervision is more likely to be based on self-report and case notes. Therefore, they found that supervision in the field was far more reflective in nature than that on campus, which focused more on skills. Kadushin's (1974) research also found little use of modern technology in field supervision. Perhaps supervisors need not only to inform their students about the form of supervision they use but also to educate them about the forms they do not use.

A supervisor's typical supervision process can be supplemented specifically for the purpose of evaluation. For example, Tomm and Wright (1982) suggested that as one part of the evaluation process, supervisors keep samples of trainees' early work to compare with their later work. They also encouraged the use of consumer satisfaction surveys. Crane, Griffin, and Hill (1986) also found client feedback helpful in estimating certain therapist strengths. (In general, client satisfaction and client improvement are considered controversial criteria for therapist skill because so many variables outside of therapy can influence client perceptions.) Additionally, Dimick and Krause (1980) offered several novel procedures for the evaluation of counselors at the practicum level.

1. Do away with courses. Describe "levels" (e.g., prepracticum, practicum, internship) and what a person must be able to do before going to the next level. Complete "training by objectives" would be the goal.
2. Since we know so little about what part of counseling is therapeutic, grade students on how well their clients do.
3. Have an instructor for all but the last two weeks of practicum. Then have a different instructor come in to evaluate.
4. Utilize student or peer group evaluation. E.g., for a group of 25 practicum students, break down into five groups. Each

week students pick the best and worst counselors. The best goes to the next group up, the worst goes to the next group down. By the end of the semester, students have grouped themselves for grading.
5. Make practicum a pass/fail class with no time limits. Some students could pass in one week, some might never pass. Students would get credit only when they passed. (pp. 249–250)

There are problems inherent in every form of evaluation. One procedure we would like to highlight, however, is the use of additional evaluators. It is very difficult for supervisors to evaluate someone they have worked with in a close supervisory relationship.

Bernard used the following evaluation format in a counseling center where doctoral students served as the supervisors for master's level counselors. One doctoral student was assigned to three master's level students. Most semesters, there were 12 counselors and 4 supervisors. In addition to working closely with the supervisees, each doctoral student was required to observe (usually through a one-way mirror) three other counselors at least twice during the semester. The doctoral students did not have to share their observations with the counselors; their charge was simply to have some knowledge of the counselor's ability. Additionally, weekly supervision-of-supervision conferences were held, which included listening to taped supervision sessions between the doctoral supervisors and their three supervisees. When it was time to evaluate the counselors, the faculty instructors for both groups (supervisors and counselors), the center coordinator (who read all of the counselors' intake and termination reports), and the group of doctoral supervisors met together. Therefore, the work of each counselor was known by at least four people, and all were encouraged to voice their opinion.

These evaluation meetings provided both a learning experience for supervisors and the opportunity to arrive at consensus evaluations of the counselors. One of the most obvious dynamics in these meetings was the investment each supervisor had in the three supervisees. There were times when the supervisor would get noticeably defensive if the supervisor's counselors were seen as weaker than some others. Such reactions were always processed, and awareness was increased that the supervisory relationship can be a powerful one and can cloud a supervisor's ability to be objective.

A secondary issue was whether the supervisor felt responsible for the counselor's level of performance. Sometimes it was thought that the supervisor might have been partially responsible, but most times this was not the case. The most important lesson, however, was appreciating that different views could be held about the same supervisee, even when objective criteria were in place.

The time when process becomes a conspicuous issue is in the unfortunate circumstance of a negative final evaluation. Miller and Rickard (1983) discussed the due process rights of students when the summative evaluation is negative. They offered a middle of the road posture regarding procedures, warning that too elaborate a process can be burdensome and time consuming and can build inflexibility into the system, which they believed can work against trainees as often as it works for them. They favored having a simple, but precise, evaluation process for all students (not just those who are in trouble) and refraining from trying to articulate a procedure for problems that are unlikely to arise. Miller and Rickard referred to J. L. Bernard's (1975) four evaluation steps, which they used to evaluate clinical psychology students.

1. *Incoming students should be presented with written material fully describing conditions under which a student may be terminated, including personal unsuitability for the profession.*
2. *All students should be routinely evaluated at least once a year, and this evaluation should include a section on personal functioning.*
3. *If inadequacies are identified, the student is so advised, a remediation plan with a time line should be put in place, and the student should be made aware of the consequences of failure to remedy.*
4. *If sufficient remediation is not accomplished in the time designated, the student should be given time to prepare a case, then this should be presented to the faculty and the faculty then make a decision. If the student is terminated, all of the above should be summarized in writing to the student. (p. 832)*

Levy (1983) reviewed the APA's statements on accreditation criteria for 1973 and 1979 and found that the former stressed "personality factors" as a reason for dismissal from the profession whereas the latter dropped both the issue of personality and the reference to dismissal and focused instead on "skill deficits." Levy noted that this reflects a general development in the helping professions to see more and more psychological problems behaviorally and, therefore, as skill deficits.

This, however, does not match our professional experience that personal unsuitability is at least a contributing factor for the majority of trainee dismissals. Because of this, it is even more important that a process for evaluation is in place, that it is clear and consistent, and that supervisors be asked to document their evaluations over time.

## Communicating Evaluations

When it comes right down to it, the clarity of supervisors' communications is primarily responsible for the effect of their evaluative efforts. Each message will either affirm, challenge, discourage, confuse, or anger a supervisee. If the meta-message is different from the stated message, the result will be an unclear communication. The most serious communication problem is when the message is dishonest, either intentionally or unintentionally. This typically happens when the supervisor is involved in denial and does not want to face up to the fact that the trainee is not meeting expectations. As a result, the supervisor is not prepared to address the critical issues.

The interaction of supervisor discomfort and lack of communication clarity is why evaluation is often considered the supervisor's weak suit (Bernard, 1981). Borders and Leddick (1987) suggested that feedback to trainees focus on specific behavior and delineate alternative behavior. They also addressed the importance of the supervisor's willingness to confront and pointed out that confrontations challenge strengths rather than weaknesses. But as Munson (1983) asserted, there will be times when the supervisor must criticize the trainee. Borrowing from the work of Weisinger and Lobsenz (1981), Munson outlined 20 suggestions for supervisors to consider when delivering criticism. Among these, Munson urged supervisors to focus only on behaviors that can be changed and to be specific in their criticism; to offer criticism as opinion, not fact; to work to separate personal feelings about the supervisee from the need to criticize; and to steer away from accusatory comments or ultimatums.

Poertner (1986) suggested that supervisor feedback be clear enough either to automatically reinforce trainees or give them direction for improvement. Directionality, therefore, is an important concept, and one that the supervisor should attend to. It might be a good idea for the supervisor to ask before each supervision conference, Do I like the direction things are going? If not, how do I help the trainee change direction?

*Feedback.* If mental health professionals were asked to identify the single activity that best characterizes supervision, we are certain most would say that it is the feedback the supervisor provides the supervisee. But although feedback is understood as being central to su-

pervision, researchers have given relatively little specific attention to it. What research there is has examined either categories of supervisor feedback given in response to particular supervisee statements (e.g., Walz & Roeber, 1962) or the effects of certain feedback that was delivered as part of the experimental manipulation (e.g., Bernstein & Lecomte, 1979a). Almost none has sought simply to study the frequency and type of feedback given in a naturalistic setting.

The study of Friedlander, Siegel, and Brenock (1989) is one that has. The working definition of feedback they developed is fairly typical of what most supervisors would understand as feedback:

> *A statement, with an explicit or implicit evaluation component that refers to attitudes, ideas, emotions, or behaviors of the trainee or to aspects of the trainee-client relationship or the trainee-supervisor relationship. Feedback does not include questions or observations that lack an explicit or implied evaluation of the trainee on the part of the supervisor. (p. 151)*

Using this definition, they trained three raters to high levels of agreement (median interjudge agreement rate: .92) about the presence or absence of feedback in a particular supervisor speaking turn. These raters then examined each speaking turn of one supervisor across nine supervision sessions (ranging from 45 to 60 minutes in length) with one supervisee. They identified only 14 speaking turns as containing feedback. Eight speaking turns occurred in the last two sessions; sessions 3, 4, and 6 had no feedback whatsoever.

The Friedlander et al. (1989) study was an intensive case study. Therefore, the results might be idiosyncratic to the particular dyad they studied and may not apply to supervision in general. But it is fair to raise the question of how frequently feedback—as most supervisors understand it—actually is provided in supervision.

*Expanded Conceptions of Feedback.* Though the definition used by Friedlander et al (1989) seems to capture the meaning most people attach to feedback, it may be too restrictive. Blocher (1983) offered an expanded perspective of feedback that can be very helpful to supervisors. He noted that supervisors have two roles in the feedback process. One role certainly is to present to the supervisee observations about the supervisee's work. He argued, however, that this, the usual conception of feedback, is insufficient.

From Blocher's perspective, the second and more important role supervisors take in the feedback process is to help the trainee attend to and interpret the most salient feedback that is coming in constantly from a variety of sources, including the client, the client's environment, colleagues, and so on. He stated that

> *[t]he total volume of information available either in the live counseling situation or in electronic playback is almost always so great as to constitute an information overload for the counselor. The major tasks of the supervisor are to help the counselor to be aware of or "hear" the most relevant cues, and to develop a manageable number of themes or constructs with which to organize this information. (p. 32)*

Perhaps a good analogy might be to a veteran bird-watcher who takes a group of children on their first outing to search for a particular species of bird. Although the woods provide many visual and auditory clues about the possible whereabouts of the bird, the children are aware only of the most obvious aspects of being in the woods (e.g., there are trees and dense underbrush). The bird-watcher's task is to help them attend to the feedback given by the woods — for example, the particular terrain or foliage in which the bird is likely to be found, tracks, the sounds of particular bird calls, nests, and bird droppings. So it is with the supervisor who helps the trainee notice the multiple sources of feedback available once they are recognized.

But useful as this expanded conception of supervision feedback is, it still seems to suggest that the feedback process is intentional and operates as an occasional event that readily can be identified as feedback by both supervisor and supervisee. A perspective that broadens our understanding of feedback even further is that of the interactional theorists (see, e.g., Claiborn & Lichtenberg, 1989). This perspective allows us to think of feedback as something ongoing and constant between the supervisor and supervisee.

Two premises are basic to understanding the interactional perspective. The first is that you can't not communicate. This premise has been suggested as an axiom of communication by Watzlawick, Beavin, and Jackson (1967). It means, for example, that even the act of ignoring another person is feedback to that person, communicating a message such as leave me alone or, perhaps, you are not important enough for me to talk with. The second premise essential to understanding the interactional perspective is that any communication to another person contains both a message about the relationship between the two parties and a message about some particular content (Watzlawick et al., 1967).

When these two premises are applied to supervision, it can be understood that feedback — especially that which concerns the supervisor-trainee relationship — *constantly* is being given the trainee. Just as important, though, is that the supervisee also is giving the supervisor constant and ongoing feedback about the relationship.

***The Importance of Feedback Clarity.*** Regardless of how feedback is conceptualized, it always involves communication, and there are many reasons that the supervisee might receive unclear, mixed, or inaccurate communications. For example, the supervisor may be uncomfortable with the power that comes with the role of evaluator; the supervisor may be unprepared for the conference; the supervisor might be intimidated, professionally or personally, by the trainee; or the supervisor might have too little experience in giving negative feedback (especially in doing so kindly and clearly). Regardless of the reasons, the consequences for the trainee are the same: incomplete or inaccurate information, leaving the trainee ill equipped to alter the course of his or her efforts.

What follows are two segments taken from summative evaluation conferences conducted by supervisors in training with counselors in training. Both supervisor and counselor are female in each case. In the first segment, the pair begins by reviewing the Evaluation of Counselor Behaviors form (see Appendix B) that the supervisor completed prior to the session. The person referred to as Dr. P. is the counselor's faculty instructor.

S: Uh, I would put this more here, I think, and more here. Now you have to do another one of these? (Referring to evaluation form on self)
C: Are you asking me or telling me?
S: I'm asking.
C: I don't know.
S: Well then, you must not have to if you don't know. (Laughs)
C: I've not . . .
S: Have you not heard the news? (Laughs)
C: I haven't seen it in my mailbox or anything. Of course, that doesn't mean that when I make contact with Dr. P., that he won't say that it has to be done.
S: And I think, you know, again, I did this here. I may go back and circle . . . if you see anything that you don't agree with, just go ahead and question it. I think you know how I look at it. I see you just having started to work.
C: Oh, I . . .
S: You know, you may not like that. I just think since that one big leap, when you started to consciously try to do things differently . . .
C: I can't even visualize 10 years down the line having you say that everything is excellent.

I don't know. To me, you're asking for close to perfection.
S: It would be hard for me to get there. (Laughs) I wouldn't want to be evaluated.
C: So much that comes to me comes through experience.
S: Yeah. I suppose, you know, maybe it's the teacher part of me . . . whenever I see the word "always," I just can't . . . we're in trouble.
C: Yeah.
S: Even for me. (Laughs)
C: I understand. You know, as I look at this, it looks like a positive evaluation because of what you've said so far.
S: Um, well, you have a lot of 2's and 1's, but "good" to me is good. Letter grade wise, I don't know. I can't tell you. Part of me says, because of what has gone on the whole semester, you know, and part of me says, "OK. What are you doing now?" So, you know, I don't assign grades. It won't be an A. I'm not too sure. I'd say probably a C+ to a B− in that area.
C: But there are no +'s or −'s in the grading schedule.
S: That's right.
C: To me, a C is a failure and I'm assuming that you are not . . .
S: I don't think I look at it as a failure. I think that maybe, you know, when you do course work and things like that, maybe you could look at it that way. But I don't look at it as a failure because failure is an F.
C: Um hum.
S: If I were to have to assess a grade by skill level, it probably would be close to a C/D. But in looking from the beginning, you know, you've come a long way. But that isn't for me to assess. That's for Dr. P. to assess and I don't know how he will do it. I definitely think that there has been a lot of improvement.
C: And to me, it seems like it's been such a short time.
S: Yes, a very short time.

It is not difficult to see that there are several communication problems in this example. Actually, four things have contributed to the ambiguity presented here: (1) the supervisor's personal style of communication is clouded. She does not finish many of her statements. She is not crisp. She would do well to practice the delivery of her feedback for clarity. (2) The process is ambiguous. Either Dr. P. has not been clear regarding procedures or neither supervisor nor counselor have attended to these details. The result is that the supervisor does not seem to know her role in the evaluation process. Another possibility is that because of her discomfort, she is playing down her role and referring the counselor to Dr. P. for the difficult task of final evaluation. From the conversation as it stands, we cannot know which of these is the case. (3) Criteria for evaluation also seem to be ambiguous to the supervisor. She vacillates from references about skill level to references about progress. It is obvious that she is not clear about how Dr. P. will weigh each of these two factors. (4) The supervisor seems to be uncomfortable with the responsibility of evaluation, especially in this case where the practicum seems to be ending on a down note. We don't know if the supervisor was not prepared adequately for this conference or whether any amount of preparation would have countered her personal discomfort. The result is a series of mixed messages:

1. "You're not a very good counselor." / ' 'C' isn't a bad grade."
2. "You've come a long way." / "You still aren't very good."
3. "I'm trying to be fair." / "I wouldn't want to be in your shoes."
4. "I'm recommending between a 'C +' and and 'B'." / "I don't assign grades."

In our second summative session, the supervisor and counselor have had a better working relationship and the results are more positive.

*S: I came up with some agenda items, things I thought we needed to touch base on. You can add to this agenda if you'd like. The concern that you expressed previously about the deadlines, wrapping up, dealing with your clients, and then talking about termination/continuation issues. Kind of finishing up, so that it concludes not only your client situations, but practicum. Again, the other issue I have down is evaluation. I am not sure how he [Dr. P.] . . . Did he mention that in class today? How he's going to handle that? Do you have a conference with him?*

*C: There will be the conference next Monday with the three of us and then it seems to me that the other was kind of nebulous as to if we had another conference with him about you. Is that what you mean?*

*S: No, no. I meant about you. See, I was not aware that we were meeting on Monday. (Laughs)*

*C: Yes, yes.*

*S: OK. (laughs) What time did he say?*

*C: We had to choose a time and I chose 2:00 next Monday afternoon.*

*S: Oh, OK. I wondered.*

*C: He sent around a piece of paper so that we could sign up for Monday or Tuesday.*

*S: Well, that's nice to be aware of. Surprise!*

*C: Yeah.*

*S: (Laughs)*

*C: So it will be the three of us for evaluation.*

*S: So I thought, depending upon if you had any concern about that, that maybe we can discuss that ahead of time. I don't know if we need to here today or not or whatever, but that was something that I had as a possibility at least.*

*C: There are other things that are more urgent.*

*S: Yes. (Laughs)*

*C: That's next week.*

*S: Uh huh.*

*[Supervisor and counselor then talk about a particularly difficult case. The following occurs later in the same session.]*

*C: You've been very supportive. I really appreciate your feedback that you give me. A lot of good supportive feedback. It's not all the positive . . . There's been good con-*

*structive criticism you give too. I appreci-
ate that.*

S: *You perceive that there has been enough of
a balance?*

C: *Um, you've been heavier on the positive,
but maybe it's just because I've done such a
good job. (Laughs)*

S: *(Laughs) I'm laughing because you're
laughing.*

C: *You very nicely have couched the constructive criticism, preceding it with a lot of positive. "I like the way you did this, and then
when you said this, it was very good, and
then this was good and now you, probably
if you had said this, perhaps you would
have . . ." You preceded criticism with
about two or three positive things, which
helps, helps the ego. I've appreciated that a
lot.*

S: *Good.*

C: *Um, you know, I just, I think that we have
learned a lot just being in the sessions, all
the counselors, that we have learned from
mistakes, and that there are times when we
just haven't seen our mistakes. I think it's
good to have them pointed out and I think
you have done it very nicely. I appreciate
that.*

S: *Kind of while we are on the subject, is there
something that you can pinpoint at all that
you think that you've learned the most
from practicum? Not necessarily from your
clients, just anything in general. Is there
something that sticks out in your mind that
you have learned a lot from?*

C: *Um, well, with my two clients who were the
most difficult, I feel that with both of
them, I needed to be more forceful, and so,
that's a lesson learned, that I'm not doing
people a favor by letting them ramble on
and on. That oftentimes I would do people
a favor by stopping them and saying, "Now
let's back up a little. Let's focus a little bit
more." I haven't been quite assertive
enough and I think I've learned that about
myself. [Counselor continues]*

S: *I've seen you do continually more intervening and trying different things, being aware
of this and trying to do things about it. Do*

*you feel like, as you go away from here,
you'll be able to take away something so
that you can do that when you get into situations like this again?*

C: *Yeah, I've really learned that, and I do feel
that I am doing it more.*

S: *Oh, yes, I think so.*

The most dramatic difference between this
pair and the previous pair is the quality of the
relationship. Apparently this has been a positive experience for both supervisor and counselor. There may or may not be some lack of
comfort for the supervisor with evaluation in
that what might have been a summative conference became a preconference by their mutual choice. But the important characteristic
of their interaction, as it appears here, is that
they seem to be current with each other. Evidently, there has been enough direct communication along the way that each person appears
to know where she stands. Notice, however,
that the same administrative problem that appeared in the first example appears here, too.
Again, we see that communication between
the instructor and the supervisor has not occurred and this leaves the supervisor at a disadvantage in the conference. Because both of
these sessions transpired in the same training
program, we could come to the conclusion
that the doctoral supervisors need more support from the faculty in the form of clearer
guidelines about their role in the evaluation
process and clearer communication down the
administrative hierarchy.

## The Subjective Element

Clinical supervisors all work hard to be fair
and reasonable in their evaluations. Without
some awareness of the pitfalls to objective
evaluation, however, supervisors are at a disadvantage for attaining that goal. But supervisors also must be continually aware that the
subjective element cannot, and should not, be
totally eliminated. There is something intrinsi-

cally intuitive about psychotherapy, this is equally true for clinical supervision. Supervisors are in a position to supervise because they have had more fine tuning of their intuitions. Evaluation is a delicate blend of subjective judgment and objective criteria. But sometimes our personal subjectivity intertwines with our professional subjectivity, and evaluation becomes cloudy and out of focus. No clinical supervisor is above this dilemma. Being aware of the possibility, however, may help the supervisor draft a checklist of personal biases and blind spots to recollect when evaluating.

Each clinical supervisor will have a separate list of subjective obstacles to navigate when facing the task of evaluation. Our list is only a partial delineation of some of the more common problems, ones that we have experienced or that have received attention in the professional literature.

*Similarity.* There is an assumption that has spawned a good deal of empirical investigation that attraction (which includes the concept of similarity) influences the therapeutic process and, likewise, the supervision process. Kaplan (1983), however, reported that findings were mixed when personality characteristics and value systems of supervisors and supervisees were the focus of research efforts. Royal and Golden (1981), on the other hand, found that attitude similarity between supervisor and employee had a significant influence on the evaluation of the employee's intelligence, personal adjustment, competence, quality of work, quantity of work, and motivation, among other things. Leaning in a similar direction, Lanning (1986) raised the subject of cognitive style similarity and whether it affects evaluation.

Similarity with one's supervisor is probably more of an advantage than a disadvantage. But there are times when this is not true. If the supervisor is suffering from a poor self-image, this may spill over to the trainee. From an-

other vantage point, dissimilarity is an advantage for the trainee if the lack of similarity has a power valence. For example, if the supervisor is young and relatively inexperienced and the trainee is older and has more life experience, such dissimilarity might translate to a better evaluation than if the supervisor were the same age as the trainee. There is evidence that females rate males higher in competence; therefore, a female supervisor might rate a male trainee higher than a male supervisor would (Goodyear, 1990). (Goodyear cited several of those studies, but in his own study found no evidence of gender bias in trainee evaluations.)

Finally, there is a situation-specific form of similarity that the supervisor should consider. When life has dealt two people the same hand, or at least some of the same cards, this tends to create a bond between them. Both supervisor and trainee might have recently been through a divorce, might have children of the same age, or might each have an alcoholic sibling. Depending on each person's comfort level about these life situations, such similarities can be an advantage or a disadvantage. Regardless, they must be considered.

*Familiarity.* "He's difficult to get to know, but he wears well." How many of us have had negative first impressions of people who we now hold in high esteem? Not all of a person's qualities are apparent in the short run, and sometimes it takes a significant amount of time (in graduate training terms) to arrive at what later would look like a balanced view of the trainee's strengths and weaknesses. In conjunction with this, when affection for someone has grown over time, it can become more and more difficult to evaluate objectively. In fact, one can come to like Charlie so much that one might have to ask How would I react if Jeff did that instead of Charlie? to have any hope of arriving at a fair judgment.

There is some empirical evidence to support the case that familiarity affects evaluation. Blodgett, Schmidt, and Scudder (1987) found that supervisors rated the same trainees differently depending on how they knew the trainees. If a supervisor had had the trainee in a class prior to the supervision experience, the supervisor was more likely to evaluate the trainee more positively. Blodgett et al. noted that the trainees who had received their undergraduate and graduate training at the same institution had a distinct advantage in this particular study. The authors warn that it would be unwise, however, to assume that familiarity always works to the trainee's advantage. Our experience supports this admonition. Just as some trainees wear well, others do not. Entry behavior can be deceiving or, at least, very incomplete.

A separate, but overlapping, phenomenon is the tendency to trust negative impressions more than positive ones. If a supervisor likes Tracey and evaluates her positively, the supervisor might be concerned that the liking for her has influenced the objective evaluation. But if the supervisor dislikes Louise, the supervisor is far more likely to assume that this *is* an objective evaluation, trusting that the negative characteristics are relevant to her role as helper. What may be closer to the truth is that Louise reminds the supervisor of someone else she dislikes, or an unresolved part of herself; the reaction to her is just as subjective as the liking of Tracey. The unfortunate ingredient in both cases is that supervisors may stop trying to learn more about the trainee once they have reached a certain level of familiarity with her. At such a point, familiarity contaminates evaluation.

A corollary to the issue of familiarity is the perseverance of first impressions (Sternitzke, Dixon, & Ponterotto, 1988). Although we have already stated that our first impressions are not always our last, it is important to mention that first impressions can be long-lasting. If supervisors attribute dispositional characteristics to their trainees early in their relationships, it may require an inordi-

nate amount of evidence for the trainee to reverse the supervisor's opinion. In this case, the trainee may be familiar to the supervisor, but the trainee might be far from known.

*Experience.* The level of experience of the supervisor is evidently somewhat of an evaluation factor regardless of the particular relationship with the trainee. Worthington (1984a) reported that experienced supervisors were less likely to project personal attributes to explain counselor behavior than were inexperienced supervisors. In other words, an experienced supervisor saw counselor behavior as either therapeutic or nontherapeutic but did not conclude that the counselor as a person was genuine, competent, submissive, etc. A supervisor with less experience was more likely to generalize behavior to such traits. Perhaps the experienced supervisor has been wrong enough times in the past to withhold judgment about personal attributes when evaluating counselors. Perhaps the difference is simply a matter of language sophistication that comes with experience. Regardless, Worthington's study suggests that trainees will hear different feedback from supervisors based on the supervisor's level of experience.

It is our belief that the experience of supervisors will surface in other ways also. Ekstein and Wallerstein (1972) commented that it is difficult for a supervisor to be invested in a trainee without being either overprotective or manipulative. We assume that the type of investment experienced by the supervisor changes with experience, with the more experienced supervisor better able to resist over investment and, perhaps, ego involvement with trainees. Finally, just as a supervisor's approach to therapy changes with time, a supervisor's experience certainly affects many of the subtleties of supervision, changing some for the better, some not. Supervisors must look at their approach over time, attempt to evaluate how experience has affected them, and attempt to accommodate this subjective element as it affects their views of trainees and their work.

*Priorities.* Each supervisor has an individual set of priorities when judging the skill of a trainee. Most often, supervisors are cognizant that their priorities are partially subjective and that an equally qualified supervisor might have a somewhat different list of priorities. All perception is selective, and we process more quickly what is familiar to us (Atwood, 1986) or what we value more.

We have some evidence (Bernard, 1982) that when viewing the same therapy session, supervisors rate the trainee differently on the same criteria, depending on the value attributed to each criterion by the different supervisors. During a pilot investigation, supervisors were first analyzed using the Discrimination Model (Bernard, 1979) to discern if they had a primary focus; that is, did they tend to approach supervision from either a process, conceptual, or personal perspective regardless of the therapy session they observed? (See Appendix B, Session 7.) In a majority of cases, a primary focus was identified. During the second stage of this investigation, the supervisors were asked to view two videotapes and to evaluate each trainee using a Likert scale for 15 items, equally divided among the three focus areas. Again, a sizable number (although not statistically significant) of supervisors rated each trainee lower on their primary focus than on the other two categories. For example, when observing trainee A, supervisor A with a process focus rated trainee A lower on process skills than on conceptual skills and personalization skills, whereas supervisor B with a conceptual focus rated trainee A lower on conceptual skills than on process skills and personalization skills. This formula was substantiated for all three focus possibilities. In other words, the trainee was rated relative to the supervisor's bias and independent of a more objective set of criteria. Yet all supervisors thought they were being quite objective and, in several cases, were not aware of having a focus bias or priority. These results are supported by attribution theory as explained by Sternitzke, Dixon, and Ponterotto (1988). Building on the work of Ross (1977), they identified egocentric bias as a common problem for supervisors when observing trainee behavior and explained the nature of the bias as follows:

> One's estimate of deviance and normalcy are egocentrically biased in accord with one's own behavioral choices, because observers tend to think about what they would have done in a similar situation and then compare their hypothesized behavior with the actor's actual behavior. If the observers believe they would have acted differently, then there is an increased tendency for them to view the actor's behavior as deviant. If the observers believe they would have acted in a similar fashion, then their tendencies are to view the actor's behavior as normal. (p. 9)

Evidence of an egocentric bias, is more reason to share the responsibility of evaluation whenever possible, rather than keep it as a private activity.

## Consequences of Evaluation

Like most activities of any importance, the process of evaluation contains some risks. There have been false positives and false negatives in the evaluation experience of most clinical supervisors. Possibly because supervisors all know that they have evaluated incorrectly in the past, the consequences of evaluations can loom before them like an unforgiving superego. Supervisors know that a positive evaluation may mean that a trainee will be competitive in the job market or an employee will be promoted, whereas a negative evaluation may result in a student being dropped from a program or an employee being the first to go. It is because of supervisors' awareness of the consequences of evaluation that they find themselves doing some extra soul searching over the evaluations of the strongest and weakest supervisees.

But even for the average evaluation, there are consequences. Levy (1983) referred to the "costs" of evaluation as the inordinate time it requires of the supervisor, the anxiety it causes the trainee, and stress it puts on the supervisory relationship. Levy noted that if the individual supervisee were all that was at stake, the costs might be inordinately high. But when the larger picture is considered, including the integrity of the program or organization and the welfare of future clients, then the costs are in line with the benefits.

There are additional consequences intrinsic to the evaluation itself. As Middleman and Rhodes (1985) pointed out, if evaluations are too formal or remote and have no relevance for advancement or professional development (as in an annual performance rating done in a perfunctory manner), then the evaluation will be resisted and not taken seriously. But if evaluations *are* used for advancement, they may be so stressful as to undermine their intent. We believe that consequences can be avoided at least partially by giving more attention in all supervision situations to formative evaluation than to summative evaluation.

In a highly practical discussion, Kadushin (1985) mentioned the administrative consequences for the supervisor when a negative evaluation is necessary. If in a work environment an employee is let go because of an evaluation, the supervisor will often be the person to feel the brunt of the extra work load until a replacement can be found. Even in a training program, a negative evaluation will typically mean more extensive documentation, the possibility of an appeal process, and at the very least, a lengthy interview with the trainee involved. It is understandable, although not acceptable, that some supervisors shy away from negative evaluations in their work in order to avoid these unattractive consequences. Such shortsightedness, however, does not acknowledge the much more significant consequences when evaluations are not done properly.

## SUPERVISOR EVALUATION

It would be supercilious to examine the topic of evaluation without addressing supervisor evaluation. Remarkably, however, evaluation of supervision effectiveness is in an even more rudimentary stage than the evaluation of psychotherapy effectiveness (Galassi & Trent, 1987; Holloway & Roehlke, 1987). One reason for this is that supervisor training is a much newer phenomenon in graduate training than the training of therapists. With the introduction of supervisor training models came the need to evaluate, at least within graduate programs. These developments are starting to influence employment settings, but at a slow pace.

Unlike the trainee, the supervisor is much more likely to be in a position of having to develop criteria for evaluation. This poses a problem because it introduces a closed system. If supervisors believe incorrectly that certain interventions are central to good clinical supervision, their request for feedback will be manipulated by these faulty assumptions. Furthermore, studies indicate that supervisors and trainees value different things and that their perceptions of what goes on in supervision do not always match.

Worthington and Roehlke (1979) found that supervisors and trainees rated different supervisor interventions as contributing to a positive evaluation of the supervisor. Trainees valued the sharing of counseling experiences, giving literature and references about therapeutic techniques, providing initial structure during supervision, calling the trainee by name, being available at other than scheduled times, and allowing trainees to listen to audiotapes or observe the supervisor as therapist. Supervisors, on the other hand, thought their competence was demonstrated by giving positive and negative feedback, confrontation, not missing appointments with the trainee, pointing out weaknesses, and being available for emergencies. In a similar study (Sleight, 1984) from the field of communication disorders, supervisors rated themselves higher on a significant number of items (from a total of 42) than did trainees. Supervisors rated themselves higher in facilitating interpersonal communication, providing a professional model, providing information and technical support, and in fulfilling supervisory responsibilities. The only area in which students rated supervisors higher than they rated themselves was in fostering student autonomy. These results were different from an earlier study done by Ulrich and Watt (1977) in which supervisors rated themselves lower than did trainees. Sleight noted, however, that in the Ulrich and Watt study, supervisors all had less than two years of experience. In the Sleight study, all had more than two years of experience. Therefore, the experience of the supervisor must be taken into account when comparative data are studied. To complicate matters, the developmental literature suggests that trainees want different things from their supervisors as they increase in competence. Therefore, a supervisor cannot generalize feedback from one level of trainee to another.

There are several scales that have been developed to evaluate supervisors (Borders & Leddick, 1987). For the most part, these are summative evaluation forms. Galassi and Trent (1987) recognized that more evaluation measures are needed that address the formative needs of supervisors. "Supervisors can benefit from measures that help them determine when it might be time to switch the content or focus of supervision to facilitate counselor development and from measures that help them monitor how a counselor is progressing across a variety of skill areas" (pp. 267–268). It is our opinion that it is difficult to

receive good formative feedback from a trainee if the relationship is going to be short-term (say, one academic semester). This is especially true if the trainee has had no prior supervision. If trainees are given information about supervision at the beginning of the supervisory experience (e.g., Bernard, 1988), however, they are in a better position to be articulate throughout the experience and are more likely to give a superior summative report. To further assist the trainee and increase the probability of useful feedback, other authors have advised, and we agree, that some feedback instrument be used. The use of an assessment tool, although vulnerable to supervisor bias, will direct the trainee's feedback and will allow the supervisor an opportunity to see if patterns emerge when several trainees complete the same form. When supervision occurs over a long period of time, regular feedback sessions about supervision are critical if supervision is to remain vital and not pro forma. But we want to emphasize once again that it is the supervisor who must provide the environment that encourages evaluation and structures a procedure to accomplish supervisor evaluation (Cohen, 1988). Otherwise, the supervisee, being the vulnerable person in the relationship, will find ways to avoid evaluating the supervisor. Cohen described the situation quite succinctly:

> *Telling a supervisee that we would appreciate feedback whenever appropriate is easy. It is as easy as telling an acquaintaince to "drop around sometime." It is also just as effective; the acquaintance never shows up and neither does the feedback. (p. 195)*

Galassi and Trent (1987) found promising two trainee self-report measures: the Supervisor Styles Inventory (SSI) (Friedlander & Ward, 1984) and the Supervision Questionnaire (Worthington & Roehlke, 1979). The SSI (see Appendix C and the discussion of it in Chapter 3) was found to differentiate among supervisors with different theoretical orientations, be sensitive to the way the supervisor's style changes with trainee development, be associated with the trainees' willingness to work with different supervision styles and their satisfaction with supervision, and be associated with supervisor's role behaviors. The Supervision Questionnaire (see Appendix C), in addition to rating the frequency of 46 supervisory behaviors on a Likert scale, includes global ratings of supervision satisfaction, supervisor competence, and supervisor contribution to improving trainee skills. Although not meant as an evaluation instrument, Lanning's (1986) Supervisor Emphasis Rating Form (see Appendix C) measures the areas of emphasis established by the supervisor with a trainee. Lanning reported that supervisors and trainees disagreed on the degree of emphasis of many items. This, then, could be used to evaluate whether the supervisor is communicating the importance of different aspects of supervision to such a degree that the trainee recognizes the emphasis. Used in this way, Lanning's form could be used as a formative evaluation tool. A similar instrument has been developed by Yager, Wilson, Brewer, and Kinnetz (1989; see Appendix C). Like Lanning's, it expands upon Bernard's (1979) Discrimination Model and allows supervisors to self-evaluate their supervision focus, role preference, and distinct personality variables. Finally, the Counselor Evaluation of Supervisor form (Bernard, 1976, 1981; see Appendix C) can be used to acquire intermittent information or as a summative form.

As Middleman and Rhodes (1985) emphasized, supervisees are in the best position to evaluate many, if not most, of clinical supervisors' interventions. Furthermore, their feedback is crucial if supervisors are to avoid becoming myopic and stagnant in their work. Because of the unfortunate isolation of many supervisors, peer feedback is less accessible, increasing the value of supervisee evaluation. At the same time that supervisors are enhanced by supervisee feedback, they model an important professional lesson for them—that helping professionals can never afford to stop asking for advice about their work.

## Self-Assessment

According to Munson (1983), there is a trend in the literature toward self-assessment of clinical skill. Because of the multiple commitments of most clinical supervisors, budgets that seem to be cut at every juncture, and practitioners with heavy caseloads, we believe that self-assessment is a critical skill for helping professionals. It is our belief also that, in general, self-assessment is overused by clinical supervisors and underused by therapists; therefore, we will focus on the latter in this section. Blodgett et al. (1987) noted that there is little being done to help clinicians and supervisors learn to self-evaluate. Assuming that their criticism is at least partially justified, the error of our practice is emphasized by the research of Dowling (1984), who found evidence that graduate student trainees were both accurate self-evaluators and good peer evaluators. Therefore, it would seem wise, if not an ethical imperative, that clinical supervisors train their supervisees to self-evaluate.

From the vantage point of the clinical supervisor, the goal is to incorporate self-assessment into the larger framework of evaluation. Kadushin (1985) argued that supervisory evaluation, in and of itself, makes learning conspicuous to the trainee and helps to set a pattern of self-evaluation. Ekstein and Wallerstein (1972) were more cautious, reminding the supervisor that asking trainees to self-evaluate will stimulate all their past experiences of being selected, rejected, praised, etc. We challenge this caution in that self-evaluation, we believe, takes some of the parental-like authority away from the supervisor rather than adding to it. If negative feelings are going to be experienced as a result of evaluation, these will be there regardless of whether the trainee is given an opportunity to contribute to the assessment. Yogev (1982) raised the important interpersonal issue of the supervisor's reaction to the trainee's self-assessment. Yogev warned the supervisor not to put trainees in a no-win situation by asking for their evaluation and then holding it against them. For example, if a trainee admits feeling overwhelmed and intimidated by the training experience, the supervisor should not later criticize the trainee for being weak and dependent. Therefore, if supervisors ask for candid disclosure as part of a self-assessment, they must be ready to handle respectfully what transpires.

There are several highly productive ways that the trainee can be involved in self-assessment while in the context of supervision. The most obvious is for the supervisor to communicate an expectation that the trainee will do some sort of self-assessment prior to each supervision session. It has been our experience that unless the supervisor follows through on this expectation, most trainees will falter in their intentions to self-assess. Bernstein and Lecomte (1979b) provided nine questions that trainees were required to address prior to presenting a videotaped session in group supervision. Their questions were aimed primarily at allowing the trainee to self-evaluate prior to receiving feedback from the group.

1. What was I hearing my client say and/or observing my client to do?
2. What was I thinking about my observations?
3. What were my alternatives to say or do at this point?
4. How did I choose from among the alternatives?
5. How did I intend to proceed with my selected response(s)?
6. What did I actually say or do?
7. What effect(s) did my response have on my client?
8. How, then, would I evaluate the effectiveness of my response?

9. What would I do differently now? (pp. 71–73)

As a result of addressing these questions, trainees would become aware if their self-perceptions were markedly different from the perceptions of their supervisor and peers. Bernstein and Lecomte argued that, without an assurance of adequate supervision in the field, one goal of all training programs must be the trainee's ability to self-evaluate.

Another useful self-evaluating exercise is to ask the trainee to periodically review a segment of a therapy session in greater depth for response patterns (Collins & Bogo, 1986). For example, we have had trainees submit a typescript of a 10-minute segment of a counseling session in which each of their responses was identified (e.g., confrontation, reflection of affect) and evaluated. If the trainee's evaluation is negative (This was inappropriate, or This accomplished nothing), the trainee is asked to replace the weak response with a stronger one. This is a time-consuming assignment and need not be done more than once during an academic semester. The results, however, are substantial for helping the trainee to recognize and break nontherapeutic response patterns.

Closely related to self-assessment is peer evaluation; it also is similar in that it is underused with trainees. As we stated earlier, when peers are asked to work together for each other's benefit, the star syndrome is diminished and a group cohesiveness is established. We have found that peers can be invaluable reviewers for each other, and it is consistently both humbling and inspiring when peers make observations that are absolutely correct and have been overlooked by the supervisor. But it is important to structure peer feedback. Often feedback is given verbally in group supervision, but we have found that the type of feedback that comes spontaneously, although valuable, is generally inferior to the type of feedback that is given in writing when a peer is asked to review an audio- or videotape between supervision sessions. When, in addition, the reviewer is evaluated by the supervisor for the critique, thoughtful and highly useful reviews are most often the result. It has been our experience that the more supervisors share the responsibility for trainee development with the trainee group, the better the students perform and the more positive the overall experience is.

## Program Evaluation

Although program evaluation has become a specialty in its own right and, as such, is far beyond the scope of this chapter, we will widen our circle for a moment to include a brief discussion about it and its implications for clinical evaluation. The position we are taking is that trainee success reflects on the supervision they have received, and both trainee and supervisor performance reflect on the program or organization of which they are a part.

There is not always a connection between service delivery, supervision, and program parameters, but systemic theory has taught us to be more sensitive to their interconnectedness. In a sense, clinical supervision cannot make up for a weak program or a weak organization, at least not entirely. Furthermore, when supervision is performed in the context of program evaluation, accountab 'ity is a more concrete concept. This benefits trainees as well as supervisors. It also promotes the viewing of clinical evaluation not as a disconnected, worrisome necessity but as an integral part of a larger whole, a system which is committed to studying the benefits and liabilities of its own actions.

Although most professionals will probably agree that program evaluation makes good sense, it has been a difficult idea to get across. One of the traditional justifications for abandoning program evaluation is that without a tangible product, it is difficult, if not impossible, to measure effectiveness. It will always

be true that the value of the helping professions will have to be inferred from other sources. But we overstate the problem when we assume that we do not have recognizable criteria because we do not have a tangible product. If we cannot evaluate, how can we train practitioners? In other words, if we can decide what people should know and be able to do, we have, in some way, identified the elements that should be targets of our evaluations.

A more palpable block to program evaluation is the relative degree of unaccountability that graduate schools and human service agencies have enjoyed. As long as students were trained and services were provided, there was a limited demand for information about the nature of what was conducted in those institutions. With consumer education and the upgrading of professional standards, some of that has changed. But as Norcross and Stevenson (1986) pointed out, it is difficult even for highly acclaimed programs to conduct program evaluations. Instead, training programs have continued to survive on "the reputation of the provider" (Byles, Bishop, & Horn, 1983).

In several studies that considered the program evaluation activities of APA-accredited clinical training programs and internship training sites (Norcross & Stevenson, 1984, 1986; Stevenson & Norcross, 1982; Stevenson, Norcross, King, & Tobin, 1984), seven blocks to evaluation were identified:

1. *Time constraints* on those persons who would be responsible for the evaluating.
2. *Inadequate methods and measures for conducting the evaluation.* There is still a significant lack of confidence in the evaluation designs thus far presented (Liddle & Halpin, 1978).
3. *Lack of personnel.* It is highly unusual for either training programs or human service agencies to have additional, appropriately

trained personnel for the purpose of evaluation.

4. *Transience of trainees.* Especially in field work sites, the trainee is not there long enough to get adequate before and after data.

5. *Insufficient funding.* Along with the lack of personnel, evaluation usually is done, if at all, out of an already small operational budget.

6. *Practical difficulties.* Issues like confidentiality of trainee evaluations as they relate to program evaluation have been stumbling blocks for some programs.

7. *Staff attitude.* Although last on our list, resistance of staff toward the activity of program evaluation rated high among clinic directors as blocks to this activity (Stevenson & Norcross, 1982). Most prior experience of supervisors with evaluation has been more negative than positive, and they perceive the task as tedious, potentially threatening, and usually an exercise in futility because little changes after it is done.

In spite of these obstacles, program evaluations are being attempted. "Clinical training evaluation appears to be in a preparadigmatic stage characterized by diversity, creativity, and informality" (Norcross & Stevenson, 1984, p. 497). At present, evaluations are characterized more by soft measures than concrete measures; qualitative procedures are more likely to be used than quantitative measures. Also, evaluations tend to be erratic, incomplete, and lacking in their impact for future decision making. There are however, some notable exceptions, and a body of literature is emerging on the topic of program evaluation, along with a concomitant list of recommendations for conducting useful evaluations. Norcross and Stevenson (1986) accumulated the following recommendations of 179 APA-accredited programs:

1. Conduct routine evaluations of trainees, supervisors, and the program, preferably in written, structured form. Some of these statements can be anonymous.

2. Invite colleagues to visit the program and offer candid feedback.

3. Complement the pervasive use of qualitative measure with numerical ratings or standardized measures.

4. Consider the follow up of graduates as another important source of data about the program's success.

5. Adopt an ongoing, internal evaluation design or plan.

Byles et. al. (1983) also stressed the importance of ongoing evaluation and suggested evaluation be built in from the inception of any academic or service delivery program. In addition to the importance of an ongoing process, Stevenson et al. (1984), in their five-year study of training clinics, found the impact of program evaluation was greatest if supported within the organization, not by an outside source. One could hypothesize that internal financial support would not occur if there were not other, perhaps more important, forms of support to keep program evaluation alive.

Finally, Middleman and Rhodes (1985) suggested that we not rule out client feedback as part of program evaluation. It is their opinion that this source of data has been overlooked and undervalued, reflecting a negative attitude about clients' ability to evaluate at a program level. Certainly, clients should be asked for input about those aspects of training that should be evident to them (e.g., Crane, Griffin, & Hill, 1986). If we cannot see the point in asking clients their perceptions, perhaps we have missed the whole point of our professional charge.

We believe that when programs are self-reflective, they are more vital and more apt to be training practitioners who will be self-reflective in their own approach to psychotherapy. The core of program evaluation is, in fact, the same core of good therapy: asking the correct questions to collect relevant data to arrive at needed solutions. When such an important process is repeated at several levels of the system, the mutual influence that results cannot help but enrich and enliven the training environment.

## CHRONIC ISSUES OF EVALUATION

We hope that this chapter has aided the supervisor in defining parameters for evaluation and in clarifying some of the issues involved in the task of evaluation. Some problems, however, are chronic and cannot be eliminated through adherence to a model, use of a form, or communicating in a certain way. As we conclude this chapter, we pose some of the issues that we believe still loom above the conscientious clinical supervisor's head and are only partially resolved by some of the guidelines we have proposed to this point.

1. What should be the relationship of admissions, retention, hiring, and so on to clinical evaluation? Should the same people be involved in administrative decisions and clinical supervision? To what extent should evaluation be used to correct admissions or hiring errors? What are the consequences when evaluation is used in this way? (Cohen [1987] argued that "supervisors who disengage themselves from the agency's evaluation process are violating their commitment to the supervisee's welfare" [p. 195]. Cohen includes the role of "advocate" as an appropriate responsibility of the clinical supervisor, especially when a talented clinician is in some political trouble with the agency.)

2. How do we work around theoretical differences between supervisor and trainee? Should the trainee be asked to adopt the supervisor's theoretical bias for the duration of supervision? Can a supervisor of a different theoretical orientation evaluate a trainee adequately?

3. When peer evaluation is used, should this evaluation even be used for administrative purposes? If it is, what are the practical and ethical consequences of such a practice?

4. How do we determine how much of a trainee's development is the result of supervision? How does this affect evaluation?

5. What is the optimum length of a supervision relationship? What are the signs that a trainee would benefit from working with a new supervisor? When does supervision become consultation? How do supervisors evaluate when their supervision style is consultative?

6. Have supervisors trained their supervisees in all the skills that they later evaluate? Have they articulated adequately (to themselves) their overall goals for the trainees? Have they communicated these goals to their trainees?

7. To what extent are clinicians supervising and evaluating in a manner that fits external reality, including client needs and certification requirements? In other words, does training reflect the employment demands trainees will eventually face? Also, are supervisors sensitive to the fact that their trainees may or may not be eligible for a variety of professional certifications and are they training and evaluating appropriately? (It is our experience that some psychologists, for example, evaluate their master's level counseling candidates using standards appropriate for psychologists, a certification for which the trainees are not eligible.)

This is only a partial list of the issues related to evaluation that make the process more complicated. They must, however, be addressed, at least as limitations to the evaluation process, if supervisors are to be balanced and to approach fairness in their clinical evaluations.

Evaluation poses the most extreme paradox for the clinical supervisor. It is at the same time the most disconcerting responsibility, the most challenging, and the most important. There are, however, conceptual and structural aids to help supervisors in this process, aids that can increase confidence and competence and can contribute to a productive evaluation process experience for the supervisee.

# CHAPTER 8

# ETHICAL AND LEGAL CONSIDERATIONS

It is perhaps a sign of the times that ethics is an increasingly visible topic in mental health literature. In part this reflects the evolution of the helping professions from theoretical exploration to professional introspection. Mabe and Rollin (1986) maintained that the development of ethical standards for each of the major helping professions reflected a maturity for that group, one that stimulated a search for professional identity. In addition to professional evolution, the focus on ethics is a natural reaction to a complex and diverse society.

If therapy was ever a sedate endeavor, it is no longer. The growth of professional literature alone is an indication of the increasing complexity of human service delivery. The therapist is bombarded with new models of therapy and new client populations with seemingly more complicated presenting concerns. Such complexity has spawned an increase in specialization, contributing to the isolation of many therapists and making it more difficult to intelligently interact with one's professional colleagues. Therefore, ethical standards become critically important to guide professionals when things feel beyond their expertise and there is no vital community of which the professional feels a part. Even if isolation is not an issue, the responsible practitioner senses that ethical practice demands commitment and vigilance.

But there is a more pressing motive for the heightened interest in ethical standards, and this is the relatively new fear of litigation. Although this relationship is understandable, there is a great deal of misunderstanding about the relationship between ethics and legal liability. Ethical principles are conceptually broad in nature, few in number, and open to interpretation (in most cases). Although they are sometimes perceived as documents to be used for the avoidance of professional liability, they are devised for a much loftier purpose, that is, a call to ethical excellence. Ethical standards are a statement from a particular group to the general public of what they stand for. Tennyson and Strom (1986) addressed the tendency for professionals to consider ethical standards legalistically. They describe this approach as one of "responsibility." In contrast, they subscribe to the concept of "responsibleness," where ethics serve as a beginning, not an end, for professional standards.

Legal liability, on the other hand, is specific in nature. The law is introduced when a specific act or series of acts leaves the professional vulnerable to litigation. Furthermore, the law is not interested in the highest standards of the profession when judging someone but in the least common denominator. As Woody (1984) stated, "the practitioner need not be superior but must possess and exercise the knowledge and skill of a member of the profession in good standing" (p. 393). Woody then referred to Prosser's (1971) definition of "in good standing": "Professional men [and women] in general, and those who undertake any work calling for special skill, are required not only to exercise reasonable care in what they do, but also to possess a standard minimum of special knowledge and ability" (p. 161).

Besides their dichotomy of purpose, ethics and the law do not overlap as often as the practitioner assumes. For example, Margolin (1982) described several potential ethical and legal dilemmas for marriage and family therapists, none of which are addressed by the AAMFT Code of Professional Ethics (1984). One of the situations described by Margolin is when a couple presents itself for marriage counseling but one wants the marriage to survive and the other wants a divorce. This can leave the therapist legally vulnerable if, for example, the husband is disappointed with the outcome of therapy and believes that his well-being was injured by therapy. A recent study conducted by Green and Hansen (1986) found that of the eight ethical dilemmas frequently faced by marriage and family therapists, six were not addressed specifically in the ethical principles. It is clear, therefore, that a working knowledge of ethical principles, whether one is a psychiatrist, psychologist, counselor, marriage and family therapist, or social worker, does not adequately prepare one for the ethical dilemmas or legal pitfalls that may be encountered.

The above notwithstanding, there is one way in which ethical standards and the law have a strong reverse relationship. Once there is a legal precedent, it usually becomes the acknowledged standard for the profession. There is perhaps no more dramatic example of this than the Tarasoff case, where the duty to warn a potential victim was upheld in the California courts *(Tarasoff v. Regents of the University of California,* 1976). Although the university psychologist warned campus police that one of his clients had threatened to kill his girlfriend (Tarasoff), and the client was questioned and later released, the court found the university staff negligent in that the potential victim was not warned personally.

This is an important case for supervisors because the supervisor in the case also was found negligent and liable. Following this landmark case, a large majority of therapists and supervisors assumed the duty to warn. Therefore, the legal system can and does have a profound effect on ethical standards of behavior. This was further demonstrated by two recent studies (Baird & Rupert, 1987; Haas, Malouf, & Mayerson, 1986). Baird and Rupert's study sought to measure psychologists' level of regard for confidentiality. Of the situations presented to 188 respondents, only two surfaced as legitimate for violating the confidentiality principle: consulting a colleague and dealing with a potentially dangerous client. In the second study, Haas et al. presented 294 seasoned psychologists with 10 ethical dilemmas and asked them to indicate their preferred resolution to each dilemma. They found a great deal of variance among the solutions, but the duty to warn potential victims of violence was one of three dilemmas for which there was at least 75 percent agreement among the respondents.

## SUPERVISORS AND ETHICAL ISSUES

As practitioners themselves, clinical supervisors will be cognizant of the ethical principles of their profession. Their attention to those principles, however, typically has been as therapists, not as supervisors. This highlights one of the two problems for supervisors concerning ethical practice. First, the codes of ethics for the AACD, AAMFT, APA, and NASW include almost no reference to the process of supervision. These documents clearly were fashioned for the service deliverer, not the clinical supervisor. Therefore, it is up to the supervisor to translate the standards to reflect the dimensions of the supervisory relationship. Second, the supervisor must be adept at multidimensional thinking and be willing to safeguard ethical practice not only at the supervisory level but also at the therapy level. As the Tarasoff case demonstrated, the concept of vicarious responsibility (Cohen, 1979) must be taken seriously by supervisors.

*According to this doctrine, someone in a position of authority or responsibility, such as a supervisor, is responsible for acts of his or her trainees or assistant. Stated another way, supervisors are ultimately legally responsible for the welfare of clients counseled by their supervisees. (Cormier & Bernard, 1982, p. 488)*

It has been our experience that supervisors who have been trained well in the area of ethical practice are cautious regarding the behavior of their trainees. Few, however, seem to be equally sophisticated regarding the ethical implications of the supervisory relationship. It must also be said that those clinical supervisors who received adequate training in ethical issues are still in the minority, although this is changing rapidly.

It behooves supervisors to make ethical practice an integral and obvious part of their work with supervisees. A discouraging study was reported by J. L. Bernard and C. S. Jara (1986) in which 170 graduate students from 25 APA-accredited clinical training programs were presented with hypothetical situations in which a peer/friend was found to be in violation of APA ethical principles (APA 1977, 1981). Although the students received high scores in being knowledgeable about what action they should take, approximately half of the students stated that they would do less than this. The authors concluded that the attitude of half of the students was "I know what I should do as an ethical psychologist, but I would not do it" (p. 315). In another study, 58 percent of doctoral-level psychologists felt "they were not well informed enough about ethical issues in psychology" (Tymchuk, Drapkin, Major-Kingsley, Ackerman, Coffman, & Baum, 1982, p. 419). Therefore, the clinical supervisor seems to be facing a problem of both ignorance and attitude about ethical therapeutic practice. Although we have no evidence that the supervisor can correct either deficiency, the stakes are high enough to warrant a serious attempt.

## Major Ethical Issues for Clinical Supervisors

What follows are the major ethical themes about which clinical supervisors should be informed. We will be presenting the implications of these themes for the practice of supervision based on our understanding and a review of the literature. We will limit our discussion to issues that have distinct and additional responsibilities for supervisors and, therefore, will not discuss topics such as advertising practices or research. At the same time, several ethical issues have implications for both the supervisory relationship and the therapy relationship that the supervisor oversees. We will attempt to address each dimension separately. It goes without saying that a flagrant abuse of ethical practice leaves the supervisor legally liable for any one of the following topics. We will address the issues of liability, negligence, and malpractice separately at the end of the chapter.

***Due Process.*** Due process is a legal term that insures one's rights and liberties. In the human services, due process has surfaced as an issue mostly around the proper route to take if a client needs to be committed to a mental health hospital (Ponterotto, 1987; Schutz, 1982). Most hospitals are aware of their due process duties, and professionals who work with volatile populations also are aware of correct procedures.

Trainees have due process rights, too, and these are more likely to be overlooked. The Code of Ethics for the NASW (1980) are most explicit in addressing the due process issue: "The social worker who has the responsibility for employing and evaluating the performance of other staff members should fulfill such responsibility in a fair, considerate, and equitable manner, on the basis of clearly enunciated criteria" (III., J., 10); and "[t]he social worker who has the responsibility for evaluating the performance of employees, supervisees, or students should share evaluations with them" (III., J., 11).

The most blatant violation of a trainee's due process rights occurs when the trainee is given a negative final evaluation or dismissed from a training program or job without having had prior warning that performance was inadequate and without a reasonable amount of time to improve. When intermittent evaluations are given, they must be specific enough to be of use to the trainee. A statement such as "We have some concerns about your performance and have decided to give you two months to improve or be dropped from the training program" is not adequate to meet due process standards. Rather, the trainee must be given a specific description of what constitutes inadequate behavior in that particular case and what behaviors constitute an improvement. Additionally, the trainee should be forewarned of what degree of improvement is expected for retention. Too many students have been told that they have improved but not enough to be allowed to continue in a training program. Finally, the wise supervisor puts all of the information in a written document that is signed and dated by all parties involved. Although this may be perceived as a sign of distrust from the supervisor to the trainee, it is in actuality a protection for everyone.

*Example: Susan is in a master's program in mental health counseling. She has completed four courses in the program. Her last course was a prepracticum laboratory in counseling skills. Susan received a C in the course. Upon completion of the prepracticum, Susan's advisor summons her to inform her that she is being dropped from the program. Her advisor explains that it is the policy of the program to use the prepracticum as a final screening process before allowing students to continue in the program. When Susan's reaction communicates that she is totally taken aback by this turn of events, the advisor refers her to the school catalog, which states that the mental health counseling program reserves the right to discontinue in the program those students whose performance is marginal, either academically or in skill development. Susan's advisor assures her that a C in a prepracticum laboratory meets the definition of marginal performance.*

In order to determine if Susan's due process rights have been violated, we must ask if a catalog disclaimer is enough to inform students of their vulnerability. Furthermore, are there steps that the program should be taking to insure that its students' rights are being protected? We believe that a graduate catalog disclaimer is insufficient unless there is an established procedure to insure that each incoming student is alerted to this condition. Iovacchini (1981) advanced two standards for safeguarding due process around the issue of dropping a student from a training program: a set of detailed written behavioral objectives or criteria issued to every student early in the program so the student knows what will be accepted as satisfactory performance; and "a rigid notification and grievance procedure to handle student dismissals for failure to meet the above objectives" (p. 169). According to Iovacchini, it is most important that students get sufficient notice of difficulty as they proceed through the program. Therefore, in our example Susan's rights were violated because she was given no warning of the faculty's displeasure with her performance and no opportunity to improve. (A more complete discussion of handling a negative evaluation is given in Chapter 7.)

From the standpoint of the clinical supervisor, a violation of due process rights is understandable but unfortunate. As we stressed in Chapter 7, Goodyear and Sinnett (1984) also noted that psychologists typically prefer the role of nurturer to that of evaluator. When therapists take on the role of supervisor, they do not automatically change their role preferences. The result sometimes is that trainees who believe they are doing adequately based on the warm responses from clinical supervisors find out later that this is not the case. We believe that the opportunity to be trained adequately as a supervisor is at least a partial solution to this dilemma.

Although due process refers to a specific process around a particular issue, it is perhaps not too farfetched to view some of the parameters of supervision as either enhancing or diminishing the probability of due process. In other words, supervisors are involved in a larger process that will determine their readiness to be sensitive to due process at each critical moment. Newman (1981, pp. 692–694) raised 10 questions for psychotherapy supervisors that we believe represent the kind of thoughtfulness that predisposes the supervisor to keep the trainee's rights in mind.

1. Is the psychologist qualified to supervise?
2. Does the psychologist accept the responsibilities associated with the various supervisory roles and functions?
3. Have the trainees' interests been sufficiently considered?
4. Has the appointment of a trainee to a supervisor been adequately considered?
5. Have the goals of supervision been adequately considered?
6. Has the choice of supervisory methods been adequately considered?
7. Have the limits of confidentiality of the supervisory relationship been specified?
8. Have the supervisor's expectations for supervision been adequately considered?
9. Has the student's progress been evaluated?
10. Has the adequacy of supervision been evaluated?

In addition to addressing the overall ethical framework for supervision, several of Newman's questions fall under the category of informed consent, which we will consider next.

***Informed Consent.*** The concept of informed consent has been handed down to us from the medical profession. Informed consent

is one in which the patient has received sufficient information from his [or her] physician concerning the health care proposed, its incumbent risks, and the acceptable alternatives to that care so that the patient can participate and make an intelligent, rational decision about [her- or] himself. (Hemelt & Mackert, 1978, p. 94)

There is perhaps no ethical standard as far-reaching as that of informed consent for the practice of psychotherapy. This is underscored by Woody (1984), who asserted that informed consent is the best defense against a charge of malpractice for the practitioner. For the supervisor, there are really three levels of responsibility: (1) The supervisor must determine that clients have been informed by the supervisee regarding the parameters of therapy; (2) the supervisor must also be sure that clients are aware of the parameters of supervision that will affect them; and (3) the supervisor must provide the supervisee with the opportunity for informed consent. We will discuss each of these separately.

*Informed Consent with Clients.* It is essential that clients understand and agree to the procedures of therapy prior to its beginning. This is not to imply that there will be no ambiguity in therapy or that the therapist should be able to predict everything that will happen during the course of therapy. But it does imply that some assessment must occur that will be shared with the clients, that goals will be determined, and that the general course of therapy will be outlined for the clients' approval. If it is determined later that a redirection of therapy would be beneficial, this process should be repeated.

Partly because of theoretical orientation, some therapists have resisted this process. But even less directive forms of therapy can and should be explained to the clients prior to their commitment to the process. As Woody (1984) stated, *[t]he professional should be the last person to object to a requirement of informed consent. If anything, the professional should reach to the maximum allowed by public policy to ensure that the service recipient does, in fact, understand and consent to the treatment. To do otherwise is to court a disciplinary action for unethical conduct and/or a legal suit for malpractice. (p. 376)*

Margolin (1982) suggested that informed consent dictates that the following types of information, which are based on the reviews of Everstine et al. (1980) and Hare-Mustin, Maracek, Kaplan, and Liss-Levinson, be given:

*(a) an exploration of the procedures and their purpose, (b) the role of the person who is providing therapy and his or her professional qualifications, (c) discomforts or risks reasonably to be expected, (d) benefits reasonably to be expected, (e) alternatives to treatment that might be of similar benefit, (f) a statement that any questions about the procedures will be answered at any time, and (g) a statement that the person can withdraw his or her consent and discontinue participation in therapy or testing at any time. (p. 794)*

Several authors have expressed concern about informed consent within several marriage and family therapy paradigms (Corey, 1986; Green & Hansen, 1986; Hines & Hare-Mustin, 1978; Keith-Spiegel & Koocher, 1985; Margolin, 1982; Willbach, 1989). One of the issues raised most frequently by these authors is that of coercion if one or more family members does not want to be involved in therapy. This issue is of concern for not only adults but children, especially teenagers who are unclear as to their legal rights of consent. Either exacting undue pressure on the reluctant family member(s) or refusing to see the family unless all members are present could be construed as coercion. Perhaps a more serious example is the case in which the family therapist refuses to continue to work with the family if one member drops out of therapy. In addition to

the problem of informed consent, if the family was not fully aware that this would happen, is the ethical and legal issue of abandonment. In either case, it seems that individuals' rights are not being honored equally.

Margolin (1982) articulated an additional concern for strategic family therapists. She aptly described some of their interventions as "mobilizing the oppositional tendencies of family members" (p. 795). Such paradoxical interventions would be difficult to explain to families beforehand, and many would argue that it would be untherapeutic to do so. "[M]anipulating a family for therapeutic reasons," however, ranked number 12 of 39 frequently encountered ethical dilemmas by family therapists (Green & Hansen, 1986). It must be acknowledged, therefore, that such interventions are perceived as troublesome at least by some family therapists, especially in terms of informed consent. Another concern mentioned by Margolin is the optimistic posture taken by the family therapist at the outset of therapy as an intervention to mobilize family energy. Her concern was that this might be, in some cases, a violation of the spirit of describing benefits reasonably to be expected from therapy. This concern can also be raised for other types of therapies.

*Example: John is a trainee in a mental health agency. He has been seeing Ellen for four months in individual counseling. It has become apparent that Ellen and her husband need marriage counseling. John has been trained in marriage and family therapy. He very much wants to follow this case to its conclusion. Without discussing alternatives, he suggests that Ellen bring her husband to the next session. Ellen says that she is relieved that he is willing to work them. She was afraid that John would refer them to another therapist. Having John work with both her and her husband is exactly what she was hoping for.*

In this example, we must ask if Ellen has been given the opportunity of informed consent. Has her husband? Is there information about the therapy process that John should have offered to help both Ellen and her husband make the best decision for their present situation? At the very least, John has erred in not discussing alternatives. John's supervisor must now help John backtrack. If the supervisor had any inkling that marital therapy might be indicated, the supervisor was negligent for not coaching John regarding the client's informed consent rights.

*Informed Consent Regarding Supervision.* The client must be aware of not only therapeutic procedures but also supervision procedures. Whether sessions will be taped or observed, who will be involved in supervision (one person or a team), how close will be the supervision — all of these need to be communicated to the client. Most training programs use written forms to alert clients of the conditions of supervision. It is also sometimes wise for the supervisor to meet with the clients personally before the outset of therapy for a number of reasons: By meeting the supervisor directly, the client usually is more comfortable with the prospect of supervision; it gives the supervisor an opportunity to model for trainees the kind of direct, open communication that is needed to insure informed consent; and by not going through the trainee to communicate with clients, it is one less way that the supervisor could be vicariously responsible should the trainee not be clear or thorough.

The most frequent and most serious breach of informed consent occurs when the client has not been made aware that therapy is totally contingent on supervision. In an attempt to make clients (or themselves) more comfortable, trainees sometimes downplay the necessity of supervision. They use ambiguous language like "If it's alright with you, I'll be audiotaping our session," when what they mean is "I am required to audiotape our sessions if I am to work with you." Later, when the client feels more comfortable with the trainee, the client might come for therapy and

say something like "I'd like to discuss something that is quite sensitive and I'd prefer that you not tape today." This leaves the trainee in the awkward position of setting an unwise precedent or having to backpedal to explain the true parameters of therapy.

We are not saying that supervision needs to be constant in every situation or with every trainee, but rather that whatever the conditions of supervision are, these need to be explained openly and clearly to the client.

> *Example: Beth is a social worker who works with battered women. She is well trained to do initial interviews with women in crisis, and her supervisor is confident in Beth's abilities to carry out these interviews without taping them. Additionally, there is the concern that the use of audiotape would be insensitive to women who are frightened and vulnerable during the interview. But if Beth is able to interest any of these women in further counseling, she is required to introduce the supervisory condition of audiotaping at the first subsequent session. Once Beth has developed her therapy skills, she will be asked to audiotape only on occasion.*

*Informed Consent with Trainees.* It goes without saying that it is as important that trainees be as well informed as clients. Trainees should enter the supervisory experience knowing the conditions that dictate their success or advancement. It also should be clear to them what their responsibilities are and what the supervisor's are. Consider the following examples:

> *Ken makes an appointment to see his academic advisor in August. He plans to do his internship in the fall. His advisor tells Ken that this is probably impossible because Ken would need to find a site, and the chances are very slim that he can find one at such a late date. This is the first time that Ken has heard that he is responsible for finding his own site.*
>
> *Ruth has been assigned to a local mental health hospital for her internship to work with patients who are preparing to be discharged. It*

is her first day at the site, and she is meeting with her site supervisor. He gives her a form to fill out, which asks for information regarding her student malpractice insurance. When Ruth tells her supervisor that she does not carry such insurance, he advises her that it is the hospital's policy not to accept any student who does not have insurance. The supervisor also expresses some surprise because this has always been the hospital's policy, and Ruth is not the first student to be assigned there from her training program.

Alexandra has received a C in her first practicum. Her instructor tells her that it is an agreement among faculty that anyone who receives a C must repeat the course in order to continue in the program (that is, if there is reasonable expectation that the student can improve the grade). Alexandra knew she was to receive a C but hoped that she could improve through her internship, which she has already set up in a local agency. She is advised to cancel these arrangements.

Pauline is in her first month of employment at a residential center for troubled youths. Most of her assignments have been what she considers babysitting rather than any serious work with her charges. When she talks to her supervisor about this, she is informed that she will not be assigned a case load for the first six months and only then if she is perceived as "ready." This is news to Pauline. She is frustrated because she turned down another job where she could have begun to work with kids immediately. Pauline is upset further because her husband has been notified by his firm that he will be transferred in nine months to another location. Had Pauline known the conditions of her present position, she would not have accepted the job.

Whiston and Emerson (1989) and Patrick (1989) addressed an additional salient issue regarding informed consent and students in training programs. Whiston and Emerson, in their discussion of dual relationships, take the generally accepted position that supervisors should not counsel their supervisees. They also stressed, however, that it is an informed consent violation if supervisors refer their trainees for therapy as a condition for continuing in a training program when their trainees were not aware of this possibility from the outset of training. In other words, if there is a possibility that personal counseling will be recommended for any trainees in a given program, all trainees should be cognizant of this policy upon entering the program. Similarly, Patrick (1989) warned against allowing trainees in a program to volunteer to be clients for a laboratory course if these trainees are not aware that exposing some types of personal information might lead to a change of status in that program. We will return to Patrick's argument under the topic of dual relationships.

These are only a few of the many types of information that trainees should be alerted to by their supervisors before they encounter any consequences. Others include the choice of supervisor, the form of supervision, the time that will be allotted for supervision, the expectations of the supervisor, the theoretical orientation of the supervisor, and the type of documentation required for supervision (Cohen, 1987). Simply put, the surprises in store for the trainee should be caused by the learning process itself and the complexity of human problems and not by oversights on the part of the supervisor.

As a final comment about informed consent, we refer to Stout's (1987) injunction that supervisors and supervisors in training also be forewarned about the parameters of supervision. "Supervisors, as such, should be allowed the prerogative of informed consent, that is, they need to be fully aware of the heavy responsibility, accountability, and even culpability involved in supervision" (p. 96).

***Dual Relationships.*** Ethical standards are clear that dual relationships of any kind between therapists and clients are to be avoided, and sexual relationships are never sanctioned. In most states, sexual intercourse with a client is grounds for the automatic revocation of the therapist's license or certification. There is consensus among the helping professions that the characteristics of a therapeutic relationship and an intimate sexual relationship are incompatible.

Pope, Keith-Spiegel, and Tabachnick (1986) argued convincingly, however, that training programs must offer trainees more than this admonition about dual relationships. Rather, supervisors should encourage honest discourse about inevitable sexual attraction to certain clients, so that trainees will not be left feeling guilty and anxious when they find themselves in such a situation. As Pope et al. noted, modeling openness and the seeking of consultation when therapists are attracted to clients will do more to enhance ethical practice than will simply passing down the ethical dictum.

As Pope, Schover, and Levenson (1980) maintained, the guidelines for dual relationships between supervisors and supervisees are far less clear. One nationwide survey (Pope, Levenson, & Schover, 1979) found that 10 percent of psychologists admitted having sexual contact with their educators when they were students, and 13 percent reported having had a sexual relationship with their students when they were educators. Therefore, research and experience tell us that supervisors sometimes form intimate relationships with trainees but not that these relationships are acceptable.

The AACD Ethical Standards (AACD, 1988) state that "[w]hen the education program offers a growth experience with an emphasis on self-disclosure or other relatively intimate or personal involvement, the member must have no administrative, supervisory, or evaluating authority regarding the participant" (Section H, 12). Although the intent of this principle is not to address personal relationships, it can be inferred that the AACD would not encourage such dual relationships for supervisors and trainees. The APA is more explicit in its principles:

> *Psychologists do not exploit their professional relationships with clients, supervisees, students, employees, or research participants sexually or otherwise. Psychologists do not condone or engage in sexual harassment. Sexual harassment is defined as deliberate or repeated comments, gestures, or physical contacts of a sexual nature that are unwanted by the recipient. (Principle 7: d)*

Sexual harassment is as indefensible as sexual relations with clients. Those supervisors who expect or request sexual favors or who take sexual liberties with their trainees are clearly in violation of the spirit, if not the letter, of all ethical codes for the helping professions. They have abused the power given them by their professional status and serve as poor role models for future therapists (Corey, Corey, & Callanan, 1988). Sexual relationships that grow from positive, caring feelings on the part of both participants, however, are more troublesome to label as clearly inappropriate. In fact, most of us know at least one dual-career couple whose relationship began while one, or both, was in training; some had unequal professional status when they became involved with one another.

When adults are working closely together in the intense world of therapy, it is understandable that intimate relationships might emerge. The question, therefore, is not always how to prevent such relationships from occurring, but how to assure that such a relationship poses no ethical compromise for the supervisor or trainee and no negative consequence for the trainee's clients. Hall (1988b) identified the two major problems with supervisory dual relationships as being impairment of judgment for the supervisor and risk of exploitation of the supervisee. Therefore, any plan to compensate for a dual relationship must keep these two potential problems in mind.

We suggest the following guidelines to handle a dual relationship within the supervisory context. If at all possible, a trainee should receive a new supervisor if an intimate relationship has evolved. This should be done in a manner that will not negatively impact upon clients being served or the professional growth of the trainee. If there is a rational reason for not replacing the present supervisor (e.g., the supervisor is the only Gestaltist on the staff and the student aspires to be a Gestalt therapist), then an additional supervisor should be involved to monitor the supervisory relationship. But there may be occasions when there is no possibility for removal of the supervisor or for an additional supervisor to be involved. In this case, we suggest that both supervisor and trainee take great pains to document their work together. Having audio- or videorecorded examples of the trainee's work will be important when it is time to evaluate. Usually it is not difficult to get a second opinion about a supervisee's abilities. The topics covered in supervision and their resolutions should all be recorded. Additionally, the supervisor should request consultation with colleagues more liberally than would be the case ordinarily. Finally, we suggest that if group supervision is one of the models being used, the group is made aware of the personal relationship between supervisor and trainee. By bringing up the issue openly and asking the group to give them feedback if any preferential treatment is observed, the couple reduces the possibility that the relationship will be insidious to the group.

The above notwithstanding, it must be noted that such dual relationships are still dangerous and difficult to manage. (Pope et al. [1980] reported that only 2 percent of their respondents believed that intimate relationships between trainees and supervisors could be "beneficial" to either party. Harrar, Vandecreek, and Knapp [1990] implied that *all* intimate relationships between a supervisor and supervisee constitute violations of professional ethics.) It is enough to negotiate personal power in a new relationship without adding the dimension of unequal professional power. When the relationship ends, the trainee is at a distinct disadvantage if the professional relationship must continue. It also is very typical for new couples to become insulated from the outside world and for each person involved to see things in a way that is very protective of the other. It is the rare person who can keep such dynamics from interfering with professional growth and service delivery.

Finally, we would like to say a few words about dual relationships that are not sexual. Goodyear and Sinnett (1984) argued that it is inevitable that supervisors and their supervisees will have dual relationships. Unlike therapy relationships, persons who work together will share other experiences with each other. Faculty and students in graduate programs often become quite close through formal and informal contacts. Additionally, the same person who serves as a trainee's clinical supervisor could be a member of the same trainee's doctoral research committee, an instructor for another course, or the supervisor for an assistantship. In an agency or school it sometimes happens that someone under supervision is the same person the supervisor learned to count on in a crisis or is someone with a personal style that allows the supervisor to be more candid than with other professional peers. Some of these relationships are very gratifying, and supervisors would not choose to avoid them. It seems to us, therefore, that supervisors should approach this matter by attempting to differentiate the dual relationships that cause no concern from those that are problematic. Those that are problematic typically involve either an abuse of power or serve to cloud our objectivity.

> *Example: Sharon is a good therapist. In her work with Jeanne, her supervisor, she has been very open and unguarded. Sharon had a very troubled past, and she has struggled hard to get where she is. A couple of times Sharon has shared some of her personal pain with Jeanne during intense supervision sessions. Sharon and Jeanne feel very close to each other. In the past couple of weeks, Sharon has not looked well. She is jumpy and short with Jeanne. When Jeanne pursues this change in behavior, Sharon begins to cry and tells Jeanne that she has recently returned to an old cocaine habit.*

*She begs Jeanne not to share her secret, promising that she will discontinue using the drug. She also asks that she be allowed to continue seeing clients.*

In this example, it is an open question as to who has the greater power in the relationship. Jeanne has position power, but Sharon has become a special person to Jeanne, giving Sharon a good deal of influence. Jeanne must determine if her objectivity is intact with Sharon or if they have already moved to a dual relationship. If Jeanne honors Sharon's request, it is likely that their professional relationship will be compromised even more.

Besides Sharon's inappropriate request, this vignette highlights the types of complications that can emerge when supervisors attempt to be therapists to their supervisees. However, because supervision can stimulate personal issues in the supervisee, it is quite likely that a supervisor will be faced with the challenge of determining where supervision ends and therapy begins (Whiston & Emerson, 1989; Wise, Lowery, & Silverglade, 1989). A recent study of the ethical choices required by psychologists (Pope et al., 1988) found this issue to be more problematic than other, clearer situations.

In spite of some confusion, most authors (e.g., Green & Hansen, 1989; Kitchener, 1988; Patrick, 1989; Stout, 1987; Whiston & Emerson, 1989; Wise et al., 1989) recommend that supervisors be clear from the outset of supervision that personal issues might be activated in supervision and that if these issues are found to be substantial, the supervisee will be asked to work through them with another professional. It is important to stress that this ethical question is not a novel one for supervisors. Green and Hansen (1989) reported that the trainee's personal issues was one of the six most important ethical dilemmas cited by AAMFT clinical members. The collective wisdom of those authors who have grappled with this issue is that supervisors have the responsibility to help supervisees identify their issues, especially as they interfere with their work as therapists; but "after the supervisor identifies the personal issues, the trainees must then be given the responsibility for resolving those issues" (Whiston & Emerson, 1989, p. 322).

Finally, as we mentioned earlier, Patrick (1989) made an interesting point that in some laboratory experiences, we can create dual relationships by asking peers to counsel other peers in order to increase their skills prior to working with a client population. Supervisors should be very cautious in such situations and should avoid pairing students who have any potential for being in contact in the foreseeable future. In fact, with Patrick's caution in mind, it may be best to avoid the inherent dangers in this type of situation altogether by relying on simulations.

*Example: Margaret is a school counselor who has been assigned a trainee from the local university for the academic year. As she observes Noah work with elementary school children, she is increasingly impressed with his skills. She asks him to work with Peter, a nine-year-old, who has not adjusted well to his parents' recent divorce. Again, she is impressed with Noah's skill, his warmth and understanding, and, ultimately, with the success he has in working with Peter. Margaret is a single parent who is concerned about her nine-year-old son. She decides to ask Noah to see him. Noah is quite complimented by her confidence in him. Margaret's son attends a different school, but she arranges to have Noah see him after school hours.*

In this case, the supervisor has initiated the dual relationship. Even though she has already decided that Noah is a skilled counselor, Noah's vulnerability is heightened by seeing Margaret's son. Furthermore, who will supervise this case? Assuming that Noah has a university supervisor also, it will be up to this person to intervene with Noah, an unenviable professional responsibility.

Kitchener (1988, p. 219) listed three guidelines to help the clinical supervisor differentiate between a relationship that could easily lead to ethical compromise and one that probably will not. First, "as the incompatibility of expectations increases between roles, so will the potential for misunderstanding and harm." A prime example of such incompatibility is the role of supervisor versus the role of therapist. Second, "as the obligations of different roles diverge, the potential for divided loyalties and loss of objectivity increases." In other words, if a supervisor and supervisee are involved in a personal relationship, the supervisor's loyalty to the supervisee's client might be compromised by the desire to have an egalitarian personal relationship with the supervisee. Finally, "as the power and prestige between the professional's and the consumer's role increase, so does the potential for exploitation and an inability on the part of the consumers to remain objective about their own best interests."

If a supervisor has significant power in one's personal life, it will be difficult for the supervisee to sort out professional feedback. The one-down position of the supervisee is either exacerbated or confused by the dual relationship. In fact, a personal relationship that should end might continue out of fear of the professional consequences.

*Competence.*    We all remember the feelings we had when we saw our first client. We might have doubted the sanity of our supervisor to trust an incompetent with someone who had a problem. And if we were observed for that session, it was even worse. (One of us recalls the nightmare of being electrocuted by the audiorecorder when trying to record the first counseling session!) For most of us, those feelings waned with time, helped by encouraging feedback from our supervisors and accumulation of experience. The feelings also lessened as we grew to appreciate that therapy is at least part art and probably a combination of many

things, only some of which we control. Finally, the feelings diminished through the authenticity of the relationships we shared with our clients and the positive results of those relationships. The issue of our own competence became less and less bothersome to us. Eventually, we felt good enough about our own abilities that we agreed to supervise the work of another. Now we are involved in the developmental process at two levels: We are the overseers of the initial steps taken by our supervisees while we continue to develop ourselves. There are times when we can appreciate how far we have come by observing the tentative work of those under our charge.

There is something very self-assuring about having some experience and being able to see from where one has come. There also is something seductive, and even dangerous, about being in such a position: Supervisors can forget to question their competence. This is not to imply that it is admirable to remain professionally insecure but that it is vital for supervisors to remember that the issue of competence is one of the most central to the process of clinical supervision. Supervisors must remain competent not only as therapists but also as judges of another's abilities, while being competent in many facets of supervision itself. In fact, the whole issue of competence, supervisors' and supervisees', is central to the most pressing ethical responsibility of all, that of monitoring client welfare.

In addition to the benefits supervisors accrue from their work as educators, clinicians, researchers, or administrators, we believe there are three additional ways to monitor supervisors' competence.

*Restricting One's Area of Expertise.*    Most supervisors realize that they cannot be all things to all people. Yet they are tempted to forget this bit of wisdom when a trainee wants to gain some experience in an area that the supervisor is unfamiliar with. As we mentioned earlier, the helping professions for better or for worse, have become a field with many specialties. There are times when it can be a difficult decision whether a supervisor's skills are sufficient to supervise in a particular area. Sometimes the theoretical orientation makes this less of a problem (e.g., a systemic family therapist would view many different disorders as variations on the same theme, that is, a problem in the family system that is being expressed by the identified patient). But more often than not, supervisors would be wise to have a clear sense of the kinds of cases that they would either not supervise or would supervise only under certain conditions (e.g., for a limited number of sessions, for the purposes of referral, or, as Hall [1988a] suggested, with the aid of a consultant). Examples of specialties that some supervisors might choose to shy away from include substance abuse, sexual or physical abuse, eating disorders, divorce counseling, or endogenous depression.

*Continuing Education.* Given the tremendous influence that supervisors have on future practitioners, it is frightening to consider the supervisor who is not actively engaged in continuing education. The various ethical codes reflect this concern: "Members recognize the need for continuing education to ensure competent service" (AACD, 1988, Section A:1); "[t]he social worker should take responsibility for identifying, developing, and fully utilizing knowledge for professional practice" (NASW, 1984, V.O.); "[p]sychologists recognize the need for continuing education and are open to new procedures and changes in expectations and values over time" (APA, 1981, Principle 2:c.). Perhaps the point was best made recently by Corey (1986) who said, "I question the ethics of practitioners who fail to keep current with new developments" (p. 330).

Although most professionals probably agree with the necessity of continuing education for all practitioners and for supervisors in particular, the task itself can be enormous. Not only should supervisors be current in their own professional specialties, but they also should be aware of the substantial developments that are being made in the area of clinical supervision. Some would add that supervisors should at least be minimally aware of specialties that dovetail with their own. Goodyear and Sinnett (1984) stated that it is an ethical responsibility for practitioners to be knowledgeable regarding social issues, including those surrounding minorities and women.

The most efficient way for supervisors to stay current is to be active members of their national organizations and to attend regional and national meetings. This is usually a more advantageous approach to continuing education than occasionally attending a workshop because it is more comprehensive and will afford supervisors an avenue to be aware of developments that might not otherwise be apparent to them. It is important to be aware of national trends for another reason: There is reason to believe that in litigation, national professional standards, not local ones, would be used to evaluate the supervisor's performance (Woody, 1984).

*Consultation.* Finally, we believe that a liberal use of consultation with professional peers is important to prevent the kind of isolation that diminishes competence. "Supervision is a serious activity and one with unforeseen challenges. It is important that a supervisor has a network of colleagues, a place to go, for consultation when needed in order to meet the complex demands of supervision" (Bernard, 1987, p. 55).

Being able to consult with a colleague seems especially important when trying to balance the client's therapy needs with the supervisee's training needs. There can be a rather narrow ban of case complexity that will challenge the trainee without jeopardizing the client. Because supervisors come to know, and sometimes care about, their trainees more than they do the trainees' clients, it is wise to occasionally monitor opinions with those of a trusted colleague. Furthermore, interactions with another supervisor can increase a supervisor's skills in ways that it may not have predicted.

*Confidentiality.* Confidentiality is the ethical principle given the most attention in most training programs. In addition to liability concerns, we believe this is so because confidentiality represents the essence of therapy (a safe place where secrets and hidden fears can be exposed) and because much of our professional status comes from being the bearer of such secrets. We earn our clients' respect and the respect of others by the posture we take toward confidentiality. There was a time when confidentiality was a sacred obligation. In recent years, however, confidentiality has become the step-sibling to safety and judicial judgment. As a result, the issues surrounding confidentiality have become more complicated. As with all therapeutic components, the implications for supervision are more complex still.

Before we consider the legal realities regarding confidentiality, we would like to outline those dimensions that must be safeguarded by the supervisor. First, the supervisor must be sure that the trainee keeps confidential all client information except for the purposes of supervision. Because supervision allows for a third-party discussion of the therapy situation, the trainee must be reminded that this type of discourse cannot be repeated elsewhere. In group supervision, the supervisor must reiterate this point and take the extra precaution of having cases presented using first names only and with as few demographic details as possible. When videotape or live supervision are employed with additional trainees present, the only recourse for the supervisor is to emphasize and reemphasize the importance of confidentiality. When students are asked to tape their sessions, they must be reminded that they have in their possession confidential documents. Notes on clients should have code numbers rather than names and be guarded with great care.

In addition to having some assurance that trainees are meeting the requirements of confidentiality, the supervisor must be sure that trainees view the information received in supervision as confidential and not as akin to something read in a textbook of case studies. There is a certain discipline required to view someone else's clients as one's own as far as privacy is concerned.

Finally, there is the trainee's right to privacy and the supervisor's responsibility to keep information confidential. It is inevitable that supervision will be an opportunity for the supervisor to hear something about the trainee that would not be discovered in a less personal learning situation. For example, the trainee might share some painful aspect of childhood as it relates to a client. The divulging of such information might come from the trainee's concern that personal history should not detract from therapy and with the request that the supervisor monitor the case more closely. We can all imagine several situations in which such an encounter could take place; the topics could range from family secrets and sexual orientation to prejudicial attitudes that the trainee believes must be divulged. With each such piece of information, the supervisor must decide if the trainee's right to privacy should be upheld. For example, it might be easy to determine that a trainee's disclosure that she was an incest victim as a child is something that no one else need know. But should one discover that a trainee is a racial bigot, is that personal information or professional information? Is confidentiality an obligation in that case? Perhaps the legal parameters of privacy and confidentiality will help us determine if there is due cause for divulging such information.

There is still some occasional confusion in the helping professions regarding the distinctions between confidentiality, privacy, and privileged communication. Confidentiality is defined by Siegel (1979) as follows: "Confidentiality involves professional ethics rather than any legalism and indicates an explicit promise or contract to reveal nothing about an individual except under conditions agreed to by the source or subject" (p. 251). Privacy is the other side of confidentiality. It is the client's right not to have private information, including the information gained in therapy, divulged without informed consent. Privileged communication is

> *a legal concept and refers to the right of clients not to have their privileged communication used in court without their consent. If a client waives this privilege, the professional has no grounds for withholding the information. Thus, the privilege belongs to clients and is meant for their protection, not for the protection of therapists. (Corey, Corey, & Callanan, 1988, p. 177)*

Although these three terms are vital in therapy and supervision, they are not absolute. In fact, knowing the limits of each is as serious a responsibility for the clinician as honoring their intent. It is ultimately an individual decision when the therapist or supervisor will decide to overturn the client's (or supervisee's) right of privacy and break confidentiality. But there are a number of cases in which either legal precedent, a law, or a value of a higher order dictates such a direction. In a court of law, the therapist cannot use confidentiality as a reason not to testify unless the client has the right of privileged communication. (This would be given to the client if the client's therapist was in a professional discipline that was specified by state statute as having privileged communication.) Even then, privileged communication may not be honored if the court believes the information held by the therapist will contribute to a just decision, such as in a contested child custody case. Likewise, the therapist must break confidentiality if there is suspected child abuse (by law) or a minor who is suicidal (by legal precedent). These are fairly clear cases to resolve. There are others that fall into grey areas. Does the minor who is using drugs have a right to privacy? If the drug is cocaine, more and more practitioners would say no. But what if the

drug is marijuana or alcohol? Here the particular values of therapists seem to vary greatly as do their actions. Some would say that it is a natural part of adolescence to experiment in one way or another, and confidentiality should be protected in order to give the teenager a safe place to talk; others would declare that adolescent suicide, in many cases, has been paired with substance abuse, and the risk is too great to take. Both positions have a body of knowledge to support them, but they lead to dramatically different decisions.

The trend in the helping professions seems to be toward a more guarded view of confidentiality. There are at least two reasons for this development: The law is increasingly specifying how the therapist should carry out this professional obligation, and therapists are becoming increasingly aware that they can proceed with the therapeutic process without the existence of absolute confidentiality (Denkowski & Denkowski, 1982). It is considered wise, therefore, to make a discussion of confidentiality and its limits a common practice in therapy.

## LEGAL ISSUES

### The Duty to Warn

As we stated earlier, the result of the Tarasoff case is that most practitioners take very seriously the duty to warn potential victims of dangerous clients. This seems like a fairly straightforward dictum. But there are at least two problems: How does one identify all potentially dangerous clients? What if there is no identified potential victim?

"The consensus of opinion by responsible, scientific authorities is that the profession is incapable of accurately predicting the dangerousness of mental patients" (Olsen, 1977, p. 288). Although it would be comforting to view Olsen's summary of the research as the definitive legal view, it is not (Fulero, 1988). The courts have often noted that helping professionals make decisions regarding dangerousness every day in child abuse cases and in making judgments about involuntary commitment (Schultz, 1982). The practitioner can, however, expect a balance between the two: the expectation that sound judgment and reasonable or due care was taken but not the expectation to see the unforeseeable. Schutz (1982) suggested that practitioners pay attention to "the level of socialization and capacity to feel and express concern for others. Attention should also be paid to the patient's level of impulsiveness and capacity for self-control" (p. 60). Additionally, Schutz and other authorities on such legal matters make the point emphatically that consultation with others and documentation of treatment is vital in any questionable case.

In other situations, there is some indication that the client might be dangerous but no potential victim has been named. In fact, there might not be a particular person in danger; rather, the hostility might be nonspecific. At present, ethical standards and legal experts seem to lean in favor of the client unless there is clear evidence that the client is immediately dangerous (Fulero, 1988; Knapp & Vandecreek, 1982; Schutz, 1982; Woody, 1984). In other words, therapists and supervisors are not expected to, nor should they, read between the lines when working with clients. Many clients make idle threats when they are frustrated. It is the therapist's job to make a reasonable evaluation of those threats. In fact, in the eyes of the law, it is more important that therapists make the evaluation than that they predict with perfect accuracy. The former is their job; the latter is their hope.

## Multiple Clients

For both group counseling and family therapy, there are problems with confidentiality and, especially, privileged communication. In group counseling, the therapist is considered to be bound to keeping information confidential (Corey, Corey, & Callanan, 1988). The

therapist also must attempt to impress upon the members of the group the importance of confidentiality. Some group leaders ask members to sign an agreement form to that effect. Confidentiality, however, is a principle that should be paired with the power to uphold it, and this might be questionable in groups. For example, should young people in a group be expected not to share the information with their peers or even with their parents? What about adults sharing information with their spouses? In short, confidentiality may be an ideal, but not an obligation, for group members. To promise confidentiality to group members would be foolhardy.

In family therapy, the issue is a different one, having mostly to do with keeping information about one or more family members away from other family members. The most common occurrences of this problem are when one spouse has been seen privately prior to the entry of the other spouse or when a child has been seen separate from his or her parents. Some family therapists believe that each family member has a right to confidentiality and would, therefore, honor secrets, whereas others inform their clients that no private communication will be considered confidential because it allows for special alliances to be formed between the therapist and individual family members. Margolin (1982) suggested a third alternative.

> *Rather than treat all information shared in individual sessions as confidential, the therapist may indicate that (1) in general, confidentiality conditions do not apply, but (2) the client has the right to request that any specific information be kept confidential and the therapist will comply with any such requests. (p. 791)*

In addition, Margolin pointed out that the therapist may choose to keep information out of family therapy (e.g., an extramarital affair) for therapeutic reasons rather than for reasons of confidentiality.

Privileged communication is another area

of concern for multiple clients. Meyer and Smith (1977) reported that in almost no jurisdiction in the United States will privileged communication be assured for group therapy clients. The issue for families is more intricate. The question in family therapy is "who holds the privilege?" (Margolin, 1982). When a couple has been seen together, can one member waive the right if the other refuses? Courts in different states have varied in their rulings about this matter. "Lacking definitive legislation on these issues, family therapists cannot comfortably assume that existing privilege statutes protect the communications that occur during family therapy" (Margolin, 1982, p. 794). As a stopgap measure, Margolin suggested that therapists have clients sign a written statement in which each agrees not to call on the therapist to testify in the case of future litigation. It must be noted, however, that courts tend not to honor a priori agreements.

In summary, the rights of clients to have their communications kept private can be compromised for a number of reasons. The responsible therapist or supervisor makes both the commitment to confidentiality and the realistic limits of confidentiality clear to clients at the outset of the therapy process.

> *Example: Mrs. Bennett makes an appointment to see a marriage and family therapy trainee. She is going through a difficult divorce, which includes a very upsetting child custody battle, and states that she needs a place where she can talk and feel safe. During the phone intake, she implies that there are a few things that her husband does not know that would add power to his case if he did.*

In supervising this case, the trainee must be helped in explaining the limits of confidentiality to Mrs. Bennett. Another supervision challenge is to consider a way that therapy could be structured so that Mrs. Bennett could have the safety she seeks without putting herself in jeopardy. To promise Mrs. Bennett complete safety, however, would be foolhardy and unethical.

Returning to our question about the trainee who is a racial bigot, we contend that this is professional information and not strictly personal. We also contend that it is not information that must be kept confidential (that is, away from others involved in this person's training), because doing so might put the trainee's future clients at risk. Additionally, all codes of ethical principles include a statement of the responsibility for the betterment of society, a responsibility called upon in this case. Once this has been determined, supervisors have several options available to them, including sharing their deep concern with the trainee, setting up a learning experience with exposure to minorities, consulting with colleagues who may have encountered the same problem, and, perhaps, counseling the trainee out of the program.

## Malpractice

As we mentioned at the beginning of this chapter, there is a peaked interest in the helping professions regarding malpractice. Therapists' vulnerability is directly linked to their assumption of professional roles. When they take the role of therapist or supervisor, they are expected to know and follow legal standards and the profession's ethical standards. According to Woody (1984), some professionals are aghast at the legal profession's intrusion into the human services professions. Yet Woody referred to Bierig's (1983) assertion that malpractice suits have resulted from faulty self-regulation systems within these professions. Recent research seems to support both therapists' great difficulty in judging each other's competence (Haas et al., 1986) and their reluctance to report known ethical violations of peers (J. L. Bernard & Jara, 1986).

There are other sociological factors that contribute to the increase of lawsuits against helping professionals. Cohen (1979) claimed that the three primary factors for the increase are a general decline in the respect afforded helping professionals by clients and society at large, an increased awareness of consumer's rights in general, and the highly publicized malpractice suits in which settlements were enormous—leading to the conclusion that a lawsuit may be a means of obtaining easy money. As the reader will note, none of these factors would spare the ethical practitioner from a potential lawsuit.

The following definitions are offered by Corey, Corey, and Callanan (1988):

> *Civil liability means that an individual can be sued for not doing right or for doing wrong to another. Malpractice can be seen as the opposite of acting in good faith. It is defined as the failure to render proper service, through ignorance or negligence, resulting in injury or loss to the client. Professional negligence consists of departing from usual practice or not exercising due care. The primary problem in a negligence suit is determining which standards of care apply to determine whether a counselor [therapist] has breached a duty to a client. (p. 230)*

Schutz (1982) described four elements necessary for malpractice: "a therapy [or supervision] relationship must be established; the therapist's [or supervisor's] conduct must fall below the acceptable standard of care; this conduct was the proximate cause of injury to the client; an actual injury was sustained by the client" (p. 2). We are not aware of any suits brought against supervisors by trainees for inadequate supervision. But in a society so litigious that children are now suing parents for inadequate parenting, such a suit does not seem farfetched. It is more likely that supervisors would be involved in legal action as a codefendant in a malpractice suit (Snider, 1985) based on the inadequate performance of the supervisee.

Slimak and Berkowitz (1983) listed the six types of malpractice suits against mental health professionals as

> *(1) faulty diagnosis; that is, diagnosis of a problem of physical origin as psychological; (2) improper certification in a commitment proceeding; (3) failure to exercise adequate precautions for a suicidal patient; (4) breach of confidentiality; (5) faulty application of therapy; and (6) promise of a cure, which may form the basis of a breach of contract. (pp. 291–292)*

Snider (1985) added "duty to warn" as the seventh type of malpractice suit. Because of the Tarasoff case, this last issue has been most identified with supervisors. But the concept of vicarious liability or respondeat supervisor (literally, let the master answer) is relevant anytime a therapist or trainee has a supervisor.

## Vicarious Liability

Slovenko (1980) defined the legal precedent that had been set in the Tarasoff case.

> *One may be held legally responsible not only for one's own faulty conduct but also for that of others. By reason of certain relationships that may exist between parties, the negligence of one may be charged against the other, though the latter has played no part in it, has done nothing whatever to aid or encourage it, and in fact has done all that he [or she] possibly can to prevent it. (p. 453)*

In addition to the supervisor's vulnerability due to the trainee's inexperience, Slovenko warned that the supervisor might be held responsible for trainee behavior that the supervisor is unaware of (e.g., having sex with a client) or when the trainee does not follow through on supervisory suggestions.

Snider (1985) offered four guidelines to supervisors to reduce the likelihood of being named as a codefendant in a malpractice suit. First, maintain a trusting relationship with supervisees. Within a context of mutual trust and respect, supervisees will be far more likely to voice their concerns about their clients, themselves, and each other. Second, keep up to date regarding legal issues that affect mental health settings and the professional in general. Additionally, supervisors need to have a healthy respect for the complexity of the law and recognize the need for competent legal aid. Third, if the supervisor is the administrative head, it is essential that the supervisor retains the services of an attorney who specializes in malpractice litigation. If this is not the supervisor's decision, the supervisor should be sure that the organization has appropriate legal support. Fourth, supervisors should have adequate liability insurance and should be sure that their supervisees also carry liability insurance. Although this final precaution does not reduce the chances of being sued, it does, obviously, minimize the damages that could accrue from such an experience.

Unfortunately, there is little comfort to offer the timid supervisor who is afraid of the tremendous responsibility and potential legal liability inherent in supervision. Short of refusing to supervise, we believe that protection for the supervisor lies in the same concepts of reasonable care and sound judgment that protect therapists. This includes an awareness of, and command of, the concepts and skills presented in this book. It includes also a commitment to investing the time and energy to supervise adequately. And perhaps above all, it includes having operational guidelines to use when having to evaluate an ethical dilemma.

## ETHICAL DECISION MAKING

In May of 1987, *Time* magazine published a cover story entitled "What's Wrong" (Shapiro, 1987). The article was a scathing review of different pockets of our society, including government, Wall Street, and TV evangelism, where morality is sorely lacking and there is "an excessively legalistic approach to defining ethical behavior" (p. 17). Shapiro's article implied that the laissez-faire attitude "at the top" must take a sizable share of the blame and that the result has been the unsettling of "the nation's soul." Unfortunately, Shapiro's article did not mark the end of our ethical crisis. The

80s ended in a manner that made Watergate look comparatively innocent.

As we said at the beginning of this chapter, we seem to be witnessing a joining of ethical behavior and liability. This is true not only for the human services, but also for society at large. The great danger of this development is the further joining of what is "right" with "what I can get away with," leaving only "what I can't get away with" as "wrong." Knowing full well that most unethical behavior is not confronted, the practitioner becomes more likely to lose sight of the moral parameters. The potential consequence is that the helping professions will become another example of the law dictating professional ethics.

The only reasonable alternative to this approach is putting ethics in the foreground. We believe that graduate programs need to include courses in ethics and professional issues or, at the very least, find several pockets for this material in the curriculum. We agree with Handelsman (1986) that supervision is not an ideal time to incorporate ethical principles. Ethical behavior should be proactive and not reactive. Waiting for ethical issues to emerge in supervision seems to set up the conditions for crisis training, not ethics training. Additionally, such a passive attitude toward ethics seems to communicate the kind of laissez-faire attitude that Shapiro found lacking in ethical rigor. On the other hand, supervisors cannot afford to assume that ethics have been taken care of if supervisees have had academic exposure to ethical principles prior to supervision. The point is, of course, that ethical practice is a way of professional existence, not a command of a body of knowledge. Anything short of this is an inadequate position for the clinical supervisor.

One aid to ethical development for both supervisors and trainees is experiential learning. Many ethical mishaps result from acts of omission, not intentional malice (Bernard, 1981). Such omissions are more likely when professionals have not had an opportunity to experience the ins and outs of a similar situation. The use of simulation and behavioral rehearsal is an excellent way to safely allow both trainees and supervisors to face difficult situations, try alternative resolutions, and evaluate outcomes. (See Appendix B for one format for experiential training in ethical dilemmas.)

Finally, ethical decision making includes a cognitive process, a map to follow, from the presentation of the ethical dilemma to its resolution. There are many models for decision making. Keith-Spiegel and Koocher (1985) borrowed Tymchuk's (1981) list of steps as they were outlined for behavioral research and revised them for the purposes of ethical decision making.

1. *Describe the parameters of the situation.*
2. *Define the potential issues involved.*
3. *Consult ethical guidelines, if any, already available that might apply to the resolution of each issue.*

4. *Evaluate the rights, responsibilities, and welfare of all affected parties.*
5. *Generate the alternative decisions possible for each issue.*
6. *Enumerate the consequences of making each decision.*
7. *Present any evidence that the various consequences or benefits resulting from each decision will actually occur.*
8. *Make the decision. (pp. 19–20)*

As gatekeepers of the profession, clinical supervisors will continue to be heavily involved with ethical standards for practice. The most comprehensive approach to this responsibility is to be well informed and personally and professionally confident. Both are accomplished by continually putting ethics in the foreground of practice, discussion, and contemplation. In this case, perhaps more than in any other, supervisors' primary responsibility is to model what they hope to teach.

# CHAPTER 9

# ADMINISTRATIVE TASKS

In the practice of supervision, there has existed a real split between that which is clinical and that which is administrative. Most supervisors identify themselves with one or the other of the two roles. The professional literature reflects this split, for certain journals are devoted to administrative supervision (e.g., *Administration in Mental Health* and *Administration in Social Work*), whereas others are more likely to publish articles on clinical supervision (e.g., *Professional Psychology: Research and Practice* and *The Clinical Supervisor*). And in those journals that attempt to bridge the gap (e.g., *Counselor Education and Supervision*), the articles clearly differentiate between the two foci of supervision. When the Association for Counselor Education and Supervision decided to publish a monograph on supervision, it eventually opted to commission two—one for the counselor supervisor (Borders & Leddick, 1987) and one for the administrative supervisor (Falvey, 1987).

As we will see in this chapter, there is some justification for such a dichotomy. Although there is overlap, the goals of each form of supervision are different from the other. The clinical supervisor has a dual investment in the quality of services offered to clients and the development of the trainee; the administrative supervisor, while concerned about service delivery, must also focus on matters such as organizational structure, personnel, and legislative and fiscal issues, to name just a few. The administrative supervisor will, by necessity, choose to view any particular piece of datum in a larger context (Falvey, 1987); the clinical supervisor will be more likely to focus on the uniqueness of the case at hand. In fact, if the same supervisor is given both administrative and clinical tasks, this will usually lead to some sense of frustration and conflict. Therefore, not only the tasks assigned to each type of supervisor but also the operational perspectives themselves are different. This has led to the position that each form of supervision is a discipline in and of itself. Several authors have noted that the human service professional who is promoted to the position of administrative supervisor will find the transition difficult and would benefit greatly from some form of retraining (Falvey, 1987; Feldman, 1980; White, 1981).

The above notwithstanding, it is our position that there is a strong and necessary component to clinical supervision that is administrative or organizational in nature. One would have a difficult time accepting the information presented in either the chapter on ethics and legal issues or the chapter on clinical evaluation without recognizing that an administrative context must exist that allows for these dimensions of supervision. Therefore, our goal in this chapter is to address the administration of clinical supervision.

There are at least three matters that complicate a discussion of the administrative tasks of clinical supervision. The first is a bias among many human service practitioners (clinical supervisors included) that organizational matters are somewhat inferior to theoretical or clinical issues. Although administrators are persons to be contended with, they are viewed essentially as political animals or paper pushers. Therefore, the element of clinical supervision that smacks of administration is given a lower priority in the scheme of things. This bias is supported, in part, by Kadushin (1985), who found that the most highly ranked stress reported by clinical supervisors was "dissatisfaction with administrative 'housekeeping' " (p. 321).

The second complicating matter is an assumption that clinical perceptiveness and administrative competence are rarely found in the same individual. This is similar to the assumption about absent minded professors—that they can be brilliant in their field but have little ability to negotiate the real world. Although there is some basis for most stereotypes, we believe that in many instances, a lack of organization is the result of systemic properties rather than a deficit of inherent individual ability. In other words, if the consequences for being disorganized are subtle or nonexistent, there is very little reason for the naturally disorganized person to change. Or viewed somewhat differently, that which often appears as disorganized behavior in fact is functional. Persons who describe themselves as incapable of any level of administration have organized their lives and their behaviors in a way that keeps this myth alive. When one thinks about it, it takes a certain amount of organization to be consistently disorganized!

The third complicating factor to our discussion is the reality that in some organizations, there is no distinction between clinical supervision and administrative supervision. Supervisors are asked to wear one blended hat, without the luxury of a clear focus in either direction. We acknowledge this dilemma as a real one and hope that having some clarity on the types of administrative activities that directly affect clinical supervision will somehow help the blended supervisor to be more deliberate in all activities.

With these complications in mind, we will begin by arguing for the importance of administrative competence for the delivery of clinical supervision. Then we will consider the differences when supervision is offered within one system (organization) versus when two systems are involved. This will be followed by an examination of administrative competency in both university settings and field settings with the hope of eliminating any mystery about what constitutes an organized approach to supervision. Finally, we will suggest additional guidelines through which a clinical supervisor can attain administrative competence.

## IMPORTANCE OF ADMINISTRATIVE COMPETENCE

Although there are many references to the importance of being organized in one's delivery of clinical supervision, there is very little direct data supporting the importance of administrative competence for clinical supervision. A distinct exception to this is a study conducted by Eisikovits, Meier, Guttman, Shurka, and Levinstein (1986), which looked at the relationship of eight factors—one of which was the administrative competence of supervisors—to both service delivery and work environment.

Conducted in Israel with social workers, the study concluded that the administrative skill factor was correlated with pressure on professionals to be actively involved with the functioning of the agency; viewing the work environment as being highly task oriented; perceiving the agency as emphasizing order, organization, and the planning of in-service provision; and perceiving the agency as encouraging free expression on the client's part. In addition, these components were interrelated with one another. One surprise of the study was that, although administrative skill was shown to effect both work environment and service delivery positively, its greatest effect was on the latter.

*It seems that workers associate the process and components of supervision more with the ecology of service provision than with the ecology of the agency as a work place. Yet, when they do relate the professional development and administrative aspects of supervision to the work environment of the agency, they associate them with an agency's climate which allows them to be autonomous and task-oriented, and thereby enhanced their personal development, and with involvement among the staff . . . This may suggest that supervisors who emphasize the workers' professional development and who are administratively competent, contribute to the workers' sense of mastery and competence in their work, and to their perception of the agency as involving them as a group in its everyday functioning (Eisikovits et al., 1986, p. 54).*

As a result of their findings, Eisikovits et al. recommended enhancing the administrative skills of clinical supervisors. They also recommended more research on this topic.

Despite the dearth of studies looking specifically at the administrative component of clinical supervision, several authors have asserted that practitioner burnout may indeed be related not only to service demands but also to poor administrative structure (Kaslow & Rice, 1985; Malouf, Haas, & Farah, 1983; Murphy & Pardeck, 1986; Stoltenberg & Delworth, 1987). Murphy and Pardeck noted that either authoritarian or laissez-faire styles of management (supervision) add to burnout and that burnout may be more organizational than psychological. Their recommendations echo Eisikovits et al. (1986) in that practitioners be involved in program planning, supervision not be viewed as oppressive by nature, and "a lack of planning is not understood to be the only method for encouraging individualism" (Murphy & Pardeck, 1986, p. 40). A study conducted by Russell, Lankford, and Grinnell (1983) suggested that the present situation in the helping professions is in great need of correction. When one large agency was surveyed, 21 of 44 clinical supervisors were perceived as exemplifying an "impoverished" management style, indicating a low concern for people and a low concern for production.

We wish to underscore the concept that burnout may be organizational as well as, if not rather than, psychological. From the supervisee's perspective, it makes intuitive sense

to us that the best of supervisory relationships or the finest of clinical insights can be sabotaged by weak administrative skills. This can be seen in training situations or in work situations in which supervisees are no longer patient or tolerant of inconveniences or frustrations caused by the supervisor who cannot maintain some level of mastery of the supervisory plan. Supervisees often realize that a lack of administrative skill not only leaves them vulnerable but also leaves the client and agency vulnerable as well. When messages are inconsistent, communication erratic, procedures unclear or not adhered to, the entire experience of service delivery under supervision becomes tainted. Because of lack of experience, trainees or new employees are hard pressed to distinguish their feelings about service delivery from their feelings about supervision. As a result of cognitive dissonance, it is very difficult for supervisees to admit their disappointment in their supervisor for two reasons: their respect for the supervisor's therapeutic skill and their appreciation of the learning that has taken place under the supervisor's tutelage; and an acknowledgement of the power differential between them and their supervisor and that any open disapproval of the supervisor might serve them poorly. Therefore, whether the supervisee is a new trainee or an ongoing employee, the supervisor must realize that signs of frustration or burnout may be feedback to the supervisor rather than about the supervisee.

To focus on burnout is to focus on the negative effects of administrative incompetence. Administrative competence, however, enhances positive experiences; or as Lowy (1983) stated, "[t]he learning and teaching transactions in supervision require an organizational structure in order to become implementable" (p. 60). The education literature is replete with studies confirming the need for structure in the learning process. Often educational theory tends to be ignored in the helping professions. Yet there is evidence that the process of acquiring clinical skill follows predictable developmental sequences. Sound educational advice, therefore, calls for a stable background (administrative structure) to ground the trainee who is being asked to take risks and meet challenges in the clinical arena.

Finally, we maintain the importance of administrative competence because certain supervisory functions are inextricably tied to such competence. Specifically, evaluating supervisees and maintaining an operation that meets minimal ethical standards requires administrative skill. Because a deficit in these areas can become threatening to supervisors and supervisees alike, we hope that the importance of administrative competence becomes self-evident. But with the minimal attention given to this topic in clinical supervision literature, it is understandable that these skills remain underdeveloped.

Once we have accepted the importance of the administrative component of clinical supervision, we begin to appreciate the importance of context to supervision. No part of supervision is more immediately affected by the environment than the part that attempts to organize the experience. The organizational structure will form the experience even before supervision begins. Every organization is maintained by a certain set of structural guidelines within which supervision must occur. Therefore, we will look at those systems and how the two major settings for supervision, universities and the field, require different administrative expertise of the clinical supervisor. But first we will consider the differences when one system is involved in clinical supervision versus when two systems are involved.

## TRAINING SYSTEMS

### One System

Although graduate training usually requires that the trainee work within at least two different systems, an increasing amount of supervision occurs within one system. Many agencies

(used generically to include schools, hospitals, pastoral settings, etc.) incorporate ongoing supervision by clinical supervisors for postgraduate or new employees. Similarly, some training institutions run counseling centers or other training clinics on campus so that students receive clinical supervision and didactic education within more or less the same system. Universities often prefer such a setup for the very reason that we will discuss in this chapter: It is much easier to negotiate one system than it is to react to two. The loss for the student, however, is that the difficult, but necessary, lesson of negotiating agency goals and methods for attaining these goals is not experienced while in training.

Even when supervision is being conducted within one agency or exclusively within the educational facility, administrative ability is paramount. As we shall see, however, the complexity of the task grows algebraically when more than one system is involved.

## Two Systems: University and Field Sites

Often there are two systems involved in the training of an individual trainee. This, of course, is by design. Departments of social work and psychiatry were perhaps the first to realize the importance of field instruction to supplement academic instruction. Counseling, psychology, and marriage and family therapy, as well as a host of others, also require the student to successfully complete a supervised field experience while still in a degree program. But there would be no reason for this field experience to occur within the degree program if the campus supervisor did not intend both to influence the experience and receive feedback from the site supervisor to be used in some sort of summative evaluation of the trainee. The site supervisor typically accepts the trainee because the supervisor enjoys influencing trainees regarding real client issues and agency circumstances (Holloway & Roehlke, 1987). Often the site supervisor also would like to influence the training program in terms of the preparation offered to trainees prior to field experience. Therefore, both systems have an investment in one another that is both practical and educational. Yet the differences between these two systems and their separate goals often are not acknowledged in a way that allows the principals to work them through. Additionally, adequate communication between the two systems is often wanting (Holtzman & Raskin, 1988; Shapiro, 1988; Skolnik, 1988). We will address goals and communication separately.

***Goals.*** Dodds (1986) delineated the major difference between the training institution and the service delivery agency as a difference in population to be served. As depicted in Figure 9.1, the training institution is invested in the education and training of its students, whereas the mental health agency is primarily invested in the delivery of quantity and quality services to a target population. Dodds warned, however, that to stereotype each system by these goals is to lose sight of each unit's investment in the other's mission. That notwithstanding, the basic goals of each system will determine the motives of that system's primary supervisor and the supervisor's administrative goals. As Figure 9.1 illustrates, the persons who have the responsibility of interfacing these two systems are the university and site supervisors

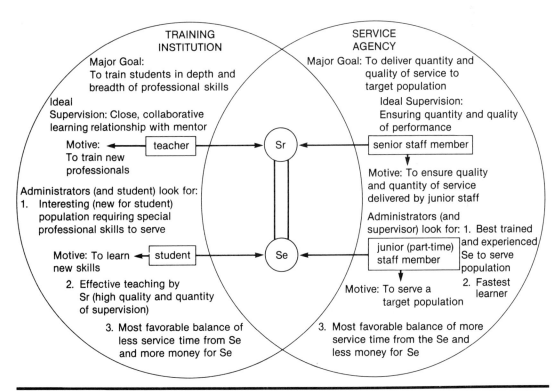

**FIGURE 9.1**   The overlapping systems of a training institution and a service agency (Sr, supervisor: Se, supervisee)*

*From Dodds, J. B. (1986). Supervision of psychology trainees in field placements. *Professional Psychology: Research and Practice, 17*(4), 296–300. Copyright © (1986) by the American Psychological Association. Reprinted by permission.

involved. But if they default on this responsibility due to time constraints, disinterest, or the absence of administrative effort, it is left to the supervisee to interface the two systems. When difficulties emerge, this leaves the least powerful individual (organizationally) to negotiate and attempt to find a resolution.

As an example of one of the many differences that grow out of each system's goals, Dodds (1986) noted the "common source of stress [that] arises when the student participates simultaneously in two institutions with differing time rhythms" (p. 299). For instance, the trainee must perform the role of junior staff member on the agency's timetable, turning in reports and so on, regardless of whether the training institution is on semester break. Furthermore, the regularity of demand at the site will not be sensitive when pressure increases from the training institution, such as during midterm or final exams.

The first step in mastering the interface between the two systems is in understanding that there will be complications whenever two systems are simultaneously involved with a trainee because of each unit's systemic properties, including their different goals. Once that fact is accepted, supervisors can begin to predict issues that may arise. A primary strategy for reducing problems either within each system or, especially, between them is to increase the quantity and quality of communication.

*Communication.* The university supervisor is often quite clear about what kinds of communication are expected from the site supervisor; however, a reciprocity of information often is lacking. Shapiro (1988) reported a high burnout rate for site supervisors when there was a significant discrepancy between what was initially communicated to them regarding expectations and the actual demands of supervision, which superseded those expectations. Another error both sides make is to keep information too limited in its focus. For example, there can be ample information

about the placement expectations from both sides. But university programs do not keep their field site current with program growth or curriculum changes (Malouf, 1983), and agencies do not let university programs know when administrative, fiscal, or programmatic changes are being planned or implemented. The result of such incomplete communication can be conflict where it could have been avoided or two systems growing less and less relevant to each other without being aware of it. We will consider the types of communications that are desirable between university and site later in this chapter.

## THE ESSENTIAL INGREDIENT: A SUPERVISION PLAN

Before we focus on the specific administrative duties of the supervisor, it is important that we give our attention to the primary administrative task of all clinical supervisors — arriving at a cohesive supervision plan. One of the greatest misconceptions of those not in administrative positions is that administration is made up of filling out forms and making on-the-spot decisions. Power and paperwork come to be identified with the administrative function of any organization. On the contrary, the essential ingredients of administrative competence are planning and foresight. Beyond these is the discipline to implement the plan in a methodical fashion, which, admittedly, often includes the creation of some paperwork. It is interesting to note, however, that Eisikovits et al. (1986) found that highly competent supervisors did not attempt to control supervisees through unusual demands for written accountability. Rather, it can be assumed that competency includes the skills of efficiency and preciseness and that this is passed on through one's expectations of others.

The primary responsibility of the clinical supervisor is to plan a training experience that will culminate in the emergence of a competent and realistic practitioner while it safeguards client welfare. This goal will be frustrated if supervision is random or repetitious throughout the trainee's program or internship. The antithesis of planning is when a supervisor accepts a trainee, sets weekly appointments with the trainee, and lets things just happen; or it is when a university instructor places students in field sites and then conducts weekly group supervision sessions that are based on self-report and little else. In both of these instances, there is no evidence of awareness of trainees' developmental needs or of the desirability of some variety of learning modes. This is supervision as you go, not planned supervision.

Leddick and Dye (1987) reported that trainees often equate supervisor effectiveness with a comprehensive supervisory plan. "Trainees expect to learn from a variety of modalities including didactic presentations, feedback and evaluation, individual and group supervision, observing the supervisor as therapist, group discussion of cases and issues and peer observation" (p. 149). This sentiment is echoed by a growing number of training programs as they experiment with different methods of supervision. For example, Liddle et al. (1985) discussed a multimodal approach to training supervisors that included live supervision of supervision, a seminar to examine supervision issues, and individual meetings between the trainer and supervisor in training to discuss developmental concerns.

One example of a supervision plan is that institutionalized by the APA through the criteria it imposes in its accrediting of internship sites. Doctoral students in psychology who take an APA-accredited internship can be assured they will have certain types of opportunities and learning experiences, which include direct service, group work, in-service training, and consultation experience. In addition, the form and amount of supervision is also determined by APA. A highly advantageous aspect of the APA plan is that it is not program specific. In other words, an APA-accredited internship has meaning nationally rather than regionally.

In short, a supervision plan begins by having a vision of what the well-trained practitioner should look like and an appreciation for the types of experiences that are most likely to produce this practitioner. From there, the clinical supervisor must create a training context within which learning can occur. This context must be ideological and structural. It is our impression that clinical supervisors to date have been much stronger in the former than the latter. Supervision was first appreciated as a conceptualizing activity. With the emergence of a variety of training models and techniques, a more active supervisor has emerged. Although more active, a more organized supervisor has not necessarily emerged.

The remainder of this chapter will outline some of the issues that can detract from the central role of supervision if they are not addressed adequately. In and of itself, well-organized supervision is not necessarily good supervision. But if clinical supervisors have addressed the categories listed that follow, they can have some confidence that supervisory efforts will not be undermined by a crumbling structural base.

## THE UNIVERSITY SUPERVISOR

Our focus in this section will be those tasks specific to the university supervisor as overseer of trainees in field placements. We do not address those aspects of clinical supervision that occur on campus in prepracticum or other training contexts. Nor do we address the role of the university supervisor when the university *is* the site. These responsibilities will be covered in the later section on the site supervisor. Because our discussion will pertain only to local field placements, we will not be examining the concerns when students (usually doctoral students) relocate to complete an internship. Finally, we remind the reader that only the administrative aspect of clinical supervision will be covered here. Therefore, we will not be addressing the clinical supervision that may be offered on campus while a trainee is out in the field.

## Preparing Students

Unless a training program has the luxury of a full-time (or even part-time) director of training or field placement coordinator, the first problem to hit university supervisors is coordinating an advising system that will determine when students will be eligible and available to take either a practicum or internship and determine if there are ample supervisory resources to cover the number of requests in any given semester. All too often, especially in large departments, students discuss such matters with their academic advisors, but no system is in place to get this information to the practicum or internship instructor. Sometimes this is no problem, but often it creates an atmosphere of rushed placements or compromises in placement. When matters are rushed, the field supervisor may think that the university program is slightly out of control and may feel less accountable to the university and the student as a result. At the very least, both the student and the campus supervisor begin the experience with nerves jangled and matters slightly off center when the practicum or internship does not enjoy some organizational planning prior to their beginning.

A solution to this dilemma is rather simple if the following procedure is followed. Some sort of registration form is required before a student is admitted to the field experience. The program faculty can decide how much notice each student should give prior to beginning a field experience (usually one semester or one-half semester). The forms should be held by one faculty member, who is typically a primary instructor of the practicum or internship. Any other faculty who will serve as instructors can check the file to determine which students are planning on a practicum or internship for a specific semester. The faculty

member in charge of the file will alert the program director if additional faculty will be needed at a certain time because the demand is high.

A second issue is how much lead time a student should allow in finding an appropriate field placement. This will be determined by the following:

1. *The amount of local competition for field sites.* If there are other universities nearby, or other programs within the university are seeking the same sites, the student must start out earlier than if the market is wide open.
2. *The specificity of the students interests.* If the student has a very specific interest not represented in a variety of sites (e.g., hospice work), then more lead time will be required.
3. *The policy of the specific agency.* Some agencies will only accept interns during a certain time period or may require a resume and more than one interview, all of which are time consuming. To be assured enough time to find a site, the student should assume that there will be some hurdles to negotiate in the selection process.
4. *The relationship established between the university and a particular site.* Some sites not only want, but expect, students every semester. Because of their past dealings with the university, they require only minimal contact with the student prior to starting the field experience.

With the above factors in mind, each campus supervisor will want to determine when an initial meeting with the student should be held to discuss practicum and internship. Once a plan is established, it should be carried out consistently.

## Selecting Sites

In some academic programs it is the training director or the faculty supervisor who makes the initial contact with a potential field site. In other programs it is the student who makes the first contact. In either case the faculty supervisor must assume a role in helping the student determine the appropriateness of a particular site based on three categories of variables: program factors, student factors, and agency factors.

Program factors are those baseline conditions that must be met before a site can be approved as meeting training goals. For example, the program may require that students not only see a variety of clients but also have continuity in their work. Therefore, a crisis center that revolves around singular client contacts would not be an appropriate placement. Or the program may require that audiotaping be allowed for the purposes of campus supervision. This may be a nonnegotiable item for some sites, and one that eliminates them.

Student factors can be introduced either by the student or determined by the supervisor. It has been suggested elsewhere (Brownstein, 1981; Wilson, 1981) that comprehensive surveys of the student be undertaken to determine the appropriateness of a particular site. Certainly the student's career goals must be the most important variable in finding an appropriate site. Many other conditions can be survived if the site will increase the student's chances of pursuing a desired career path. Other student characteristics include whether the student is a self-starter or someone who needs a structured atmosphere, whether the student has the background or interest to work with a variety of ethnic or economic groups, and whether the student prefers urban or rural settings (Brownstein, 1981). The student's schedule may also be a limiting factor. If the student is working in addition to attending graduate school, the site might have to be one that serves clients in the evening or on weekends. All such variables must be considered before selecting one or two sites that may be appropriate.

Agency factors are the third consideration and include the atmosphere of the work envi-

ronment (Stoltenberg & Delworth, 1987), the interest of the agency to work with students, the variety of opportunities within the agency, and the theoretical orientation of the supervisor, to name a few. The agency factors may or may not be known by the campus supervisor or the student if the site has not been used before. Therefore, the student should be assisted in determining a list of things to look for when making contact with the site.

Raskin (1985) surveyed twelve accredited social work programs to determine the importance of different variables in choosing placement sites. Although Raskin supported Wilson (1982) in her belief that student needs should be primary in the selection process, Raskin found that this was not the case, as can be seen in Table 9.1. In fact, when all factors were ranked, student concerns rated lowest in their impact on the placement decision, while school factors and environmental factors rated highest. This could be construed as the reality of the situation in which many students compete for a few good placements, and this, of course, is true in many geographical locations. It is disheartening, however, to note that the educational needs of the student rated 13 of 15 in importance when university field directors were seeking sites for their students. It would seem that this represents some breakdown of program goals. The solution might be a process that is more methodical in taking student factors into account as field placements are considered.

Hamilton and Else (1983) outlined 18 dimensions, shown in Table 9.2, that might be considered in making decisions regarding the appropriateness of a field placement site. It is doubtful that many sites will be optimal on all 18 dimensions, but such an outline could serve to raise students' awareness of which items are most important to them.

## Communication With the Site

It is up to the university supervisor to communicate the program's expectations to the site

**TABLE 9.1**   Fifteen Variables Ranked as Most Important by Field Directors*

| Factor | Variable | Rank Within Factor | Mean† | Rank All Variables |
|---|---|---|---|---|
| School | Quality of agencies and field instructors available | 1 | 1.75 | (3) |
| | Availability of agencies | 2 | 2.33 | (5) |
| | Availability of supervision | 3 | 2.68 | (6) |
| Field | Interest in supervising | 1 | 1.47 | (1) |
| Instructor | Previous supervision | 2 | 3.60 | (9) |
| | Degree | 3 | 4.90 | (12) |
| Environmental | Professional support system | 1 | 1.58 | (2) |
| | Number of agencies available | 2 | 2.08 | (4) |
| | Supplemental opportunity | 3 | 3.00 | (7) |
| Agency | Provides social work supervision | 1 | 3.41 | (10) |
| | Type of experience agency provides | 2 | 4.33 | (8) |
| | Educational commitment | 3 | 6.00 | (14) |
| Student | Placement preference | 1 | 4.70 | (11) |
| | Education needs | 2 | 5.70 | (13) |
| | Transportation | 3 | 6.60 | (15) |

*From Raskin, M. S. (1985). Field placement decision: Art, science or guesswork? *The Clinical Supervisor, 3*(3), 55–67. Copyright (1985) by The Haworth Press, Inc., 10 Alice Street, New York, NY. Reprinted by permission.

†Based on responses from a 7 point Likert scale ranging from Always (1) taken into consideration as a placement variable to Never (7) taken into consideration as a placement variable.

**TABLE 9.2**   Eighteen Dimensions to Aid in Choosing Appropriate Social Work Field Placements*

Learning Opportunities
1. Administrative Structure and Location
   a. agency
   b. teaching
   c. service
   d. campus
2. Field of Practice of Social Problem Area
   a. one field of practice/social problem area
   b. multiple fields of practice/social problem areas
3. Theoretical Orientation of the Agency
   a. one theoretical perspective
   b. two or more theoretical perspectives
4. Methods of Practice
   a. one practice method
   b. one primary, other secondary methods of practice
   c. multiple practice methods with relatively equal emphasis (generalist orientation)

**TABLE 9.2**   Eighteen Dimensions to Aid in Choosing Appropriate Social Work Field Placements* (*cont.*)

5. Interdisciplinary Potential
   a. social workers only
   b. limited interdisciplinary exchange
   c. extensive interdisciplinary teamwork
6. Primary Service Area
   a. rural
   b. small city
   c. metropolitan area: inner city
   d. metropolitan area: suburban
7. Diversity of Population Served
   a. service assignments exclusively or primarily with people of one group, e.g., age, class, race, sex, religion
   b. service assignments with people of diverse groups
8. Breadth of Service Assignments
   a. one unit of one agency
   b. several service/program units of one agency

**TABLE 9.2** Eighteen Dimensions to Aid in Choosing Appropriate Social Work Field Placements* (*cont.*)

c. primary assignment in one agency with supplementary assignments in other agencies

9. Potential for Student Innovation
   a. work only with existing client groups using existing service approaches
   b. develop alternative service approaches and/or extend services to new constituencies

Field Instruction†

10. Sources of Field Instruction
    a. single (exclusive) field instructor
    b. primary instructor plus secondary (supplementary) instructors
    c. multiple instructors

11. Number of Students Jointly in Placement
    a. one
    b. two to five
    c. teaching unit of six to twelve students

12. Teaching Format
    a. individual conferences
    b. group sessions
    c. both individual and group

13. Teaching Methods
    a. direct (during service) instruction (supervision) only
    b. post service instruction only
    c. both direct and post service instruction

Field Instructor

14. Theoretical Orientation of Field Instructor
    a. one theoretical perspective
    b. one primary theoretical perspective with understandings and techniques from other perspectives integrated into practice
    c. several theoretical perspectives

15. Education and Experience as Practitioner
    a. BA in social work with limited or extensive specialized training, professional experience, professional standing
    b. MSW plus limited or extensive specialized training, professional experience, professional standing
    c. degree in another discipline plus social work experience or orientation with limited or extensive specialized training, professional experience, professional standing

**TABLE 9.2** Eighteen Dimensions to Aid in Choosing Appropriate Social Work Field Placements* (*cont.*)

16. Education and Experience as Field Instructor
    a. no formal education in field instruction and limited experience as an instructor
    b. no formal education in field instruction and extensive experience as an instructor
    c. formal seminar in field instruction and limited experience
    d. formal seminar in field instruction and expensive experience

17. Field Instructor's Employer
    a. agency
    b. educational institution

18. Time Committed to Field Instruction
    a. full-time
    b. part-time

---

*From Hamilton, N., & Else, J. F. (1983). *Designing field education: Philosophy, structure and process.* Courtesy of Charles C. Thomas, Publisher, Springfield, Illinois.

†The word *supervisor* can be substituted for *instruction* wherever it appears.

supervisor, not up to the student. Under the best of circumstances, this is done both in writing and in person. Personal contact allows the university supervisor to determine whether there is any resistance to meeting the program's requirements. It has been our experience that student trainees are typically not good judges of a site when the site is ambivalent about meeting program requirements. Perhaps they are too eager to find an appropriate site to be discriminating. Even when they do discern ambivalence, they are in a vulnerable position regarding the site and are uncertain about asserting themselves with potential site supervisors. Clearly this is something the university supervisor can and should do.

Once a site has been chosen, it is important that the campus supervisor stay in touch with the site supervisor. A phone call a couple of weeks after the student has been placed is a good idea to be sure that things are going reasonably well. Additionally, there should be a plan for formal contacts in order to evaluate the student's progress. These can be done in person at the site or through written evaluations from the site. The site supervisor should know, however, when these will occur and what form they will take.

Leonardelli and Gratz (1985) addressed another important occasion for communication between campus and site, and that is when there is some conflict between the student and the site. Although it is important for students to have experience in resolving conflicts, the power differential between them and their site supervisors may make this difficult in some cases. In such instances the campus supervisor has a legitimate role to play. Leonardelli and Gratz outlined three sources of conflict for which it is appropriate for the campus supervisor to become involved:

1. *Inconsistency in performance expectations.* An example of this type of conflict is when the student understood that he or she would be spending the majority of time at the site in direct service and finds instead that the site supervisor expects a sizable amount of time to be spent in meetings, outreach activities, written work, etc.
2. *Incompatibility between expectations and reality of the facility.* Recently, one of our students experienced this kind of conflict. She was placed in a community center that offered a program for high-risk children. She was advised that she would be working with the parents while the children were in group therapy. Parent involvement, however, was very low, and the student spent the majority of her time assisting in play therapy, not one of her career goals. In a review of unsuccessful field placements, Holtzman and Raskin (1988) found that a major contributing factor to placement failure was "limited exploration and monitoring by the school of the learning opportunities in different

agencies" (p. 131). Obviously, the faculty supervisor cannot be held accountable if an agency misrepresents itself, but it is probably more common that the faculty's investigation prior to the placement of the student is incomplete.

3. *Inconsistency between expectations of the educational facility and the field site.* A prime example of this would be when the educational facility expected that clinical supervision would occur primarily on the site, but the site expected the reverse.

Leonardelli and Gratz suggested the use of a social systems model, based on the work of Getzels and Guba (1957), to negotiate these and similar sources of conflict. As can be seen in Figure 9.2, the university supervisor would take on the role of coordinator and collaborator between the site and the individual. The site encompasses the nomothetic, or normative, dimension, representing roles and expectations within the site; the individual represents the ideographic, or personal, dimension, including the personality and needs of the student. The observed behavior "that results as an interaction of these two dimensions is the attempt of the individual to cope with the expectation of the institution and its roles in ways consistent with that person's own needs" (Leonardelli & Gratz, p. 18). In conflict situations, therefore, the campus supervisor would attempt to mediate and find the best compromise between the nomothetic and ideographic dimensions, with either dimension potentially being asked to adjust to the other.

The final types of communication that should occur between campus and site are informational and educational. When sites have become regular placements for students from a particular program, there should be an effort to keep the site abreast of changes within the program and even with the everyday workings of the program. Meetings on campus for site supervisors can be planned for this purpose, or gestures as simple as sending copies of the

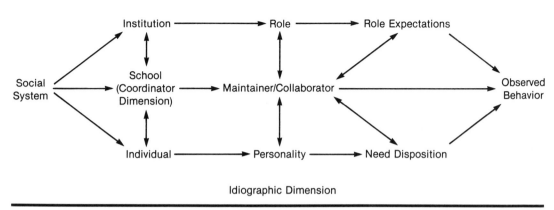

Nomothetic Dimension

FIGURE 9.2   Modification of social behavior model with addition of coordinator dimension*

*From Leonardelli, C. A., & Gratz, R. R. (1985). Roles and responsibilities in fieldwork experience: A social systems approach. *The Clinical Supervisor*, 3(3), 15–24. Copyright © (1985) by The Haworth Press, Inc., 10 Alice Street, New York, NY. Reprinted by permission.

minutes of program staff meetings could accomplish this goal. This type of communication not only aids students but also enhances the overall relationship between the program and field sites.

Finally, training programs should attempt to communicate new developments in the area of supervision to their site supervisors. Although site supervisors have a wealth of practical knowledge, traditionally they have not stayed as current as university supervisors in terms of the research on supervision, new models and techniques, and supervision literature in general. Therefore, in-service training for site supervisors or seminars in which both campus and site supervisors share their ideas and experiences comprise a special kind of communication activity (Beck, Yager, Williams, Williams, & Morris, 1989; Brown & Otto, 1986).

### Contracts

Supervision contracts are often drawn up between supervisors and trainees (Munson,

1983). Yet, as Munson pointed out, it is very difficult for the trainee to demand that the agency keep its end of the bargain. The contract, in that case, becomes a job description for the trainee and little more. This leads us to the conclusion that the only realistic use of contracts is between the training program and the field placement. Such a contract should include:

1. The activities that the trainee will be performing
2. The responsibilities of the site supervisor
3. The responsibilities of the university supervisor
4. The expectations of the site supervisor for the trainee
5. The expectations of the university supervisor for the trainee
6. Goals of the trainee above and beyond each supervisor's expectations
7. An outline of the evaluation plan

Although these contracts are mostly gentlepersons' agreements, they raise everyone's consciousness about what is to transpire and how things are to evolve. Furthermore, they can decrease the amount of discomfort when confrontation is justified because one party is not living up to the contract.

## Quality Control

In terms of meeting program expectations, it is only reasonable that the university supervisor, as the invested party, monitor quality control (Rosenblum & Raphael, 1987; York, 1985). This is done throughout the field experience by means of personal contact with the site, careful reading of student documentation of site activities, and individual or group supervision on campus during which sites are discussed.

A special kind of quality control issue is assuring that standards that are tied to accreditation, certification, or licensure are met. Among the items that might need to be monitored are the credentials of the site supervisor, the type of supervision conducted (individual or group), the amount of supervision offered, the ratio between service delivery hours and supervision, and the ratio between service delivery and other related professional activities. While a trainee is enrolled in an academic training program, it is the responsibility of the university supervisor to know that standards are being met or to reject a field placement if it is not able to meet standards.

## Evaluation

Finally, it is the prerogative and the responsibility of the university supervisor to develop an evaluation plan and to conduct all summative evaluations. As Rosenblum and Raphael (1987) noted, site supervisors dread evaluating university students. When the supervisor's experience has been positive, the evaluation tends to be glowing; when the trainee has not met expectations, the evaluation is sometimes avoided. It is our belief that site supervisors, because their relationships with trainees are

short term and because their relationships with the universities are rarely mandated, should not be asked to carry out discriminating summative evaluations. For example, the site supervisor should not be asked to grade the student except to give a pass or fail recommendation. On the other hand, it is important for site supervisors to give feedback, both to the trainee and to the university supervisor. But the task of translating feedback into a final grade is clearly the charge of the program faculty. (Evaluation procedures were delineated in Chapter 7.)

## THE FIELD SITE SUPERVISOR

Although it is clear that the campus supervisor does not relinquish all responsibility to the site supervisor during a practicum or internship, there are some administrative tasks that can only be accomplished by the site supervisor. These will be the focus of this section.

## The Interview

It is the goal of the university supervisor to place all students; it is the goal of the site supervisor to make a judgment about the individual student's fit with the goals and work of the agency. Although background information is sometimes requested, the basis for the decision is usually the placement interview. It is essential that the site supervisor has a grasp of the attributes that are necessary for the student to take full advantage of the placement. It is equally essential that the supervisor is able to perceive what a time-limited experience in the agency will be like and communicate this realistically to the candidate.

Trainees should receive feedback about these interviews whether or not a site accepts them. Hearing the supervisor's perception of why one was seen as appropriate is a good beginning for a working relationship with the site supervisor. When the trainee is not accepted, it is important to know if the decision was made based on a negative evaluation of the student's competence or because of a perceived lack of fit. If the feedback is not given directly to the student, it should at least be given to the campus supervisor.

The interview may serve as a metaphor for the agency. In other words, if the agency is unstructured and requires a great deal of creativity from the staff, the interview should mirror this situation. If, on the other hand, the agency is highly structured with clear guidelines for each staff member's role, the interview should be handled similarly. This type of consistency serve two purposes: It becomes a first-level orientation for the student to the agency and its expectations; it allows the site supervisor the opportunity to gain relevant data about the student on which to base a decision.

## Orientation

Because of the relatively short duration of both practicum and internship situations, the trainee must be oriented to the organization and service delivery issues as efficiently as possible. There are some lessons that only a learn as you go approach can accomplish. But many more things can be learned through an orientation. Unfortunately, many trainees believe they are just getting a handle on procedures and policy issues when they  rap up their field experience. At least some of this can be attributed to an inadequate orientation process.

If an agency accepts trainees on a regular basis, the site supervisor would be wise to develop a trainee manual covering the major agency policies that must be mastered. (A good resource for such a manual is the trainees who are at the end of their field experience; they can usually be quite precise about what information would have made their adaptation easier.) If written orientation materials are not available, the site supervisor might schedule more intensive supervision the first week or so to cover orientation matters with

the trainee. The supervisor would be wise to use simulations of situations and ask the trainee to provide the correct procedure to be followed in order to determine if the policies are clear.

Malouf et al. (1983) devised a questionnaire to reflect information they considered important to cover in orientation to APA-approved internships. Their questionnaire includes items about policies, fees, referrals, procedures, supervision, case management, and ethical and legal matters. As the following three questions extracted from the Malouf et al. questionnaire demonstrate, orientation should cover not only nuts and bolts issues but also dilemmas that are more subtle. (We have retained their item numbers.)

> 5. *What do you need to do when seeing a client for the first time? What information do you need to obtain? What paperwork do you need to do, etc.?*
> 10. *What do you do if you think one of your clients may need to be hospitalized?*
> 16. *With whom can you ethically discuss your clients? Can you use your clients at the agency as examples in university classes, either identified by name or anonymously? (p. 626)*

## Reducing Burnout

As we stated earlier, a good administrative structure can help in reducing burnout among supervisees. The site supervisor has considerable control over the atmosphere within which the trainee (and all supervisees) work. The trainee is not likely to refer to an initial experience as one of burnout, but trainees often have referred to being overwhelmed and too busy to be able to integrate the experience (Kaslow & Rice, 1985). Stoltenberg and Delworth (1987) suggested that supervisors attempt to mold the setting to the developmental needs of the trainee, including determining numbers of direct service hours, amount of supervision, and contact between the training program and the site. In other words, there should be a sense of being weaned from the training program while being oriented into a professional setting. Too quick an emersion may be counterproductive for the trainee.

One advantage of when a site supervisor attempts to control the environment for the benefit of trainees is that the necessity of a similar strategy for *all* employees becomes evident. Counselors, social workers, and therapists need time to regroup and consult if they are to remain vital in their direct service responsibilities. Structuring time so that supervisees have variety and the opportunity for collegial support in their day will raise not only the quality of the work environment but also the quality of service delivery (Falvey, 1987). Protecting supervisees from overload communicates a respect for the practitioner and respect also for the work that needs to be done, work that should be done by persons who can perform at their optimum level.

### Communication

Just as it is critical for the university supervisor to keep the site supervisor abreast of program developments, it is equally important for the site supervisor to keep the university current. Political, organizational, and fiscal developments may affect trainees both in their field experiences and in their employment search. When campus supervisors are kept current about what is going on in their sites, they are better able to advise students about the professions they are entering.

An invaluable contribution site supervisors can make to training programs is to communicate their opinion of the training the student has received prior to their field placement. Once a site supervisor has overseen several trainees from the same program, the supervisor is in a position to see thematic strengths and weaknesses. In order to do this, however, site supervisors must have a structure

that allows them to view the trainee in a variety of ways so that this type of appraisal can be accomplished in a valid manner.

Finally, the site supervisor must organize communication within the agency to benefit the trainee. It happens occasionally that a trainee has contact only with the supervisor and feels isolated from the rest of the agency. In some instances, trainees are made to feel disloyal if they happen to ask some advice from an employee other than their supervisors. This always leads to a negative outcome. The supervisor should have a plan as to how the trainee will be integrated into the agency, including attendance at staff meetings and joint projects with other staff members.

### Supervisor as Agency Representative

One function that the site supervisor is less likely to acknowledge as an administrative task is to serve as a liaison between supervisees and agency administration. (Even if the supervisor wears two hats, when in the role of clinical supervisor, the supervisor must communicate administrative issues to supervisees.) This function is often carried out in an informal manner, sharing bits and pieces of both spoken and unspoken rules, agency politics, etc. When done in an informal fashion, however, the trainee is more likely to get incomplete information and/or become triangulated in organizational power struggles. It is far better for the interface between service delivery and organizational realities to be covered in supervision in a deliberate way. Perhaps part of each supervision session could be reserved for organizational issues, not as a gripe session but as a learning process. Munson (1983) stated that interns may avoid certain interventions because they perceive them as being contrary to organizational policy. Whether or not the trainee is correct, this is an important area of discussion for the trainee and supervisor.

It is far more likely, however, that trainees

will be naive about organizations (Munson, 1983). Every person who has worked in an organization knows that there are unspoken rules that must be understood in order to succeed in the environment. Some of these must be learned through experience. But how the ecology of an agency affects each branch of its operation is something that can be addressed during the field experience. Furthermore, if supervisors are thinking in ecological terms, they are less likely to be totally reflexive in supervision. In other words, if the supervisor is not pulling back to see the larger picture, supervision can become a mindless arm of administrative whim. When this occurs, everyone is frustrated; but aside from some finger pointing, no one has a good handle on what is going on and how one can extricate oneself from the situation. Therefore, structuring systemic lessons into supervision will help supervisors carry out their clinical supervisory functions in a more thoughtful manner. In summary, the trainee should leave the field experience with some systemic understanding of the site and how this affected the trainee's particular role in that site.

Another liaison function of the site supervisor is to structure some way that other agency personnel can give input about the performance of the trainee. Again, it is too common for this to occur informally and, therefore, inconsistently. The site supervisor can devise a short form and ask colleagues to complete it once or twice during the field placement. This kind of overture can have several positive effects.

1. It lessens the trainee's isolation by involving additional personnel in the trainee's experience.
2. It can provide the trainee with additional feedback from different perspectives or role positions.
3. It can confirm or confront the supervisor's own evaluation of the trainee.

## TASKS COMMON TO ALL SUPERVISORS

Thus far, we have discriminated between administrative tasks relevant to the university supervisor and those relevant to the site supervisor. As the reader might have assumed, however, there are several tasks common to all clinical supervisors and we will consider these now.

### Time Management

Supervisors are busy people. Whether at the university or in the human service agency, there are many obligations that compete with supervision. Because supervision is an enjoyable role for many professionals, they often take it on even when they really have no extra time. Time management, therefore, becomes a crucial skill; one that needs to be exercised and modeled for trainees who themselves are juggling several roles. Falvey (1987) listed several simple time-management strategies for administrative supervisors that include coordinating activities to maximize one's productivity (e.g., tackling difficult tasks when one's energy is high), avoiding escapists behaviors (e.g., doing an unpleasant task first thing in the morning rather than allowing it to bear on one's mind all day), and dividing difficult tasks so that they do not appear overwhelming.

Perhaps the most central time-management skill is the ability to set priorities and keep to them. It is virtually impossible to end one's work day with absolutely no work left over for the following day. Rather, supervisors who can manage time have addressed the most important concerns immediately and have learned to pace themselves in accomplishing less pressing tasks. For some supervisors, it is a seemingly natural ability to take control of one's schedule; for others, it is a constant struggle that can be supplemented by, for example, time management self-help books. Regardless of how the supervisor accomplishes the goal of finding and protecting time for supervision, the supervisor must realize that making time must be a deliberate choice and is not something that will take care of itself.

Assuming that one has found the time to dedicate to supervision, the issue of timing emerges. When is it best to supervise? How often should trainees be monitored? Does it matter? We discussed the training issues imbedded in the timing of supervision in Chapter 4. Based on these, the supervisor should attempt to devise the most productive supervision schedule for the trainee.

## Form

Chapters 4, 5, and 6 outlined a variety of ways in which the process of supervision can be conducted. Deciding on the form that supervision will take and implementing the desired process can be an administrative task of significant proportion. For example, the supervisor might decide that using Interpersonal Process Recall (Kagan, 1976) would be desirable with a particular trainee because of difficulties the trainee is having with a client. Using the technique, however, will require that videotape equipment be made available and that arrangements are made for videotaping the next therapy session. It is understandable, although regrettable, that supervisors often default on their supervision plans because the form that supervision should take becomes administratively too complicated. If the supervisor is convinced that a particular process (e.g., IPR or live supervision) is essential for the trainee's learning, it is incumbent upon the supervisor to work out the administrative details. When supervisors continue to put aside their teaching instincts because of the time and care they require, the quality of supervision eventually deteriorates. Perhaps there is no administrative responsibility so essential to clinical supervision as the choreography required to ensure that the form of supervision matches the learning needs of supervisees.

## Record Keeping

In a litigious era the process of record keeping has gained in importance for helping professionals of all disciplines. Schutz (1982) identified record keeping as one of five areas in therapy management that relate to the risk of liability suits. Snider (1987) and Soisson, Vandecreek, and Knapp (1987) have taken the next step in suggesting that keeping good client records serve as a desirable defense against litigation.

Whether supervising from campus or on site, it is the supervisor's responsibility to be sure that client records are complete. Most agencies and university professors have established record-keeping procedures that have evolved over time. But with an ever changing professional and legal climate, the wise supervisor reviews the record-keeping system occasionally to be sure that it is current with national trends.

Schultz (1982) determined that an adequate client record contains:

1. Written and signed informed consents for all treatment
2. Written and signed informed consents for all transmissions of confidential information
3. Treatment contracts, if used
4. Notes on all treatment contacts made, either in person or by telephone, including descriptions of significant events
5. Notes on all contacts or consultation with significant others, including correspondence
6. A complete history and symptom picture leading to diagnosis, with regular review and revision of the diagnosis
7. A record of all prescriptions and a current drug use profile

8. A record of the therapist's reasons for diagnosis and direction of treatment
9. Any instructions, suggestions, or directives made to the client that he or she failed to follow through on

Beis (1984) suggested that a record of termination and an aftercare plan also be part of a record. We would add that, depending on the form of supervision used, there be signed informed consents for any taping or observation practices that occur. The trainee should also have a record of any consultations with other professionals about the case. Of course, a trainee will be discussing each case with the supervisor. If the supervisor seeks consultation, this should be part of the supervisor's records.

Most supervisors are far more careful about client records than about supervision records. Yet as the Tarasoff case pointed out (*Tarasoff v. Regents of the University of California,* 1974), supervision records can be equally important in a liability suit. On a more optimistic note, supervision records discipline supervisors to pause and consider the supervision with each trainee. As we have said to our trainees over and over, written records offer the writer moments of insight that would not otherwise occur. Therefore, for legal and instructional reasons, supervisors must keep accurate and complete supervision records.

Munson (1983) suggested that supervision records include the following:

1. The supervisory contract, if used or required by the agency.
2. A brief statement of supervisee experience, training, and learning needs.
3. A summary of all performance evaluations.
4. Notation of all supervisory sessions.
5. Cancelled or missed sessions.
6. Notation of cases discussed and significant decisions.
7. Significant problems encountered in the supervision and how they were resolved, or whether they remain unresolved and why (p. 184).

**Planning Ahead**

We have come full circle and end where we began, with a discussion about planning. The exemplary supervisor has a blueprint of what the well-trained practitioner looks like and how supervision can contribute to developing that picture in a systematic way. The best supervisors have planned ahead for situations that may or may not occur but which demand that a process be in place. It is frustrating, if not frightening, for a trainee to face an emergency with a client—for example, the need to hospitalize—and have no idea how the situation is to be handled. Emergency procedures should be in document form, given to the trainee during orientation, and placed in a convenient place for reference should an emergency occur.

Another time when planning ahead is crucial is when the supervisor will be away. For example, it is not unusual for all clinical supervisors in a training program to attend the same convention, leaving a university-based clinic either in the hands of doctoral students or fill-in supervisors. With the rush to prepare the paper that will be presented at the convention or the arrangements that must be made to cover one's classes, it often happens that a colleague from another department is asked to cover supervision with little or no information about the operations of the clinic, the status of any worrisome clients, or information about the student staff. This could easily be a case where the lack of administrative foresight takes on the characteristics of questionable ethical practice.

By planning ahead we do not mean to suggest that the supervisor compulsively worry about every possible way that things may go wrong. "The sky is falling" is not a productive supervisory posture. Rather, we urge supervisors to take reasonable care regarding their responsibilities and, especially, to give themselves the time to plan well and to put their plans into action.

### Working Toward Administrative Competence

Short of receiving training in management and/or administrative supervision, what can the clinical supervisor do to achieve administrative competence? This chapter has presented many of the goals that the clinical supervisor might set for him or herself. The following are five simple guidelines that can be of use as one sets out to achieve these goals.

*Get Support.* Before clinical supervisors commit themselves to the substantial task of supervising either on or off a university campus, they should be sure that they have administrative support for their activity. Beck et al. (1989) found that clinical supervision was compromised when the agency director did not support having trainees on site. This position was reiterated by Holloway and Roehlke (1987), regarding APA-accredited internship sites. Likewise, an academic program director must appreciate the time it takes to develop good field sites, to organize the operation of practicum and internship, and to serve as an ongoing liaison with sites. If, as Skolnik (1988) and others have suggested, the faculty supervisor also offers to train site supervisors, the responsibilities can begin to grow algebraically. The grater the support offered by superiors, the more that can be accomplished and the better the quality of the supervision. If support is limited, the clinical supervisor must decide if minimal standards can be met. If not, the supervisor must decline an offer to supervise on ethical grounds.

*Know Yourself.* As simple as it sounds, there seems to be a relatively high degree of unawareness among clinical supervisors about their ability to organize themselves and those in their charge. Perhaps supervisors assume that they should already have the skills of a competent administrator and, therefore, resist admitting that this is an area in which they need to grow. Perhaps the expectation that they already have all the skills they need to do the job comes from others around them, leaving them little room to be tentative. Regardless of the source, a cycle of assuming, followed by denying, can keep a clinical supervisor operating at a less than satisfactory level in the administrative responsibilities of the supervisor's position.

Organization comes far more naturally to some than to others. When supervisors believe that they fall in the latter category, they should find a member of their staff or a professional colleague who they believe can help develop a plan or, more likely, help implement a plan. The beginning of implementation is a critical point that calls for different abilities than those required for arriving at the original plan. This is the point at which many clinical supervisors could use assistance.

*Gather Data.* There is nothing particularly virtuous about reinventing the wheel. As supervisors approach the task of organizing a training program or the clinical operation of an agency, they might contact other training programs or agencies and ask for samples of policy statements, supervision forms, and other materials relevant to their tasks. When a specific issue arises, consulting with colleagues and determining how they have managed the issue is a sound strategy. Isolating oneself is a common supervisor flaw, both in terms of clinical work and administrative work. Supervisors have a tremendous amount to learn from each other, and they need to model for their trainees the ability to consult with others as part of good clinical practice.

The professional literature is another source for data collection. As we stated earlier, there is less about the administration of clinical supervision in the literature than there might be, but the careful reader will gather important information from the research on supervision and from others' investigations and descriptions of the process of supervision.

*Get Feedback.* Any new procedure should be considered a pilot study of sorts. An administrative strategy may work well from the supervisor's vantage point but be untenable for supervisees. The administratively competent supervisor knows how to manipulate procedures to work for people and the program, not the other way around. Part of this competence is demonstrated by seeking the opinions of others. The result is an administrative structure that is always being fine-tuned without continually starting over from scratch.

*Go Slow.* One way to avoid having to scrap one plan for another (and thereby keeping those under supervision in a state of turmoil) is for supervisors to give themselves permission to build the administrative plan slowly. No one who is supervising for the first time will be totally organized in the first year. Rather, one should begin with those aspects of supervision that are most critical for ethical and safe practice and eventually pay heed to items that add to convenience and expediency of communication, among other things. In addition to being practical, going slow encourages the supervisor to hone in immediately on those things that are absolutely essential to any supervisory operation. Discriminating between issues that are essential and those that are desirable is the beginning and the core of administrative competence.

# CHAPTER 10

# SUPERVISION ISSUES AND DILEMMAS

A consistent theme through most of what we have presented in this book is that supervision is a complex process, characterized by interplay among a wide array of variables. These certainly include such external factors as setting, client population served, and treatment modalities. They include also the epistemology, history, values, expectations, and personality that the supervisor and supervisee each bring to the relationship. The number of ways these and other variables can combine is virtually infinite. Consequently, each supervisory relationship is unique and follows its own course.

Even so, certain issues, problems, and dilemmas occur with almost predictable frequency across supervisory dyads. The purpose of this chapter is to consider several of these that we believe have particular importance for the supervisor. Discussed here are the effects on supervisees and supervisors of anxiety, supervisees' need for adequacy, supervisors' countertransference, supervisor-supervisee conflict, issues of interpersonal power, and harmful influences of supervision. Although the manner of presentation might give the impression, we do not intend to imply these issues and dilemmas are discrete or mutually exclusive. In fact, they often overlap with and influence one another.

## SUPERVISEE ANXIETY

Anxiety is natural in supervision. It is pervasive and affects both the supervisor and supervisee. But although supervisors experience anxiety, it is perhaps a more serious matter for the supervisee. It is the supervisee who is under continual scrutiny and evaluation, including self-evaluation. Also, the supervisee experiences anxiety on *two* fronts, in work with both the client and the supervisor. But on either of these fronts, the supervisor's actions—or lack thereof—can affect the level and type of the supervisee's anxiety.

Although anxiety is a fact of life for the supervisee, there is no simple or uniform way to characterize it. This is so because a supervisee's anxiety may arise from any of a number of sources and is moderated by such factors as the supervisee's maturity, experience level, personality, and relationships with clients and the supervisor.

Most discussions of the effects of anxiety on the supervisee have focused on its undesirable consequences. For example, Schauer, Seymour, and Geen (1985) briefly summarized selected empirical literature on the effects of anxiety on therapists. Among the negative effects they found documented were that anxiety activates speech productivity while disrupting its flow, reduces the accuracy of the therapist's perception of the client, decreases the therapist's recall of words and feelings expressed in a session, and elicits overelaboration or argumentative behavior from the therapist. Unfortunately, a focus on these and other negative consequences of anxiety could lead to the premature conclusion that trainees' anxiety is always to be avoided or minimized. In fact, Rioch (in Rioch et al., 1976) is among those who have observed that, within limits, the more anxiety counselors are able to allow themselves, the more they will learn.

In other words, then, anxiety is not always something to ward off. As counselors or therapists, we know that much of the time it is unhelpful to rush in to attempt to diminish a client's anxiety. The same rule pertains to supervisee anxiety. Likely there is a parallel here for supervisors' handling of their own anxiety as well.

Although we are aware of questions Neiss (1988) recently raised about it, the inverted-*U* hypothesis that Yerkes and Dodson (1908) advanced at the turn of the century remains a useful way to think of anxiety: It is an arousal state that, in moderate amounts, serves to motivate the individual and facilitate task performance. Performance suffers, however, when the individual experiences either *too little* and *too much* anxiety—too little, one lacks sufficient motivation to perform; too much, one is debilitated. It is not difficult, then, to extrapolate this general law of human learning to supervision and conclude that there is an optimal level of anxiety for trainees to experience.

This suggests that supervisors should have the simultaneous goals of helping to keep their supervisees from engaging in anxiety-avoidant behaviors *and* of helping to keep their anxiety in bounds so that it works in the service of performance. Kell and Burow (1970) noted, for example, that they work "not only to facilitate . . . an awareness of the anxiety associated with the seriousness of learning, but also to leaven and help control the anxious experience" (p. 184).

## Supervision Styles and Trainee Anxiety

But if leavening and controlling the supervisee's anxiety is a special responsibility of the supervisor, there are particular supervisory styles that have quite the opposite effect. Rosenblatt and Mayer (1975) identified from written narrative accounts by social work students four different kinds of supervisory behavior that the students found to be objectionable. The

three that they labeled *amorphous, unsupportive,* and *"therapeutic"* supervisions seemed in one way or another to serve to increase the supervisee's anxiety level. These types of supervision, therefore, merit consideration.

***Amorphous Supervision.*** In this style of supervision, supervisors offer too little clarity about what they expect. They also offer the supervisee too little structure and/or guidance.

Anxiety is a natural response for anyone in a new situation. So, too, with supervisees entering a new supervisory relationship. This anxiety generally will dissipate as supervisees orient to their new environment. It will be maintained, however, to the extent that supervisors fail to provide clear structure and expectations. This is the characteristic of amorphous supervision.

It is important to remember also that the experience level of supervisees will moderate the amount of structure they perceive themselves as needing. Beginning supervisees perceive themselves as needing more structure than those who are more advanced (e.g., Heppner & Roehlke, 1984; McNeill, Stoltenberg, & Pierce, 1985; Reising & Daniels, 1983; Stoltenberg, Pierce, and McNeill, 1987; Tracey, Ellickson, & Sherry, 1989; Wiley & Ray, 1986). But across all levels of trainee experience, a general rule to consider is that ambiguity in itself is a root cause of trainee anxiety. There are many ways in which the relationship between supervisor and supervisee can be ambiguous. But supervisors should be sensitive to some of the other possible sources of ambiguity in the training situation. Hollingsworth and Witten (1983) suggested, for example, that a source of anxiety for some supervisees centers on their uncertainty about the roles they are expected to fill in their field placements. Ambiguity about the criteria and procedures by which supervisees will be evaluated is yet another source of anxiety.

Because these last two types of ambiguity can be anticipated by supervisors, it is easy enough for them to take steps intended to reduce that ambiguity. For example, prior to their placements, trainees can be oriented to agency policies and role expectations. If the source of ambiguity should reside with some misunderstandings or lack of clear communication between the training institution and agency, dialogue between the two units should be initiated (see Chapter 9). As we discussed in Chapter 7, supervisors have an obligation to establish clearly the procedures and criteria of evaluation at the very outset of the supervision experience.

Some supervisors, such as those at the University of Missouri-Columbia's counseling center (Roehlke, personal communication, July 13, 1989), have adopted a role induction, or presupervision training procedure, as one means of minimizing trainee ambiguity and anxiety. As we discussed in Chapter 3, beginning trainees especially can profit from meeting as a group prior to the beginning of the supervision experience to discuss expectations (theirs, the supervisors', the training institution's, and the agency's), roles, and procedures.

***Unsupportive Supervision.***    This type of supervision is characterized by a supervisor who is cold, aloof, and perhaps even hostile. The following account by a respondent in the Rosenblatt and Mayer (1975) study is illustrative:

> *After the first couple of sessions [my supervisor] began to grow increasingly critical and unsupportive, and as a result I became more anxious and insecure . . . When we tried to talk about my clients, I would be so anxious that I couldn't think and would end up staring miserably at her, trying not to cry. My self-esteem hit rock bottom. I remember becoming almost sick with anxiety before a supervisory session because I was so sensitive to her criticism. (p. 186)*

It is true, as Blocher (1983) asserted, that it is not possible to make supervision "idiot proof or bastard resistant" (p. 30). We would like to believe, however, that the unsupportive supervision Rosenblatt and Mayer described is less likely to occur with supervisors who have received formal supervision training.

Kell, Morse, and Grater (undated) discussed the importance of providing support to supervisees, particularly new ones, as a means of keeping their anxiety from hindering their work.

> *What form this support takes will depend to a large degree on our diagnosis of the trainee. In the case of the person who doubts his [sic] abilities we lend support and reassurance relating to no small degree [sic] to the strengths of this individual. Perhaps we make mention of such a person's sensitivity and how valuable this can be to a therapist. We might suggest techniques we feel might better free him in this new interpersonal relationship. Perhaps above all, with every trainee we attempt to give a great deal of permission, perhaps even our expectation that he will make errors. We hope to reduce for them the threat of failure and the need to strive for success, allowing him to admit that he knows little and thus might learn a lot.*

***"Therapeutic" Supervision.***    In this form of supervision, shortcomings in the supervisee's work are attributed to some deficiencies in personality, which the supervisor then attempts to address in detail within supervision. Significantly, supervisees who were surveyed often did not object to the labeling of their work as somehow inappropriate. What they found objectionable was, first, the causal attribution given by the supervisor (i.e., that the supervisee's behavior was a function of some personal deficit) and, second, the supervisor's attempt then to remedy it in supervision. Liddle (1988) seems to have been speaking of this type of supervision when he alluded to those whose focus is that of a "deficit detective."

An example recounted by a student illustrates this style of supervision.

*My supervisor wanted to know why I didn't get into a discussion of sexual matters more rapidly with my clients in cases when it would be appropriate . . . My supervisor insisted that I held back because I did not want to reawaken memories of the loss of such activities due to my husband's recent death. Later on, whatever criticism she had of my work with clients, she managed to attribute to my personal circumstances. I did not object to her criticism of my performance, only to the reasons she gave for it. When I disagreed with her reasons, she said that I could not be objective — that I was being defensive. I still felt she was wrong, but how could I argue with her? (Rosenblatt & Mayer, 1975, p. 186)*

A second such example is provided in an anecdote Goin and Kline (1976) took from their study of supervisor-supervisee interactions.

*[The supervisee] was having difficulty understanding a case and saw the patient's dynamics differently than the supervisor did. The supervisor attributed these difficulties to the resident's psychological makeup, saying, "You keep responding to the patient as if he is anxious. What you don't hear is his anger. I realize you have a problem handling your own anger, so that must be interfering with your appreciation for what is going on." (p. 431)*

Rosenblatt and Mayer (1975) found that students who received this form of supervision were more distraught than those who received any of the other objectionable types of supervision they had identified. In part this may be because no matter how obviously wrong the supervisor's construction of the situation may seem to the supervisee, the supervisee may be left with the secret worry that the supervisor is right. To compound the matter, the problems being identified in this type of supervision typically are difficult to remedy; they also tend to be central to the supervisee's sense of personal adequacy.

Supervisees who attempt to challenge their supervisor's wrong attributions may find

themselves in something of a double-bind situation: Their objections may be construed as resistance, which itself then is confirming of the supervisor's belief about the supervisee. Remember, too, that one necessary condition for a double-bind is that the recipient cannot easily exit the relationship in which it is occurring (Sluzki, Beavin, Tarnopolski, & Vernon, 1967); this typically is a characteristic of supervision.

We conclude this section by speculating that the tendency to make such attributions is not limited to one particular type of supervisor. In fact, there are data to suggest that there may be reliable attributional differences between supervisors and supervisees. Dixon and Kruczek (1989), for example, found that trainees were more likely to explain their behaviors with clients in terms of external, situational variables, whereas supervisors were more likely to perceive those same behaviors as being more within the trainees' control and reflecting stable, dispositional aspects of the trainees. But regardless of supervisors' accuracy in these instances, they should remain sensitive to the likelihood that these attributions, when offered as the primary supervision intervention, will most assuredly heighten trainee anxiety — perhaps to a debilitating level.

## Supervisor Style and Trainee Anxiety: Further Data

More information on the relationship between supervisory styles and trainee anxiety was provided in a phenomenological study by Hutt, Scott, and King (1983). They concluded from their examination of the supervisory experiences of a small sample of counselor education, social work, and clinical psychology students that positive and negative supervision are not opposite ends of the same continuum. Rather, each has its own unique structure, its own balance of focus on the tasks of supervision and on the supervisory relationship itself.

All trainees approach supervision expecting to be judged and, therefore, are anxious. The experience of *positive* supervision, however, is such that the trainee's anxiety does not raise to such a level that the work of supervision is hindered. This occurs because the supervisor is able to be simultaneously supportive and encouraging—which seems to us to echo Blocher's (1983) argument that effective supervision demands an optimal balance between *support* (including structure) and *challenge*. This seems reflected also in the findings of Worthington and Roehlke (1979), whose factor analysis of supervisors' behaviors yielded two factors that they labeled *support* and *evaluation* (which certainly is a form of challenge).

In positive supervision, then, the supervisee is given permission to make mistakes and then not to experience them as failure. The supervisor is respectful of the supervisee, including the need for autonomy. The supervisor self-discloses to the supervisee, which, in turn, encourages appropriate self-disclosure from the supervisee. Evaluation of the supervisee occurs as a shared process between supervisor and supervisee.

Hutt et al. (1983) found that the most critical aspect of *negative* supervision is the supervisor-supervisee relationship itself. The total emotional tone is negative, and supervision is focused on the relationship, diverting attention and focus from the appropriate goals and tasks of supervision. That is, the supervisee comes to expect the supervisor to offer criticism but no support. This leads to the supervisee's feelings of vulnerability and threat. As a self-protective stance, the supervisee then carefully censors what is told the supervisor and manages anxiety through various forms of resistance.

The supervisor, in turn, does not take responsibility for his or her role in the impasse that has occurred in the supervisory relationship. If the supervisee attempts to resolve the impasse by expressing negative reactions to the supervisor, the supervisee is met with a defensive or impassive reaction.

### Anxiety-Avoidant Maneuvers

We already have argued that anxiety in moderate amounts can be a positive element of supervision. But because the experience of anxiety can be so unpleasant, there is a particularly insidious aspect of it that can affect supervision. In their efforts to avoid or manage their anxiety, supervisees may implement maneuvers with their clients and/or with their supervisors that are counterproductive. Such strategies might take the form, for example, of not addressing directly erotic undercurrents occurring with the client or perhaps simply of censoring in an exceptionally careful manner the material presented to the supervisor. But not only do such anxiety-avoidant strategies hinder the therapeutic process, they also ultimately limit the supervisee's learning.

Our primary focus so far in this chapter has been on trainee anxiety. Supervisors, however, are not immune to anxiety and its effects. In fact, they may collude with their supervisees at some unspoken level to engage in behaviors that will minimize the anxiety experienced by either or both of them.

One primary anxiety-avoidant strategy that is not always successful and almost always exacts a cost to the supervisory relationship (and/or to the outcome of the work in it) is for the supervisor and supervisee to engage in games of the sort Berne (1964) described. By this, we mean a series of transactions that are to some extent stylized. That is, the dyad's transactions emanate from roles that are interlocking or complementary, roles that each participant understands and accepts with greater or lesser degrees of conscious awareness.

Kadushin (1968) identified a series of such games that occur in supervision. Most of those are summarized in Table 10.1. Our experience is that most therapists and supervisors

**TABLE 10.1** Summary of Selected Supervision "Games"

| | Participant roles | |
| --- | --- | --- |
| *Game* | *Supervisee* | *Supervisor* |
| "Be nice to me because I am nice to you." | Flatters the supervisor ("You are the best supervisor I've had"; "You're so perceptive.") | Colludes with the supervisee, accepting the praise, supervisor then finds it difficult to hold supervisee to legitimate demands. |
| "Evaluation is not for friends." | Takes coffee breaks with the supervisor, invites him or her to lunch, walks him or her to parking lot, and so on | Begins redefining the relationship as friendship; finds it increasingly hard to monitor and impose limits on the "friend" |
| "If you knew Dostoyevsky like I know Dostoyevsky" | In discussing clients, makes allusions to how they remind him or her of certain literary characters—which the supervisor, of course, *must* remember; the content varies and often may focus on the latest therapy theorists (especially when the supervisor may not have read their work). | Colludes in the conspiracy not to expose ignorance about the subject matter; in the process, teacher-learner roles are covertly changed; power disparities are reduced. |
| "I have a little list" | Comes prepared with a list of questions (often carefully chosen to correspond to areas of the supervisor's greatest interest and/or expertise); each is presented, in turn, for the supervisor's response. | Given this opportunity to help the supervisee by demonstrating knowledge, supervisor responds to each question with a short lecture. |
| "Little old me" | Presents self as dependent on the supervisor's detailed prescription for how to proceed ("What would you do next?"; "Then what would you say?") | Responds as the capable parent; then can take pleasure in vicariously doing therapy with the client |
| "I did like you told me" | Often—though not always—the outcome of "little old me"; scrupulously follows supervisor's suggestions, then comes to report that it didn't work (confirms to self that supervisor can be of no help) | Responds defensively, but with feelings of inadequacy; forced to adopt a one-down position in relationship to the supervisee |
| "It's all so confusing." | In the face of advice from the supervisor, mentions that in similar situations former supervisor(s) gave different advice; consequently, she or he is confused. (Note: When the supervisee has more than one supervisor at one time, each also can be played off the other this way.) | Responds by defending his or her approach against this competitor; finds sense of authority with the supervisee shaken |
| "Heading them off at the pass" | Ancitipating criticism of his or her work, opens the supervision by freely admitting mistakes, self-flagellating to excess | Responds with reassurance and praise for what the supervisee did well; finds self uneasy about focusing on mistakes the supervisee already has pointed out and is so miserable about |
| "Treat me, don't beat me" | Prefers to expose self rather than his or her work; therefore, raises personal problems that are affecting his or her | Trained initially as a therapist and still being motivated to help people in pain, supervisor crosses boundary between |

**TABLE 10.1**   Summary of Selected Supervision "Games" (*cont.*)

| Game | Participant roles | |
| --- | --- | --- |
| | *Supervisee* | *Supervisor* |
| | work and invites the supervisor's help in solving them | supervision and therapy; nature and extent of demands on supervisee change |
| "I wonder why you really said that." | Disagrees with supervisor and expresses it; later, accepts the premise of the supervisor's response (that the disagreement was prompted by some underlying—hence, unknown—personal problem in his or her self) | Redefines honest disagreement (with the necessity that he or she defend position) as supervisee's psychological resistance—prompted by motives and needs outside his or her awareness |
| "One good question deserves another" | Asks a question of the supervisor; later, does not challenge or confront the supervisor's response | Responds to the supervisee's question with another (i.e., what he or she thinks about it) (Note: A further ploy in case a satisfactory answer is not forthcoming is to suggest they think about it and discuss it next session.) |

*Material in this table was adapted from Kadushin (1968).

readily recognize one or more of these interaction patterns as something they have experienced themselves in either a supervisor or supervisee role. We acknowledge also that although anxiety management is basic to most of these games, these maneuvers also allow the supervisor and supervisee to meet other needs as well. We do, however, offer an important caveat. One person may *initiate* the particular game, but it always requires the collusion of both parties to make it a game. It is inappropriate (and counterproductive), therefore, for the supervisor to scold or blame the supervisee for initiating games in which both of them have participated. Each party shares responsibility for the interaction pattern.

Note, too, that we are not suggesting here specific strategies for supervisors to employ in avoiding or dissolving these games. We believe that for the supervisor simply to have an awareness of these frequent interaction patterns can be sufficient to suggest alternative responses.

**Anxiety Reduction Through Metaphor**

Anxiety reduction through interpersonal games of the sort discussed by Kadushin (1968) derails the supervision process and interferes with the attainment of goals. Barnat (1977), however, has suggested a more effective means by which supervisors can address supervisee anxiety. The use of metaphors that capture the essence of the situation might be considered something of a microintervention that supervisors could employ. Barnat gives some examples: "If you're acting, it will be dust and ashes in your mouth," or "You're a surfer on a board and the client is the wave" (p. 307).

One metaphor he related occurred in response to an intake he did with a female client, in which there was mutual sexual magnetism and which concluded with her asking him for his phone number—he found himself flustered and gave her the number. The event was discussed during supervision, along with the issues of control (or lack thereof) implicit in someone having your number. Then, when the supervisor asked, metaphorically, whether it would be possible to get his number back, Barnat reported experiencing this as a statement that he hadn't lost his adequacy in this situation; he only thought he had.

In fact, metaphor use of this sort seems to be used by many supervisors and to good effect. An excellent example occurs in Rudolph Ekstein's videotaped supervision of Dick Hackney (Goodyear, 1982; see transcript in Appendix D). Hackney had commented to the client that she seemed always to have to "smoke out" her husband whenever she wanted something from him. In the supervision he provided based on this session of Hackney's work, Ekstein adopted this metaphor himself and employed it repeatedly throughout the supervision session. At one point, for example, he observed to Hackney that in this, their first meeting, each was attempting to smoke the other out.

Of course, the use of metaphors in supervision requires specific competence that not all supervisors have or perhaps ever will have. Those supervisors who will be able to use metaphors successfully have perhaps already discovered their usefulness in therapy. We do not intend to suggest that that deliberate use of metaphorical language in supervision is for everyone.

## SUPERVISEES' NEED FOR ADEQUACY

One specific cause of supervisee anxiety that merits its own attention stems from the supervisee's need to feel adequate. Developmental psychologists (e.g., White, 1959) have spoken to the need for competence (which we will use interchangeably with adequacy) that affects all of us and becomes especially salient at a particular stage of childhood. Whether or not supervisees actually recapitulate developmental issues of childhood, adolescence, and

adulthood, we agree with Stoltenberg and Delworth (1988) that it is a useful orienting metaphor to employ. In fact, adequacy does seem to become a salient issue for supervisees, just as is the case with children.

The obverse side of this same phenomenon is that supervisees may experience themselves much of the time as imposters (Harvey & Katz, 1985) who are vulnerable to being found out. Although they go through the motions of acting as therapists, they worry that they are acting charade—that it will be only a matter of time before they are found out to be the impostors they believe themselves to be. Significantly, then, Kell and Mueller (1966) contended that supervision is "a process of mobilizing [the supervisee's] adequacy" (p. 18).

Bordin (1983) has offered some personal observations about supervisees' need for reassurance about their competence. He noted that he contracts with his trainees about goals they especially want to accomplish with his help. Typically, their *explicit* request is for fairly limited, focused goals (e.g., "learning to deal more effectively with manipulative clients"; "becoming more aware of when my own need to nurture gets in my way of being therapeutic"). Yet Bordin observed that supervisees almost always seem to have as an *unstated* agenda the wish to have global feedback about how he perceives them to be functioning.

*At first, I thought that this goal would be satisfied by the feedback I was giving in connection with the more specifically stated ones. But I soon learned such feedback was not enough. Despite our reviews of what the therapist was doing or not doing and of its appropriateness and effectiveness, the supervisee seemed uncertain how I evaluated him or her. Only as I offered the remark that I saw him or her as typical of (or even above or below) those of his or her level of training and experience was that need satisfied. (p. 39)*

Competence was one of the eight domains of supervisee development that Loganbill, Hardy, and Delworth (1982) identified. Data suggest, though, that the manner in which this issue is manifest is experience related. For example, Rabinowitz, Heppner, and Roehlke (1986) had supervisees at three levels of training rate the importance of 12 supervisory issues. Statistically significant *(p < .01)* differences were obtained between students in their first practicum and psychology interns when they rated the issue *Believing that I have sufficient skills as a counselor or psychotherapist to be competent in working with my clients.* The beginning practicum students rated it significantly higher.

Stoltenberg (1981) hypothesized that supervisees at Level 2 (of a four-level model in which level 4 is the most advanced) move from the strong dependency that is characteristic of beginning level supervisees to a dependency-autonomy conflict. Correspondingly, "there is a constant oscillation between being over confident in newly learned counseling skills and being overwhelmed by the increasing responsibility" (p. 62). In short, this is very similar to the struggle any adolescent experiences as he or she enters that middle ground between childhood and adulthood. Kell and Mueller (1966) captured graphically the essence of this conflict around adequacy by employing what they referred to as a topographic analogy. According to them, it can be characterized as

> *an effort to stay on a highway which is bordered on one side by the beautiful and inviting "Omnipotence Mountains" and on the other side by terrifying "Impotence Cliff." Clients can and often do tempt counselors to climb to the mountain tops. Sometimes the counselor's own needs and dynamics can push him into mountain climbing. More often, the complex, subtle interaction of counselor and client dynamics together lead to counselor trips into the rarified mountain air.*
>
> *Yet the attainment of a mountain top may stir uneasy and uncomfortable feelings. From*

> *a mountain top, what direction is there to go except downward? The view to the bottom of the cliff below may be frightening and compelling. The trip down the mountain may well not stop at the highway. The momentum may carry our counselor on over the cliff where he [or she] will experience the crushing effects of inadequacy and immobilization . . . It seems that either feeling state [omnipotence or impotence] carries the seeds of the other . . . Rapid oscillation between the two kinds of feeling can occur in such a short time span as a five minute segment of an interview. (pp. 124–125)*

**Skill Mastery, Scrutiny, and Felt Competence**

A trainee's sense of competence is, of course, ultimately linked to the quality of the skills the trainee is able to demonstrate. But trainees often are dismayed to find that their therapeutic skills become quite fragile and vulnerable to deterioration under conditions of observation.

Schauer, Seymour, and Green (1985) drew from social psychological research to offer a hypothesis that seems intuitively true even though it has not yet been empirically supported in the specific context of clinical supervision. Being observed will impair the performance of a person who has not fully mastered a skill; on the other hand, when that skill has been overlearned (i.e., highly developed), observing will facilitate that person's performance. In fact, there are data to suggest that inexperienced trainees are more anxious than those who are more experienced and that videotape reviews of their work may stimulate trainee anxiety (e.g., Gelso, 1974; Hale & Stoltenberg, 1988; Yenawine & Arbuckle, 1971).

An excellent example of this is the performance of Olympic athletes, individuals who have overlearned their particular athletic skill through thousands of hours of practice. Under conditions of competition and close scrutiny, their performance often attains record-breaking levels. In contrast, consider the beginning practicum student who has attained adequate levels of basic interviewing skills under conditions of loosely observed practice. When this same student is observed by a supervisor behind one-way glass, the student's performance deteriorates.

Miller (1989) drew from the work of Patterson (1988) to suggest one possible mechanism, that of *automaticity,* to explain this performance vulnerability. The concept of automaticity is that, through practice, counselor behaviors such as reflections of feeling or restatements that were techniques—that is, behaviors that may not have felt entirely comfortable or natural and which required some conscious attention—eventually become automatic and are performed without effort. As this automaticity begins to occur, the counselor needs to engage in less and less internal dialogue ("What response should I give now?" or even, "If I were in a situation like that, how would I feel? What then should I do with that information?"). This auotmaticity therefore has the effect of freeing up the counselor to attend to other dynamics going on in the client-counselor interaction.

In a very related vein, Hillerbrand (1989) discussed the supervisory implications of Anderson's (1982) information processing model, in which he discussed the distinction between *procedural* and *declarative* knowledge. Hillerbrand noted that declarative knowledge is factual knowledge stored in memory (e.g., "depressed people have flat affect"), whereas procedural knowledge is knowledge of how to engage in complex tasks, such as reflection of feelings.

According to Anderson, complex skills are developed first through the acquisition of factual (declarative) knowledge about the skill. The beginner initially is slow in executing the skill because it must first recall the declarative knowledge about the skill, then translate it to action.

*With practice, smaller procedures are transformed into larger procedures that are used au-* *tomatically. Through feedback the novice learns discrimination and generalization cues that dictate when the procedures are used (Anderson, 1982), behavior sequences, and efficient ways of hierarchically organizing knowledge into memory. (Hillerbrand, 1989, p. 294)*

In summary, then, supervisees have a particular need to feel competent but too often experience themselves as impostors instead. As they gain in skills, they often will fluctuate between the extreme positions of feeling exceptionally competent and of feeling totally incompetent. It is important that supervisors be aware of and responsive to this trainee need. We believe that it is especially important that the supervisor not lose sight of the fact that the portion of the supervisee's work that the supervisor observes may not be representative. That is, because the supervisee may not have attained procedural knowledge of one or more of the skills being demonstrated, those skills may be vulnerable to disruption when the supervisee is functioning under conditions of evaluation. Furthermore, in many instances communicating this awareness of performance disruption to the supervisee can itself be an effective supervision intervention to lower trainee anxiety.

## SUPERVISOR COUNTERTRANSFERENCE

Discussions of supervision often seem to take the supervisor's self-awareness for granted. As Gizynski (1978) noted, however, this is "a comforting but unwarranted assumption" (p. 203). In their work with supervisees, supervisors are prone to the same types of blind spots and lapses of objectivity that therapists experience in their work with clients.

It is important, then, to consider the matter of supervisor countertransference. The literature on this topic is relatively small, and empirical investigations of it are virtually nonexistent. Nevertheless, there seems general recognition that the phenomenon is not only real but important. For example, Ekstein and Wallerstein (1972) noted that the process of mutual evaluation and reevaluation that occur in supervision does not occur on strictly an intellectual level. It will "be accompanied by interactions on every level, which would be described, were they to occur in a therapeutic context, as transference reactions of the one and countertransference reactions of the other" (p. 284). Lower (1972) observed that "the learning alliance . . . is threatened continuously by resistances that derive from immature, neurotic, conflict-laden elements of the personality" (p. 70).

Identifying their own countertransference reactions and, then, the possible sources is difficult enough for therapists. But once a supervisor has recognized that his or her response to the trainee might, indeed, be tainted by one or another type of countertransference, the supervisor has the sometimes difficult task of isolating its origins. That is, to what extent do these reactions have their origins in the supervisory dyad alone versus in the client-therapist dyad? A particular characteristic of supervision is that what is occurring between the supervisor and supervisee may have bubbled up from the client-therapist interactions as a parallel process (see Chapter 2). This adds an element not present in therapy, in which the therapist is reacting only to the dynamics present in the therapy room.

As an illustrative example of this point, consider the supervisor who experienced irritation in the face of the trainee's self-presentation of confusion and indecision. Eventually, they both come to recognize that the trainee was mirroring the confusion and indecision of the client. Although the supervisor's reaction was to the trainee's behavior, its root cause was the client. This and similar examples make it clear why it is important that supervisors have available to them a colleague who can serve as a supervisor or consultant.

Lower (1972) suggested that supervisors' countertransference might be categorized into four areas: general personality characteristics, inner conflicts reactivated by the supervision situation, countertransference reactions to the individual trainee, and countertransference reactions to the trainee's transference. These categories seem to provide a useful way to organize an examination of the origins of supervisor countertransference. Therefore, each will be considered in turn.

## Categories of Supervisor Countertransference

*General Personality Characteristics.* This type of countertransference stems from the supervisor's own characterological defenses, which then affect the supervisory relationship. Lower noted that one of the most common manifestations of this occurs in the supervisor's wish to foster the supervisee's identification with the supervisor at the expense of the therapeutic process; perhaps this extends even to having fantasies of developing a following among the supervisees. The result of this is to encourage the supervisee to be passive and dependent.

Another frequent manifestation of this occurs with the supervisor's tendency to over-identify with the student. Lower (1972) discussed this as motivated by the supervisors' wish to protect him- or herself in the supervisee. As a consequence, the supervisor becomes indulgent of the supervisee and does not offer clear feedback, particularly about problems the supervisee may be having.

Gizynski (1978) seemed to be speaking of the same phenomenon when she discussed the supervisor who is "personally possessive" of the trainee. She saw it as especially manifesting itself in the supervisor's advocacy for the supervisee in relationship to other members of the agency or training program. The message — overt or covert — is that the supervisor is the one who really understands the trainee. The trainee therefore can discount feedback from other faculty or staff because they are unduly critical and/or in error. "Students become a narcissistic extension of the supervisor; loyalty issues tend to override expectations of clinical performance and the supervisor loses his [or her] objectivity in evaluation and freedom in teaching" (p. 206).

### Inner Conflicts Reactivated by the Supervisory Situation.

Lower's first category of supervisor countertransference focused on supervisors' characteristic ways of expressing themselves. The second category focused on supervisors' inner conflicts that are triggered by the supervision. Although some of the supervisor behaviors might resemble those of the first category, they have different origins.

Lower, who wrote from a psychoanalytic perspective, argued that many of the conflicts aroused in the supervisor are oedipal in nature. This is so because the supervisor's role is essentially that of a parent; moreover, the many latent triangles among the supervisor, trainee, client, agency, colleagues, and so on also contribute to the reactivation of oedipal issues. There are many ways such reactivated conflicts can intrude in supervision. For example, the supervisor may attempt to be the good parent and attempt to offer more of a favorable supervisory environment than that which was offered the supervisor. Or, alternatively, the supervisor (parent) may behave sadistically to defend against an anticipated challenge from the trainee (child).

The following list of other supervisor responses suggest the myriad ways supervisors' own inner conflicts can be manifest in supervision. Lower (1972) suggested that they may

1. Play favorites with the trainees;
2. Covertly encourage the supervisee to act out his or her own conflicts with other colleagues or encourage rebellion against the institution;
3. Compete with other supervisors for supervisees' affection;
4. Harbor exaggerated expectations of the

trainee that, when unmet or rejected by the trainee, lead to frustration and perhaps even aggression;
5. Have narcissistic needs to be admired that divert the supervisor from the appropriate tasks of supervision.

### Reactions to the Individual Trainee.

The types of supervisor countertransference discussed so far have been triggered by the supervisor's response to the supervisory *situation*. In addition to these, there may be aspects of the individual supervisee that themselves serve to stimulate conflicts in the supervisor. For example, if the trainee seems brighter (or more socially successful, or financially better off, etc.) than the supervisor, this may elicit from the supervisor competitive impulses to engage in one-up behaviors. Alternatively, in the face of these same supervisee attributes, the supervisor might feel compelled to take a one-down position in relation to the apparently stronger trainee. The trainee who appears too normal or too healthy may be discounted as being shallow and unable to respond to the needs of clients.

### Sexual/Romantic Attraction.

Sexual or romantic attraction is one type of supervisor countertransference reactions to the individual supervisee that merits specific mention. At the same time, though, we need to acknowledge that countertransference is not the only possible source of such attraction. In commenting on this, Goodyear and Sinnett (1984) have observed that one aspect of interpersonal attractiveness is shared interests and values, a condition that prevails among people within any particular occupation. Therefore, it is not surprising that supervisors and supervisees occasionally may find themselves drawn to one another.

But regardless of the source of the attraction and whether it fits the strict definition of transference and countertransference, it is important that the supervisor and supervisee not act on it while they are in their supervisory relationship. Whether the supervisor chooses to address his or her attraction directly to the supervisee, the supervisor should not attempt to deny it to him- or herself. Attending to it may be useful in understanding the supervisee or perhaps even the client.

Hall (1988b) adopted a different perspective of this general issue, discussing the problems posed by preexisting supervisor-supervisee socio-sexual relationships (e.g., in husband-wife supervisory dyads). The transference and countertransference problems these supervision relationships pose are sufficient reason to avoid them. To illustrate, she offered a vignette in which a woman was supervising her husband. Hall noted two transference-related issues likely to emerge with this particular relationship. First, the wife, because of her relationship with her husband, might be inclined to be relaxed in her monitoring of his work, *assuming* he was doing a competent job—whether or not this was true. Second, the wife very likely would be reluctant to acknowledge or confront transference and countertransference issues in her husband's work.

*Cultural Countertransference.*    Another type of countertransference reaction the supervisor may have to the individual supervisee may reside in cultural differences between the two. Vargas (1989) differentiated between this type of countertransference and prejudice: "Whereas prejudice refers to an opinion for or against someone or something without adequate basis, the sources and consequences of cultural countertransference are far more insidious and are often repressed by the therapist" (p. 3). Although his discussion centered on *therapists'* countertransference reactions, we will extrapolate his ideas to a consideration of possible sources of supervisors' cultural countertransference.

Vargas (1989) noted that cultural countertransference reactions can originate in either

of two ways. The first, and more common instance, occurs when the supervisor has limited experience with members of the ethnic minority group to which the supervisee belongs. Vargas argues that a frequent response in this situation would be for the supervisor to engage in overgeneralization. For example, the supervisor might expect all Asian-American supervisees to find it difficult to engage in directly confrontive behaviors. Vargas maintains that this typically is a relatively easy consequence of cultural countertransference with which to deal. There are less direct consequences that are more problematic. For example, mental health professionals may deal with their own unresolved issues toward a particular minority group—including, perhaps, possible guilt feelings about societal oppression that group has experienced—by romanticizing that group. This provides the supervisor a mechanism to reduce possible ethnic tensions with the supervisee. Its manifestations in supervision might include perceiving most of the supervisee's behavior through the lens of culture. This effectively can blind the supervisor to issues and problems of the supervisee that actually are individual to the supervisee and that should be addressed in supervision.

The second source of cultural countertransference Vargas (1989) discussed stems from potent feelings associated with *non-*minority people in the supervisor's past with whom the current minority supervisee is associated. Although the example he gave illustrated a *therapist's* countertransference, it does suggest how similar dynamics might occur between supervisor and supervisee of different ethnic groups. He discussed the hypothetical situation of a white male therapist having

*intensely negative feelings about the raw expression of anger as a result of his own unresolved experiences regarding his own anger at this father who left him and his mother when the therapist was very young. When confronted with a belligerent and sadistically taunting Black adolescent, the therapist expe-*

*riences intense disgust and hostility toward the patient which the therapist considers as disturbing evidence of his prejudice. In reality, it is not prejudice in the true sense of the word but rather a type of cultural countertransference misconstrued as prejudice. (p. 4)*

### Countertransference to the Trainee's Transference.

Perhaps the area in which supervisors are at the greatest risk of experiencing countertransference reactions to the supervisee is when the supervisee manifests transference responses to the supervisor. It is important to note here that Ekstein and Wallerstein (1972) have argued that supervisees do not actually experience transference reactions toward the supervisor in the same sense that clients do toward therapists. This is so because, in contrast to therapy, the supervisory relationship does not encourage regression but instead encourages the supervisee to think independently; also, the supervisor and supervisee are in constant, task-focused dialogue. Carl Rogers probably spoke for most supervisors when he observed, similarly, that one distinction between supervision and counseling was that in supervision he shared more of his own thoughts and reactions than in therapy (Hackney & Goodyear, 1986).

But whether supervisees experience transference in the classical sense, there is little question that they do experience distortions in their perceptions of the supervisor and that they behave in accordance with those distortions. As with the other types of supervisor countertransference, there are numerous ways in which this form may be expressed. Lower (1972) offered an example that illustrates one such manifestation.

*A resident had been working in psychotherapy with a . . . young woman for about six months when a new supervisor questioned his formulation and treatment goals and suggested that they follow the patient in supervision over a period of time. The resident responded as though the supervisor were intruding upon his*

*relationship with the patient and became more and more vague in his presentation of material. In reaction, the supervisor became increasingly active in suggesting what the therapist should pursue with the patient and at last asked to see the patient together with the resident in order to make his own assessment. Only after the supervisor began the interview by asking the patient, "Well how are you and Doctor—ah— what's his name here getting along" did he recognize the oedipal conflict within both himself and the resident that had interfered with the learning alliance. (p. 74)*

### Countertransference as Theme Interference

The consultation literature suggests one possibly useful way to think about supervisors' countertransference or what Caplan (1970) would refer to as "lapses in professional objectivity." A specific type of transference is what Caplan called "theme interference," in which an unfortunate consequence is anticipated as the outcome for the particular case—and for all other cases in which this category of individuals is involved. Consider, for example, Joan Smith, a supervisor in a publicly funded social service agency that serves a low-income population. She has been assigned to supervise a field placement student from a local, private, and very expensive university; at their first meeting, the supervisee comes dressed in what are obviously very expensive, stylish clothes. Joan takes an immediate dislike to the trainee, believing that he is spoiled and incapable of empathy for the population with which they work.

According to Caplan, there is an *initial category* (in Joan's case, stylish, wealthy students) and an *inevitable outcome* (such students are shallow, self-centered, and incapable of responding effectively with low-income clients). Caplan invoked psychoanalytic explanations of this phenomenon (e.g., that it stems from the supervisee's repressed impulses). But although Heller and Monahan (1983) shared Caplan's belief that theme interference is a valid phenomenon, they argued that it might more usefully be considered an instance of stereotyping. They argued that the helping professional who has lost objectivity in this manner is responding either to cultural experiences learned in early socialization or to some unfortunate personal experience that has been blown out of proportion and overgeneralized.

Heller and Monahan (1983) agree with Caplan (1970) that there are two general strategies for helping someone experiencing such stereotyping to regain objectivity. The first, and less desirable of these, is *unlinking*. In this strategy, the supervisee would be helped to change its perception of the particular client; the client would thereby be unlinked from the supervisee's stereotype, but the stereotype itself would persist intact. The more desirable strategy is to help the supervisee overcome the stereotype itself.

Although theme interference has been discussed as a consultation issue, there is utility in also considering it as one that pertains to supervision. Therefore, Joan, the supervisor who believes her supervisee to be spoiled, might be helped to see that what she was operating from was a stereotype and that the stereotype is in many cases unwarranted, a point central to our discussion of cultural countertransference.

## SUPERVISOR-SUPERVISEE CONFLICT

Supervision occurs in the context of a relationship. For this reason alone it is difficult enough to manage. *Any* relationship is fraught with difficulties. In fact, a central thesis of Mueller and Kell's (1972) supervision book, *Coping with Conflict,* was that in any relationship, whether personal or professional, there will occur conflict; the manner in which the parties involved resolve (or fail to resolve) that conflict will dictate whether the relationship continues to grow and develop or to stagnate. This certainly is true in supervision.

A particular issue that pervades supervisory relationships, however, is the power differential between the parties. Therefore, in addition to the normal relationship conflicts that occur, there is another, contaminating layer of conflict that results from that power differential. As in any such relationship where there is a real power differential, there is the possibility for abuse of that power.

Robiner (1982) pointed out that the unequal power between the supervisor and supervisee is a constant obstacle to the attainment of the mutual trust that is so important in supervision. He suggested that mutual respect is one important means of overcoming the impasse that this can present. The supervisor's position of power suggests that he or she must model that respect if both the supervisor and supervisee are to attain it.

Moskowitz and Rupert (1983) surveyed 158 supervisees, asking them to describe conflicts they had experienced with their supervisors. Three categories of conflictual situations were reported. In frequency, 20 percent, 30 percent, and 50 percent of these conflictual situations, respectively, fell into the following categories:

1. Conflicts due primarily to differences between the supervisor and trainee in theoretical orientation or in their views on appropriate therapeutic approaches or techniques. For example, the dynamically-oriented supervisor might discourage the supervisee from using behavioral techniques.
2. Conflicts that seemed to center on the supervisor's style of supervision. For example, the supervisor provided the supervisee with too little (or, conversely, too much) direction, or the supervisor was not free enough in acknowledging accomplishments (the occasional, well-timed "great job" can be very important to supervisees). Significantly, the examples of

problematic supervisor styles that were obtained in this study seemed to coincide with those of Rosenblatt and Mayer (1975), which we summarized earlier in this chapter.

3. Conflicts that related directly to a personality clash or personality issues on the part of the supervisor or trainee. The range of possible specific conflicts in this category is as broad as the possible range of ways in which two people, especially two between whom there are power differentials, might have difficulties.

Interestingly, 76.9 percent of the supervisees in the Moskowitz and Rupert study reported that they discussed with their supervisors the conflict they had reported; of those who did not, 66.7 percent reported that it was because they feared that raising the issue would make matters worse. Of those who did discuss the conflict, 83.8 percent reported that *they* had initiated the discussion. This seems a really interesting result that might mean that supervisees more readily recognize and/or are more eager to resolve conflicts with their supervisors than the reverse. At the same time, though, these were self-report data gathered from supervisees; the results might be quite different if their supervisors were surveyed.

## RELATIONSHIP PARAMETERS: INTERPERSONAL POWER

In the section above we asserted that although conflict is inherent in any relationship, the power differential between supervisor and supervisee both enhances the potential for that conflict and also may affect the manner in which the conflict is resolved. Therefore, there is merit in considering some possible issues surrounding interpersonal power.

In this section, we will address two specific conceptions of interpersonal power. The first speaks to the importance of both involve-

ment and power in interpersonal influence. The second, although also social psychological, deals with the very different phenomenon of people relating to each other in three-person systems.

### Power and Involvement

Penman (1980) developed a system of categorizing interpersonal interactions so that they were arrayed along the two dimensions of *power* and *involvement*. At least three studies (Abadie, 1985; Holloway, Freund, Gardner, Nelson, & Walker, 1989; Martin, Goodyear, & Newton, 1987) have employed Penman's system to analyze supervisory interactions. Only that of Holloway et al. (1989), however, has highlighted the results strongly in terms of the power and involvement dimensions.

Another model of interpersonal interaction is that of Strong et al. (1988) who have adapted Leary's (1957) circumplex model of behavior. In their model, presented in Figure 10.1, interpersonal behavior is arrayed along the two dimensions of *status* and *affiliation*. This model has been employed in at least two studies of supervisory interactions (Friedlander, Siegel, & Brenock, 1989; Harris & Goodyear, 1990).

It is noteworthy that these two models—Penman's and Strong's—arrive at such a similar two-dimensional structure, for there does seem a virtual equivalence between status and power and between involvement and affiliation. This similarity has occurred despite the models' origins in independent research programs in different countries (Penman's, in Australia to describe marital interaction; Strong's, in the United States to describe counseling interaction). Together they suggest—to use Penman's language—the importance of supervisors thinking in terms simultaneously of the power they may exert with supervisees *and* of the degree of involvement they might have with them. Each is an important compo-

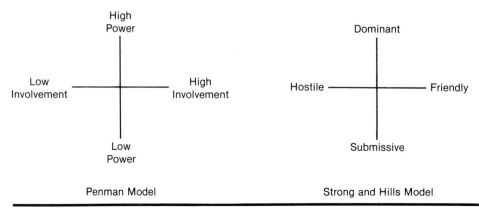

**FIGURE 10.1**    The axes of the Penman (1980) and the Strong and Hills (1986) models of interpersonal behavior

nent of the supervisory relationship and, ultimately, the supervisory outcome.

### Three-Person Systems

Bowen (1978) has done much to sensitize counselors to the role of three-person systems, or triangles, in human interaction. Although it seems customary to think of the dyad as the most elemental interpersonal unit, he asserts that the triangle is the basic "molecule" of social interaction; a given dyad is stable only in relationship to another person. We believe this contains important implications for supervisors and supervisees.

Caplow's (1968) book devoted to the subject shows just how long theorists have been considering human interaction in terms of triangles. He traced the essential ideas back to the theorizing Simmel began in about 1890 (e.g., Spykman, 1966). He also reviewed empirical studies (Vinacke, 1959) that help to inform us of the nature of triangles.

Caplow maintained that triangles constitute a type of social geometry in which there is a tendency for two members to form a coalition against a third. He asserted further that the patterns of coalitions for any given triangle can be predicted with some accuracy by an observer, based on the observer's knowledge of the relative power of the individuals involved;

that is, coalitions are a means for redistributing power. In fact, Caplow (1968) maintained that the most distinctive feature of triadic social systems is "the transformation of strength into weakness and weakness into strength" (p. 3).

The following is an illustrative example from Caplow:

> *Ahab, Brutus, and Charlie are smugglers who divide their goods on a lonely island far from civil authority. Brutus and Charlie are equally matched. Ahab is slightly more dangerous. He could overpower either Brutus or Charlie in a fight but could easily be overpowered by the two of them together.*
>
> *Ahab will probably try to form a coalition with Brutus or with Charlie, but neither of them would have any reason to accept him as a partner. The predicted coalition is Brutus-Charlie. If Brutus chooses Charlie, he has a partner who does not threaten to dominate him and who needs him for protection against the superior strength and guile of Ahab.*
>
> *If Brutus were to choose Ahab as a coalition partner, his position would be much less favorable, for he would remain subordinate to Ahab and entirely at his mercy if Charlie were removed from the scene. (p. 2)*

In his book Caplow surveyed the variety of ways in which triangles occur in our day-to-day living, ranging from the nuclear family and the oedipal triangle to the triangles that occur within governments (e.g., with liberal, moderate, and conservative groups) and even among nations. We all can think back to relationships with friends growing up in which, of three friends, there was one dyad that was particularly close. During times of tension between these two, however, the third member was drawn into an alliance with one of them against the other.

One characteristic of triangles that is particularly interesting is that they seem to have what Caplow refers to as a *catalytic effect;* that is, although coalitions can occur between two members of a triangle without the third member present, his or her presence almost always modifies the relationship of the other two. He offers as an illustrative example the common playground situation in which the presence of a mutual antagonist enhances the affection between two friends and their felt hostility toward the antagonist.

The three possible functions of the third member within the triangle seem to be those of mediator, *tertius gaudens,* and oppressor. The *tertius gaudens,* or "enjoying third," is one who is able to profit from dissension between the other two members of the triangle. It is the member of the triangle wanted by both of the other members when they have rejected each other. Certainly it is possible that a given person in a particular triangle may, over time, serve all three of these functions—perhaps even over and over.

Bowen (1978) would maintain that a coalition exists when two members discuss a third in privacy. Certainly we all have seen this in our families. Most of us also have experienced it in work settings when two colleagues meet to express to each other their concerns about the behavior of a third colleague.

It is easy to see these dynamics in the work of mental health professionals. For example, anyone who has provided counseling to couples can see how the counselor might fulfill any of the three functions of the third member; that is, the natural tendency of many

couples is to cast the counselor in the role of negotiator. It also is frequent in times of escalating tension between the members of the couple to begin competing for the counselor's support. It is even possible that, with the use of certain interventions, the counselor could come to be perceived as the oppressor.

One reason it is so difficult for counselors to begin with an individual client and then later bring in the spouse is that a coalition typically already has been formed between the counselor and the original client. The spouse who later joins the counselor and client who have been working together is likely to feel ganged up on, usually for good reason. The person who was seen initially already has discussed the spouse with the counselor, who probably has become swayed to view the situation from the original client's perspective. This initial counselor-client interaction is an instance of the sort of secrecy about which Bowen spoke as definitive of a coalition.

In supervision the most obvious triangle is that of the client, the counselor, and the supervisor. It does, however, have its own characteristics that constrain the possible coalitions. Two of these are the way in which power is arrayed (the least powerful member of this group is the client; the most powerful, the supervisor) and the fact that the supervisor and client rarely will have an ongoing face-to-face relationship with each other. Strategically oriented family therapists sometimes use this to their advantage in supervision. The supervisor is deliberately set up in the oppressor role as a means both of enhancing the strength of the client-counselor bond and of steering the client toward a desired behavior. (For example, the counselor might say something like this to the client: "My supervisor is convinced that your problem is _____ and that I should be doing _____ about it. Just between us, though, I think she's off base. In fact, I think she's pretty insensitive to the issues you are facing.") The discussion between two people of a third person most often occurs between the counselor and the supervisor. This, of course, suggests a counselor-supervisor coalition with the client as the third member. When this occurs, especially at a time when the counselor and client are experiencing some relationship difficulties, it is easy for the supervisor to become pulled in and to experience countertransference reactions. On the other hand, it *is* possible for the counselor and client to discuss the supervisor, as in the manner just suggested. In this instance, the coalition is between counselor and client.

Supervision, of course, occurs in a larger context, and there are many other possible triangles that can come into play. For example, as discussed earlier in the section on games (see Table 10.1), the supervisee might triangle in another supervisor (either present or past) by saying something like, "I'm feeling confused: You are saying this, but the supervisor I had last semester [or, the supervisor I have in my other setting] has been telling me something really different." In this case, the coalition is between the trainee and another supervisor who may not even realize he or she has become a member of this particular triangle. Because coalitions—even with a phantom member such as this—are used to redistribute power, it is easy to recognize the purpose for the supervisee doing this.

The point of this is not to suggest that triangles are bad and, therefore, to be avoided. They exist in any human interaction, including those that occur between and among professionals. It is, however, useful for the supervisor to have some awareness of them and their effects on the dynamics of supervision.

## HARMFUL CONSEQUENCES OF SUPERVISION

In closing this chapter, we will suggest that the manner in which the supervisor works with the supervisee has the potential to result in actual harm to the supervisee. If supervisors' actions are powerful enough to have positive conse-quences, it stands to reason that they are powerful enough to cause harm as well.

Harm to the trainee can be in the form of skill deterioration, psychological damage, or both. As Blocher (1983) noted, "The possibility always exists that an immature, inadequate, and insensitive supervisor may intimidate, bully, and *even damage* [italics added] a supervisee" (p. 30).

Our particular concern here is not with the sometimes transitory "de-skilling" that may occur during supervision. Trainees may conclude during supervision that their favored interventions are not having the effects they had believed, drop those interventions from their repertoire, and then go through a period in which they temporarily regress. They have had something taken from them on which they had relied; until they develop an alternative to replace it, they may experience a period of being de-skilled. This phenomenon is similar to what Loganbill, Hardy, and Delworth (1982) described as the stage of "confusion."

Being de-skilled or confused, however, typically is relatively short-lived. Moreover, most trainees understand it to be a normative experience and, therefore, do not respond strongly to it. As is the case with any other psychological intervention, outcomes of supervision vary. This variability seems to be the result of a number of either supervisee characteristics (e.g., motivation, personal maturity, skill level) or supervisor characteristics (e.g., supervision experiences, type of supervision environment provided ); often, though, it is a function of interactions among characteristics of the two. We believe these same supervisor and supervisee factors contribute also to *some* supervisees being harmed by the supervision. Interestingly, this phenomenon has been virtually ignored in supervision literature.

The iatrogenic (literally, disease caused by the physician) consequences of counseling or psychotherapy have been recognized for some time. Whether called the "deterioration effect" (Bergin, 1966), "negative effect" (Strupp,

Hadley, & Gomes-Schwartz, 1977), or "negative outcome" (Mays & Franks, 1980, 1985), there seems general agreement that some clients who seek help leave therapy worse off than when they arrived.

Lambert, Shapiro, and Bergin (1986) reviewed empirical literature on this phenomenon. They also alluded to the "variety of 'horror stories' of the type that often are shared privately among clients and professionals but are rarely published" (p. 184). It is primarily on this latter sort of data that we currently have to rely regarding the existence and types of harmful effects of supervision. It may seem curious that a phenomenon that actually may be fairly widespread has not been better documented. It is important to realize, however, that research bearing on *any* type of outcome of supervision is less developed than is research on counseling or therapy outcomes.

Certainly we have horror stories to recount, as we suspect is the case with many experienced supervisors. To illustrate, we provide the following (composite) case:

*Joyce was an excellent and well-liked student whose first counseling practicum was one in which clients were seen in several consecutive time blocks under observation behind one-way glass; then, the practicum group convened to provide group supervision in which members offered critical feedback to one another based on what they had observed. Although the class members all perceived Joyce as among the better counselors in the class, the instructor saw her quite differently. In the name of "genuineness," he offered his criticism—alone and publicly in the group—in a direct, unsupportive style. He ignored any comment on her strengths and focused instead on what he perceived to be her weaknesses; any protestations on her part were labeled as resistance. He gave her an unsatisfactory grade at the end of the semester.*

*Joyce decided to wait a semester before retaking practicum. During this period she showed stress-related weight loss and sought counseling for issues of self-confidence. When she eventually retook the practicum with another instructor, she initially behaved in a constricted and guarded manner with her clients, demonstrating excessive preoccupation with the evaluation aspect of supervision she was receiving.*

In Joyce's second practicum, therefore, her new supervisor might assess her as inaccessible to her clients and to supervision—unless, of course, Joyce is fortunate enough to have a second supervisor who is sufficiently perceptive and talented to undo the damage done by her first supervisor.

The fact is that supervisees often may be at greater risk for harm as a function of supervision than are clients as a function of therapy. This is so for several reasons.

1. Evaluation is an ever-present issue. No matter how well it is conducted, supervisees often have difficulty discerning the fine line between evaluation of self-as-person and the evaluation of self-as-counselor. We speculate, incidentally, that it is in the more humanistically oriented models that supervisees are at particular risk in this regard, for these models often blur the distinction between self and skills.

2. Trainees certainly are invested in the process of supervision, for it is concerned with the development of their professional selves. When it does not go well, it could be a barrier to their entry to the field in which they have invested so much time, money, and personal commitment.

3. As we noted in Chapter 1, a trainee usually has less choice about participating in supervision than does the client who seeks counseling. Moreover, trainees often are assigned to their supervisor rather than having the opportunity to work with someone they deliberately seek out.

In closing this section, we note that Rioch, Coulter, and Weinberg (1976) discussed another, particular form of risk faced by supervisees. They maintained that supervisees must be willing "to face unpleasantness, evil, and even terror as part and parcel of their own make-up" (p. 3). The question for the supervisor is how to accomplish this with " 'healthy, clean' young people without bringing about at the same time debasement and self-hatred" (p. 4). They acknowledge that supervision of the type they were describing carries risks. We suspect that this is true of *any* supervision.

## CONCLUDING COMMENT

We have discussed in this chapter several of the most frequent problems and dilemmas that face supervisors. As readers likely will have noticed, we offered few solutions. We believe that other chapters in this book offer guidelines that, if followed, should reduce some of the pitfalls posed by these dilemmas and problems.

# CHAPTER 11

# SUPERVISION IN
# A MULTICULTURAL CONTEXT

No two people are identical. Therefore, we cannot avoid the issue of difference if we are to approach the tasks of therapy and supervision seriously. Yet until recently, our training as therapists and our melting pot society have reinforced a particular understanding of difference, one reflecting an individualistic bias (Bellah, Madsen, Sullivan, Swidler, & Tipton, 1985). We have been trained to focus our attention on individual differences. Family therapists have expanded the focus to include the systemic uniqueness of each family. Helping professionals, however, have just begun to struggle with the larger and more subtle (for some) force of group identity. For those who were brought up not to notice group identity, it can still feel like prejudice to address the issue directly. We are in the midst of a paradigmatic shift that often leaves us awkward and inadequately prepared to address group identity. The decade of the '80s marked a serious attempt by mental health practitioners and writers to catch up with societal changes. In true Western, linear fashion, the literature first addressed client characteristics based on group identity, moved on to therapist characteristics that were culturally sensitive, and, for the most part, only recently addressed cross-cultural supervision.

In part this chapter will mirror the progress that the field as a whole has witnessed; that is, we will rely on concepts offered by authors concerned with therapy as some basis for our discussion of supervision. We will, of course, additionally stress the current under-

standing of multicultural supervision. As another parallel to the field, we will use the terms multicultural and cross-cultural interchangeably.

This chapter is limited by the relatively few empirical examinations of multicultural therapy and supervision. Most contributions to date that address cultural issues have been theoretical in nature. We approach our topic, therefore, with an awareness that (1) future research efforts may challenge, if not discount, some of our present assumptions because (2) cultural bias can be extremely subtle and has infiltrated our cognitive constructs in ways of which we are only partially aware.

Before we consider some of the supervision issues with persons who have different group identities, it is important to realize that there is an up side and a down side to our topic. The up side can be described (albeit simplistically) by the word *pluralism,* whereas the down side focuses on the concept of discrimination. To embrace the assumptions of pluralism is to affirm that "the dominant culture benefits from coexistence and interaction with the cultures of adjunct groups" (Axelson, 1985, p. 13). From the standpoint of pluralism, helping professionals celebrate diversity and welcome the viewpoints from different groups because they recognize the gain for themselves. Conversely, the down side of respecting difference stems from the social conscience and assertion that persons who deviate from the norm should not suffer from this deviation. Therefore, any person whose group identity puts him or her in a minority category should be protected from being bullied by the majority culture, both in obvious and subtle ways.

Professional helpers are more accustomed to fighting discrimination than to celebrating pluralism. This has led, unfortunately, to the reinforcing of social stereotypes that it is bad or unfortunate to be a minority. For this and many other reasons, helping professionals have been criticized for contributing to the one-down position many minorities continue to experience in this culture. But it is our belief that the pluralistic view alone also is flawed because it can be construed as a "Pollyanna" position that diminishes the real hardships encountered by minorities when they attempt to prosper in this society. The only desirable option, as we see it, is to adopt a position that keeps both the up and down sides in focus. When working with trainees or when helping trainees to work with their clients, supervisors must look for opportunities to enrich each other by a sharing and accepting of different perspectives; however, they must also stand guard lest a person's group identity becomes a rationale for less than acceptable treatment.

An academic point: There is no basis for the argument that one can ignore differences. Although this was perceived as a liberal posture (Larson, 1982) in years past, it was never credible. As Allport (1958) postulated over thirty years ago, the mind is prone to categorize and to group in order to reduce the stress on the brain in its attempt to comprehend its surroundings. Therefore, there is a "normality of prejudgment" (p. 19). But this is not the problem. The problem, as Allport understood it and as we understand it, is that we become partisan. We start to attach "rightness," or in our profession, normality, to the group of which we are members. In order to feel safe by virtue of group membership, we determine that other groups must be somehow defective. The overall task, then, if we are to support pluralism, is to redefine safety to include a pluralistic orientation. Otherwise we are only fooling ourselves in our attempts to be more aware. As Ibrahim (1985) stated,

> [i]f counselors and psychotherapists insist on analyzing and examining clients, they are persisting in setting up barriers by creating an unequal situation. Counseling (learning) relationships would be greatly enhanced if each counselor (facilitator) considered the client as a cultural equal and set about establishing a "relationship" between two equivalent beings. (p. 635)

Although our overall attitude is important, it is just the beginning. Minority groups are many, and the issues are complex. "Indeed, to some it may seem that the proliferation of minority groups has outpaced the ability of many professionals to assimilate all the calls for change" (Larson, 1982, p. 843). We will begin by considering some concepts or models that apply to a variety of minority groups before we attempt to take a more focused look at several distinct groups.

## DEFINITIONS AND ISSUES

### Definition of Minority

Larson (1982) made the salient point that before we attempt to understand *different,* we must identify *same.* This is crucial because it affects our definition of *minority.* Larson concludes, as have many others, that the beginning of a definition of *majority* must revolve around the overrepresentation of white males of European descent in positions of relative power in our society. Larson defined minorities, therefore, in terms of power, not numbers. He asserted that the central feature to being a minority is the potential of being stigmatized. Therefore, women can legitimately be included as a minority in this country whereas the very wealthy cannot, regardless of the number in each group. A poignant example of this concept is South Africa, where blacks have been the numerical majority but are minorities by this definition because of their reduced status.

## Myth of Sameness

One of the many factors that contributes to the complexity of appreciating difference and sameness is that each is a partial truth. Smith (1981) referred to the "myth of sameness" as the error of most helping professionals who were convinced that their skills were generic and could be applied to individuals of varying backgrounds. Larson (1982) developed Smith's ideas and defended the position that all individuals carry within themselves an individual identity, a group identity, and a universal identity.

> *If viewed only in the context of his or her universality, a his or her universality, a person loses his or her individuality; if viewed only in the context of individuality, the person loses a sense of connectedness with humanity; if viewed only in the context of group membership, an individual is stereotyped. The delicate task in counseling is to integrate all three views when working with clients. Although this task is important in dealing with any client, it is paramount in dealing with a client whose minority background makes the group membership dimension take on more importance. (p. 844)*

There is yet another way that helping professionals deny difference, and this can be seen among those who are white and share a professional identity. Because most helping professionals continue to represent the dominant culture, it is easy to adopt an us-them mentality regarding minority clients. We believe it is very important in training activities to discourage this us-them mentality when introducing multicultural issues. When our classes or supervision groups are composed of persons who appear more similar than dissimilar, we have found it useful to begin by taking time to study our own ethnic and regional differences

as a backdrop to exploring the cultures of others. We use McGoldrick's (1982) outline and ask our trainees to

1. *describe themselves ethnically;*
2. *describe who in their family experience influenced their sense of ethnic identity;*
3. *discuss which groups other than their own they think they understand best;*
4. *discuss which characteristics of their ethnic group they like most and which they like least;*
5. *discuss how they think their own family would react to seeking the services of a helping professional. (p. 27)*

Often the answers to these items are stilted at first and become more animated as more trainees get involved, beginning to compare and contrast experiences. The wide diversity of assumptions and opinions, use of food and drink, acceptance or rejection of religion, regard for education and upward mobility, etc., among white middle-class helping professionals is an eye-opening experience for many trainees. Therefore, the myth of sameness is challenged within the majority culture group before it is seen as wanting in the work with minority clients. Additionally, we find it helpful to have trainees discover and react to differences among themselves as a way to desensitize them to making similar observations about cultures they see as further away from their experience. Finally, because we are likely to have several ethnic groups well represented in a training situation, the relativity of ethnic characteristics can be observed, some following traditional patterns more than others. This serves as a reminder of levels of acculturation and intragroup differences when we attempt to examine cultures with only a single representative or no representative in the training group.

## World View

Ibrahim (1985) and Sue (1981) stressed the importance of world view as the basis for relating to each other. It should be noted that world view is similar to Friedlander and Ward's (1984) assumptive world discussed in Chapter 3.

Ibrahim asserted that an understanding of our own world view and that of others is key to enhancing multicultural effectiveness. Structures of reasoning are central to one's world view. Ibrahim and Kahn (1987) developed the existential work of Kluckhohn and Strodtbeck (1961) and incorporated into their model an investigation of one's ideas about human nature, human relationships, the relationship between people and nature, time orientation, and level of activity. Ibrahim and Kahn challenged the assumption of pronounced intergroup differences and minimal intragroup differences. Their research supported both intergroup and intragroup differences.

Therefore, in a country with perhaps the greatest cultural complexity and variety on earth, helping professionals must become adept at refining and redefining generic knowledge. Furthermore, therapists and supervisors must be willing to discard hard earned cultural knowledge when it is not a good fit for the client or supervisee being encountered.

In another highly regarded world view model, Sue (1978, 1981, 1990) merged the concepts of locus of control (Rotter, 1966) and attribution theory (Jones et al., 1972) to arrive at a model of four quadrants: internal locus of control—internal responsibility (IC-IR); internal locus of control—external responsibility (IC-ER); external locus of control—internal responsibility (EC-IR); and external locus of control—external responsibility (EC-ER) (see Figure 11.1). Sue's model described not only the world view of the person in each quadrant but also the counseling implications for each and the likelihood of the client being able to tolerate a person representing another world view. For example, clients who fall into the IC-IR quadrant rely on themselves to accomplish their ends. If they are not yet succeeding, they will try harder (IC). If others do not accept

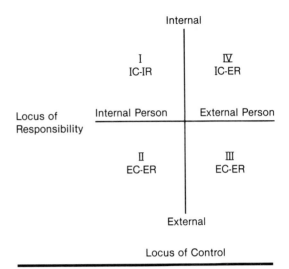

**FIGURE 11.1** Graphic representation of world views*
*From Sue, D. W. (1978). Eliminating cultural oppression in counseling: Toward a general theory. *Journal of Counseling Psychology, 25,* 422. Copyright © (1978) by the American Psychological Society. Reprinted by permission.

them even when they are doing nothing to earn their disdain, they will still blame themselves (IR). Therefore, if these clients are minorities, it will be upsetting for them to have white therapists because they would feel the burden of rectifying any discrepancy between the cultures. Although these clients need help in understanding the limits of their responsibility, a good therapist of any race could be effective given their world view. So basic is the concept of world view that those studying the development of minority identity suggest that as the minority becomes more personally integrated, it is more important that the therapist share the client's world view than the client's race or cultural identity (Larson, 1982). We perceive Sue's model to be equally relevant to the process of supervision.

Mokuau (1987) also explored the world view theme. Analyzing the results of a study where no differences were found when Asian American and white American social workers evaluated counseling effectiveness where there was variation of ethnicity, counseling style, and the presenting problem, Mokuau concluded that what seemed to be critical was an understanding of the client's world view and values. Mokuau noted that "ethnic similarity between counselor and client does not ensure attitudes and values similarity, and ethnic dissimilarity does not preclude a mutual understanding of another's value and cultural orientation" (pp. 334–335).

One of the paradoxes of world view theory is that it is best applied as an overlay to sound cultural information. In other words, an appreciation of the idiosyncratic nature of world views does not negate the need to understand cultural differences among groups. It is, rather, the interplay of these complimentary positions that puts helping professionals in a position to react astutely and knowledgeably to their clients and trainees. There is no easy way to become more culturally sensitive. The place to begin, however, is to understand what the literature has come to call the majority culture.

## Assumptions of the Majority Culture

Pedersen (1987) identified 10 common assumptions that reflect a Western bias in the helping professions. These, he argued, help to reinforce "institutional racism, ageism, sexism, and other forms of cultural bias" (p. 16), and are as follows (the italicized material is Pedersen's):

1. *Assumptions regarding normal behavior.* What we define as normal is culturally, politically, and economically defined.
2. *Emphasis on the individual as opposed to emphasis on family, community, and/or society.*
3. *Fragmentation by academic disciplines.* We tend to identify the problem differently based on whether we are psychologists, anthropologists, sociologists, priests, or physicians. Clients don't necessarily experience their problems in such compartmentalized ways.
4. *Dependence on abstraction.* The dominant culture in this country has relied heavily on abstract concepts without reference to a context. As a result, there is a false assumption that these words mean something to most other persons regardless of their cultural identity. As we have become more aware of context in recent years, we have become more appreciative of the relativity of all cognitive constructs.
5. *Overemphasis on independence.* Our strength and weakness as a culture is our confidence in the individual. This makes us disregard the opinions of others who seem to be overly dependent on family, community, church, etc. Lee (1984) also addressed this issue and pointed to our sophistication in the area of individual development as one indication of our bias.
6. *Neglect of client's support systems.* One of the strange idiosyncrasies of our profession is that we are often more comfortable with the concept of paid friendship than of deliberately involving the client's natural group, familial or social, in treatment.
7. *Dependence on linear thinking.* Systemic therapies have become more sensitive to interactive paradigms but, by and large, most of our paradigms revolve around cause-effect thinking. Other cultures appreciate far more the interconnectedness of seemingly separate events.
8. *Focus on changing the individual, not the system.* As a profession, we are still more in the camp of person-blame, than system-blame. We tend not to challenge institutions and we accept as necessary that the client must accommodate the system.
9. *Neglect of history.* As an uninspired part of our here-and-now philosophy, we tend to neglect the historical context of our clients. If we collect data on the client's immediate family, we believe we have been thorough. Torrey's (1972) statement that we do not adequately understand our own

majority culture is a commentary on our disregard for our own history. This disregard is magnified when we encounter persons different from ourselves.

10. *Dangers of cultural encapsulation.* Pedersen highlighted all of his previous insights by reminding the helping professional that the most dangerous assumption is to think that one is already aware of all of one's assumptions. We are only at the edge of the frontier of appreciating cultural diversity. We needn't be concerned about admitting our ignorance. On the other hand, we communicate a much more uninformed posture if we become self-satisfied with our cultural awareness prematurely.

Pedersen's 10 cultural pitfalls are as important to keep in mind in supervision as in therapy. For example, the supervisor is guilty of fragmentation when multicultural information that is offered in a didactic course is not integrated into work with clients. The supervisor can be critical of a trainee's intervention because it is unorthodox (not "normal") although it is highly effective with a minority youth; the supervisor ignores the supervisee's history when a middle-class African American is sent into a high crime area for internship in order to work with other blacks (Gutierrez, 1982). Furthermore, there is the additional danger in supervision of making one or several of these assumptions because supervisors tend to view their trainees as extensions of themselves, even if their cultural identity is different. By virtue of the trainees' identification with the profession, supervisors can mistakenly assume that trainees identify with them culturally as well.

## Political Nature of Therapy

Another important notion to consider as part of professional context is that the helping professions are "sociopolitical" in nature (Katz, 1985). As was stated earlier, we are not a cul-

turally articulate society. Because we are not sensitive to our majority culture per se, we are equally insensitive to its effects on minority cultures in this country. Katz described this insensitivity as an "invisible veil" that affects our interactions with others, often outside of our awareness. Perhaps this blind spot would be acceptable, except for the diagnostic and evaluative component of our work that requires that we judge our clients and our trainees. We cannot judge without having power. If we judge from the standpoint of one culture to the detriment of a client (or trainee) of another, we have committed a political act.

## The Therapy Culture

Not only is therapy reflective of the majority culture in the United States, it makes up a culture in and of itself, "with its own belief systems, language, customs, governance, and norms" (Holiman & Lauver, 1987, p. 184). Holiman and Lauver made the excellent point that client-centered practice is perhaps far more difficult to achieve than is commonly assumed because of the counselor's enmeshment with the therapy culture. "To the extent that practitioners are acculturated within the counseling culture, their relationships with clients from outside of this culture are subject to barriers of cross-cultural understanding" (p. 185). The simple assessment that someone is behaving defensively is an example of the therapy culture at work in that this commonly used term is rooted in Freudian psychodynamic theory. Therefore, we are all in the business of cross-cultural counseling and cross-cultural training regardless of whether our clients or trainees represent a different group identity from ourselves.

This issue of the many nuances of culture brings us to our last point before we address specific minority groups. McGoldrick et al. (1982) used the metaphor of a snapshot to describe the kind of information we may gain about another culture. It is an image of the real thing, not the real thing itself. In addition to the quality of the focus (fuzzy or sharp), the snapshot can be a good or a distorted image of a person within a culture. (Think of all the perfectly clear photos we have described as not a good likeness of so and so.) The snapshot is also frozen in time, as can be our understanding of another's culture. The snapshot metaphor is similar to observations made by Holiman and Lauver (1987), Blocher (1966), and Haley (1987b) that the real client (or supervisee) is someone different from the hypothetical model that exists in our minds. Just as we are prone to categorize, we are prone also to simplify. Not only is this natural, it is necessary if we are going to do therapy or train others to do so. Real people are too complex to treat or to train. But a person with a phobia (a snapshot) or a family with a disruptive child (the family photo) is within our grasp. This is true not only for diagnostic categories but also for cultural phenomena. Therefore, our understanding of *Hispanic* or *gay* or *physically disabled* becomes a cognitive shorthand for a variety of constructs. To return to the metaphor, we can find ourselves working with a variety of negatives as we attempt to discern what the picture really looks like. But even when we have developed our negatives, our pictures of our clients and the cultures they represent are no more who they are than the pictures of a wonderful vacation are the vacation itself. The trap, of course, is for us to stop searching for new perspectives, updated snapshots, and to close the album on ourselves and on the people we serve.

For the remainder of this chapter, we will be considering several distinct minority groups. One problem we have encountered is that issues relating to one minority group often relate to others as well. This, of course, makes intuitive sense because a society that is intolerant of any minority will be predisposed to be intolerant of all minorities. Therefore, many comments made to underscore one group's obstacles could be made about other groups as well. We appeal to our readers to see the following sections as overlapping and not discrete. Many points that are made about counseling with racial minorities, for instance, also can be made about counseling across generations or sexual orientations. We have focused on the literature specific to each group and have attempted not to repeat issues within the chapter. We hope, however, that the reader will feel the permission to expand upon statements made about one minority and to look for applications for all minority groups.

We also have followed a reverse pyramid format in the amount of attention we give to each group. In one way, this parallels the attention being given to each group in the literature. In another way, it exemplifies our attempt not to be redundant in our discussion.

## RACIAL AND ETHNIC MINORITIES

Twenty-five years ago there was very little awareness that what seemed like a political reality only (minority status in this country) could affect the helping process. The helping professions were an accurate mirror of society at large. Believing in the melting pot, we assumed that the culture we embraced was attractive to everyone. The fact that we benefited from our intimacy with our culture and others did not never seemed to cast doubt on the "rightness" of our assumptions. When minorities did not fare well, we referred to our ancestors and noted how they thrived in this society, never acknowledging that the cultural gap between one Western ethnic group and another did not equal the paradigmatic shift that was being required of those of a more "foreign" ancestry. The legacy of slavery and forced migration was equally ignored. We lived in a tidy world where deviants were considered personally guilty for their plights. We were self-righteous. Helping professionals were, for the most part, self-righteously helpful.

Then came the civil rights movement. Concepts such as "black power" and "black is beautiful" chilled the country to its bone. Our unidimensional view of the world was threatened. For those with insight and conscience, the future held out possibilities for a richness not available in the past. Many of our society's axioms seemed likely for the first time. For those of us in the helping professions at the time, the spirit of the '60s seemed to mirror our own mission to help each person develop his or her potential, unburdened by emotional and psychological problems. There was no better time to be a helper. We would be freed up and encouraged to do what came naturally to us. At the time, we had no idea of our cultural encapsulation and our unpreparedness to meet our goals. Culturally immature, we could not appreciate our limits. Unfortunately, there were very few among us more mature than ourselves to show us the way. We began to flounder vigorously.

Now in the '90s, our professional journals reflect the needs of racial and ethnic minorities. Our collective wisdom, however, deems that we have just begun to appreciate the enormity of our task. It took us this long to shed our innocence, an enormous task in its own right, given our cultural insensitivity. The result, however, is that most white, middle-class therapists and supervisors are still intimidated about the implications of working with persons of different color or culture. In short, we have our work cut out for us.

Before we look at therapy and supervision issues, we need to appreciate once more our own cultural history—that is, the therapy culture and its enmeshment with the dominant white culture. We must start by reminding ourselves that the major theoretical orientations to therapy were devised to work with persons of relative privilege, not the socially disenfranchised. Copeland (1983) noted that in our work with minorities, we adopted terms such as *disadvantaged* and *culturally deprived* to guide us in our efforts. These terms obviously used the dominant culture as the norm. Gardner (1980) traced the history of psycho-

therapy and, more specifically, the use of "scientific" research to perpetuate stereotypes. To help make his point, Gardner referred to Kamin's (1974) work, which examined the results of IQ tests given to immigrants on Ellis Island. "83% of Jews, 80% of Hungarians, 79% of Italians, and 87% of the Russians were [found to be] 'feeble-minded' " (Gardner, 1980, p. 477). Equally "scientific" inquiry has been made more tenacious in its quest to find racial minorities to be intellectually or morally inferior. In the post-civil rights era the language of discrimination is far more subtle. Our legacy, however, remains the same: Academic psychology (and much of practicing psychology, social work, and counseling) has been a strong supporter of upper-class, respectable bigotry (Lerner, 1969).

Even when bigotry is not the motivating force, we refer the reader back to Pedersen's 10 cultural assumptions inherent in the helping professions. If a therapist has learned that problem solving is an active process, then the passive client will be seen as functioning at an inadequate level regardless of the appropriateness of the passivity within the client's cultural group. If the family therapist has learned that adults must be differentiated from their families of origin, then the adult who seeks out the approval of parents will be seen as undifferentiated, a diagnostic label. There is no overt bigotry here, just unawareness that therapeutic concepts are not, nor can be, universal. Therefore, it is important that we are aware of the pitfalls within the therapy culture itself.

Presently, the professional literature reflects three different layers of specificity around the topic of racial and ethnic minorities. Some authors reflect an interest in a particular cultural group connected to a particular geography or environment (e.g., urban blacks, Puerto Ricans). Sometimes this is made more specific by including gender as a variable (e.g., urban black males). A second group focuses on a more generic cultural group (e.g., Asian Americans, Hispanics). Finally, a more recent thrust is an attempt to find models that are applicable to several different racial and ethnic groups. Although we will make some reference to distinct minority groups, we will focus primarily on the larger context of multicultural counseling in its generic sense. Much is lost in such an approach because each minority group interfaces the white dominant culture differently. To do justice even to the largest minority groups in the United States, however, is beyond the scope of this chapter.

A first step in grappling with multicultural counseling and supervision is to determine what makes up a distinct cultural group. Copeland (1983), in her review of the literature, suggested that

> [d]ifferent groups of individuals who share a common experience, history, and language or dialect, and who also reside in the same geographic location are referred to as members of a particular cultural group. Although members of a particular nationality may share a common culture, culture should not be equated with nationality or race . . . since experiences and patterns of behavior and language may vary among members of a particular race. (p. 11)

Sue (1981) followed a similar framework when he defined cross-cultural counseling as a helping relationship in which two or more persons differ with respect to cultural background, values, norms, roles, life styles, and methods of communication. In an interview with Jackson (1987), Vontress made the point that cross-cultural therapy is in the eyes of the beholder:

> For example, White Americans and Black Americans are more culturally similar than are White Americans and Russians, even though the former may not perceive it, because for them race reduces the social attractiveness of Blacks and enhances that of the Russians, even though they and the Russians have little in common, culturally speaking. (p. 22)

Vontress went on to say that "if the counselor and client perceive mutual cultural similarity, even though in reality they are culturally different, the interaction should not be labeled cross-cultural counseling" (p. 22). By definition then, according to Vontress, multicultural therapy must be in the foreground for client and therapist. The same condition would apply for multicultural supervision. Although we agree that cross-cultural issues should be addressed by both therapists and supervisors, we are not willing to concede that perception makes it so. There are many ways that clients, therapists, and supervisors can miss one another; culturally is but one possibility. As with other therapeutic or supervision errors, however, lack of awareness that the error has been made, we believe, does not constitute an eradication of the error.

Wohl (1981) outlined the most obvious occurrences of cross-cultural counseling: (a) The therapist is a member of the dominant white culture, and the client is a member of a racial or ethnic minority; (b) the therapist is from a Western-oriented country and conducts therapy in a non-Western country; (c) the therapist is a member of the dominant white culture and works with clients from other countries; (d) the therapist is a member of a racial or ethnic minority, and the client is a member of the dominant white culture. Typically we think of multicultural counseling following the power dynamics of the society at large, as in (a); the situation would be equally, if not more, complex when the reverse is true, as in (d).

As a reflection of the research available to us to date, most of our comments will address the situation where the person with more power in the relationship is white and the client or trainee is a racial or ethnic minority. Because cross-cultural therapy has been a concern of the mental health field longer than cross-cultural supervision, there is much more information in the literature about the former than the latter. We have chosen to look at the therapy relationship specifically for two reasons: because supervisors are vicariously responsible for the therapy relationship and because a consideration of multicultural issues between the therapist and the client can parallel those of the supervisee and supervisor in multicultural supervision. Later in the section, we will review what has been reported in the literature on multicultural supervision.

## Therapy Issues

As we have already stated, having similar beliefs and values makes conducting therapy across cultures significantly easier. Usually, however, a therapy relationship is quite advanced before such attitudes and values are known by both parties. At the beginning of therapy all parties make assumptions that are attempts to acclimate to the situation. Culture becomes a shorthand for understanding one another. This is not a problem unless stereotyping replaces cultural knowledge, or the shorthand becomes a replacement for each client's unique story. Even under the best of conditions, however, the therapist must consider a sizable number of variables that may be literally foreign. These variables are not just cultural, they are uniquely intertwined into the therapeutic constructs that the therapist must consider. In other words, therapy cannot take place outside of culture. It will either transpire within the client's culture or will be aborted. The following are some questions that the therapist might consider when working with a client of a different racial or ethnic culture:

What is the racial (ethnic) identity of the client? What is the history of the client's race (ethnic group) in this country? What is most likely to be the client's experience with persons of the therapist's race (ethnic group)?

What is the primary language spoken by the client? If English is a second language for the client, how difficult is it for the client to comprehend subtle nuances of the English language? In what ways can the therapist be sure that the client understands what is said? In what ways can the therapist be sure that he or she understands the client?

Even if the client and therapist speak English, are communication patterns different? Does silence mean the same thing to the therapist and client? Are questions experienced by the client in ways that the therapist intends? Do families have a particular hierarchy through which all communication must flow?

Do client and therapist define family membership similarly? What are the boundaries for the client's family? How important are members of extended family to the client? Are nonrelatives considered family to the client? What are the child-rearing practices within the culture? What roles do elderly family members play?

What is the client's level of acculturation? To what degree does the client identify with cultural heritage? How mainstream American is the client? Does the client aspire to be? Are the client's parents acculturated into American society? Are there issues within the family regarding acculturation?

What is the role of religion in this client's life? Does religion mean the same to the client as it does to the therapist? How does the client understand his or her problems? Bad luck? Result of sin? God's wrath? As separate from his or her beliefs?

What is the socioeconomic status of the client? Is socioeconomic status the main source of the client's problems? Is the client's socioeconomic status significantly different from the therapist's? From the majority of the members of the client's cultural group? To what does the client attribute socioeconomic status?

What are predominant gender roles within the client's culture? Does the gender of the therapist pose dissonance for the client? Is the client congruent with gender roles for his or her cultural group?

Does the client's culture enhance readiness for the therapeutic encounter? What is the value of self-disclosing in the client's culture?

Does the client understand his or her role in therapy?

What is the client's concept of time? Do problems seem imminent or more diffuse? What value does the client place on the past? The present? The future? What value does the client place on timeliness?

Not all of these questions are equally important. For instance, Sanchez and Atkinson (1983) studied Mexican Americans and found that the critical variables in terms of self-disclosure to a white therapist were the clients' commitment to their culture to the exclusion of the therapist's culture (making the clients less disclosive) and the sex of the client (females being more likely to self-disclose). Therefore, the cross-cultural therapist must put some valence on each question as it relates to each particular client or family. As the reader can surmise, this alone is a sizable task.

The ultimate purpose of considering the questions listed above, however, is for the therapist to be able to accomplish the basic tasks of therapy. These tasks are an outgrowth of Torrey's (1972) suggestions: identifying and understanding the problem, communicating an acceptance of the client, achieving a status that will allow the therapist to help the client, finding appropriate alternatives for resolution of the client's problems, helping the client implement the most acceptable alternative, and terminating therapy in such a way that therapy will be considered a viable option for the client in the future.

Rogler, Malgady, Costantino, and Blumenthal (1987) considered the different ways in which mental health services can be culturally sensitive and found three distinct patterns, at least in regards to counseling Hispanics: rendering traditional treatments more accessible to Hispanics, selecting available therapeutic models according to the perceived features of the Hispanic culture, and extracting elements from Hispanic culture to modify traditional treatments or to use as an innovative treatment tool. It seems to us that any of these

levels could be a therapist's choice once a more basic cross-cultural understanding is achieved between the client and the therapist. We hope, however, that the client would be given some voice in the therapist's choice.

***The Client's Perspective.*** Sue and Zane (1987) discussed two conditions that must be present from the client's perspective if multicultural therapy is to be successful: The client must perceive the therapist as a credible, effective, and trustworthy helper, and the client must perceive almost immediately some direct benefit from therapy. The latter does not mean giving the client instant cures. Rather, what is given to the client might be a feeling of being understood or a feeling of hope that the problem will be addressed adequately.

Copeland (1983) reported that those minorities who also are of low socioeconomic status (variables that are often confounded in the research literature) have expectations that therapists will be authority figures who will give adequate advice and guidance. They do not seem prepared for a more participatory form of therapy. There is an assumption that in reality, they cannot afford the luxury of the slower, participatory style. This assumption, however, has been challenged (Gardner, 1980) as another form of discrimination. It seems that because therapy reflects the values of the dominant culture, clients who are not members of this culture need to receive preparation to participate in therapy. Once they have been prepared (thus making them more attractive clients to their therapists), attrition goes down, and the clients report greater satisfaction with the process (Gardner, 1980).

***The Therapist's Perspective.*** If minority clients are wary of psychotherapy with white therapists, the literature seems to support their apprehensions. There are documented therapist biases that affect diagnosis and treatment of both racial minorities and the poor. Schofield (1964) coined the acronym *YAVIS* (young, attractive, verbal, intelligent, and successful) to describe the best candidates for therapy. *Attractive* has been defined elsewhere as meaning like me, an obvious drawback in cross-cultural therapy. It seems, then, that the therapist's perspective regarding minorities and working with them accounts for a great deal of the difficulty in cross-cultural therapy.

Webb (1983) used attribution theory to explain our tendency to translate behavior into a trait. He used the theory to describe the cross-cultural counselor's discouragement when attempting to reach across cultures. We believe that attribution theory also can work against the client if the client represents a minority group unfamiliar to the counselor. For example, if we have a colleague of our own ethnic group who is dishonest, we attribute this as a characteristic of the individual. But if the colleague is from an ethnic group that we are unfamiliar with, we are more likely to assume that all Frenchmen, or Jews, or African Americans, or Iranians are dishonest. Finally, Gardner (1980) noted five common blind spots for therapists working with black clients that could be applied to work with other minorities as well. Gardner used psychodynamic terminology to describe these blind spots. Restated in more generic terms, they are

1. Culturally conditioned interaction tendencies that influence the course of therapy but are independent of it
2. Tendency of the therapist to avoid the client because of the therapist's racial or social class aversion
3. Failure to deal with subcultural differences that play a role in the client's conflicts due to a need to deny such differences
4. Assuming the "I love everyone. I'm not prejudiced" posture as a way to deny the therapist's unconscious hostility or aversion toward the client's race or social status
5. Minimizing or overlooking severe psychopathology in the client because of a ten-

dency to attribute the source of the client's problems to environmental stress, discrimination, or intercultural conflict (p. 499)

Although most of the literature refers to a negative bias from the therapist to the client, we assert that there are therapists (and trainees) who are suffering more from lack of information and fear of the unknown than latent hostility. The supervisor is perhaps in the best position to identify this problem and help the supervisee work it through, if the supervisor is sensitive to multicultural issues.

*Therapeutic Approaches.* As we stated earlier, part of therapy's cultural history was to assume that the progressive approach regarding minorities was to find one theoretical approach (usually behaviorism) that would fit their concerns. In fact, the diversity among minorities is as great as that of the majority culture. Therefore, if as practitioners, we believe we perform best using a particular approach, this should be true for our work with minorities as well. On the other hand, if we believe a directive form of therapy is a good fit for minorities because it is more efficient and will be effective before we lose them, then why are we not using this form of therapy for everyone?

Copeland (1983) reported that most cross-cultural theoreticians favor eclecticism for the therapist working with minorities. This can be viewed as more of the same, that is, trying to fit a therapy based on preconceived notions about the client's cultural group. Or it can be seen as a dictum to therapists to be creative in all their therapy, allowing them to choose their approach based on a variety of variables, one being the client's group identity and how this affects the client's problem.

Along with creativity, the multicultural literature often uses the word *flexibility*. If the therapist is determined to work with all clients effectively, then the therapist might need to take cultural variables into account. For example, Nishio and Bilmes (1987) suggested visiting the client's ethnic community in order to understand the client's environmental context. This is not an extreme recommendation. It is more extreme to consider oneself able to help another when that person's culture is totally foreign. Another suggestion Nishio and Bilmes made is to match Asian clients to therapists by gender. Their very salient point is that Asian males, if not very acculturated, may not see a female as enough of an authority figure to be helpful; a female client with a male therapist may be too intimidated to self-disclose, especially if the therapist is bearded! Presently, the professional literature has many suggestions for culturally sensitive interventions. The problem is that training programs are just beginning to acknowledge the need for such specialized knowledge, and seasoned practitioners are unlikely to have been exposed to the rationale for such in their training.

### Supervision Issues

There is only modest attention given in the literature to the dynamics and experiences of multicultural supervision. This is a testimony primarily to the dearth of minorities in the helping professions, a situation perpetuated by poor recruiting efforts (Bernal, Barron, & Leary, 1983). In contrast, there is a sizable body of information that describes training criteria to prepare (presumably) white, middle-class students to work with racial and ethnic minorities. We will begin with the latter. If supervisors are working independent of a training program, they might consider ways in which they can incorporate the information offered in the following paragraphs for their culturally naive supervisees.

*Training for Cross-Cultural Therapy.* What types of experiences will prepare the mental health professional to work effectively with a minority population? As Ponterotto and Casas (1987) asserted, therapists will not become culturally sensitive until training programs are

culturally sensitive. Christensen (1989) described five stages, shown in Table 11.1, that both majority and minority trainees will experience as they develop in cross-cultural awareness. As a means to achieving cross-cultural awareness, the following foci represents the collective opinions of several authorities in the field:

1. *A pluralistic philosophy* (Axelson, 1985; Katz, 1985; Larson, 1982; Paradis, 1981; Ponterotto & Casas, 1987). No amount of training will undo the determined or frightened trainee who is not willing to discard the melting pot myth. Gardner (1980) suggested that we include open-mindedness and freedom from bias as an admissions standard for training programs.

2. *Cultural knowledge* (Gardner, 1980; Hood & Arceneaux, 1987; Ivey, 1987; Paradis, 1981; Parker, 1987; Parker, Bingham, & Fukuyama, 1985; Parker, Valley, & Geary, 1986; Ponterotto & Casas, 1987; Sue, Akutsu, & Higashi, 1985; Webb, 1983). Being open-minded is not enough when we are ignorant of the basic underpinnings of a particular minority culture. The criticism of learning about the culture is that it clouds individuality, that it is closely related to stereotyping (Lloyd, 1987). As Hood and Arceneaux (1987) stated, however, most of the cultural knowledge acquired in training programs barely eliminates "the false information about different cultural groups that has been developed in a student's background and through the media" (p. 174).

3. *Consciousness raising* (Parker, 1987; Parker & McDavis, 1979; Parker et al., 1985; Webb, 1983). Being open-minded and welcoming diversity are imperative preconditions to consciousness raising, but they are not the same thing. Unless the trainee is a minority, many of the experiences of minorities in the society will

**TABLE 11.1**    Stages in the Development of Cross-Cultural Awareness*

### STAGE 1: UNAWARENESS

**Serious thought has never been given to cultural, ethnic, or racial differences or their meaning and influence for individuals and groups.**

*Majority Individual*
Glibly accepts idea of equality, multiculturalism, or the superior/inferior position of his or her own/other groups in the society without speculation. Oblivious to all but the most blatant acts of racism or ethnic discrimination and often relabels such acts as being something else.

*Minority Individual*
Believes in equality of all people or has accepted the position of his or her group in society without speculation. Able to deny or negate even glaring forms of racism or ethnic discrimination, relabeling such acts as possibly due to something else.

*Transition:* A precipitating event of undeniable personal import, forcing the individual to reevaluate beliefs and world view relating to ethnicity, culture, or race.

### STAGE 2: BEGINNING AWARENESS

Accompanied by uneasiness and beginning sense of cognitive dissonance.

*Majority Individual*
Begins to be aware of ethnic and racial stereotypes and to wonder if, and how, these relate to discriminatory acts. Begins to question assumptions and beliefs previously accepted about societal positions of various cultural, ethnic, and racial groups. Accompanied by attempts to disassociate self from sharing responsibility for suffering and harm of disadvantaged and oppressed minority groups.

*Minority Individual*
Begins to be aware of covert and overt ethnic and racial prejudice and discrimination and to wonder if, and how, these impact on minority people's lives. Begins to question reasons for societal position of his or her own and other cultural, ethnic, and racial groups. Accompanied by beginning sense of shared experience with members of own and other disadvantaged or oppressed minorities, but with ambivalence.

*Transition:* A meaningful personal relationship, providing intimate and intense opportunities to learn about a dissimilar group.

### STAGE 3: CONSCIOUS AWARENESS

Evidence of sometimes conflicting preoccupation with cultural, ethnic, and racial differences and their possible meanings in historical and present-day context.

*Majority Individual*
Fully aware of impact of culture, ethnicity, and race, but unsure of how to integrate and use emerging knowledge and understanding in daily life. The following phases may be expected: curiosity, denial, guilt, fear, powerlessness, anger.

*Minority Individual*
Fully aware of impact of ethnicity and race, but unsure of how to integrate and use emerging knowledge and understanding in daily life. The following phases may be experienced: excitement, denial, rejection, sadness, powerlessness, anger.

*Transition:* The working-through of feelings and responses relating to powerful and prolonged soul-searching and continued cross-cultural learning.

### STAGE 4: CONSOLIDATED AWARENESS

Characterized by involved commitment to seek positive societal change and promote intergroup understanding. Experiences differences as positive and rewarding.

*Majority Individual*
Positive acceptance and integration of self-identity and acceptance of other cultures, ethnic groups,

*Minority Individual*
Positive acceptance and integration of his or her own cultural, racial, and ethnic identity and accept-

and races. Accompanied by desire to help other majority group members to reach this new level of understanding. Actively seeks cross-cultural experiences and ways to promote cross-cultural understanding in self and others.

ance of other groups. Accompanied by desire to help others of his or her own minority group to reach this new level of understanding. Actively seeks cross-cultural experiences and ways to promote cross-cultural understanding in self and others.

*Transition:* Graduate and imperceptible shift in allegiance from *own* group to humankind. An affair of the heart.

### STAGE 5: TRANSCENDENT AWARENESS

Beyond limitations of societal dictates regarding appropriate and acceptable manner for relating to various cultural, racial, and ethnic groups.

Cross-cultural awareness is a *way of life* and need no longer be consciously sought. The individual is comfortable in all human environments, responding appropriately, but effortlessly and spontaneously. Although the individual is aware of how others, be they of majority or minority background may perceive his or her actions and responses, this is not a major factor determining behavior in cross-cultural situations.

*From Christensen, C. P. (1989). Cross-cultural awareness development: A conceptual model. *Counselor Education and Supervision, 28*(4), 270–287. Copyright (1989) by the American Association for Counseling and Development. Reprinted by permission.

be out of the trainee's awareness. In effect, we must know ourselves, including our learned cultural reactions, before we can attempt to understand another from a different culture. Stewart (1981) noted that our culture is more prone to sympathy than empathy. One might say that consciousness-raising is the beginning of empathy.

4. *Experiential training* (Gardner, 1980, Ivey, 1987; Parker et al., 1986; Stadler & Rynearson, 1981; Webb, 1983). Cognitive learning cannot be bypassed, but it should be complemented with some trial-and-error opportunities prior to direct work with minorities. Use of videotape and role-plays to monitor communication patterns that might hinder cross-cultural therapy are quite useful. Larson (1982) recommended that trainees be given an opportunity to observe a supervisor working with members of a minority group for whom the trainee is preparing to work. (Of

course it is important to remember that each minority is an individual with individual ways of interfacing the culture. Therefore, the types of techniques that are important for the supervisor to model are ways of addressing race or ethnicity in the therapy session, checking out cultural information, etc.)

Another type of experiential learning is depicted by Neimeyer and Fukuyama (1984). They developed the Cultural Attitudes Repertory Test (CART), which can be used for trainee self-exploration of private knowledge about a number of different minority groups. CART allows trainees the opportunity to appreciate cultural variations among groups (differentiation) and aids trainees in bringing variations together into a more comprehensive understanding of their private understanding of a particular group (integration).

5. *Contact with minorities* (Parker et al.,

1985; Parker et al., 1986; Parker & Mc-Davis, 1979; Sue et al., 1985). In a pluralistic society it is less and less congruous for a therapist to work with a minority when the therapist has had no social experiences with members of the minority's cultural group. Ethnic neighborhoods abound, and some training programs require that their students spend some time in such neighborhoods or in minorities' homes.

6. *Practicum or internship with minorities* (Parker et al., 1985; Sue et al., 1985). Prior to leaving a training program the student should have supervised, direct contact with minorities. Even if solid cognitive content is presented and appropriate attitudinal changes occur, when trainees work only with members of their own culture during practicum and internship, they cannot be considered trained as a multicultural therapists. This especially is true because the field has not determined what approaches and techniques are crucial for cross-cultural therapy (Parker, 1987). Therefore, supervised experience is imperative to help trainees integrate their new knowledge with actual experience, sometimes in a trial-and-error fashion. Of course, the trainee's experience will be partially determined by the cross-cultural expertise of the supervisor. With so few minority supervisors in the field, this in itself can be a precarious situation. As Gardner (1980) stated,

*[w]ithout scientifically tested procedures those who would . . . engage in direct supervision of work with nontraditional patients will have to rely upon an underdeveloped literature, unvalidated personal experience and knowledge, and a variety of trial-and-error experiences guided by keenly attuned empathy and clinical wisdom. (pp. 493–494)*

*Nagging Problems.*    Even the most progressive programs (Ponterotto & Casas, 1987) cannot undo social ills, nor can they produce better than state of the art helping professionals. Among our nagging problems in multicultural training are the following:

1. Our training programs are still culturally deprived in that most educators and supervisors represent the majority culture. In addition, we have done little to seriously address the underrepresentation of minorities in our training programs.
2. Larson (1982) commented that cross-cultural training has the potential of missing two important groups: those referred to as marginal, that is, identifying neither with the dominant culture nor with their minority culture; and those who are multilabeled, e.g., poor Hispanic, physically disabled Asian.
3. Until all minorities have equal access to power and influence, real pluralism will be beyond our reach (Sue, 1983). We must encourage trainees not only to be therapeutic but also to be political. In order to be credible, we must approach our supervisory roles in a political fashion.
4. Our training is not empirically based. Christensen (1984) reported that trainees were no more effective with African American clients after cross-cultural training than before. (However, trainees' performance was no different with white clients.) We do not know the relative importance of race in therapy; we only infer from the importance our society has put on race.
5. A little knowledge is a dangerous thing. With increased exposure to minorities, graduates of our programs can presume cultural values when they do not apply (Sue & Zane, 1987). The ability to be discriminating among similar persons and situations requires experience and more than just a smattering of information.

*The Supervision Process.*    In his frank and thoughtful chapter, Bradshaw (1982) addressed the implications of race in the supervisory relationship. He asserted that race is a highly charged catalyst in our society, one that is bound to emerge, even if not addressed, in supervision. Bradshaw addressed situations where blacks and whites interact, but his comments are relevant to other cross-cultural situations as well.

Bradshaw noted that a black client seeing a white therapist who is supervised by a white supervisor is the most common occurrence in mental health practice. In this circumstance both therapist and supervisor must be diligent that preconceived notions do not negatively affect therapy. For example, Bradshaw suggested that ignorance of the appropriateness of "black paranoia" would affect the diagnostic process negatively when the client seemed initially distrustful. On the other hand, the therapist's own discomfort with blacks might encourage the therapist to patronize the black client for fear of stimulating strong feelings in the client (as if patronizing would not!). Finally, both supervisor and therapist might attribute too much of the client's problem to race out of discomfort with racial issues. Underdiagnosis is, therefore, another common problem when the helping professionals are all white and the client is a minority (Vargas, 1989). Often minorities can feel this and play it to their (supposed) advantage (Montalvo & Gutierrez, 1984).

Although as supervisors we often communicate our desire to have more minority trainees, we are often caught unprepared to work with our minority trainees. Douce (1989) offered the astute insight that minority trainees are experiencing their own multicultural developmental process, one that may or may not dovetail with the supervisor's. She recounted the following anecdote:

> I remember a Black psychology intern from a few years ago. She arrived having experienced a fair amount of blind discrimination and oppression from her clinical academic program where she had been one of very few Blacks. We were a safe place; we talked about appreciation of differences and provided training in it; we

have three Black professionals on staff. We expected her to respond appreciatively to all this nurturance. She spent the whole year angry — angry at Black and White senior staff and colleagues alike. The real surprise came when she had a hard time leaving and told everyone in her next position what a wonderful internship she had had. I saw this same process repeated with a gay man. I had never felt so judged by an intern on my own commitments and actions. I was hurt and sometimes angry. He thinks it was the best, most growthful year he has ever had. (p. 13)

According to Christensen's (1989) stages, both of these interns seem to have spent the majority of their internship at Stage 3 (conscious awareness) but moved on to some form of Stage 4 (consolidated awareness) at its conclusion.

Supervisors inadvertently can put the minority supervisee in a double bind by being oversolicitous on the one hand and never addressing the supervisee's race on the other. Such behavior effectively isolates the supervisee even if the supervisor's intention is very different from this. As Bradshaw (1982) noted, another form of the supervisor's discomfort is to express to a black supervisee that the supervisee is not thought of as black. Bradshaw emphasized that this "hallucinatory whitening" can hardly be taken as a compliment.

On the other hand, minority supervisees can be deemed experts regarding all clients of their cultural group when working with a white supervisor. Although the minority's perspective is assuredly valuable, to assume that a supervisee understands all clients of that culture is another form of "all _____'s are alike." The supervisee knows that he or she cannot adequately fill such a role but may not know how to renege without being seen as uncooperative (Bradshaw, 1982).

Gutierrez (1982) underscored this issue by challenging the insensitivity of supervisors when they ask middle-class Latinos to complete field placements in economically deprived environments because the students share an ethnic identity with the clients served in these areas. Although certainly not always a problem, trainee fear (especially female trainees who must work evening hours) and guilt about their fear can complicate the training experience. Gutierrez also noted that supervisors sometimes appear flexible but become highly resistant if trainees introduce nontraditional techniques in their work. In other words, the supervisor is communicating a willingness to work with a minority trainee as long as it involves no change on the supervisor's part.

As a counterpoint to the above issues Zuniga (1987) reported a pilot project with Mexican-American supervisees in which supervision focused on ethnic identity, family history, acculturation, and racism experiences. When trainees vacillated between feelings of competence and feelings of inadequacy, these were processed within a cultural context. "As they talked about painful school experiences, they could comprehend how they had introjected the negative expectations of former teachers and school peers who assumed they would perform poorly because they were Mexican American" (p. 18). These insights were used not only for the interns' own growth but also as a vehicle for them to work with Mexican-American clients. On a positive note, supervision also focused on the strong survival attributes of these interns to negotiate their former hostile environments.

A related issue surfaces when all Hispanics, for example, are referred to a Puerto Rican supervisee. There is some wisdom and some empirical data to suggest that clients tend to prefer someone of their own race as therapists. But there are several problems with this practice: (1) It is naive to assign clients on the most global of group characteristics. For example, a Cuban client will more than likely be no more satisfied with a Puerto Rican therapist than an Anglo therapist, unless, of course, language is a serious barrier. (2) The supervisee's experi-

ence will be limited if he or she is not allowed to work with white clients. (3) The supervisee might not even be party to the decision to assign minority clients to him or her. This, then, becomes another example of making race the primary focus but not necessarily addressing race with the supervisee. (4) The supervisee and the clients alike might resent this type of stereotyping. For example, an interesting anecdote was told by one African-American trainee who said that often when a black client was referred to him in the university counseling center where he interned, he had to prove to the client that he knew what he was doing. "They just assumed that they were assigned to me because I was black and that I mustn't be good enough to see white clients." We reiterate Bradshaw's sentiments; race is a powerful force in our society.

Another complication for the minority supervisee who works with a white supervisor is that the supervisor may lean on the supervisee's insights more than is usual or appropriate. If a supervisor has not worked with many minority supervisees, the supervisor often will not know what to expect in supervision. One black doctoral student reported that she was taken aback in her final interview with her supervisor when the supervisor said, "You know, I was really worried about working with you since I've never supervised a black student before, but it really went well." The student had no idea that this was going on with the supervisor during the internship and had to wonder how things might have gone if she had encountered some trouble in her clinical work. As a buffer to this possibility, Vargas (1989) recommended that the supervisor seek consultation with a minority-group colleague rather than turn to the supervisee for consultation.

In an excellent review of salient issues in cross-cultural supervision of Asian and Hispanic social workers by nonminority supervisors, Ryan and Hendricks (1989) identified five differential characteristics that may become sources of conflict: cognitive orientation, motivational orientation, communication styles, value orientations, and sensory orientation. In the first category, Ryan and Hendricks noted that the Japanese are more likely to trust nonverbal information than verbal analysis to solve a problem. This might put them at a disadvantage in a traditional case conference. Representative of motivational orientation is the supervisor who might experience the Hispanic trainee as not paying enough attention to planning for therapy sessions, which is a behavior that might be linked to the traditional Hispanic belief that much of life is beyond one's control and planning does not change that basic premise.

The third category, communication styles, has received more attention elsewhere in the literature. Both Asians and male Hispanics, for different reasons, are unlikely to willingly admit to having trouble in their clinical work. Additionally, Asians are likely to view excessive talking as indication of narcissism and attention seeking. This may be paired with a tendency to cut off the process of supervision and case conceptualization too soon. Reflecting the value of orientation of humility is an Asian intern who was told by her supervisor that she lacked self-confidence. She had to explain to him that she had often minimized her achievements so as not to appear boastful. In relationship to the relative value given to either hierarchical or egalitarian approaches, Ryan and Hendricks noted that both Asian and Hispanic societies embody a hierarchical structure. "In supervision, it is helpful to watch for nonverbal cues, such as facial expression or changes in body posture, in order to know if the supervisee is angry or disagreeing with the supervisor" (p. 36).

Finally, it was noted that Asians are more visual, whereas Hispanics are more verbal. Hispanics might be resistant to writing out comprehensive case notes, whereas some Asians have difficulty with the auditory sense, making the audiotape a difficult vehicle for learning. Ryan and Hendricks's contribution

of classifying some of the inherent obstacles in cross-cultural supervision is significant. However, acculturation and intragroup differences always should be kept in mind.

It is the rare white supervisee who has the opportunity to work with a minority supervisor. If the supervisee is then assigned minority clients, it will be imperative that race and culture be a topic openly addressed. According to Vargas (1989), the supervision process may easily go awry if the minority supervisor does not introduce the issue of cultural manifestations both in therapy and in supervision. Once this becomes a permissible topic, however, the majority culture supervisee stands to learn a great deal in this context.

We will conclude by reviewing two empirical studies that addressed the issue of cross-cultural supervision. Cook and Helms (1988) studied 225 Asian, black, Hispanic, or native American supervisees to examine their satisfaction with cross-cultural supervision. Of the variables they considered, supervisor's liking and conditional interest were found to contribute to greater satisfaction. About the second variable the authors hypothesized that

> supervisees may value conditional supervisory relationships as long as they perceive that the conditions occur in an atmosphere of caring. Perhaps in such a context supervisees are able to use the information communicated by the supervisor's conditions to help them figure out what is expected of them in this particular cross-cultural environment. (p. 273)

Overall, the supervisees tended to report guarded relationships with their supervisors; additionally, native-American and African-American supervisees were least satisfied with cross-cultural supervision, and Asian Americans were most satisfied.

In a provocative examination of field instructors and supervisees' working relationships within a cross-cultural context, McRoy, Freeman, Logan, Blackmon (1986) found that actual problems were few but that both supervisors and supervisees expected more problems than benefits in such relationships. Several black supervisors reported that white supervisees had questioned their competence and resisted their supervision. Hispanic supervisors also noted experiences that were related to a lack of acceptance of their authority on the supervisee's part. Despite these responses, the actual number of supervisors (12, or 28 percent) and supervisees (7, or 16 percent) who reported having directly experienced a cross-cultural problem was quite low. When problems did occur, those supervisees who addressed the problem with their supervisors were satisfied with the outcome. Of the seven students who had experienced difficulty, however, only two chose to approach their supervisors about it. The others felt it was too threatening to do so because of the power differential in supervision. This study points to the vital issue of supervisor and supervisee expectations that influence cross-cultural encounters. Despite some recent progress, cross-cultural relationships are still approached with trepidation by minorities and nonminorities alike.

## GENDER ISSUES

The status of women in our society has been a tenacious problem that has affected women economically and psychologically. Because of its pervasiveness, helping professionals must take gender into account both in therapy and in training and supervision. As with all minority issues, it must be remembered that the problem of gender not only is something we must be sensitive to in service delivery but also is something we must live with (and confront) within our own profession (Fitzgerald & Nutt, 1986). Because the vast majority of persons with a master's degree (and many of those with doctorates) in the helping professions are female, the issue of gender hits close to home for many of us.

At the very root of gender issues is the distribution of power. In our society power is most often paired with money. It is well known that women generally earn less than their male counterparts. The helping professions are no exception. York, Henley, and Gamble (1987) found that female social workers in one state were underrepresented in higher paying administrative positions but not in supervisory positions. In fact, it was easier for women than for men to find themselves in supervisory slots but more difficult to secure an administrative post. (This might be interpreted as one way to give women responsibility without giving them power. It might also be a testimony to the fit between the skills of many women and the supervisory role.) Questioning whether women were less interested in the responsibility of administration, the authors controlled for this factor in their study. Yet even when they were in similar positions, women earned only 70 percent of what men earned. Job position was found to be a better predictor of salary for men than for women, even when desire to advance, experience, and education were controlled. This is but one example of a pervasive problem.

Psychology has addressed the gender issue with two somewhat dichotomous concepts: androgyny, or the development of both male and female characteristics, and the "different voices" of men and women perspective (Gilligan, 1982). Would our society be better off and individuals and families better served if we encouraged males and females to develop the opposite-sex part of themselves? Or should we come to terms with real differences (in addition to those that are biological) between men and women and attempt to shape society to appreciate and use fully the perspective each gender can offer? A decade ago, the helping professions seemed to be in support of androgyny. Although still a viable and useful concept, androgyny is less likely to be put forth as the single solution to the gender problem (Deau, 1984). Perhaps androgyny, while expanding the options for men and women, did not cut deep enough into our consciousness to change the foundation on which we stood. While men and women were encouraged to be more alike behaviorally, the inferior position held by females was not altered. In fact, the only hope for women that their status would be elevated was if men found their feminine side useful. Therefore, women again found their status intrinsically connected to men. (It is interesting to note that the root of the word *androgyny* is *androgen,* a male sex hormone.) Gilligan (1982), instead, addressed the psychological theories by which we defined normality for men and women and found that our most basic premises were male oriented. Against such odds, androgyny rings hollow.

> *Implicitly adopting the male life as the norm, they [psychological theorists] have tried to fashion women out of a masculine cloth . . . [i]f you make a woman out of a man, you are bound to get into trouble. In the life cycle, as in the Garden of Eden, the woman has been the deviant. (p. 6)*

The problem in theory, therefore, becomes a problem in women. As they have with other minority groups, the helping professions have represented societal bias in the treatment of women better than they have represented their clientele. We must approach the gender issue knowing we have helped perpetuate it.

All data are not yet in. As with much of our work, we are more aware of the problem than the solution. Therefore, as we consider gender issues in therapy and supervision, we must proceed tentatively. Perhaps the danger surrounding the gender issue is that therapists and supervisors feel more secure in their assumptions about gender than they do in their assumptions about other minority issues. As a result they can help drive the finishing nail into a sexist and limiting solution to the client's problem or the supervisee's training.

As we briefly consider gender issues in therapy and supervision, we will not include the demeaning problem of sexual harassment. It is our view that, although related to gender issues, this is an ethical and legal matter and one that we hope our readers will see as self-evident. In addition, in order to isolate gender issues, we will assume that there are no other minority issues operating as there would be if the therapist and supervisor, for example, represented different racial groups. Finally, as we hope will be evident in what follows, we see sexism as a problem that hurts men as well as women. The female's plight is more dramatic; the male's, perhaps, more insidious.

## Therapy Issues

Operating within our framework that the supervisor must oversee therapy as well as stay attuned to the supervisory relationship, we will begin by considering briefly some of the therapeutic dilemmas generated by gender issues and some alternative routes the therapist can take.

*The Client's Perspective.* Therapy can be an intimidating enterprise for the client. This is often exacerbated by gender. The female client with an overbearing, rigid father enters therapy with a male therapist, hoping this time to gain approval; the male client who expresses no emotion to his male friends and colleagues enters therapy with a male therapist; the couple who have become frightened because the man has become physically abusive enters therapy with a female therapist; the male client who has not been successful establishing an intimate relationship with a female enters therapy with a female therapist. The implications of gender are fairly apparent for each of these somewhat stereotypical cases. But even when they are not so apparent, gender issues are operating at some level because gender is one of our societal markers.

Unfortunately, we do not have data on the complaints of male clients about gender issues in therapy. We do have such data for women, however, and the complaints break down into four categories (APA, 1975):

1. Fostering traditional sex roles
2. Bias in expectations and devaluation of women
3. Sexist use of psychoanalytic concepts
4. Responding to women as sex objects, including seduction of women

As we all know, gender or sex role issues do not begin in therapy. More and more, we are becoming aware of the power of sex role stereotyping to bring conflict into our lives. Women returning to work in midlife, divorcing couples, dual career couples, men physically ill from stressful work environments—these are only a few examples of the many cases where our rigid views of men's and women's roles have made life more difficult. Often these men and women will seek therapy for answers. Therapists who are congruent regarding the issue of sex roles are of paramount importance to such clients. Cook (1985) provided a list of additional problems that have sex role issues at their base:

1. *Overconformity to prevailing sex role standards.*
2. *Dissonance between self-perceptions and sex role-related standards for behavior.*
3. *Disjunctions between personal sex role standards and present environmental and life stage demands [e.g., a newly divorced male who must be a full-time parent on weekends or who receives custody of a child for whom he has not been the primary caregiver].*
4. *Possession of an inadequate behavioral repertoire to cope with present environmental and life stage demands [e.g., the new widow who is unprepared to handle her own finances].*
5. *Inhibition of behavioral skills because of sex role standards [e.g., the new father who considers it unmasculine to be too nurturant but who wants to be close to his*

*child; the young woman who wants a career in business but is afraid of being perceived as unfeminine].*
6. *Ambiguity about appropriate behavior and possible consequences in an upcoming situation [e.g., the first male in a school of nursing, or the first woman hired in a particular law firm].*
7. *Coping with actual, externally imposed sanctions incurred [i.e., sexism being played out].*
8. *Conflicts ensuing from overly rigid attitudes about others [e.g., a father who cannot cope with a son who has decided to become a nurse, or a daughter who has decided to enter the military, etc.]. (pp. 255–256)*

Cook's list is probably not exhaustive, but it gives the therapist an anchor with which to conceptualize client problems that revolve around gender issues. In several examples given above, the client may be unaware that part of the problem is self-imposed (with great help from society) limits. We will look at interventions to help clients once we have considered the therapist's perspective.

***The Therapist's Perspective.***    For the ardent feminist therapist, there is no alternative but to use therapy as an instrument for change. As an example of this position, Dworkin (1984) maintained that the female client must be assessed as a by-product of a patriarchal society. She further maintained that the therapist has the responsibility to intervene, directly or indirectly, into the client's value system if it reflects a patriarchal bias. Along with many other authors, Dworkin's position was that relief is not enough for clients who have suffered discrimination. Rather, women must unlearn old attitudes and learn new ones.

Most therapists take a more moderate view of the role of therapy to influence women and men in terms of their sex role issues. Therapists and their supervisors, however, should keep their antennae out for sexist overtones in therapy, whether these work against women, men, or both. They also need to continually challenge their own therapeutic assumptions to see if they camouflage gender issues. For example, when Freud first introduced his theories, they were accepted as valid, in part, because they reflected the socially accepted views of sex roles of the times. In more recent years, psychoanalysis as Freud put it forth has been attacked by feminists as sexist. Similarly, the DSM III was challenged (Kaplan, 1983) as reflecting masculine-based assumptions regarding normality and, thus, codifying these biases into its diagnostic categories. Taggart (1985) is one of the feminist family therapists who challenged the sexist element in systemic therapy. She asserted that the female client's "context" must reach beyond the family to the broader social context where her behavior may have a different meaning. Taggart was particularly offended when dynamics such as spouse abuse were explained within the family only, disregarding society's overall messages to men and women about appropriate sex role behavior.

As in Freudian times, therapists continue to reflect societal views. It bears repeating that when we live in a society that discriminates against any group, the extent to which therapy mirrors society is the extent to which we help perpetuate the problem. As Pittman (1985) stated, we are both "culture brokers" and "gender brokers" (p. 29). The Broverman, Broverman, Clarkson, Rosenkrantz, and Vogel (1970) research raised the consciousness of helping professionals when it was found that therapists saw men and women in very stereotypical ways and, moreover, found that the behavior of men only was equivalent to "adult" behavior. More recently, O'Malley and Richardson (1985) repeated the study to see if attitudes had changed since the early '70s. They found that counselors still viewed men and women stereotypically but that male and female behaviors were both seen as "adult."

O'Malley and Richardson concluded that "each counselor needs to assess his or her own beliefs in relationship to counseling different-sex clients in an attempt to provide unbiased support and assistance in allowing individuals to grow and develop in their own way" (p. 299).

Although gender issues can contaminate therapy regardless of the sex of the therapist or the client, there has been more concern when the therapist is male and the client is female. The male therapist must be diligent when working with a female client to present to his client the same breadth of alternatives that he would give a male client. The APA's Task Force on Sex Bias and Sex Role Stereotyping in Psychotherapeutic Practice published "Guidelines for Therapy With Women" (1978), listed in Table 11.2, to help the therapist with this task. Additionally, Division 17 (counseling psychology) of the APA approved "Principles Concerning the Counseling/Psychotherapy of Women," which have been examined thoroughly in a more recent publication (Fitzgerald & Nutt, 1986).

From another perspective, Hare-Mustin (1978) seemingly discouraged even the most "liberated" male from working with traditional female clients. Her point was that if one assumes that what the client needs is an egalitarian male therapist as part of treatment, this reinforces stereotypes because it presupposes that female clients need a special male to treat them differently. "What a woman needs to learn is not that some men are different but how can she become a different woman" (p. 190).

Finally, gender issues have received a good deal of attention in the family therapy field. Therapists have at least one additional degree of complication if they are doing couples therapy in that they must deal with the couple's gender issues as well as their gender issues with the couple. Reese-Dukes and Reese-Dukes (1983) argued that cotherapy teams (male and female) are the only rational way around this issue because the politics of sex will be operating whether the lone therapist is male or female. Furthermore, a cotherapy team can model egalitarian behavior and be a "potent implicit catalyst to therapeutic change" (p. 99).

**TABLE 11.2**    Guidelines for Therapy with Women*

1. The conduct of therapy should be free of constrictions based on gender-defined roles, and the options explored between client and practitioner should be free of sex role stereotypes.
2. Psychologists should recognize the reality, variety, and implications of sex discriminatory practices in society and should facilitate client examination of options in dealing with such practices.
3. The therapist should be knowledgeable about current empirical findings on sex roles, sexism, and individual differences resulting from the client's gender-defined identity.
4. The theoretical concepts employed by the therapists should be free of sex bias and sex role stereotypes.
5. The psychologist should demonstrate acceptance of women as equal to men by using language free of derogatory labels.
6. The psychologist should avoid establishing the source of personal problems within the client when they are more properly attributable to situational or cultural factors.
7. The psychologist and a fully informed client mutually should agree upon aspects of the therapy relationship such as treatment modality, time factors, and fee arrangements.
8. While the importance of the availability of accurate information to a client's family is recognized, the privilege of communication about diagnosis, prognosis, and progress ultimately resides with the client, not with the therapist.
9. If authoritarian processes are employed as a technique, the therapy should not have the effect of maintaining or reinforcing stereotypic dependency of women.
10. The client's assertive behaviors should be respected.
11. The psychologist whose female client is sub-

jected to violence in the form of physical abuse or rape should recognize and acknowledge she is the victim of a crime.
12. The psychologist should recognize and encourage exploration of a woman client's sexuality and should recognize her right to define her own sexual preferences.
13. The psychologist should not have sexual relations with the client, nor treat her as a sex object.

*From "Guidelines for Therapy with Women," Task Force on Sex Bias and Sex Role Stereotyping in Psychotherapeutic Practice, October 1, 1976. Copyright (1978) by the American Psychological Association. Reprinted by permission.

In general, family therapists have been found to be more liberal in their views of sex roles than individually trained therapists, and female therapists have been found to be more liberal than male therapists (Hare-Mustin & Lamb, 1984). Liberal attitudes, however, can pose their own threat. Having grown through the era of women's liberation and beyond, we have arrived at a place where "overlooking sex role issues, whether it takes the form of reinforcing traditional values or automatically assuming that an egalitarian relationship [between a married couple] exists, communicates a lack of respect and appreciation for clients' life-style choices" (Margolin, Talovic, Fernandez, & Onorato, 1983, p. 143).

*Therapeutic Interventions.*    As with all social issues, the position the therapist takes on sex role is more important than the theoretical model the therapist employs (Margolin et al., 1983). Beyond theory, however, Cook (1987) advised any therapist who is sensitive to the androgyny literature to consider the following when contemplating a therapeutic intervention:

*(a) the value of both masculine and feminine characteristics for both sexes; (b) the existence of between and within sex differences regarding sex-role differences; (c) the importance of*

*individual differences in sex-role adjustment; (d) the complexity of sex-role phenomena; and (e) the occurrence of changes in sex-role perceptions, norms, attitudes, and behaviors over time. (p. 503)*

Consciousness raising in a group setting has long been considered an ideal form of treatment for sex role issues (Cook, 1985; Croteau & Burda, 1983). Both men and women often need support from same-sex group members to delve into uncharted waters. According to Gilligan (1982), men need to increase their ability to attach and to arrive at a wider range of emotional responses (Croteau and Burda, 1983); women need to increase their ability to separate and assert their own needs and wants. Obviously, the supervisor must be sure that the therapist has group skills as well as a clear perception of sex role matters to serve clients adequately.

Lastly, we return again to the subject of power and the recommendation made by Beamish and Marinelli (1983) that female clients should be taught different bases of power (referent, expert, legitimate and coercive), taught how to discriminate among different power bases, and encouraged to practice responses that reflect each power base. If, for instance, a woman overuses coercive power to get her needs met, it is not enough to be told this. Knowing what *not* to do does not always make what one *should* do obvious. Furthermore, the strategy suggested by Beamish and Marinelli should also take into consideration the context in which coercive power is effective. Skill building can be a weak response to a systemic problem.

These are only some of the interventions the therapist can use to address gender issues with clients. The supervisor's task, in addition to being sure that the trainee has the skills to deliver these interventions, is to be aware of the trainee's own sex role identity and how this might interact with these or any other interventions. Finally, supervisors must keep watch over sex role issues that might be emerging between themselves and their supervisees.

**Supervision Issues**

Students often enter training programs (and occasionally supervision) no more sophisticated about the implications of gender on the therapeutic process than their clients. It falls on trainers and supervisors to offer the kinds of experiences and knowledge that will help bridge the gap from where the trainees' socialization has brought them to where the trainees need to be in order to be helpful to others.

*Training in Sex Role Issues.* There is some indication that the androgynous therapist is in the best position to work with a variety of clients (Borders & Fong, 1984; Fong, Borders, & Neimeyer, 1986; Foxley, 1979). Borders & Fong (1984) found androgynous counselors to be more "flexible, self-assured, adaptive, accepting and competent in interpersonal interactions" (p. 65). Furthermore, these authors made the critical point that it is not the behavior of an androgynous trainee per se that makes a difference but the fact that the androgynous person thinks differently. Therefore, they warn trainers to watch for behavior that is mimicked but not representative of an androgynous attitude. In their later study (Fong et al., 1986), the authors concluded that the personality characteristics of androgyny might be as important as counseling skills for working with clients.

It seems appropriate that androgyny be considered as part of training. Therapists in training should be asked to look at their own sex role histories and be given a chance to consider the consequences of stereotypical responses in different therapeutic situations. Building on the work of Gilligan (1982), Hotelling and Forrest (1985) suggested that men need to learn that they are not good listeners (in general). Because their primary position is to separate, men may listen just long enough to find a solution or figure out what the other wants, without ever really hearing the subtleties of the message.

Moore and Nelson (1981) proposed a model for increasing awareness of sex role bias that is simple and would be easy to implement in most settings. They presented trainees with a minilecture about sex role issues. They then played videotaped vignettes (audiotapes could be used) of clients of different ages with counselors, all showing some gender bias. The trainees were then asked to identify the sex role bias in each vignette, address possible contingencies, and suggest alternative counselor behaviors. The matter of contingencies is crucial to such a process because it underlines the fact that sex role biases come from somewhere in the social makeup of the trainee. It is not just trainee responses that need to be changed; rather, as was stated earlier, it is the attitudes underlying the behavior that are of utmost concern.

Brodsky (1980) also suggested an experiential method of sensitizing trainees to sex role issues. She recommended a group mode so interactions can be observed by others. Among the training strategies she recommended are guided fantasy, role reversals, and therapy simulations.

*The Supervision Process.*    Gender is one of the issues that must be considered in the relationship between supervisors and supervisees. Among the many relationship issues are the following possibilities:

— A female supervisee does not think her male supervisor takes her seriously.
— A male supervisee states that he expected his female supervisor to be more nurturant (Brodsky, 1980).
— A male supervisor finds his most talented supervisee to be the only female he is supervising. The male supervisees assume that the supervisor is sexually attracted to her.

— A female supervisor gives her male supervisee feedback that he is treating his female client in a sexist manner. The supervisee feels ganged up on and requests a male supervisor.

These are only a few of the complications around the issue of gender in the supervision process. Petty and Odewahn (1983) reported a study conducted with 144 social workers and their supervisors. Male social workers responded negatively to female supervisors initiating structure and positively to male supervisors doing the same. Female social workers responded more positively to female supervisors initiating structure than to males doing so. All supervisors in the study (male and female) were found to be equally "considerate." Clearly there seems to be a gender issue operating in this study. Yet the numbers are so small in most supervisory situations (by design) that such dynamics are often attributed to individual personalities. It is important for supervisors to attempt to step back and see the broader picture.

Stoltenberg and Delworth (1987) advised supervisors to watch out for female supervisees who might overidentify with client affect and "wallow in the confusion," whereas male supervisees might avoid affect and "escape the necessary ambivalence" by focusing on cognition primarily (p. 176). This pattern might also be true for supervisors. It is possible that female supervisors, relying on their intuitive strength of connecting with others (Gilligan, 1982), might overidentify with their supervisees and appear confused at times. Male supervisors may arrive at their perceptions more quickly but may be employing less data to do so. Female supervisors may also take feedback from supervisees more to heart (Reid, McDaniel, Donaldson, & Tollers, 1987) than do their male counterparts.

As was put forth earlier, the need for power is generic to clients, therapists, and supervisors alike, men and women. The type of power utilized, however, will vary and may or may not be functional. Robyak, Goodyear, and Prange (1987) considered the topic of power and whether male and female supervisors were different in their use of power. They categorized power as either expert (the display of such resources as specialized knowledge and skills, confidence, and rationality), referent (derived from interpersonal attraction and based on trainees perceiving that they hold in common with supervisors relevant values, attitudes, opinions, and experiences), or legitimate (a consequence of perceived trustworthiness in that a supervisor is a socially sanctioned provider of services who is not motivated by personal gain). Contrary to what one might expect, male supervisors reported greater preference for referent power than did female supervisors. Robyak et al. also found that referent power was preferred by supervisors with relatively little experience. They noted that there is an inherent danger in using referent power in that initial similarities might dissipate as supervisees and supervisors get to know each other better. These differences might seem more extreme if the relationship is based on perceived similarities. Also, the evaluation process can become more complicated when supervisees have been given the impression that they share important characteristics with their supervisors.

Robyak et al. (1987) hypothesized that male supervisors might lean on referent power in an attempt to compensate for the male tendency to separate rather than to "attach" (Gilligan, 1982). One can hypothesize similarly that female supervisors try to compensate by using a power base that does not overly depend on relationship.

In a similar study that focused on supervisee behavior (Goodyear, 1990), both supervisees and their supervisors perceived female supervisees as more likely to employ a personal-dependent influence style in a conflict situation with their supervisors. This was the only significant finding of the study that ex-

amined eight different influence strategies for supervisees of both genders interacting with supervisors of both genders. It is interesting to note that both male and female supervisors perceived the female supervisees similarly. Furthermore, when we compare this study to that done by Robyak et al. (1987), it seems that female supervisees behave in a more stereotypical manner than female supervisors.

Another modest research effort has been to consider gender pairings in individual supervision. There is some evidence that the gender of the supervisor will have some bearing on the satisfaction of the supervisee with supervision (Behling, Curtis, & Foster, 1982, 1988), but not all studies (i.e., Raskin, 1982) support these findings. In general, same-sex role combinations are more positive in their effect than other combinations. Furthermore, the female-female dyad resulted in the most positive experience. The most troublesome combination reported was the female supervisee with a male supervisor, which was attributed to the sexist attitudes on the part of the supervisor (Behling et al., 1988). Although these results make sense intuitively, Thyer, Sowers-Hoag, and Love (1988) argued that although their findings were similar, the gender issue accounted for only five percent of the variance in supervisee satisfaction. Furthermore, there is some argument that insulating supervisees within same-sex role pairs does not provide an opportunity to address some of the more subtle gender issues that can occur in therapy and supervision. Therefore, although the level of androgyny of the supervisor remains extremely important, the supervisor's gender per se might not be a crucial enough variable to demand manipulation.

We will close this section with a statement about termination, which Stoltenberg and Delworth (1987) argued is also a gender-related issue. Relying once more on the foundation laid by Gilligan (1982), Stoltenberg and Delworth speculated that female supervisors and trainees have a difficult time saying good-bye, whereas males have a difficult time saying hello.

> *For female supervisors with female supervisees, the danger is that the crucial "good-bye" may not be said, leaving both participants in a sort of limbo regarding their relationship and the work they did together. For male trainees, the "good-bye" may come too easily, thus creating a pseudo termination in which affect is suppressed rather than acknowledged. (p. 177)*

## GAYS AND LESBIANS

Although it is estimated that homosexuals represent approximately 10 percent of our population, they are a relatively hidden and neglected minority. The biggest reason for this is homophobia, the fear of homosexuality. Although it causes no alarm for a white person to choose to work primarily with Hispanics, or blacks, or women, it is quite a different story to identify oneself as working with a gay population. The assumption is that one is homosexual oneself if one chooses to work with gays and lesbians. As many gays know, this is a professionally dangerous admission.

This is yet another instance in which the helping professions reflect our society at large. In one study where the researchers presented trainees with an ambiguous situation, 83 percent of the trainees assumed that the client was heterosexual (Glenn & Russell, 1986). Our trainees reflect the social value that it is derogatory to assume that another is homosexual. We can, however, decrease homophobia by making a concerted effort to train new therapists to be aware of the gay person's issues and, especially, to investigate and confront their own fears and biases.

Other than an occasional article (e.g., Buhrke, 1989; Graham, Rawlings, Halpern, & Hermes, 1984), there is scant literature on gay or lesbian issues in supervision. In many instances, then, supervisors will be learning along with their trainees. Although this is not optimal, ignoring gay and lesbian issues is indefensible.

## Therapy Issues

As is true for members in any minority group, it is difficult for gays and lesbians to be diagnosed and treated correctly. Casas, Brady, and Ponterotto (1983) investigated whether counselors would process information with equal precision for heterosexual men, heterosexual women, and gay or lesbian clients if the information went contrary to commonly held stereotypes. They found that more errors were made when information was incongruent (did not match stereotypes) than when it was congruent.

> *This finding exemplifies the fact that even mental health professionals, whom one might expect to be more sensitive to the need of processing information accurately, given the responsibility inherent in their roles, are unable to accurately process information that goes contrary to commonly held stereotypes ascribed to specific groups. (p. 143)*

Furthermore, counselors made more errors when processing information about gays and lesbians *even when information was congruent with stereotypes.* One might assume that counselors were expending some energy dealing with their own internal processes, which distracted them from their task. The authors noted that the situations given to the counselors in the study were quite simple all the more reason to suspect that the heterosexual counselor might miss relevant information when assessing the homosexual client.

## Training and Supervision Issues

It is not uncommon in the final stages of training, when trainees first encounter a gay or lesbian client, for trainees to express concern over their lack of preparation to work with a gay population (Glenn & Russell, 1986; Graham, Rawlings, Halpern, & Hermes, 1984). When one of us teaches a course entitled "Counseling Diverse Populations," a disproportionate number of students do their final paper on gays or lesbians with the comment that this is the minority group about which they believe they have the greatest amount of misinformation. Like most heterosexuals, initial discussions tend to revolve around the etiology of homosexuality. Eventually, however, the student group moves on to issues more consequential to gay and lesbians, including relationship issues, dealing with their families of origin and their children, employment issues, and the homosexual's plight in dealing with the larger social system (Roth, 1985).

Graham et al. (1984) suggested the following as the minimum amount of training that should be provided in therapy programs:

1. Information about lesbian and gay life-styles and support networks
2. Information about homophobia and heterosexism
3. Issues around self-esteem in lesbian and gay clients or couples
4. Discussion of appropriate and inappropriate therapeutic goals

Graham et al. suggested also that training be done by gays whenever possible and that trainees work with gay supervisors. As is the case with other minority groups we have discussed in this chapter, the trainee who has an opportunity to work with a gay supervisor will be better prepared to work with any minority if part of what is learned is to accept and validate group identity while respecting individual differences presented by the individual client. Unfortunately, only a few trainees will have a gay supervisor. What is even more unfortunate is that virtually no supervisors have been trained to address issues of life-style in the supervisory context.

In her singular article, Buhrke (1989) addressed lesbian-related issues within supervision. She identified two nonconflictual situations and two conflictual situations that might arise as a function of who in the triad (client, supervisee, or supervisor) might be lesbian. In the most productive situation, neither supervisor nor supervisee is homophobic. When this is the case, the following examples

are possible: the lesbian supervisor can serve as a positive role model for her supervisees; the lesbian supervisor can openly discuss the appropriateness of coming out to a particular client; and mutual attraction between supervisor and supervisee (and the need to avoid a dual relationship) can be discussed openly and professionally.

Ironically, the second situation that poses no conflict is "the worst of possible supervisory scenarios" (p. 200), according to Buhrke. This is when both supervisor and supervisee are homophobic. Buhrke described mutual homophobia as blocking many productive interactions (including either supervisor and supervisee coming out). Because supervisor and supervisee will reinforce each other's biases, a lesbian client either will be underserved (i.e., references to a lesbian life-style will be ignored) or will be badly served (e.g., her lesbianism will be viewed as pathological).

Buhrke (1989) similarly saw one conflict situation as potentially positive and one as far more difficult. When the supervisor is not homophobic but the supervisee is, there is the potential for the supervisee to deal with its attitudes under the tutelage of the supervisor. Buhrke noted, however, that the supervisor must make a careful judgment call regarding the degree of homophobia (or the milder form of homophobia, heterosexual bias) and the supervisee's ability to work productively with a lesbian client. When the supervisee is free from homophobia but the supervisor is not, the power differential may make it difficult for the former to "challenge the supervisor's irrational beliefs about homosexuality" (p. 202). Furthermore, the lesbian supervisee might feel the necessity to conceal her life-style preference, a tragic outcome given the context in which it occurs.

With Buhrke's (1989) contribution in mind, it is obvious that the homophobic supervisor is the most powerful and potentially the most destructive in the therapy system. Therefore, any supervisor who is aware of negative attitudes toward homosexuality should seek the consultation of a colleague to deal with such attitudes. Short of that, the supervisor should help supervisees find additional supervision when the issue of homosexuality is unavoidable.

When the supervisor has a positive view of alternative lifestyle, the supervisor can be an important role model for supervisees, homosexual and heterosexual alike. Furthermore, when the supervisor takes such a posture, it is more likely that homosexual supervisees will come out to the supervisor.

In the context of an open and healthy atmosphere regarding homosexuality, we suggest the following when supervising a gay supervisee or a supervisee who is working with a gay client:

1. Homophobia and heterosexual bias should be discussed. No assumptions should be made about the supervisee or the client being comfortable with a homosexual lifestyle.
2. If the supervisor is heterosexual and the supervisee is gay or lesbian, the supervisee's feelings of vulnerability in coming out should be discussed fully. If the supervisee feels very vulnerable, it would be good for the supervisor to explore past experiences that have contributed to the supervisee's feeling.
3. The supervisor should share his or her own experience with gays and feelings about homosexuality. The supervisor should attempt to foster a situation in which there can be mutual learning through honest feedback. As in all pluralistic circumstances, there should be a sense of opportunity that is not possible when sameness is the norm.
4. The wishes of the supervisee regarding case load should be determined. Would the supervisee like to work with all gay or lesbian clients who present themselves? With gays only? With lesbians only? To be assigned clients with no regard for sexual preference?

We are advocating that the supervisor adopt as open a style as possible with supervisees around the issue of sexual preference. We believe that most minority issues can be diffused with time when openness is encouraged and there is good faith. As we already have stated, in the therapy system it is the supervisor who has the most power to establish this kind of atmosphere.

## OTHER MINORITY GROUPS

We have chosen to focus on particular groups because their numbers are larger in training programs than are other minority groups. Each supervisee (and each client), however, whether that person is a member of the dominant culture, a large minority, or a smaller minority, deserves supervisors who are equipped to handle the supervisee as an individual, first, and as a person who has a special identity by virtue of group membership, second. The largest task, it seems to us, is to avoid making careless assumptions about others. For example, a physically disabled trainee recently said to one of us that one of the things that most bugs him is that peers assume that he wants to be a rehabilitation counselor because of his physical impairments.

As well as the physically disabled, training programs may begin to see another minority group, those of retirement age. With the growth of gerontology, which parallels the growth of the elderly population in this country, it is quite conceivable that more and more retired persons will want to work with their peers as counselors. As an 80-year-old man who took an adult development and aging course from one of us said recently, "I'm not here because I'm old. I'm here because I'm a peer counselor."

As we stated earlier, much of what was

said in this chapter about one minority group could easily be transferred to other minorities. Also, as embryonic as our field is as a whole, we are unsophisticated in merging individuality and group membership into our working constructs. While we are learning and reshaping our views, we believe it is imperative that we underscore the importance of the concepts of pluralism and world view. This must be the foundation of our supervision if we are to train therapists who can be models in their work settings and in their communities.

# CHAPTER 12

# SUPERVISION RESEARCH ISSUES AND METHODS

A couple of decades ago, Kell, Morse, and Grater (undated) asserted that

> [t]he training of counselors and psychotherapists can perhaps be described by the old epigram, "the blind leading the blind." It is an attempt to teach, using methods about which we know practically nothing, a process about which we know far too little.

More recently, Holloway and Hosford (1983) picked up on that same theme, arguing that one remedy for this state of affairs would be develop a science of supervision.

It is true that research on counseling and psychotherapy is fraught with its own problems and that its relatively short history dates only from approximately the end of World War II (Garfield, 1983). But even this short history is longer than that of supervision research. Harkness and Poertner (1989) reported, for example, that the first published study of social work supervision appeared in 1958. It was at about that time also when *Counselor Education and Supervision* was founded (1961) to provide a journal outlet for articles on counselor training and supervision.

Although a number of researchers have conducted an occasional study of supervision during the past several decades (many of them doctoral students who focus their dissertations on a topic very central to their academic lives at the time they are choosing a research topic),

Particular thanks are due to DiAnne Borders, P. Paul Heppner, Elizabeth Holloway, and Everett Worthington for their valuable input on this chapter.

fewer than a score are engaged in any programmatic investigations of supervision. Even so, the science of supervision for which Holloway and Hosford (1983) called seems to have healthy forward momentum. Moreover, as researchers develop instrumentation (e.g., Friedlander & Ward, 1984) and models (e.g., Stoltenberg, 1981) unique to supervision, this science increasingly is becoming independent of psychotherapy theory and research. That independence, however, is far from complete. In fact, Lambert and Arnold (1987) make the strong assertion that research on the effects of supervision "will not progress faster than knowledge about the effective ingredients of psychotherapy" (p. 222). Because this assertion relates directly to the very purpose of this chapter, we will digress briefly to address some of the issues involved.

Supervision models often have developed as extensions of therapy theories (see, for example, Bartlett, Goodyear, & Bradley, 1983; Hess, 1980; also, see Chapter 2). On one level this type of extrapolation makes excellent sense, for Shoben (1962) and others have argued that each counselor or therapist works from an implicit theory of human nature that also must influence how the therapist construes reality (through, for example, epistemology) and interpersonal behavior. It is reasonable to assume that this same theory of human nature is present whether the professional is offering therapy, supervision, or some other intervention (see, for example, data from Friedlander & Ward, 1984; Goodyear, Abadie, & Efros, 1984; and, Holloway,

Freund, Gardner, Nelson, & Walker, 1989). It also is true that much of the *content* of supervision (e.g., the teaching of specific counseling techniques) inevitably is grounded in particular counseling models. For example, attention to the supervisee's working alliance with clients derives from psychodynamic counseling models; skills in using an empty-chair technique follow from a Gestalt therapy perspective.

On the other hand, there are drawbacks to such extrapolations. Russell, Crimmings, and Lent (1984) have suggested at least three:

1. To the extent that supervision remains anchored in theories of therapy, no full-blown, formal theory specific to supervision is developed.
2. This therapy-theory-to-supervision-theory linkage fosters an atmosphere of parochialism that hinders attempts to view supervision in an integrative, cross-theoretical manner.
3. Therapy theorists too often have failed either to translate their hypotheses into testable propositions or to operationalize their constructs.

To these points, Worthington has added:

> In counseling, a client is often involved in stable personal interactions and personality and mood states. In supervi ion, the supervisee usually is not rigidly bound into the same personality dynamics across situations and further, at least in the beginning, the supervisee does not know how to counsel. Thus, supervision is better described by a teaching metaphor than by a counseling metaphor. (Personal communication, 1990)

In short, despite the adverse consequences, it is natural for supervisors to use therapy as the lens through which they view supervision. The tendency to do so, however, likely will weaken as supervision research grows in both volume and sophistication.

Some of this growing volume of research

on supervision has been summarized in critiques and reviews. Anyone interested in conducting serious research on supervision should begin by reading commentaries such as those of Borders (1989a); Ellis, Ladany, Krengel, and Schult (1988); Holloway (1984); Holloway and Hosford (1983); Lambert (1980); Lambert and Arnold (1987); Russell, Crimmings, and Lent (1984); and Worthington (1987).

In Chapter 1, we cited Schön's (1983) belief that professional training is a process of inculcating in trainees two distinct realms of knowledge: formal theories and observations that have been confirmed, or are confirmable, by research; and knowledge that has been accrued from the professional experience of practitioners. In our attempts to be true to our scientist-practitioner orientation, we have drawn from both these realms in writing this book. We, therefore, will have failed in our intent if readers have not found in the first 11 chapters at least some research questions that would interest them to pursue. In fact, the placement of this chapter at the end of the book reflects our hope that at this point readers will have been stimulated to consider ways they could expand the empirical base of supervision.

We anticipate that readers of this chapter will vary widely in their sophistication about research in general and supervision research specifically. Consequently, we have attempted to steer a middle course that we hope will provide virtually all readers with some useful material.

## METHODOLOGICAL CONSIDERATIONS

It seems logical to begin coverage of supervision research by examining conceptual and practical issues relevant to the conducting of that research. Accordingly, that will be the focus of this first major section of the chapter.

Perhaps the first point to be made in this section should be that no study in the behavioral sciences is without limitations. Gelso

(1979) vividly captured this issue in his discussion of the "bubble hypothesis."

> *A few years ago, a graduate student in a seminar I teach on counseling and psychotherapy research . . . proposed that the conduct of science was analogous to the placement of a sticker on a car windshield. During the placement, a bubble would appear. The owner presses the bubble in an attempt to eliminate it, but it reappears in another place. The only way to get rid of it is to eliminate the entire sticker. The student termed this phenomenon the "bubble hypothesis." . . . [t]he idea behind it is obvious, ubiquitous—and all too infrequently in the awareness of students and researchers. (p. 12)*

Thus, a study with a very rigorous design might have high internal validity but at the expense of external validity (generalization). To redesign the study to have greater external validity, the researcher likely would have to sacrifice internal validity. Gelso discussed this tension as one between *rigor* and *relevance*.

But the fact that all investigations have limitations is not an excuse for inattentiveness to methodology. In fact, there is considerable room for improvement in the state of supervision research. Holloway and Hosford (1983) reported that several reviewers of supervision research literature had found such pervasive design shortcomings as

> *(a) non-random assignment to experimental groups, (b) inadequate sample size, (c) global and imprecisely defined variables, (d) lack of specificity in design procedures and treatment conditions, (e) invalid and/or unreliable scales of measurement, (f) criterion measures that do not accurately represent actual supervisory behaviors, and (g) unjustified generalization from findings of analogue studies. In fact, the majority of research in counselor supervision threatens the integrity of basic principles of internal, external, and construct validity. (p. 74)*

Other reviewers of supervision research (e.g., Ellis et al., 1988) have reached similar conclusions. In the following subsections, we

will address some of these methodological issues in greater depth.

## Research Strategies for a Science of Supervision

### Stage One of Supervision Science: Descriptive Studies.

If we are to develop a science of supervision, it is important to consider Holloway and Hosford's (1983) point that scientific endeavor is progressive and should proceed through three stages: (1) one of descriptive observation in which a phenomenon is observed in its natural environment; (2) one in which important, specific variables are identified and relationships between and among them are clarified; and (3) one in which a theory is developed, based on the empirically derived evidence about variables and their interrelationships. Holloway and Hosford (1983) then stated that

> *[u]nfortunately, in counselor supervision we have ignored the groundwork of phases one and two in favor of spawning "theories" that have more relevance to counseling than to supervision. Our theories need to predict what types of supervision techniques will result in what types of trainee outcomes for which type of trainee. When such a prescriptive model is developed and tested, we will have a science of supervision. (p. 75)*

In supervision, much of phase one (i.e., descriptive observation) has been accomplished via extrapolations from counseling and psychotherapy and from the clinical (i.e., subjective) observations of supervision practitioners. Increasingly, however, a body of literature has begun to evolve that provides essential descriptive data for this stage. Because no one methodological approach has been uniquely suited for providing these data, we believe it is essential to assert the importance of methodological diversity. Invoking a metaphor to comment on this issue, Harmon

(1989) noted that when a car does not run, the problem can be explained

> *by either a mechanic or a physicist without either of them necessarily understanding what the other was talking about. The point to be made here is that neither level of abstraction is wrong, it just depends on what your needs are.* (p. 87)

What follows are summaries of four different research strategies, all of which would be consistent with what Mahrer (1988) called a "discovery oriented" approach. Although critics can identify problems and limitations with each of these strategies, many of those complaints are attenuated when they are considered in relation to the one specific stage of science (i.e., description) for which they are especially appropriate.

1. *Qualitative research.* Although few in number, there are some in this category. An example is the phenomenological study of Hutt, Scott, and King (1983); Doehrman's (1976) study also might be considered qualitative. Although such studies may seem unacceptably soft by empirically oriented scholars, they can provide a rich source of information about the subjective experiences of supervisors and supervisees.

2. *Case study research.* A case study is a useful vehicle to address the first, descriptive, stage of science, for it provides "a holistic methodology for studying how multiple variables interact to affect the process and outcome of psychotherapy for an individual" (Hill, 1989, p. 17). Early case studies (e.g., Freud's cases of Dora and of Ratman), although perhaps clinically useful, were retrospective accounts by the therapist. For that reason, and because there was no corroborating evidence, they inevitably were limited by the subjectivity and omissions of the person who recounted the case.

Doehrman's (1976) multiple-case study of parallel processes in supervision constituted a methodological improvement. In that study she employed structured interviews and an observer's perspective to gather and interpret data. Further rigor has been possible through innovations Hill and her colleagues have made to case studies in counseling research (e.g., Hill, 1989; Hill, Carter, and O'Farrell, 1983). By employing multiple measures that include psychometric data, the evaluations of trained raters, and the observations of the involved parties, she has brought rigor to the case study. That approach to case studies has much to offer supervision researchers and already has been employed in at least one study (Martin et al., 1987).

The videotape series Goodyear (1982) developed (see Appendix E) have allowed for between-supervisor comparisons that actually are multiple case studies (e.g., Abadie, 1985; Friedlander & Ward, 1984; Harris & Goodyear, 1990; Holloway, Freund, Gardner, Nelson, & Walker, 1989). These have in common a focus on supervisor-supervisee interactions and employ the research strategy covered in the following section.

3. *Interactional research.* Because supervision is largely a verbal endeavor, there is merit in examining the verbal discourse between the supervisor and supervisee and, perhaps, between the supervisee and client. Studies of this nature have been conducted for some time (e.g., Dodenhoff, 1981; Lambert, 1974; Pierce & Schauble, 1970). The sophistication with which supervisor-supervisee interactions have been analyzed, however, has increased considerably during the past decade, largely through the research program of Holloway and her colleagues (e.g., Holloway, 1982; Holloway et al., 1989; Holloway & Wampold, 1983; Holloway & Wolleat, 1981).

Like any other methodology, of course, interactional analyses have limitations. For example, they are concerned with moment-to-moment interactions, and these patterns cannot easily be linked to behaviors occurring later. Moreover, the use of interactional analyses in naturalistic settings results in correlational data that preclude the making of causal inferences. Despite these and other limitations, however, interactional research is a very promising way to begin addressing the descriptive stage of science. A useful overview of interactional research methods can be found in Lichtenberg and Heck (1986) and in Wampold (1986).

4. *An "Events Paradigm."* A fourth approach has been suggested by Stiles, Shapiro, and Elliott (1986) as the "events paradigm." Heppner and Claiborn (1989) summarize it as follows:

*The events paradigm has three components: first, the identification of a specific context for examining the process of interest. . . ; second, the manipulation of specific interventions to set the process in motions (such as different interpretation styles or levels of discrepancy); and, third, the measurement of effects (that is, attitude change in the direction of the interpretation). All of this can be done in a single session or series of sessions in ongoing counseling. The approach is based on the ideas that sessions themselves have outcomes and that the processes leading to them ought to be the focus of process research. (p. 375)*

Before concluding this section on descriptive research, we should mention the potential value of examining unintended consequences of supervision. Most supervision research has focused either on *successful* supervision or on supervision that is assumed to be in some way *typical.* For the descriptive stage of a science, however, mistakes and failures can be a rich source of hypotheses. Yet very little has been done to examine these unintended consequences of supervision (one exception is a

chapter in Rioch, Coulter, & Weinberger, 1976). Although attention to this issue may dictate a case study or intensive single-subject approach, this would provide a more rigorous alternative to the small anecdotal literature that exists.

***Stages Two and Three of Supervision Science: Methodological Issues.*** For those researchers who wish to undertake studies intended to examine relationships between and among supervision-related variables (i.e., stage two in the development of a science of supervision), we intend first to argue for a consideration of aptitude-treatment interactions as a model for supervision research. Then, we will list eight specific issues important to the conducting and reporting of supervision research.

*ATI Research.* In a now-classic article, Kiesler (1966) argued against what he called the "uniformity myth" in psychotherapy research: The implicit idea that all clients with a particular disorder constitute a homogeneous group. Unfortunately, the uniformity myth too often has applied as well to psychotherapists in training. It is true that some, particularly those concerned with a developmental perspective on supervision, have attended to person-environment matches, that is, the interaction between the developmental level of supervisees' and their training environments. Others, however, have persisted in adhering to the uniformity myth in supervision to one degree or another.

It is but a short step from acknowledging the uniformity myth to acknowledging the discrepancies that occur between what we intend to teach versus what trainees actually learn (a distinction made by, among others, Ekstein & Wallerstein, 1972; Zaphiropoulos, 1984). Specifically, it is important to recognize that much of what we *intend* to teach does not result in new learnings and that trainees often learn from supervisors that which is unintended. It is not uncommon, for example, for a supervisee to adopt a personal mannerism of the supervisor, of which the supervisor may have only minimal awareness.

It is possible, of course, to view this discrepancy between what is intended to be taught and what actually is learned as an undesirable factor that complicates the supervisor's work. Reflection, however, suggests otherwise; that is, to have a perfect congruence between what is intended to be taught and what is learned would required the validity *both* of the uniformity myth *and* of the implicit belief that trainees are empty vessels to be filled by their instructors. The latter view is one that suggests a passivity among our trainees that is contrary to what we would expect of the therapists they will become.

All this leads to our suggesting the aptitude-treatment interaction model (Cronbach & Snow, 1977). This model suggests that learning occurs as a function of interaction between the treatment environment (including the supervisor) and individual characteristics of the learner. Although the term *aptitude* is used, it need not refer only to a measure of ability but to any personality dimension or trait. This is consistent, for example, with the work of Dance and Neufeld (1988), who reviewed aptitude-treatment interaction clinical studies.

Research on aptitude-treatment interactions seems to provide a con.pelling means for advancing our knowledge of supervision processes and effects. Nevertheless, this research approach has been employed regularly only by those investigating variants of conceptual systems theory (Harvey, Hunt, & Schroeder, 1961; conclusions about this research are summarized in Holloway & Wampold, 1983). In fact, this model, covered later in the chapter, explicitly embraces an interactionalist perspective. (We include in this category research on developmental models such as that of Stoltenberg [1981], which are based on conceptual systems theory.) In summary, then, the aptitude-treatment interaction approach clearly

has been underutilized by supervision researchers.

*Selected Practical and Procedural Issues in Methodology.* Unfortunately, space limitations constrain the coverage of supervision research methodology that we can offer. Therefore, we will conclude this first section of the chapter with passing coverage of eight methodological issues that we believe are partricularly important for supervision researchers.

**I. Sample sizes:** The first issue is the practical one of obtaining sufficiently large subject samples to conduct supervision research. This is a greater difficulty in supervision research than it is in research on counseling or psychotherapy. Whereas clients — or people who might be reasonably construed as potential clients — are readily accessible, the same is not true of supervisors and/or supervisees.

There *are* training programs with large numbers of trainees spread across the various levels of preparation. But these are few in number, and the many researchers who are not in such settings often must consider such strategies as the following, each of which imposes certain constraints on the types of research questions that can be examined.

1. Researchers can extend the time of their work to enable them to perform their interventions over longer periods of time (in universities, for example, data can be gathered across two or more semesters). This, of course, can be a substantial hurdle for the doctoral student who is eager to complete dissertation research.

2. Researchers can employ mailed surveys or questionnaires. Although such studies have been the source of much of our empirical knowledge of supervision, they do not allow observation of actual supervision events. Also, return rates in typical studies of this sort pose interpretive problems. For example, if 40 percent of a sam-

ple does not respond to a survey, the investigator is left to speculate about the representativeness of the 60 percent of the sample who did return their materials. For example, did they return their materials because of a special investment in the issue being addressed—a type of investment that may bias results in a particular fashion?

3. Researchers can develop analogue studies that employ as subjects nonsupervisors (or nonsupervisees). An example of this is the study by Stone (1980), who used introductory psychology students as "inexperienced supervisors." Studies of this sort may be of special value in the preliminary stages of investigations of previously unexamined phenomena. They must of necessity, however, be analogues.

**II. Cross-sectional versus other designs:** Researchers, especially those interested in investigations of developmental models, should employ other designs than cross-sectional designs (see Holloway, 1987). The use of the (too infrequent) longitudinal study (e.g., Hill, Charles, & Reed, 1981) adds an important dimension. But it, too, has limitations (e.g., cohort effects). Ellis et al. (1988) recommended instead a sequential design that combines aspects of both cross-sectional and longitudinal designs.

**III. Information about raters:** "When using raters and rating procedures, provide sufficient information about the raters and their training for the reader to evaluate the raters' qualifications, potential for biases [e.g., blind to experimental conditions], standardization of ratings, and how rating materials were assigned to raters" (Ellis et al., 1988, p. 9).

**IV. Demographics report:** "In case of nonrandomized studies, full reporting of participant demographics (e.g., age, sex, degree program) and other data germane to the study (e.g., amount of supervised counseling experience, theoretical orientation, types of clients seen)

are needed to assess for differences among groups" (Ellis et al., 1988, p. 10).

**V. Multiple roles for participants:** "Avoid using participants in multiple roles (e.g., as both supervisor in one group and supervisee in another). If this is unavoidable, control for this confound methodologically and statistically" (Ellis et al., 1988, p. 11).

**VI. Clear working definitions:** Basic to social science is that phenomena being investigated have well-accepted and clear operational definitions. It is our impression, for example, that one reason there are not more investigations of parallel processes is that although they are intuitively compelling to practitioners, it is difficult to arrive at an appropriately circumscribed working definition of them. On another front, it is only recently that those studying developmental processes in supervision have begun to define developmental level in terms other than the level of practicum at which the trainee is working. For a given study, the researcher has a responsibility for clarity of working definitions. For an entire field of study, however, it is important that there is uniformity among those definitions. If 10 different researchers each arrived at a clear, but idiosyncratic, working definition of parallel processes, for example, it would be very difficult to make between-study comparisons.

**VII. Self-reports of satisfaction:** In her discussion of the future research agenda in supervision, Borders (1989a) called for a moratorium on the use of self-reports of supervisee satisfaction as an outcome measure. Just as it is in counseling, satisfaction often is imperfectly correlated with effectiveness. For example, during periods of confrontation by and conflict with the supervisor, the supervisee may find himself or herself quite dissatisfied and even angry, even though the effects on his or her functioning as a therapist or practitioner eventually may be very positive.

On the other hand, Worthington (personal communication, 1990) made the point that satisfied supervisees might be expected to learn better than those who are dissatisfied. He argued that, as an alternative to imposing a moratorium on the use of satisfaction data, supervision researchers give more empirical attention to determining the actual link between supervisees' satisfaction and supervision outcome.

**VIII. Analogue studies:** Analogue studies can provide high internal validity (rigor). Moreover, they can be of particular value in the first stages of attempting to extrapolate the implications of a particular theory (see, for example, Stone, 1984). For this reason, they can be of particular value in Stages Two and Three of supervision science. Also, analogue designs can be useful as a means of safeguarding clients when researchers are investigating some potentially dangerous situations (e.g., the effects of breaches of confidentiality). But in keeping with the theme we have adopted in this chapter, researchers should regard analogue studies as *especially* useful at an early stage in a science. (Although they can be useful at any time as a means of testing theory, there comes a time in counseling and supervision research when real-life situations must be employed.) For example, the research on the social influence model (which will be discussed briefly later) has been based primarily on analogue research. In their recent review of this model, Claiborn and Heppner (1989) urged "researchers to move away from analogue methodologies . . . [i]t seems absolutely essential that the social influence process be examined in realistic counseling situations" (p. 383).

The foregoing might seem to imply that research is either analogue, or it is not. In fact, a study may vary in its degree of "analogness," that is, the degree to which it represents the real world (Munley, 1974; Strong, 1971). Strong (1971) proposed useful criteria for gauging the degree of artificiality of a particular analogue study. Specifically, he suggested that researchers meet as many of five "boundary conditions" as possible in designing analogue research. These are that (1) counseling (as well as supervision) is a conversation between two or more people; (2) the interactants (supervisor and supervisee; supervisee and client) have clearly defined roles that constrain conversation; (3) supervision exists in varying (though usually extended) durations; (4) clients (and supervisees) are motivated to change; and (5) many clients are psychologically distressed and heavily invested in the behaviors they wish to change (the parallel here to supervisees should be obvious).

**Assessing Supervision Process and Outcome**

Holloway and Hosford's (1983) proposed three-stage model for supervision science provides researchers with a useful blueprint. Practical and strategical issues necessary for implementing this blueprint were considered in the immediately preceding material. The material that follows will consider two issues that, although necessary for a supervision science, are not linked specifically to one or another of the Holloway and Hosford stages.

The first issue is the substantial one of the criteria to employ in assessing supervision outcomes. That will be followed by a consideration of the instruments used to assess supervision process and outcome. The logic of this order is that the construct and perspective to be employed in assessment must drive the choice of a measurement device.

*Choice of Outcome Criteria.* The root question in supervision research is Does supervision work? Although there are encouraging data to support an affirmative answer, several aspects of supervision research handicap those who seek reassurance on the issue. One such aspect has been the problem of selecting appropriate criteria. For example, should the index of supervision's effectiveness be some facet of trainees' functioning—or, alternatively, some facet of the functioning of clients seen by that trainee? And if trainees (or clients), then which specific facet(s) of their functioning?

Gelso (1979) noted that although the selection of appropriate criteria has been a problem for researchers since the beginning of psychology, it has been especially troublesome for counseling and psychotherapy researchers. In supervision, this problem becomes even more troublesome. One source of frustration has been the sometimes very low intercorrelations among various criteria "such as client self-evaluations, counselor judgments, observer ratings, etc." (p. 19).

Gelso found promise in the position of Strupp and Hadley (1977), who argued for what they called a tripartite model of mental health. Their position was that any assessment of mental health (and, thus, therapy) outcomes would include the perspectives of the therapist, the client, and society (including people significant in the life of the client). Strupp and Hadley suggested eight different outcome combinations that might be judged from the three vantage points. "The critical point for the present discussion is these researchers' demonstration of a variety of ways in which outcome criteria can be conflicting when the three vantage points are combined (as they need to be)" (Gelso, 1979, p. 19).

Compared to psychotherapy, supervision has both more people involved and more contexts in which the evaluations might be conducted. Holloway (1984) has argued that the traditional criteria of supervision effectiveness, supervisees' skill acquisition and client change, are overly restrictive. She stated also that "design for outcome evaluation in supervision has primarily grown out of isolated experimental needs" (p. 168). Analogous to Strupp and Hadley (1977), she recommended that researchers instead employ multiple criteria that evolve from the perspectives of the supervisor, the supervisee, the client (or client system), and an external observer, each of whom might evaluate the supervisor, the supervisee, and the client in the contexts of either counseling or supervision.

Table 12.1 depicts the 24 possible data points this would yield. As can be seen, 6 of those (marked with dashes) make no conceptual sense to employ. It also is interesting to note that Holloway was able to locate no studies that employed 6 of the remaining 18 perspectives.

Holloway's suggested framework should be very helpful both to researchers planning investigations of supervision and to those who attempt to make sense of that research. An important point to underscore is the usefulness of more than one perspective. Borders (1989a), for example, urged caution in relying only on self-reports of perceptions by *either* supervisees or supervisors. For example, supervisors have an investment in perceiving

**TABLE 12.1**   Summary of Holloway's (1984) Survey of Studies Addressing Possible Measures of Supervision Outcome

| Evaluator | EVALUATION CONTEXT: SUPERVISION INTERVIEW | | | EVALUATION CONTEXT: COUNSELING INTERVIEW | | |
|---|---|---|---|---|---|---|
| | *Person Evaluated* | | | *Person Evaluated* | | |
| | *Supervisor* | *Trainee* | *Client* | *Supervisor* | *Trainee* | *Client* |
| Supervisor | X | X | — | O | X | O |
| Trainee | X | X | — | O | X | O |
| Client | — | — | — | O | X | X |
| Observer | X | X | — | X | X | O |

Note: X signifies that studies addressing this type of outcome were cited; O signifies that no such studies were located; — signifies that these combinations would not be sensible to use in outcome research.

positive change in their trainees; moreover, their perceptions easily can be colored by theoretical orientation or individual traits. To illustrate her point, Borders noted the observation of Martin, Goodyear, and Newton (1987) that supervisees, when *surveyed,* reported that they perceived their supervisors to be supportive (e.g., Rabinowitz, Heppner, & Roehkle, 1986; Worthington & Roehlke, 1979); but at least some studies that focused on actual verbalizations of supervisors found supervisors use relatively few supportive verbalizations (e.g., Holloway & Wampold, 1983; Martin et al., 1987). But rather than argue against using self-reports as Borders did, we argue that self-reports should be used in conjunction with *other* sources of data. Contradictions that emerge between and among various perspectives (e.g., supervisees' perceptions of support versus what actually seems to be offered; Holloway & Wampold, 1983) are important to know of and can suggest directions for additional, second generation research.

This last point bears underscoring, for researchers are not always clear about how to handle the multiple perspectives yielded when they conduct multivariate outcome investigations. Worthington (personal communication, 1990) argued that "simply trying to combine measures across raters (e.g., insider versus outsider perspectives) does not necessarily reveal *more* truth about what is going on. It may, in fact, obscure truth."

### Measures of Supervision Process and Outcome.
After reviewing seven years (1981–1987) of published research on supervision, Ellis et al. (1988) made a number of recommendations for supervision researchers. One of those was "for psychometrically sound measures for supervision" (p. 9).

Almost all instruments that have been used to assess supervision process and outcomes variables are ones that originally were developed for other purposes, such as psychotherapy or (occasionally) classroom instructional research. When used in supervision

research, these measures have been modified. For example, the Counselor Rating Form (Barak & LaCrosse, 1975)—designed to measure counselors' expertness, attractiveness, and trustworthiness—has been used in a number of supervision studies after simply substituting the word *supervision* or *supervisor* for *counseling* or *counselor* and retitling it the Supervision Rating Form.

There are at least two problems with a practice such as this. First, tinkering with an instrument through word changes and so on, without then checking its psychometric properties, results in an instrument that has been changed in unknown ways. Second, using such instruments can perpetuate the use of roles and metaphors from interventions *other* than supervision (e.g., therapy, teaching). Ellis et al. (1988) recommended that when using such measures, the researcher should, at minimum, conduct a pilot study to examine the psychometric properties of the measure in the new setting and report internal consistency (e.g., Cronbach's alpha) based on the entire sample.

Increasingly, instruments such as some of those found in Appendix C have been developed for supervision research. Although homegrown instruments have allowed supervision research to advance, few of them have undergone rigorous instrument development with all the necessary psychometric analyses. One notable exception is the Supervisory Styles Inventory (Friedlander & Ward, 1984). This instrument, intended expressly for supervision research, was developed carefully and stands as a model to be emulated by other supervision researchers.

### Concluding Remark About Methodology

Russell et al. (1984) stated that

> *as we see it, there have been four primary obstacles to progress in supervision research: (1) the failure of theory in most cases to offer clear-cut directions for supervisory research,*

*(2) the small sample sizes of trainees and supervisors available at most training sites, (3) the difficulty, in both pragmatic and ethical terms, of manipulating independent variables in real-life training settings, and (4) the "criterion problem," which includes such issues as how best to measure change, from whose perspective, and on what dimensions. (pp. 667–668)*

At the same time, they concluded that these obstacles may not be insurmountable. We agree and hope that aspiring researchers will rise to the challenge.

## ISSUES AND TOPICS FOR FUTURE RESEARCH

Although we already have pointed to some of the limitations of relying exclusively on psychotherapy theory and research for developing a science of supervision, we do not intend to suggest that a supervision science should be created from scratch. Any science of supervision inevitably will be an *applied* science. As such, it will have to draw from more basic theory and research for its fundational assumptions and concepts.

The purpose of the remainder of this chapter is to single out several broad strands of research that seem especially promising as vehicles for extending our thinking about supervision. Although we are tempted to offer a laundry list of research issues that merit attention, we believe this strategy would be unnecessarily redundant with the earlier chapters: Many provocative research questions are suggested in the material of those chapters. A second factor in our decision to avoid the laundry list approach was that the more specific the questions we offer, the shorter their shelf life. For that reason, such a list likely is more appropriate for journal articles than for a book.

The broad intellectual strands that we will address are those of cognitive science, relationship variables, and social psychological contributions to practice. Because of space

limitations and our wish only to point to the general topics, our coverage of them necessarily will be cursory and incomplete.

## Cognitive Science and Supervision

Stone (1988) noted that cognitive researchers "have been chastised for employing trivial tasks and inadequate models in describing human cognition" (p. 2). He argued that because supervision overcomes these objections, it provides an ideal vehicle for cognitive research.

*Supervision provides a domain involving such nontrivial factors as human context, affective experience, and personal beliefs, requiring more complex models of cognition; while a cognitive approach offers an appealing and heuristic alternative conceptualization of trainee experience. (p. 3)*

There are at least three different lines of cognitive research that seem to have current implications for supervision. Although they inevitably intertwine, we will treat them independently. They concern (1) cognitive structure and style, (2) discrete cognitions of supervisors and supervisees, and (3) ways in which experts process information differently than novices.

*Cognitive Structures and Styles: How People Process Information.* In response to a query about important areas for future research in supervision, Heppner (personal communication, 1989) suggested the following questions to guide investigators:

*How does supervision affect the supervisee's ability to arrange information cognitively about counseling? In particular, how does the supervisee begin to conceptualize clients differently or more effectively, diagnose clients, learn intervention strategies and so on?*

In raising these questions, Heppner is speaking to the issue of cognitive schemata. To understand this concept—one that is central in current research on social cognition — consider that we constantly are bombarded with overwhelming amounts of information about our social environments; at any given moment, we have available to us far more information than we can register, much less process. Consequently, we attend selectively to that information. The selective encoding, representing, and recalling of information is guided by internal cognitive structures, or *schemata,* that provide us with some efficiency in our processing of information (see, for example, Heppner & Krauskopf, 1987; Markus, 1977).

Martin (1985), in particular, has helped us to understand cognitive schemas. He and his colleagues have provided us with concepts and methods that have been employed in a number of recent studies (e.g., Martin, Slemon, Hiebert, Hallberg, & Cummings, 1989).

*Cognitive Developmental Models.* The notion of cognitive schema is central to the cognitive developmental theorists such as Harvey, Hunt, and Schroeder (1961), Piaget (Piaget & Inhelder, 1969), Perry (1970), and Loevinger (1976). Cognitive-developmental models, however, should be considered a separate category because of their central assumption that there is a predictable pattern in the manner in which people will attend to and process information; moreover, these models assume a hierarchical, or stage, sequence through which people move. In general, these models all maintain that people progress from concrete, simple, and externally focused ways of processing information to ways that are more abstract, complex, and internally focused.

In counseling and supervision literature, the cognitive developmental model that has been employed most often is Harvey, Hunt, and Schroeder's (1961) conceptual systems theory (CST). A central tenet of this system is that optimal learning and performance depends on the degree of matching between the learner and its environment. The key personal variable in this model is that of conceptual

level (CL), which usually is considered to exist on a continuum from low (concrete) to high (abstract). Note that CL is unreliably related to intelligence.

> As individuals progress in their acquisition of abstract functioning, they increase the availability of multiple alternatives in evaluation and behavior, responding more relativistically and less dichotomously. Hunt's (1971) developmental hierarchy is often depicted on a concrete-abstract continuum. The concrete types, referred to as low *CL,* exhibit conceptual simplicity and external, dependent orientations to interpersonal affairs. The abstract types, referred to as high *CL,* demonstrate conceptual complexity and internal, interdependent orientations. (Holloway & Wampold, 1986, p. 310)

That model has been used frequently as a means of considering the matching of classroom environments and students. For example, it would predict that low CL students would learn best in a more structured environment (e.g., one in which an instructor had a detailed syllabus that logically flowed from one topic to another; in class the instructor would stay close to the outline, discourage tangents away from it, and minimize ambiguous material). High CL students, on the other hand, would function better in less structured environments.

Holloway and Wampold (1986) noted that during the 1970s researchers began to apply CST to counselor training and the counseling process. They maintained that it has been Stone and his associates (e.g., Berg & Stone, 1980; Stein & Stone, 1978) who have been most involved in systematically investigating CST in counseling and counselor training. But other researchers have conducted research in this domain as well. For example, Holloway and Wolleat (1980) found that higher CL trainees produced more effective clinical hypotheses. Employing Loevinger's related model of ego development, Borders, Fong, and Neimeyer (1986) found that trainees at lower ego levels were more likely to describe their clients in simplistic concrete terms, whereas those at higher levels used more sophisticated, interactive descriptions. Holloway and Wampold (1986) reviewed the findings about the CST model; although their focus was primarily on counseling studies, many of their conclusions generalize to supervision.

Stoltenberg's (1981) developmental model of supervision (see Chapter 2) employs CST as one of its foundational bases. According to this model, beginning supervisees are more likely to function at low conceptual levels and, therefore, demand more structured learning environments. As they progress in their training, supervisees move to higher conceptual levels and, therefore, require corresponding training environments. Blocher's (1983) developmental model of supervision also is based on cognitive developmental models, including that of Harvey, Hunt, and Schroeder (1961). (See Holloway [1987] for a thoughtful critique of the actual congruence between the CST model and those of Stoltenberg and Blocher.)

Stoltenberg (1981) and Blocher (1983) drew different conclusions about the implications of cognitive development for an optimal training environment. Whereas Stoltenberg maintained that the environment should be deliberately *matched* with the supervisee's level of cognitive functioning, Blocher argued for an intentional *mismatch* intended to force the supervisee to grow to a higher level of functioning. Quarto and Tracey (1989) have suggested that research designed to compare these contrasting assumptions should be examined.

*Attributions and Self-efficacy.* Because much of current social psychological theory and research focuses on individuals' cognitions, we will address briefly here attributions, which as easily could appear in the section on social psychological theory and research. Despite an imperfect fit, we include this as a subpart of cognitive structure, reasoning that the issue of this entire section is one of *how* people

process information. Attributions are a particular type of information.

One important finding of attributional research in supervision is that the perspective of the observer determines the types of attributions he or she will make about another's behaviors. For example, Dixon and Kruczek (1989) found in an analogue study that supervisors were more likely to attribute effects of therapy to the therapist's *actions;* therapists, on the other hand, were more likely to attribute those effects to environmental factors. In a test of the actor-observer hypothesis, Worthington (1984a) found that the experience level of supervisors affected attributions they made of supervisees' behaviors. Specifically, he found that supervisors with greater experience were *less* likely to explain their supervisees' behaviors in terms of enduring traits (such as empathy, genuineness, etc.).

Self-efficacy beliefs (e.g., Bandura, 1977, 1984, 1986), a specific type of attribution, have particular implications for supervision. Bandura (1977) maintained that self efficacy is "the conviction that one can successfully execute [a particular] behavior" (p. 205). He hypothesized that behavior and behavior change is mediated by expectations of personal efficacy. Such expectations determine whether or not a behavior will be initiated, how much effort will be expended, and how long the behavior will be sustained in the face of obstacles. According to the model, a person's self efficacy regarding a particular behavior is influenced by four basic factors: actually having done the behavior, vicariously observing another person perform the behavior, being persuaded by an influential other that one can perform the behavior, and physiological responses in the face of performing the behaviors (e.g., bodily concomitants of anxiety, which usually have an inhibiting effect on self-efficacy).

The earliest work on self-efficacy was clinical, focusing, for example, on the degree to which individuals with snake phobias perceived themselves to be able to approach and handle snakes after having undergone desensitization. The model since has been expanded to such other areas as education and vocational choice. In supervision, it has been a variable in at least three studies (Friedlander, Keller, Peca-Baker, & Olk, 1986; Johnson & Seem, 1989; Johnson, Baker, Kopala, Kiselica, & Thompson, 1989). The model seems promising as both an independent and a dependent variable for additional supervision research. For example, to what extent — and in what ways — does self-efficacy influence supervisee performance? In what way does the self-efficacy of a trainee change over time (e.g., is it linear or does it show some other pattern of development)? In what ways do certain supervisory styles of interventions affect trainee self-efficacy? What links exist between supervisees' self-efficacy and their affective experience of supervision and therapy they are doing?

***Discrete Cognitions: What Information People Process.*** Perhaps corresponding with the rise of cognitive-behavioral models, mental health professionals and educators have become particularly interested in what people think (whereas cognitive structure or schemas speak more to how people process information). This interest has extended to supervision, with some promising lines of research. With the knowledge we gain from this research, we will be in a better position to develop "prescriptions on how supervisors and counselors ought to think, plan, and decide" (Stone, 1989, p. 6).

There are a number of ways to assess a person's cognitions (see, e.g., Merluzzi, Glass, & Genest, 1981). Among the most promising of these is the thought-listing technique proposed by Cacioppo and Petty (1981). In this technique, respondents are asked to record their thoughts about some event (e.g., an upcoming therapy session, a recent supervision session). Cacioppo and Petty suggested that

these thoughts then be classified on the three dimensions of *polarity* (favorable, neutral, or unfavorable), *origin* (internal or external), and *target*. Tarico, Van Zelzen, and Altmaier (1986) have since demonstrated that respondents themselves can rate the thoughts with no sacrifice of reliability or validity (as compared to the more expensive trained raters).

Related to thought listing is the thinking aloud technique (Genest & Turk, 1981), and Dole et al. (1984) developed a recall procedure that was an adaptation of Kagan's (1980) Interpersonal Process Recall, designed to elicit and score the therapist's actual internal dialogue. Data are beginning to suggest that thinking aloud and thought-listing techniques yield different information (e.g., Blackwell, Galassi, Galassi, & Watson, 1985). Supervision studies that have used one or another of these cognitive assessment procedures include Friedlander, Keller, Peca-Baker, and Olk (1986), Kurpius, Benjamin, and Morran (1985), and Borders (1989d). Also, a couple of potentially useful exploratory studies have used the thinking aloud technique. In what they called a "methodological pilot," Etringer and Claiborn (1986) examined how supervisees processed feedback, and Ricke and Peterson (1988) compared the thinking of two expert and two novice counselors.

***The Information Processing of Novices Versus Experts.*** The particular focus of this entire section on cognitive science is on how people process information. Knowing about information processing can help us to know better the manner in which clinicians attend to and process data about people in order to form judgments about them (see, for example, Faust, 1986). In fact, there is emerging literature that shows that experts and novices do this differently.

Recent learning models have employed studies contrasting novices and experts. Hilerbrand (1989) discussed possible supervisory implications for this work, especially the work of Anderson (1982, 1985; briefly summarized in Chapter 10). Glaser (1990) described the essence of Anderson's work as follows:

> The major mechanism in Anderson's ACT* theory is knowledge compilation, *which accounts for the transition process that turns declarative knowledge, initially encoded from text or from the teacher's instruction, into proceduralized, use-oriented knowledge (i.e., converting "knowing what" into "knowing how")*. . . . *First, during solution, it is assumed that learners draw on declarative knowledge as they apply general problem-solving processes, using domain-general methods, such as means-ends search or analogy to an example. Subsequently, the process of knowledge compilation creates efficient, domain-specific productions from the trace of the initial problem-solving episode*. . . . *Knowledge compilation results in automaticity of application and in proficient execution of previously acquired declarative knowledge. It frees working memory, leaving more capacity for the processing of new knowledge. (p. 31)*

But there are others in addition to Anderson (1982, 1985) who have developed learning models intended to draw implications from differences between the ways experts and novices solve problems (several are summarized in Glaser, 1990). What these models have in common is an assumption that information processing and metacognition will change with experience; as a person's knowledge about an area increases, there are concomitant changes in how the person thinks and reasons about problems connected with that knowledge base. For example, experts are more able to chunk information into large blocks that more quickly can be processed. If applied to therapy, it could be assumed that as a therapist gains experience, the therapist will

> *begin to see that all problems [raised by clients] are not new and independent of each other. He [or she] learns to ignore the irrelevant patterns of activity and concentrate on the critical ones. Eventually, he [or she] begins to group the rele-*

> *vant patterns together as a chunk of understanding and to link that chunk to others.*
>
> *Once chunked, the linked patterns are viewed as a single unit (thus taking up less working memory and attention) and as automatically activating any related knowledge chunks from long-term memory for use in working memory. . . . Patterns invoke chunks which invoke chunks and so forth. (Prietula & Simon, 1989, p. 121)*

This superior information processing works with familiar patterns. When confronted with unfamiliar situations, the expert will resort to the same information processing strategies as the novice. With the familiar situation, however, the expert often processes information rapidly in what appears to the observer to be intuition.

> *Intuition grows out of experiences that once called for analytic steps. As experience builds, the expert begins to chunk the information into patterns and bypasses the steps. A pattern of [client behavior confusing to the inexperienced therapist] leads to thought of possible causes which calls for deep analysis.*
>
> *Eventually, the [therapist] uncovers the cause. If the same pattern of information is encountered again, it will be less confusing. The person will know what data are relevant and what are not. Possible answers generated from experience will pop up intuitively. . . . Over time, as more patterns are chunked and linked, the hunches become better and better. (Prietula & Simon, 1989, p. 122)*

One potentially negative aspect of expert-novice differences in information processing is that they may use different language to describe their experiences. This sometimes can lead to difficulties in communication as the expert (e.g., the supervisor) and the novice (e.g., the trainee) strive to find common language to describe their respective experience of the same phenomena (e.g., Isaacs & Clark, 1987).

There are recent studies contrasting expert and novice therapists (e.g., Cummings, Hallberg, Martin, Slemon, & Hiebert, 1989; Martin, Slemon, Hiebert, Hallberg, & Cummings, 1989; Ricke & Peterson, 1988), some of which have invoked these promising learning models. We believe these models are promising in their possible implications for both supervisor and trainee development and for the supervisory process itself.

***Cognitive Science: Concluding Comments.***
A number of authors have observed that psychology has been in the midst of a cognitive revolution. Perhaps for that reason, the domains of cognitive science considered here are characterized by considerable intellectual energy; supervision researchers should find rich material in each. As Borders (personal communication, 1990) has pointed out, hypothesis generation is enhanced even more when material from two or more of these domains are integrated. She pointed out, for example, that both Stoltenberg (1981) and Blocher (1983) imply that conceptual level has a "ceiling effect": What might be the implication of this for expert versus novice thinking processes? Cognitive science should provide fertile material for supervision researchers for some years to come.

## Relationship Issues in Supervision

In psychotherapy, there has been a sometimes-heated discussion about the relative contributions of *specific* versus *nonspecific* factors that may account for outcomes. Two of the most frequently discussed nonspecific factors are the expectations for change that people bring with them; and the positive, caring relationship that some (e.g., Rogers, 1957; Patterson, 1984) have maintained is in itself curative. Specific factors are the actual interventions that therapists employ. The emerging consensus seems to be that *both* are operative.

This same debate over specific versus nonspecific factors has not taken place in supervision. Implicit in much of the supervision literature is that the effects of supervision derive primarily from specific factors. Although relationship factors have been considered central in supervision, they have not been framed as having the same singular effects as some have argued are present in counseling and therapy (e.g., Patterson, 1984).

Research on the supervisor-supervisee relationship paralleled and was based on the research on the therapist-client relationship. During the late 1960s and early 1970s, for example, the operationalization of Rogers's (1957) relationship variables, especially by Carkhuff (1969), contributed to the dominance of that relationship paradigm. This same approach was apparent in supervision research. Illustrative of this are studies such as those of Pierce and Schauble (1970) and Lambert (1974), which were intended to examine the extent to which supervisors' levels of empathy, regard, genuineness, and concreteness (i.e., "facilitative conditions") influenced the development of those same conditions in their trainees. Summaries of this and related research were written by Lambert and Arnold (1987) and Matarazzo and Patterson (1986).

Gelso and Carter (1985), however, suggested that this Rogers-based relationship paradigm may have taken the field as far as it can go. Although the therapeutic relationship is regarded as important in virtually all models of therapy (and of supervision), Gelso and Carter argued that perhaps it is now time to develop new paradigms for understanding it. They found promise, for example, in Bordin's (1979) thinking about the working alliance. Bordin suggested that the working alliance is composed of three elements: the *bond* between therapist and client, the extent to which they agree on *goals,* and the extent to which they agree on *tasks.* Central to his concept of working alliances also is that any relationship will experience periods of weakening and repair (not unlike Mueller and Kell's [1972] notion of the inevitability of conflict in supervisor-supervisee relationships).

Bordin (1983) later extended his working alliance model to include supervision. This seems to have provided several recent researchers (e.g., Baker, 1990; Efstation, Patton, & Kardash, 1990) with a fresh way of thinking about supervisory relationships. The development of the Working Alliance Inventory (Horvath & Greenberg, 1989; see Appendix C for Baker's [1990] modification of it) has provided a useful tool for such studies. So, too, has the Efstation et al. (1990) Supervisory Working Alliance Inventory (see Appendix C).

Both because shared goals are an important aspect of the working alliance and because expectations are an important aspect of social influence (see the following section), it also is reasonable to examine the congruence of supervisor and supervisee expectations for supervision. Tinsley and his associates (e.g., Tinsley, Workman, & Kass, 1980; Tinsley, Bowman & Ray, 1988) have conducted programmatic research on clients' expectations for counseling and have developed an instrument for assessing expectations. There is promise in extending this work to the area of supervision.

## Social Influence Models

Supervision occurs in a social context. For that reason, there is utility in looking to the social psychology literature for hypotheses and concepts to employ in supervision theory and research.

Literature applying social psychological concepts to counseling and psychotherapy is three decades old and continues to grow in vitality. In fact, there now is the *Journal of Social and Clinical Psychology* devoted to encouraging this interface. Heppner and Claiborn (1989) suggested that "formal articulation of the social influence point of view probably began with the publication of Frank's (1961) *Persuasion and Healing"* (p. 365). Further articulation of that point of view

occurred in such other works as that of Goldstein, Heller, and Sechrest (1966) and of Strong (1968). In fact, Strong's article, presenting a two-stage model of change, probably was most directly instrumental in stimulating what now has become a substantial amount of research.

In Strong's view, we as individuals give interpersonal power (or influence) to those in our lives who we perceive to have resources necessary to meet our needs. These are the people with whom we form relationships of a personal or professional nature. By the same token, any relationship is reciprocal, and we, therefore, exert influence on others even as they influence us. When our needs or the needs of the other people either cease to exist or no longer are met, the relationship will end.

Strong (in press) noted that "[w]hen one person affects another's behavior, social influence has occurred" (p. 2). In his original work (Strong, 1968), he drew from French and Raven (1959) to suggest that the basis of this influence resided in three basic resources that clients (or trainees) will seek from therapists (or supervisors). A therapist or supervisor will have interpersonal influence to the extent that he or she is perceived by the client or trainee as having *expertness, attractiveness* (i.e., perceived similarity in values, goals, etc.), and *trustworthiness*. Applying Strong's two-stage social influence model to supervision, we can understand that the supervisor's first task is to establish him- or herself as a credible resource (i.e., possessed of expertness, attractiveness, and trustworthiness). Once the trainee has come to perceive the supervisor as credible, the supervisor's second task is to begin attempts to influence the supervisee to make changes (skill, conceptual, etc.).

The first decade of research on this basic model was summarized in separate reviews by Corrigan et al. (1980) and Heppner and Dixon (1981). More recently, Heppner and Claiborn (1989) reviewed the second decade of that research, and Dixon and Claiborn (1987) reviewed research on social influence processes in supervision.

***Bidirectional Influence.*** The primary focus of most of this book has been on the *supervisor's* responsibility in the supervisory process. Perhaps an unfortunate consequence has been to imply a one-way process in which supervisors influence trainees, but not necessarily vice versa. This emphasis is consistent with an aspect of social influence research that has been criticized (Heppner & Claiborn, 1989); most studies have been based on Strong's (1968) original model, placing primary emphasis on the counselor's (or supervisor's) role in the change process. Extensions of the model (e.g., Strong & Matross, 1973; Strong & Claiborn, 1982) that recognize the bidirectional nature of social processes have been relatively overlooked. Just as the supervisor influences the trainee, the trainee *also* influences the supervisor. Heppner and Claiborn (1989) recommend that more attention be given to the manner in which the client and the supervisee process information about the counseling and supervision processes. In particular, what are some of the affective and cognitive responses of these participants that, together, mediate the change process?

The concept of strategic self-presentation bears directly on this issue of bidirectional influence. According to this concept, a person will modify his or her behavior to elicit a particular behavior from another person (Claiborn & Lichtenberg, 1989). Self-presentation (also called *impression management*) certainly is an important area in supervision because it has bearing both on how supervisors attempt to manage trainees' impressions of them and of how trainees attempt to manage impressions clients and supervisors have of them.

Because of the threat of evaluation, supervisees' attempts to manage the impressions su-

pervisors have of them are likely of particular importance. Interestingly, only a couple of studies have been done to examine this phenomenon in supervision (Friedlander & Schwartz, 1985; Ward, Friedlander, Schoen, & Klein, 1985). Those wishing to consider ways of extending this work should examine the article by Leary and Kowalski (1990), who usefully break impression management into two processes: *Impression motivation* (i.e., the desire to control how others see them) and *impression construction* (i.e., the choice of impression to convey and the strategy implemented to convey it).

***Social Influence: Concluding Comments.*** Blocher (1987) and Martin (1988) both distinguished between theories that are scientific and guide inquiry and those that are personal or process oriented and guide practice. Heppner and Claiborn (1989) asserted that the social influence model is of the former type, intended to guide scientific inquiry. Perhaps as a result, many practitioners would find it "experience far" (Gelso, 1985), that is, foreign to their usual ways of understanding. This does not, however, negate its potential for leading eventually to findings with practical implications. In fact, the social influence area likely will remain a fertile source for hypotheses about supervision.

We have noted repeatedly throughout the book that one aspect of supervision that distinguishes it from counseling or therapy is its evaluative aspects. This suggests that French and Raven's (1957) *coercive power,* not invoked in Strong's (1968) original formulations of counseling, might be a source of supervisor influence. This has not been examined in supervision research.

Extensions of social psychological theory to practice continue to be proposed (e.g., Brehm & Smith, 1986; Claiborn & Lichtenberg, 1989; Dorn, 1986; Maddux, Stoltenberg,

& Rosenwein, 1987; McNeill & Stoltenberg, 1989; Strong, in press; Strong & Claiborn, 1982; Strong et al., 1988). For that reason, supervision researchers will continue to have fresh hypotheses to test for some time to come.

## CONCLUDING THE BOOK

It might be instructive to consider an assertion Raimy (1950) made about psychotherapy. In many ways, it seems to capture the current status of clinical supervision (and echoes the quote with which we began this chapter). He stated that "[p]sychotherapy is an undefined technique applied to unspecified problems with unpredictable outcomes. For this technique we recommend rigorous training" (p. 93).

An initial reaction might be that it is inappropriate to extrapolate from this statement about psychotherapy to apply it to supervision because few have recommended rigorous training of supervisors; until recently, *any* training for supervisors was rare. Yet professional associations and credentialing groups now have begun to stipulate standards for the preparation of supervisors. As mental health professionals come to appreciate the extent to which this important intervention is unique, the importance and quality of such training increasingly will come to be appreciated.

Although supervision is a newer area of science than is psychotherapy and, therefore, has a smaller literature, its literature is not negligible. In fact, the recent growth in quantity and quality of supervision research is noteworthy although not uniform across the various supervision modalities and models. The body of research on family therapy training and supervision, for example, remains quite small (see our coverage of it in Chapter 6). In their short review of this literature, Gurman, Kniskern, and Pinsof (1986) asserted that "to date little formal evaluation of training practices or programs has been forthcoming" (p. 595).

But this very unevenness in the literature is cause for excitement: Because supervision is a young field, practitioners and researchers alike have much yet to learn. It is our hope that this book will play a small role in contributing to this discovery process.

# REFERENCES

Abadie, P. D. (1985). *A study of interpersonal communication processes in the supervision of counseling.* Unpublished doctoral dissertation, Kansas State University.

Abels, P. A. (1977). Group supervision of students and staff. In F. W. Kaslow (Ed.), *Supervision, consultation, and staff training in the helping professions.* San Francisco: Jossey-Bass, pp. 175–198.

Abroms, G. M. (1977). Supervision as metatherapy. In F. W. Kaslow (Ed.), *Supervision, consultation, and staff training in the helping professions.* San Francisco: Jossey-Bass, 81–99.

Akamatsu, T. J. (1980). The use of role-play and simulation techniques in the training of psychotherapists. In A. K. Hess (Eds.), *Psychotherapy supervision: Theory, research, and practice.* New York: John Wiley and Sons. 209–225.

Albee, G. W. (1970), The uncertain future of clinical psychology. *American Psychologist, 25,* 1071–1080.

Alderfer, C. (1983). *The supervision of the therapeutic system in family therapy.* Unpublished manuscript.

Allen, G. J., Szollos, S. J., & Williams, B. E. (1986). Doctoral students' comparative evaluations of best and worst psychotherapy supervision. *Professional Psychology: Research and Practice, 17,* 91–99.

Allen, J. (1976). Peer group supervision in family therapy. *Child Welfare, 55,* 183–189.

Allport, G. W. (1958). *The nature of prejudice.* Garden City, NY: Doubleday Anchor Books.

Alonso, A. (1983). A developmental theory of psychodynamic supervision. *The Clinical Supervisor, 1,* 23–36.

Alonso, A. (1985). *The quiet profession: Supervisors of psychotherapy.* New York: Macmillan.

Altucher, N. (1967). Constructive use of the supervisory relationship. *Journal of Counseling Psychology, 14,* 165–170.

American Association for Counseling and Development. (1988). *Ethical standards* (rev. ed.). Alexandria, VA: Author.

American Association for Marriage and Family Therapists. (1984). *Ethical principles for family therapists* (Pamphlet). Washington, DC: Author.

American Psychological Association. (1973). *Accreditation procedures and criteria.* Washington, DC: Author.

American Psychological Association. (1975). Report of the task force on sex bias and sex role stereotyping in psychotherapeutic practice. *American Psychologist, 30,* 1169–1175.

American Psychological Association. (1978). Guidelines for therapy with women. *American Psychologist, 33,* 1122.

American Psychological Association. (1979). *Criteria for accreditation of doctoral training programs and internships in professional psychology.* Washington, DC: Author.

American Psychological Association. (1981). *Ethical principles of psychologists* (rev. ed.). Washington, DC: Author.

American Psychological Association. (1986). *Accreditation handbook.* Washington, DC: Author.

Anderson, J. R. (1982). Acquisition of cognitive skill. *Psychological Review, 38,* 396–406.

Anderson, J. R. (1985). *Cognitive psychology and its implications* (2nd ed.). San Francisco: W. H. Freeman.

Atwood, J. D. (1986). Self-awareness in supervision. *The Clinical Supervisor, 4,* 79–96.

Axelson, J. A. (1985). *Counseling and development in a multicultural society.* Monterey, CA: Brooks/Cole.

Baird, K. A., & Rupert, P. A. (1987). Clinical management of confidentiality: A survey of psychologists in seven states. *Professional Psychology: Research and Practice, 18,* 347–352.

Baker, D. E. (1990). *Relationship of the supervisory working alliance, supervisor and supervisee narcissism, and theoretical orientation.* Unpublished doctoral dissertation. University of Southern California.

Bandura, A. (1977). Self-efficacy: toward a unifying theory of behavior change. *Psychological Review, 84,* 191–215.

Bandura, A. (1984). Recycling misconceptions of perceived self-efficacy. *Cognitive Therapy and Research, 8,* 231–256.

Bandura, A. (1986). *Social foundations of thought and action: A social cognitive theory.* Englewood Cliffs, NJ: Prentice-Hall.

Barak, A., & LaCrosse, M. B. (1975). Multidimensional perception of counselor behavior. *Journal of Counseling Psychology, 22,* 471–476.

Barnat, M. R. (1977). Spontaneous supervisory metaphor in the resolution of trainee anxiety. *Professional Psychology, 8,* 307–315.

Bartlett, W. E., Goodyear, R. K., & Bradley, F. O. (Eds.). (1983). Supervision in counseling II [Special issue]. *The Counseling Psychologist, 11*(1).

Baum, L. F. (1956). *The wizard of Oz.* Chicago: Reilly & Lee Co.

Bauman, W. F. (1972). Games counselor trainees play: Dealing with trainee resistance. *Counselor Education and Supervision, 11,* 251–256.

Beamish, P. M., & Marinelli, R. P. (1983). A power-base training model for women. *The Personnel and Guidance Journal, 61,* 542–544.

Beck, A. T. (1976). *Cognitive therapy and the emotional disorders.* New York: International Universities Press.

Beck, T. D., Yager, G. G., Williams, G. T., Williams, B. R., & Morris, J. R. (1989, March). *Training field supervisors for adult counseling situations.* Paper presented at the annual meeting of the American Association for Counseling and Development, Boston.

Behling, J., Curtis, C., & Foster, S. A. (1982). Impact of sex-role combinations on student performance in field instruction. *Journal of Education for Social Work, 18,* 93–97.

Behling, J., Curtis, C., Foster, S. A. (1988). Impact of sex-role combinations on student performance in field instruction. *The Clinical Supervisor, 6,* 161–168.

Beis, E. (1984). *Mental health and the law.* Rockville, MD: Aspen.

Bellah, R. N., Madsen, R., Sullivan, W. M., Swidler, A., & Tipton, S. M. (1985). *Habits of the heart.* New York: Harper & Row.

Berg, K. S., & Stone, G. L. (1980). Effects of conceptual level and supervision structure on counselor skill development. *Journal of Counseling Psychology, 27,* 500–509.

Berger, M., & Dammann, C. (1982). Live supervision as context, treatment, and training. *Family Process, 21,* 337–344.

Bergin, A. E. (1966). Some implications of psychotherapy research for therapeutic practice. *Journal of Abnormal Psychology, 71,* 235–246.

Bernal, M. E., Barron, B. M., & Leary, C. (1983). Use of application materials for recruitment of ethnic minority students in psychology. *Professional Psychology: Research and Practice, 14,* 817–829.

Bernard, J. L. (1975). Due process in dropping the unsuitable clinical student. *Professional Psychology, 6,* 275–278.

Bernard, J. L., Jara, C. S. (1986). The failure of clinical psychology graduate students to apply understood ethical principles. *Professional Psychology: Research and Practice, 17,* 313–315.

Bernard, J. M. (1979). Supervisor training: A discrimination model. *Counselor Education and Supervision, 19,* 740–748.

Bernard, J. M. (1981). Inservice training for clinical supervisors. *Professional Psychology, 12,* 740–748.

Bernard, J. M. (1982). *Laboratory training for clinical supervisors: An update.* Paper presented at the annual meeting of the American Psychological Association, Washington, DC.

Bernard, J. M. (1987). Ethical and legal considerations for supervisors. In L. D. Borders & G. R. Leddick, *Handbook of Counseling Supervision.* Alexandria, VA: Association for Counselor Education and Supervision, 52–57.

Bernard, J. M. (1988). Receiving and using supervision. In H. Hackney and L. S. Cormier, *Counseling strategies and interventions* (3rd. ed.). Englewood Cliffs, NJ: Prentice Hall, 153–169.

Bernard, J. M. (1989). Training supervisors to examine relationship variables using IPR. *The Clinical Supervisor, 7,* 103–112.

Berne, E. (1964). *Games people play.* New York: Grove Press.

Bernstein, B. L., & Lecomte, C. (1979a). Supervisory feedback effects: Feedback discrepancy level, trainee psychological differentiation, and immediate responses. *Journal of Counseling Psychology, 26,* 295–303.

Bernstein, B. L., & Lecomte, C. (1979b). Self-critique technique training in a competency-based practicum. *Counselor Education and Supervision, 19,* 69–76.

Bernstein, R. M., Brown, E. M., & Ferrier, M. J. (1984). A model for collaborative team processing in brief systemic family therapy. *Journal of Marital & Family Therapy, 10,* 151–156.

Bierig, J. R. (1983). Whatever happened to professional self-regulation? *American Bar Association Journal, 69,* 616–619.

Biggs, D. A. (1988). The case presentation approach in clinical supervision. *Counselor Education and Supervision, 27,* 240–248.

Bion, W. (1961). *Experience in groups.* New York: Basic Books.

Blackwell, R. T., Galassi, J. P., Galassi, M. D., & Watson, T. E. (1985). Are cognitive assessment methods equal: A comparison of think aloud and thought listing. *Cognitive Therapy and Research, 9,* 399–413.

Blaney, P. H. (1986). Affect and memory: A review. *Psychological Bulletin, 99,* 229–246.

Blocher, D. H. (1966). *Developmental counseling.* New York: Ronald Press.

Blocher, D. H. (1983). Toward a cognitive developmental approach to counselor supervision. *The Counseling Psychologist, 11*(1), 27–34.

Blocher, D. H. (1987). On the uses and misuses of the term *theory. Journal of Counseling and Development, 66,* 67–68.

Blodgett, E. G., Schmidt, J. F., & Scudder, R. R. (1987). Clinical session evaluation: The effect of familiarity with the supervisee. *The Clinical Supervisor, 5,* 33–43.

Bloom, B. L. (1984). *Community mental health: A general introduction.* Monterey, CA: Brooks/Cole.

Blum, A. F., & Rosenberg, L. (1968). Some problems involved in professionalizing social interaction: The case of psychotherapeutic training. *Journal of Health and Social Behavior, 9,* 72–85.

Blumberg, A. (1970). A system for analyzing supervisor-teacher interaction. In A. Simon & G. Boyer (Eds.), *Mirrors for behavior* (Vol. 3). Philadelphia: Research for Better Schools.

Borders, L. D. (1986). Facilitating supervisee growth: Implications of developmental models of counseling supervision. *Michigan Journal of Counseling and Development, 17*(2), 7–12.

Borders, L. D. (1989a). A pragmatic agenda for developmental supervision research. *Counselor Education and Supervision, 29,* 16–24.

Borders, L. D. (1989b, March). *Structured peer supervision.* Paper presented at the annual convention of the American Association for Counseling and Development, Boston.

Borders, L. D. (1989c, August). *Learning to think like a supervisor.* Paper presented at the annual meeting of the American Psychological Association, New Orleans.

Borders, L. D. (1989d). Developmental cognitions of first practicum supervisees. *Journal of Counseling Psychology, 36,* 163–169.

Borders, L. D. (1989e). [Review of *Supervising counselors and therapists: A developmental approach*]. *The Clinical Supervisor, 7,* 161–166.

Borders, L. D., Bernard, J. M., Dye, H. A., Fong, M. L., Henderson, P., & Nance, D. Curriculum guide for training counseling supervisors: Rationale, development, and implementation. Unpublished manuscript.

Borders, L. D., & Fong, M. L. (1984). Sex-role orientation research: Review and implications for counselor education. *Counselor Education and Supervision, 24,* 58–69.

Borders, L. D., Fong, M. L., & Neimeyer, G. J. (1986). Counseling students' level of ego development and perceptions of clients. *Counselor Education and Supervision, 26,* 36–49.

Borders, L. D., & Leddick, G. R. (1987). *Handbook of counseling supervision.* Alexandria, VA: Association for Counselor Education and Supervision.

Borders, L. D. & Leddick, G. R. (1988). A nationwide survey of supervision training. *Counselor Education and Supervision, 27,* 271–283.

Bordin, E. S. (1979). The generalizability of the psychoanalytic concept of the working alliance. *Psychotherapy: Theory, Research, and Practice, 16,* 252–260.

Bordin, E. S. (1983). A working alliance model of supervision. *The Counseling Psychologist, 11*(1), 35–42.

Boscolo, L., & Cecchin, G. (1982). Training in systemic therapy at the Milan Centre. In R. Whiffen and J. Byng-Hall (Eds.), *Family therapy supervision: Recent development in practice.* New York: Grune & Stratton. 153–166.

Bowen, M. (1978). *Family therapy in clinical practice.* New York: Aronson.

Bowman, J. T., & Roberts, G. T. (1979). Effects of taperecording and supervisory evaluation on counselor trainee anxiety levels. *Counselor Education and Supervision, 19,* 20–26.

Boyd, J. (1978). *Counselor supervision: Approaches, preparation, practices.* Muncie, IN: Accelerated Development, Inc.

Bradley, L. J. (1989). *Counselor supervision: Principles, process, practice.* Muncie, IN: Accelerated Press.

Bradley, J. R., & Olson, J. K. (1980). Training factors influencing felt psychotherapeutic competence of psychology trainees. *Professional Psychology, 11,* 930–934.

Bradshaw, W. H., Jr. (1982). Supervision in black and white: Race as a factor in supervision. In M. Blumenfield (Ed.), *Applied supervision in psychotherapy.* New York: Grune & Stratton, 199–220.

Brehm, S. S., & Smith, T. W. (1986). Social psychological approaches to psychotherapy and behavior change. In S. L. Garfield & A. E. Bergin (Eds.), *Handbook of psychotherapy and behavior change* (3rd ed.). New York: John Wiley and Sons, 69–115.

Breunlin, D., Karrer, B., McGuire, D., & Cimmarusti, R. (1988). Cybernetics of videotape supervision. In H. Liddle, D. Breunlin, & R. Schwartz (Eds.), *Handbook of family therapy training and supervision.* New York: The Guilford Press. 194–206.

Broder, E., & Sloman, L. (1982). A contextual comparison of three training programmes. In R. Whiffen & F. Byng-Hall (Eds.), *Family therapy supervision: Recent developments in practice.* New York: Grune and Stratton, Inc. 229–242.

Brodsky, A. (1980). Sex role issues in the supervision of therapy. In A. K. Hess (Ed.), *Psychotherapy supervision: Theory, research and practice.* New York: John Wiley and Sons. 509–524.

Brodsky, S., & Myers, H. H. (1986). In vivo rotation: An alternative model for psychotherapy supervision. *The Clinical Supervisor, 4,* 95–104.

Bromberg, P. M. (1982). The supervisory process and parallel process in psychoanalysis. *Contemporary Psychoanalysis, 18,* 92–111.

Broverman, I. K., Broverman, D. M., Clarkson, F. E., Rosenkrantz, P. S., & Vogel, S. (1970). Sex role stereotypes and clinical judgments of mental health. *Journal of Counseling and Clinical Psychology, 38,* 1–7.

Brown, R. W., & Otto, M. L. (1986). Field supervision: A collaborative model. *Michigan Journal of Counseling and Development, 17*(2), 48–51.

Brownstein, C. (1981). Practicum issues: A placement planning model. *Journal of Education for Social Work, 17,* 52–58.

Bubenzer, D. L., Mahrle, C., & West, J. D. (1987). *Live counselor supervision: Trainee acculturation and supervisor interventions.* Paper presented at the annual convention of the American Association for Counseling and Development, New Orleans.

Buhrke, R. A. (1989). Lesbian-related issues in counseling supervision. *Women and Therapy, 8,* 195–206.

Byles, J., Bishop, D. S., & Horn, D. (1983). Evaluation of a family therapy training program. *Journal of Marital and Family Therapy, 9,* 299–304.

Cacioppo, J. T., & Petty, R. E. (1981). Social psychological procedures for cognitive response measurement: The thought listing technique. In T. V. Merluzzi, C. R. Glass, & M. Genest (Eds.), *Cognitive assessment.* New York: The Guilford Press. 309–342.

Cade, B. W., Speed, B., & Seligman, P. (1986). Working in teams: The pros and cons. *The Clinical Supervisor, 4,* 105–117.

Caplan, G. (1970). *The theory and practice of mental health consultation.* New York: Basic Books.

Caplow, T. (1968). *Two against one: Coalitions in triads.* Englewood Cliffs, NJ: Prentice-Hall.

Carkhuff, R. R. (1969). *Helping and human relations: A primer for lay and professional helpers* (vols. 1 & 2). New York: Holt, Rinehart, and Winston.

Casas, J. M., Brady, S., & Ponterotto, J. G. (1983). Sexual preference biases in counseling: An information processing approach. *Journal of Counseling Psychology, 30,* 139–145.

Chaiklin, H., & Munson, C. E. (1983). Peer consultation in social work. *The Clinical Supervisor, 1,* 21–34.

Chickering, A. W. (1969). *Education and identity.* San Francisco: Jossey-Bass.

Christensen, C. P. (1984). Effects of cross-cultural training on helper response. *Counselor Education and Supervision, 23,* 311–320.

Christensen, C. P. (1989). Cross-cultural awareness development: A conceptual model. *Counselor Education and Supervision, 28,* 270–287.

Claiborn, C. D. (1987). Science and practice: Reconsidering the Pepinskys. *Journal of Counseling and Development, 65,* 286–288.

Claiborn, C. D., & Lichtenberg, J. W. (1989). Interactional counseling. *The Counseling Psychologist, 17,* 355–453.

Cohen, B. Z. (1987). The ethics of social work supervision revisited. *Social Work, 32,* 194–196.

Cohen, R. J. (1979). *Malpractice: A guide for mental health professionals.* New York: Free Press.

Cohen, R. J., & DeBetz, B. (1977). Responsive supervision of the psychiatric resident and the clinical psychology intern. *American Journal of Psychoanalysis, 37,* 51–64.

Cohen, M., Gross, S., & Turner, M. (1976). A note on a developmental model for training family therapists through group supervision. *Journal of Marital and Family Counseling, 2,* 48–56.

Collins, D., & Bogo, M. (1986). Competency-based field instruction: Bridging the gap between laboratory and field learning. *The Clinical Supervisor, 4,* 39–52.

Constantine, J., Piercy, F., & Sprenkle, D. (1984). Live supervision-of-supervision. *Journal of Marital and Family Therapy, 10,* 95–97.

Cook, E. P. (1985). A framework for sex role counseling. *Journal of Counseling and Development, 64,* 253–258.

Cook, E. P. (1987). Psychological androgeny: A review of the research. *The Counseling Psychologist, 15,* 471–513.

Cook, D. A., & Helms, J. E. (1988). Visible racial/ethnic group supervisees' satisfaction with cross-cultural supervision as predicted by relationship characteristics. *Journal of Counseling Psychology, 35,* 268–274.

Cooper, L., & Gustafson, J. P. (1985). Supervision in a group: An application of group theory. *The Clinical Supervisor, 3,* 7–25.

Copeland, E. J. (1983). Cross-cultural counseling and psychotherapy: A historical perspective, implications for research and training. *Personnel and Guidance Journal, 62,* 10–15.

Corey, G. (1986). *Theory and practice of counseling and psychotherapy* (3rd ed.). Monterey, CA: Brooks/Cole.

Corey, G., Corey, M. S., & Callanan, P. (1988). *Issues and ethics in the helping professions* (3rd ed.). Monterey, CA: Brooks/Cole.

Corey, M. S. & Corey, G. (1987). *Groups: Process and practice* (3rd ed.). Monterey, CA: Brooks/Cole.

Cormier, L. S., & Bernard, J. M. (1982). Ethical and legal responsibilities of clinical supervisors. *Personnel and Guidance Journal, 60,* 486–491.

Corrigan, J. D., Dell, D. M., Lewis, K. N., & Schmidt, L. D. (1980). Counseling as a social influence process: A review [Monograph]. *Journal of Counseling Psychology, 27,* 395–441.

Corsini, R. J. (Ed.). (1981). *Handbook of innovative psychotherapies.* New York: John Wiley and Sons.

Couchon, W. D., & Bernard, J. M. (1984). Effects of timing of supervision on supervisor and counselor performance. *The Clinical Supervisor, 2,* 3–21.

Crane, D. R., Griffin, W., & Hill, R. D. (1986). Influence of therapist skills on client perceptions of marriage and family therapy outcome: Implications for supervision. *Journal of Marital and Family Therapy, 12,* 91–96.

Cronbach, L. J., & Snow, R. E. (1977). *Aptitudes and instructional methods.* New York: Irvington.

Cross, E. G., & Brown, D. (1983). Counselor supervision as a function of trainee experience: Analysis of specific behaviors. *Counselor Education and Supervision, 22,* 333–341.

Croteau, J. M., & Burda, P. C., Jr. (1983). Structured group programming on men's roles: A creative approach to change. *Personnel and Guidance Journal, 62,* 243–245.

Cummings, A. L., Hallberg, E. T., Martin, J., Slemon, A. G., & Hiebert, B. (1989, August). *A qualitative analysis of the conceptualizations of novice and experienced psychotherapists.* Paper presented at the annual meeting of the American Psychological Association, New Orleans.

Dance, K. A., & Neufeld, W. J. (1988). Aptitude-treatment interaction research in the clinical setting: A review of attempts to dispel the "patient uniformity" myth. *Psychological Bulletin, 104,* 192–213.

Danskin, D. G. (1957). A role-ing counselor gathers no moss. *Journal of Counseling Psychology, 4,* 41–43.

Deau, K. (1984). From individual differences to social categories: Analysis of a decade's research on gender. *American Psychologist, 39,* 105–116.

Delaney, D. J. (1972). A behavioral model for the practicum supervision of counselor candidates. *Counselor Education and Supervision, 12,* 46–50.

Denkowski, K. M., & Denkowski, G. C. (1982). Client-counselor confidentiality: An update of rationale, legal status, and implications. *Personnel and Guidance Journal, 60,* 371–375.

deShazer, S. (1984). The death of resistance. *Family Process, 23,* 11–17.

deShazer, S. (1985). *Keys to solution in brief therapy.* New York: W. W. Norton & Co.

Dimick, K. M., & Krause, F. H. (1980). *Practicum manual for counseling and psychotherapy.* Muncie, IN: Accelerated Development Press.

Dixon, D. N., & Claiborn, C. D. (1987). A social influence approach to counselor supervision. In J. E. Maddux, C. D. Stoltenberg, & R. Rosenwein (Eds.), *Social processes in clinical and counseling psychology.* New York: Springer-Verlag, 83–93.

Dixon, D. N., & Kruczek, T. (1989, August). *Attributions of counseling by counselor trainees and supervisors.* Paper presented at the annual meeting of the American Psychological Association, New Orleans.

Dodds, J. B. (1986). Supervision of psychology trainees in field placements. *Professional Psychology: Research and Practice, 17,* 296–300.

Dodenhoff, J. T. (1981). Interpersonal attraction and direct-indirect supervisor influence as predictors of counselor trainee performance. *Journal of Counseling Psychology, 28,* 47–52.

Doehrman, M. J. (1971). Parallel processes in supervision and psychotherapy (Doctoral dissertation, University of Michigan, 1971). *Dissertation Abstracts International,* 7214845.

Doehrman, M. J. (1976). Parallel processes in supervision and psychotherapy. *Bulletin of the Menninger Clinic, 40,* 3–104.

Dole, A. A., Nissenfeld, M., Browers, C., Herzog, L., Levitt, D., McIntyre, P., Wedeman, S., & Woodburn, P. (1984, April). *Counselor retrospections and supervisor cognitions: A case study.* Paper presented at the annual meeting of the American Educational Research Association, New Orleans.

Dorn, F. J. (1986). *Social influence processes in counseling.* Springfield, IL: Charles C Thomas.

Douce, L. (1989, August). *Classroom and experiential training in supervision.* Paper presented at the annual meeting of the American Psychological Association, New Orleans.

Dowling, S. (1984). Clinical evaluation: A comparison of self, self with videotape, peers, and supervisors. *The Clinical Supervisor, 2,* 71–78.

Dworkin, S. (1984). Traditionally defined client, meet feminist therapist: Feminist therapy as attitude change. *Personnel and Guidance Journal, 62,* 301–305.

Efstation, J. F., Patton, M. J., & Kardash, C. M. (1990). Measuring the working alliance in counselor supervision. *Journal of Counseling Psychology, 37,* 322–329.

Eisenberg, S. (1956). *Supervision in the changing field of social work.* Philadelphia: The Jewish Family Service of Philadelphia.

Eisikovits, Z., Meier, R., Guttman, E., Shurka, E., & Levinstein, A. (1986). Supervision in ecological context: The relationship between the quality of supervision and the work and treatment environment. *Journal of Social Service Research, 8,* 37–58.

Ekstein, R. (1964). Supervision of psychotherapy: Is it teaching? Is it administration? Or is it therapy? *Psychotherapy: Theory, Research, and Practice, 1,* 137–138.

Ekstein, R., & Wallerstein, R. S. (1972). *The teaching and learning of psychotherapy* (2nd ed.). New York: International Universities Press, Inc.

Ellis, A. (1974). *The techniques of Disputing Irrational Beliefs (DIBS).* New York: Institute for Rational Living.

Ellis, M. V., & Dell, D. M. (1986). Dimensionality of supervisor roles: Supervisors' perceptions of supervision. *Journal of Counseling Psychology, 33,* 282–291.

Ellis, M. V., Dell, D. M., & Good, G. E. (1988). Counselor trainees' perceptions of supervisor roles: Two studies testing the dimensionality of supervision. *Journal of Counseling Psychology, 35,* 315–324.

Ellis, M. V., Ladany, N., Krengel, M., & Schult, D. (1988, August). *An investigation of supervision research methodology: Where have we gone wrong?* Paper presented at the annual meeting of the American Psychological Association, Atlanta.

Etringer, B. D., & Claiborn, C. (1986, August). *Processing of feedback in supervision: A methodological pilot.* Paper presented at the annual meeting of the American Psychological Association, Washington, DC.

Everett, C. A. (1980). Supervision of marriage and family therapy. In A. K. Hess (Ed.), *Psychotherapy supervision: Theory, research and practice.* New York: John Wiley and Sons. 367–380.

Everett, C. A., & Koerpel, B. J. (1986). Family therapy supervision: A review and critique of the literature. *Contemporary Family Therapy, 8,* 62–74.

Everstine, L., Everstine, D. S., Heymann, G. M., True, R. H., Frey, D. H., Johnson, H. G., & Seiden, R. H. (1980). Privacy and confidentiality in psychotherapy. *American Psychologist, 35,* 828–840.

Falvey, J. E. (1987). *Handbook of administrative supervision.* Alexandria, VA: Association for Counselor Education and Supervision.

Faust, D. (1986). Research on human judgment and its application to clinical practice. *Professional Psychology: Research and Practice, 17,* 420–430.

Feldman, S. (1980). The middle management muddle. *Administration in Mental Health, 8,* 3–11.

Fenell, D. L., Hovestadt, A. J., & Harvey, S. J. (1986). A comparison of delayed feedback and live supervision models of marriage and family therapist clinical training. *Journal of Marital and Family Therapy, 12,* 181–186.

Fisher, B. (1989). Differences between supervision of beginning and advanced therapists: Hogan's hypothesis empirically revisited. *The Clinical Supervisor, 7*(1), 57–74.

Fitzgerald, L. F., & Nutt, R. (1986). The division 17 principles concerning the counseling/psychotherapy of women: Rationale and implementation. *The Counseling Psychologist, 14*(1), 180–216.

Fitzgerald, L. F., & Osipow, S. H. (1986). An occupational analysis of counseling psychology: How special is the specialty? *American Psychologist, 41,* 535–544.

Fleming, J., & Benedek, T. (1966). Psychoanalytic supervision: A method of clinical teaching. New York: Grune & Stratton.

Fong, M. L., Borders, L. D., & Neimeyer, G. J. (1986). Sex role orientation and self-disclosure flexibility in counselor training. *Counselor Education and Supervision, 25,* 210–221.

Forsyth, D. R., & Ivey, A. E. (1980). Micro-training: An approach to differential supervision. In A. K. Hess (Ed.), *Psychotherapy supervision: Theory, research and practice.* New York: John Wiley and Sons, 242–261.

Fox, R. (1983). Contracting in supervision: A goal oriented process. *The Clinical Supervisor, 1,* 37–49.

Foxley, C. H. (1979). *Nonsexist counseling: Helping women and men redefine their roles.* Dubuque, IA: Kendall/Hunt Publishing Co.

Frank, J. D. (1961). *Persuasion and healing.* Baltimore: Johns Hopkins University Press.

Frank, J. D. (1973). *Persuasion and healing* (rev. ed.). Baltimore: Johns Hopkins University Press.

French, J. R. P., Jr., & Raven, B. (1959). The bases of social power. In D. Cartwright (Ed.), *Studies in social power.* Ann Arbor: Institute for Social Research.

Friedlander, M. L. (1984). Hill counselor verbal response category system—revised. *Tests in microfische.* Princeton, NJ: Educational Testing Service (Test Collection, No. 012397, Set I).

Friedlander, M. L., Keller, K. E., Peca-Baker, T. A., & Olk, M. E. (1986). Effects of role conflict on counselor trainees' self-statements, anxiety level, and performance. *Journal of Counseling Psychology, 33,* 73–77.

Friedlander, M. L., & Schwartz, G. S. (1985). Toward a theory of strategic self-presentation in counseling and psychotherapy. *Journal of Counseling Psychology, 32,* 483–501.

Friedlander, M. L., Siegel, S., & Brenock, K. (1989). Parallel processes in counseling and supervision: A case study. *Journal of Counseling Psychology, 36,* 149–157.

Friedlander, M. L., & Ward, L. G. (1984). Development and validation of the supervisory styles inventory. *Journal of Counseling Psychology, 31,* 541–557.

Friedlander, S. R., Dye, N. W., Costello, R. M., & Kobos, J. C. (1984). A developmental model for teaching and learning in psychotherapy supervision. *Psychotherapy, 21,* 189–196.

Friedman, R. (1983). Aspects of the parallel process and counter-transference issues in student supervision. *School Social Work Journal, 8,* 3–15.

Froehle, T. C. (1984). Computer-assisted feedback in counseling supervision. *Counselor Education and Supervision, 24,* 168–175.

Fulero, S. M. (1988). Tarasoff: 10 years later. *Professional Psychology: Research and Practice, 19,* 184–190.

Fuller, F. F., & Manning, B. A. (1973). Self-confrontation reviewed: A conceptualization for video playback in teacher education. *Review of Educational Research, 43,* 469–528.

Galassi, J. P., & Trent, P. J. (1987). A conceptual framework for evaluating supervision effectiveness. *Counselor Education and Supervision, 26,* 260–269.

Gallant, J. P., & Thyer, B. A. (1989). The "bug-in-the-ear" in clinical supervision: A review. *The Clinical Supervisor, 7,* 43–58.

Gardner, L. H. (1980). Racial, ethnic, and social class considerations in psychotherapy supervision. In A. K. Hess (Ed.), *Psychotherapy supervision: Theory, research and practice.* New York: Wiley. 474–508.

Garfield, S. L. (1983). Effectiveness of psychotherapy: The perennial controversy. *Professional Psychology: Theory, Research, and Practice, 14,* 35–43.

Garfield, S. L. (1986). Research on client variables in psychotherapy. In S. L. Garfield & A. E. Bergin (Eds.), *Handbook of psychotherapy and behavior change* (3rd ed.). New York: John Wiley and Sons.

Garfield, S. L., & Kurtz, R. M. (1976). Clinical psychologists in the 1970s. *American Psychologist, 31,* 1–9.

Garfield, S. L., & Kurtz, R. M. (1977). A study of eclectic views. *Journal of Consulting and Clinical Psychology, 45,* 78–83.

Gelso, C. J. (1974). Effects of recording on counselors and clients. *Counselor Education and Supervision, 13,* 5–12.

Gelso, C. J. (1979). Research in counseling: Methodological and professional issues. *The Counseling Psychologist, 8*(3), 7–36.

Gelso, C. J. (1985). Rigor, relevance, and counseling research: On the need to maintain our course between Scylla and Charybdis. *Journal of Counseling and Development, 63,* 551–553.

Gelso, C. J. & Carter, J. (1985). The relationship in counseling and psychotherapy. *The Counseling Psychologist, 13*(2), 155–243.

Genest, M., & Turk, D. C. (1981). Think-aloud approaches to cognitive assessment. In T. V. Merluzzi, C. R.

Glass, & M. Genest (Eds.), *Cognitive assessment*. New York: Guilford. 233–269.

Gershenson, J., & Cohen, M. (1978). Through the looking glass: The experiences of two family therapy trainees with live supervision. *Family Process, 17,* 225–230.

Getzel, G. S., & Salmon, R. (1985). Group supervision: An organizational approach. *The Clinical Supervisor, 3,* 27–43.

Getzels, J. W., & Guba, E. G. (1957). Social behavior and the administration process. *The School Review, 65,* 423–441.

Gilligan, C. (1982). *In a different voice*. Cambridge, MA: Harvard University Press.

Gizynski, M. (1978). Self awareness of the supervisor in supervision. *Clinical Social Work Journal, 6,* 203–210.

Glaser, R. (1985). *The nature of expertise* (Occasional Paper No. 107). Columbus, OH: Ohio State University, The National Center for Research on Vocational Education.

Glaser, R. (1990). The reemergence of learning theory within instructional research. *American Psychologist, 45,* 29–39.

Glenick, D. S., & Stevens, E. (1980). In A. K. Hess (Ed.), *Psychotherapy supervision: Theory, research, and practice*. New York: John Wiley and Sons. 226–241.

Glenn, A. A., & Russell, R. K. (1986). Heterosexual bias among counselor trainees. *Counselor Education and Supervision, 25,* 222–229.

Glidden, C. E., & Tracey, T. J. (1989, August). *The structure of perceived differences in supervision across developmental levels*. Paper presented at the annual meeting of the American Psychological Association, New Orleans.

Goin, M. K., & Kline, F. (1976). Countertransference: A neglected subject in clinical supervision. *American Journal of Psychiatry, 133,* 41–44.

Goldberg, D. A. (1985). Process notes, audio, and video tape: Modes of presentation in psychotherapy training. *The Clinical Supervisor, 3,* 3–13.

Goldstein, A. P., Heller, K., & Sechrest, L. B. (1966). *Psychotherapy and the psychology of behavior change*. New York: John Wiley and Sons.

Goodman, R. W. (1985). The live supervision model in clinical training. *The Clinical Supervisor, 3,* 43–49.

Goodyear, R. K. (1982). *Psychotherapy supervision by major theorists* [Videotape series]. Manhattan, KS: Instructional Media Center. (Note: For further information, contact the author at the University of Southern California.)

Goodyear, R. K. (1990). Gender configurations in supervisory dyads: Their relation to supervisee influence strategies and to skill evaluations of the supervisee. *The Clinical Supervisor, 8,* 67–79.

Goodyear, R. K., Abadie, P. D., & Efros, F. (1984). Supervisory theory into practice: Differential perception of supervision by Ekstein, Ellis, Polster, and Rogers. *Journal of Counseling Psychology, 31,* 228–237.

Goodyear, R. K., & Robyak, J. E. (1982). *Psychological Reports, 51,* 978.

Goodyear, R. K., & Sinnett, E. R. (1984). Current and emerging ethical issues for counseling psychologists. *The Counseling Psychologist, 12*(3), 87–98.

Graham, D. L. R., Rawlings, E. I., Halpern, H. S., & Hermes, J. (1984). Therapists' needs for training in counseling lesbians and gay men. *Professional Psychology: Research and Practice, 15,* 482–496.

Grann, I., Hendricks, B., Hoop, L., Jackson, G., & Traunstein, D. (1986). Competency-based evaluation: A second round. *The Clinical Supervisor, 3,* 81–91.

Green, S. L., & Hansen, J. C. (1986). Ethical dilemmas in family therapy. *Journal of Marital and Family Therapy, 12,* 225–230.

Green, S. L., & Hansen, J. C. (1989). Ethical dilemmas faced by family therapists. *Journal of Marital and Family Therapy, 15,* 149–158.

Grinder, J., & Bandler, R. (1976). *The Structure of Magic II*. Palo Alto, CA: Science and Behavior Books.

Gurk, M. D., & Wicas, E. A. (1979). Generic models of counselor supervision: counseling/instruction dichotomy and consultation metamodel. *Personnel and Guidance Journal, 57,* 402–407.

Gurman, A. S., Kniskern, D. P., & Pinsof, W. M. (1986). Research on the process and outcome of marital and family therapy. In S. L. Garfield & A. E. Bergin (Eds.), *Handbook of psychotherapy and behavior change.* New York: John Wiley and Sons, 565–624.

Gutierrez, F. J. (1982). Working with minority counselor education students. *Counselor Education and Supervision, 21,* 218–226.

Haas, L. J., Malouf, J. L., & Mayerson, N. H. (1986). Ethical dilemmas in psychological practice: Results of a national survey. *Professional Psychology: Research and Practice, 17,* 316–321.

Hackney, H. L. (1971). Development of a pre-practicum counseling skills model. *Counselor Education and Supervision, 11,* 102–109.

Hackney, H. L., & Goodyear, R. K. (1984). Carl Rogers' client-centered supervision. In R. F. Levant and J. M. Shlien (Eds.), *Client-centered therapy and the person-centered approach: New directions in theory, research, and practice.* New York: Praeger. 278–296.

Hale, K. K., & Stoltenberg, C. D. (1988). The effects of self-awareness and evaluation apprehension on counselor trainee anxiety. *The Clinical Supervisor, 6,* 49–69.

Haley, J. (1987a). *Problem solving therapy* (2nd ed.). San Francisco: Jossey-Bass.

Haley, J. (1987b, June). *Strategic Family Therapy.* Presented at the master therapist workshop, University of Connecticut School of Medicine, Farmington, CT.

Halgin, R. P. (1986). Pragmatic blending of clinical models in the supervisory relationship. *The Clinical Supervisor, 3,* 23–46.

Hall, J. E. (1988a). Protection in supervision. *Register Report, 14,* 3–4.

Hall, J. E. (1988b). Dual relationships in supervision. *Register Report, 15,* 5–6.

Hamilton, N., & Else, J. F. (1983). *Designing field education: Philosophy, structure, and process.* Springfield, IL: Charles C. Thomas.

Hamlin, E. R., II, & Timberlake, E. M. (1982). Peer group supervision for supervisors. *Social Casework, 67,* 82–87.

Handelsman, M. M. (1986). Problems with ethics training by "osmosis." *Professional Psychology: Research and Training, 17,* 371–372.

Hare-Mustin, R. T., & Lamb, S. (1984). Family counselors' attitudes toward women and motherhood: A new cohort. *Journal of Marital and Family Therapy, 10,* 419–421.

Hare-Mustin, R. T., Marecek, J., Kaplan, A. G., & Liss-Levinson, N. (1979). Rights of clients, responsibilities of therapists. *American Psychologist, 34,* 3–16.

Harkness, D., & Poertner, J. (1989). Research and social work supervision: A conceptual review. *Social Work, 34,* 115–119.

Harmon, L. W. (1989). The scientist/practitioner model and choice of research paradigm. *The Counseling Psychologist, 17*(1), 86–89.

Harrar, W. R., Vandecreek, L., & Knapp, S. (1990). Ethical and legal aspects of clinical supervision. *Professional Psychology: Research and Practice, 21,* 37–41.

Harris, S., & Goodyear, R. K. (1990, April). *The circumplex model in four supervisory dyads: A study of interaction.* Paper presented at the annual meeting of the American Educational Research Association, Boston.

Hart, G. M. (1982). *The process of clinical supervision.* Baltimore: University Park Press.

Harvey, C., & Katz, C. (1985). *If I'm so successful, why do I feel like a fake? The impostor phenomenon.* New York: St. Martin's Press.

Harvey, O. J., Hunt, D. E., & Schroeder, H. M. (1961). *Conceptual systems and personality organization.* NY: Holt, Rinehart, and Winston.

Hawthorne, L. S. (1987). Teaching from recordings in field instruction. *The Clinical Supervisor, 5*(2), 7–22.

Heath, A. W. (1982). Team family therapy training: Conceptual and pragmatic considerations. *Family Process, 21,* 187–194.

Heath, A. W. & Storm, C. L. (1985). From the institute to the ivory tower: The live supervision stage approach for teaching supervision in academic settings. *The American Journal of Family Therapy, 13*(3), 27–36.

Heller, K., & Monahan, J. (1983). Individual process consultation. In S. Cooper & W. F. Hodges (Eds.), *The mental health consultation field*. New York: Human Sciences Press. 57–69.

Hemelt, M. D., & Mackert, M. E. (1978). *Dynamics of law in nursing and health care*. Reston, VA: Reston Publishing.

Hennessy, T. C. (1970). A model of clinical supervision of counseling. *ERIC Reports*, CG 01450C.

Henry, W. E., Sims, J. H., & Spray, L. S. (1971). *The fifth profession*. San Francisco: Jossey-Bass.

Heppner, P. P., & Claiborn, C. D. (1989). Social influence research in counseling: A review and critique [Monograph]. *Journal of Counseling Psychology, 36,* 365–387.

Heppner, P. P., & Dixon, D. N. (1981). A review of the interpersonal influence process in counseling. *Personnel and Guidance Journal, 59,* 542–550.

Heppner, P. P., & Handley, P. G. (1981). A study of the interpersonal influence process in supervision. *Journal of Counseling Psychology, 28,* 437–444.

Heppner, P. P., & Krauskopf, C. J. (1987). An information-processing approach to personal problem solving. *The Counseling Psychologist, 15,* 371–447.

Heppner, P. P., & Roehlke, H. J. (1984). Differences among supervisees at different levels of training: Implications for a developmental model of supervision. *Journal of Counseling Psychology, 31,* 76–90.

Hess, A. K. (Ed.). (1980a). *Psychotherapy supervision: Theory, research and practice*. New York: John Wiley and Sons.

Hess, A. K. (1980b). Training models and the nature of psychotherapy supervision. In A. K. Hess (Ed.), *Psychotherapy supervision: Theory, research, and practice*. New York: John Wiley and Sons. 15–28.

Hess, A. K. (1986). Growth in supervision: Stages of supervisee and supervisor development. *The Clinical Supervisor, 4,* 51–67.

Hess, A. K. (1987). Psychotherapy supervision: Stages, Buber, and a theory of relationship. *Professional Psychology: Research and Practice, 18,* 251–259.

Hess, A. K., & Hess, K. A. (1983). Psychotherapy supervision: A survey of internship training practices. *Professional Psychology, 14,* 504–513.

Hill, C. E. (1989). *Therapist techniques and client outcomes: Eight cases of psychotherapy*. Newbury Park, CA: Sage Publications.

Hill, C. E., Carter, J. A., & O'Farrell, M. K. (1983). A case-study of the process and outcome of time-limited counseling. *Journal of Counseling Psychology, 30,* 3–18.

Hill, C. E., Charles, D., & Reed, K. G. (1981). A longitudinal analysis of changes in counseling skills during doctoral training. *Journal of Counseling Psychology, 28,* 428–436.

Hill, R. (1958). Generic features of families under stress. *Social Casework, 39,* 139–150.

Hillberbrand, E. (1989). Cognitive differences between experts and novices: Implications for group supervision. *Journal of Counseling and Development, 67,* 293–296.

Hines, P. M., & Hare-Mustin, R. T. (1978). Ethical concerns in family therapy. *Professional Psychology, 9,* 165–171.

Hofstadter, D. (1979). *Godel, Escher, Bach: An eternal golden brain*. New York: Basic Books.

Hogan, R. A. (1964). Issues and approaches in supervision. *Psychotherapy, Theory, Research, and Practice, 1,* 139–141.

Holiman, M., & Lauver, P. J. (1987). The counselor culture and client-centered practice. *Counselor Education and Supervision, 26*(3), 184–191.

Hollingsworth, D. K., & Witten, J. (1983). Clarification of the counselor-trainee and supervisor roles in clinical education. *The Clinical Supervisor, 1,* 47–56.

Holloway, E. L. (1982). Interactional structure of the supervision interview. *Journal of Counseling Psychology, 29,* 309–317.

Holloway, E. L. (1984). Outcome evaluation in supervision research. *The Counseling Psychologist, 12*(4), 167–174.

Holloway, E. L. (1987). Developmental models of supervision: Is it supervision? *Professional Psychology: Research and Practice, 18,* 209–216.

Holloway, E. L. (1988a). Instruction beyond the facilitative conditions: A response to Biggs. *Counselor Education and Supervision, 27,* 252–258.

Holloway, E. L. (1988b). Models of counselor development or training models for supervision? Rejoinder to Stoltenberg and Delworth. *Professional Psychology: Research and Practice, 19,* 138–140.

Holloway, E. L., Freund, R. D., Gardner, S. L., Nelson, M. L., & Walker, B. R. (1989). Relation of power and involvement to theoretical orientation in supervision: An analysis of discourse. *Journal of Counseling Psychology, 36,* 88–102.

Holloway, E. L., & Hosford, R. E. (1983). Towards developing a prescriptive technology of counselor supervision. *The Counseling Psychologist, 11*(1), 73–77.

Holloway, E. L., & Johnston, R. (1985). Group supervision: Widely practiced, but poorly understood. *Counselor Education and Supervision, 24,* 332–340.

Holloway, E. L., & Roehlke, H. J. (1987). Internship: The applied training of a counseling psychologist. *The Counseling Psychologist, 15,* 205–260.

Holloway, E. L., & Wampold, B. E. (1983). Patterns of verbal behavior and judgments of satisfaction in the supervision interview. *Journal of Counseling Psychology, 30,* 227–234.

Holloway, E. L., & Wolleat, P. L. (1980). Relationships of counselor conceptual level to clinical hypothesis formation. *Journal of Counseling Psychology, 27,* 539–545.

Holloway, E. L., & Wolleat, P. L. (1981). Style differences of beginning supervisors: An interactional analysis. *Journal of Counseling Psychology, 28,* 373–376.

Holtzman, R. F., & Raskin, M. S. (1988). Why field placements fail: Study results. *The Clinical Supervisor, 6*(3), 123–136.

Hood, A. B., & Arceneaux, C. (1987). Multicultural counseling: Will what you don't know help you? *Counselor Education and Supervision, 26,* 173–175.

Horvath, A. O., & Greenberg, L. S. (1989). Development and validation of the working alliance inventory. *Journal of Counseling Psychology, 36,* 223–233.

Hosford, R. (1981). Self-as-a-model: A cognitive social learning technique. *The Counseling Psychologist, 9,* 45–62.

Hotelling, K., & Forrest, L. (1985). Gilligan's theory of sex-role development: A perspective for counseling. *Journal of Counseling and Development, 64,* 183–186.

Hovestadt, A., Fenell, D., Piercy, F. (1983). Integrating marriage and family therapy within counselor education: A three level model. In B. Okun & S. Gladding (Eds.), *Issues in training marriage and family therapists.* Ann Arbor, MI: ERIC/CAPS, 29–42.

Howard, G. S., Nance, D. W., & Myers, P. (1986). Adaptive counseling and therapy: An integrative, eclectic model. *The Counseling Psychologist, 14*(3), 363–442.

Hunt, D. E. (1971). *Matching models in education: The coordination of teaching methods with student characteristics.* Toronto, Ont. Canada: Ontario Institute for Studies in Education.

Hutt, C. H., Scott, J., & King, M. (1983). A phenomenological study of supervisees' positive and negative experiences in supervision. *Psychotherapy: Theory, Research, and Practice, 20,* 118–123.

Ibrahim, F. A. (1985). Effective cross-cultural counseling and psychotherapy: A framework. *The Counseling Psychologist, 13*(4), 625–638.

Ibrahim, F. A., & Kahn, H. (1987). Assessment of world views. *Psychological Reports, 60,* 163–167.

Iovacchini, E. V. (1981). The impact of recent academic due process decisions on counselor education programs. *Counselor Education and Supervision, 20,* 163–171.

Isaacs, E., & Clark, H. (1987). References in conversation between experts and novices. *Journal of Experimental Psychology, 116,* 26–37.

Ivey, A. E. (1971). *Microcounseling: Innovations in interviewing training.* Springfield, IL: Thomas.

Ivey, A. E. (1987). Cultural intentionality: The core of effective helping. *Counselor Education and Supervision, 26,* 168–172.

Ivey, A. E., & Authier, J. (1978). *Microcounseling: Innovations in interviewing, counseling, psychotherapy, and psychoeducation.* Springfield, IL: Thomas.

Jackson, M. L. (1987). Cross-cultural counseling at the crossroads: A dialogue with Clemmont E. Vontress.

*Journal of Counseling and Development, 66,* 20–23.

Jakubowski-Spector, P., Dustin, R., & George, R. L. (1971). Toward developing a behavioral counselor education model. *Counselor Education and Supervision, 11,* 242–250.

Johnson, E., Baker, S. B., Kopala, M., Kiselica, M. S., & Thompson, E. C. (1989). Counseling self-efficacy and counseling competence in prepracticum training. *Counselor Education and Supervision, 28,* 205–218.

Johnson, E., & Moses, N. C. (1988, August). *The dynamic developmental model of supervision.* Paper presented at the annual convention of the American Psychological Association, Atlanta.

Johnson, E., & Seem, S. R. (1989, August). *Supervisory style and the development of self-efficacy in counselor training.* Paper presented at the annual meeting of the American Psychological Association, New Orleans.

Jones, E. E., Kanouse, D., Kelley, H. H., Nisbett, R. E., Valins, S., & Weiner, B. (Eds.). (1972). *Attribution: Perceiving the causes of behavior.* Morristown, NJ: General Learning Press.

Kadushin, A. (1968). Games people play in supervision. *Social Work, 13,* 23–32.

Kadushin, A. (1974). Supervisor-supervisee: A survey. *Social Work, 19,* 288–297.

Kadushin, A. (1976). *Supervision in social work.* New York: Columbia University Press.

Kadushin, A. (1985). *Supervision in social work* (2nd ed.). New York: Columbia University Press.

Kagan, D. M. (1988). Research on the supervision of counselors- and teachers-in-training: Linking two bodies of literature. *Review of Educational Research, 58,* 1–24.

Kagan, N. (1976). *Influencing human interaction.* Mason, MI: Mason Media; or Washington, DC: American Association for Counseling and Development.

Kagan, N. (1980). Influencing human interaction—eighteen years with IPR. In A. K. Hess (Ed.), *Psychotherapy supervision: Theory, research and practice.* New York: John Wiley and Sons. 262–286.

Kagan, N., & Krathwohl, D. R. (1967). *Studies in human interaction: Interpersonal process recall stimulated by videotape.* East Lansing, MI: Michigan State University.

Kagan, N., Krathwohl, D. R., & Farquhar, W. W. (1965). *IPR—Interpersonal process recall by videotape: Stimulated recall by videotape.* East Lansing, MI: Michigan State University.

Kagan, N., Krathwohl, D. R., & Miller, R. (1963). Stimulated recall in therapy using videotape—a case study. *Journal of Counseling Psychology, 10,* 237–243.

Kamin, L. J. (1974). *The science and politics of I.Q.* New York: John Wiley and Sons.

Kaplan, I. M. (1983). Current trends in practicing supervision research. *Counselor Education and Supervision, 22,* 215–226.

Kaplan, M. (1983). A woman's view of DSM-III. *American Psychologist, 38,* 786–792.

Kaplan, R. (1987). The current use of live supervision within marriage and family therapy programs. *The Clinical Supervisor, 5*(3), 43–52.

Kaslow, F. W. (Ed.). (1977). *Supervision, consultation, and staff training in the helping professions.* San Francisco: Jossey-Bass.

Kaslow, N. J., & Rice, D. G. (1985). Developmental stresses of psychology internship training: What training staff can do to help. *Professional Psychology: Research and Practice, 16,* 253–261.

Katz, J. H. (1985). The sociopolitical nature of counseling. *The Counseling Psychologist, 13*(4), 615–624.

Kaul, T. J., & Bednar, R. L. (1986). Research on group and related therapies. In S. L. Garfield & A. E. Bergin (Eds.), *Handbook of psychotherapy and behavior change* (3rd ed.). New York: John Wiley and Sons. 671–714.

Keith-Spiegel, P., & Koocher, G. P. (1985). *Ethics in psychology: Professional standards and cases.* New York: Random House.

Kell, B. L., & Burow, J. M. (1970). *Developmental counseling and therapy.* Boston: Houghton Mifflin.

Kell, B. L., Morse, J., & Grater, H. (undated). *The supervision and training of counselors and psychotherapists: An instance of ego-evaluation, support and development.* Unpublished paper.

Kell, B. L., & Mueller, W. J. (1966). *Impact and change: A study of counseling relationships.* New York: Appleton-Century-Crofts.

Kennard, B. D., Stewart, S. M., & Gluck, M. R. (1987). The supervision relationship: Variables contributing to positive versus negative experiences. *Professional Psychology: Research and Practice, 18,* 172–175.

Kiesler, D. J. (1966). Some myths of psychotherapy research and the search for a paradigm. *Psychological Bulletin, 65,* 110–135.

Kitchener, K. S. (1988). Dual role relationships: What makes them so problematic? *Journal of Counseling and Development, 67,* 217–221.

Kluckhohn, F. R., & Strodtbeck, F. L. (1961). *Variations in value orientations.* Evanston, IL: Row, Peterson.

Knapp, S., & Vandecreek, L. (1982). Tarasoff: Five years later. *Professional Psychology, 13,* 511–516.

Kopp, S. (1971). *Guru: Metaphors from a psychotherapist.* Palo Alto, CA: Science and Behavior Books.

Krause, A. A., & Allen, G. J. (1988). Perceptions of counselor supervision: An examination of Stotenberg's model from the perspectives of supervisor and supervisee. *Journal of Counseling Psychology, 35,* 77–80.

Kruger, L. J., Cherniss, C., Maher, C. A., & Leichtman, H. M. (1988). A behavioral observation system for group supervision. *Counselor Education and Supervision, 27,* 331–343.

Kurpius, D. J., Benjamin, D., & Morran, D. K. (1985). Effects of teaching a cognitive strategy on counselor trainee internal dialogue and clinical hypothesis formulation. *Journal of Counseling Psychology, 32,* 263–271.

Lambert, M. J. (1974). Supervisory and counseling process: A comparative study. *Counselor Education and Supervision, 14,* 54–60.

Lambert, M. J. (1980). Research and the supervisory process. In A. K. Hess (Ed.), *Psychotherapy supervision: Theory, research, and practice.* New York: John Wiley and Sons. 423–450.

Lambert, M. J., & Arnold, R. C. (1987). Research and the supervision process. *Professional Psychology: Research and Practice, 18,* 217–224.

Lambert, M. J., Shapiro, D. A., & Bergin, A. E. (1986). The effectiveness of psychotherapy. In S. L. Garfield & A. E. Bergin (Eds.), *Handbook of psychotherapy and behavior change* (3rd ed.). New York: John Wiley and Sons.

Landau, J., & Stanton, M. D. (1983). Aspects of supervision with the "Pick-a-Dali-Circus" model. *Journal of Strategic and Systemic Therapies, 2,* 31–89.

Lanning, W. (1986). Development of the supervisor emphasis rating form. *Counselor Education and Supervision, 25,* 191–196.

Larson, P. C. (1982). Counseling special populations. *Professional Psychology, 13,* 843–858.

Lazarus, A. A. (1976). *Multimodal behavior therapy.* New York: Springer.

Leary, M. R., & Kowalski, R. M. (1990). Impression management: A literature review and two-component model. *Psychological Bulletin, 107,* 34–47.

Leary, T. (1957). *Interpersonal diagnosis of personality: A theory and a methodology for personality evaluation.* New York: Ronald Press.

Leddick, G. R., & Bernard, J. M. (1980). The history of supervision: A critical review. *Counselor Education and Supervision, 19,* 186–196.

Leddick, G. R., & Dye, H. A. (1987). Effective supervision as portrayed by trainee expectations and preferences. *Counselor Education and Supervision, 27,* 139–154.

Lee, D. J. (1984). Counseling and culture: Some issues. *Personnel and Guidance Journal, 62,* 592–597.

Leonardelli, C. A., & Gratz, R. R. (1985). Roles and responsibilities in fieldwork experience: A social systems approach. *The Clinical Supervisor, 3*(3), 15–24.

Lerner, M. (1969). Respectable bigotry. *American Scholar, 38,* 606–617.

Levenson, E. A. (1984). Follow the fox. In L. Caligor, P. M. Bromberg, & J. D. Meltzer (Eds.), *Clinical perspectives on the supervision of psychoanalysis and psychotherapy* (pp. 153–168). New York: Plenum Press.

Levine, F. M. & Tilker, H. A. (1974). A behavior modification approach to supervision and psychotherapy. *Psychotherapy: Theory, Research and Practice, 11,* 182–188.

Levy, L. H. (1983). Evaluation of students in clinical psychology programs: A program evaluation perspective. *Professional Psychology: Research and Practice, 14,* 497–503.

Lewin, K. (1952). Group decision and social change. In T. Newcomb & E. Hartley (Eds.), *Readings in social psychology.* New York: Holt, Rinehart and Winston.

Lewis, G. J., Greenburg, S. L., & Hatch, D. B. (1988). Peer consultation groups for psychologists in private practice: A national survey. *Professional Psychology: Research & Practice, 9,* 81–86.

Lewis, W. (1988). A supervision model for public agencies. *The Clinical Supervisor, 6*(2), 85–91.

Lewis, W., & Rohrbaugh, M. (1989). Live supervision by family therapists: A Virginia survey. *Journal of Marital and Family Therapy, 15,* 323–326.

Lichtenberg, J. W., & Heck, E. J. (1986). Analysis of sequence and pattern in process research. *Journal of Counseling Psychology, 33,* 170–181.

Liddle, B. J. (1986). Resistance in supervision: A response to perceived threat. *Counselor Education and Supervision, 26,* 117–127.

Liddle, H. A. (1988). Systemic supervision: Conceptual overlays and pragmatic guidelines. In H. A. Liddle, D. C. Breunlin, & R. C. Schwartz (Eds.), *Handbook of family therapy training and supervision.* New York: Guilford. 153–171.

Liddle, H. A., Breunlin, D. C., Schwartz, R. C., & Constantine, J. A. (1984). Training family therapy supervisors: Issues of content, form and context. *Journal of Marriage and Family Therapy, 10,* 139–150.

Liddle, H. A., & Halpin, R. (1978). Family therapy training and supervision literature: A comparative review. *Journal of Marital and Family Counseling, 4,* 77–98.

Liddle, H. A., & Saba, G. W. (1982). Teaching family therapy at the introductory level: A conceptual model emphasizing a pattern which connects training and therapy. *Journal of Marital and Family Therapy, 8,* 63–72.

Liddle, H. A., & Saba, G. W. (1983). On context replication: The isomorphic relationship of family therapy and family therapy training. *Journal of Strategic and Systemic Therapies, 2,* 3–11.

Liddle, H. A. & Schwartz, R. (1983). Live supervision/consultation: Conceptual and pragmatic guidelines for family therapy training. *Family Process, 22,* 477–490.

Linehan, M. M. (1980). Supervision of behavior therapy. In A. K. Hess (Ed.), *Psychotherapy supervision: Theory, research and practice.* New York: John Wiley and Sons. 148–180.

Littrell, J. M., Lee-Borden, N., & Lorenz, J. A. (1979). A developmental framework for counseling supervision. *Counselor Education and Supervision, 19,* 119–136.

Lloyd, A. P. (1987). Multicultural counseling: Does it belong in a counselor education program? *Counselor Education and Supervision, 26,* 164–167.

Loevinger, J. (1976). *Ego development.* San Francisco: Jossey-Bass.

Loganbill, C., Hardy, E., & Delworth, U. (1982). Supervision: A conceptual model. *The Counseling Psychologist, 10*(1), 3–42.

Loganbill, C., & Stoltenberg, C. (1983). The case conceptualization format: A training device for practicum. *Counselor Education and Supervision, 22,* 235–242.

Lower, R. B. (1972). Countertransference resistances in the supervisory relationship. *American Journal of Psychiatry, 129,* 156–160.

Lowy, L. (1983). Social work supervision: From models to theory. *Journal of Education for Social Work, 19*(2), 55–62.

Mabe, A. R., & Rollin, S. A. (1986). The role of a code of ethical standards in counseling. *Journal of Counseling and Development, 64,* 294–297.

Maddux, J., Stoltenberg, C., & Rosenwein, R. (Eds.). (1987). *Social processes in clinical and counseling psychology.* New York: Springer-Verlag.

Mahrer, A. R. (1988). Discovery oriented psychotherapy research: Rationale, aims, and methods. *American Psychologist, 43,* 694–702.

Mahoney, M. J. (1974). *Cognition and behavior modification.* Cambridge, MA: Ballinger.

Mahoney, M. J. (1977). Reflections on the cognitive-learning trend in psychotherapy. *American Psychologist, 32,* 5–13.

Malouf, J. L., Haas, L. J., & Farah, M. J. (1983). Issues in the preparation of interns: Views of trainers and trainees. *Professional Psychology: Research and Practice, 14,* 624–631.

Margolin, G. (1982). Ethical and legal considerations in marital and family therapy. *American Psychologist, 37,* 788–801.

Margolin, G., Talovic, S., Fernandez, V., & Onorato, R. (1983). Sex role considerations and behavioral marital therapy: Equal does not mean identical. *Journal of Marital and Family Therapy, 9,* 119–145.

Marikis, D. A., Russell, R. K., & Dell, D. M. (1985). Effects of supervisor experience level on planning and in-session verbal behavior. *Journal of Counseling Psychology, 32,* 410–416.

Markowski, E. M., & Cain, H. I. (1983). Live marital and family therapy supervision. *The Clinical Supervisor, 1*(3), 37–46.

Marks, J. L., & Hixon, D. F. (1986). Training agency staff through peer group supervision. *Social Casework, 67,* 418–423.

Markus, H. (1977). Self-schemata and processing information about the self. *Journal of Personality and Social Psychology, 35,* 63–78.

Martens, B. K., Lewanddowski, L. J., & Houk, J. L. (1989). Correlational analysis of verbal interactions during the consultative interview and consultees' subsequent perceptions. *Professional Psychology: Research and Practice, 20,* 334–339.

Martin, J. M. (1985). Measuring clients' cognitive competence in research on counseling. *Journal of Counseling and Development, 63,* 556–560.

Martin, J. M. (1988). A proposal for researching possible relationships between scientific theories and the personal theories of counselors. *Journal of Counseling and Development, 66,* 261–265.

Martin, J. M. (1990). Confusions in psychological skills training. *Journal of Counseling and Development, 68,* 402–407.

Martin, J. S., Goodyear, R. K., & Newton, F. B. (1987). Clinical supervision: An intensive case study. *Professional Psychology: Research and Practice, 18,* 225–235.

Martin, R. M., & Prosen, H. (1976). Psychotherapy supervision a life tasks: The young therapist and the middle-aged patient. *Bulletin of the Menninger Clinic, 40,* 125–133.

Martin, J. M., Slemon, A. G., Hiebert, B., Hallberg, E. T., & Cummings, A. L. (1989). Conceptualizations of novice and experienced counselors. *Journal of Counseling Psychology, 36,* 395–400.

Matarazzo, R. G., & Patterson, D. R. (1986). Methods of teaching therapeutic skill. In S. L. Garfield & A. E. Bergin (Eds.), *Handbook of psychotherapy and behavior change* (3rd ed.). New York: John Wiley and Sons, 821–843.

Mathews, G. (1986). Performance appraisal in the human services: A survey. *The Clinical Supervisor, 3*(4), 47–61.

Mays, D. T., & Franks, C. M. (1980). Getting worse: Psychotherapy or no treatment. The jury should still be out. *Professional Psychology, 11,* 78–92.

Mays, D. T., & Franks, C. M. (1985). *Negative outcomes in psychotherapy and what to do about it.* New York: Springer.

McCarthy, P., DeBell, C., Kanuha, V., & McLeod, J. (1988). Myths of supervision: Identifying the gaps between theory and practice. *Counselor Education and Supervision, 28,* 22–28.

McColley, S. H., & Baker, E. L. (1982). Training activities and styles of beginning supervisors: A survey. *Professional Psychology 13,* 283–292.

McCubbin, I., & Patterson, J. (1983). The family stress process: The double ABCX model of adjustment and adaptation. *Marriage and Family Review, 6,* 7–38.

McDaniel, S., Weber, T., & McKeever, J. (1983). Multiple theoretical approaches to supervision: Choices in family therapy training. *Family Process, 22,* 491–500.

McGoldrick, M. (1982). Ethnicity and family therapy: An overview. In M. McGoldrick, J. K. Pearce, & J. Giordano (Eds.), *Ethnicity and family therapy.* New York: Guilford. 3–30.

McKenzie, P., Atkinson, B., Quinn, W., & Heath, A. (1986). Training and supervision in marriage and family therapy: A national survey. *American Journal of Family Therapy, 14,*(4).

McNeill, B. W., & Stoltenberg, C. D. (1989). Reconceptualizing social influence in counseling: The elaboration likelihood model. *Journal of Counseling Psychology, 36,* 24–33.

McNeill, B. W., Stoltenberg, C. D., & Pierce, R. A. (1985). Supervisee's perceptions of their development: A test of the counselor complexity model. *Journal of Counseling Psychology, 32,* 630–633.

McNeill, B. W., & Worthen, V. (1989). The parallel process in psychotherapy supervision. *Professional Psychology: Research and Practice, 20,* 329–333.

McRoy, R. G., Freeman, E. M., Logan, S. L., & Blackmon, B. (1986). Cross-cultural field supervision: Implications for social work education. *Journal of Social Work Education, 22,* 50–56.

Meichenbaum, D. H. (1977). *Cognitive-behavior modification.* New York: Plenum.

Merluzzi, T. V., Glass, C. R., & Genest, M. (1981). *Cognitive assessment.* New York: Guilford.

Meyer, R., & Smith, S. A. (1977). A crisis in group therapy. *American Psychologist, 32,* 638–643.

Miars, R. D., Tracey, T. J., Ray, P. B., Cornfeld, J. L., O'Farrell, M., & Gelso, C. J. (1983). Variation in supervision process across trainee experience levels. *Journal of Counseling Psychology, 30,* 403–412.

Middleman, R. R., & Rhodes, G. B. (1985). *Competent supervision: Making imaginative judgments.* Englewood Cliffs, NJ: Prentice-Hall.

Miller, M. J. (1989). A few thoughts on the relationship between counseling techniques and empathy. *Journal of Counseling and Development, 67,* 350–351.

Miller, H. L., & Rickard, H. C. (1983). Procedures and students' rights in the evaluation process. *Professional Psychology: Research and Practice, 14,* 830–836.

Minuchin, S., & Fishman, C. (1981). *Family therapy techniques.* Cambridge, MA: Harvard Press.

Mokuau, N. (1987). Social workers' perceptions of counseling effectiveness for Asian American clients. *Social Work, 32,* 331–335.

Moldawsky, S. (1980). Psychoanalytic psychotherapy supervision. In A. K. Hess (Ed.), *Psychotherapy supervision: Theory, research, and practice.* New York: John Wiley and Sons. 126–135.

Montalvo, B. (1973). Aspects of live supervision. *Family Process, 12,* 343–359.

Montalvo, B., & Gutierrez, M. (1984). The mask of culture. *The Family Therapy Networker, 8,* 42–46.

Moore, H. B., & Nelson, E. S. (1981). A workshop model for developing awareness of sex-role bias in counseling students. *Counselor Education and Supervision, 20,* 312–316.

Morran, D. K. (1986). Relationship of counselor self-talk and hypothesis formation to performance level. *Journal of Counseling Psychology, 33,* 395–400.

Moskowitz, S. A., & Rupert, P. A. (1983). Conflict resolution within the supervisory relationship. *Professional Psychology: Research and Practice, 14,* 632–641.

Moy, C. T., & Goodman, E. O. (1984). A model for evaluating supervisory interactions in family therapy training. *The Clinical Supervisor, 2*(3), 21–29.

Mueller, W. J. (1982). Issues in the application of "Supervision: A conceptual model" to dynamically oriented supervision: A reaction paper. *The Counseling Psychologist, 10*(1), 43–46.

Mueller, W. J., & Kell, B. L. (1972). *Coping with conflict: Supervising counselors and psychotherapists.* New York: Appleton-Century-Crofts.

Munley, P. H. (1974). A review of counseling analogue research methods. *Journal of Counseling Psychology, 21,* 320–330.

Munson, C. E. (1983). *An introduction to clinical social work supervision.* New York: Haworth Press.

Murphy, J. W., & Pardeck, J. T. (1986). The "burnout syndrome" and management style. *The Clinical Supervisor, 4*(4), 35–44.

Muslin, H. L., Singer, P. R., Meusea, M. F., Leahy, J. P. (1968). Research and learning in psychiatric interviewing. *Journal of Medical Education, 43,* 398–404.

National Association of Social Workers. (1984). *Code of ethics.* Washington, DC: Author.

Neimeyer, G. J., & Fukuyama, M. (1984). Exploring the content and structure of cross-cultural attitudes. *Counselor Education and Supervision, 23,* 214–224.

Neiss, R. (1988). Reconceptualizing arousal: Psychobiological states in motor performance. *Psychological Bulletin, 103,* 345–366.

Newman, A. S. (1981). Ethical issues in the supervision of psychotherapy. *Professional Psychology, 12,* 690–695.

Nichols, M. (1984). *Family therapy: Concepts and methods.* New York: Gardner Press.

Nishio, K., & Bilmes, M. (1987). Psychotherapy with Southeast Asian American clients. *Professional Psychology: Research and Practice, 18,* 342–346.

Norcross, J. C., & Stevenson, J. F. (1984). How shall we judge ourselves? Training evaluations in clinical psychology programs. *Professional Psychology: Research and Practice, 15,* 497–508.

Norcross, J. C., & Stevenson, J. F. (1986). Evaluation of internship training: Practices, problems, and prospects. *Professional Psychology: Research and Practice, 17,* 280–282.

Olsen, T. A. (1977). Imposing a duty to warn on psychiatrists—a judicial threat to the psychiatric profession. *University of Colorado Law Review, 48,* 283–310.

Olson, U. J., & Pegg, P. F. (1979). Direct open supervision: A team approach. *Family Process, 18,* 463–470.

O'Malley, K. M., & Richardson, S. (1985). Sex bias in counseling: Have things changed? *Journal of Counseling and Development, 63*(5), 294–299.

Paradis, F. E. (1981). Themes in the training of culturally effective psychotherapists. *Counselor Education and Supervision, 21,* 136–151.

Paravonian, S. D. (1981). Evaluating and grading preservice counseling students. *Counselor Education and Supervision, 20,* 276–284.

Parihar, B. (1983). Group Supervision: A naturalistic field study in a specialty unit. *The Clinical Supervisor, 1*(4), 3–14.

Parker, W. M. (1987). Flexibility: A primer for multicultural counseling. *Counselor Education and Supervision, 26,* 176–180.

Parker, W. M., Bingham, R. P., & Fukuyama, M. (1985). Improving cross-cultural effectiveness in counselor training. *Counselor Education and Supervision, 24,* 349–352.

Parker, W. M., & McDavis, R. J. (1979). An awareness experience: Toward counseling minorities. *Counselor Education and Supervision, 18,* 312–317.

Parker, W. M., Valley, M. M., & Geary, C. A. (1986). Acquiring cultural knowledge for counselors in training: A multifaceted approach. *Counselor Education and Supervision, 26,* 61–71.

Patrick, K. D. (1989). Unique ethical dilemmas in counselor training. *Counselor Education and Supervision, 28,* 337–341.

Patterson, C. H. (1964). Supervising students in the counseling practicum. *Journal of Counseling Psychology, 11,* 47–53.

Patterson, C. H. (1983). A client-centered approach to supervision. *The Counseling Psychologist, 11*(1), 21–25.

Patterson, C. H. (1984). Empathy, warmth, and genuineness in psychotherapy: A review of reviews. *Psychotherapy, 21,* 431–438.

Patterson, C. H. (1986). *Theories of counseling and psychotherapy* (4th ed.). New York: Harper & Row.

Patterson, L. W. (1988). The function of automaticity in counselor information processing. *Counselor Education and Supervision, 27,* 195–202.

Pederson, P. (1987). Ten frequent assumptions of cultural bias in counseling. *Journal of Multicultural Counseling and Development, 9,* 16–24.

Penman, R. (1980). *Communication processes and relationships.* London: Academic Press.

Perry, W. G., Jr. (1970). *Forms of intellectual and ethical development in the college years.* New York: Holt, Rinehart, and Winston.

Petty, M. M., & Odewahn, C. A. (1983). Supervisory behavior and sex role stereotypes in human service organizations. *The Clinical Supervisor, 1*(2), 13–20.

Piaget, J., & Inhelder, B. (1969). *The psychology of the child.* New York: Basic Books.

Pierce, R. M., & Schauble, P. G. (1970). Graduate training of facilitative counselors: The effects of individual supervision. *Journal of Counseling Psychology, 17,* 210–215.

Piercy, F. P., Sprenkle, D. H., & Constantine, J. A. (1986). Family members' perceptions of live, observation/supervision: An exploratory study. *Contemporary Family Therapy, 8,* 171–187.

Pittman, F. (1985). Gender myths. *The Family Therapy Networker, 9*(6), 24–33.

Poertner, J. (1986). The use of client feedback to improve practice: Defining the supervisor's role. *The Clinical Supervisor, 4*(4), 57–67.

Ponterotto, J. G. (1987). Client hospitalization: Issues and considerations for the counselor. *Journal of Counseling and Development, 65,* 542–546.

Ponterotto, J. G., & Casas, J. M. (1987). In search of multicultural competence within counselor education programs. *Journal of Counseling and Development, 65,* 430–434.

Ponterotto, J. G., & Zander, T. A. (1984). A multimodal approach to counselor supervision. *Counselor Education and Supervision, 24,* 40–50.

Pope, K. S., Keith-Spiegel, P., & Tabachnick, B. (1986). Sexual attractice to clients: The human therapist and the (sometimes) inhuman training system. *American Psychologist, 41,* 147–152.

Pope, K. S., Levenson, H., & Schover, L. R. (1979). Sexual intimacy in psychology training: Results and implications of a national survey. *American Psychologist, 34,* 682–689.

Pope, K. S., Schover, L. R., & Levenson, H. (1980). Sexual behavior between clinical supervisors and trainees: Implications for professional standards. *Professional Psychology, 10,* 157–162.

Pope, K. S., Tabachnick, B. G., & Keith-Spiegel, P. (1988). Good and poor practices in psychotherapy: National survey of beliefs of psychologists. *Professional Psychology: Research and Practice, 19,* 547–552.

Prietula, M. J., & Simon, H. A. (1989, January-February). The experts in your midst. *Harvard Business Review,* 120–124.

Prosser, W. L. (1971). *Handbook of the law of torts* (4th ed.) St. Paul, MN: West.

Protinsky, H., & Preli, R. (1987). Interventions in strategic supervision. *Journal of Strategic and Systemic Therapies, 6*(3), 18–23.

Quarto, C. J., & Tracey, T. J. (1989, August). *Factor structure of the supervision level scale.* Paper presented at the annual meeting of the American Psychological Association, New Orleans.

Quinn, W. H., Atkinson, B. J., & Hood, C. J. (1985). The stuck-case clinic as a group supervision model. *Journal of Marital & Family Therapy, 11,* 67–73.

Rabiner, W. N. (1982). Role diffusion in the supervisory relationship. *Professional Psychology, 13,* 258–265.

Rabinowitz, F. E., Heppner, P. P., & Roehlke, H. J. (1986). Descriptive study of process and outcome variables of supervision over time. *Journal of Counseling Psychology, 33,* 292–300.

Raimy, V. C. (Ed.). (1950). *Training in clinical psychology.* New York: Prentice-Hall.

Raphael, R. D. (1982). *Supervisee experience: The effect on supervisor verbal responses.* Paper presented at the annual meeting of the American Psychological Association, Washington, DC.

Raskin, M. S. (1982). Factors associated with student satisfaction in undergraduate social work field placements. *Arete, 7,* 44–54.

Raskin, M. S. (1985). Field placement decisions: Art, science or guesswork? *The Clinical Supervisor, 3*(3), 55–67.

Reese-Dukes, J. L., & Reese-Dukes, C. (1983). Pairs for pairs: A theoretical base for co-therapy as a nonsexist process in couple counseling. *Personnel and Guidance Journal, 62,* 99–101.

Reid, E., McDaniel, S., Donaldson, C., & Tollers, M. (1987). Taking it personally: Issues of personal authority and competence for the female in family therapy training. *Journal of Marital and Family Therapy, 13,* 157–165.

Reising, G. N., & Daniels, M. H. (1983). A study of Hogan's model of counselor development and supervision. *Journal of Counseling Psychology, 30,* 235–244.

Resnikoff, R. O. (1981). Teaching family therapy: Ten key questions for understanding the family as patient. *The Journal of Marital and Family Therapy, 7,* 135–142.

Rice, L. N. (1980). A client-centered approach to the supervision of psychotherapy. In A. K. Hess (Ed.), *Psychotherapy Supervision: Theory, research, and practice.* New York: John Wiley and Sons. 136–147.

Richardson, B. K., & Bradley, L. J. (1984). Microsupervision: A skill development model for training clinical supervisors. *The Clinical Supervisor, 2*(3), 43–54.

Richardson, B., & Stone, G. L. (1981). Effects of a cognitive adjunct procedure within a microcounseling situation. *Journal of Counseling Psychology, 28,* 168–175.

Rickards, L. D. (1984). Verbal interaction and supervisor perception in counselor supervision. *Journal of Counseling Psychology, 31,* 262–265.

Ricke, J., & Peterson, G. W. (1988, August). *Comparing perceptual processes in clinical judgment: Novice versus expert counselors.* Paper presented at the annual meeting of the American Psychological Association, Atlanta.

Rickert, V. L., & Turner, J. E. (1978). Through the looking glass: Supervision in family therapy. *Social Casework, 59,* 131–137.

Riessman, F. (1965). The "helper" therapy principle. *Social Work, 10,* 27–32.

Rioch, M. J., Coulter, W. R., & Weinberg, D. M. (1976). *Dialogues for therapists.* San Francisco: Jossey-Bass.

Ritchie, A., & Storm, C. (1983). Personal Communication.

Roberts, J. (1983). Two models of live supervision: Collaborative team and supervisor guided. *Journal of Strategic and Systemic Therapies, 2,* 68–78.

Robiner, W. N. (1982). Role diffusion in the supervisory relationship. *Professional Psychology, 13,* 258–267.

Robyak, J. E., Goodyear, R. K., & Prange, M. (1987). Effects of supervisors' sex, focus, and experience on preferences for interpersonal power bases. *Counselor Education and Supervision, 26,* 299–309.

Rogers, C. R. (1951). *Client-centered therapy.* Boston: Houghton-Mifflin.

Rogers, C. R. (1957). The necessary and sufficient conditions of therapeutic personality change. *Journal of Consulting Psychology, 21,* 95–103.

Rogler, L. H., Malgady, R. G., Costantino, G., & Blumenthal, R. (1987). What do culturally sensitive mental health services mean? *American Psychologist, 42,* 565–570.

Rosenblatt, A., & Mayer, J. E. (1975). Objectionable supervisory styles: Students' views. *Social Work, 20,* 184–189.

Rosenblum, A. F., & Raphael, F. B. (1987). Students at risk in the field practicum and implications for field teaching. *The Clinical Supervisor, 5*(8), 53–63.

Ross, L. (1977). The intuitive psychologist and his shortcomings: Distortions in the attribution process. In L. Berkowitz (Ed.), *Advances in experimental social psychology, 10,* 174–220.

Roth, S. (1985). Psychotherapy with lesbian couples: Individual issues, female socialization, and the social context. *Journal of Marital and Family Therapy, 11,* 273–286.

Roth, S. A. (1986). Peer supervision in the community mental health center: An analysis and critique. *The Clinical Supervisor, 4*(2), 159–168.

Rotter, J. B. (1966). Generalized expectations for internal versus external control of reinforcement. *Psychological Monographs, 80*(1, Whole No. 609).

Royal, E., & Golden, S. (1981). Attitude similarity and attraction to an employee group. *Psychological Reports, 48,* 251–254.

Rubinstein, M., & Hammond, D. (1982). The use of videotape in psychotherapy supervision. In M. Blumenfield (Ed.), *Applied Supervision in Psychotherapy.* New York: Grune & Stratton. 143–164.

Russell, R. K., Crimmings, A. M., & Lent, R. W. (1984). Counselor training and supervision: Theory and research. In S. D. Brown & R. W. Lent (Eds.), *Handbook of Counseling Psychology.* New York: John Wiley and Sons. 625–681.

Russell, P. A., Lankford, M. W., & Grinnell, R. M., Jr. (1983). Attitudes toward supervisors in a human service agency. *The Clinical Supervisor, 1*(3), 57–71.

Ryan, A. S., & Hendricks, C. O. (1989). Culture and communication: Supervising the Asian and Hispanic social worker. *The Clinical Supervisor, 7*(1), 27–40.

Sanchez, A. R., & Atkinson, D. R. (1983). Mexican-American cultural commitment, preference for counselor ethnicity, and willingness to use counseling. *Journal of Counseling Psychology, 30,* 215–220.

Sansbury, D. L. (1982). Developmental supervision from a skill perspective. *The Counseling Psychologist, 10*(1), 53–57.

Schauer, A. H., Seymour, W. R., & Green, R. G. (1985). Effects of observation and evaluation on anxiety in beginning counselors: A social facilitation analysis. *Journal of Counseling and Development, 63,* 279–285.

Schmidt, J. P. (1979). Psychotherapy supervision: A cognitive-behavioral model. *Professional Psychology, 10,* 278–284.

Schofield, W. (1964). *Psychotherapy, the purchase of friendship.* Englewood Cliffs, NJ: Prentice-Hall.

Schön, D. A. (1983). *The reflective practitioner: How professionals think in action.* New York: Basic Books.

Schreiber, P., & Frank, E. (1983). The use of a peer supervision group by social work clinicians. *The Clinical Supervisor, 1*(1), 29–36.

Schutz, B. M. (1982). *Legal liability in psychotherapy.* San Francisco, CA: Jossey-Bass.

Schwartz, R. (1981). The conceptual development of family therapy trainees. *American Journal of Family Therapy, 2,* 89–90.

Schwartz, R. C., Liddle, H. A., & Breunlin, D. C. (1988). Muddles in live supervision. In H. A. Liddle, D. C. Breunlin, & R. C. Schwartz (Eds.), *Handbook of family therapy training and supervision.* New York: Guilford. 183–193.

Searles, H. (1955). The informational value of the supervisor's emotional experiences. *Psychiatry, 18,* 135–146.

Shapiro, C. H. (1988). Burnout in social work field instructors. *The Clinical Supervisor, 6*(4), 237–248.

Shapiro, W. (1987, May 25). What's wrong. *Time, 129*(21), 14–17.

Sharon, D. (1986). The ABCX model—implications for supervision. *The Clinical Supervisor, 4,* 69–94.

Shoben, E. J. (1962). The counselor's theory as personal trait. *Personnel and Guidance Journal, 40,* 617–621.

Shulman, L. (1982). *Skills of supervision and staff management.* Itasca, IL: F. E. Peacock.

Siegel, M. (1979). Privacy, ethics and confidentiality. *Professional Psychology, 10,* 249–258.

Simon, R. (1982). Beyond the one-way mirror. *Family Therapy Networker, 26*(5), 19, 28–29, 58–59.

Skolnik, L. (1988). Field instruction in the 1980s—Realities, issues, and problem-solving strategies. *The Clinical Supervisor, 6*(3), 47–75.

Sleight, C. C. (1984). Supervisor self-evaluation in communication disorders. *The Clinical Supervisor, 2*(3), 31–42.

Slimack, R. E., & Berkowitz, S. R. (1983). The university and college counseling center and malpractice suits. *Personnel and Guidance Journal, 61,* 291–295.

Slovenko, R. (1980). Legal issues in psychotherapy supervision. In A. K. Hess (Ed.), *Psychotherapy Supervision: Theory, research, and practice.* New York: John Wiley and Sons. 453–473.

Sluzki, C. E., Beavin, J., Tarnopolski, A., & Vernon, E. (1967). Transactional disqualification: Research on the double-bind. *Archives of General Psychiatry, 16,* 494–504.

Smith, E. J. (1981). Cultural and historical perspectives in counseling blacks. In D. W. Sue (Ed.), *Counseling the culturally different.* New York: John Wiley and Sons. 141–185.

Smith, H. D. (1984). Moment-to-moment counseling process feedback using a dual-channel audiotape recording. *Counselor Education and Supervision, 23,* 346–349.

Snider, P. D. (1985). The duty to warn: A potential issue of litigation for the counseling supervisor. *Counselor Education and Supervision, 25,* 66–73.

Snider, P. D. (1987). Client records: Inexpensive liability protection for mental health counselors. *Journal of Mental Health Counseling, 9,* 134–141.

Soisson, E. L., Vendecreek, L., & Knapp, S. (1987). Thorough record keeping: A good defense in a litigious era. *Professional Psychology: Research and Practice, 18,* 498–502.

Speed, B., Seligman, P. M., Kingston, P., & Cade, B. W. (1982). A team approach to therapy. *Journal of Family Therapy, 4,* 271–284.

Sperling, M. B., Pirrotta, S., Handen, B. L., Simons, L. A., Miller, D., Lysiak, G., Schumm, P., & Terry, L. (1986). The collaborative team as a training and therapeutic tool. *Counselor Education and Supervision, 25,* 183–190.

Spice, C. G., & Spice, W. H. (1976). A triadic method of supervision in the training of counselors and counseling supervisors. *Counselor Education and Supervision, 16,* 251–258.

Spykman, N. J. (1966). *The social theory of Georg Simmel.* New York: Atherton.

Stadler, H. A., & Rynearson, D. (1981). Understanding clients and their environments: A simulation. *Counselor Education and Supervision, 21,* 153–162.

Stanton, J. L., & Stanton, M. D. (1986). Family therapy and systems supervision with the "Pick-a-Dali Circus" model. *The Clinical Supervisor, 4,* 169–182.

Stein, M., & Stone, G. L. (1978). Effects of conceptual level and structure on initial interview behavior. *Journal of Counseling Psychology, 25,* 96–102.

Stenack, R. J., & Dye, H. A. (1982). Behavioral descriptions of counseling supervision roles. *Counselor Education and Supervision, 22,* 295–304.

Stenack, R. J., & Dye, H. A. (1983). Practicum supervision roles: Effects of supervisee statements. *Counselor Education and Supervision, 23,* 157–168.

Sternitzke, M. E., Dixon, D. N., & Ponterotto, J. G. (1988). An attributional approach to counselor supervision. *Counselor Education and Supervision, 28,* 5–14.

Stevenson, J. F., & Norcross, J. C. (1982). *Survey of evaluation activity in psychology training clinics.* Unpublished manuscript, University of Rhode Island.

Stevenson, J. F., Norcross, J. C., King, J. T., & Tobin, K. G. (1984). Evaluating clinical training programs: A formative effort. *Professional Psychology: Research and Practice, 15,* 218–229.

Stewart, E. C. (1981). Cultural sensitivities in counseling. In P. B. Pedersen, J. Draguns, W. J. Lonner, & J. Trimble (Eds.), *Counseling across cultures.* Honolulu: University Press of Hawaii.

Stiles, W. B., Shapiro, D. A., & Elliott, R. (1986). "Are all psychotherapies equivalent?" *American Psychologist, 41,* 165–180.

Stoltenberg, C. D. (1981). Approaching supervision from a developmental perspective: The counselor complexity model. *Journal of Counseling Psychology, 28,* 59–65.

Stoltenberg, C. D., & Delworth, U. (1987). *Supervising counselors and therapists: A developmental approach.* San Francisco: Jossey-Bass.

Stoltenberg, C. D., & Delworth, U. (1988). Developmental models of supervision: It is development—Response to Holloway. *Professional Psychology: Research and Practice, 19,* 134–137.

Stoltenberg, C. D., Pierce, R. A., & McNeill, B. W. (1987). Effects of experience on counselor needs. *The Clinical Supervisor, 5,* 23–32.

Stone, G. L. (1980). Effects of experience on supervision planning. *Journal of Counseling Psychology, 27,* 84–88.

Stone, G. L. (1984). Reaction: In defense of the "artificial." *Journal of Counseling Psychology, 31,* 108–110.

Stone, G. L. (1988, August). *Clinical supervision: An occasion for cognitive research.* Paper presented at the annual meeting of the American Psychological Association, Atlanta.

Storm, C. L. & Heath, A. W. (1982). Strategic supervision: The danger lies in discovery. *Journal of Strategic and Systemic Therapies, 1,* 71–72.

Storm, C. L., & Heath, A. W. (1985). Models of supervision: Using therapy as a guide. *The Clinical Supervisor, 3*(1), 87–96.

Stout, C. E. (1987). The role of ethical standards in the supervision of psychotherapy. *The Clinical Supervisor, 5*(1), 89–97.

Strong, S. R. (1968). Counseling: An interpersonal influence process. *Journal of Counseling Psychology, 15,* 215–224.

Strong, S. R. (1971). Experimental laboratory research in counseling. *Journal of Counseling Psychology, 18,* 106–110.

Strong, S. R. (in press). Social influence and change in therapeutic relationships. In C. R. Snyder and D. R. Forsyth (Eds.), *Handbook of social and clinical psychology.* New York: Pergamon.

Strong, S. R., & Claiborn, C. D. (1982). *Change through interaction: Social psychological processes of counseling and psychotherapy.* New York: Wiley-Interscience.

Strong, S. R., Hills, H. I., Kilmartin, C. T., DeVries, H., Lanier, K., Nelson, B. N., Strickland, D., & Meyers, C. W. (1988). The dynamic relations among interpersonal behaviors: A test of complementary and anticomplementarity. *Journal of Personality and Social Psychology, 54,* 798-810.

Strong, S. R., & Matross, R. P. (1973). Change process in counseling and psychotherapy. *Journal of Counseling Psychology 20,* 25-37.

Strupp, H. H., & Hadley, S. W. (1977). A tripartite model of mental health and therapeutic outcomes. *American Psychologist, 32,* 187-196.

Strupp, H. H., Hadley, S. W., & Gomes-Schwartz, B. (1977). *Psychotherapy for better or worse.* New York: Jason Aronsen.

Sue, D. W. (1978). Eliminating cultural oppression in counseling: Toward a general theory. *Journal of Counseling Psychology, 25,* 419-428.

Sue, D. W. (1981). *Counseling the culturally different: Theory and practice.* New York: John Wiley and Sons.

Sue, S., Akutsu, F. O., & Higashi, C. (1985). Training issues in conducting therapy with ethnic-minority-group clients. In P. Pedersen (Ed.), *Handbook of cross-cultural counseling and therapy.* Westport, CT: Greenwood Press, 275-280.

Sue, D. W., & Sue, D. (1990). *Counseling the culturally different: Theory and Practice* (2nd edition). New York: John Wiley and Sons.

Sue, S., & Zane, N. (1987). The role of culture and cultural techniques in psychotherapy. *American Psychologist, 42,* 37-45.

Sullivan, H. S. (1953). *The interpersonal theory of psychiatry.* New York: Norton.

Taggart, M. (1985). The feminist critique in epistemological perspective: Questions of context in family therapy. *Journal of Marital and Family Therapy, 11,* 113-126.

Tarasoff v. Regents of the University of California, 118 Cal. Rptr. 129, 529 P. 2d. 533 (1974).

Tarico, V. S., Van Zelzen, D. R., & Altmaier, E. M. (1986). Comparison of thought-listing rating methods. *Journal of Counseling Psychology, 33,* 81-83.

Tennyson, W. W., & Strom, S. M. (1986). Beyond professional standards: Developing responsibleness. *Journal of Counseling and Development, 64,* 298-302.

Thyer, B. A., Sowers-Hoag, K., & Love, J. P. (1988). The influence of field instructor-student gender combinations on student perceptions of field instruction quality. *The Clinical Supervisor, 6*(3), 169-179.

Tinsley, H. E. A., Bowman, S. L., & Ray, S. B. (1988). Manipulation of expectancies about counseling and psychotherapy: A review and analysis of expectancy manipulation strategies and results. *Journal of Counseling Psychology, 35,* 99-108.

Tinsley, H. E. A., Workman, K. R., & Kass, R. A. (1980). Factor analysis of the domain of client expectancies about counseling. *Journal of Counseling Psychology, 27,* 561-570.

Todtman, D. A., Bobele, M., & Strano, J. D. (1988). An inexpensive system for communication across the one-way mirror. *Journal of Marital and Family Therapy, 14,* 201-203.

Tomm, K., & Wright, L. (1982). Multilevel training and supervision in an outpatient service programme. In R. Whiffen & J. Byng-Hall (Eds.), *Family therapy supervision: Recent developments in practice.* New York: Grune & Stratton.

Torrey, E. F. (1972). *The mindgame: Witch doctors and psychiatrists.* New York: Emerson Hall.

Tracey, T. J., Ellickson, J. L., & Sherry, P. (1989). Reactance in relation to different supervisory environments and counselor development. *Journal of Counseling Psychology, 36,* 336-344.

Truax, C. B., & Carkhuff, R. R. (1967). *Toward effective counseling and psychotherapy: Training and practice.* Chicago: Aldine.

Tymchuk, A. J. (1981). Ethical decision making and psychological treatment. *Journal of Psychiatric Treatment and Evaluation, 3,* 507-513.

Tymchuk, A. J., Drapkin, R. S., Major-Kingsley, S., Ackerman, A. B., Coffman, E. W., & Baum, M. S. (1982). Ethical decision making and psychologists' attitudes toward training in ethics. *Professional Psychology, 13,* 412-421.

Ulrich, S. R., & Watt, J. (1977, November). *Competence of clinical supervisors: A statistical analysis.* Paper presented at the annual meeting of the American Speech, Language and Hearing Association, Chicago.

Vanderkolk, C. (1974). The relationship of personality, values, and race to anticipation of the supervisory relationship. *Rehabilitation Counseling Bulletin, 18,* 41–46.

Vargas, L. A. (1989, August). *Training psychologists to be culturally responsive: Issues in supervision.* Paper presented at the annual meeting of the American Psychological Association, New Orleans.

Vinacke, W. E. (1959). The effects of cumulative scores on coalition formation in triads with various patterns of internal power. *American Psychologist, 14,* 381.

Vygotsky, L. S. (1978). *Mind in society: The development of higher psychological processes.* (M. Cole, V. John-Steiner, S. Scribner, & E. Souberman, Eds. and Trans.). Cambridge, MA: Harvard University Press.

Walz, G. R., & Roeber, E. C. (1962). Supervisors' reactions to a counseling interview. *Counselor Education and Supervision, 1,* 2–7.

Wampler, L. D., & Strupp, H. H. (1976). Personal therapy for students in clinical psychology: A matter of faith. *Professional Psychology, 7,* 195–201.

Wampold, B. E. (1986). State of the art in sequential analysis: Comment on Lichtenberg and Heck. *Journal of Counseling Psychology, 33,* 182–185.

Ward, L. G., Friedlander, M. L., Schoen, L. G., & Klein, J. G. (1985). Strategic self-presentation in supervision. *Journal of Counseling Psychology, 32,* 111–118.

Ward, G. R., Kagan, N., & Krathwohl, D. R. (1972). An attempt to measure and facilitate counselor effectiveness. *Counselor Education and Supervision, 11,* 179–186.

Watkins, C. E., Lopez, F. G., Campbell, V. L., & Himmell, C. D. (1986). Contemporary counseling psychology: Results of a national survey. *Journal of Counseling Psychology, 33,* 301–309.

Watzlawick, P., Beavin, J. H., & Jackson, D. D. (1967). *Pragmatics of human communication: A study of interactional patterns, pathologies, and paradoxes.* New York: Norton.

Webb, M. W. (1983). Cross-cultural awareness: A framework for interaction. *Personnel and Guidance Journal, 61,* 498–500.

Webb, N. B. (1983). Developing competent clinical practitioners: A model with guidelines for supervisors. *The Clinical Supervisor, 1*(4), 41–51.

*Webster's new world dictionary of the American language.* (1966). New York: World Publishing.

Weisinger, H., & Lobsenz, N. M. (1981). *Nobody's perfect: How to give criticism and get results.* Los Angeles: Stratford.

Wendorf, D. J. (1984). A model for training practicing professionals in family therapy. *Journal of Marital and Family Therapy, 10,* 31–41.

Wendorf, D. J., Wendorf, R. J., & Bond, O. (1985). Growth behind the mirror: The family therapy consortium's group process. *Journal of Marital and Family Therapy, 11,* 245–255.

West, J. D., Bubenzer, D. L., & Zarski, J. J. (1989). Live supervision in family therapy: An interview with Barbara Oken and Fred Piercy. *Counselor Education and Supervision, 29,* 25–34.

Whiffen, R. (1982). The use of videotape in supervision. In R. Whiffen & J. Byng-Hall (Eds.), *Family Therapy Supervision: Recent Developments in Practice.* London: Academic Press.

Whiston, S. C., & Emerson, S. (1989). Ethical implications for supervisors in counseling of trainees. *Counselor Education and Supervision, 28,* 318–325.

White, R. W. (1959). Motivation reconsidered: The concept of competence. *Psychological Review, 66,* 297–323.

White, S. L. (1981). *Managing health and human service programs.* New York: The Free Press.

Wilbur, M. P., & Roberts-Wilbur, J. (undated). Schemata of the steps of the SGS model. Unpublished table.

Wilbur, M. P., Roberts-Wilbur, J., Hart, G. M., & Betz, R. L. (undated). Structured group supervision: Integrating supervision models and group modalities. Unpublished manuscript.

Wiley, M. O. (1982). Developmental counseling supervision: Person-environment congruency, satisfaction, and learning. Paper presented at the annual meeting of the American Psychological Association, Washington, DC.

Wiley, M. & Ray, P. (1986). Counseling supervision by developmental level. *Journal of Counseling Psychology, 33,* 439–445.

Willbach, D. (1989). Ethics and family therapy: The case management of family violence. *Journal of Marital and Family Therapy, 15,* 43–52.

Williams, A. (1987). Parallel process in a course on counseling supervision. *Counselor Education and Supervision, 26,* 245–254.

Williams, A. J. (1988). Action methods in supervision. *The Clinical Supervisor, 6*(2), 13–27.

Wilson, S. (1981). *Field instruction techniques for supervisors.* New York: The Free Press.

Wise, P. S., Lowery, S., & Silverglade, L. (1989). Personal counseling for counselors in training: Guidelines for supervisors. *Counselor Education and Supervision, 28,* 326–336.

Wohl, J. (1981). Intercultural psychotherapy: Issues, questions, and reflections. In P. B. Pedersen, J. G. Draguns, W. L. Lonner, & J. Trimble (Eds.), *Counseling across cultures* (2nd ed.). Honolulu: University of Hawaii.

Wolpe, J., Knopp, W., & Garfield, Z. (1966). Postgraduate training in behavior therapy. *Exerta Medica International Congress Series, No. 150.* Proceedings of the IV World Congress of Psychiatry, Madrid, Spain.

Woody, R. H. and Associates. (1984). *The law and the practice of human services.* San Francisco: Jossey-Bass.

Worthington, E. L., Jr. (1984a). Use of trait labels in counseling supervision by experienced and inexperienced supervisors. *Professional Psychology: Research and Practice, 15,* 457–461.

Worthington, E. L. (1984b). An empirical investigation of supervision of counselors as they gain experience. *Journal of Counseling Psychology, 31,* 63–75.

Worthington, E. L. (1987). Changes in supervision as counselors and supervisors gain experience: A review. *Professional Psychology: Research and Practice, 18,* 189–208.

Worthington, E. L., & Roehlke, H. J. (1979). Effective supervision as perceived by beginning counselors-in-training. *Journal of Counseling Psychology, 26,* 64–73.

Worthington, E. L., Jr., & Stern, A. (1985). Effects of supervision and supervisee degree level and gender on the supervisory relationship. *Journal of Counseling Psychology, 32,* 252–262.

Wright, L. M. (1986). An analysis of live supervision "phone-ins" in family therapy. *Journal of Marital and Family Therapy, 12,* 187–190.

Yager, G. G., Wilson, F. R., Brewer, D., & Kinnetz, P. (1989, March). *The development and validation of an instrument to measure counseling supervisor focus and style.* Paper presented at the annual meeting of the American Educational Research Association, San Francisco.

Yenawine, G., & Arbuckle, D. (1971). Study of the use of video-tape and audio-tape as techniques in counselor education. *Journal of Counseling Psychology, 28,* 1–6.

Yerkes, R. M., & Dodson, J. D. (1908). The relation of strength of stimulus to rapidity of habit formation. *Journal of Comparative Neurology and Psychology, 18,* 459–482.

Yogev, S. (1982). An eclectic model of supervision: A developmental sequence for beginning psychotherapy students. *Professional Psychology, 13,* 236–243.

Yogev, S., & Pion, G. M. (1984). Do supervisors modify psychotherapy supervision according to supervisees' levels of experience? *Psychotherapy, 21,* 206–208.

York, R. O. (1985). Applying the exception principle to the field instruction program. *The Clinical Supervisor, 3*(3), 77–86.

York, R. O., Henley, H. C., & Gamble, D. N. (1987). Sexual discrimination in social work: Is it salary or advancement? *Social Work, 32,* 336–340.

Zaphiropoulos, M. L. (1984). Educational and clinical pitfalls in psychoanalytic supervision. In L. Caligor, P. M. Bromberg, & J. D. Meltzer (Eds.), *Clinical perspectives on the supervision of psychoanalysis and psychotherapy.* New York: Plenum, 257–273.

Zimmerman, N., Collins, L. E., & Bach, J. M. (1986). Ordinal position, cognitive style, and competence: A systemic approach to supervision. *The Clinical Supervisor, 4*(3), 7–23.

Zucker, P. J., & Worthington, E. L., Jr. (1986). Supervision of interns and postdoctoral applicants for licensure in university counseling centers. *Journal of Counseling Psychology, 33,* 87–89.

Zuniga, M. E. (1987). Mexican-American clinical training: A pilot project. *Journal of Social Work Education, 23*(3), 11–20.

# APPENDIX A

# THE ASSOCIATION FOR COUNSELOR EDUCATION AND SUPERVISION STANDARDS FOR COUNSELOR SUPERVISION*

## Core Areas of Knowledge and Competency

The proposed Standards include a description of eleven core areas of personal traits, knowledge and competencies that are characteristic of effective supervisors. The level of preparation and experience of the counselor, the particular work setting of the supervisor and counselor and client variables will influence the relative emphasis of each competency in practice.

These core areas and their related competencies have been consistently identified in supervision research and, in addition, have been judged to have face validity as determined by supervisor practitioners, based on both select and widespread peer review.

1. Professional counseling supervisors are effective counselors whose knowledge and competencies have been acquired through training, education, and supervised employment experience.

    The counseling supervisor:

    1.1 demonstrates knowledge of various counseling theories, systems, and their related methods;

    1.2 demonstrates knowledge of his/her personal philosophical, theoretical and methodological approach to counseling;

    1.3 demonstrates knowledge of his/her

assumptions about human behavior; and

    1.4 demonstrates skill in the application of counseling theory and methods (individual, group, or marital and family and specialized areas such as substance abuse, career-life, rehabilitation) that are appropriate for the supervisory setting.

2. Professional counseling supervisors demonstrate *personal traits and characteristics* that are consistent with the role.

    The counseling supervisor:

    2.1 is committed to updating his/her own counseling and supervisory skills;

    2.2 is sensitive to individual differences;

    2.3 recognizes his/her own limits through self-evaluation and feedback from others;

    2.4 is encouraging, optimistic and motivational;

    2.5 possesses a sense of humor;

    2.6 is comfortable with the authority inherent in the role of supervisor;

    2.7 demonstrates a commitment to the role of supervisor;

    2.8 can identify his/her own strengths and weaknesses as a supervisor;

*These standards were authored by the ACES Supervision Interest Network and were adopted by the American Association for Counseling and Development in 1989.

2.9  can describe his/her own pattern in interpersonal relationships.

3. Professional counseling supervisors are knowledgeable regarding *ethical, legal and regulatory aspects* of the profession, and are skilled in applying this knowledge.

The counseling supervisor:

3.1  communicates to the counselor a knowledge of professional codes of ethics (e.g., AACD, APA);

3.2  demonstrates and enforces ethical and professional standards;

3.3  communicates to the counselor an understanding of legal and regulatory documents and their impact on the profession (e.g., certification, licensure, duty to warn, parents' rights to children's records, third party payment, etc.);

3.4  provides current information regarding professional standards (NCC, CCMHC, CRC, CCC, licensure, certification, etc.);

3.5  can communicate a knowledge of counselor rights and appeal procedures specific to the work setting; and

3.6  communicates to the counselor a knowledge of ethical considerations that pertain to the supervisory process, including dual relationships, due process, evaluation, informed consent, confidentiality, and vicarious liability.

4. Professional counseling supervisors demonstrate conceptual knowledge of the *personal and professional nature of the supervisory relationship* and are skilled in applying this knowledge.

The counseling supervisor:

4.1  demonstrates knowledge of individual differences with respect to gender, race, ethnicity, culture and age and understands the importance of these characteristics in supervisory relationships;

4.2  is sensitive to the counselor's personal and professional needs;

4.3  expects counselors to own the consequences of their actions;

4.4  is sensitive to the evaluative nature of supervision and effectively responds to the counselor's anxiety relative to performance evaluation;

4.5  conducts self-evaluations, as appropriate, as a means of modeling professional growth;

4.6  provides facilitative conditions (empathy, concreteness, respect, congruence, genuineness, and immediacy);

4.7  establishes a mutually trusting relationship with the counselor;

4.8  provides an appropriate balance of challenge and support; and

4.9  elicits counselor thoughts and feelings during counseling or consultation sessions, and responds in a manner that enhances the supervision process.

5. Professional counseling supervisors demonstrate conceptual knowledge of *supervision methods and techniques,* and are skilled in using this knowledge to promote counselor development.

The counseling supervisor:

5.1  states the purposes of supervision and explains the procedures to be used;

5.2  negotiates mutual decisions regarding the needed direction of learning experiences for the counselor;

5.3  engages in appropriate supervisory interventions, including role-play, role-reversal, live supervision, modeling, interpersonal process recall, micro-training, suggestions and advice, reviewing audio and video tapes, etc.;

5.4  can perform the supervisor's functions in the role of teacher, counselor, or consultant as appropriate;

5.5  elicits new alternatives from counselor for identifying solutions, techniques, responses to clients;

5.6 integrates knowledge of supervision with his/her style of interpersonal relations;

5.7 clarifies his/her role in supervision;

5.8 uses media aids (print material, electronic recording) to enhance learning; and

5.9 interacts with the counselor in a manner that facilitates the counselor's self-exploration and problem solving.

6. Professional counseling supervisors demonstrate conceptual knowledge of the *counselor developmental process* and are skilled in applying this knowledge.

The counseling supervisor:

6.1 understands the developmental nature of supervision;

6.2 demonstrates knowledge of various theoretical models of supervision;

6.3 understands the counselor's roles and functions in particular work settings;

6.4 can identify the learning needs of the counselor;

6.5 adjusts conference content based on the counselor's personal traits, conceptual development, training, and experience; and

6.6 uses supervisory methods appropriate to the counselor's level of conceptual development, training, and experience.

7. Professional counseling supervisors demonstrate knowledge and competency in *case conceptualization and management*.

[The counseling supervisor:]

7.1 recognizes that a primary goal of supervision is helping the client of the counselor;

7.2 understands the roles of other professionals (e.g., psychologists, physicians, social workers) and assists with the referral process, when appropriate;

7.3 elicits counselor perceptions of counseling dynamics;

7.4 assists the counselor in selecting and executing data collection procedures;

7.5 assists the counselor in analyzing and interpreting data objectively;

7.6 assists the counselor in planning effective client goals and objectives;

7.7 assists the counselor in using observation and assessment in preparation of client goals and objectives;

7.8 assists the counselor in synthesizing client psychological and behavioral characteristics into an integrated conceptualization;

7.9 assists the counselor in assigning priorities to counseling goals and objectives;

7.10 assists the counselor in providing rationale for counseling procedures; and

7.11 assists the counselor in adjusting steps in the progression toward a goal based on ongoing assessment and evaluation.

8. Professional counseling supervisors demonstrates [*sic*] knowledge and competency in client *assessment and evaluation*.

The counseling supervisor:

8.1 monitors the use of tests and test interpretations;

8.2 assists the counselor in providing rationale for assessment procedures;

8.3 assists the counselor in communicating assessment procedures and rationales;

8.4 assists the counselor in the description, measurement, and documentation of client and counselor change; and

8.5 assists the counselor in integrating findings and observations to make appropriate recommendations.

9. Professional counseling supervisors demonstrate knowledge and competency in

*oral and written reporting and recording.*
The counseling supervisor:

9.1  understands the meaning of accountability and the supervisor's responsibility in promoting it;

9.2  assists the counselor in effectively documenting supervisory and counseling-related interactions;

9.3  assists the counselor in establishing and following policies and procedures to protect the confidentiality of client and supervisory records;

9.4  assists the counselor in identifying appropriate information to be included in a verbal or written report;

9.5  assists the counselor in presenting information in a logical, concise, and sequential manner; and

9.6  assists the counselor in adapting verbal and written reports to the work environment and communication situation.

10. Professional counseling supervisors demonstrates [*sic*] knowledge and competency in the *evaluation of counseling performance.*
The counseling supervisor:

10.1  can interact with the counselor from the perspective of evaluator;

10.2  can identify the counselor's professional and personal strengths, as well as weaknesses;

10.3  provides specific feedback about such performance as conceptualization, use of methods and techniques, relationship skills, and assessment;

10.4  determines the extent to which the counselor has developed and applied his/her own personal theory of counseling;

10.5  develops evaluation procedures and instruments to determine program and counselor goal attainment;

10.6  assists the counselor in the description and measurement of his/her progress and achievement; and

10.7  can evaluate counseling skills for purposes of grade assignment, completion of internship requirements, professional advancement, and so on.

11. Professional counseling supervisors are knowledgeable regarding *research in counseling and counselor supervision* and consistently incorporate this knowledge into the supervision process.
The counseling supervisor:

11.1  facilitates and monitors research to determine the effectiveness of programs, services and techniques;

11.2  reads, interprets, and applies counseling and supervisory research;

11.3  can formulate counseling or supervisory research questions;

11.4  reports results of counseling or supervisory research and disseminates as appropriate (e.g., inservice, conference, publications); and

11.5  facilitates an integration of research findings in individual case management.

## The Education and Training of Supervisors

Counseling supervision is a distinct field of preparation and practice. Knowledge and competencies necessary for effective performance are acquired through a sequence of training and experience which ordinarily includes the following:

1. Graduate training in counseling;

2. Successful supervised employment as a professional counselor;

3. Certification as a National Certified Counselor, Certified Clinical Mental Health Counselor, Certified Rehabilitation Counselor, or Certified Career Counselor;

4. Certification by a state department of education or licensure by a state as a professional counselor;

5. Graduate training in counseling supervision including didactic courses, seminars, laboratory courses, and supervision practica;
6. Continuing educational experiences specific to supervision theory and practice (e.g., conferences, workshops, self-study); and
7. Research activities related to supervision theory and practice.

The supervisor's primary functions are to teach the inexperienced counselor and to foster their professional development, to serve as consultants to experienced counselors, and to assist at all levels in the provision of effective counseling services. These responsibilities require personal and professional maturity accompanied by a broad perspective on counseling that is gained by extensive, supervised counseling experience. Therefore, training for supervision generally occurs during advanced graduate study or continuing professional development. This is not to say, however, that supervisor training in the pre-service stage is without merit. The presentation of basic methods and procedures may enhance students' performance as counselors, enrich their participation in the supervision process, and provide a framework for later study.

August 1988

# STRUCTURED WORKSHOP IN CLINICAL SUPERVISION*

## STRUCTURED WORKSHOP IN CLINICAL SUPERVISION

This workshop has been developed to give participants an opportunity to observe and practice distinct supervision approaches as well as to consider primary supervision issues. The desired outcomes of the workshop are to equip novice supervisors with some breadth of practice, as well as to instruct seasoned supervisors in alternatives to their present approach. Because of its brevity, the workshop only introduces the participants to relevant supervision models and issues. Therefore, in the optimal training situation, the workshop is followed by extensive supervision of supervision.

## Session 1

*Topic:* Obtaining baseline behavior on supervisor *focus.*

*Rationale and Assumptions:* Counseling is a complex activity which weaves many different behaviors into its cloth. The observer (supervisor), however, must simplify this pattern into conceptual units that can be communicated back to the counselor/therapist for the purposes of supervision. Each supervisor has an idiosyncratic style of observing, and will focus on certain behaviors to the exclusion of others. It is important for the supervisor to know his/her natural affinity to certain focus areas in order to compensate, if necessary. For this laboratory session, the three focus areas are defined as: (1) process skills, (2) conceptualization skills, and (3) personalization skills (Bernard, 1979).

*Activities:*

1. Participants are shown a 30-minute counseling videotape and are asked to take notes on the counselor's performance as if they were the counselor's supervisor and would be giving feedback after the session.
2. When the tape is finished, participants are asked to study their notes and choose five items they would *most want* to cover in supervision. After the items have been identified, the participants rank-order them by importance.
3. From the same observation notes, participants are also asked to choose three items they would use in the *first few minutes* of

---

*Developed in 1980 by J. M. Bernard. Revised in 1989.

a supervision session (not necessarily from the list of five obtained above).

4. Referring to number 2, participants report their most important items to be covered in supervision (no. 1 on their list of 5). These are written on a blackboard and the group discusses the focus of each item (process, conceptualization or personalization using Bernard's [1979] Discrimination Model). All participants are taught to discriminate between categories at this time.

5. The large group is broken down into groups of three or four. Each small group categorizes each member's first five items. In addition, the items obtained in number 3 are categorized.

6. Back in the large group, each participant identifies his or her *primary* focus category (obtained from items participant had deemed as most important), and his or her entry behavior (initial items). The implications of these for supervision are discussed.

*Comments*: Most supervisors are not aware of their baseline focus behaviors although they generally think that the results of the exercise are representative of their general style. They also find it interesting to consider the effect of their entry style on the process of supervision. (For instance, often supervisors want to focus on counselor feelings at the beginning of supervision but then switch to process issues. Later, they realize that this might leave the counselor at a disadvantage if the switch is done abruptly). In addition to identifying baseline focus behavior, there are two additional advantages to this first session. First, participants are forced to condense their observation notes into five important feedback items. This is an important activity because many supervisors attempt to give counselors too much feedback per session. Second, by comparing each supervisor's most important five items, participants become sensitized to

the fact that any counseling session can be viewed in a variety of ways. This increases their motivation to move beyond their baseline focus behavior.

### Session 2

*Topic* Obtaining baseline behavior on supervisor *role*.

*Rationale and Assumptions* Once supervisors are aware of their primary focus, they superimpose role behavior in an attempt to communicate their perceptions to the counselor. As with focus behavior, there is a tendency for supervisors to favor certain roles over others when working with counselors. This baseline behavior becomes the target of Session 2 using the labels of Teacher, Counselor and Consultant (Bernard, 1979) as discriminate role categories. Again, the assumption is that if supervisors are made aware of their baseline role behavior, they will be in a more strategic position to choose other roles when appropriate.

*Activities* The large group is divided into dyads for an exercise.

1. Using observation notes taken during Session 1, 30-minute role plays are conducted where one person plays the role of supervisor while the other plays the counselor in the tape viewed earlier. These sessions are audiotaped.

2. A second round of simulations follows in order to give every participant an opportunity to perform in the role of supervisor. (However, dyads should be varied so that the same two participants are not in more than one role play with each other.)

3. The large group is reassembled. One of the participants' audiotapes is used as a demonstration tape. The group is instructed to focus on the supervisor only and to note the role the supervisor is using as the tape proceeds. The instructor monitors on a blackboard so that participants

can check their ability to identify each of the roles. The tape is stopped whenever there is a question about the role being used. At the end of this activity, participants should be able to identify the three different supervisor roles. If time permits, a second tape is reviewed. (Depending upon the ability of the participants to recognize different supervisor roles, the audiotapes can be analyzed simultaneously for focus behaviors with a discussion of different combinations.)

4. An assignment is given for participants to analyze their own audiotapes for role behavior before Session 3.

   *NOTE* If the training is being done as a two-day workshop, a 30 minute time slot is needed here for individual analysis of tapes.

*Comments* Although some participants are not surprised with their baseline role behavior, others are. One participant had been pegged as a "counselor type"; his responses, however, were almost exclusively in the teacher category. This was important information for him in order to avoid confusion in his relationship with counselors. Some participants have made the comment that they were finding out as much about themselves as they had in their counselor training. This surprised them.

## Session 3

*Topic* The Discrimination Model
*Rationale and Assumptions* A major assumption of this entire training laboratory is that supervisors need practice in different supervisor behaviors before they can use them competently with counselors. Therefore, recognizing their baseline focus and role behaviors must be followed by practicing those behaviors which come less easily. Session 3 is designed to give supervisors practice in all three focus behaviors and all three role behaviors. As a result,

their repertoire will be increased beyond their baseline abilities.
*Reference* Bernard, J. M. (1979)
*Activities*

1. First, participants are asked whether they had any difficulty in completing the assignment at the end of Session 2. Questions are answered and another audiotape is analyzed if necessary. Participants share the results of their tape analysis.

2. A different 30-minute counseling videotape is viewed by the group. Participants are asked to divide a piece of paper in thirds and take notes on the counselor's performance in the three different categories of process skills, conceptualization, and personalization. (By asking participants to take notes in this manner, they learn to discriminate among categories while viewing a counseling session.)

3. Using a fishbowl format, role plays follow with one participant playing the counselor in the videotape and the other playing the supervisor. The supervisor must give feedback in all three focus areas while being given role changes with flash cards (out of the counselor's view). Role plays are 10 to 15 minutes in length and are followed by feedback from the counselor and discussion in the group.

4. More role plays follow until several participants have had an opportunity to use the Discrimination Model on cue.

*Comments* As with pre-practicum training for counselors, participants often complain at this point in the training that they are becoming overly conscious of their behavior to the detriment of the supervision process. It is important that the instructor support this reaction as an accurate reflection of the learning process. Participants are over-learning behaviors so that they can surface more naturally in the future. The comparison between counselor training and supervisor training is usually sufficient to handle this protest.

## Session 4

*Topic* Interpersonal Process Recall (IPR)
*Rationale and Assumptions* IPR is an important supervision model especially when there are interpersonal issues in the counselor/client relationship and the counselor has conceptual realizations that he or she is not translating into process. IPR is also important for the supervisor because it stresses the consultant and counselor roles, and most supervisors find it difficult to screen out the teacher role. Also, inherent in this model is a respect for the counselor as his or her own authority, which adds an important dimension to the supervisor/counselor relationship.
*References* Kagan, N. (1980); Bernard, J. M. (1989)
*Activities*

1. Prior to this session, 3 volunteers must be used to make training videotapes. One 30-minute counseling session (simulated) is made using two of the volunteers, one as client, the other as counselor. Following this simulation, the third volunteer who has observed the former videotape as it is being taped, acts as supervisor with the counselor in a 15-minute taped supervision session.
2. The first activity in the lab is an IPR demonstration with the counselor from the simulation, with the instructor taking the role of "inquirer." Once the role has been demonstrated, the supervisor volunteer from #1 continues with the IPR session. Halfway through the tape, other participants are invited to take the role of inquirer.
3. Following the IPR segment is a discussion of the process with counselor and client giving feedback to the different inquirers and remarking on the learning involved in the IPR process.
4. The next activity is a supervisor/counselor IPR session using the 15-minute supervision tape made prior to the lab. A volunteer from the group acts as inquirer. Similar relationships or conceptual issues between supervisor and counselor are targeted as was done between counselor and client.
5. A discussion similar to that in item 3 with feedback given by counselor and supervisor follows. The use of IPR for training counselors and supervisors is discussed.

*Comments* Participants find it helpful to follow the usual counselor/client IPR session with the supervisor/counselor IPR session. Participants typically are of the opinion that IPR has the potential of magnifying a relationship and comment on the advantages and potential disadvantages of such a potential. Participants especially find it valuable to experience the model in the supervisor/counselor IPR session because it gives them insight as to how this model might be received by counselors. IPR is viewed as most helpful when interpersonal dynamics between counselor and client, or between supervisor and counselor, are subtle and thus need magnification. For more obvious relationship issues, the model is viewed as having potential drawbacks if magnification would result in distortion. Also, the role of inquirer is a good exercise for any supervisor who needs to do less teaching in supervision.
*Note* If #1 is not possible, the IPR demonstration can be done if one or two participants can bring an audiotape of one of their therapy sessions to the workshop. However, the supervisor/therapist dimension will not occur using this option.

## Session 5

*Topic* Microtraining
*Rationale and Assumptions* The Microtraining (MT) model offers an excellent balance to IPR because it emphasizes the teacher role and stresses process skills. Thus, MT is an essential part of supervisor training since the supervisor

is often put in the position of teaching new or more advanced skills or strategies to the counselor. Indeed, if teaching were not a component of supervision, professional growth for the counselor would be limited. Microtraining is the most direct and efficient form of teaching.

*References* Akamatsu, T. J. (1980); Forsyth, D. R., & Ivey, A. E. (1980).

*Activities*

1. A 30-minute counseling videotape is viewed by the group.
2. The large group is divided into smaller groups of 3 or 4 and these smaller groups decide on two or three strategies or skills which could be taught to the counselor in the videotape to improve the counseling session. It is important that suggestions be limited to *observable behaviors* which are very specific.
3. Back in the large group and using the MT format, a participant volunteers (as supervisor) to teach one of the skills or strategies, using modeling and practice, to another participant (counselor) from another small group. This MT session is videotaped. The counselor then attempts to use this learning in a five-minute role play with yet another participant (client) and this is also videotaped.
4. The large group watches the videotape and feedback follows which focuses on the supervisor's skills and clarity in teaching. The counselor's ability to translate the supervisor's teaching into behavior is the best feedback. If the original teaching was not complete, accurate, or skillful, the process is repeated. (Obviously, the last activity is more meaningful when the skill being taught is new to the "counselor." Although most participants are familiar with the techniques that are suggested, it is best if the "counselor" has not attempted them in actual practice. When this is the case, this activity can

offer some welcomed practice with unique therapeutic interventions.)
5. Items 3 and 4 are repeated with a different pair of volunteers and different content.

*Comments* Supervisors appreciate the immediate feedback they receive on their skills as teachers. They also find it very helpful repeating the process until they have mastered teaching any one skill. For the purposes of the laboratory, it is assumed that if the volunteer counselor does not accurately perform the skill as the supervisor wished, the supervisor did not instruct in a clear or concise enough manner. The videotape playback also gives supervisors information about assumptions they make in their instructions. Supervisors discover the value of taping their supervision sessions as well as having counselors practice new skills in simulation, rather than attempting them in a subsequent counseling session without the benefit of prior practice. Although initially more time consuming, they feel this is more efficient in the long run.

### Session 6

*Topic* Live Supervision

*Reference* Haley, J. (1987)

*Rationale and Assumptions* Live supervision is important for a variety of reasons. For training purposes, live supervision allows a counselor to work with a client that is too difficult for him or her to counsel without live supervision. Another training advantage is that live supervision gives the supervisor an opportunity to pace the counselor through counseling strategies which ultimately produces a more reinforcing and supportive atmosphere for learning. This eliminates a mutually frustrating situation where the supervisor sees major errors midway through a session but must wait until later to tell the counselor — when it is too late to do anything about it! One major condition and assumption for using live supervision is a positive relationship between supervisor and counselor. Live supervision is a delicate paradigm and will not be successful if the counselor feels criticized or threatened by the supervisor.

On another level, live supervision is important as an ethical safeguard for the supervisor. Most supervisors can remember a time when they wanted to, or should have, interrupted a counseling session for a number of reasons, most of which center around the well-being of the client. It is very disrupting for supervisor, counselor and client if this kind of delicate or emergency situation is the first time a supervisor uses an active role as a supervisor during a counseling session. Therefore, training and regular, or even intermittent, use of a live supervision model allows for more flexibility which tends to minimize the possibilities of ethical breaches occurring.

It is assumed also that the use of live supervision causes no major discomfort for clients if the counselor and supervisor are comfortable and competent in its use. Although there are several forms of live supervision (e.g., bug in the ear, telephone systems, etc.), training is centered around calling the counselor out of the session by means of a light knock on the observation window since this requires no additional facilities and allows for maximum application by the participants.

Finally, it should be noted that live supervision can look deceptively simple when, in fact, it is a complex model. Therefore, the following exercises take some components of live supervision out of context, moreso than for other models. The participant should be alerted to the need for both additional training and follow-up if live supervision is to be used effectively.

*Activities*

1. A major skill in live supervision is the ability to give brief, clear, and helpful "directives" to the counselor. Although directives should have a sound rationale, they should be delivered in behavioral or process language so the counselor can translate the directive into counseling behavior easily. In order to acquire skill in directive giving, participants watch a videotape of a counseling session which is stopped at several pre-determined times. Participants jot down a directive each time the tape is stopped. Several directives are then read to the group and a discussion follows analyzing the directives for their precision, clarity and helpfulness.

2. Practice in composing directives is followed by a simulated counseling session viewed by the participants on a TV monitor. During the counseling session, each participant is required to interrupt the session at least once with a directive. All directives are audiorecorded in the observation room. The counselor must attempt to implement each directive upon returning to the counseling room.

3. In addition to the immediate feedback which the participant receives by observing how the directive is translated by the counselor and received by the client, all directives are reviewed after the simulation is over and discussed by the entire group with specific attention given to the counselor's feedback.

4. Because activities 2 and 3 serve almost as a caricature of live supervision (because of the frequency of interruptions), rather than a "typical" live supervision session, they are followed by a simulation where observers are asked to be conservative and call for a directive only when they think one will be helpful to the therapist. This activity can be aided by giving the client a very resistant or manipulative role, one which would cause most therapists to welcome some help.

*Comments* Of all the models taught in the lab, live supervision typically earns the strongest reaction. It is common for some participants to be very cautious, if not skeptical, about the possible gains in using this model. However, the workshop experience usually dispels such concerns. Those who volunteer to be be counselors in the simulations remark that they felt a great deal of support in the form of directives, and not the criticism they had expected to experience. It is usually the general consensus that the team effort experience of live supervision, and the potential of changing the direction of a session, more than compensate for the interruption of the counseling process.

### Session 7

*Topic* Evaluation

*Rationale and Assumptions* Evaluation is one of the most crucial responsibilities of the supervisor. It is important for the supervisor to have an evaluation plan, including objective criteria, while remaining sensitive to subjective issues. Without specific training in evaluation, this responsibility often is handled in a random fashion. Connecting this with Session 8, it is also important that the supervisor be a discriminating and clear evaluator for ethical reasons. This lab session is based on three distinct evaluation skills: 1) identifying criteria for evaluation; 2) recognizing the relative strengths and deficits of the counselor; and 3) communicating these in clear, concrete language.

*Activities*

1. Prior to this session (or in the session in groups), participants are asked to identify ten to fifteen criteria they consider important for counselor effectiveness. In small groups they discuss their criteria and, perhaps, refine them.

2. In the large group, participants view a 20–30 minute counseling tape of a novice counselor. Participants then rate the counselor on their criteria (using a Likert scale). In addition, participants rate the counselor using the Evaluation of Therapist Performance: Short Form. (The short form has 15 items divided equally between process skills, conceptualization, and personalization.)

3. Participants return to small groups to discuss their evaluations. The instructor presents the key for the Short Form so participants can see if they were more critical of process skills, for example, than for the other two areas of counselor performance. Any differences among participants are discussed. Participants are also asked to discuss any difficulty in rating a counselor on the criteria they have chosen. It is at this point that participants may realize that they have selected too few criteria that lend themselves to observation.

4. Participants are then asked to take their criteria and translate them into behaviors that are observable. The instructor may need to take one participant's items and do this with the whole group. Once this is accomplished (might be too time-consuming to do in one session), participants can again rate the counselor seen on videotape using the revised criteria.

5. Depending on the time taken for steps 1–4, role plays can follow in which participants practice giving feedback (positive and negative) to volunteers who play the part of the counselor in the videotape. Feedback is given to the supervisor regarding the clarity and conciseness of the feedback by both the counselor and the larger group.

*Comments* There are several insights that seem to develop from this workshop session. First, participants begin to appreciate the importance of selecting criteria that can be evaluated with some accuracy. This almost requires that the criteria (or some of them) be observable. Second, occasionally some information related to the first session emerges as a result of completing the Short Form. If a participant had a strong conceptualization theme in the first session, it is possible that he or she may be more critical of the counselor on this theme. If participants with other themes (e.g., process skills) are not as critical on the conceptualization items, this is important information. The instructor can help participants realize that their investment in part of the counseling process may compromise their ability to carry out objective (relatively speaking) evaluations. Finally, participants also find that receiving feedback on how they communicate their impressions to the counselors reveals new information for them. For instance, some participants are surprised that they receive more constructive feedback on their delivery of negative feedback than positive feedback. By this point in the workshop, participants are fairly confident and trust their critical perceptions. They can remain, however, somewhat ambiguous and unclear regarding positive impressions.

**Session 8**

*Topic* Ethical and Legal Issues
*References:* Cormier, L. S., & Bernard, J. M. (1982); Bernard, J. M. (1987).
*Rationale and Assumptions* First, it must be noted that all of the above training is considered vital for avoiding ethical and legal problems. Assuming that the supervisor is able to evaluate counselors and clients accurately, and perform in a variety of appropriate ways, ethical and legal situations most often arise as a result of avoidance, oversight, or discomfort on the part of the supervisor rather than malice or a deliberate disregard of professional ethical guidelines. This workshop assumes that training must take two forms to adequately prepare the participant: (1) Because most supervisors in counseling or psychotherapy are primarily trained as practitioners, they are less apt to be prepared to accept the power and authority inherent in the role of supervisor. If they refuse to accept the responsibility to evaluate, they are more likely to find themselves in unethical situations. It is important that supervisor training not assume that this issue will work itself out naturally. Supervisors are much more comfortable and confident if they have had prior practice in asserting themselves in a direct and responsible manner; (2) Even if supervisors are generally comfortable with their roles, there might be particular situations which they are unprepared for or that they avoid because they make them uncomfortable. These particular situations tend to be those which can lead most often to ethical and legal problems. For instance, a supervisor might be neglectful in referring a client to another counselor even though s/he believes that the present counselor is not sufficiently skilled to handle the case. Supervisor training should include experiences in confronting uncomfortable situations so that supervisors have a repertoire of skills and alternatives which will enable them to be responsible and ethical without undue stress.
*Activities:*

1. Participants view a videotape of a counseling session in which the counselor has performed poorly. After about 20 minutes of viewing, the group divides into smaller units and a volunteer in the role of supervisor gives direct, negative feedback to a volunteer in the role of counselor. The supervisor is instructed to be supportive when possible, but to be clear about what must take place for counseling to improve and the necessity of the latter. Observers and the counselor then give feedback to the supervisor.

2. In emergency situations, the supervisor is most likely to be the person called upon to deal with a very distraught client. Using a fishbowl format, one participant assumes the stance of a client in need of hospitalization (the diagnosis can be agreed upon by the group depending upon the client population most participants serve). Another volunteer (as supervisor) works with

this client to inform him/her that it is his/her opinion that hospitalization is necessary. After a short while, feedback is given to the supervisor on his/her ability to communicate authority, caring, and important, specific information to the client.

3. Item 2 is followed by another brief simulation of the supervisor making contact with a professional in a discipline other than his or her own in order to make the referral. The instructor usually plays the part of the other professional. The purpose of this activity is to determine whether the supervisor obtained all necessary information from the client in order to make a referral and to tap stereotypes and difficulties in working with other professionals. A discussion follows.

4. The final exercise is designed around the particular needs of the group. Vignettes are presented which depict different ethical and/or legal dilemmas for the supervisor. Several vignettes are acted out in the following fashion. Each vignette has two roles. Depending on the situation, there is often missing information in each role. Although observers are given a description of both roles, those volunteering to be in the vignette are only given one of the roles. How each person communicates his or her information to the other is part of the exercise. The following is an example of a vignette:

Counselor: You are seeing a woman as a client who has seen another therapist in town. When you ask her if she is currently seeing this person she is vague. You inform her that you must contact her former therapist before you can continue to see her. You call the therapist but she is not in. You make another attempt with the same result. Since then you have made no further attempts to contact the former therapist. There has been no further mention of this therapist in your sessions with your client and you assume that the issue

is past. In your past counseling session with your client, she talks about being very depressed. You want to talk to your supervisor about the possibility of recommending her to a physician in conjunction with counseling since you believe that her depression is interfering with counseling progress. She has not been sleeping or eating well. This is your major concern as you enter the upcoming supervision session. Your supervisor was not able to observe your last session so she is dependent on your self report for supervision.

Supervisor: One of your counselors is seeing a female client and there is some question whether the client is also seeing another therapist. The counselor informs the client that he must contact the other therapist and the client does not resist. Three weeks later you receive a very cold phone call from the therapist who was to be contacted. She has just learned that her client has been seeing your counselor. She makes clear that professional courtesy (if not ethics) has been violated by your agency since she was not contacted by you or the counselor concerning his last session with this client. You were not able to observe this session so you will have to rely on self report for supervision purposes. Your most urgent intent, however, is to discuss this breach of professional ethics.

*Comments* This last session is particularly enjoyable because it involves a bit of drama. The best of some participants comes out as they work creatively through the role plays. Also, because of the type of information being covered, group cohesiveness usually occurs which adds to the final session. The last activity has, at times, stimulated the use of constructive humor—a positive attribute for a supervisor. This last session should serve to integrate some of the concepts learned earlier in the workshop. For instance, in the vignette given above, one supervisor was attempting to get the counselor to "fess up" relying heavily on the consultant role. However, he had a hidden, somewhat punitive, alternative if the counselor didn't share the critical information. In the feedback session that followed the supervisor and the observers agreed that a much more straightforward teacher role as an initial style would have been more helpful and more honest. Several participants said that they became aware of how they hid behind the consultant role when uncomfortable and how this could develop into an ethical dilemma.

Evaluation of Counselor Behaviors
Long Form*

| The Counseling Session | Poor Never | | Good Often | | | Excellent Always |
|---|---|---|---|---|---|---|
| Rate the counselor's ability to: | | | | | | |
| 1. Begin and end sessions smoothly | 1 | 2 | 3 | 4 | 5 | 6 | 7 |
| 2. Convey warmth to the client | 1 | 2 | 3 | 4 | 5 | 6 | 7 |
| 3. Convey competence to client | 1 | 2 | 3 | 4 | 5 | 6 | 7 |
| 4. Conduct a systematic and complete intake interview | 1 | 2 | 3 | 4 | 5 | 6 | 7 |
| 5. Use a variety of counselor responses (reflection, summary, confrontation, ability potential, etc.) | 1 | 2 | 3 | 4 | 5 | 6 | 7 |
| 6. Explain the nature and objectives of counseling when appropriate | 1 | 2 | 3 | 4 | 5 | 6 | 7 |
| 7. Be flexible in the session | 1 | 2 | 3 | 4 | 5 | 6 | 7 |
| 8. Focus on the client's primary concern | 1 | 2 | 3 | 4 | 5 | 6 | 7 |
| 9. Integrate client's secondary concerns into counseling | 1 | 2 | 3 | 4 | 5 | 6 | 7 |
| 10. Facilitate client expression of thought and feeling | 1 | 2 | 3 | 4 | 5 | 6 | 7 |
| 11. Help the client set appropriate goals | 1 | 2 | 3 | 4 | 5 | 6 | 7 |
| 12. Help the client work towards established goals | 1 | 2 | 3 | 4 | 5 | 6 | 7 |
| 13. Follow client (nondirective) when client is working or needs some flexibility | 1 | 2 | 3 | 4 | 5 | 6 | 7 |
| 14. Be directive and create a structured atmosphere when needed | 1 | 2 | 3 | 4 | 5 | 6 | 7 |
| 15. Pace client to arrive at a good tempo | 1 | 2 | 3 | 4 | 5 | 6 | 7 |

Evaluation of Counselor Behaviors
Long Form* (*cont.*)

| The Counseling Session | Poor Never | | | Good Often | | | Excellent Always |
|---|---|---|---|---|---|---|---|
| 16. Interject counseling knowledge into the interview when appropriate (can teach the client) | 1 | 2 | 3 | 4 | 5 | 6 | 7 |
| 17. Use different tests to enhance the counseling process | 1 | 2 | 3 | 4 | 5 | 6 | 7 |
| 18. Arrive at a balance between implementing planned strategies and remaining spontaneous in the counseling session | 1 | 2 | 3 | 4 | 5 | 6 | 7 |
| 19. Monitor reactions to client when appropriate | 1 | 2 | 3 | 4 | 5 | 6 | 7 |
| 20. Resist client manipulation | 1 | 2 | 3 | 4 | 5 | 6 | 7 |
| 21. Respond to client affect when appropriate | 1 | 2 | 3 | 4 | 5 | 6 | 7 |
| 22. Address interpersonal dynamics between self and client | 1 | 2 | 3 | 4 | 5 | 6 | 7 |
| 23. React quickly to important developments in the counseling session | 1 | 2 | 3 | 4 | 5 | 6 | 7 |
| 24. Keep control of the session | 1 | 2 | 3 | 4 | 5 | 6 | 7 |
| 25. Be aware of client's nonverbal and verbal behaviors | 1 | 2 | 3 | 4 | 5 | 6 | 7 |
| 26. Recognize and skillfully interpret client's covert messages | 1 | 2 | 3 | 4 | 5 | 6 | 7 |

*Supervision*

Rate counselor's ability to:

| | Poor Never | | | Good Often | | | Excellent Always |
|---|---|---|---|---|---|---|---|
| 27. Conceptualize a case accurately | 1 | 2 | 3 | 4 | 5 | 6 | 7 |
| 28. Arrive at appropriate goals as a result of conceptualization | 1 | 2 | 3 | 4 | 5 | 6 | 7 |
| 29. Understand interplay between strategies and goals | 1 | 2 | 3 | 4 | 5 | 6 | 7 |
| 30. Plan a session to enhance overall goals | 1 | 2 | 3 | 4 | 5 | 6 | 7 |
| 31. Understand the relationship between process goals and outcome goals | 1 | 2 | 3 | 4 | 5 | 6 | 7 |
| 32. Implement a series of planned responses (strategy) | 1 | 2 | 3 | 4 | 5 | 6 | 7 |
| 33. Be honest with self | 1 | 2 | 3 | 4 | 5 | 6 | 7 |
| 34. Recognize his or her own defensive behavior | 1 | 2 | 3 | 4 | 5 | 6 | 7 |

Evaluation of Counselor Behaviors
Long Form (*cont.*)*

| The Counseling Session | Poor Never | | Good Often | | | Excellent Always |
|---|---|---|---|---|---|---|
| 35. Accept feedback from supervisor | 1 | 2 | 3 | 4 | 5 | 6 | 7 |
| 36. Use feedback in future session | 1 | 2 | 3 | 4 | 5 | 6 | 7 |
| 37. Trust own insights and state these when they differ from supervisor's | 1 | 2 | 3 | 4 | 5 | 6 | 7 |
| 38. Use supervision time to learn about counseling and him or herself | 1 | 2 | 3 | 4 | 5 | 6 | 7 |
| 39. Exhibit a balance between self assuredness and awareness of the value of supervision | 1 | 2 | 3 | 4 | 5 | 6 | 7 |
| 40. Write concise and complete intake and/or termination reports | 1 | 2 | 3 | 4 | 5 | 6 | 7 |

*Professional Development*

Rate the counselor on the following criteria:

| | | | | | | | |
|---|---|---|---|---|---|---|---|
| 41. Is a reliable member of the staff | 1 | 2 | 3 | 4 | 5 | 6 | 7 |
| 42. Turns in report and logs promptly | 1 | 2 | 3 | 4 | 5 | 6 | 7 |
| 43. Behaves in a professional manner on site | 1 | 2 | 3 | 4 | 5 | 6 | 7 |
| 44. Communicates responsibility for self | 1 | 2 | 3 | 4 | 5 | 6 | 7 |
| 45. Exhibits professional values | 1 | 2 | 3 | 4 | 5 | 6 | 7 |
| 46. Is a helpful colleague | 1 | 2 | 3 | 4 | 5 | 6 | 7 |
| 47. Is sensitive to ethical issues and/or legal issues | 1 | 2 | 3 | 4 | 5 | 6 | 7 |
| 48. Is respectful of differences among people | 1 | 2 | 3 | 4 | 5 | 6 | 7 |
| 49. Conveys a respect for the power of counseling and an awareness of its limits | 1 | 2 | 3 | 4 | 5 | 6 | 7 |
| 50. Overall, exhibits the behaviors and attitudes of a competent and professional counselor | 1 | 2 | 3 | 4 | 5 | 6 | 7 |

Additional comments:

*Developed by Janine M. Bernard, April, 1976; Revised, January, 1981

*Evaluation of Therapist Performance*
*Short Form\**

| | Poor<br>Never | | | Good<br>Often | | | Excellent<br>Always |
|---|---|---|---|---|---|---|---|
| Rate the therapist's ability to: | | | | | | | |
| 1. Comprehend the client's issues. | 1 | 2 | 3 | 4 | 5 | 6 | 7 |
| 2. Facilitate client expression of thought and feeling. | 1 | 2 | 3 | 4 | 5 | 6 | 7 |
| 3. Keep control of the therapy session. | 1 | 2 | 3 | 4 | 5 | 6 | 7 |
| 4. Recognize and skillfully interpret client's covert messages. | 1 | 2 | 3 | 4 | 5 | 6 | 7 |
| 5. Identify relationship among conceptual themes as expressed by the client. | 1 | 2 | 3 | 4 | 5 | 6 | 7 |
| 6. Respond to important developments in the session. | 1 | 2 | 3 | 4 | 5 | 6 | 7 |
| 7. Trust his or her insights during therapy session. | 1 | 2 | 3 | 4 | 5 | 6 | 7 |
| 8. Appear comfortable in the role of therapist. | 1 | 2 | 3 | 4 | 5 | 6 | 7 |
| 9. Allow the client to see the *person* behind the *role* of therapist. | 1 | 2 | 3 | 4 | 5 | 6 | 7 |
| 10. Recognize the significance of client statements in relation to the presenting problem. | 1 | 2 | 3 | 4 | 5 | 6 | 7 |
| 11. Keep the session moving toward some therapeutic outcome. | 1 | 2 | 3 | 4 | 5 | 6 | 7 |
| 12. Help the client identify appropriate outcome and/or process goals. | 1 | 2 | 3 | 4 | 5 | 6 | 7 |
| 13. Convey competence to client. | 1 | 2 | 3 | 4 | 5 | 6 | 7 |
| 14. Resist being threatened by, or defensive with, the client. | 1 | 2 | 3 | 4 | 5 | 6 | 7 |
| 15. Convey warmth and caring to the client. | 1 | 2 | 3 | 4 | 5 | 6 | 7 |
| 16. Overall, the therapist seems to know what he or she is doing. | 1 | 2 | 3 | 4 | 5 | 6 | 7 |
| 17. Overall, the therapist seems to have conceptualized the case correctly. | 1 | 2 | 3 | 4 | 5 | 6 | 7 |
| 18. Overall, the therapist seems congruent as a therapist. | 1 | 2 | 3 | 4 | 5 | 6 | 7 |

Evaluation of Therapist Performance
Short Form* *(cont.)*

KEY
EVALUATION OF THERAPIST PERFORMANCE: SHORT FORM

Process skills items: 2, 3, 6, 10, and 13.

Conceptualization skills items: 1, 4, 5, 11, and 12.

Personalization skills items: 7, 8, 9, 14, and 15.

*Developed by Janine M. Bernard, 1982

# APPENDIX C

# SUPERVISION INSTRUMENTS

## SUPERVISORY STYLES INVENTORY*

**For trainees' form:**  Please indicate your perception of the style of your current or most recent supervisor of psychotherapy/counseling on each of the following descriptors. Circle the number on the scale, from 1 to 7, which best reflects your view of him or her.

**For supervisors' form:**  Please indicate your perception of your style as a supervisor of psychotherapy/counseling on each of the following descriptors. Circle the number on the scale, from 1 to 7, which best reflects your view of yourself.

|  | 1<br>not<br>very | 2 | 3 | 4 | 5 | 6 | 7<br>very |
|---|---|---|---|---|---|---|---|
| 1. goal-oriented | 1 | 2 | 3 | 4 | 5 | 6 | 7 |
| 2. perceptive | 1 | 2 | 3 | 4 | 5 | 6 | 7 |
| 3. concrete | 1 | 2 | 3 | 4 | 5 | 6 | 7 |
| 4. explicit | 1 | 2 | 3 | 4 | 5 | 6 | 7 |
| 5. committed | 1 | 2 | 3 | 4 | 5 | 6 | 7 |
| 6. affirming | 1 | 2 | 3 | 4 | 5 | 6 | 7 |
| 7. practical | 1 | 2 | 3 | 4 | 5 | 6 | 7 |
| 8. sensitive | 1 | 2 | 3 | 4 | 5 | 6 | 7 |
| 9. collaborative | 1 | 2 | 3 | 4 | 5 | 6 | 7 |
| 10. intuitive | 1 | 2 | 3 | 4 | 5 | 6 | 7 |
| 11. reflective | 1 | 2 | 3 | 4 | 5 | 6 | 7 |
| 12. responsive | 1 | 2 | 3 | 4 | 5 | 6 | 7 |
| 13. structured | 1 | 2 | 3 | 4 | 5 | 6 | 7 |
| 14. evaluative | 1 | 2 | 3 | 1 | 5 | 6 | 7 |
| 15. friendly | 1 | 2 | 3 | 4 | 5 | 6 | 7 |
| 16. flexible | 1 | 2 | 3 | 4 | 5 | 6 | 7 |
| 17. prescriptive | 1 | 2 | 3 | 4 | 5 | 6 | 7 |
| 18. didactic | 1 | 2 | 3 | 4 | 5 | 6 | 7 |
| 19. thorough | 1 | 2 | 3 | 4 | 5 | 6 | 7 |
| 20. focused | 1 | 2 | 3 | 4 | 5 | 6 | 7 |
| 21. creative | 1 | 2 | 3 | 4 | 5 | 6 | 7 |
| 22. supportive | 1 | 2 | 3 | 4 | 5 | 6 | 7 |
| 23. open | 1 | 2 | 3 | 4 | 5 | 6 | 7 |
| 24. realistic | 1 | 2 | 3 | 4 | 5 | 6 | 7 |
| 25. resourceful | 1 | 2 | 3 | 4 | 5 | 6 | 7 |

*Developed by M. L. Friedlander and L. G. Ward (1984). Unpublished instrument.

| | | | | | | |
|---|---|---|---|---|---|---|
| 26. invested | 1 | 2 | 3 | 4 | 5 | 6 | 7 |
| 27. facilitative | 1 | 2 | 3 | 4 | 5 | 6 | 7 |
| 28. therapeutic | 1 | 2 | 3 | 4 | 5 | 6 | 7 |
| 29. positive | 1 | 2 | 3 | 4 | 5 | 6 | 7 |
| 30. trusting | 1 | 2 | 3 | 4 | 5 | 6 | 7 |
| 31. informative | 1 | 2 | 3 | 4 | 5 | 6 | 7 |
| 32. humorous | 1 | 2 | 3 | 4 | 5 | 6 | 7 |
| 33. warm | 1 | 2 | 3 | 4 | 5 | 6 | 7 |

Scoring Key for SSI

Attractive:     Sum items 15, 16, 22, 23, 29, 39, 339; divide by 7.
Interpersonally sensitive:     Sum items 2, 5, 10, 11, 21, 25, 26, 28; divide by 8.
Task oriented:     Sum items 1, 3, 4, 7, 13, 14, 17, 18, 19, 20; divide by 10
Filler items:     6, 8, 9, 12, 24, 27, 31, 32

## COUNSELOR EVALUATION OF SUPERVISORS*

| | Strongly disagree | | Somewhat agree | | Strongly agree | | |
|---|---|---|---|---|---|---|---|

My supervisor:

1. Provides me with useful feedback regarding counseling behavior.    1 2 3 4 5 6 7
2. Helps me feel at ease with the supervision process.    1 2 3 4 5 6 7
3. Makes supervision a constructive learning process.    1 2 3 4 5 6 7
4. Provides me with specific help in areas I need to work on.    1 2 3 4 5 6 7
5. Addresses issues relevant to my current concerns as a counselor.    1 2 3 4 5 6 7
6. Helps me focus on new alternative counseling strategies that I can use with my clients.    1 2 3 4 5 6 7
7. Helps me focus on how my counseling behavior influences the client.    1 2 3 4 5 6 7
8. Encourages me to try alternative counseling skills.    1 2 3 4 5 6 7
9. Structures supervision appropriately.    1 2 3 4 5 6 7
10. Adequately emphasizes the development of my strengths and capabilities.    1 2 3 4 5 6 7
11. Enables me to brainstorm solutions, responses, and techniques that would be helpful in future counseling situations.    1 2 3 4 5 6 7
12. Enables me to become actively involved in the supervision process.    1 2 3 4 5 6 7
13. Makes me feel accepted and respected as a person.    1 2 3 4 5 6 7
14. Deals appropriately with the affect in my counseling sessions.    1 2 3 4 5 6 7
15. Deals appropriately with the content in my counseling sessions.    1 2 3 4 5 6 7

*Developed by Janine M. Bernard, 1976; Revised 1981.

| | Strongly disagree | | Somewhat agree | | | Strongly agree | |
|---|---|---|---|---|---|---|---|
| 16. Motivates me to assess my own counseling behavior. | 1 | 2 | 3 | 4 | 5 | 6 | 7 |
| 17. Conveys competence. | 1 | 2 | 3 | 4 | 5 | 6 | 7 |
| 18. Is helpful in critiquing report writing. | 1 | 2 | 3 | 4 | 5 | 6 | 7 |
| 19. Helps me use tests constructively in counseling. | 1 | 2 | 3 | 4 | 5 | 6 | 7 |
| 20. Appropriately addresses interpersonal dynamics between self and counselor. | 1 | 2 | 3 | 4 | 5 | 6 | 7 |
| 21. Can accept feedback from counselor. | 1 | 2 | 3 | 4 | 5 | 6 | 7 |
| 22. Helps reduce defensiveness in supervision. | 1 | 2 | 3 | 4 | 5 | 6 | 7 |
| 23. Enables me to express opinions, questions and concerns about my counseling. | 1 | 2 | 3 | 4 | 5 | 6 | 7 |
| 24. Prepares me adequately for my next counseling session. | 1 | 2 | 3 | 4 | 5 | 6 | 7 |
| 25. Helps me clarify my counseling objectives. | 1 | 2 | 3 | 4 | 5 | 6 | 7 |
| 26. Provides me with opportunity to adequately discuss the major difficulties I am facing with my clients. | 1 | 2 | 3 | 4 | 5 | 6 | 7 |
| 27. Encourages me to conceptualize in new ways regarding my clients. | 1 | 2 | 3 | 4 | 5 | 6 | 7 |
| 28. Motivates me and encourages me. | 1 | 2 | 3 | 4 | 5 | 6 | 7 |
| 29. Challenges me to accurately perceive the thoughts, feelings and goals of my client and myself during counseling. | 1 | 2 | 3 | 4 | 5 | 6 | 7 |
| 30. Gives me the chance to discuss personal issues related to my counseling. | 1 | 2 | 3 | 4 | 5 | 6 | 7 |
| 31. Is flexible enough for me to be spontaneous and creative. | 1 | 2 | 3 | 4 | 5 | 6 | 7 |
| 32. Focuses on the implications and consequences of specific behaviors in my counseling approach. | 1 | 2 | 3 | 4 | 5 | 6 | 7 |
| 33. Provides suggestions for developing my counseling skills. | 1 | 2 | 3 | 4 | 5 | 6 | 7 |
| 34. Encourages me to use new and different techniques when appropriate. | 1 | 2 | 3 | 4 | 5 | 6 | 7 |
| 35. Helps me to define and achieve specific concrete goals for myself during the practicum experience. | 1 | 2 | 3 | 4 | 5 | 6 | 7 |
| 36. Gives me useful feedback. | 1 | 2 | 3 | 4 | 5 | 6 | 7 |
| 37. Helps me organize relevant case data in planning goals and strategies with my client. | 1 | 2 | 3 | 4 | 5 | 6 | 7 |
| 38. Helps me develop increased skill in critiquing and gaining insight from my counseling tapes. | 1 | 2 | 3 | 4 | 5 | 6 | 7 |
| 39. Allows and encourages me to evaluate myself. | 1 | 2 | 3 | 4 | 5 | 6 | 7 |
| 40. Explains the criteria for evaluation clearly and in behavioral terms. | 1 | 2 | 3 | 4 | 5 | 6 | 7 |
| 41. Applies criteria fairly in evaluating my counseling performance. | 1 | 2 | 3 | 4 | 5 | 6 | 7 |

Additional comments:

*Note.* There are no scales to be scored for this instrument. Individual items are used for feedback to the supervisor.

**SUPERVISION QUESTIONNAIRE-REVISED***

Name _____ Supervisor's Name _____

This semester's practicum is my (circle one): 1st   2nd   3rd   4th   Intern

Site of practicum (University and agency): _____

This questionnaire is designed to evaluate the supervision you received this semester. It has two parts. The first part asks you to rate the effectiveness of the supervision you have received. The second part of the questionnaire is designed to measure more specifically the behaviors of your supervisor. Please consider each item carefully on its own merits. Try to avoid the "halo effect" in which a good supervisor tends to receive "high marks" on everything. Do not mark this second part according to how frequently you think your supervisor "should" have done each behavior; rather, rate the actual frequency of behavior. This form is used at a number of universities and agencies. It is highly likely that your supervisor never did (rating 1) some of the behaviors. Marking a 1 or 2 (or any rating for that matter) is not an indictment of or testimony for your supervisor.

I. *Effectiveness of supervision.*
   1. Satisfaction with supervision.

| Totally unsatisfied; it could not have been worse. | Mostly unsatisfied; it could have been a little worse. | More unsatisfied than not. | So-so; not really satisfied or unsatisfied. | More satisfied than not. | Mostly satisfied; could have been a little better. | Totally satisfied; it could not have been better. |
|---|---|---|---|---|---|---|

   2. How competent was your supervisor at giving good supervision?

| Totally incompetent | Mostly incompetent | More incompetent than not | So-so | More competent than not | Mostly competent | Totally competent |
|---|---|---|---|---|---|---|

   3. How much did interactions with your supervisor contribute to improvement in your counseling ability?

| Had almost no effect | Had a small effect | Had somewhat of an effect | Had a moderate effect | Had a substantial effect | Had a large effect | Had a very large effect |
|---|---|---|---|---|---|---|

II. *Description of your supervisor's behavior*
   Please rate each of the following items as to how descriptive it is of your supervisor's behavior. Use the following 5-point scale to make your ratings.

   5 — perfectly descriptive of my supervisor's behavior
   4 — usually descriptive of my supervisor's behavior
   3 — descriptive of my supervisor's behavior
   2 — occasionally descriptive of my supervisor's behavior
   1 — never (or very infrequently) descriptive of my supervisor's behavior
   My supervisor was (check one): _____Pre Ph.D. (Intern or Practicum Assistant)
                                   _____Ph.D. (Faculty or Staff)

*Originally developed by Worthington, E. L., & Roehlke, H. J. (1979): Revised by Worthington (1983). Unpublished instrument.

PLEASE RATE EVERY ITEM!

| Behavior (or Pseudo Behavior) of Supervisor | | Rating (circle one) | | | | |
|---|---|---|---|---|---|---|

1. Established good rapport with you.      1   2   3   4   5
2. Established clear goals conjointly with you against which progress in supervision was measured.      1   2   3   4   5
3. During the initial sessions the supervisor provided more structure than during later sessions.      1   2   3   4   5
4. Observed you counsel (live observation) at a minimum of one time this semester.      1   2   3   4   5
5. Observed at least three videotapes of your counseling this semester.      1   2   3   4   5
6. Listened to at least three audiotapes of your counseling this semester.      1   2   3   4   5
7. Provided relevant literature or references on specific treatment techniques or assessment techniques.      1   2   3   4   5
8. Gave appropriate feedback to you
    a. About positive counseling behaviors      1   2   3   4   5
    b. About non-facilitative behaviors      1   2   3   4   5
9. Was sensitive to the differences between how you talk about your actions and how you really behave with clients.      1   2   3   4   5
10. Modeled within the supervision session good task-oriented skills.      1   2   3   4   5
11. Gave direct suggestions to you when appropriate.      1   2   3   4   5
12. Supervisor allowed you to observe him or her, do co-counseling with him or her, listen to audiotapes of his or her counseling, or view videotapes of his or her counseling.      1   2   3   4   5
13. Supervisor was available for consulting at times other than regularly scheduled meetings.      1   2   3   4   5
14. Used the relationship between supervisor and supervisee to demonstrate principles of counseling.      1   2   3   4   5
15. Helped you to conceptualize cases. Worked together with you to evolve a joint conceptualization for clients.      1   2   3   4   5
16. Encouraged you to experiment with different assessment and intervention techniques to discover your own unique style.      1   2   3   4   5
17. Suggested specific ways to help you get your client(s) to accept your conceptualization of the client's problems.      1   2   3   4   5
18. Used humor in supervision sessions.      1   2   3   4   5
19. Labeled counselor behavior as effective or ineffective rather than right or wrong.      1   2   3   4   5
20. Helped you develop self-confidence as an emerging counselor.      1   2   3   4   5
21. Helped you realize that trying new skills usually seems awkward at first.      1   2   3   4   5
22. Confronted you when appropriate.      1   2   3   4   5
23. Helped you assess your own:
    a. strengths      1   2   3   4   5
    b. weaknesses      1   2   3   4   5
24. Evaluated you at mid-semester.      1   2   3   4   5
25. Re-negotiated goals with you at mid-semester.      1   2   3   4   5
26. Called you by name at least one time per session.      1   2   3   4   5
27. Provided suggestions for alternative ways of conceptualizing clients.      1   2   3   4   5
28. Provided suggestions for alternative ways of intervening with clients.      1   2   3   4   5
29. Discussed with you experiences in the practicum class in addition to clients.      1   2   3   4   5
30. Gave emotional support to you when appropriate.      1   2   3   4   5

31. Supervisor taught you specific counseling behaviors intended to facilitate your style. 1 2 3 4 5
32. Encouraged you to find your own style of counseling. 1 2 3 4 5
33. Helped you with personal problems that may interfere with your counseling. 1 2 3 4 5
34. Supervisor demonstrated, by role playing, techniques of intervention. 1 2 3 4 5
35. Helped you deal with your own defensiveness when it arose in supervision. 1 2 3 4 5
36. Supervisor shared his or her own experiences with clients with you. 1 2 3 4 5
37. Supervisor consulted with you when emergencies arose with your clients. 1 2 3 4 5
38. Supervisor missed no more than one supervisory session per semester. (If a missed session was rescheduled and made up, it is not counted as missed.) 1 2 3 4 5
39. Supevisory sessions lasted at least 50 minutes. 1 2 3 4 5
40. At least 45 minutes of each supervisory session were spent discussing counseling and/or clients. 1 2 3 4 5
41. Focus of most supervision sessions was on the relationship between supervisor and supervisee. 1 2 3 4 5
42. Focus of most supervision sessions was on content of counseling sessions. 1 2 3 4 5
43. Focus of most supervision sessions was on conceptualizing the dynamics of the client's personality. 1 2 3 4 5
44. Supervisor made it easy to give feedback about the supervision process. 1 2 3 4 5
45. Helped you develop skills at intake interviews. 1 2 3 4 5
46. Helped prepare you for consultation and case disposition after intake interviews.

*Note.* There are no scales to be scored for this instrument. Individual items are to be used for feedback to the supervisor. However, results of a factor analytic study of the instrument are available from Professor Workington, Department of Psychology, Virginia Commonwealth University.

## SUPERVISOR EMPHASIS RATING FORM*

*Directions:* Below are listed a number of skills and behaviors that many supervisors consider important for counselors to exhibit in counselor training. Please read each carefully and then decide which of the skills of behaviors you *most emphasize* in supervision with trainees *at the beginning Master's level.* Please respond to what you emphasize, *not wh t* you consider to be desirable counselor behaviors. Use the following scale to respond to each item.

| 7 | 6 | 5 | 4 | 3 | 2 | 1 |
|---|---|---|---|---|---|---|
| strong emphasis | | moderate | | some emphasis | little | no emphasis |

_____ 1. The counselor is on time for client appointments.
_____ 2. The counselor exhibits appropriate eye contact.
_____ 3. The counselor is aware of socio-economic and/or cultural factors that may influence the counseling session.
_____ 4. The counselor understands how people are the same even though they may be worked with differently.
_____ 5. The counselor communicates his/her sincerity and genuineness to the client.

*From Lanning, W. (1986). Development of the supervisor emphasis rating form. *Counselor Education and Supervision,* 25(3), 191–196, 207–208. Copyright (1986) by the American Association for Counseling and Development. Reprinted by permission.

_____ 6. The counselor actively participates in professional organizations.

_____ 7. The counselor conceptualizes a client accurately within a theoretical frame of reference.

_____ 8. The counselor recognizes when a client needs help in continuing to cope.

_____ 9. The counselor engages in adequate preparation for counseling sessions.

_____ 10. The counselor reinforces appropriate client behavior.

_____ 11. The counselor communicates his/her respect and positive regard to the client.

_____ 12. The counselor appropriately summarizes client statements.

_____ 13. The counselor allows him/herself the freedom to be wrong in the counseling session.

_____ 14. The counselor is able to prioritize client problems.

_____ 15. The counselor maintains appropriate conduct in personal relationships with clients.

_____ 16. The counselor engages in appropriate non-verbal expressions.

_____ 17. The counselor recognizes and admits when he/she enters into a "power struggle" with the client.

_____ 18. The counselor is able to set attainable goals in line with client readiness.

_____ 19. The counselor is aware of his/her personal needs for approval from the client.

_____ 20. The counselor accurately reflects the content of a client's speech.

_____ 21. The counselor maintains appropriate relationships with professional colleagues.

_____ 22. The counselor is able to identify client themes.

_____ 23. The counselor maintains confidentiality of client information.

_____ 24. The counselor uses open-ended questions and allows the client maximum freedom of expression.

_____ 25. The counselor demonstrates the use of open-ended questions.

_____ 26. The counselor maintains a non-judgmental attitude despite value differences with a client.

_____ 27. The counselor makes appropriate use of additional information obtained from other professional sources.

_____ 28. The counselor is able to identify and manage personal feelings that are generated in counseling.

_____ 29. The counselor maintains a receptive and appropriate posture during the session.

_____ 30. The counselor dresses appropriately.

_____ 31. The counselor is able to choose and apply techniques appropriately.

_____ 32. The counselor is able to manage a strong expression of client's feelings.

_____ 33. The counseling is aware of the effects of his/her own anxiety in the counseling process.

_____ 34. The counselor understands which techniques are compatible and consistent with his/her stated theoretical model.

_____ 35. The counselor makes appropriate referrals of clients.

_____ 36. The counselor formulates specific plans and strategies for client behavior change.

_____ 37. The counselor takes advantage of opportunities for additional training.

_____ 38. The counselor can affectively manage his/her frustrations with lack of progress with clients.

_____ 39. The counselor is aware of how his/her attraction to the client is effecting the counseling process.

_____ 40. The counselor engages in appropriate confrontation with the client.

_____ 41. The counselor is able to risk self in counseling with a client.

_____ 42. The counselor maintains her/his office neatly and orderly.

_____ 43. The counselor is able to interpret client behavior within a coherent theoretical framework.

_____ 44. The counselor identifies the need for and uses immediacy appropriately.

_____ 45. The counselor is able to develop short and long term goals with a client.

_____ 46. The counselor recognizes when he/she needs consultative help from another professional.

_____ 47. The counselor is able to tolerate ambiguity in the counseling sessions.

_____ 48. The counselor responds to client non-verbal behavior.

_____ 49. The counselor keeps appointments with clients.

_____ 50. The counselor receives feedback in a non-defensive fashion.
_____ 51. The counselor is knowledgeable about ethical codes of behavior.
_____ 52. The counselor engages in adequate note-keeping on clients.
_____ 53. The counselor uses appropriate reflection of feeling with a client.
_____ 54. The counselor prepares clients for termination.
_____ 55. The counselor shows a commitment to personal growth.
_____ 56. The counselor is able to predict the effects on a client of the techniques applied in counseling.
_____ 57. The counselor recognizes his/her personal limitations and strengths.
_____ 58. The counselor is aware of the client's potential for successful counseling progress.
_____ 59. The counselor is aware of his/her own needs and conflicts.
_____ 60. The counselor is able to keep personal problems out of the counseling session.

Key
Supervisor Emphasis Rating Form

**SUPERVISION FOCUS**
**ITEMS BY CATEGORY**

|  | Professional Behavior | Process | Personal | Conceptual |
|---|---|---|---|---|
| 1. | 1 | 2 | 13 | 3 |
| 2. | 6 | 5 | 17 | 4 |
| 3. | 9 | 10 | 19 | 7 |
| 4. | 15 | 11 | 26 | 8 |
| 5. | 21 | 12 | 28 | 14 |
| 6. | 23 | 16 | 33 | 18 |
| 7. | 30 | 20 | 38 | 22 |
| 8. | 35 | 24 | 39 | 27 |
| 9. | 37 | 25 | 41 | 31 |
| 10. | 42 | 29 | 47 | 34 |
| 11. | 46 | 32 | 50 | 36 |
| 12. | 49 | 40 | 55 | 43 |
| 13. | 51 | 44 | 57 | 45 |
| 14. | 52 | 48 | 59 | 56 |
| 15. | 54 | 53 | 60 | 58 |

## THE SUPERVISORY FOCUS AND STYLE QUESTIONNAIRE*

### Personality Subscales

AFFECTION = Affection Needs expressed or desired
INCLUSION = Inclusion Needs expressed or desired
CONTROL = Control Needs expressed or desired

*From Yager, G. G., Wilson, F. R., Brewer, D., & Kinnetz, P. (1989). *The development and validation of an instrument to measure counseling supervisor focus and style.* Paper presented at the annual meeting of the American Education Research Association, San Francisco. Unpublished instrument.

## Supervisory Focus Subscales

PROCESS = Supervisor focus on process skills and issues
CONCEPTUALIZATION = Supervisor focus on conceptualizing the concerns of the client
PERSONALIZATION = Supervisor focus on the personal issues of the counselor, as these relate to counseling

## Supervisory Style Subscales

TEACHING = Supervisory style is didactic/instructional
COUNSELING = Supervisory style is therapeutic/experiential
CONSULTATION = Supervisory style is collegial/peer-to-peer

Supervision Questionnaire

### PART I: ATTRIBUTES OF THE SUPERVISORS

*Directions:* Please read each of the items in this questionnaire carefully. Taking into account the specific characteristics (e.g., background and training) of the counselor described in the short vignette you have just read, indicate your level of agreement with each statement below. Use the following scale to respond to each item:

1 — Strongly Agree (SA)
2 — Agree (A)
3 — Disagree (D)
4 — Strongly Disagree (SD)

|  | SA | A | D | SD |
|---|---|---|---|---|
| 1. I would be friendly with the supervisee. | 1 | 2 | 3 | 4 |
| 2. I would like my supervisee to maintain a professional distance during supervision. | 1 | 2 | 3 | 4 |
| 3. I would like the supervisee to invite me to join in informal discussions. | 1 | 2 | 3 | 4 |
| 4. I would decide what topics to discuss during supervision. | 1 | 2 | 3 | 4 |
| 5. I would like my supervisee to feel comfortable to confide in me regarding personal concerns and issues. | 1 | 2 | 3 | 4 |
| 6. I would like to be asked to help with the supervisee's educational development. | 1 | 2 | 3 | 4 |
| 7. I would make strong attempts to influence the supervisee's case conceptualization and the choice of counseling strategies. | 1 | 2 | 3 | 4 |
| 8. I would disclose issues of a deeply personal nature with my supervisee. | 1 | 2 | 3 | 4 |
| 9. I would allow the supervisee to evaluate the effectiveness of the on-going counseling sessions. | 1 | 2 | 3 | 4 |
| 10. I would try to be included in the supervisee's other educational experiences. | 1 | 2 | 3 | 4 |
| 11. I would let the supervisee take the lead in supervision sessions. | 1 | 2 | 3 | 4 |
| 12. My relationship with the supervisee would be strictly professional. | 1 | 2 | 3 | 4 |
| 13. I would invite the supervisee to participate in some of my own professional activities. | 1 | 2 | 3 | 4 |
| 14. I would let the supervisee influence strongly my view of the conceptualization of the counseling case and the selection of counseling strategies to be used. | 1 | 2 | 3 | 4 |
| 15. I would take charge of evaluating the success of the supervisee's on-going counseling. | 1 | 2 | 3 | 4 |
| 16. I would like the supervisee to invite me to join in his/her professional activities. | 1 | 2 | 3 | 4 |
| 17. I would initiate informal contacts with the supervisee. | 1 | 2 | 3 | 4 |
| 18. I would like my supervisee to act in a friendly manner toward me. | 1 | 2 | 3 | 4 |

## PART II: FOCUS OF THE SUPERVISION

*Directions:* In this section of the questionnaire, please indicate (using the same four-point rating scale) the level of your agreement with each of the following statements. These statements concern issues that you might or might not be likely to address during a supervision session with the individual described in the written vignette you have just read.

I WOULD EMPHASIZE DURING MY SUPERVISORY SESSIONS WITH THIS SUPERVISEE:

|  | SA | A | D | SD |
|---|---|---|---|---|
| 19. The supervisee's communication of sincerity, genuineness, respect and positive regard for the client. | 1 | 2 | 3 | 4 |
| 20. The supervisee's ability to conceptualize a client accurately within a theoretical frame of reference. | 1 | 2 | 3 | 4 |
| 21. The supervisee's ability to prioritize client problems. | 1 | 2 | 3 | 4 |
| 22. The supervisee's recognition and admission of possible "power struggles" with a client. | 1 | 2 | 3 | 4 |
| 23. The supervisee's awareness of personal needs for approval from the client. | 1 | 2 | 3 | 4 |
| 24. The identification of general themes within the client's on-going presentations. | 1 | 2 | 3 | 4 |
| 25. The use of open-ended questions to allow the maximum freedom of expression for the client. | 1 | 2 | 3 | 4 |
| 26. The identification and management of personal feelings that are generated in counseling. | 1 | 2 | 3 | 4 |
| 27. An understanding of techniques compatible and consistent with the supervisee's stated theoretical model. | 1 | 2 | 3 | 4 |
| 28. Awareness of how attraction to the client can affect the counseling process. | 1 | 2 | 3 | 4 |
| 29. Appropriate methods to confront a client. | 1 | 2 | 3 | 4 |
| 30. The willingness and ability to risk oneself in the process of counseling a client. | 1 | 2 | 3 | 4 |
| 31. Interpretation of client behaviors within a coherent theoretical framework. | 1 | 2 | 3 | 4 |
| 32. The ability to tolerate ambiguity in the counseling sessions. | 1 | 2 | 3 | 4 |
| 33. The supervisee's response to client nonverbal behavior. | 1 | 2 | 3 | 4 |
| 34. Appropriate reflection of feeling within a client session. | 1 | 2 | 3 | 4 |
| 35. Preparation for client termination. | 1 | 2 | 3 | 4 |
| 36. The supervisee's commitment to personal growth and self-knowledge. | 1 | 2 | 3 | 4 |
| 37. The ability of the supervisee to predict the effects on a client of the techniques applied to counseling. | 1 | 2 | 3 | 4 |
| 38. The awareness of the client's potential for successful counseling progress. | 1 | 2 | 3 | 4 |
| 39. The ability to keep supervisee personal problems out of the counseling session. | 1 | 2 | 3 | 4 |

### Part III: Supervisor Style

*Directions:* In this section, please indicate, again using the same four-point scale, the extent of your agreement with each of the following statements relating to your potential actions toward or direction of the supervisee described in the vignette you have read.

|  | SA | A | D | SD |
|---|---|---|---|---|
| 40. I would refer the supervisee to appropriate readings from counseling/psychotherapy texts. | 1 | 2 | 3 | 4 |

| | SA | A | D | SD |
|---|---|---|---|---|
| 41. I would want to establish mutually-determined goals for the content of each supervisory session. | 1 | 2 | 3 | 4 |
| 42. I would devote considerable attention to the supervisee's feelings about this client case. | 1 | 2 | 3 | 4 |
| 43. I would answer the supervisee's questions about the client sessions as directly and as clearly as possible. | 1 | 2 | 3 | 4 |
| 44. I would give supervisee examples of possible ways to handle client concerns. | 1 | 2 | 3 | 4 |
| 45. I would focus on the counselor's interpersonal dynamics as illustrated in the relationship with this client. | 1 | 2 | 3 | 4 |
| 46. I would remain flexible during this supervision to give advice and direct feedback or to explore personal issues. | 1 | 2 | 3 | 4 |
| 47. I would suggest we role-play the counseling interaction that the supervisee has described. | 1 | 2 | 3 | 4 |
| 48. I would use empathy as an important supervisory tool. | 1 | 2 | 3 | 4 |
| 49. I would brainstorm with this supervisee concerning possible conceptualizations of the client's concern. | 1 | 2 | 3 | 4 |
| 50. I would encourage the supervisee to ask questions about whatever information I conveyed during the supervision session. | 1 | 2 | 3 | 4 |
| 51. I would direct attention to the supervisee's relationship with me and would try to draw parallels between our relationship and the client/counselor relationship. | 1 | 2 | 3 | 4 |
| 52. I would encourage the supervisee to speak about his/her past history and learning experiences. | 1 | 2 | 3 | 4 |
| 53. I would treat supervision relatively informally, much like a discussion between two colleagues. | 1 | 2 | 3 | 4 |
| 54. I would give examples from both readings and from my own experience to illustrate the points I wish the supervisee to remember. | 1 | 2 | 3 | 4 |
| 55. I would listen to the audiotape of the counseling session and, on occasion, I would offer my reactions and feedback. | 1 | 2 | 3 | 4 |
| 56. I would be certain to mention at least several reactions/ideas/suggestions regarding what might be done in the next counseling session. | 1 | 2 | 3 | 4 |
| 57. I would behave in much the same manner with this supervisee as I behave with most of my clients. | 1 | 2 | 3 | 4 |
| 58. I would use self-disclosure of my own client cases and my own emotional reactions with clients. | 1 | 2 | 3 | 4 |
| 59. I would attempt to aid this counselor to feel more adequate during subsequent counseling contacts. | 1 | 2 | 3 | 4 |
| 60. I would allow the supervisee to reject or accept my feedback; the supervisee would be allowed to choose how/if my ideas might be implemented with the client. | 1 | 2 | 3 | 4 |

## Key
## The Supervisory Focus and Style Questionnaire

*Personality Subscales:*

Affection: 1, 2, 5, 8, 12, 18.
Inclusion: 3, 6, 10, 13, 16, 17.
Control: 4, 7, 9, 11, 14, 15.

Key
The Supervisory Focus and Style Questionnaire *(cont.)*

*Supervisory Focus Subscales:*

Process: 19, 22, 25, 29, 33, 34, 35.
Conceptualization: 20, 21, 24, 27, 31, 37, 38.
Personalization: 23, 26, 28, 30, 32, 36, 39.

*Supervisory Style Subscales:*

Teaching: 40, 44, 47, 50, 54, 55, 56.
Counseling: 42, 45, 48, 51, 52, 57, 59.
Consultation: 41, 43, 46, 49, 53, 58, 60.

## SUPERVISORY WORKING ALLIANCE INVENTORY*

Supervisor Form

### INSTRUCTIONS

Please indicate the frequency with which the behavior described in each of the following items seems characteristic of your work with your supervisee. After each item, check (X) the space over the number corresponding to the appropriate point on the following seven-point scale:

| | 1 | 2 | 3 | 4 | 5 | 6 | 7 |
|---|---|---|---|---|---|---|---|
| | Almost Never | | | | | | Almost Always |

1. I help my trainee work within a specific treatment plan with his/her client.

   1   2   3   4   5   6   7

2. I help my trainee stay on track during our meetings.

   1   2   3   4   5   6   7

3. My style is to carefully and systematically consider the material that my trainee brings to supervision.

   1   2   3   4   5   6   7

4. My trainee works with me on specific goals in the supervisory session.

   1   2   3   4   5   6   7

5. In supervision, I expect my trainee to think about or reflect on my comments to him or her.

   1   2   3   4   5   6   7

6. I teach my trainee through direct suggestion.

   1   2   3   4   5   6   7

*The supervisor and supervisee forms of the Supervisory Working Alliance are reprinted with permission by the American Psychological Association. From: Efstation, J. F., Patton, M. J., & Kardash, C. M. (1990). Measuring the working alliance in counselor supervision. *Journal of Counseling Psychology, 37,* 322–329.

| | 1<br>Almost<br>Never | 2 | 3 | 4 | 5 | 6 | 7<br>Almost<br>Always |
|---|---|---|---|---|---|---|---|

7. In supervision, I place a high priority on our understanding the client's perspective.

   1    2    3    4    5    6    7

8. I encourage my trainee to take time to understand what the client is saying and doing.

   1    2    3    4    5    6    7

9. When correcting my trainee's errors with a client, I offer alternative ways of intervening.

   1    2    3    4    5    6    7

10. I encourage my trainee to formulate his/her own interventions with his/her clients.

   1    2    3    4    5    6    7

11. I encourage my trainee to talk about the work in ways that are comfortable for him/her.

   1    2    3    4    5    6    7

12. I welcome my trainee's explanations about his/her client's behavior.

   1    2    3    4    5    6    7

13. During supervision, my trainee talks more than I do.

   1    2    3    4    5    6    7

14. I make an effort to understand my trainee.

   1    2    3    4    5    6    7

15. I am tactful when commenting about my trainee's performance.

   1    2    3    4    5    6    7

16. I facilitate my trainee's talking in our sessions.

   1    2    3    4    5    6    7

17. In supervision, my trainee is more curious than anxious when discussing his/her difficulties with me.

   1    2    3    4    5    6    7

18. My trainee appears to be comfortable working with me.

   1    2    3    4    5    6    7

19. My trainee understands client behavior and treatment techniques similar to the way I do.

   1    2    3    4    5    6    7

20. During supervision, my trainee seems able to stand back and reflect on what I am saying to him/her.

   1    2    3    4    5    6    7

21. I stay in tune with my trainee during supervision.

   1    2    3    4    5    6    7

22. My trainee identifies with me in the way he/she thinks and talks about his/her clients.

   1    2    3    4    5    6    7

| | 1 | 2 | 3 | 4 | 5 | 6 | 7 |
|---|---|---|---|---|---|---|---|
| | Almost | | | | | | Almost |
| | Never | | | | | | Always |

23. My trainee consistently implements suggestions made in supervision.

|  | 1 | 2 | 3 | 4 | 5 | 6 | 7 |
|---|---|---|---|---|---|---|---|

---

## SCORING

The supervisor form of the SWAI has three scales, Rapport, Client Focus, and Identification. They are scored as follows.

Rapport: Sum items 10–16, then divide by 7.
Client Focus: Sum items 1–9, then divide by 9.
Identification: Sum items 17–23, then divide by 7.

---

Trainee Form

---

## INSTRUCTIONS

Please indicate the frequency with which the behavior described in each of the following items seems characteristic of your work with your supervisee. After each item, check (X) the space over the number corresponding to the appropriate point on the following seven-point scale:

| | 1 | 2 | 3 | 4 | 5 | 6 | 7 |
|---|---|---|---|---|---|---|---|
| | Almost | | | | | | Almost |
| | Never | | | | | | Always |

1. I feel comfortable working with my supervisor.

| | 1 | 2 | 3 | 4 | 5 | 6 | 7 |
|---|---|---|---|---|---|---|---|

2. My supervisor welcomes my explanations about the client's behavior.

| | 1 | 2 | 3 | 4 | 5 | 6 | 7 |
|---|---|---|---|---|---|---|---|

3. My supervisor makes the effort to understand me.

| | 1 | 2 | 3 | 4 | 5 | 6 | 7 |
|---|---|---|---|---|---|---|---|

4. My supervisor encourages me to talk about my work with clients in ways that are comfortable for me.

| | 1 | 2 | 3 | 4 | 5 | 6 | 7 |
|---|---|---|---|---|---|---|---|

5. My supervisor is tactful when commenting about my performance.

| | 1 | 2 | 3 | 4 | 5 | 6 | 7 |
|---|---|---|---|---|---|---|---|

6. My supervisor encourages me to formulate my own interventions with the client.

| | 1 | 2 | 3 | 4 | 5 | 6 | 7 |
|---|---|---|---|---|---|---|---|

7. My supervisor helps me talk freely in our sessions.

| | 1 | 2 | 3 | 4 | 5 | 6 | 7 |
|---|---|---|---|---|---|---|---|

8. My supervisor stays in tune with me during supervision.

| | 1 | 2 | 3 | 4 | 5 | 6 | 7 |
|---|---|---|---|---|---|---|---|

| | 1 Almost Never | 2 | 3 | 4 | 5 | 6 | 7 Almost Always |
|---|---|---|---|---|---|---|---|

9. I understand client behavior and treatment technique similar to the way my supervisor does.

|   | 1 | 2 | 3 | 4 | 5 | 6 | 7 |

10. I feel free to mention to my supervisor any troublesome feelings I might have about him/her.

|   | 1 | 2 | 3 | 4 | 5 | 6 | 7 |

11. My supervisor treats me like a colleague in our supervisory sessions.

|   | 1 | 2 | 3 | 4 | 5 | 6 | 7 |

12. In supervision, I am more curious than anxious when discussing my difficulties with clients.

|   | 1 | 2 | 3 | 4 | 5 | 6 | 7 |

13. In supervision, my supervisor places a high priority on our understanding the client's perspective.

|   | 1 | 2 | 3 | 4 | 5 | 6 | 7 |

14. My supervisor encourages me to take time to understand what the client is saying and doing.

|   | 1 | 2 | 3 | 4 | 5 | 6 | 7 |

15. My supervisor's style is to carefully and systematically consider the material I bring to supervision.

|   | 1 | 2 | 3 | 4 | 5 | 6 | 7 |

16. When correcting my errors with a client, my supervisor offers alternative ways of intervening with that client.

|   | 1 | 2 | 3 | 4 | 5 | 6 | 7 |

17. My supervisor helps me work within a specific treatment plan with my clients.

|   | 1 | 2 | 3 | 4 | 5 | 6 | 7 |

18. My supervisor helps me stay on track during our meetings.

|   | 1 | 2 | 3 | 4 | 5 | 6 | 7 |

19. I work with my supervisor on specific goals in the supervisory session.

|   | 1 | 2 | 3 | 4 | 5 | 6 | 7 |

## SCORING

The trainee form of the SWAI has two scales, Rapport and Client Focus. They are scored as follows.
    Rapport:  Sum items 1–12, then divide by 12.
Client Focus:  Sum items 13–19, then divide by 6.

**WORKING ALLIANCE INVENTORY***

Supervisor Form

---

**INSTRUCTIONS**

---

The following sentences describe some of the different ways a person might think or feel about his or her supervisee. As you read the sentences, mentally insert the name of your supervisee in place of _____ in the text.

With each statement there is a seven-point scale:

---

| 1 | 2 | 3 | 4 | 5 | 6 Very | 7 |
|---|---|---|---|---|---|---|
| Never | Rarely | Occasionally | Sometimes | Often | Often | Always |

---

If the statement describes the way you *always* feel (or think), circle the number "7;" if it *never* applies to you, circle the number "1." Use the numbers in between to describe the variations between these extremes.

This questionnaire is confidential. Neither your supervisee nor the agency will see your answers.

Please work fast: Your first impressions are the ones we would like to have. PLEASE DO NOT FORGET TO RESPOND TO *EVERY* ITEM

Thank you for your cooperation.

1 — Never
2 — Rarely
3 — Occasionally
4 — Sometimes
5 — Often
6 — Very Often
7 — Always

---

1. I feel uncomfortable with _____ 1  2  3  4  5  6  7
2. _____ and I agree about the steps to be taken to improve his/her work as a therapist. 1  2  3  4  5  6  7
3. I have some concerns about the outcome of these sessions. 1  2  3  4  5  6  7
4. _____ and I both feel confident about the usefulness of our current activity in supervision. 1  2  3  4  5  6  7
5. _____ and I have a common perception of her/his goals. 1  2  3  4  5  6  7
6. I feel I really understand _____. 1  2  3  4  5  6  7
7. _____ finds what we are doing in supervision confusing. 1  2  3  4  5  6  7
8. I believe _____ likes me. 1  2  3  4  5  6  7
9. I sense a need to clarify the purpose of our sessions for _____. 1  2  3  4  5  6  7
10. I have some disagreements with _____ about the goals of these sessions. 1  2  3  4  5  6  7
11. I believe that the time _____ and I are spending together is not spent efficiently. 1  2  3  4  5  6  7
12. I have doubts about what we are trying to accomplish in supervision. 1  2  3  4  5  6  7
13. I am clear and explicit about what _____'s responsibilities are in supervision. 1  2  3  4  5  6  7

---

Reprinted with permission: Horvath, A. O. (1982). *Working Alliance Inventory* (Revised Edition). Vancouver, BC: Simon Fraser University. Additional psychometric information on the WAI can be found in Horvath and Greenberg (1989).

*Note* that these item stems were modified by Baker (1990) for use in supervision research.

| 1 | 2 | 3 | 4 | 5 | 6<br>Very | 7 |
|---|---|---|---|---|---|---|
| Never | Rarely | Occasionally | Sometimes | Often | Often | Always |

14. The current goals of these sessions are important for _____ _____. 1  2  3  4  5  6  7

15. I find that what _____ and I are doing in supervision is unrelated to his/her current concerns. 1  2  3  4  5  6  7

16. I feel confident that the things we do in supervision will help _____ to accomplish the changes he/she desires. 1  2  3  4  5  6  7

17. I am genuinely concerned for _____'s welfare. 1  2  3  4  5  6  7

18. I am clear as to what I expect _____ to do in these sessions. 1  2  3  4  5  6  7

19. _____ and I respect each other. 1  2  3  4  5  6  7

20. I feel that I am not totally honest about my feelings toward _____. 1  2  3  4  5  6  7

21. I am confident in my ability to help _____. 1  2  3  4  5  6  7

22. We are working towards mutually agreed-upon goals. 1  2  3  4  5  6  7

23. I appreciate _____ as a person. 1  2  3  4  5  6  7

24. We agree on what is important for _____ to work on. 1  2  3  4  5  6  7

25. As a result of these sessions, _____ is clearer as to how he/she might be able to improve his/her work as a therapist. 1  2  3  4  5  6  7

26. _____ and I have built a mutual trust. 1  2  3  4  5  6  7

27. _____ and I have different ideas on what his/her learning needs are. 1  2  3  4  5  6  7

28. Our relationship is important to _____. 1  2  3  4  5  6  7

29. _____ has some fears that if she/he says or does the wrong things, I will stop working with him/her. 1  2  3  4  5  6  7

30. _____ and I have collaborated in setting goals for these sessions. 1  2  3  4  5  6  7

31. _____ is frustrated by what I am asking him/her to do in supervision. 1  2  3  4  5  6  7

32. We have established a good understanding between us of the kind of changes that would be good for _____. 1  2  3  4  5  6  7

33. The things that we are doing in supervision don't make much sense to _____. 1  2  3  4  5  6  7

34. _____ doesn't know what to expect as the result of supervision. 1  2  3  4  5  6  7

35. _____ believes the way we are working with his/her issues is correct. 1  2  3  4  5  6  7

36. I respect _____ even when she/he does things I do not approve of. 1  2  3  4  5  6  7

---

Supervisee Form

### INSTRUCTIONS

The following sentences describe some of the different ways a person might think or feel about his or her supervisor. As you read the sentences, mentally insert the name of your supervisor in place of _____ in the text.

With each statement there is a seven-point scale:

| 1 | 2 | 3 | 4 | 5 | 6<br>Very | 7 |
|---|---|---|---|---|---|---|
| Never | Rarely | Occasionally | Sometimes | Often | Often | Always |

If the statement describes the way you *always* feel (or think), circle the number "7;" if it *never* applies to you, circle the number "1." Use the numbers in between to describe the variations between these extremes.

This questionnaire is confidential. Neither your supervisor nor the agency will see your answers.

Please work fast: Your first impressions are the ones we would like to have. PLEASE DO NOT FORGET TO RESPOND TO *EVERY* ITEM

Thank you for your cooperation.

1 – Never
2 – Rarely
3 – Occasionally
4 – Sometimes
5 – Often
6 – Very Often
7 – Always

---

1. I feel uncomfortable with _____. 1 2 3 4 5 6 7
2. _____ and I agree about the things I will need to do to improve my abilities as a therapist. 1 2 3 4 5 6 7
3. I am worried about the outcome of these sessions. 1 2 3 4 5 6 7
4. What I am doing in supervision gives me new ways of looking at how I approach my work as a therapist. 1 2 3 4 5 6 7
5. _____ and I understand each other. 1 2 3 4 5 6 7
6. _____ perceives accurately what my goals are. 1 2 3 4 5 6 7
7. I find what I am doing in supervision confusing. 1 2 3 4 5 6 7
8. I believe _____ likes me. 1 2 3 4 5 6 7
9. I wish _____ and I could clarify the purpose of our sessions. 1 2 3 4 5 6 7
10. I disagree with _____ about what I ought to get out of supervision. 1 2 3 4 5 6 7
11. I believe that the time _____ and I are spending together is not spent efficiently. 1 2 3 4 5 6 7
12. _____ does not understand what I am trying to accomplish in supervision. 1 2 3 4 5 6 7
13. I am clear on what my responsibilities are in supervision. 1 2 3 4 5 6 7
14. The goals of these sessions are important to me. 1 2 3 4 5 6 7
15. I find that what _____ and I are doing in supervision is unrelated to my concerns. 1 2 3 4 5 6 7
16. I feel the things I do in supervision will help me to improve as a therapist. 1 2 3 4 5 6 7
17. I believe _____ is genuinely concerned my welfare. 1 2 3 4 5 6 7
18. I am clear as to what _____ wants me to do in these sessions. 1 2 3 4 5 6 7
19. _____ and I respect each other. 1 2 3 4 5 6 7
20. I feel that _____ is not totally honest about his/her feelings toward me. 1 2 3 4 5 6 7
21. I am confident in _____'s ability to help me. 1 2 3 4 5 6 7
22. _____ and I are working towards mutually agreed-upon goals. 1 2 3 4 5 6 7
23. I feel that _____ appreciates me. 1 2 3 4 5 6 7
24. We agree on what is important for me to work on. 1 2 3 4 5 6 7
25. As a result of these sessions, I am clearer as to how I might be able to improve my work as a therapist. 1 2 3 4 5 6 7
26. _____ and I trust one another. 1 2 3 4 5 6 7
27. _____ and I have different ideas on what my difficulties are. 1 2 3 4 5 6 7
28. My relationship with _____ is very important to me. 1 2 3 4 5 6 7
29. I have the feeling that if I say or do the wrong things, _____ will stop supervising me. 1 2 3 4 5 6 7

| 1 | 2 | 3 | 4 | 5 | 6<br>Very | 7 |
|---|---|---|---|---|---|---|
| Never | Rarely | Occasionally | Sometimes | Often | Often | Always |

30. _____ and I collaborate on setting goals for my supervision. 1  2  3  4  5  6  7

31. I am frustrated by the things I am doing in supervision. 1  2  3  4  5  6  7

32. We have established a good understanding of the kind of changes that would be good for my work as a therapist. 1  2  3  4  5  6  7

33. The things that _____ is asking me to do don't make sense to me. 1  2  3  4  5  6  7

34. I don't know what to expect as the result of my supervision. 1  2  3  4  5  6  7

35. I believe the way we are working in supervision is correct. 1  2  3  4  5  6  7

36. I feel _____ cares about me even when I do things that he/she does not approve of.
1  2  3  4  5  6  7

Scoring key: ***Working Alliance Inventory***
**(both supervisor and supervisee forms)**

| Scale | Items to be summed |
|---|---|
| Task: | 2, 4, 7*, 11*, 13, 15*, 16, 18, 24, 31*, 33*, 35 |
| Bond: | 1*, 5, 8, 17, 19, 20*, 21, 23, 26, 28, 29*, 36 |
| Goal: | 3*, 6, 9*, 10*, 12*, 14, 22, 25, 27*, 30, 32, 34* |

*Note:* Items marked with asterisk (*) are scored in reverse direction

# TRANSCRIPTS OF GOODYEAR'S SUPERVISION TAPES

## INTRODUCTION

These transcripts are based on a supervision videotape series developed by Goodyear (1982). Harold (Dick) Hackney served as supervisee. Material for the supervision he received was based on counseling he provided an anonymous female client.

Ina Carlson, then a doctoral student in counseling at Purdue University, had listened to audiotapes of Hackney's first four sessions with this client. Then, in a TV studio at Purdue, Hackney counseled Carlson in the role of the client — as she imagined the client might be in the fifth session. This procedure, deemed necessary to safeguard the client's privacy, did add some artificiality to the project. But even with this apparent artificiality, meaningful material was generated.

We should note also that all this was done with the full knowledge and consent of the client. In fact, the client viewed the Hackney-Carlson studio tape and verified that it seemed to capture with some accuracy the material with which she was dealing.

The sessions with Polster, Rogers, Kagan, and Ekstein all were done in a three day period in August, 1981. The tape with Ellis was done the following April. With the exception of Kagan (whose IPR technique dictated a different procedure), all supervision was based on the supervisors having watched approximately the same brief portion of the videotape of Hackney with Carlson. The first of the following transcripts is of the segment of the therapy session that most supervisors had watched. It is followed by the supervision sessions in the following order: Polster, Rogers,* Kagan, Ekstein, and Ellis. This is the order in which supervision was provided to Hackney.

All supervision sessions except Kagan's are in response to common material — the segment of the videotape captured on the Hackney-Carlson therapy transcript. For that reason, they are especially useful in making comparisons between supervisors. For example, it is interesting to note the portion of time each supervisor spends talking (calculated by dividing the number of supervisor utterances by the total number of utterances), which is an index of supervisor activity level: Ekstein, 72.6 percent; Ellis, 82.2 percent; Polster, 46.8 percent; Rogers, 46.8 percent (this calculation has not been made for the Kagan session). Other data on the sessions are reported by Abadie (1985), Friedlander and Ward (1984), Goodyear, Abadie, and Efros (1984), Harris and Goodyear (1990), and Holloway et al. (1989).

It is interesting to see how a different picture of the client and her relationship with Hackney emerges across sessions. It also is interesting to see how two portions of the Hackney-Carlson therapy session are addressed by the supervisors: the one in which Carlson

---

*Note that the transcript of the Rogers-Hackney session originally was published in "Carl Rogers' client-centered approach to supervision," by H. Hackney and R. K. Goodyear, in *Client centered therapy and the person centered approach*, R. F. Levant and J. M. Shlien (Eds.). New York: Praeger Publishers. Reprinted with permission.

states that Hackney is the only person who listens to her, and the one in which Hackney notes that Carlson has to "smoke out" her husband.

Notice that these transcripts originally were developed by Abadie (1985) and then refined by Holloway, Freund, Gardner, Nelson, and Walker (1989). Speech disfluencies and interruptions have been retained in the transcripts for researchers who might wish to use them for supervision research.

## THERAPY SESSION: DICK HACKNEY AS COUNSELOR

**CO** = Hackney    **CL** = Client

[This segment begins midway through the 50 minute session.]

**CL:** Mmm. Yeah. I feel stuck, and if I'm going to be stuck here I want to at least like where I am.

**CO:** Yeah, yeah. So I guess what you're saying is that what you would like is to really enjoy feeling stuck.

**CL:** Well, I think if I enjoyed it I wouldn't feel stuck.

**CO:** OK.

**CL:** I mean, if I'm going to stay married to John, I'd really like to feel good about it. I'd like to feel good about not going out with other guys. Or, I don't mean going out with other guys. Or, if I want to talk to another guy, you know, I want to know that it's just because that person's a friend and not someone I have this big dream about.

**CO:** Mm hmm.

**CL:** Do you know what I mean?

**CO:** Yeah, I think what you'd like is to feel free in this relationship, and feel that you're in this relationship because it's the right place for you to be.

**CL:** Mmm. I've never felt free. I mean, maybe when I was four, but never, you know . . . I wouldn't know what that was like. I wouldn't know what that was like.

**CO:** But you're trapped right now and you don't like that, too.

**CL:** No.

**CO:** You know, we've been talking the last few minutes, mostly about John and your relationship with him, and I'm wondering if you're saying this is the relationship you'd most like to work on. Yes, there's always your mother in the background, and-uh Don, of course, is coming and going but not the dominant character so much. But John is very central. Is that where you think you'd like to put your energies?

**CL:** Mmm hmm. Yeah.

**CO:** What would you like to have happen this week between you and John? Do you have any dream of how it might all get started?

**CL:** I'd like him to talk to me. Not just like who's going to cut the grass, but I'd like him to talk to me.

**CO:** OK. Say some more.

**CL:** I'd like him to listen to me. I mean . . . it's really weird . . . I was thinking about this this week . . . I feel a little embarrassed to tell you, but the only place anybody listens to me is here. And I just don't want to have this be the only place.

**CO:** Mmm hmm.

**CL:** Because I can't come here forever.

**CO:** Mm hmm. I hope not.

**CL:** But I really wanted to come today . . . cause I wanted someone to listen to me. And it felt . . . well, I'd sure like somebody else in my life to listen to me. And to talk to me like I was a really . . . person . . . I mean, I understand why he doesn't do this. I mean I really know this. You know, he's . . . well, I've told you how things were for him when he was growing up. So I understand and so maybe I'm asking too much. But, I'd listen to him. If he'd ever talk to me, I'd listen to him. It's not that I just want something for me that I wouldn't give back. Maybe he doesn't need that.

**CO:** OK, let's . . . ummm . . . just play a game for a moment. If you were to be fortunate enough to have a meaningful conversation with John this week, can you fantasize where it might take place? Would it be at home? Would it be in the truck going from work to home? Or, would it be down in the tavern?

**CL:** No, no, not there. Gosh, no. Probably out on the back porch.

**CO:** Out on the back porch.

**CL:** Yeah, I mean, it's got screens and sometimes I like to just go out there and listen to the crickets, and you know, if he would come and sit with me . . .

**CO:** You would be out there, hoping that he would show up.

**CL:** Yeah, but he's always busy. He'd probably be fixing things around the house, and painting and stuff, so he probably wouldn't.

**CO:** OK, so there probably would not be any way that he would come out there on his own.

**CL:** Well, no . . . no, not this week. No, not this week.

**CO:** What would bring him out on the back porch?

**CL:** Well, I suppose I could ask him. I mean, he does about what I want.

**CO:** Short of asking him.

**CL:** The house caught fire?

**CO:** Well, that would probably bring him out. Smoke him out. . . . That's part of the problem, isn't it, that anytime you feel you get what you want from him, it's because you had to smoke him out.

**CL:** Mmm hmm. Mmm hmm. I'm sure I could beg him and he'd sit beside me. And I'd start to talk, and then he'd pat my arm, and say, "Oh, you want a beer?"

**CO:** That's the scene we want to avoid, isn't it? You've tried that before and it just didn't work.

**CL:** Well, I haven't tried all that hard before. I mean, because I haven't even been sure,

I mean, if I'm going to do something else.

**CO:** What would it be like, uh, if you-uh . . . do you ever have lunch out on the back porch, or dinner, or . . . ? He would come out to eat, I would think. Is that — can you imagine doing that ever?

**CL:** Well, you know, we have a little grill. I haven't used it much this summer. Just because, I mean, I never get around to buying charcoal and stuff like that. I would have to, you know, maybe get some steaks and some, well, probably hamburger . . . I would, yeah, I suppose I could cook out there. It's just a little job . . .

**CO:** Yeah, I was thinking of eating out there. You know, setting up a TV tray or two and just eating out there.

**CL:** Yeah, I suppose I could do that. I don't fuss a lot with cooking and usually . . . you know, we'll just run out and get a bag of something, you know, like some chicken or something like that, you know. But, I like to do stuff like that once in a while.

**CO:** I don't necessarily know that that's the way to do it, but it seemed to me that something as natural as eating wouldn't-uh-would be a little different than just sitting down with John and saying, "All right, John, now we're going to have a meaningful conversation."

**CL:** Well, he would, I mean, he just gets real antsy, and then I'd get mad, and say something nasty.

**CO:** Right. Maybe you need to have something to focus your attention on, or maybe John needs to have something to focus his attention on, because you said how shy he was, and I can imagine that, just from my contact with him . . . that he would get to feeling so self-conscious that minute he thought he had to perform . . .

**CL:** Or, he'd go, "Here she goes again."

**CO:** Right, right.

**CL:** I mean, I haven't done this, and I haven't, you know, but I'd get, yeah, you mean like, if he had a fork to focus on on . . .

**CO:** Or a Big Mac . . . or whatever . . .

**CL:** Well, you know, I guess I could try it, but I might chicken out. I could certainly fix the food, but . . .

**CO:** And, it wouldn't surprise me if you chickened out. I guess I want to say that. This is a, this is not an easy thing to do.

**CL:** Well, it's not. But I do things that I decide to do.

**CO:** Yeah. Oh, I think you are very good at doing things that you decide to do. I think that's part of your strength.

**CL:** Yeah, but the things that, I mean, I'm not sure I'm very, I mean, some people think I'm . . . I mean my family's so shitty that maybe in comparison, but . . .

**CO:** Well, part of who you are, Ina, is the fact that you survived your family.

**CL:** Yeah, but I get scared that I'm going to blow it. I just really do. And I'll just be down there with all the rest of them. And I'm so scared, I'm scared it's like fate. It's almost like I gotta keep on, like I can't . . . like if I relax for a second, everything's just going to go. And that's sort of like what I felt.

**CO:** That must be part of what John feels too, from you. When you want to have a closer relationship with him, the intensity that you feel must be part of that.

[The session continues.]

## SUPERVISION SESSION 1: ERVING POLSTER SUPERVISING DICK HACKNEY

**H = Hackney  P = Polster**

**H:** It's a pleasure to-to be here. And-uh-I'm not . . . I'm not sure what we're going to be doing, I guess, in terms of-uh-the supervision session.

**P:** Well, that's one of the things we'll have to find out.

**H:** Right.

**P:** I'm not sure either; but I'd like to know something of-uh . . . what you'd like.

**H:** I think the-uh . . . one of the things that I experience with this client is-is that there are times when I feel some real inertia in the case. Uh-and . . . part of my temptation is to try to create some kind of an incident or a crisis to get the case going again. Uh-especially-uh . . . does she seem to be-uh-in-she's really almost totally dependent upon a crisis happening over the week. If she comes in and has a week that hasn't had any particular crisis, then she doesn't do very much, that-she doesn't have much that she wants to work on.

**P:** Yeah.

**H:** So that's one-one of the problems I have with this case.

**P:** Well, it's a little drastic to have to go from crisis to crisis in order to get anyplace.

**H:** Yes.

**P:** And-uh-what I noticed as I watched part of your tape . . . uh-was that-uh-there were a lot of opportunities for a heightening of experience.

**H:** Uh-huh

**P:** A heightening that would-might not have led into a crisis but would, nevertheless, have-uh-raised the tone of your engagement with her. What I experienced was that you were really-uh-marvelously-uh-uh-uh-friendly and strong and-uh . . .

**H:** Yeah.

**P:** understanding . . .

**H:** OK.

**P:** wise. Uh-I felt like you were giving her-uh-a very important experience.

**H:** Right. There have been times when I've felt like I was being too supportive. I don't know if that hooks in to what you're saying or not.

**P:** Well-uh . . . supportiveness has a lot of dimensions to it. I felt you were being supportive; I didn't feel-I didn't think you were being vapid or-uh-or-uh . . . or patting her on the shoulder and such.

**H:** Yeah.

**P:** I didn't feel that kind of support. I felt the support of your . . . attention?

**H:** Uh-huh.

**P:** And-uh-your voice was-had authorship.

**H:** Yeah.

**P:** You cared about her, as it seemed to me.

**H:** Yeah.

**P:** And so on.

**H:** Yeah.

**P:** Uhm. So I don't think it was a matter of reducing support, but increasing your engagement. I can't tell you exactly what I mean by that . . .

**H:** Yeah

**P:** right away. I-I hope to be able to as we talk.

**H:** Good.

**P:** Like right now, as you smiled at me, I felt you increase your engagement with me.

**H:** Right.

**P:** Did you feel that?

**H:** I felt that, too. Yes.

**P:** Yes. Fantastic.

**H:** You really hooked me, as a matter of fact.

**P:** Right. Fantastic.

**H:** Right. Yeah.

**P:** Yeah.

**H:** Yeah. Ok.

**P:** Now you're going to recede a little bit, I think.

**H:** (Laughs)

**P:** Right?

**H:** Right.

**P:** OK. Now can you say what was going on there when the . . . led you to recede some after?

**H:** Yeah. I think you're touching on something that I do know about me-uh-and that is that I-I have a reserve that I-that-I wear and pull back into. And-uh-as soon as you first said that there was a-uh-kind of a continuous level-uh-I realized that

probably in-my reserve was running that case-that session.

**P:** Oh, your reserve was running.

**H:** My reserve was running that session.

**P:** Say more. I'm curious about . . .

**H:** Uh . . .

**P:** what reserve you're referring to.

**H:** It's-it's a safe kind of-uh-it's really, I guess, it's controlling-uh-more than anything else. But it's-uh . . . there's not a whole lot of personal contact in it . . .

**P:** Yeah.

**H:** to connect it to what you just said. Now I-I think I do it-I wasn't getting very personally involved with her.

**P:** I see. Well, how about right now? What's it like, your personal involvement with me, at this point?

**H:** Well, it went up just a few minutes ago, just two . . .

**P:** Yeah. Yeah.

**H:** or three minutes ago. And now I'm-I'm intellectualizing again.

**P:** Your-your words are interfering here.

**H:** Yeah. Yeah. That's true.

**P:** So wouldn't it be something if your words would-could be added on to that . . .

**H:** I'd love that.

**P:** aliveness?

**H:** Yeah.

**P:** Can you find some way-can you feel the aliveness now? I can feel it, not as full as full as before, but still somewhat.

**H:** Right.

**P:** How would your words sound if they fit that aliveness?

**H:** Well, I think I'd be a lot more excited. How would my words sound?

**P:** Well, try it out instead of trying to figure it out.

**H:** OK.

**P:** Just talk to me.

**H:** OK. Good.

**P:** Talk-talk to me as though you're fascinated with me.

**H:** Well, just a moment ago . . .

P: Pretend I'm fascinating.

H: Well, you are . . .

P: (Laughs)

H: as a matter of fact.

P: Well, let me see it.

H: OK. I felt some-some magnetism . . .

P: She was fascinating.

H: Yes. Yes.

P: She was really quite fascinating.

H: Yes, she was.

P: OK.

H: Uh-I'm aware how easy you are; and yet-uh-just a moment ago when you said . . . uh-"Where was I?"-uh . . . I think I got a little scared.

P: Scared?

H: Yeah.

P: Ah. Good. Well, tell me about it.

H: Well. (Laughs) How far back?

P: (Laughs) Now you're laughing. Now you're laughing. So where do you feel your laughter?

H: Right there. (Gestures inches in front of face)

P: Oh-uh-right there?

H: Yes.

P: Your face is rosy.

H: I think . . .

P: Feel the rosiness?

H: No.

P: No. OK, fine.

H: OK.

P: So the laughter's right here?

H: Yeah. I think that was . . . (Pause) You're hitting something that I . . . really would like to get through. And-uh . . . I'm-it makes me nervous because I think I've a very long history of it. Uh-I think it's a real deep habit I have; so it might not be easy, and that worries me a little.

P: History? Long history?

H: Ok.

P: You smiled at me. Every time you get a chance to go into something like that, you smile; but then you don't actually do it.

H: Yeah.

P: But it's like a pleasure to be recognized, isn't it?

H: Yes, it is.

P: Even though you're not quite ready yet to tell me all about it.

H: Yeah.

P: But just to be recognized.

H: Right. That's true.

P: Uh-huh. Your face is a little bit softer now.

H: You're-you're really right about that. (Pause)

P: So what is this history you're referring to?

H: Well, you may have said it all just now, I think-uh . . . being recognized, and still having some control; maybe being recognized in some of the ways I'd like to be recognized.

P: Oh, yeah. Yeah. Which would be how? What kind of recognition?

H: Uhm. (Pause) I think just being let in. Uh-granted there are times when I love to be recognized for something I did-uh-but those-those are fleeting moments. And-uh-I think being let in; friendship-uh . . . being known, maybe.

P: Yeah.

H: (Pause) It helps when you smile. (Laughs)

P: OK, so you get some feeling about your mutual recognition . . .

H: Yeah.

P: Like right now, you feel some power in that. Right? I mean . . .

H: Yeah, but I'm not as much aware of power as that.

P: I mean-OK-what word would you prefer?

H: Uh . . . (Pause) I think-uh-I feel safer.

P: Safer. Yeah. (Pause) All right. Now, I think you recognize your patient. I saw a lot of recognition.

H: Yeah.

P: That is, I-uh . . . inferred a lot of recognition.

H: Yeah.

P: Now, what would you like to say to her, if

you-your heart were involved in it? What would you say to her about the session you just had, or about some part of what she wants?

**H:** Uh.

**P:** Turn. Imagine she's over there.

**H:** OK.

**P:** And turn to her.

**H:** "I think, Ina, the thing I'd really like to say to you is how much I-uh-how much confidence I have in you; how much I think . . . how much I think you can change your world, and how much I would like that, if you did."

**P:** Uh-huh. And how does it feel for you to say that to her?

**H:** It feels good, you know, speaking personally. Uh-I . . .

**P:** Yes, that's how I'm asking you to.

**H:** (Laughs) When I think about saying it as a therapist-uh-I say-should I say how much I like that, you know?

**P:** OK. Well, for the moment, fortunately, here you don't have to worry about that because . . .

**H:** Right.

**P:** you don't have to do it with her.

**H:** That's true.

**P:** But you can begin to get a feeling for your inner . . .

**H:** Yeah.

**P:** self. OK, so you know what you said to her a moment ago and how it felt, right?

**H:** Yeah. And, you know, what I wonder is, should I put that on her, to let her know how much of an investment I have in her?

**P:** Not necessarily, you see. But you mustn't wipe out your inner experience so as not to tell her.

**H:** Ok, Right. Yeah, I cheat her.

**P:** It would be better to have all the experience and then you make your choice . . . about what you say or you don't say . . .

**H:** Yeah.

**P:** although I must say, in many instances, it

would be . . .

**H:** Yeah.

**P:** salutary.

**H:** It sure would give me a lot wider range of things to say.

**P:** Yeah. It would open up your . . . your face and your mind.

**H:** Yeah.

**P:** OK. Well, let's go back for a moment, all right? Now you remember what you said to her?

**H:** Yes.

**P:** All right. Now I'd like you to go over and be her responding.

**H:** OK. That's the easy part. I do think I know what she'll say.

**P:** Fantastic.

**H:** I think she'll say-uh-"That's exactly what I'm wanting from you, Dick."

**P:** Uh-huh.

**H:** Uhm. "I sense-uh-what you're saying to me."

**P:** Did you notice how she just called you "Dick"?

**H:** Yeah.

**P:** She never did in the session-in what I observed.

**H:** That's true.

**P:** That just came naturally . . .

**H:** Yeah.

**P:** didn't it?

**H:** Uh-huh.

**P:** Uh-huh.

**H:** Uh-I think she would-uh-I think she senses . . .

**P:** No. Just-just be her and . . .

**H:** OK. "I sense everything you're saying, but hearing it from you-uh . . . makes it real for me." And I think that's really what she'd say. I think she'd also say, "There are times when I don't have that trust in me. And-uh-I'm not sure I would be able to use it when I heard it from you, but . . . basically, I know that is what you're thinking, and-uh-and it will-and it gives me strength." (Pause) Uhm. I'm-I'm also aware that I'm not even speaking to the personal statement-uh-about the investment. Uhm . . . uh . . .

**P:** But she wasn't all that-uh-concerned with that aspect, was she?

**H:** Right. Right.

**P:** OK, come over here now . . . and be Dick. What do you feel like saying to her now?

**H:** Uhm. "It's really silly that I haven't done this before. Uh-it's a lot easier than I thought it would be. Uh-it makes sense to me. And-uh-I'm really glad I got around to saying it." (Pause) It is-uh-it's an amazing block that I have had on that.

**P:** Uh-huh. Well, tell me more about what you're saying is a block.

**H:** Uh-well, I guess the thing I want to say is that I've just never thought it through in those terms. Uh . . . I've never addressed it. I just haven't ever addressed it; an-uh-realized what I was not saying, or what I was not doing.

**P:** Haven't ever addressed-uh-what? The feelings you had inside?

**H:** My feelings in the relationship, yeah.

**P:** Yeah.

**H:** Right. You know, that . . . I haven't owned my feelings in the relationship with her.

**P:** Yeah.

**H:** I feel them. I anticipate her coming in for a session.

**P:** Oh, you do?

**H:** Oh, yeah. I really enjoy working with her.

**P:** Fantastic.

**H:** She's a-she's a fine person . . .

**P:** Yes.

**H:** fun person.

**P:** Yes.

**H:** And-uh . . . it is one of those-it is a case that I-uh-don't prepare much for, I mean, mentally.

**P:** Yeah.

**H:** And I think, in a lot of ways, I'm more natural in that-in that case . . . (Laughs)

than in a lot of the others that I do. Which is a-that's a statement.

**P:** What sort of statement.

**H:** Well, I guess, I brought one of my best cases along. (Laughs). And-uh-I wonder what I'm like in some of my other relationships with my clients.

**P:** Well, I must say to you in-in . . . all thoroughness, that I experienced this warmth in you when you were working with her. I experienced your really liking her.

**H:** Uh-huh.

**P:** But you seemed like a-uh . . . a Dutch uncle who really wanted to take care of whatever she needed to have taken care of.

**H:** Oh, yeah. Oh, yeah, that's me.

**P:** Yeah. You weren't going to be around too much; but, while you were around, you were going to really take care of her.

**H:** Yeah.

**P:** Yeah.

**H:** Yeah, I feel a lot of responsibility with-uh-working with her.

**P:** Yeah; but it felt very friendly and warm.

**H:** Uh-huh.

**P:** And what we're dealing with now is a question of-uh . . . what might add to that in terms of your appreciation of your warmth and your lubrication for . . .

**H:** Yeah.

**P:** Your mind flow.

**H:** Yeah, it certainly-I know what the lubrication is. I get to feeling a lot more fluid . . . in just the last few minutes.

**P:** Uh-huh.

**H:** (Pause) I'd like to take this into that case. (Pause)

**P:** Well, you could still do it.

**H:** OK. Uh. (Pause) Let me ask you a question . . .

**P:** Indeed.

**H:** in that regard.

**P:** Yeah.

**H:** Uh . . . part-part of my reaction when you said that would be to-uh . . . to-to raise the problem with Ina, and say,

"Look, here is what I'm feeling and here's what I hope to be able to accomplish"-uh . . . in other words, to let her in on what I-uh-would like to accomplish in the relationship.

**P:** What-which is what?

**H:** That I would like to become more comfortable and more fluid in our case. (Pause) I'm realizing when I say that, too, that it shifts responsibility over on her, and . . .

**P:** Yeah.

**H:** I don't know that she would know what to do with that.

**P:** Yeah. I-I-I don't-uh-I know that there are many instances where a simple statement of the-of your truth . . .

**H:** Yeah.

**P:** will open up-uh-new avenues . . .

**H:** Yeah.

**P:** there, and . . .

**H:** OK. What I worry about is, once I get it started, can I keep it going. I think that's . . .

**P:** But the question is, what is the "it" that you're referring to? What do you think is going to happen?

**H:** Oh.

**P:** You see? It's almost as though you're making a confession to her.

**H:** Yeah. Yeah.

**P:** Whereas actually . . . all you have to do is do it; you don't even have to tell about it.

**H:** That sounds a lot easier. (Laughs)

**P:** Well sure, I mean, you know, why-why would you have to suddenly make everything so drastically different from your nature? If you can bring your blood into your face . . .

**H:** Yeah.

**P:** and your interest out front, and your sense of relationship clear . . .

**H:** Yeah.

**P:** then it may not be necessary to make any confession about it.

**H:** I think that-I can see that.

**P:** Yeah.

**H:** Perhaps my worry is, can I keep doing that?

**P:** Well, chances are you can't . . .

**H:** Yeah.

**P:** right away; but this takes a while to develop.

**H:** Uh-huh.

**P:** You can't expect all of a sudden . . . to get to a different place. Yeah, I feel like you know what we're talking-what I'm talking about.

**H:** You know, I feel like I do, to. And-uh . . . I'm gonna try.

**P:** Yeah. Let me give you a couple of-uh-a other observations about what I saw there.

**H:** Good.

**P:** It might be . . . it might permit you a more gradual entry into the feeling of what . . .

**H:** Yeah.

**P:** But like, for example, there's a particular point in the session where she seemed quite shy.

**H:** Uh-huh. Yeah.

**P:** She'd said something warm to you.

**H:** Right. She'd . . . she'd got embarrassed.

**P:** Yes; and it was really a lovely moment.

**H:** Uh-huh.

**P:** She appreciated you. And-uh-somehow it got slid over, rather than an appreciation of the appreciation, or an acceptance of it.

**H:** OK. Yeah.

**P:** So some remark like, "Well, you seem very shy now. Uh-is it too difficult to say how you appreciate me?" You see?

**H:** OK. Yeah.

**P:** Why is that so difficult?

**H:** I mean, to say that to her?

**P:** Yeah. I mean, you know, something. I'm not saying those would be the words . . .

**H:** Yeah.

**P:** but something on the order of dealing with the events as they happen . . .

**H:** Uh-huh.

**P:** rather than looking for the major event that may come to happen.

**H:** Right. Right.

**P:** Every moment has it's own . . . drama.

**H:** Uh-huh. Yeah.

**P:** I think you may be waiting for the major . . .

**H:** I haven't paid very much attention to those moments in the session, that's true. That's one example; I-I can think of others, too.

**P:** Tell-tell me about some of the others.

**H:** Uhm. I don't know whether it was apparent on the tape, she's a beautician.

**P:** Yeah; I didn't know.

**H:** And-uh . . . a couple of sessions back, I had just got my hair cut, or had had it styled; and she came in, and uh-about a third of the way through the session, she said-uh, "You know, you look better than I've ever seen you look."

**P:** Huh.

**H:** Well, I got embarrassed . . .

**P:** Yeah.

**H:** and I just really kind of brushed that aside.

**P:** You're-you're . . . yeah. You're a very handsome man, you know.

**H:** Well, thanks.

**P:** I feel it. You got embarrassed?

**H:** Yes.

**P:** I'd like to know about your embarrassment.

**H:** (Pause) Huh.

**P:** Also, how did you feel about my saying you were handsome?

**H:** I appreciated it. Uh . . . and-uh-yeah, I-I think I had a little embarrassment just then.

**P:** Yeah. Yeah, you sort of heard it, but slid . . .

**H:** Yeah.

**P:** over it a little bit.

**H:** But I'll-I'll come back, later . . .

**P:** OK.

**H:** and remember it. (Laughs) It won't get thrown in the trash can. (Laughs)

**P:** (Inaudible)

**H:** Right. Right.

**P:** Can you feel the color coming . . . to your face now?

**H:** Yeah.

**P:** Fantastic! You look like you got a suntan.

**H:** Yeah; well, I think, you know, once again I got discovered.

**P:** Yes.

**H:** And-uh-that's . . . that's manipulative, I suppose.

**P:** What is?

**H:** To wait until I get discovered.

**P:** Manipulative sounds like a very bad word.

**H:** That's how I was using it.

**P:** Yeah. What'd you mean by it?

**H:** (Pause) Well, I think it's-uh-it's probably not showing as much responsibility or ownership to-uh-to sit back and-uh-get noticed, and then come out. (Pause) It's something like some of the fish I try to catch.

**P:** Some of the fish you try to catch?

**H:** (Laughs) Who I-that I can see down there, but they won't come out . . .

**P:** Uh-huh.

**H:** until I throw out the right bait.

**P:** Oh, you're sort of a benign fisher?

**H:** Oh, very benign. Yes. (Pause) I've really gotten something here-uh-in terms of the relationship. In fact, I'm a little surprised at how little attention I've been paying to the relationship. And-uh. (Pause) And I think it really is quite important in this case. Maybe-I don't mean just in this case, but as I think about the case, I think-uh-I could have been moving more; I think I could have been better with her had I been coming out more. (Pause) I'm not quite sure how to get started, but I-that's-that's OK, too.

**P:** There's no demand.

H: Uh-OK.

P: See, I'm wondering whether you're turning something into a demand on yourself.

H: Oh, I think so. Yeah, I definitely was, just now.

P: Yeah.

H: Right. (Pause) It would be very difficult for me to walk into a case without having some demand.

P: What sort of demands are you familiar with?

H: Uhm. (Pause) Well. (Pause) One of my big demands is to try to screen out whatever else is going on and-so that I-so that I can really direct myself to my client.

P: Yeah.

H: That is a big demand I've got on myself. Uh . . . and I-I feel like that's what they're paying their money for . . .

P: Sure.

H: and they have-at the very least, they should get that from me.

P: Sure.

H: Uhm. (Pause) I think I have-feel some honesty demand, too, in a case. I might try to couch it, you know, but I-I think-I really do think that there-that I feel some need to-to be honest with my clients.

P: That's certainly understandable.

H: Yeah.

P: What I am wondering is, how you . . . how you manage to satisfy these demands? Like how do you manage . . . to screen out everything but what's happening?

H: (Pause) How do I manage to screen out everything but what's happening?

P: Yeah, you said that's what you wanted to do, that-uh-you owed her . . .

H: OK.

P: your full attention.

H: I think I go on automatic pilot sometimes . . .

P: (Laughs)

H: (Laughs) to do it. Yeah, I probably do

click in to a different level of functioning. And I imagine it is-there-there has to be some mechanical-uh-treatment to that.

P: Uh-huh. Well, say more about the mechanical treatment possibilities there.

H: Well, I know how to begin a session. I know how to get a client started; I know how to make a client explore. And if I'm really trying to tune in to that, generally-uh-within ten minutes of a session beginning, I'm very much tuned in to a client, and not into whatever happened just before the session . . .

P: Yeah.

H: the fact that something happened. I-I can immerse myself in the content of the session . . .

P: Yeah.

H: that way. And that's-that is what I do; I immerse myself in the content.

P: Uh-huh. Well, it's beautiful to be able to immerse yourself. What you're saying is that you immerse yourself in the content, and the implication is that-uh-the process or the form would not be as much in . . . in your attention.

H: It comes following along. That's right. I'll have moments where that is just-that's bursting into my attention, but-uh-it's not the way I get it.

P: Yeah. Yeah.

H: (Pause) I'm kind of gathering from you that maybe the way you would do it would be through process.

P: Well, no-no, not-uh-just process. The way I would-the way I get in is that I get-uh-uh-I get fascinated with what's happening.

H: OK.

P: It might be content, it might be process; but I have no barriers to my being fascinated.

H: Yeah.

P: You see? So like I think-I think, you know, something somebody says to me, I would think of it almost like a writer would a story line.

**H:** Yeah.

**P:** Like in wh-in what context is that the most interesting thing that could have been said?

**H:** Yeah.

**P:** And I think of everybody's life as being worth a novel.

**H:** Yes.

**P:** So once I have that perspective, and I don't make demands about-uh-goals, 'cause that's always a complication . . .

**H:** Uh-huh.

**P:** which I'm never free from, because I believe in goals in therapy, not just . . .

**H:** Yes. Yeah.

**P:** the experience itself. But it is-so it's a complication, because if what's happening doesn't seem like it fits my goals, then I might lose interest in it.

**H:** Yeah. OK. Right.

**P:** You see?

**H:** Right.

**P:** If I can get the right rhythm between my goals and what's actually happening, then I am free to be fascinated all the time.

**H:** Yeah, and the thing which hits me with that is, I would love to be that accessible. Uh-it's almost uncluttered. I think that's how I would experience me, it. I could do something like that . . .

**P:** Yeah.

**H:** and I would love that.

**P:** Well, let's-let's look at it for a moment. Are you fascinated now?

**H:** Very. Oh, yeah.

**P:** What-what are you fascinated with?

**H:** Well-uh-with what you've said; and with how you might, you know, I-I-there's no doubt in my mind that that's exactly how you function, and that intrigues me. Uh-I guess I think I could perhaps do that at some point, and that intrigues me. Uh. (Pause)

**P:** OK. Now tell me what fascinates you about what she does and what she says? You can either tell me . . .

**H:** Right.

**P:** or tell her, imagining she's there. Either way's OK with me.

**H:** OK. I-the thing-I'll tell her.

**P:** OK.

**H:** Uh.

**P:** Now, I'm not saying, and mind you, I'm not suggesting that you tell her this in therapy.

**H:** Right.

**P:** This is just you and me now.

**H:** Right.

**P:** The whole thing that we're doing now is just you and me . . .

**H:** Yeah.

**P:** and it has no immediate certainty about how it will be applied in your actual work.

**H:** OK.

**P:** It will have to evolve.

**H:** Right.

**P:** OK?

**H:** Yeah.

**P:** So then, there will be no demand; I mean, we can do what we want here, and you don't have to feel a demand that you're going to have to do that in your next session.

**H:** Good.

**P:** OK.

**H:** Yeah, that helps.

**P:** OK.

**H:** "I think the thing I would say-uh-that facinates me about you, Ina . . ."

**P:** Look, try-try it a little differently. Not the thing that you would say . . .

**H:** Uh-huh.

**P:** because that's a prediction . . .

**H:** Right.

**P:** but rather what you feel like . . .

**H:** OK.

**P:** saying right now . . .

**H:** OK.

**P:** that fascinates you about her. And you may never want to say it again. Just right now.

**H:** "The thing that fascinates me most, I think, is what a good juggler you are. Uh-you have-uh-a way of taking almost all the-any kind of experiences that come your way and-and you keep 'em going in the air. And-uh-and . . ."

**P:** May I interrupt you for just a minute?

**H:** Sure.

**P:** I'd like you to sound a little more fascinated.

**H:** OK. (Laughs)

**P:** (Laughs) Like-like you really . . .

**H:** And I wouldn't be saying it this way? (Laughs)

**P:** Not to her. (Laughs) Well, I don't know how you'd say it. But, you see, I'm not saying you should say it to her . . .

**H:** Yeah.

**P:** this way. Just for our sake here, I want to hear how you'd sound if you really sounded fascinated.

**H:** Oh, OK. OK, fine. Uh-you're-it fascinates me how you can keep things juggling in the air. I never have seen anyone who can take so many different events and keeping them going all at the same time."

**P:** Terrific. Can you feel-can you feel the difference, you see?

**H:** Yeah.

**P:** There's less monotone.

**H:** Yeah. Yeah.

**P:** There's more meaning of-each word has a certain place in your sentence . . . emphasizes a certain something?

**H:** Yeah, it . . .

**P:** Were you able to feel that?

**H:** Oh, yeah.

**P:** Yeah.

**H:** Yeah. As soon as I started saying it, I felt it.

**P:** Yeah. Yeah. Try it some more.

**H:** OK. Well, I know what she's going to say right back is-uh, "What do you mean?"

**P:** All right. OK.

**H:** She's going to for . . . uh. (Pause) "Well, when I-when I think about how you han-

dle your husband, and how you handle your mother, and how you handle your sister who is a drug addict, and-uh-how you handle your boss at work; all these things-it's, from what you say, they all hit you at the same time, and you just keep them going, and you never really let anyone of them land so that it creates a uh-uh-a catastrophe for you. Uh-what I think is bad about that, when you keep them going in the air, you-you also never have any ending to them. And-uh-that's the part that-uh-that I really wish that you could do something with."

**P:** How did that seem to you?

**H:** That felt good. Yeah. Yeah, that really is a-a statement that I have felt and thought about, generally after a session.

**P:** I could feel the struggle between your fascination and your trying to form the right words.

**H:** Yeah. Yeah.

**P:** You . . .

**H:** Yeah, it-it . . .

**P:** (Inaudible)

**H:** it didn't feel quite authentic, especially the second time.

**P:** The first time you didn't care; the words just came out.

**H:** Yeah. Right.

**P:** Yeah. Yeah.

**H:** (Pause) Yeah, I think I wouldn't have liked her to ask me, "What do you mean?"

**P:** (Laughs)

**H:** (Laughs) Rather've just left it there.

**P:** Uh-huh. Yeah. Yeah.

**SUPERVISION SESSION 2: CARL ROGERS SUPERVISING DICK HACKNEY**

**H = Hackney   R = Rogers**

**H:** Would you start? (Laughs)

**R:** Well, I'd like to have you start because I'm not sure-uh-uh-what you'd like to . . . what you'd like to learn.

**H:** Good. There are several things I've thought about in going over this case, but I think perhaps the thing that-that bothers me the most as I work with her and this-I've seen her five times-uhm . . . the thing I think . . .

**R:** Is this the fifth time?

**H:** This was the fifth time, yes. The thing which bothers me the most is that-uh . . . I'm unable to anticipate her motivation to change from one session to another. She comes in one session, and if there's been a crisis that week then she's really motivated to try to work on that. Then-uh . . . if she's had a good week, she doesn't have very much motivation, then it's-I really feel like I'm pulling teeth and I-that's-that's pretty much what it is: I think I work harder than she does on that week.

**R:** You feel a responsibility for getting her to move.

**H:** Right. I think I do. Uh-I think related to that is some confusion that I have in terms of . . . what we are working toward because she originally came into counseling concerned about her-uh-marriage and her relationship to her husband, and then in the second session he came and joined her, but hasn't-he-he hasn't been able to make it since that time. Uhm . . . and one week she's dealing with how she can-uh-adjust to being newly married. The next week she's saying, "I-he's dragging me down, and I'm really trying-I'm wondering if I'd be better off outside the marriage, or not to be married." So I've-I've been having some trouble in that regard, too, of following to-uh . . . really to know what to do with what-what focus to take in the-uh-in the-uh therapy.

**R:** And-and that focus is really up to you?

**H:** I've been assuming some responsibility for it, yes. (Pause) Uh-I think I get different . . .

**R:** Have you expressed that to her?

**H:** Not in so many words. I-I-'m aware that-uh . . . on a couple of different occasions I've asked her, you know, I've asked her "What do you want to be working on? What-what is it that you would really like to see happen as a result of counseling?" Uh . . . but I think I've done that indirectly. I . . .

**R:** It looks like you've been trying to draw the answers from her, rather than express some of your own feelings of uncomfortableness.

**H:** I think that's fair. Yes. I think that is what I've been doing. Uh . . .

**R:** Sort of wish she would answer your questions for you.

**H:** (Pause) Probably that's part of it; I think part of me also-uh-would like her to-uh-discover some self-direction, maybe. Uh-maybe I'm believing in that too much, at this point. Uhm . . . but, yes, I've been trying to pull it out of her . . . rather than to express myself. And I think what you're hitting on there may be one of the-the qualities of this relationship that we have-that I'm removed in it a bit.

**R:** Uh-huh. What, in the portion that we saw of the interview, any particular things trouble you there or-uh-haven't you . . .

**H:** (Pause) I felt she was working well there in that part. Uh . . . I wish it were like that more often.

**R:** What did you feel about your own functioning?

**H:** I felt pretty good about it then. I-uh-there were a couple of times when I thought I was putting words in her mouth. Uh . . . when she didn't seem to be-uh . . . they didn't ring true for her. But-uh . . . I felt pretty good about that particular segment that we looked at.

**R:** I had the feeling as the-as the interview went on that-uh . . . you were giving more and more direction to it.

**H:** That's right. And I think that is part of my tendency. I think I . . . I will start out slowly in-in an interview . . .

**R:** Uh-huh.

**H:** and this-maybe this is-uh-an agenda that I have; but as a session wears on, I'm beginning to feel more and more of a need to-uh-have some-the client take something away that she can do during the week. Uh . . . there is a desire for-for some homework there, something for her to-uh-to extend the therapy session . . . with. And I think that was the direction I was going.

**R:** What did you feel her response to that was?

**H:** (Pause) Well, I think she had-I think she had some-uh-she was-her interest was teased just a little bit with it; but I think she also had some fear with it.

**R:** Uh-huh.

**H:** Uh . . . I think she-I think she was afraid to take a risk of-uh . . . trying to . . . deal with her relationship with her husband.

**R:** It seems as though-uh-what you succeeded in doing was teasing her a bit further than she might have gone otherwise.

**H:** Uh-huh. (Pause) Yeah. (Laughs) That doesn't sound exactly like therapy.

**R:** Well, it-uh . . .

**H:** I think you're right.

**R:** It-uh and I-I-my estimate of her response was that it was a fairly dubious response as to whether she could do, "Yeah . . ."

**H:** Right. (Pause)

**R:** Any-any other comments of yours on that segment that we saw?

**H:** (Pause) I-I think that . . . perhaps the part that we haven't seen or that we didn't see following that was-uh-maybe an important point. Uh-it feels to me like all of that was laying groundwork-what we have seen. Uh-just a little bit later-uh-she said, "I'm not sure I can do it", and I said, "I'm not sure you could either." And she bristled when I said that; and she said, "Well, I don't know-uh; when I make up my mind to do something, I can usually do it." And my comment then was-uh, "Yeah, I've seen that in you, and I know

you can do it when you make up your mind to do it." And she looked at me suspiciously at that point, because I think she-I think she felt trapped. I think she thought I had set her up. And I don't think I really meant . . . (Laughs) to set her up. Uh-but that seemed to be the moment of the-if there was anything that was going to-to be meaningful to her, it-may be what-it became at that point.

**R:** Would you like me to say some of the things that I felt I saw in that segment?

**H:** I'd really, really like that. Yes.

**R:** Uhm. Some of the time I felt that-uh-you-you-you did-you did well in responding to her feelings and understanding her. Uh-a few times I felt it would be possible to have gone more deeply, but that's-that happens to all of us all the time. Uh-one thing that had meaning to me because I look for metaphors, and when she spoke about the marriage and she couldn't move this way and she couldn't move that way, you responded that she felt stuck-uhm . . . for whatever it's worth, my-my-uh-vision at that time was of prison bars; I-I would have responded, "You feel-uh-that you're really in a-in a prison; that you can't get out."

**H:** Uh-huh.

**R:** And-uh . . . that might have enabled her to use that metaphor more. Uh . . . then-uh . . . then she seemed like a person who, as you say, has a hard time-uh-deciding what she wants, and it's sort of this way, "Well, it's-uh . . . sort of a laid back-uh-attitude, and uh . . . I guess it seemed to me that you were-uh-uh-fitting into that pattern. She wished . . . I don't know what she wished; she-she acted as though-uh-she didn't quite know what she wanted or where she wanted to go. And then you began suggesting things as directions where she could go.

**H:** Yeah.

**R:** And-uh-I-I-uh . . . I would have gambled

on-on responding to her where she was . . . uh-with the possibility that that would lead her to take a firmer stand.

**H:** Uh-huh. Uh-huh.

**R:** You're-you're-as you say, the fact that she-uh-as I said, that she made up her own mind and she did what she-uh . . .

**H:** Yeah.

**R:** Uhm . . . it wasn't . . .

**H:** So I kind of took that away from her?

**R:** Yeah, a little bit, I think.

**H:** Yeah.

**R:** Uhm-and it interests me that she said, "When I make up my mind to do it, I'll go ahead and do it."

**H:** Yeah.

**R:** And when you responded accurately to that . . . that threatened her . . .

**H:** Uh-uh.

**R:** which I think means that that was a very important statement for her.

**H:** Uh-huh.

**R:** I've often noticed that if a person takes quite a positive step-uh-expresses a feeling quite positively, and you understand it accurately, God, that's almost too much for them.

**H:** Huh.

**R:** They tend to draw away from what they just said.

**H:** Right. Right. That was the reaction I got from her when I said that.

**R:** (Pause) The-uh . . . when you say she has a sort of differing type of motivation, different . . . reason for motivation each time she comes in-uhm . . . that wouldn't bother me. I-I would-I would-uh . . . go with whatever . . . shred of feeling she would let me have at the time.

**H:** Uh-huh. (Pause) I'd like to be able to do that. (Laughs)

**R:** (Laughs) Well, I'm saying what I would do; that doesn't mean that's necessarily what you should do.

**H:** Well, I don't think what I'm doing is working for me. Uh . . . and I don't think it really is working for her either, so-uhm . . . and I think it would be-I think I'd be better-uh . . . in this case if I-uh . . . could feel a little bit less responsible when she comes in with less motivation.

**R:** She came in of her own accord. She asked to see you.

**H:** That's right. That's right. And she's been very faithful-uh . . . so far in the case.

**R:** Wonderful. So then anything that you do that takes any responsibility away from her is really quite unnecessary.

**H:** Uh-huh.

**R:** She did decide to come; and she comes.

**H:** Right.

**R:** (Pause) An interesting, mixed-up, modern young woman, it seems like.

**H:** Yes, it is. Uh . . . and a delightful young woman, too. She really is. Uh . . . she's the person I think I like most among the people I'm working with.

**R:** OK. OK, that's important. That's one reason why you want it to go well.

**H:** That's right. Right.

**R:** (Pause) My feeling of her is very . . . good . . . feeling, and I like that. It means you will get somewhere, but-uh . . . (Pause) But if you like her enough to want her to go your way, that's-that's a different matter.

**H:** Yeah. Well . . . you-that's especially true because I'm not really sure . . . what way it would be if it was going my way. And I-I'm not clear there either, so . . .

**R:** Well, you were-you were somewhat clear toward the end of the interview as to a step that you clearly thought was advisable for this coming week.

**H:** Right. I had an agenda at that point; I was wanting to set up . . . an opportunity for her and-and her husband to-uh-to have a conversation. Whether that came off or not was another matter. But part of the sense that I was picking up at that point was that because of the pace of their lives they never even really had the opportunity.

And then she got-uh ignored or missed-uh . . .

**R:** Well, that's where you did feel a responsibility for helping set up something that would make that come off.

**H:** Oh, I was-I was taking care of it all. Yes. (Pause) Where do you think it might go if-if I were to-uh . . . that-that's maybe an impossible question to ask.

**R:** Uh-huh.

**H:** If I were to-uh . . . to try to follow what her inclinations were-uh-as far as . . . her trying to find a moment with her husband, where do you think that might go? Do you think-do you think she would bring the initiative out of that?

**R:** I haven't any idea where it would go, but to me that's the fascination of-of therapy, is not knowing; and yet-uh-connecting just as deeply as I can with the, in this case, the confusion, the-uh . . . "Maybe I will; maybe I won't. Maybe I like Don; maybe I like John." Uh . . . just connecting as deeply as possible with that feeling, and following it wherever she leads me . . .

**H:** Uh-huh.

**R:** uh-because she already feels your companionship in the relationship. That's important to her . . .

**H:** Yes.

**R:** and so-uh-and she trusts you and trusts you enough to be completely open . . .

**H:** Uh-huh.

**R:** so that I think her own-uh-feelings would move in some direction. When you ask what direction, I don't know. I don't know. To me that's-that's the fascination of a relationship that, once in it, I don't have any idea where it will go, and yet . . .

**H:** Right.

**R:** uh . . . I-I'm more-uh . . . the way that I work, I would have less of an agenda than you do. My agenda would be, Can I get so connected that I can feel every particle of what she's feeling . . .

**H:** Uh-huh.

**R:** whether it's-uh-wishiwashiness or whether she's-or whether-one thing that I did notice that I probably would have responded to, her eyes lit up twice in the interview; once was when she, I think, got a little angry. And-uh-you responded to that, but I-I would have responded also to the gleam in her eye that . . .

**H:** Uh-huh.

**R:** that-uh-"Boy, that really makes you light up."

**H:** Yeah.

**R:** Uh-and I forgot just what the other one was, but she lit up at another time, too. And-uh-so that's that's the kind of thing I like to do is-is just be so much with their person, their-their expression, their intonation-uh-their words, their metaphors, that-uh . . . they get excited and want to move further. That's-uh . . .

**H:** Uh-huh. Uh-huh. Yeah, I think I know what you mean about catch-letting them catch your excitement-uh-too. I can see where that would work with her. Uh-I don't mean that the way it sounds, as-as a technique, but I've seen her get excited and-uh-I know that that . . . when she does get excited, that's when she really is being-uh-very good for herself and . . . (Pause) Well, I think I'll-uh-see what I can do about laying back just a little. And I think it's going to be hard to . . . let go of some goals.

**R:** And I'm-I'm saying very sincerely that I was describing the way I would tend to go about it. You've got to be sure that that's the way you really want to go about it . . .

**H:** Uh-huh.

**R:** or else it would be-come across as a form of (Unclear)

**H:** Right. I'm aware-uh . . . I guess that's where I'm testing myself a little bit, too, because I'm not sure if that-uh . . . that drive only part is-uh . . . manufactured or if that is me, too. Probably-uh . . . I suppose if it could be me-uh-at this point in time, maybe that's me. Uh-

**R:** Uh-huh. Yeah. At this moment in time, you know that's the way you feel . . .

**H:** Right.

**R:** Uh-huh.

**H:** Right.

**R:** Whether you'll feel that way when you next see her, that's . . .

**H:** Right.

**R:** up to that point in time.

**H:** I'm going to be looking for it, though.

**R:** Uh-huh.

**H:** And that's . . . uh-and that part I would-I'm looking forward to that part.

**R:** Well, it-uh . . . I sometimes say that when I see a client in demonstration interviews or something like that, I'm like an old fire horse responding to the bell; I-I-I would like to work with her, too. (Laughs) I can see why-why you would like to work with her.

**H:** Yeah.

**R:** (Pause) OK. Is that-uh?

**H:** I think that will do it.

## SUPERVISION SESSION 3: NORMAN KAGAN SUPERVISING DICK HACKNEY

**H** = Hackney  **K** = Kagan

**K:** Dick, Uhm-you want to try the Recall Process as one more approach to supervising you, uh-in this series. Uhm-the way I would work with you and would like to work with you now—I know this tape is about a week old, but my guess is that much of it will still be fresh for you. Uhm-as you interacted with your client—you told me her name was Ina . . .

**H:** Right.

**K:** Uhm—I go on the assumption that a heck of a lot was going on under the surface for you. Thoughts, feelings, impressions you were having of her. Or, impressions you thought she was having of you. Uhm-you know the mind works a heck of a lot faster

than the voice does, so that there were lots of things that there couldn't possibly have been time for you to say or deal with, but perhaps more important for you, there may have been a lot of things you only vaguely perceived and couldn't find the words for, or weren't sure if you dared to deal with, or . . .

**H:** . . . or didn't trust.

**K:** Or didn't trust. And-uhm-when you listen to the tape and I know you could now probably talk about a lot of those things, but when you listen to the tape I think you'll find that a lot of that kind of process, the things that were going on inside you, things you thought were going on inside her, uh-a lot of that will come back to you. Whenever you remember any of it, just stop the tape. My role will be to pursue the story.

**H:** Uh-huh.

**K:** That you tell, that will always be your story because you know what was going on. You were there, you know what was going on in your head. My task is going to be to help you get as much of that out, put it in the form of language so that you can look at it, think about it. Uhm-you may also get in touch with things that you were thinking of saying and, and this will be an opportunity for you to-to say what you were thinking of saying . . .

**H:** Right.

**K:** . . . and listen to the sound of it.

**H:** OK.

**K:** OK, so whenever you remember anything at all, relevant or irrelevant, stop the tape and talk about what was going on.

**H:** OK, fine. Uh-just by way of introduction to this session, there-it was really like there were two sessions in this session. The first half of the session-uh-was awkward-uh-I was uncomfortable. The second half of the session, we seemed to get into a groove and I felt good. I saw her relax. Uh-but I also got resistance from her in the second half of the session when I started uh-try-ing to plant some suggestions. So there's something to work on with both-in both halves of the session. And I just turned to a place in the first half of the session to start . . .

**K:** Uh-huh.

**H:** . . . and I uh-I have to play it to see just where it is. (Plays audio tape)

**H:** (Stops tape) OK, uh-she's been married four months and her husband is John. However, in the last two or three weeks a new man has entered on the scene. Uh-and it's strange how he has entered because he has suddenly become friends of her hus-band, and uh-he and Ina had a soiree just a week earlier, and much to her surprise and I think to her delight. And so she hasn't uh-mentioned him yet in the session so this is where I decide that I wanted to get his name into the session at this point, uh-so let me go from there.

**K:** What did you want to do with . . . ?

**H:** . . . that . . . I wanted her to acknowledge that uh-or to at least make me current that he was in her world at this point. Uh-at this early moment in the session, she is talking about what a terrible week she's had. She's talking about everything except this new man. And I'm curious, partly, is this new man still in the scene, if not — and if he is, I'm sure that he's part of the com-plication. If he's not in the scene, then I would guess that's part of the complica-tion. But she's not speaking to him.

**K:** Uhm-huh.

**H:** And she's not acknowledging him and-and so I'm kind of forcing the issue there.

**K:** OK. How did she react to . . . ?

**H:** I think that she was a little bit relieved. I think she was waiting for me to make that move, because I-I think she's a little un-comfortable to talk about him. Uh-but as I remember, uhm-there was just a little bit of relief in her face when I brought his name up.

**K:** Uhm-huh. How did that influence what followed?

**H:** Oh, I was delighted (Laughs), of course.

**K:** Uh-uh.

**H:** I thought that, "Yeah, you were right that time." Uhm-I'm going to have to play it to see what follows. I can't recall right now. (Plays tape)

**H:** (Stops tape) Ok, I-I laughed at that point because everything I was reading was "Here I put myself out on the porch where he would be sure-sure to see me, uh-yet I was nervous about that but I-I didn't want to miss the chance, and then the sucker didn't even uh-say anything to me."

And I thought, uh-well, all right I-I think I thought, "Yeah, you probably de-served that. You're playing a game with him and-uh it's not a bad game, but you're playing a bit of a game with him, and he decided not to play it. So maybe you got your natural consequences in that."

**K:** Uh-huh.

**H:** So there's a little bit of satisfaction, I think, in my-in my reaction.

**K:** Dick, did you get any sense of what she wanted from you at that point. Did you get any . . .

**H:** Well . . .

**K:** . . . glint in her eyes?

**H:** This has been troubling me all through this case, uh-because one minute I have a sense of what she's wanting and then 10 minutes later uh-what I'm getting from her is just the opposite.

Uh-in that particular moment, what I think she was wanting uh . . . well, let me think. (Pause) In a way, I think she was wanting me to react the way I did, because I think she recognizes the game. I think if I had uh-taken her too seriously uh-that it would have eventually led her into a trap.

**K:** Uhm-hm.

**H:** But I don't think she's that serious.

**K:** Do you have any sense of how she feels about you at that point?

**H:** Very comfortable with me. This is uh-probably-probably my biggest sense in-in this case-that she likes me, she's comfortable with me, she will let me confront her. Uh-sometimes I get a little too close with something and she gets embarrassed. She gets nervous. She will pull back. Uhm-in that moment I think she-I-I do think she felt good about uh-how I was reacting to her. She did smile . . .

**K:** Uh-huh.

**H:** . . . following my laugh, she smiled.

**K:** Any risks that you're sensing, any cautions on your part, any sense of being on a tightwire, uh . . . ?

**H:** Not yet.

**K:** Late . . .

**H:** Later. (Mutual laughs)

**H:** Right. (Plays tape)

**H:** (Stops tape) I didn't believe her uh-when she said that I thought she ought to be embarrassed. But I didn't really quite trust that embarrassment. I think she was really just saying, "You're getting awfully close right now."

**K:** What did you think you were getting close to?

**H:** Uhm-the crisis of her indecision I-I is about the only way I know to say that. I think what she really wants is to be confronted by her—what she's doing in her world right now. Because I think she is really not quite sure what she wants, whether she wants to stay in her marriage or whether she wants to get out of her marriage, but she's very good at uh-protecting herself from that question. At any given moment, she gets immediately into the moment and doesn't have to face the other half of the issue.

Uh-like when Don came up uh-to the house, she wasn't dealing with what will John's reaction be at all. Uh-when Don is out of the scene, John is there. She's not dealing with Don's existence at all, so what I was trying to do was to bring those

two-what I am trying to do is to bring those two worlds together.

**K:** OK. Is there anything that you're tempted to do or say that you're holding back? (Pause)

**H:** Well, I think there is a part of me uh-that thinks she's uh-uh-being unrealistic and uh-playing games with herself, playing some dangerous games with herself, uh-maybe being a little bit under-responsible in her behavior.

**K:** You're tempted to say that but you don't?

**H:** I-yeah, right. (Laughs)

**K:** What keeps you from saying that . . . ?

**H:** I don't know if it would be therapeutic to say that. I guess I'm-if I-I'd like to uh-I'd like to think that it was therapeutic. But I am-I'm not convinced of that, and-uh-I'd-there's-there's the tight wire that you asked earlier. I think-on this particular issue I am walking a tight wire. Uh-sometimes I-it feels to me like I'm coaxing her right up to the edge of her risks, and I don't want to push her too far there, because I think I could lose her.

**K:** Do you have a fantasy of what would happen if you lost her?

**H:** Well, the only real concern I have is that uh-it would do some uh-damage to the relationship and we would have to rebuild. Uh-I don't have any greater fantasy than . . .

**K:** When you're on this tight wire, what does it feel like for you physically? Is it in any part of your body, particularly?

**H:** Ah.

**K:** A physiological concomitant?

**H:** Uh-I might . . . I-I-I'm having trouble locating where that might be. (Pause) I think I show it in my face more than anywhere else. I-I-may face uh-(Pause) my facial reactions probably start to uh-to reflect that discomfort.

**K:** Do you think she's aware of your discomfort?

**H:** I don't. Uh-and maybe I'm misreading her

completely. Uhm-she's uh-in terms of psychotherapy, she's very naive. And uh-in some ways she's really kind of a model client because she is uh-uh-so amenable to the process. I don't experience her as being critical of the process though.

**K:** Anything else you're aware of at this point in time?

**H:** No, that's about . . .

**K:** Uh-huh.

**H:** . . . that's about it.

**K:** (Unclear)

(Hackney plays tape)

**H:** (Stops tape) I'm confused at that point. I really don't know what she's trying to say to me. Uhm-and I've—and I don't know that she knew what she was trying to say at that point. So I-I-I remember at the time trying to figure out where-where are we going with this? Uhm-what is it she's . . . it seemed to me she'd made a jump at that point in her thinking and I couldn't catch up with it to figure out where she was.

**K:** Uh-uhm.

**H:** And I can't remember where we went from this. Uh-that does happen in our-in our sessions. There are times-there are often times when-uh I have to catch up to her. She's-she's made a kind of jump and . . .

**K:** At those moments, is there anything that you're tempted to say that you don't?

**H:** Well, yes. Yeah. I-I think I have been uh-when I'm in one of those moments, I feel like I have been doing too much following. And maybe I ought to be getting more active, and maybe I ought to be confronting a little more, or just asking her "Where-where are you right now?"

**K:** OK and what keeps you from doing that?

**H:** Uh, well, basically what keeps me from doing that, I think, is that uh-I-I'm working out of a uhm-model that I use of uh-trying to get really grounded with the client in the first part of the session. Uh-maybe I'm-maybe I'm saying that I'm be-

ginning to question my model a little bit. Because I do feel some impatience uhm-to become involved. I-later in the session I, in any session I tend-tend to get a bit more active. Uh-maybe I'm having trouble with my model here.

**K:** Is there anything about her age, sex, physical appearance uh-that's having an impact on you? Or I should say what is her age, sex, physical appearance . . . ?

**H:** Uhm-she's attractive. She's just a little bit overweight. Uh-her personality is delightful. And uh-I guess I'd have to say she's my-my favorite among my client's that I'm working with now. Uhm-and I really do look forward to the session because it's—they're fresh. Each session really is a fresh sesion. Uh-and I have a good sense, you know, almost always at the end of a session, I feel good about the session.

Uh-it's the first half of that session that is the struggle for me. May I'm-maybe I'm too invested. I don't know. Uh-maybe I . . .

**K:** How do want-how do you want her to perceive you. How do you want her to feel about you?

**H:** Well, uh-that's-there's several different things, I think. I want her to like me. Uh-I want her to feel that she is getting her money's worth. Uh-I want her to feel that I have compassion, that I-that I do understand uh-the world she's operating in. Uhm-and I want her to-to feel that, ultimately, that she doesn't need me.

Uh-we talk about that just a little bit later in the session, in fact. But uh-(Pause) I think those are basically the things I'd-I'd like to have her feel.

**K:** Anything else (unintelligible)?

**H:** No, I think that's that. Uh-let me-let me advance it some now.

**K:** Sure.

**H:** I get into a strategy just a little bit later, and uh-halfway in I'm not sure if it's the right strategy to choose. So maybe that-if

I can find that here.

**K:** Uh-huh.

(Plays tape)

**H:** (Stops tape) Ok.

(Plays tape)

**H:** (Stops tape) That's still too far in.

(Plays tape)

**H:** (Stops tape) This is her mother she's talking about.

(Plays tape)

**H:** (Stops tape) Here I'm starting to . . .

(Plays tape)

**H:** (Stops tape) I'm pushing her at this point because she really doesn't want to accept, my sense of-of her reaction is that she really doesn't want to accept responsibility for uh-making things happen. I think she-she's still kind of sees herself as a victim.

Or maybe it's uh-maybe she just can't see any alternative to being a victim at this point, and I'm-I realize as I'm suggesting to her "You might be able to make some things happen differently." And I feel resistance from her. This is where the resistance starts to uh-build.

**K:** Ok, so this is your strategy for her at this point.

**H:** This? Yeah.

**K:** Do you recall what your feelings are as this is going on? What's going on inside you?

**H:** I'm-I-at this moment, I'm feeling like I'm right on.

**K:** Uh-huh.

**H:** Uhm-uh-but I'm not sure how she's going to react to it. I'm feeing pretty good about my-in my head this is what I want to do.

**K:** What reaction are you hoping for? What do you want her to say in your favorite fantasy?

**H:** Uh-oh I think in my fantasy it-it comes-it comes as a revelation, you know, an "aha" . . .

**K:** Uh-huh.

**H:** . . . experience to her. And she says, "Well, of course, and I'm going to go right out and do it." (Laughs)

**K:** Do you get that?

**H:** No. No. I get a lot of reservation, a lot of, lot of guardedness. And a little bit later, I decide that I can't push it frontally any more and that the most I can hope for is to plant the suggestion and uh-in fact I paradox her at that point. Tell her that I'm not at all sure she can do it. Uhm . . .

**K:** The-the feeling that you have when you don't get what you want from her, what happens to you at that moment? Wh-what's happening to you here when she's not giving you what you hope for?

**H:** I'm doing a lot of reading, to trying to read. I'm trying to read her reactions in her face, in her facial gestures, ' n-her body movement. Uhm-I'm-I'm t₁ying to measure her resistance to me. That's what I'm trying to do.

**K:** Ok, when you don't get the response, what feelings do you have as you're doing all that? What happens to you?

**H:** When I'm active like I am at the moment, uhm-my reaction is that "You've pushed too far. You-you need to back off a little bit."

**K:** Ok. To what extent do you think at that moment she's aware of what's going on in you?

**H:** I don't think she's very aware at all of what's going on in me. I think that may be uh-I think that definitely is one of the characteristics of our relationship. She doesn't have-I don't give her much sense of what's going on with me.

**K:** Do you want her to know what's going on with you?

**H:** Well, uh-I've been dealing with that just lately. I-I am beginning to entertain the-the possibility that that would be good. But until just recently, I haven't seen that as particularly necessary. Uh-

**K:** As you contemplate sharing what's going on with you with her, are there risks involved for you?

**H:** Perhaps there are risks-well yeah, sure there are risks involved. Uh-I think as I let her get to know what I'm doing, uhm-what I'm reacting to, I think I'm going to give up a little control in the session. And-uh-I'm not sure where that will go.

**K:** What-what's your fantasy?

**H:** (Laughs)

**K:** What's the nightmare?

**H:** My best one or my worst one?

**K:** Yeah. (Laughs) I like the worst, that's . . .

**H:** Well, I think in my worst fantasies, she will have uh-she'll have seen my cards. And uh-I won't have uh-anymore cards to play.

**K:** And what happens then?

**H:** Oh, I-I suspect at that point, it's up for grabs. No seriously . . .

**K:** (Laughs)

**H:** Uh . . . (Laughs) Probably nothing very serious would happen then. Uh . . .

**K:** What's it feel like to . . . what's the other process for you?

**H:** Uhm-(Pause) Huhm. I suppose uh-there's a clutching, and uh-maybe that would bring on some of my uncertainties. Uhm-where would I go from there? Just uh-I think part of what I tend to use is my anticipation. And where the session might be going next.

**K:** Uh-huh.

**H:** And I think I would give up that-that potential, maybe. And uh-I'd probably have to be a whole lot more uh-available to uh-what was happening in each moment . . .

**K:** Uh-huh.

**H:** . . . if I did that. I know I would. And, that's not a style I have used. Uhm-that may be good or bad, I don't know, but uh-I feel some discomfort with it.

**K:** Anything else?

**H:** That's all I can think of at the moment.

**K:** Ok, let's go back to the tape.
(Plays tape)

**H:** That gives me away, doesn't it?

**K:** (Laughs) What's happening for you at this point on the tape?

**H:** Uhm-I've got a strategy at this point. I-I'm starting to lay some groundwork that uh-

you know maybe we need to uh-make our plans for the coming week and this time let's try uh-submit that-those plans just a little bit more by uh-not only know what to do, but how to do it. So I'm really-I'm-I'm just really trying to hold the mirror up and say "Look, here's what you wanted to do last week and you didn't get it done. Maybe this is why that you didn't get it done."

**K:** Uh-huh. Do you have any sense at this point of what she wants from you also?

**H:** I don't think I do. No, I really don't. I think I'm into my own strategy at this point.

**K:** You don't feel any pressures from her of any sort or kind of . . .

**H:** No. And this is uh-this is part of her characteristics, I think. She is inclined to treat me like the doctor. And uh-I think when I accept that and go with that, she's very comfortable.

**K:** And you feel how when you accept that and go with that?

**H:** When I think I know what I'm doing and where I'm going, I'm-I do very good with it, I go with it-uhm-up to a point of encountering resistance, and then I-then I have to back up and reassess.

**K:** And how does she-how does the resistance occur?

**H:** Gen-well in her case, the resistance uh-occurs when she starts-typically, she will say, "Yeah, I-I see the point of that uh-and that makes sense to me and I'd like to do that" and then she says, "But I'm not sure." And then she-she'll start giving me reasons why it might not work. And when she gets into that, then I don't-that for me is her own resistance. When she starts looking for the flaw. It may be low-level resistance, but still I think it's uh . . .

**K:** And again, the impact on you when that happens?

**H:** Ok. The impact on me is to-my-my first response is, "Have I pushed too far?" You know. I-I take resistance-that resistance really very seriously. I think that uh-Ok, my reaction is if I give her something to push against . . .

**K:** Uh-huh.

**H:** . . . when she resists . . .

**K:** Uh-huh.

**H:** . . . then that is not going to be therapeutic.

**K:** Uh.

**H:** Ok.

(Plays tape)

**H:** (Stops tape) I think that's the high point of the session. I think-I think it's the high point because she came to that. Uh-she made that connection.

**K:** Uh-huh.

**H:** And I didn't strategize to get her to come to that . . .

**K:** Uh-huh.

**H:** . . . connection. I felt really good about that one.

**K:** What enables it to happen as you were-as you were in that mode?

**H:** I think I uh-a key question I asked, "Uhm-how would you like him to treat you?"

**K:** Uh-huh. What enabled you to do that?

**H:** I have no idea. I-I-when I heard that question I was su-I didn't know where it came from. It kind of surprised me, too.

**K:** And you were pleased.

**H:** Oh, yeah. Yeah, as soon as I heard it, I knew it was a—"that's a crackerjack of a question." (Laughs)

**K:** (Laughs)

**H:** And as I'm saying that I'm aware that-that there's no strategy at all behind that. That's pure intuition which is what I was saying a while ago I was a little bit worried about using.

**K:** Uh-huh.

**H:** So I-I hear the contradiction of my own statements there.

**K:** You said before that one of your struggles was the issue of maintaining control . . .

**H:** Yeah.

**K:** What's happening to that at this point in time?

**H:** I'm going with the flow. I'm not-I'm not at all thinking of control. What happened-the way I put it together at the moment I remember was things were in a groove now. It's-it's like you go out on a sail boat and for a while you can't catch a breeze, and all of a sudden you catch a breeze, and the sails fill and, you know, you're not worried about breezes anymore. Now I'm not worried about breezes any more.

**K:** Anything else arise?

**H:** Uhm, no. To tell you the truth, I think I got-I've gotten what I came for. Uh . . .

**K:** (Laughs) It's been exciting.

**H:** Yeah. I'm, uh-I'm rather pleased with what I-I think we just found there in terms of uh-of letting go a little bit maybe.

**K:** It's been exciting. I uh-also wanted to learn something about how you think, about what your struggles are and uh-I'm delighted to have been able to share that.

**H:** Well, I really enjoyed it.

**K:** Good.

**H:** Thanks.

**SUPERVISION SESSION 4: RUDOLPH EKSTEIN SUPERVISING DICK HACKNEY**

**H** = Hackney    **E** = Ekstein

**E:** It takes courage to start the supervision; to let me really direct in on it; to not change it around to give me an indirect report or interpret it, but rather show, here it is. And as I was trying to see what is here, I tell you, the first thing that occurred to me, she says, "I'm unhappy, and I'm in an unhappy marriage."

**H:** Uh-huh.

**E:** She starts out with a bit flirtatious at the moment . . .

**H:** Yes.

**E:** as if she was seductive.

**H:** Yes.

**E:** And then she says, "But I can't live with him," and-uh-you say to her, "In the end, I guess it looks like the only way you get something going with him is to smoke him out." And the main impression that I had, if I were to consider what is wrong with this woman, what is her problem, her problem . . .

**H:** Uh-huh.

**E:** not a marital problem, I would say, "What could I do to smoke her out?" So that it looked to me like a-a kind of triangle: The husband in the background, the two of you in the foreground. She complains about him, and says, "I've got to work so hard to get anything out of him; I'm not happy."

**H:** Yes.

**E:** "I've got to get it going."

**H:** Yes.

**E:** And the impression that you gave was to convey indirectly to me by showing how it was-how does one smoke her out, so that one can get to the inner self of this person. And the question that I have: Did I observe it correctly, or was it just too short for me to capture what goes on now and, from what I suspect, will continue to be the slant of that session?

**H:** Yes. That's-that's pretty much the-uh-the-tempo that session took. And-and I'd have to say that-uh-that really is . . . better than some of the sessions.

**E:** With her?

**H:** Yes.

**E:** What does she do otherwise?

**H:** Uh-there are some sessions that I feel-uh-a lot of resistance from her. She-she's there by choice, but she's-she's not there to work.

**E:** What was the-the original purpose; what brought her in?

**H:** OK. She came in-this-this was . . .

**E:** Her claim?

**H:** Her claim was-uh-anxiety attacks that she

was having-uh . . . periodically . . . some maybe two or three weeks apart. And she associated them-uh-with one of two things-uh-an auto accident she has ss-uh-six months earlier or her marriage which was-is four months old. But she says sometime around that time she started having these anxiety attacks. And-uh . . . they got so bad that she can't drive. Uh . . . at work, she's a beautician, at work, when she has one of these, she feels like she has to run out of the beauty shop. And-uh . . . if she's at home and has one of these anxiety attacks, all she wants to do is to go into her room-er-into the bedroom, close the door, turn out the lights, and just stay in bed . . . until it passes.

**E:** I heard you make a remark, there is somewhere a mother in the background.

**H:** Yes.

**E:** Another triangle situation.

**H:** That's right.

**E:** As if to say—again I'm . . . trying to think with you—to sense-I sense to leave mother, to leave the original family, and to go into a new situation and go to that man, is something deeply anxiety arousing. It would be like an auto accident; something terrible will happen.

**H:** You are absolutely right on, because-uh-she comes from a family where the father left when they were all very young. She was the oldest of three children. Mother oftentimes is the-a child. And she, in one of the earlier sessions, was reporting how she felt like she was the most mature member of the family growing up; and she still is the one that they all turn to when they have problems. So she does feel like the responsible person.

**E:** You get an absent father . . .

**H:** Uh-huh.

**E:** a triangle with an invisible father, a phantom father . . .

**H:** Yes.

E: And the original idea, "Someday I have a life of my own; I will find a man . . ."

H: Uh-huh.

E: "Can I smoke father out; where is he hidden?"

H: He's . . .

E: "Can I find him . . . or if I met him, can I get to him and say, 'Why did you leave us?' "

H: Yes.

E: " 'Why did you die; why did you leave; how come you're not here?' Can I smoke him out, or will he be like that father? Why should I get into that situation?"

H: You really are hitting several buttons for me, because about a year ago she went to find her real father in Florida; and it was a catastrophe. Uh-she drove down there. It was so bad she flew back and left her car there. Uh-she had to-to fly so fast to get out.

E: But you understand, it doesn't take much symbolism to say, "I am afraid to take care of my own life. I cannot . . ."

H: Yes.

E: "run my own car. I cannot go my direction. Somebody should go with me." Here we have an auto phobia instead of the fear of flying.

H: Yes.

E: We could just as well-could have had a fear of flying. But, "I must be taken care of by someone. I cannot trust him whom I cannot find. I cannot smoke him out of his hiding place."

H: Uh-huh.

E: "And here I am with this man, and constantly feel he's not there. I do not understand him. I have no relationship. Whenever I try, I do not get the response that I want. I get more and more anxious. What is wrong with him? Why does he not change?" And, of course here comes now your question, "What could I, the therapist, do to smoke her out?"

H: Yes.

E: "Because it's almost as if she invited me, try to pin me down, and say, 'What is wrong with you?' rather than, 'What is wrong with the father? What is wrong with the husband?' You choose . . ."

H: Uh-huh.

E: "In the search for the father you became paralyzed, and in the search for the man you're paralyzed once more; and you come to me." And you will not say now, but you will think: In the moment, there was a flirtatious moment in the beginning, as if she would say to you, "Well, if it would be you, that would be another story."

H: Yes.

E: As if she now, in the transference, makes a play for the more ideal person. But at the same time, cannot talk, because she says, "I don't trust you, either."

H: That's true.

E: And here you see, I believe, the-the-the-the ambivalence between the yearning for the father . . .

H: Uh-huh.

E: and the desperate fear that, "I will never smoke him out of his hiding." And, of course, psychotherapy is an interesting situation because we want to know the secret of her life. We are not in treatment; we don't want to give her the secret of our life. And it is now the struggle between the secret-taker, who wants to find the secret of a patient's life, and the one, however, in order to find the secret remains in some-way anonymous, because if it is not anonymous, he starts to search for her in a completely different way; and counter-transference overwhelms him.

H: Yes.

E: At the same time, if he's stymied because she doesn't come through . . . we see the other side of the countertransference: "What am I to do to smoke her out?"

And, now that we-we agree on that, play with a few solutions. (Pause) You see her tomorrow, again?

**H:** I'll see her Monday. (Pause) I-uh . . . I'm intrigued with that, and I'm not sure-I'm not sure I really do know how to-uh-to handle that because I have been feeling a-a heavy responsibility . . .

**E:** Let me ask you. This is the first time we meet.

**H:** Yes.

**E:** We smoke each other out, too. You want to find out about me; and I want to find out about you.

**H:** Well, that's true.

**E:** And I think I let on pretty well . . . how I think about such material.

**H:** Yes.

**E:** With your usual patients . . . I only know that you've finished your studies; I've got no kind of a-no idea what kind of tools or what kind of thinking you usually use.

**H:** Yes.

**E:** What would be your usual way of working with somebody?

**H:** Uh . . . my preferred way would be . . .

**E:** Give me the-uh-a label.

**H:** Uh-I would prefer to use a systemic approach . . . if-if I . . .

**E:** Tell me what you mean by that.

**H:** Uh-I would like to-uh-try to work within the social system that she has which would . . . basically, be she and her husband. I would like-I would prefer to work with the two of them together. If the opportunity ever came up, I'd like to bring her mother in.

**E:** In other words, the idea-the tendency would be to turn it into family counseling.

**H:** That's true. Yes.

**E:** Which is, of course, a very heavy decision for this reason, isn't it? You have a person who has-uh-panic states?

**H:** Yes.

**E:** Not just anxiety neurosis; she has panic states. And, you do not know, at least I wouldn't know, at that moment, whether these panic states are panic breakdown, or whether they're phobic reaction.

**H:** Right.

**E:** If they're panic breakdown . . .

**H:** That could necessitate . . .

**E:** What is this, because you could then say to yourself-uh, "Do I have a patient, or am I in a counseling situation?"

**H:** Right.

**E:** And I feel-I think that these five minutes are very interesting diagnostically . . .

**H:** Uh-huh.

**E:** because at that moment we have to deal, you know, just like I would-uh-I would-uh-if it were one way, the task that you have would be entirely different than if you go the other way.

**H:** Right.

**E:** And-uh-I say what can you do but be, at first, cautious?

**H:** Right.

**E:** As if to say, "I'm not yet ready to make that either into marital counseling or into-uh-bringing in all family members, let's say, the way Murray Bowen would do, who works with the whole family . . .

**H:** Yes. Yes.

**E:** or whether you could simply see her as a therapeutic patient.

**H:** Yes.

**E:** And-uh . . . How?

**H:** Well, in some-to some degree she has made that choice herself.

**E:** Uh-huh.

**H:** Because I did see her hus-she brought her husband in once. Uh . . . he . . . and following that session, she really did not want to have him there. Uhm . . .

**E:** If almost feels maybe the-what she needed was

**H:** That's right.

**E:** marital counseling.

**H:** Right. (Laughs) She's alluded to that. I

**have**-uh-had a sense that-that her response is a phobic one, but I'm also . . . really been reluctant yet to move on that, because I-I guess I'm not fully convinced myself of . . .

**E:** I should tell you, you know, I've seen a few phobic patients in my time. You never know what's behind the phobia.

**H:** Yes.

**E:** You know-uh-if it's a-a childhood phobia, it seems to be one of the most, you know, most frequent things that we get.

**H:** Yeah.

**E:** And usually, we assume a phobic structure and know how to handle it well. When it comes to adults . . . it-you absolutely don't instantly know.

**H:** Uh-huh.

**E:** Takes a long time.

**H:** Uh-huh. Uh-huh.

**E:** Did-did this lady get tests?

**H:** Not with me, no.

**E:** Uh-huh. No tests available?

**H:** No tests have been made with me. Uh-she was in psychotherapy two years earlier, and-uh-I had requested that-uh-the records; and I haven't received those records.

**E:** You haven't got, yet?

**H:** No.

**E:** Did she tell you why she was in therapy then?

**H:** She said she had a phobic-I mean she had a-she was having anxiety attacks then.

**E:** Uh-huh.

**H:** But they-uh-they went away, she said. And-uh . . . she was in therapy only very briefly. The psychiatrist she saw-uh . . . saw her only four or five times, and prescribed medication and prescribed . . . uh-some vitamin-uh-treatment, and that was it.

**E:** Huh. So she tried you, too.

**H:** (Laughs)

**E:** (Inaudible) . . . a completely different one this time.

**H:** Right. Right. Uh-one of the things which is . . . as I watched that segment of tape-uhm-my relationship to her. Uhm . . . there-there is a point there where she says-uh-"This is the only place, you are the only person who really listens to me." And-and I know that's a statement of transference, or of relationship, or of whatever; and I don't think I respond very well to that. I don't know that I know what I want to do with that. Uhm . . .

**E:** Well-uh . . . I just go with those five minutes.

**H:** Yes.

**E:** And it's again general with this situation because you know more; but, if it were those five minutes, I would say . . . it's good to have someone to listen to . . .

**H:** Uh-huh.

**E:** but sometimes it's difficult to tell, because there's the struggle between the wish to be-to have someone who listens . . . and the other wish . . . nobody should know.

**H:** Uh-huh.

**E:** Because, at this moment, the inner self is unprepared.

**H:** Uh-huh.

**E:** You can see the dif-she struggles with changing. Except you mentioned, later, she then said the husband will come as well. Then she had a meeting with the husband, she said, "I'd rather come alone."

**H:** Right

**E:** Which I believe is the first concession where she says, "Maybe not he has to change, but I."

**H:** Right.

**E:** "I want psychotherapy." But, that is a very interesting con-uh-con-con-concession or confession, because then she says, "You listen to me. It's so nice to be with you; you listen to me." Well, then "I come alone" is now not only the declaration of the wish for psychotherapy, it is also, as it were, the idea, "Let's be alone, and have no third person speak into that." Just like,

"I really don't want the mother to speak into the marriage."

**H:** Right.

**E:** "I don't want my husband to know what goes on between the the two of us. Why don't you stop asking me questions? Tell me what to do," she might say. And sooner or later, I would say . . .

**H:** Uh-uh-I think that is exactly right. I-I really do think that's where . . . I expect to hear that from her.

**E:** Yeah. It's almost predictable, isn't it?

**H:** Yes. Yes. (Pause) Part of my . . . wish in this case is-has been-uh-to have her discover her strength; and yet, when I do something that would lead her to that kind of a conclusion, she invariably side-steps me.

**E:** Because it's a demand at this moment, you know? You-you think it's a discovery.

**H:** Yes, that's how I framed it.

**E:** How wonderful is it to-to show that; how wonderful better to discover that I leave in my pocket 10 dollars.

**H:** Yes.

**E:** But the way that I experience it is the fact which tells me . . . that to go and discover, perhaps, you have some hidden money somewhere, isn't it, or some hidden ideas, some hidden secrets? The problem is, constantly, that she expects a demand, when really she wants to make a counter-demand. The relationship with that husband . . . I do not know, but I could sort of imagine a quiet, a not very interesting man . . .

**H:** Right.

**E:** whose idea of living together with another person is to not reveal too much about himself; somebody who is some-what close up, who does, so to speak, mysterious; and he wants a home; and he wants a woman.

**H:** Right.

**E:** This one says, "I don't know what goes on in my head" — your patient. "I don't know what goes in your head. Talk to me."

**H:** Uh-huh.

**E:** "Tell me."

**H:** Uh-huh.

**E:** "I can never talk to you. It's like we have an empty relationship."

**H:** Yes.

**E:** And she constantly tries to discover the inner world of the other, her own inner world; and I would imagine, like a girl might do who would say, "Where is my father? Maybe he lives in Florida. Do you think I could find him? And if I did find him would he tell me what happened? Would I find out the secret of the family?"

**H:** Uh-huh.

**E:** I hear this terrible thing; over and over, I hear such stories. Just talked this morning in private practice with someone. "My parents never told me. It's my sister who finally told me, the older sister, that my father was married before. Why didn't they tell me?"

**H:** Uh-huh.

**E:** They-he also didn't know that his mother grew up in an orphanage. All he knows that they're successful Beverly Hills people who have a house that comes very expensive.

**H:** Yeah.

**E:** But he didn't know that his mother grew up in an orphanage. I happened to know by chance. He didn't know his father was married before. He feels like someone who's given immensely except the one thing that he really wants . . .

**H:** Uh-huh.

**E:** "What gives with you? What's in you?" He never gets. This girl never gets. She seeks now, and you would imagine, she would not only seek in Florida, she must also seek with the therapist. That's after all, what we call transference.

**H:** Yes.

**E:** "Are you married? Do you have children? Are you free? I notice that you have a ring, or you don't have a ring. And the way that you looked at me, and I couldn't understand it. You have . . . (Unclear) to let me wait." And she would get more involved-more involved in the transference struggle. But the struggle would be, "Can I be safe enough with him to allow myself, in his presence, to tell him about me?" rather than to complain-to complain about the husband. Because to complain about the husband, true enough, it is something about her; it's the whiny, deserted child.

**H:** Yes. (Pause) I-I really like that. I haven't been thinking of the case in those terms at all. And it makes a great deal of sense.

**E:** (Inaudible) Excuse me. Whatever I said, it's your material.

**H:** That's true. That's true.

**E:** It's all your material.

**H:** Right, and I don't know why I didn't see it.

**E:** And that's always funny, isn't it? Uh-no super-no psychotherapist really ever tells a patient something new.

**H:** That's right.

**E:** All you do is you reword it. You show the meaning a little clearer. It's like you had a magnifying glass that magnified. And no supervisor ever tells a suspervisee something new. You just . . . from the outsides, it's always easier to see.

**H:** Yes.

**E:** You know that it's-it's so interesting. I guess you would have the same feeling, if you look at that tape by yourself; you could almost supervise your work, you know.

**H:** If I could back enough far.

**E:** Yeah.

**H:** And see . . .

**E:** That's right. It's excellent, if you do. And it becomes, after awhile, clear. So that there's no magic to psychotherapy; nor is there to supervision. It's sometimes good to have an outsider.

**H:** Yes.

**E:** The question is, how does one ever remain an outsider.

**H:** Right.

**E:** Because the smiling invitation, "Will you be that pleasant to me?" (Laughs) No, no.

**H:** Yes.

**E:** You told me, before the lights went on, how nice my paper was, in the beginning. (Laughs) [Allusion to a convention paper Ekstein had just presented.]

**H:** (Laughs) All right. (Laughs) True. Well, I appreciate this. I-I think I've gotten something from this, and I . . .

**E:** Good. When we meet next time, we'll see the case will go great.

**H:** Great. I will be going into it . . . (Inaudible)

**E:** (Inaudible)

**H:** Thanks.

## SUPERVISION SESSION 5: ALBERT ELLIS SUPERVISING DICK HACKNEY

**H** = Hackney   **E** = Ellis

**H:** Well, Dr. Ellis, this is-uh . . . you've seen the tape of a session that I . . . was-uh-doing with Ina. Uh-I'm not quite sure how to start. Uh-I'm wondering if there were things that you saw there that you'd like to pick up on, first.

**E:** Well, yes. But I want to explain first that-uhm-I'm naturally going to supervise from my own standpoint which is Rational Emotive Therapy, and this tape was almost the opposite . . .

**H:** Yes.

**E:** of what RET would be. So . . . uhm-I'm going to . . . get you on points which are illegitimate to some degree, you see.

**H:** That's fine because what we-our purpose is to bring out RET.

**E:** Right. So I'm going to assume wrongly that you . . . were trying to do some kind of RET session . . .

H: Good.

E: and criticize it from that . . . standpoint, because actually I wasn't quite clear what-uhm . . . you were trying to do at points. Uh . . . sort of general psychotherapy, but I wasn't quite sure. But, as I said, I'll ignore that. Now, the first thing that I noticed from RET standpoint was . . . too much emphasis on the situation, what we call the "A" activating event . . .

H: Uh-huh.

E: and then we have a "B," a belief about it; and then a "C," a consequence. Now-uh-a feeling in our gut. Now, I assume the consequence was . . . sort of came in along the side, that she's upset about the fact that her husband doesn't talk the way she wanted him . . .

H: Right.

E: to. But I wasn't sure what her feeling . . . was. We first make clear that it was an inappropriate feeling, because she might just be sorry and regretful . . .

H: Right.

E: about it, and that we wouldn't consider an emotional problem. So if she were depressed, or anxious, or real . . . upset about it, that would be different. And I think she was.

H: That's-that's right.

E: Yeah.

H: Yes.

E: So let's assume that she's . . . anxious about that and certain other things-it was obvious-that she was anxious about. So the "C" was fairly clear; we'll say she was depressed or anxious about his not-they've been married for quite a while, is that right? She doesn't . . .

H: Well-uh . . . not as long as it might seem. They've been married six months.

E: Oh, I see. Yeah. Because she mentioned twenty-seven years. Is he twenty-seven years of age?

H: She was saying that-yes, he was twenty-seven years of age. And-uh-his style has

taken twenty years to-twenty-seven years to develop.

E: Yeah.

H: That's what the reference was.

E: All right. So the first thing that came in was-uh . . . you said to her, earlier in the session, "You had to . . . smoke him out." And she sort of agreed to it. But we would be looking for the upsetting factor which, in my head, would be immediately, "as you shouldn't have to."

H: Right.

E: And now I would try to confront her: "Are you saying that that's unfortunate, that you had to smoke him out?" which is really . . .

H: Uh-huh.

E: But she's really angry and upset because she shouldn't have to . . .

H: Right.

E: smoke him out.

H: And if she smokes him out, then she feels that she didn't get what she wanted anyhow, because it should have happened spontaneously.

E: Yes, that's right. So she's in a box there, and also she didn't get what she thinks she needs, her wants were. In RET, any want, even an unrealistic want, is not too bad.

H: Uh-huh.

E: You want a million dollars right now, as long as you say you don't need it. And then you were rightly, which is part of RET, giving her a little skill training . . .

H: Yeah.

E: which we'd go back to "A," the activating event . . .

H: Uh-huh.

E: and show her very simple techniques of maybe handling it better. We wouldn't consider that of paramount importance, but we'd do it along with the changing of her belief system, and "C," her consequences or feeling.

H: Yes.

E: But while doing that we might give her

some skill training. And for a while, you were . . . doing that. That was OK. But then the crux . . . arrived pretty soon. She said, "I'm scared I'm going to blow it."

**H:** Uh-huh.

**E:** And . . . I would almost immediately confront her and saying, "What are you telling yourself when . . . you're scared you're going to blow it?" And I know it, in my own head, that she's saying something like she said a little later, "That if I blow it, as I must not, that would be awful."

**H:** Uh-huh.

**E:** So I would quickly interrupt, and suppose we implode it, saying, "Suppose you did blow it?"

**H:** Uh-huh.

**E:** "So you blew it?"

**H:** You mean even rehearse blowing it?

**E:** Well, we would . . . but we would implode it in the sense, we might do it in role-playing or something like that, but we'd implode it in her head, "Let's suppose the worst . . ."

**H:** I see.

**E:** "would happen," which is one of our main techniques.

**H:** Yeah.

**E:** "You really blew it, and he ran away screaming . . ."

**H:** Uh-huh.

**E:** "and you ended up in the loony bin."

**H:** Uh-huh.

**E:** "Why is that so awful?" Because, you see, we're trying to get an elegant solution, so when she finishes, nothing in the world-if the world came to an end-she wouldn't upset herself. She'd say, "Too damn bad. Isn't that interesting that the world is coming to an end." But you wouldn't whine and scream, because that's what we think emotional disturbance is, is nothing but whining.

**H:** OK.

**E:** You see.

**H:** OK.

**E:** She's a whiner.

**H:** Yes.

**E:** So we would try to make the whining explicit, and say, "Well, suppose that . . . happened?" and then immediately . . . uh-well-uh-as an aside, I'm just doing the sequence-I would have gotten her to see that she's telling herself, and who knows what might come out of that, but almost certainly she'd say, "Isn't it awful to blow it?" or something like that. But then . . . you were doing skill training with her-her and her husband, as I said . . .

**H:** Uh-huh.

**E:** and on the side; but we would have gone deeper than that. We would have had her do therapy with her husband, because if I hear this case accurately, he has an emotional problem.

**H:** Uh-huh.

**E:** He's unable to . . .

**H:** Right.

**E:** express himself. Now maybe not; maybe he's just the wrong type and she stupidly married him.

**H:** Yeah.

**E:** And-uh-he has a right to not be expressive. But let's assume he has an emotional problem, so I would get her to ask him, "When you don't express yourself, dear, what are you telling yourself . . ."

**H:** Yeah. OK.

**E:** "making yourself afraid of? not just . . ."

**H:** You'd teach her some therapy skill to use with him?

**E:** Yeah, because we say in RET, the more you use therapy on other people, the better it is. When I was an analyst, I used to tell my clients, "Don't analyze your friends and relatives; that's what helps screw them up." So they analyzed them, and they did. But now I tell everybody practically, "Do therapize your friends and relatives with RET because among other things it's a teaching device . . . and frequently, and I don't know in the case of her husband, you have nothing to lose if he listens and changes his mind; if he doesn't, she's still taught herself how to use . . .

**H:** Right.

**E:** the RET.

**H:** Right.

**E:** You see. So our skill training would include . . . the skill, not just of handling him, but of showing him what he's been doing.

**H:** Uh-huh.

**E:** To be a therapist.

**H:** Uh-huh.

**E:** This is in my groups, we get people to therapize each other, to treat-to practice themselves, not just to help the other. That's one of the goals of . . . though I-but that's just parenthetical. Then she says very succinctly, "I'm afraid to blow it; I'll screw everything up." Well, first, that's an overgeneralization . . .

**H:** Yes.

**E:** that you were sort of . . . I think, mildly trying to show her.

**H:** Yeah.

**E:** And we would have (Unclear) at one point.

**H:** Yes.

**E:** "Would you screw everything up, or some of the things up?" But then I would also implode them, you see. We have two levels: one is the realistic level, "Would you really blow it that badly?" and the answer is, "No."

**H:** Uh-huh.

**E:** But then, after doing that, I'd say, "Well, now let's suppose the worst, if you really did screw everything up." Again, I'm going to confront the basic problem, that if the worst comes to worst, so she ruins her relationship with him, and she spends a little time in the loony bin . . .

**H:** Uh-huh.

**E:** "What's so awful about that?"

**H:** Yeah.

**E:** You see.

**H:** Yeah.

**E:** To really get . . . the po-possible, that we call the elegant solution. So she takes new learning about herself and how not (Unclear) and kind of situation, including this one which she's dreaming up, that she's going off the wall like her sister who's apparently a drug . . . addict.

**H:** Yeah. Yeah.

**E:** And there was some mention of her mother. I wasn't clear, was her mother disturbed too?

**H:** Her mother is-uh-her child really. Her mother . . . uh-has become the child. She has become the mother, Ina has. So . . .

**E:** Yeah.

**H:** she feels just a role reversal has happened there.

**E:** Right. But that means the mother is disturbed too.

**H:** Yes.

**E:** And she may be afraid to be somewhat childish like her mother.

**H:** Right.

**E:** I'd (Unclear) what to do so she can get over it; but you don't awfulize about it.

**H:** Uh-huh.

**E:** And then she says, "I'm afraid I'll be like my sister, go to bed and not get up, and John will hate me . . . too, for doing that," Now, this implicitly gives me the information which I suspected . . .

**H:** Uh-huh.

**E:** from the moment she opened her mouth, that she has, among other things, and maybe primarily, a dire need for love.

**H:** Uh-huh.

**E:** She's not really (afraid) of going to the loony bin.

**H:** Yes.

**E:** She's afraid she's going to lose his love. Not that he sounds like a doll . . .

**H:** Right.

**E:** or anything. Uh . . . but it would go with probably any person she picked.

**H:** I-I really think that's true.

**E:** Yeah. So I would try to get her, "Aren't you saying you couldn't accept yourself at all, if he didn't love you, especially if he didn't love you because you were off the wall." (Unclear) And I would try to get her to see that that is one of her central problems-a dire need to be approved, loved, accepted. And that again, it's not necessary. It's nice to be loved; it's a delight. It's only a pleasure; it's not a necessity. She might practically want humans to take their desires and preferences and make them into dire necessities; and that is nonsense.

**H:** Uh-huh.

**E:** Whining and screaming about it if they're not getting what they have to.

**H:** Fine.

**E:** You see, so I would try to, with a few questions, at least get her to admit, probably, that she does have this dire need which she probably would admit (Unclear). Then she says, "If one little piece falls out, everything is gone." That's all or nothing.

**H:** Yeah.

**E:** How does that happen?" And then she says something interesting, "I really want that piece of pie." Now I would question that; she means "needs."

**H:** OK.

**E:** You see. I translate this in my own head. Every therapist goes in with his own bigotries and prejudices. When she says "want," people practically never mean "want" because they wouldn't be disturbed.

**H:** Uh-huh.

**E:** So I'd say, "Don't you really need that piece of pie?" This is her . . . uh-needs love.

**H:** Yeah.

**E:** When she says "wants," she's just . . . covering up.

**H:** Yeah.

**E:** You see. It's nice to want, and anybody will say (Unclear). It's nothing to criticize.

**H:** So you really don't-you wouldn't-uh-trust that wanting it was just on a level of wanting?

**E:** No, because in our theory if you really wanted anything and didn't get it, you'd be sorry, or regretful, frustrated.

**H:** But go on.

**E:** Yeah; but you wouldn't be emotionally disturbed.

**H:** Right.

**E:** You see. The must, the need, the necessitizing is what leads to it. So we always have something to look for . . .

**H:** OK.

**E:** right away . . . in the very first session, we would look for those things, and see if they're so. It might not be so.

**H:** Uh-huh.

**E:** And she says, again, "What if I do something really crazy?" And I'd say, "Well, what would you do?" you see, again imploding . . .

**H:** Yeah.

**E:** "really off the wall, and doing some really asinine act, and they're thinking of locking you up, why couldn't you still accept yourself, and say, 'Well, shit, this is inconvenient . . .' "

**H:** Yeah.

**E:** " 'being in the loony bin, but that's all of it. That's all there is in life.' " You see. I would start teaching her to only think what's obnoxious in life is only an inconvenience, and we define that as something horrible, awful, terrible. But that's our nonsense. (Unclear)

**H:** Right.

**E:** so people would like you. Then you almost gave her a homework assignment, but I was not clear . . . about that. It looked like you were giving her a homework assignment.

**H:** Yes.

E: I thought you were going to nail her to do something specific, which we would have done.

H: Right.

E: We would invariably, not invariably, but almost always give her a homework assignment. And it was not bad getting somewhere in between (Unclear) but it seemed to get vague, and I never got clear if she ended up . . .

H: She did end up with a homework assignment . . .

E: Yeah.

H: which was what you saw on the tape of having-uh-a meal with him out on the porch, out there eating it with him.

E: Yeah; but it seemed to be a sort of deeper homework assignment. You were hinting at (Unclear)

H: (Unclear)

E: not more one extreme or another; try to get some balance . . .

H: Right.

E: in between, while you're that. So that-that was OK. I just wasn't clear on the point I heard. And then you said to her, "You have fear of loss of control, and yet you're so controlling."

H: Yes.

E: But we would say that's inevitable. In almost anybody with a horror . . . of loss of control, ironically, wı ¹ be controlling. (Unclear) suppose I go out of control; wouldn't that be horrible, et cetera. So then they'll very frequently, in fact, go to the other extreme . . .

H: Yeah.

E: and . . . be that. And I would explain to her that's where her overcontrollingness comes from, not from the desire to control, but from the dire necessity to control.

H: Right.

E: Her idea of control happens to be (Unclear), then we have to be in control, the more rigid . . . you are, and then you will

. . . because your fear of lack of control to be too . . . controlling.

H: Uh-huh.

E: And then you very correctly said, I thought that was very good, because she might have been too unrealistic, that, "John isn't going to change fast, and-uh-even getting him to sit down the way you want him to sit down with you may be pie in the sky," which I thought was good, because she could easily . . . go and build up all kinds of unrealistic . . .

H: Uh-huh.

E: conclusions . . .

H: Uh-huh.

E: about, now you accept her, you've gone over certain things with her, now all I have to do is have a few talks with him, and he's going to change.

H: Yeah.

E: And again I would go back to even, "It's very unlikely that he's going to change," because either he naturally is that way, in a healthy manner, which could be that's his nature . . .

H: Sure. Right.

E: or he disturbedly is that way, and then you're going to have one hell of a time except through pounding away with RET to get him moving.

H: Yeah.

E: That-uh . . . caveat you gave her was good, that she better not think it's going to be easy.

H: Uh-huh. Right.

E: So those were the main things. But, as I said, a lot of these criticisms were unfair since you weren't trying to do it within our framework, and most of the people I supervise would have this framework in mind.

H: Right.

E: And that they would follow it. And I'd show them how they go off the framework which, ostensibly, they're following.

H: OK. Uh . . . let's just say I'm a very bad RET therapist . . .

E: Yeah.

H: at this point, and I'd like to, in my next session, I'd like to . . . build some improvement into that. Uh-one of the things I guess I'm hearing is that I could really be listening for is more of the self-statements, the point "B."

E: And . . .

H: That my ears aren't tuned in to that.

E: Right. And the philosophy behind them. And the-really the self-statement . . .

H: OK.

E: we call them self-statements because most people most of the time tell it to themselves, but they could imagine it . . .

H: Right.

E: through imagery. They could feel it even.

H: Yeah.

E: But it's a philosophy. And her two main philosophies that I hear there: one, "I absolutely need certain people's approval, maybe everybody." That might come out, but especially her husband's approval.

H: Uh-huh.

E: And two: "I must not act crazy." She has phreniphobia, really, loss of control.

H: Yeah.

E: And those two would usually be in implicit self-statements. Freud would have called them "preconscious," not deep in the id where we don't think they might be.

H: Yeah.

E: You would look for those first in your head, you see. You have an hypothesis that she has these statements, and you just ask her.

H: Yes.

E: "Aren't you doing this, or doing that?"

H: Yeah.

E: (Unclear)

H: OK. I-I think that-uhm-really trying to listen for that, I think would help, in that regard. The other thing is that . . .

E: Which incidentally is an extra form of effort, you see.

H: Yes.

E: You see, we go further than (name of therapist deleted) in empathy. He's listening to their feelings . . .

H: Yeah.

E: and their actions, and things like that; and we're looking for and listening to very acutely the self-statements that make them feel and act. So it's . . .

H: OK.

E: and, therefore, at the end of the session, they frequently say, "I've never felt so understood in my life," because we're not just reflecting.

H: Because you're hearing what was not said.

E: That's right.

H: Yeah.

E: And then we question them, "Isn't-didn't you put in those shoulds?" or whatever it was, and they almost always say, "Yeah;" they don't deny it.

H: Uh-huh. The other thing that you said which I'm-uh-interested in is the eloquent . . . uh-extreme of this, is how it sounded to me. Uh-to take her fear and build that up or in-uh-implode that . . .

E: Implode. Right.

H: into an eloquent-uh-exaggeration that would be so impossible. I-I certainly . . .

E: That's what we call the elegant solution which means that under all conditions, at all times, if we succeed, whatever happens she's not going to upset herself.

H: OK.

E: You see, not just the presenting symptom, that's nice (Unclear) and not just even a series of symptoms; but new symptoms which she would . . . dream up in the future, if she has these basic philosophies.

H: OK. Now, is the point there that if she-uh-really grasps that elegant ex-extreme . . .

E: Yeah.

H: that almost anything that she would do

would fall short of it and she wouldn't have to panic with that, is that it?

E: That's one point, but always there's a statistical probability that John might die and a few other really gruesome things might . . .

H: Yeah.

E: happen. Those usually don't. She might, as you said, lose her job and a couple . . .

H: Right.

E: of things at once; but we're saying that even then she very-she better feel very sorry and regretful. That goes from 1 to 99.

H: Uh-huh.

E: But not 101, which is depression, anxiety, despair.

H: Uh-huh.

E: Two continua. And we want her to feel very much when something goes wrong; we're not trying to get calmness and serenity . . . as some Rational people do. So we want her to feel, but appropriate within the preference continuum, and not . . .

H: Yeah.

E: jump over to the necessitized; "Because I want it very much, ergo it should be."

H: Right.

E: Which is what . . .

H: Right.

E: she's doing very clearly, as I hear.

H: Yeah, and I-you're speaking to something there that-uh-I have a concern about with Ina, in that it's almost as though she hasn't-uh-she really doesn't have a sense of what her norms could be in terms of feelings. She doesn't know-she doesn't have a baseline for her feelings, so she doesn't . . .

E: Because she's an extremist.

H: Yes. She . . .

E: She probably would feel either very lightly or all the way . . .

H: Right.

E: and feel nothing; and, therefore, she

doesn't (Unclear) until she gets rid of the extreme, that I must not be unloved and feel like that would be awful, she won't know what her preferences are, whether . . .

H: Right

E: they're needs, necessities; you don't know it.

H: Right. (Pause) OK.

E: 'Cause they drive you-you are all needs.

H: Right. Right. Now, I have some-uh-concerns that that could take a while with her to-to-uh-get that across to her because . . .

E: That's right.

H: in some ways she's resistant . . . to me.

E: Right. But we would say that unless you take the while, you're wasting your time.

H: OK. I'm-I'm just trying to get . . .

E: If you were helping her, and what you did, incidentally, was very good from one framework of therapy; that she's going to like you, and trust you, et cetera; and I say it's almost a complete waste of time; she'll get sick of it.

H: OK.

E: You see, because you haven't really changed-help change her basic philosophy. And she can take her philosophy with dire need for love and use it toward you, Sigmund Freud, or anybody. But . . . so . . . we would want you to try to see what her basic assumptions are. And-uh . . .

H: Yeah.

E: work commonly. I would say you're correct. She's bright enough, and she sees when she resists seeing it. But actually feeling it, working against it, is going to take a while.

H: That was what I was wondering.

E: Yeah.

H: Is there a while . . . is there time there, from an RET perspective, that I would have in working on that?

E: Well, we would assume that somebody like

her wouldn't take-uh-several years, but . . .

**H:** Right.

**E:** would take 20 or 30 sessions.

**H:** Right.

**E:** You gradually . . .

**H:** That's . . . OK.

**E:** see it, and maybe around the tenth or twelfth session, in a sort of, "Yeah, that's right. I can see that I'm responsible for my feelings. John's not making me feel this. I'm responsible, and I could control it. I can control my emotional destiny."

**H:** Uh-huh.

**E:** But it would take time and practice.

**H:** Right.

**E:** You see, that's why we would give her the homework assignments, things like that. So . . . looks simple-it's very simple; but simple doesn't mean easy.

**H:** Yeah.

**E:** It's simple to diet . . .

**H:** Yeah.

**E:** but look at how many people fall on their faces.

**H:** Yeah. What I was talking about in the way of homework I can see wasn't at all the kind of homework that you'd be talking about.

**E:** Well, it was partially so, 'cause I thought philosophically you said, and I may have misunderstood it, to try to get her to get some balance.

**H:** Right.

**E:** You see, so you (Unclear) and a little implied. But we would give first the activity homework, like "talk to your husband." That's OK.

**H:** Yeah.

**E:** "But while talking to your husband, look for what you're telling yourself, and try to change it . . ."

**H:** Right.

**E:** "if it's upsetting."

**H:** Huh. And I wasn't at all explicit with that; so . . .

**E:** No.

**H:** Well . . . I appreciate this. I-uh . . . can see that the-uh-the point of the-uh-the imagery or the self-statements is a whole dimension that isn't in this tape.

**E:** Yeah. Fine. And in the vast majority of therapy. That's why we think that therapy is often iatrogenic. It doesn't do any good, because it misses the essence. It gets a lot of feeling out, a lot of insight at one point . . . insight . . .

**H:** Right.

**E:** That's somewhat irrelevant to seeing your own ideas and working your ass off to change those ideas over a period of time.

**H:** Right. Well, I appreciate it. Thank you, very much.

**E:** Thank you.

# INDEX

Accrediting bodies, 2
Administrative
    competence, importance of,
        152–153
    working toward, 170–171
American Association for Marriage
    and Family Therapy, 3
Amorphous supervision, 173–174
Anxiety
    reduction through metaphor,
        178–179
    avoidant maneuvers, 176–178
Art and science, 51
Association for Counselor Educa-
    tion and Supervision
    (ACES), 3
Assumptive world, 35
Attributions and self-efficacy,
    236–237
Audiotapes, the written critique of,
    58
Audiotaping, 55–56

Behavioral supervision, 16
Bug-in-the-ear, 88–89
Burnout, reducing, 165–166

Catalytic interventions, 65
Client, 5
    cares, monitoring of, 6
    perspective, 203, 213–214
Clinical supervision, 10
Cognitions, discrete, 237
Communication, 166
Competence, 142–145
    felt, 180–181
Competency and knowledge, core
    areas of, 269–272
Conceptual interventions, 65
Confrontive interventions, 65
Consultation
    break, 91–92
    versus supervision, 6
    breaks and phone-ins, 90
Contracts, 163–164
Counseling versus supervision, 5
Counselor, evaluation of supervi-
    sors, 289–290

Countertransference
    supervisor, 181–186
        categories, 181–185
        as theme interference, 185–186
        to trainee's transference, 185
Credentialing, 2
Cross-cultural therapy, training for,
    205–212

Definitions and issues, 194–199
Developmental
    approach, conclusions about, 24
    models, cognitive, 235–236
    techniques derived from, 64–65
Discrimination
    model, 26, 40
        conclusions about, 43–46
Dual
    channel supervision, 58
    relationships, 138–142
Due process, 133–135
Duty to warn, 145–146
Dynamics
    in-session, 98–99
    team, 98

Eclectic supervision, 18
Education versus supervision, 5
Ending stage, 82–83
Ethical decision making, 149–150
    issues, major, for clinical supervi-
        sors, 133–135
    and supervisors, 132–133
Evaluation, 8, 164
    communicating, 114–115
    consequences of, 122–123
    criteria for, 110–112
    favorable conditions for, 106–110
    issues of, chronic, 129–130
    process of, 112–113
    program, 127–129
    supervisor, 123–129
Experience, 121

Facilitative interventions, 65
Familiarity, 120–121
Feedback, 115–116
    clarity, importance of, 116–119
Field-site supervisor, 164–167

Form, 168
Format, 35

Gay men and lesbians, 220–222
Gender issues, 212–220
Group
    minority, others, 222–223
    peer, supervision, 83–86
    process of, 72–83
    stages of, 82–83
    supervision of, limitations of, 76

Influence
    bidirectional, 241
    concluding comments, 241–242
    social, models, 240–241
Information processing: novices
    versus experts, 237–239
Informed consent, 135
    with clients, 135–137
    with trainees, 137–138
Initial stage, 77
Instruction, 66
Integrative supervision, 18
Interpersonal process recall (IPR),
    26, 61
Interventions
    catalytic, 65
    conceptual, 65
    confrontive, 65
    facilitative, 65
    group supervision, criteria for
        choosing, 49–50
    live supervision, 90
    therapeutic, 216–217
Interview, the, 164–165
In vivo, 89
Isomorphism, 29, 32–33
    conclusions about, 33
    as focus of supervision, 29
Issues
    and definitions, 194–199
    gender, 212–220
    methodological: stages two and
        three of supervision science,
        228–231
    sex role, training in, 217–218
    supervision, 217–220